Lecture Notes in Computer Science

Lecture Notes in Artificial Intelligence   14268

Founding Editor

Jörg Siekmann

T0155681

The series Lecture Notes in Artificial Intelligence (LNAI) was established in 1988 as a topical subseries of LNCS devoted to artificial intelligence.

The series publishes state-of-the-art research results at a high level. As with the LNCS mother series, the mission of the series is to serve the international R & D community by providing an invaluable service, mainly focused on the publication of conference and workshop proceedings and postproceedings.

Huayong Yang · Honghai Liu · Jun Zou ·
Zhouping Yin · Lianqing Liu · Geng Yang ·
Xiaoping Ouyang · Zhiyong Wang
Editors

Intelligent Robotics and Applications

16th International Conference, ICIRA 2023
Hangzhou, China, July 5–7, 2023
Proceedings, Part II

 Springer

Editors
Huayong Yang
Zhejiang University
Hangzhou, China

Honghai Liu 🆔
Harbin Institute of Technology
Shenzhen, China

Jun Zou 🆔
Zhejiang University
Hangzhou, China

Zhouping Yin
Huazhong University of Science
and Technology
Wuhan, China

Lianqing Liu 🆔
Shenyang Institute of Automation
Shenyang, Liaoning, China

Geng Yang 🆔
Zhejiang University
Hangzhou, China

Xiaoping Ouyang 🆔
Zhejiang University
Hangzhou, China

Zhiyong Wang
Harbin Institute of Technology
Shenzhen, China

ISSN 0302-9743   ISSN 1611-3349 (electronic)
Lecture Notes in Artificial Intelligence
ISBN 978-981-99-6485-7   ISBN 978-981-99-6486-4 (eBook)
https://doi.org/10.1007/978-981-99-6486-4

LNCS Sublibrary: SL7 – Artificial Intelligence

This Springer imprint is published by the registered company Springer Nature Singapore Pte Ltd.
The registered company address is: 152 Beach Road, #21-01/04 Gateway East, Singapore 189721, Singapore

Paper in this product is recyclable.

Preface

With the theme "Smart Robotics for Sustainable Society", the 16th International Conference on Intelligent Robotics and Applications (ICIRA 2023) was held in Hangzhou, China, July 5–7, 2023, and designed to encourage advancement in the field of robotics, automation, mechatronics, and applications. It aimed to promote top-level research and globalize quality research in general, making discussions and presentations more internationally competitive and focusing on the latest outstanding achievements, future trends, and demands.

ICIRA 2023 was organized and hosted by Zhejiang University, co-hosted by Harbin Institute of Technology, Huazhong University of Science and Technology, Chinese Academy of Sciences, and Shanghai Jiao Tong University, co-organized by State Key Laboratory of Fluid Power and Mechatronic Systems, State Key Laboratory of Robotics and System, State Key Laboratory of Digital Manufacturing Equipment and Technology, State Key Laboratory of Mechanical System and Vibration, State Key Laboratory of Robotics, and School of Mechanical Engineering of Zhejiang University. Also, ICIRA 2023 was technically co-sponsored by Springer. On this occasion, ICIRA 2023 was a successful event after the COVID-19 pandemic. It attracted more than 630 submissions, and the Program Committee undertook a rigorous review process for selecting the most deserving research for publication. The Advisory Committee gave advice for the conference program. Also, they help to organize special sections for ICIRA 2023. Finally, a total of 431 papers were selected for publication in 9 volumes of Springer's Lecture Note in Artificial Intelligence. For the review process, single-blind peer review was used. Each review took around 2–3 weeks, and each submission received at least 2 reviews and 1 meta-review.

In ICIRA 2023, 12 distinguished plenary speakers delivered their outstanding research works in various fields of robotics. Participants gave a total of 214 oral presentations and 197 poster presentations, enjoying this excellent opportunity to share their latest research findings. Here, we would like to express our sincere appreciation to all the authors, participants, and distinguished plenary and keynote speakers. Special thanks are also extended to all members of the Organizing Committee, all reviewers for peer-review, all staffs of the conference affairs group, and all volunteers for their diligent work.

July 2023

Huayong Yang
Honghai Liu
Jun Zou
Zhouping Yin
Lianqing Liu
Geng Yang
Xiaoping Ouyang
Zhiyong Wang

Organization

Conference Chair

Huayong Yang   Zhejiang University, China

Honorary Chairs

Youlun Xiong   Huazhong University of Science and Technology, China

Han Ding   Huazhong University of Science and Technology, China

General Chairs

Honghai Liu   Harbin Institute of Technology, China

Jun Zou   Zhejiang University, China

Zhouping Yin   Huazhong University of Science and Technology, China

Lianqing Liu   Chinese Academy of Sciences, China

Program Chairs

Geng Yang   Zhejiang University, China

Li Jiang   Harbin Institute of Technology, China

Guoying Gu   Shanghai Jiao Tong University, China

Xinyu Wu   Chinese Academy of Sciences, China

Award Committee Chair

Yong Lei   Zhejiang University, China

Publication Chairs

Xiaoping Ouyang   Zhejiang University, China
Zhiyong Wang   Harbin Institute of Technology, China

Regional Chairs

Zhiyong Chen   University of Newcastle, Australia
Naoyuki Kubota   Tokyo Metropolitan University, Japan
Zhaojie Ju   University of Portsmouth, UK
Eric Perreault   Northeastern University, USA
Peter Xu   University of Auckland, New Zealand
Simon Yang   University of Guelph, Canada
Houxiang Zhang   Norwegian University of Science and Technology, Norway
Duanling Li   Beijing University of Posts and Telecommunications, China

Advisory Committee

Jorge Angeles   McGill University, Canada
Tamio Arai   University of Tokyo, Japan
Hegao Cai   Harbin Institute of Technology, China
Tianyou Chai   Northeastern University, China
Jiansheng Dai   King's College London, UK
Zongquan Deng   Harbin Institute of Technology, China
Han Ding   Huazhong University of Science and Technology, China
Xilun Ding   Beihang University, China
Baoyan Duan   Xidian University, China
Xisheng Feng   Shenyang Institute of Automation, Chinese Academy of Sciences, China
Toshio Fukuda   Nagoya University, Japan
Jianda Han   Nankai University, China
Qiang Huang   Beijing Institute of Technology, China
Oussama Khatib   Stanford University, USA
Yinan Lai   National Natural Science Foundation of China, China
Jangmyung Lee   Pusan National University, Korea
Zhongqin Lin   Shanghai Jiao Tong University, China

Hong Liu   Harbin Institute of Technology, China
Honghai Liu   University of Portsmouth, UK
Shugen Ma   Ritsumeikan University, Japan
Daokui Qu   Siasun Robot and Automation Co., Ltd., China
Min Tan   Institute of Automation, Chinese Academy of
                            Sciences, China
Kevin Warwick   Coventry University, UK
Guobiao Wang   National Natural Science Foundation of China,
                            China
Tianmiao Wang   Beihang University, China
Tianran Wang   Shenyang Institute of Automation, Chinese
                            Academy of Sciences, China
Yuechao Wang   Shenyang Institute of Automation, Chinese
                            Academy of Sciences, China
Bogdan M. Wilamowski   Auburn University, USA
Ming Xie   Nanyang Technological University, Singapore
Yangsheng Xu   Chinese University of Hong Kong, China
Huayong Yang   Zhejiang University, China
Jie Zhao   Harbin Institute of Technology, China
Nanning Zheng   Xi'an Jiaotong University, China
Xiangyang Zhu   Shanghai Jiao Tong University, China

Contents – Part II

Wearable Sensors and Robots

**Wearable Robots for Assistance, Augmentation and Rehabilitation of
Human Movements**

Perception and Manipulation of Dexterous Hand for Humanoid Robot

Vision-Based Human Robot Interaction and Application

Object Tracking Algorithm Based on Dual Layer Attention

Ziwan Li[1,2,3], Shiben Liu[2,3,4], Zhuxuan Cheng[1,2,3], Zhencheng Yu[2,3,4], and Huijie Fan[2,3,4(✉)]

[1] School of Information Engineering, Shenyang University of Chemical Technology, Shenyang 110142, China
[2] State Key Laboratory of Robotics, Shenyang Institute of Automation, Chinese Academy of Sciences, Shenyang 110016, China
[3] Institutes for Robotics and Intelligent Manufacturing, Chinese Academy of Sciences, Shenyang 110169, China
[4] University of Chinese Academy of Sciences, Beijing 100049, China
`fanhuijie@sia.cn`

Abstract. The attention mechanism is an important part of the Transformer trackers. But the attention mechanism has some limitations in calculating the correlation. When the attention mechanism calculates the wrong correlation, it affects the quality of the final correlation and affects the overall tracking performance. To solve the above problems, we designed a dual layer attention module to improve the accuracy of correlation by dual layer attention, so that the attention mechanism can accomplish feature augmentation and fusion more effectively, thus improving the performance of the tracking algorithm. The proposed algorithm consists of a Swin-Transformer-based backbone network, a dual layer attention-based fusion module and a prediction branch. Experiments indicate that our algorithm achieves robust results on five publicly available datasets, running at approximately 35 FPS on the GPU, allowing for real-time tracking.

Keywords: Attention · Transformer · Feature fusion · Object tracking

1 Introduction

Visual object tracking is one of the important tasks in computer vision, It is receiving increasing attention in areas such as automatic driving and security [6, 7,12]. The aim of visual object tracking is to predict the position and shape of that given target on a sequence of video frames. The major challenges of tracking include rotation and deformation, etc. In the past few years, Many people make a lot of effort. For example, [1,13,14,23,27] Siamese-based trackers treat visual target tracking as a one-shot matching problem and provide an effective balance of speed and accuracy. Recently, Transformer [24] is on the rise, some trackers [3,19,25,28] have started to explore the use of the Transformer in the field of target tracking.

H. Yang et al. (Eds.): ICIRA 2023, LNAI 14268, pp. 3–14, 2023.
https://doi.org/10.1007/978-981-99-6486-4_1

Currently, the most critical module in the Transformer-based tracking framework [3,19] is the attention mechanism. In Transformer [24], the template region and search region features are enhanced by the self-attention, and the interaction between the template region and the search region is achieved by the cross-attention. This approach introduces global relationships in the feature fusion module, effectively improving the performance of tracking. The Transformer attention enter queries and a set of key-value pairs and outputs a linear combination of values, with the correlation between queries and the corresponding key as its weight. However, this calculation of correlation ignores computational errors, which can be exacerbated in cases of complex scenes or severe occlusions, thus drastically reducing the usefulness of the attention mechanism.

Therefore, in order to solve the above problems, we propose a dual layer attention module and design a target tracking algorithm based on dual layer attention (DATrack). It is an improvement on the attention in the Transformer, where the attention in the Transformer [24] is improved into an outer attention and inner attention module, with the inner attention adjusting the correlation of the outer attention calculation to reduce correlation errors. This dual layer attention module effectively improves the accuracy of correlations, allowing for more effective feature augmentation and fusion. This module is divided into two structures, including a dual layer attention self-augmentation module and a dual layer attention cross-fusion module, which are described in detail in Sect. 3.2.

In addition, current algorithms only consider the association between a single frame or two frames, ignoring the association of the entire frame sequence. The idea that the tracking result of the current frame is also influenced by the tracking result of the previous frame is largely ignored in current algorithms, and this neglect limits the performance of visual target tracking to a large extent. Therefore, to prevent our tracking algorithm from falling into this loop, we introduced an SLT [11] strategy into our algorithm to simulate realistic tracking scenarios in training, shifting the vision of the tracking task back to a sequence-level task.

The rest of this paper is arranged as follows: In Sect. 2, we present some related work on target tracking, including Siamese tracking and Transformer tracking. In Sect. 3, we present the structure of our proposed algorithm and the dual layer attention module. In Sect. 4, we present the performance of the algorithm and some ablation experiments.

2   Related Work

2.1   Visual Object Tracking

Target tracking is one of the most important research topics in computer vision and has been the subject of a great deal of active research [9,18]. The VOT algorithm based on deep learning has effectively improved the performance of the tracking algorithm. Currently, there are two main types of research in the field of target tracking, namely Siamese based target tracking algorithms [13,27] and DiMP based target tracking algorithms [2,25]. The Siamese tracking algorithms [1,14] rely on a template matching mechanism that are trained offline using a large dataset. This approach performs well in short-term tracking, but is limited by offline training and performs poorly in long-term tracking. The DiMP tracking algorithms [2,25] learn an online model predictor for target-centric regression and update the target model online during the tracking process. Recently, with the rapid development of the Transformer, the Transformer has been introduced to both methods [3,19,25], allowing for effective performance improvements in target tracking.

2.2 Siamese Tracking and Transformer Tracking

The Siamese tracking framework [1,13,27] describes target tracking as a matching problem between the template and the search area. Algorithm [1] introduces a fully convolutional network in its work to implement the tracking task and achieves a good balance of accuracy and speed [14]. In this work propose an anchor-based tracker that integrates the area suggestion network into the Siamese network, achieving an increase in tracking speed and accuracy. In subsequent work, many strategies have been proposed, such as deeper backbone network [13] and multi-level structures [5], all of which have been effective in improving the performance of the target tracking algorithm.

2.3 Transformer Tracking

Recently, Transformer trackers have proliferated. These methods [3,25,28] were the first trackers to introduce the Transformer to visual target tracking [3]. This approach introduces the Transformer into the Siamese tracking framework and designs Transformer-based feature modules ECA and CFA to replace the traditional intercorrelation modules [25]. This approach uses Transformer to design feature augmentation modules to improve the correlation operation and DiMP-based tracking algorithms [28]. This method explores the Temporal Transformer by adding a template update operation to the Transformer.

3 Method

Our tracker is shown in Fig. 1and consists of a backbone network, a feature fusion network and a prediction head. The backbone network is used to extract templates and search for regional features. The extracted features are fed into a feature fusion network to enhance and fuse the features. Finally, the prediction head performs binary classification and bounding box regression on the features to generate the final tracking results. During the training phase, using the SLT [11] training strategy fine-tuned the network.

3.1 Feature Extraction

As with the Siamese based tracker, our method takes a pair of image patches (template image patch $Z \in \mathrm{R}^{3 \times H_0 \times W_0}$ and search image patch $X \in \mathrm{R}^{3 \times H_0 \times W_0}$)

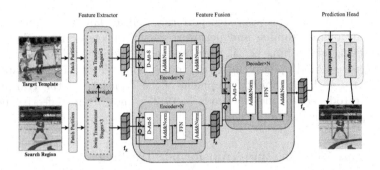

Fig. 1. Our algorithmic tracking framework. This framework consists of a feature extraction backbone network, a feature fusion model and a prediction head. The feature fusion model is constructed based on dual layer attention.

as input to the backbone network. Specifically, as shown in the Fig. 1, we use a modified Swin-Transformer [16] for feature extraction. In order to reduce the computational effort, we removed the final stage of the Swin-Transformer and used the output of the third stage as the output. Therefore, the step size is $s = 16$. The feature extraction network processes the template and search region to get their feature maps $\mathbf{F}_z \in \mathrm{R}^{C \times H \times W}$ and $\mathbf{F}_x \in \mathrm{R}^{C \times H \times W}$, $H = H_0/16, W = W_0/16, C = 384$.

3.2   Feature Fusion Network

We design a dual layer attention-based feature fusion network to enable effective augmentation and fusion of feature representations. Specifically, as shown in the Fig. 1, first, we use a 1×1 convolution to reduce the channel dimension of the feature F and then flatten the features in spatial dimension to obtain a set of feature vectors $\mathbf{f}_z \in \mathrm{R}^{d \times H \times W}$ and $\mathbf{f}_x \in \mathrm{R}^{d \times H \times W}$ of length d, $d = 256$. In the feature fusion network, a sequence of feature vectors is used as input to a template branch and a search branch. Dual layer attentional self-augment (DSA) module enhances feature with dual layer attentional adaptive attention to useful semantic contextual information. Dual layer attention cross-fusion (DCF) module receives two branch features, completes the information propagation and fusion augmentation of the two feature maps through dual layer attention, and then decodes a feature map $\mathbf{f} \in \mathrm{R}^{d \times H \times W}$. DSA and DCF are each repeates N times (we set N = 6 in this work).

Dual Layer Attention. Dual layer attention is an important part of designing feature fusion modules. As shown in the Fig. 2, dual layer attention structure consists of an outer attention and an inner attention. The feature vector of the template or search region input to outer attention as queries $\mathbf{Q}^o$, keys $\mathbf{K}^o$ and values $\mathbf{V}^o$ and calculate the correlation Y between Q and K. And then Y input to inner attention as queries $\mathbf{Q}^I$, keys $\mathbf{K}^I$ and values $\mathbf{V}^I$ of inner attention. And then, the scale of Q and K is converted to $HW \times D$ after a linear transformation. And after normalisation, adding a sinusoidal position code gives it the ability

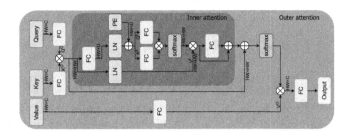

Fig. 2. Dual layer attention structure. The green area represents the outer attention and the purple area represents the inner attention. (Color figure online)

to differentiate spatial position information. We also normalize V to generate a normalized vector. Inner attention calculate to obtain a residual correlation map. Passing the residual correlation map back into outer attention. Outer attention adjusts the correlation between Q and K using inner attention in the form of residuals. Dual layer attention is described as Eq. 1

$$\text{DAttention}\left(\mathbf{Q}^o, \mathbf{K}^o, \mathbf{V}^o\right) = \left(\left(\text{Soft max }\left(\mathbf{Y} + InAttention\left(\mathbf{Y}\right)\right)\mathbf{V}^o\right)\mathbf{W}^o_o\right.$$

$$\text{IAttention}\left(\mathbf{Y}\right) = \left(Soft\max\left(\frac{\mathbf{Q}^I(\mathbf{K}^I)^{\mathrm{T}}}{\sqrt{d_{\mathbf{K}}}}\right)\mathbf{V}^I\right)\left(1 + \mathbf{W}^o_I\right) \tag{1}$$

where $\mathbf{W}^o_o$ and $\mathbf{W}^o_I$ are parameter matrices. Note that dual layer attention is divided into two structures, and inner attention is the same in both structures. The difference is that in the dual layer attention self-augmentation module, outer attention is self-attention. In the dual layer attention cross-fusion module, the outer attention is cross-attention.

Dual Layer Attention Self-augmentation. The DSA structure is shown as Encoder in Fig. 1. DSA uses dual layer attention in the form of residuals. DSA adjusts the correlation between queries and keys and adaptively integrates information from different locations of the feature map. And DSA uses a fully connected feedforward neural network (FFN) to enhance the fit of the model. We have added a spatial position encoding $p_x \in \mathrm{R}^{d \times N_x}$ generated using a sine function to give the attention mechanism the ability to distinguish between the position information of the input feature sequences. DSA is expressed as follows Eq. 2

$$\mathbf{X}_{DSA} = \tilde{\mathbf{X}}_{DSA} + \text{FFN}\left(\tilde{\mathbf{X}}_{DSA}\right)$$

$$\tilde{\mathbf{X}}_{DSA} = \mathbf{X} + \text{DAttention}\left(\mathbf{X} + \mathbf{P}_x, \mathbf{X} + \mathbf{P}_x, \mathbf{X}\right) \tag{2}$$

where $\mathbf{X} \in \mathrm{R}^{d \times N_x}$ is the spatial positional encodings and $\mathbf{X}_{DSA} \in \mathrm{R}^{d \times N_x}$ is the output of DSA.

Dual Layer Attention Cross-Fusion. The DCF structure is shown as Decoder in Fig. 1. Similar to the DSA structure, DCF fuses the two input feature vectors in the form of residuals using a dual layer attention and uses spatial location coding and an FFN module. DCF is expressed as follows Eq. 3

$$\mathbf{X}_{DCF} = \tilde{\mathbf{X}}_{DCF} + \mathrm{FFN}\left(\tilde{\mathbf{X}}_{DCF}\right)$$

$$\tilde{\mathbf{X}}_{DCF} = \mathbf{X}_q + D\mathit{Attention}\left(\mathbf{X}_q + \mathbf{P}_q, \mathbf{X}_{kv} + \mathbf{P}_{kv}, \mathbf{X}_{kv}\right) \tag{3}$$

where $\mathbf{X}_q \in \mathbb{R}^{d \times N_x}$ or $\mathbf{X}_{kv} \in \mathbb{R}^{d \times N_x}$ represents the input to the template or search branch and $p_q \in \mathbb{R}^{d \times N_x}$ or $p_{kv} \in \mathbb{R}^{d \times N_x}$ represents the spatial location code corresponding to it. $\mathbf{X}_{DCF} \in \mathbb{R}^{d \times N_x}$ is the output of DCF.

3.3 Prediction Head Network

The prediction head consists of a classification branch and a regression branch. Each branch consists of a three-layer perceptron of hidden dimension d and a ReLU activation function. To make our whole tracking framework more concise, we predict normalized coordinates directly, discarding anchor points and anchor frames based on a priori knowledge. The prediction head directly predicts the feature vectors $\mathbf{f} \in \mathbb{R}^{d \times H \times W}$ generated by the feature fusion network to obtain the classification results of the foreground/background and the normalised coordinates of the search region.

3.4 Training Loss

Prediction head receives feature vectors and outputs binary classification results and regression results. We use the feature vector predictions corresponding to the pixels in the goundtruth bounding box as positive samples and the rest as negative samples. Positive samples can lead to classification loss and regression loss, negative samples can lead to classification loss and we reduce the negative samples by a factor of 16. The classification loss uses the standard binary cross-entropy loss, which is expressed as follows Eq. 4

$$\mathcal{L}_{cls} = -\sum_j \left[y_j \log\left(p_j\right) + (1 - y_j) \log\left(1 - p_j\right)\right] \tag{4}$$

where y_j denotes the true bounding box of the j-th sample, $y_j = 1$ denotes the foreground, and p_j denotes the probability of belonging to the foreground as predicted by the model.

The regression loss uses a linear combination of L1 loss and Giou loss [22], which is expressed as follows Eq. 5

$$\mathcal{L}_{reg} = \sum_j 1_{\{y_j=1\}} \left[\lambda_G \mathcal{L}_{GIoU}\left(b_j, \hat{b}\right) + \lambda_1 \mathcal{L}_1\left(b_j, \hat{b}\right)\right] \tag{5}$$

where $y_j = 1$ denotes a positive sample, b_j denotes the j-th predicted bounding box, $\hat{b}$ denotes the normalized true bounding box, λ_G and λ_1 denote the regularization parameters, which are set to $\lambda_G = 2$ and $\lambda_1 = 5$ in the experiment.

4   Experiments

4.1   Implementation Details

Our tracking framework is implemented using Python 3.7 and PyTorch 1.11.0. The training are conducted on a server with four 48GB RTX A6000 GPUs with the batch size of 128.

Offline Training. We train the model in two stages. The size of the template and search area patches is set to 256×256. In the first stage, we train the model using the COCO [15], TrackingNet [21], LaSOT [4] and GOT-10k [8] datasets and scale up the COCO dataset using data augmentation methods such as panning. We trained the model using AdamW [17]. The learning rate of the backbone network is 1e-5 and the other parameters is 1e-4 and the weights decay to 1e-4. We train 300 epochs and after 210 epochs the learning rate decreases by a factor of 10. In the second stage, we draw on sequence-level training methods (SLT is described in detail in paper [11].) to fine-tune the model using the LaSOT, TrackingNet and GOT-10k datasets, training a total of 120 epochs.

Online Tracking. We follow the common scheme of the Siamese tracker. During the tracking process, prediction head outputs 1024 bounding boxes containing confidence scores and then uses the Hanning window of size 1616 to process the confidence scores. The final score can be defined as Eq. 6

$$score_\omega = (1 - \omega) \times score + \omega \times score_h \tag{6}$$

where score(score) is the original score output by the tracker, scoreh(scoreh) is the value of the corresponding position on the Hanning window, ω is set to 0.49. Based on the window penalty, the confidence of the feature points in the previous frame that are far away from the target will be penalized. Finally we select the prediction box with the highest confidence score as the tracking result.

4.2   Evaluation on Datasets

We validate the effectiveness of our proposed algorithm by a one-time evaluation (OPE) on the TrackingNet, LaSOT, UAV123 and NFS datasets. We compared our experimental results with nine currently representative target tracking algorithms. We give detailed results for success (AUC%), precision (P%) and normalised precision (NP%), where "-" indicates that the experimental results are not given in the original text.

TrackingNet [21]. TrackingNet is a large-scale target tracking dataset covering a wide range of scenarios in natural scenes, including various frame rates, resolutions, contextual scenes and target categories containing 30643 video clips, divided into a training set and a test set. We submitted our algorithm tracking results to the official online evaluation server and reported AUC, NP and P. As shown in Table 1, our tracker results for AUC, NP and P were 82.0, 87.4 and 80.7. Compared with other algorithms, our algorithm results show a strong competitive edge, which is the improvement brought by the dual layer attention module. The ability to achieve better metrics on a large-scale dataset such as TrackingNet proves that our algorithm is able to cope with a wide range of complex and challenging scenarios with strong generalisation capabilities.

Table 1. Tracking results on TrackingNet, LaSOT, UAV123 and NFS dataset.

Methods	TrackingNet			LaSOT			UAV123	NFS
	AUC%	NP%	P%	AUC%	NP%	P%	AUC%	AUC%
SiamFC	57.1	66.3	53.3	33.6	42.0	33.9	49.8	37.7
SiamFC++	75.4	80.0	70.5	54.4	62.3	54.7	–	–
SiamRPN++	73.3	80.0	69.4	49.6	56.9	49.1	61.3	50.2
C-RPN	66.9	74.6	61.9	45.9	–	–	–	–
DiMP50	74.0	80.1	68.7	56.9	65.0	56.7	65.3	62.0
ToMP50	81.2	86.2	78.6	67.6	–	–	69.0	66.9
TrSiam	78.1	82.9	72.7	62.4	–	60.0	67.4	65.8
StarkST50	81.3	78.1	86.1	66.4	76.3	71.2	69.1	65.2
TransT	81.4	86.7	80.3	64.9	73.8	69.0	69.1	65.7
Ours	82.0	87.4	80.7	68.0	77.2	72.3	69.5	66.5

LaSOT [4]. LaSOT is a large scale, high quality target tracking dataset which contains 1120 training sequences and 280 test sequences. As shown in Table 1, We show the results of the trace comparison with other algorithms, and that our algorithm achieves optimality in all three evaluation metrics compared to other algorithms, reaching 68.0, 77.2 and 72.3. In addition, as shown in Table 2, we give separate comparison results with other representative algorithms on 14 different challenge attributes (including light variation (IV), deformation (DEF), etc.), all of which were achieved optimally. It can thus be demonstrated that our algorithm can cope with the challenges of various complex scenarios. Thus, our design of a dual layer attention can effectively improve the accuracy of the attention mechanism in computing similarity and equip the algorithm to cope with a variety of complex scenarios.

UAV123 [20] **and NFS** [10]. UAV123 is a collection of 123 fully annotated HD video datasets captured from the perspective of low-altitude drones, consisting of 103 stabilised video sequences, 12 unstabiliser video sequences and 8 composite sequences. The NFS is a sequence of 100 videos captured from real world scenes by the higher frame rate cameras now commonly used, incorporating challenges such as lighting changes. As shown in Table 1, we show the results of the trace comparison with other algorithms. Except for being slightly lower than ToMP on the NFS dataset, our algorithm achieves optimality on two datasets with 9.5 and 66.5 respectively. And our algorithm runs at 35FPS and therefore has greater potential for real-world application scenarios.

OTB2015 [26]. OTB2015 is a tracking dataset containing 100 fully annotated sequences. Each video sequence in the dataset is annotated with attributes, including challenging attributes such as occlusion, non-rigid object distortion and motion blur. As shown in Fig. 3, in order to demonstrate the robustness of our method in complex scenarios such as target deformation, occlusion, similar object confusion and fast movement, we selected three representative video sequences in

Table 2. Tracking results of different attributes on LaSOT dataset.

	C-RPN	SiamRPN++	DiMP50	TrSiam	TransT	Ours
Illumination Variation	48.7	52.8	57.7	63.6	65.2	69.0
Deformation	47.9	52.9	57.4	63.7	67.0	69.2
Rotation	43.8	48.3	54.9	61.9	64.3	67.4
Background Clutter	40.9	44.9	50.1	54.8	57.9	62.2
Aspect Ratio Change	43.5	47.1	55.8	61.1	63.2	66.4
Scale Variation	45.2	49.4	56.0	62.4	64.6	67.2
Viewpoint Change	40.5	45.4	55.3	60.6	62.6	65.5
Fast Motion	29.0	31.9	46.7	49.9	51.0	54.7
Low Resolution	35.5	38.7	51.0	55.8	56.4	60.4
Full Occlusion	34.8	37.4	49.5	54.2	55.3	59.1
Camera Motion	48.2	52.1	60.6	65.5	67.2	69.8
Motion Blur	41.3	44.8	55.9	61.0	63.0	64.1
Partial Occlusion	43.2	46.5	53.7	59.9	62.0	65.0
Out-of-View	36.5	40.6	51.8	58.9	58.6	61.6

the OTB2015 dataset, namely biker, motor-rolling and singer sequences. As can be seen from the figure, our approach has a clear advantage over other algorithms in dealing with the various challenges.

4.3 Ablation Study

To verify the effectiveness of our propose method, we conduct ablation experiments on the LaSOT dataset and show the results of AUC and NP, the specific ablation experimental results are shown in Table 3. For the sake of fairness of the experimental results, the training methods of the variants we design and the algorithms in this paper are identical.

Table 3. Tracking results on NFS and UAV123 dataset.

Methods	AUC%	NP%
DATrack	68.1	77.2
Model1	66.9	76.3
Model2	67.4	76.6

Compared with Traditional Attention. To demonstrate the effectiveness of our design for dual layer attention, we design different variants, where DATrack is our algorithm.

Fig. 3. Visualisation of tracking results. Red for our method, green for groundtruth, black for SiamFC method and blue for SiamRPN method. (Color figure online)

Model 1 represents the replacement of dual layer attention with traditional attention in the dual layer attention self-augmentation module. As shown in Table 3, the results of the comparison between Model 1 and DATrack showed that the use of dual layer attention self-augmentation module was better than the traditional attention self-augmentation, with a 1% and 1% improvement in AUC and NP. It can be demonstrated that the dual layer attention structure we designed can work effectively in the self-augmentation phase of the features, allowing the feature representation of the target to be effectively augment.

Model 2 represents the replacement of the dual layer attention in the dual layer attention cross-fusion module with traditional attention. As shown in Table 3, from the comparison results of Model 2 and DAtrack, the fusion module using dual layer attention can propagate the feature information of the template frame more accurately and efficiently than traditional attention, making the target features of the search frame more accurate.

Combining the experimental results of Model 1 and Model 2, it can be demonstrated that the dual layer attention module plays an important role both in the self augmentation and cross fusion phases of the features.

5   Conclusions

We propose a simple and efficient dual layer attention-based target tracking algorithm, and design a dual layer attention self augment module and a dual layer attention cross-fusion module. The dual layer attention uses inner attention to adjust the correlation calculated by outer attention, removing noise from the calculation process and making the correlation more accurate as a way to achieve better augmentation and fusion of features. Broad experiments demonstrate the effectiveness of our proposed method, which effectively improves tracking performance, and our tracker has great potential to track up to 35FPS in end-to-end tracking situations, enabling real-time tracking.

Acknowledgements. This work was supported by the National Natural Science Foundation of China under Grant U20A20200 and 62273339, in part by the Youth Innovation Promotion Association of the Chinese Academy of Sciences under Grant 2019203.

References

1. Bertinetto, L., Valmadre, J., Henriques, J.F., Vedaldi, A., Torr, P.H.S.: Fully-convolutional Siamese networks for object tracking. In: Hua, G., Jégou, H. (eds.) ECCV 2016. LNCS, vol. 9914, pp. 850–865. Springer, Cham (2016). https://doi.org/10.1007/978-3-319-48881-3_56
2. Bhat, G., Danelljan, M., Gool, L.V., Timofte, R.: Learning discriminative model prediction for tracking. In: Proceedings of the IEEE/CVF International Conference on Computer Vision, pp. 6182–6191 (2019)
3. Chen, X., Yan, B., Zhu, J., Wang, D., Yang, X., Lu, H.: Transformer tracking. In: Proceedings of the IEEE/CVF Conference on Computer Vision and Pattern Recognition, pp. 8126–8135 (2021)
4. Fan, H., et al.: Lasot: a high-quality benchmark for large-scale single object tracking. In: Proceedings of the IEEE/CVF Conference on Computer Vision and Pattern Recognition, pp. 5374–5383 (2019)
5. Fan, H., Ling, H.: Siamese cascaded region proposal networks for real-time visual tracking. In: Proceedings of the IEEE/CVF Conference on Computer Vision and Pattern Recognition, pp. 7952–7961 (2019)
6. Henschel, R., Zou, Y., Rosenhahn, B.: Multiple people tracking using body and joint detections. In: Proceedings of the IEEE/CVF Conference on Computer Vision and Pattern Recognition Workshops (2019)
7. Hu, H.N., et al.: Joint monocular 3d vehicle detection and tracking. In: Proceedings of the IEEE/CVF International Conference on Computer Vision, pp. 5390–5399 (2019)
8. Huang, L., Zhao, X., Huang, K.: Got-10k: a large high-diversity benchmark for generic object tracking in the wild. IEEE Trans. Pattern Anal. Mach. Intell. **43**(5), 1562–1577 (2019)
9. Javed, S., Danelljan, M., Khan, F.S., Khan, M.H., Felsberg, M., Matas, J.: Visual object tracking with discriminative filters and siamese networks: a survey and outlook. IEEE Trans. Pattern Anal. Mach. Intell. (2022)
10. Kiani Galoogahi, H., Fagg, A., Huang, C., Ramanan, D., Lucey, S.: Need for speed: a benchmark for higher frame rate object tracking. In: Proceedings of the IEEE International Conference on Computer Vision, pp. 1125–1134 (2017)
11. Kim, M., Lee, S., Ok, J., Han, B., Cho, M.: Towards sequence-level training for visual tracking. In: Computer Vision-ECCV 2022: 17th European Conference, Tel Aviv, Israel, 23–27 October 2022, Proceedings, Part XXII, pp. 534–551. Springer (2022)
12. Lee, K.H., Hwang, J.N.: On-road pedestrian tracking across multiple driving recorders. IEEE T Multim. **17**(9), 1429–1438 (2015)
13. Li, B., Wu, W., Wang, Q., Zhang, F., Xing, J., Yan, J.: Siamrpn++: evolution of Siamese visual tracking with very deep networks. In: Proceedings of the IEEE/CVF Conference on Computer Vision and Pattern Recognition, pp. 4282–4291 (2019)
14. Li, B., Yan, J., Wu, W., Zhu, Z., Hu, X.: High performance visual tracking with Siamese region proposal network. In: Proceedings of the IEEE Conference on Computer Vision and Pattern Recognition, pp. 8971–8980 (2018)

15. Lin, T.-Y., et al.: Microsoft COCO: common objects in context. In: Fleet, D., Pajdla, T., Schiele, B., Tuytelaars, T. (eds.) ECCV 2014. LNCS, vol. 8693, pp. 740–755. Springer, Cham (2014). https://doi.org/10.1007/978-3-319-10602-1_48
16. Liu, Z., et al.: Swin transformer: hierarchical vision transformer using shifted windows. In: Proceedings of the IEEE/CVF International Conference on Computer Vision, pp. 10012–10022 (2021)
17. Loshchilov, I., Hutter, F.: Decoupled weight decay regularization. arXiv preprint arXiv:1711.05101 (2017)
18. Marvasti-Zadeh, S.M., Cheng, L., Ghanei-Yakhdan, H., Kasaei, S.: Deep learning for visual tracking: a comprehensive survey. IEEE Trans. Intell. Transp. Syst. (2021)
19. Mayer, C., et al.: Transforming model prediction for tracking. In: Proceedings of the IEEE/CVF Conference on Computer Vision and Pattern Recognition, pp. 8731–8740 (2022)
20. Mueller, M., Smith, N., Ghanem, B.: A benchmark and simulator for UAV tracking. In: Leibe, B., Matas, J., Sebe, N., Welling, M. (eds.) ECCV 2016. LNCS, vol. 9905, pp. 445–461. Springer, Cham (2016). https://doi.org/10.1007/978-3-319-46448-0_27
21. Muller, M., Bibi, A., Giancola, S., Alsubaihi, S., Ghanem, B.: Trackingnet: a large-scale dataset and benchmark for object tracking in the wild. In: Proceedings of the European Conference on Computer Vision (ECCV), pp. 300–317 (2018)
22. Rezatofighi, H., Tsoi, N., Gwak, J., Sadeghian, A., Reid, I., Savarese, S.: Generalized intersection over union: a metric and a loss for bounding box regression. In: Proceedings of the IEEE/CVF Conference on Computer Vision and Pattern Recognition, pp. 658–666 (2019)
23. Tao, R., Gavves, E., Smeulders, A.W.: Siamese instance search for tracking. In: Proceedings of the IEEE Conference on Computer Vision and Pattern Recognition, pp. 1420–1429 (2016)
24. Vaswani, A., et al.: Attention is all you need. Adv. Neural Inf. Process. Syst. **30** (2017)
25. Wang, N., Zhou, W., Wang, J., Li, H.: Transformer meets tracker: exploiting temporal context for robust visual tracking. In: Proceedings of the IEEE/CVF Conference on Computer Vision and Pattern Recognition, pp. 1571–1580 (2021)
26. Wu, Y., Lim, J., Yang, M.H.: Object tracking benchmark. IEEE Trans. Pattern Anal. Mach. Intell. **37**(9), 1834–1848 (2015)
27. Xu, Y., Wang, Z., Li, Z., Yuan, Y., Yu, G.: Siamfc++: towards robust and accurate visual tracking with target estimation guidelines. In: Proceedings of the AAAI Conference on Artificial Intelligence, vol. 34, pp. 12549–12556 (2020)
28. Yan, B., Peng, H., Fu, J., Wang, D., Lu, H.: Learning spatio-temporal transformer for visual tracking. In: Proceedings of the IEEE/CVF International Conference on Computer Vision, pp. 10448–10457 (2021)

Realtime 3D Reconstruction at Scale and Object Pose Estimation for Bin Picking System

Nianfeng Wang[✉], Weida Lin, Junye Lin, and Xianmin Zhang

Guangdong Key Laboratory of Precision Equipment and Manufacturing Technology, School of Mechanical and Automotive Engineering, South China University of Technology, Guangzhou 510641, China
menfwang@scut.edu.cn

Abstract. Obtaining high-precision, real-time 3D data of the scene surface is beneficial in many fields. As 3D reconstruction technology develops, the 6D pose estimation algorithm based on 3D point cloud data is widely used in bin picking systems. This paper presents a real-time 3D reconstruction and object pose estimation method for bin picking, and builds a robot grasping system, which mainly consists of the following aspects: 1) A GPU-based dense 3D point cloud reconstruction method is proposed for the sorting scenes. 2) An improved PPF object recognition algorithm is proposed, including optimization steps such as preprocessing, model feature construction, and positional result optimization. In addition, an improved voting weight and a composite index based on distance and normal vector are proposed. The final experiment verifies that the reconstruction and object recognition algorithm of this paper achieves better application results.

Keywords: 3D reconstruction · bin picking · 6D pose estimation · robot grasping system

1 Introduction

Robotic arm grasping is an important research topic in robotic automation and has a wide range of applications in sorting, assembly, loading, welding, and painting. The uncertainty of the spatial position of the object target, the low resolution of the acquired point cloud, the slow reconstruction speed, the complexity of the scene, and the occlusion increase the difficulty of the robotic arm to grasp the object target. This poses a serious challenge to existing robotic arm sorting technology.

With the rapid development of 3D vision technologies such as TOF, structured light, and LIDAR, 3D point clouds are becoming more accessible, and 3D vision systems are being used in more and more fields. Object recognition is one of the classic problems in robotics and machine vision. The problem of

H. Yang et al. (Eds.): ICIRA 2023, LNAI 14268, pp. 15–26, 2023.
https://doi.org/10.1007/978-981-99-6486-4_2

accurately locating the position and pose of objects in cluttered and occluded scenes has attracted the attention of many researchers. The RANSAC method [1] can be used to identify predefined geometries, using random sampling, to determine the interior and outlier points of the target model. LINEMOD features [2] fuse RGBD and normal information to achieve bit-pose calculation in occluded and cluttered scenes and solve the problem of texture-free target recognition. The 3DSC (3D shape contexts) algorithm [3] creates a 3D spherical grid at key points and generates feature vectors by calculating the weighted values of the votes within the grid. The FPFH feature description [4] uses the spatial feature histogram between neighboring points as the local surface descriptor and accelerates the computation process by weighting the computation and decomposing the array. The SHOT descriptor [5] combines histograms and identification marks, divides the neighborhood into blocks, and generates a local histogram in each block. The VFH method [6] extends the ideas and features of the FPFH method by introducing an additional viewpoint variance to fuse the viewpoint orientation with the surface shape. The CVFH method [7] optimizes the VFH method and applies the region growth algorithm to obtain a stable target region.

ICP matching [8] is a rigid matching algorithm that matches based on the location of points and has a high-accuracy matching performance. The Point Pair Feature (PPF) method [9] combines the respective advantages of local and global features for point pair feature construction, which is a model-based point cloud feature descriptor that uses a large number of point pair features, enhances the capability of point cloud feature description by feature stacking and combining, and applies a Hoff voting scheme. Many researchers have tried to use it for various types of object recognition. The performance of the original four-dimensional PPF and its optimization is discussed in the literature [10] and compared with other 3D feature description methods. The literature [11] proposes a PPF-based 6-degree-of-freedom pose estimation method for a robotic sorting task that uses adaptive threshold segmentation matching to accelerate target recognition and matching. For the visibility problem of PPF features, the literature [12] uses the rendering of models from different viewpoints to generate stable visible point pairs features. The literature [13] uses points on surfaces and geometric edges to estimate planar industrial targets, and this algorithm provides higher recognition rates and faster speeds than the original PPF. This paper presents a real-time large-scale 3D reconstruction and target pose estimation system for robot sorting.

2 Realtime Structured Light Reconstruction

2.1 GPU's and Parallel Processing Pipelines

As the number of structured light projected images increases, the number of pixels for reconstruction processing also increases. In this paper, 22 images need to be captured to reconstruct the scene. Reconstruction of large-scale point clouds using traditional CPU serial computing has limitations in time and efficiency and cannot meet the industrial requirements of real-time. This paper investigates the acceleration method of the GPU parallel approach based on CUDA programming to achieve the acceleration of the dense point cloud processing algorithm. Compared with CPU serial computing, the parallelized acceleration of GPU can significantly reduce the running time of the reconstruction algorithm and improve the efficiency and feasibility of the algorithm in industrial applications.

The overall flow of the algorithm based on GPU parallelization in this paper is shown in Fig. 1. All the algorithms of 3D reconstruction are run on the GPU, including the decoding core function, the coordinate calculation core function, and the denoising core function. The main function is run on the CPU platform, including allocating memory, copying data, and releasing memory. This 3D reconstruction algorithm and program have good parallel optimization performance.

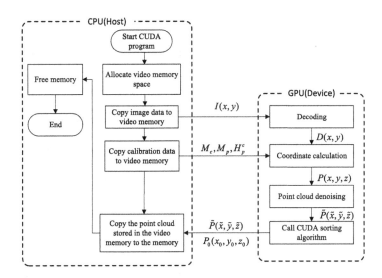

Fig. 1. Flow chart of GPU parallelized 3D reconstruction algorithm.

In this paper, the 3D point cloud is spatially gridded, and outlier points are determined based on the number of point clouds in the grids where the points are located and the surrounding grids, as shown in Fig. 2. In order to speed up the hash search process on the GPU, this paper optimizes the hash array design for parallelization. For the problem that different points have the same hash value, this paper creates four auxiliary arrays in addition to the original hash array: the no-repeat hash array, the data index array, the starting hash index array, and the ending hash index array.

2.2   3D Reconstruction Algorithm Performance Test

To verify the efficiency of the GPU-accelerated 3D reconstruction algorithm, point cloud reconstruction experiments are conducted for ROI regions of different image sizes, and the number of reconstructed point clouds approximates the

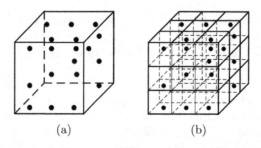

(a)   (b)

Fig. 2. Point cloud space grid structure. (a) point cloud; (b) grid structure.

number of pixels in the ROI region. The input images are 11-bit coded patterns, and each bit pattern contains both positive and negative images, totaling 22 images. The same algorithm is also run on the CPU platform for comparison, and the experimental comparison results are shown in Table 1.

Table 1. CPU and GPU Algorithm Time Comparison

ROI	Platform	Memory copy time (ms)	Decoding time (ms)	Coordinate calculation time (ms)	Total time (ms)	Acceleration ratio
600×400	CPU	\	44	8.7	52.7	1.67
	GPU	29.5	2	0.1	31.6	
1200×800	CPU	\	78	26	104	3.16
	GPU	30	2.4	0.5	32.9	
1920×1200	CPU	\	191	134	325	9.26
	GPU	29	5.2	0.9	35.1	

The experimental results show that as the reconstructed ROI area increases, the algorithm processing time on the GPU platform does not change much. However, the algorithm processing time on the CPU platform increases significantly. When a larger image ROI area is selected for 3D reconstruction, the more pixel points are processed, the more pronounced the performance advantage of the GPU platform and the greater the algorithm speedup ratio. The experimental results show that the algorithm of this paper has a significant efficiency improvement in reconstructing large-scale point clouds, and the algorithm time is 35.1ms when reconstructing a point cloud of about 2 million. In contrast, the traditional CPU parallel algorithm takes 325ms, and the acceleration ratio of GPU reconstruction reaches about nine times.

In this paper, the reconstruction accuracy of the structured light system is tested using standard objects, and the experimental results are shown in Fig. 3. The Z-axis error of the structured light sensor and reconstruction algorithm designed and studied in this paper is less than 0.5mm, which can meet the requirements of industrial 3D reconstruction.

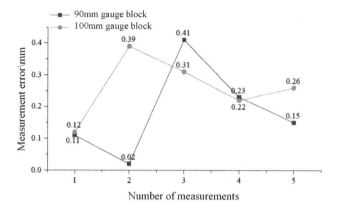

Fig. 3. Error distribution of precision test.

3   Object Pose Estimation Based on PPF

Based on the real-time 3D reconstruction of the scene, the target to be grasped must be accurately identified and located from the scene. The target recognition algorithm process proposed in this paper can be divided into offline training and online matching stages, as shown in Fig. 4. The offline stage uses the CAD model for feature extraction and training, and the online stage uses the point cloud of the scene for accurate object recognition of scattered stacked objects.

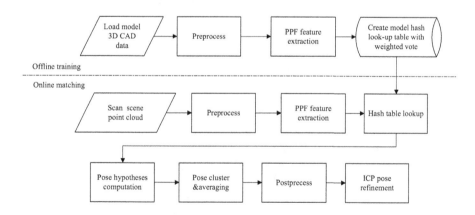

Fig. 4. Flow chart of target identification method.

3.1   Weighted Hough Voting Scheme

In the offline training phase of the original PPF algorithm, all point pair features of the model are extracted and stored in a hash table to create a global model point pair feature. However, this offline global model feature computation will contain redundant point pair features that do not appear in the scene. This paper performs offline training based on model visibility from different perspectives to address this situation. The visibility of the object point cloud is affected by the observation point of view and the shape of the object itself. This paper adopts the way of setting the virtual camera to compute the point cloud visibility, setting the virtual camera from different viewpoints and then observing the point cloud, as shown in Fig. 5.

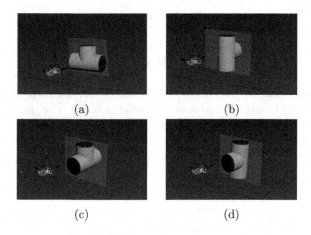

(a)   (b)

(c)   (d)

Fig. 5. Rendering of models by virtual cameras with different perspectives.

In the original PPF method, all model feature points are assigned the same vote value, which is unreasonable because some model points contain more feature information and have greater discriminative power. Point pairs that contain more information should be assigned more weights. For industrial objects composed of planes, the original PPF feature is not suitable for matching because the planar objects have insufficient DOF. Pairs of points in the plane have the same PPF value, as shown in Fig. 6, resulting in erroneous results for the generated poses.

In order to perform accurate model point-pair-feature calculations, it is necessary to reduce the flat voting weight of the surface feature. Defining two points' normal vectors n_1 and n_2, and the voting weight w of the point-pair-feature based on the consistency of the normal vectors is defined by Eq. (1):

$$w = 1 - \lambda |\boldsymbol{n_1} \cdot \boldsymbol{n_2}|. \tag{1}$$

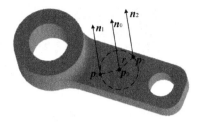

Fig. 6. Pairs of points in the plane have the same PPF eigenvalue.

3.2   Postprocessing

With the pose-clustering and sorting methods, the most likely recognition results can be filtered, and the number of votes received by the poses can be used as a scoring condition for the credibility of the pose results. However, the votes of pose clustering may not accurately represent the matching degree between model objects and scenes. Some wrong poses get high votes, while the correct ones get lower votes. At the same time, there will be a loss of efficiency if ICP finely matches all poses. The matching degree of the positional results is usually measured by the distance approximation of the model point cloud to the field point cloud after the positional transformation. However, this distance-based method has some limitations because the matching of point clouds is not only the matching of spatial positions but also includes the alignment of normal vectors of the point cloud. For randomly stacked scenes, the point cloud of an object is incomplete due to the presence of occlusion, and this occlusion reduces the accuracy of distance scoring.

In this paper, we propose an evaluation method based on the accuracy of distance and normal vector matching. Given a scene point cloud S and a model point cloud M after a position transformation, for each point $m_i \in M$ in the model point cloud M, search for the nearest point $s_i \in S$ in the scene point cloud S. The distance d_i between m_i and s_j can be expressed by Eq. (2):

$$d_i = \min\{\| \, m_i - s_j \, \|, m_i \in M, s_j \in S\}. \tag{2}$$

For a set of corresponding nearest neighbor pairs $c_i = (m_i, s_j)$, the normal vector similarity n_i of the m_i and s_j is defined by Eq. (3),

$$\eta_i = 1 - |n_i^m \cdot n_j^s|, \tag{3}$$

where n_i^m is the normal vector of m_i and n_j^s is the normal vector of s_j.

When the normal vectors n_i^m and n_j^s have the same direction, n_i will reach the minimum value. In summary, for a given pose result $P \in SE(3)$, its accuracy score of matching f_a is defined by Eq. (4),

$$f_a = \frac{1}{n} \sum_{i=1}^{n} \lambda d_i + \eta_i d_i, \tag{4}$$

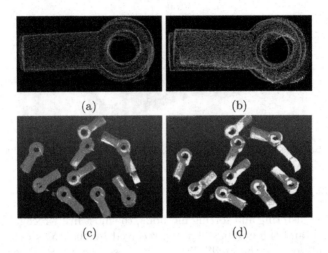

(a)   (b)

(c)   (d)

Fig. 7. Multi-instance filtering results. (a)–(b) different colors indicate duplicate poses results; (c) duplicate poses in the scene; (d) results after multi-instance filtering.

where n is the number of model point cloud and λ is the weighting factor. The smaller the accuracy error score f_a of the pose result, the higher the accuracy of target recognition is indicated. This error-scoring method has high accuracy and robustness for noisy and occluded point cloud data. After the accuracy error scoring of the poses, the poses with smaller f_a values can be selected as the matching results for subsequent ICP matching.

For a scattered stacked object sorting task, there will be multiple object instances in the environment, and it is necessary to distinguish the poses of multiple different object instances and remove the duplicate poses. The same object to be recognized will produce duplicate poses, as shown in Fig. 7. The best result for a single recognition process is the ability to recognize multiple instances in a scene. At the same time, it would be a waste of resources and time to perform fine alignment on all duplicate pose results. For each point m_i^1 in the position result p_1, find the nearest point m_i^2 in the position result p_2 and calculate the distance between m_i^1 and m_i^2. The distance between p_1 and p_2 is defined by Eq. (5),

$$dis = \frac{1}{n} \sum_{i=1}^{n} \left\| m_i^1 - m_i^2 \right\|, \tag{5}$$

where n is the number of model point cloud.

4   Experimental Results and Analysis

4.1   Data Set Object Recognition Results

Object recognition experiments are performed on the dataset, and in order to verify the effectiveness of the method in this paper, the experiments compare the original PPF method and the recognition method in this paper in terms of recognition rate and algorithm time, respectively (Tables 2 and 3).

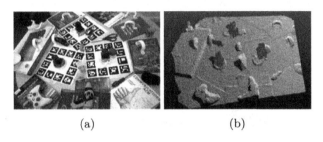

(a)   (b)

Fig. 8. Data set scene identification. (a) scenes to be recognized; (b) identification results.

Table 2. Data set experimental results

Methods	Recognition rate	Algorithm time (s)
Original PPF	98%	5.67
Our Approach	**98%**	**3.62**

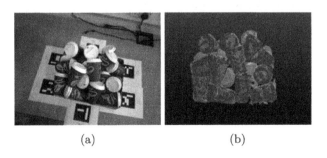

(a)   (b)

Fig. 9. Data set scene identification. (a) scenes to be recognized; (b) identification results.

Table 3. Data set experimental results

Methods	Recognition rate	Algorithm time (s)
Original PPF	76.1%	1.51
Our Approach	**82.6%**	**0.67**

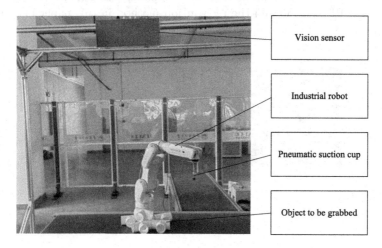

Fig. 10. Grabbing scene.

4.2 Actual Scene Reconstruction and Recognition Results

The vision-based robot arm grasping system consists of a structured light sensor, a robot, and a grasping actuation module. The system is divided into a structured light vision module, a point cloud processing module, and a grasping control module, as shown in Fig. 10.

To verify the effectiveness of the robot recognition and sorting system in this paper, sorting experiments are conducted for different objects and scenes. The experimental scenes are shown in Fig. 11, and the experimental results are shown in Table 4.

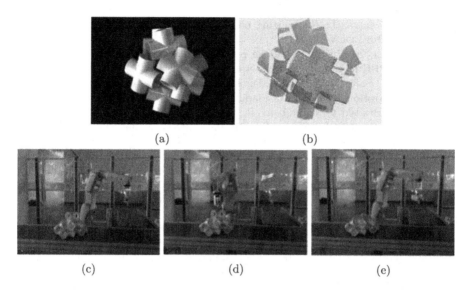

(a)   (b)

(c)   (d)   (e)

Fig. 11. Object recognition and robot sorting process in real scene. (a) actual captured image; (b) reconstructed point cloud and identification result; (c) scene of stacking objects; (d) robot moves to the grabbing position; (e) robot places object into the material frame.

Table 4. Actual scene experiment results

Object Type	Number of experiments	Number of failed recognitions	Number of failed grasps	Recognition success rate
Tee pipe	63	0	3	100
Four-way pipe	60	0	0	100
Oblique tee pipe	62	1	2	98.34
success rate				99.45

Acknowledgment. The authors would like to gratefully acknowledge the reviewers comments. This work is supported by National Natural Science Foundation of China (Grant No. 52075180), and the Fundamental Research Funds for the Central Universities.

References

1. Fischler, M.: Random sample consensus: a paradigm for model fitting with applications to image analysis and automated cartography. Commun. ACM **24** (1981)
2. Hinterstoisser, S., et al.: Model based training, detection and pose estimation of texture-less 3d objects in heavily cluttered scenes. In: Asian Conference on Computer Vision (2012)

3. Pajdla, T., Matas, J.: Recognizing objects in range data using regional point descriptors. In: ECCV (2004)
4. Zheng, L., Li, Z.: Virtual namesake point multi-source point cloud data fusion based on FPFH feature difference. Sensors **21**(16), 5441 (2021)
5. Tombari, F., Salti, S., Stefano, L.D.: Unique signatures of histograms for local surface description. Lect. Notes Comput. Sci. **6313**, 356–369 (2010)
6. Rusu, R.B., Bradski, G.R., Thibaux, R., Hsu, J.: Fast 3d recognition and pose using the viewpoint feature histogram. In: 2010 IEEE/RSJ International Conference on Intelligent Robots and Systems, 18–22 October 2010, Taipei, Taiwan (2010)
7. Fukatsu, R., Sakaguchi, K.: Automated driving with cooperative perception based on CVFH and millimeter-wave v2i communications for safe and efficient passing through intersections. Sensors **21**(17), 5854 (2021)
8. Fu, K., Liu, S., Luo, X., Wang, M.: Robust point cloud registration framework based on deep graph matching. In: Proceedings of the IEEE/CVF Conference on Computer Vision and Pattern Recognition, pp. 8893–8902 (2021)
9. Drost, B., Ulrich, M., Navab, N., Ilic, S.: Model globally, match locally: efficient and robust 3d object recognition. In: IEEE Computer Society Conference on Computer Vision and Pattern Recognition, vol. **2010**, pp. 998–1005. IEEE (2010)
10. Kiforenko, L., Drost, B., Tombari, F., Krüger, N., Buch, A.G.: A performance evaluation of point pair features. Comput. Vis. Image Underst. **166**, 66–80 (2018)
11. Yan, W., Xu, Z., Zhou, X., Su, Q., Li, S., Wu, H.: Fast object pose estimation using adaptive threshold for bin-picking. IEEE Access **8**, 63055–63064 (2020)
12. Li, D., Wang, H., Liu, N., Wang, X., Xu, J.: 3d object recognition and pose estimation from point cloud using stably observed point pair feature. IEEE Access **8**, 44335–44345 (2020)
13. Choi, C., Christensen, H.I.: 3d pose estimation of daily objects using an rgb-d camera. In: 2012 IEEE/RSJ International Conference on Intelligent Robots and Systems, pp. 3342–3349. IEEE (2012)

Large-Parallax Multi-camera Calibration Method for Indoor Wide-Baseline Scenes

Dongchen Wang[1(✉)], Jialing Liu[2], Xianglong Xu[1], Yubao Chen[1], Qingyang Hu[1], and Jianhua Zhang[1]

[1] School of Computer Science and Engineering, Tianjin University of Technology, Tianjin 300384, China
rontjut1209@hotmail.com

[2] College of Computer Science and Technology, Zhejiang University of Technology, Hangzhou, China

Abstract. Multi-camera calibration plays a crucial role in enabling efficient vision-based human-robot interaction and applications. This paper introduces a novel approach for multi-camera calibration, specifically tailored for indoor wide-baseline scenes, by leveraging 3D models. The task of multi-camera calibration in such scenarios is particularly challenging due to significant variations in camera perspectives. The limited and distant common view area of multiple cameras further exacerbates the difficulty in performing feature point matching. Traditional multi-camera calibration methods rely on matching 2D feature points, such as structure-from-motion, or employing large-area common view calibration plates, as seen in stereo camera calibration. In contrast, our proposed method eliminates the need for calibration boards or feature point pairs. Instead, we calibrate the external parameters of the multi-camera system by computing the optimal vanishing point through the extraction of orthogonal parallel lines within each camera's view. This approach begins by extracting orthogonal parallel lines from the image to establish an accurate indoor 3D model. Furthermore, we incorporate the easily obtainable camera height as a prior, enhancing the estimation of the transformation matrix among the cameras. Extensive experiments were conducted in both real and simulated environments to evaluate the performance of our method. The experimental results validate the superiority of our approach over manual marker-based structure-from-motion methods, establishing its effectiveness in multi-camera calibration.

Keywords: Wide-baseline · Multi-camera calibration · Vanishing point

1 Introduction

With the increasing demand for integrating multi-camera perspectives to enable vision-based human-robot interaction and applications, the market for multi-camera calibration technology is expanding. However, solving multi-camera poses is a challenge in scenarios with large parallax and wide baselines. To

H. Yang et al. (Eds.): ICIRA 2023, LNAI 14268, pp. 27–38, 2023.
https://doi.org/10.1007/978-981-99-6486-4_3

(a) match points   (b) extract lines

Fig. 1. Match points and extract lines.

address this, calibrating the internal parameters becomes necessary. We employ Zhang's calibration method [22], which requires only one calibration plate and provides high accuracy and robustness in obtaining camera internal parameters. Traditionally, camera pose estimation is accomplished using structure-from-motion (SFM) methods. These methods typically involve extracting key points using feature extraction algorithms such as SIFT [15]. Subsequently, the kd-tree model is utilized to match the feature points by calculating the Euclidean distance between them [11], thus obtaining point correspondences. Finally solve the camera pose [5] using multi-view geometry.

SFM methods are limited to scenes with small parallaxes and narrow baselines. Our goal is to tackle the 3D pose estimation problem in multi-camera networks that involve wide baselines and large parallaxes. In industrial environments, cameras are often static and sparsely distributed to save costs. This leads to significant parallax and wide baselines between camera views. In indoor settings like gymnasiums or lecture halls, SFM methods fail to perform well. As shown in Fig. 1, in (a), the points of the same color in the left and right figures represent matching points, wide-baseline camera networks face difficulties in detecting and matching feature points due to varying lighting conditions and textures across different camera viewpoints. In (b), the LSD algorithm remains effective in extracting orthogonal parallel lines. We leverage these lines to compute external parameters and project 3D points onto the graph, points of the same color are projections of the same 3D point. To address this, we consider placing the calibration board in the overlapping area of the cameras to provide image feature points during joint calibration. However, positioning such a calibration board can be challenging, and non-professionals may struggle to accurately record calibration data.

Perhaps, we can determine the camera pose based on the vanishing point in the image. Indoor scenes exhibit standard Manhattan world characteristics, Manhattan world is an idealized fictional world where objects and scenes follow right angles and grid structures, detecting line segments in the image is easier than matching features. As illustrated in Fig. 2, our method proceeds as follows: Firstly, given a set of images, we employ the method proposed by Lu [8] to extract and classify line segments. By cross-multiplying line segments, we can obtain the vanishing point. Arth [3] proposed that the vertical axis of the camera can be estimated using line segments, we estimate the pitch and roll angles using the

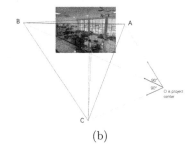

(a)   (b)

Fig. 2. Method overview: extracting orthogonal line segments to build indoor 3D model (a) and camera pose estimation with vanishing points (b).

vertical vanishing points. Next, by aligning the normal of the elevation with the vertical axis, we determine the horizontal vanishing point to estimate the yaw angle. To solve for the translation estimates, we utilize the indoor 3D model to determine vertical segments and corner points, which are then used to construct constraints. Point O represents the camera pose.

Based on the findings of J.M. [6], it is observed that the majority of indoor and outdoor (city) scenes adhere to a Manhattan three-dimensional grid structure. Our method assumes that the scene follows the standard Manhattan world configuration. Each facade of the scene contains extractable two-dimensional line segments, eliminating the need for additional features requiring calibration. We conducted experiments using both simulated and studio scenes to evaluate our approach. The results demonstrate that our method significantly outperforms SFM methods.

Our approach has several key advantages:

– We eliminate the need for a calibration board. Placing a calibration board in a large indoor scene, such as a swimming pool, can be challenging. It may require submerging the calibration board in water to ensure simultaneous viewing by two cameras. Moreover, obtaining a customized large calibration board increases costs, is inconvenient to transport, and is prone to deformation.
– Our approach reduces the need for matching a large number of feature points. In visually similar environments, matching feature points across multiple cameras becomes challenging. Instead, our method utilizes indoor 3D models and vanishing points, eliminating the requirement for feature point detection and matching.
– We conducted extensive experiments in both simulated and real scenes. The results demonstrate the high accuracy of our method.

2   Related Work

Although multi-camera calibration has been studied for over a decade, it remains a challenging problem. Existing multi-camera calibration methods can be categorized into two types. The first type is feature matching. Traditional methods typically rely on local features. For example, in the wide-baseline stereo pipeline, SIFT [15] (or BRIEF [14], ORB [19]) is used to extract local features. Recently, many deep learning methods (SuperPoint [9], UR2KiD [20], D2 net [10], LIFT [21]) employ neural networks to address the problem of feature point detection and description. There are also well-established methods that utilize semantic information [4,7] to solve the matching problem, and their accuracy in a general narrow-baseline setting is typically not low. However, our specific task presents challenges in matching feature points across multiple cameras using these methods.

The second type of method is an end-to-end solution, such as PoseNet [12]. These methods utilize convolutional neural networks for camera pose regression. They train the network using datasets from a standard SFM pipeline, extracting depth features and regressing camera poses from them. Since then, several papers have proposed methods to enhance PoseNet, including using different network architectures [17,18] and optimizing loss functions [12,13]. However, to the best of our knowledge, most end-to-end solutions do not surpass the geometric methods in terms of performance.

Since feature matching is challenging for multi-camera calibration in wide-baseline scenes, we try utilizing information from individual images to estimate the camera's external parameters relative to the world coordinate system. Antunes introduced a novel global approach for detecting vanishing points and sets of mutually orthogonal vanishing directions using line segments extracted from images of man-made environments [2]. We can leverage the orthogonal information in Manhattan world scenes to identify vanishing points. Arth proposed a method to estimate the absolute camera direction using straight line segments. They divided the façades in the input image into segments and matched them with the corresponding segments in the reference map to estimate camera displacement, resulting in an accurate and globally aligned camera pose [3]. In indoor environments, extracting orthogonal line segments is relatively straightforward based on the orthogonal information. Inspired by their work, we aim to construct indoor 3D models using indoor conditions and utilize orthogonal line segments to identify vanishing points for multi-camera calibration. This approach addresses the challenges associated with placing and matching calibration boards in complex indoor scenes.

3   Method

This section will describe our method in detail. In the initial stage of our experiment, for the internal reference matrix and distortion matrix, we use Zhang's [22] calibration method to directly calibrate. For the extrinsic parameters, We consider the use of calibration boards to provide feature descriptors to enable multi-camera calibration. Since the multi-camera network in our experimental scenes is stationary and sparse, this results in highly similar scenes from each camera's viewpoint but also very different viewpoints. Under such

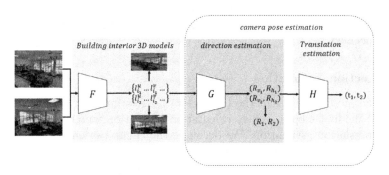

Fig. 3. System pipeline.

wide-baseline and large parallax conditions, our feature matching and extraction become very difficult, and the feature point descriptors extracted from the calibration plate have a large error.

To solve the problem of camera pose estimation in Large-parallax, wide-baseline scenes, we propose to use orthogonal vanishing points in the image to solve orientation and translation estimation. Figure 3 illustrates the flow of our algorithm, the system flow of our method, which consists of two modules: 1) building an indoor 3D model, 2) camera pose estimation. Where F function is line segment extraction and classification function, G is rotation estimation function, H is translation estimation function. l is line segment, R is the rotation estimate, t is translation estimation.

3.1 Building Indoor 3D Models

First, the first module of our method is to build indoor 3D models. To extract the orthogonal line segments on the indoor façade, we used the method of Lu. [16] to get the orthogonal line segment group in three directions. In order to ensure the accuracy of the line segment, we need to filter out the line segments that are not up to standard. Firstly, we have to filter out the line segments with excessive angular errors. In the group of three orthogonal line segments, we take the angle at which the directions of the line segments in the group are gathered to set the angle interval, and the line segments outside the angle interval are considered to have excessive angular error and removed. Secondly, We cannot determine the direction of relatively short line segments and cannot guarantee that they are suitable for us to calculate the vanishing point, so we specify a length threshold d and only keep line segments exceeding this threshold. Line segments that lie on the ground or soft objects will be removed. Filtered set of orthogonal line segments is the 2D information we use to build the indoor 3D models.

Then we have to get the 3D information for the indoor. We define the origin of a world coordinate system and define the directions of X, Y and Z (z-axis is the vertical direction). Finally, build an indoor 3D model based on the two-dimensional information extracted at the beginning and the coordinate system we specified.

3.2   Direction Estimation

The second module of our method is camera pose estimation. It is divided into two steps: the first step is camera orientation estimation, and the second step is camera translation estimation. We decouple the camera orientation estimation into two steps: Calculating the vertical rotation R_v (pitch and roll angles) and horizontal rotation R_h (yaw angle), Final rotation $R = R_v \cdot R_h$. We calculate R_v by aligning the vertical vanishing point with the z-axis of the world coordinate system, There are two specific steps. First step, we need to find the main vertical vanishing point p_v, which we dingo by taking the set of vertical line segments $\mathbf{l_v} = \{l_1^v, l_2^v, \ldots, l_n^v\}$, and Cross-multiplying their homogeneous coordinates to get the vanishing point p_{ij}.

$$p_{ij} = l_i \times l_j \ i, j \in (0, 1, \ldots n) \tag{1}$$

In the large parallax and wide-baseline environment, the adjacent lines on the image are quite different from the actual world coordinate system. The extracted vertical line segments, which are not exactly parallel to the Real-world coordinate system, can negatively affect the Manhattan world model. In order to suppress the influence of this error on the calculation of the position of the vertical vanishing point, for every vertical vanishing point p_{ij}, calculate the error between every vanishing point and other perpendicular lines l_o. The specific calculation is as follows:

$$err\,(p_{ij}, l_o) = \arccos \left(\frac{p_{ij} \cdot l_o}{(\|p_{ij}\| \cdot \|l_o\|)} \right) \ (o \neq i, j) \tag{2}$$

where p_{ij} is each vertical vanishing point, l_o is all vertical line segments except l_i and l_j, We use the arc cosine function to calculate the angle and set the angle error threshold D_v. As long as the value of $err(p_i, l_i)$ is less than the D_v, Then we add one to the weight of p_{ij} as the interior point. Finally, the p_{ij} with the greatest weight is chosen as the primary vertical vanishing point p_{vimg}. Then translate p_{vimg} to the camera coordinates system $p_v = K^{-1} \cdot p_{vimg}$, and normalize it. We specify the direction of vertical in the world coordinate system is $z = \begin{bmatrix} 0 & 0 & 1 \end{bmatrix}^T$.

The main vertical vanishing point p_v is aligned with the z-axis of the world coordinate system by crossing p_v with z, where the rotation axis is $u = z \times p_v$ and the rotation angle is $\theta = \arccos(u)$. Finally, the rotation matrix is obtained by Lee algebra to Lee Group:

$$R_v = exp_{SO(3)} \left(u \cdot \frac{\theta}{\|u\|} \right) \tag{3}$$

Next we calculate R_h, We take a horizontal line l_r and a vertical line l_h on the façade f. if there are multiple façades, take multiple pairs of horizontal and vertical lines. We cross-multiplying l_r and l_h to get façade normal vector n_f.

$$n_f = l_r \times l_h \tag{4}$$

Then we normalize n_f, cross-multiplying n_f and the vertical axis z. The result of the multiplication is the horizontal vanishing point p_h of the façade f:

$$p_h = n_f \times z \tag{5}$$

Then we traverse the set of horizontal line segments $l_h = \{l_1^h, l_2^h, \ldots, l_n^h\}$ on the façade f. We use the rotation matrix R_v to correct the direction of these horizontal lines, Get the corresponding three-dimensional horizontal line $l_{3D}^h = R_v^T l_n^h$, The set of horizontal lines l_h on the façade f is corrected in direction by R_v, intersects p_v. the l_{3D}^h obtained here consists of the Three-dimensional coordinates of the two endpoints. The cross product of the two endpoints $l_3 = l_{3_{end}} \times l_{3_{st}}$ to obtain the expression of this line. Next, calculate the rotation matrix R_h around the vertical axis, and align the horizontal axis of the camera with the horizontal vanishing point p_h.

R_h has one degree of freedom in rotation, ϕ_z. We make $a = \tan\frac{\phi_z}{2}$. We parameterize the solution of the rotation matrix according to the linear formula:

$$R_h = \frac{1}{1 + a^2} M \tag{6}$$

By separating the coefficients of the rotation matrix Rh, we define the matrix M:

$$M = \begin{bmatrix} 1 - a^2 & -2a & 0 \\ 2a & 1 - a^2 & 0 \\ 0 & 0 & 1 + a^2 \end{bmatrix} \tag{7}$$

where the root of a has two solutions, leading to two possible rotations. We choose a rotation that satisfies the alignment of the camera's orientation vector with the inverse normal $-n_f$.

The horizontal vanishing point p_h should be on the Three-dimensional horizontal line l_{3D}^h corrected by R_h. Therefore, We remove irrelevant coefficients, the intersection constraint between l_{3D}^h and the horizontal vanishing point p_h is as follows:

$$p_h \cdot \left(M \cdot l_{3D}^h \right) = 0 \tag{8}$$

Each horizontal line can be used to calculate R_h once, and using the constraint, the angular error evaluation is done with R_h and the set of horizontal line segments in the façade. Here we set the angle error threshold D_h, and when the angle error meets the threshold, we increase the current R_h's as the weight of the final result. Finally, we find the R_h with the largest weight. The rotation matrix R is decomposed into three components: R_y, R_p, and R_r. By aligning the vertical axes, R_v is obtained, which includes R_p and R_r. And Rh corresponds to R_y. Therefore, based on Eq. (9), R is calculated.

$$R = R_v \cdot R_h \tag{9}$$

3.3   Translation Estimation

The translation of the camera in the world coordinate system can be estimated from the vertical line segments on the façade. This step is detailed below.

When building the indoor 3D model, we already defined the origin of the world coordinate system. The coordinates of the line segment in the façade can be obtained from the indoor 3D model. We select two vertical line segments. Then we take the angular points on these line segments and establish constraints on the points on the line to estimate the camera translations. The height of the camera is easy to obtain. We set translation estimation $t = [t_x, t_y, t_z]$, where t_z is the camera height, it can be obtained from the indoor 3D model. We define the translation from the world coordinate system to the camera coordinate system as t_r, as shown in Eq. (10).

$$t_r = -R^{-1} \cdot t \tag{10}$$

Finally, based on Eq. (11), we construct an optimization problem and solve it by Ceres [1] to obtain high-precision translation t_r.

$$\begin{cases} l_1 \cdot (p_1 + t_r) = 0 \\ l_2 \cdot (p_2 + t_r) = 0 \end{cases} \tag{11}$$

where l_1 and l_2 are two vertical lines in the image, and p_1 and p_2 are 3D points on the vertical line.

4   Experiment

To report the evaluation results of the proposed method in this section, we first describe the dataset in Sect. 4.1, comparison with Baselines in Sect. 4.2.

4.1   Datasets

Few datasets are currently available with absolute 3D coordinates. Moreover, most of these datasets cannot provide intrinsic data from calibrated cameras or indoor 3D models. To evaluate the performance of the proposed method, we build virtual indoor scenes Lattice House and shot real indoor scenes in Exhibit Hall. For Lattice House, Unity3D wraps functions that can directly print the camera's

Table 1. Re-Projection Error

Method	Re-Projection Error (RPE, pixel)	
	Lattice House	Exhibit Hall
SIFT [33] + BFM [22]	505.86	180.07
SuperGlue [3] + SuperPoint [2]	187.11	54.24
Oracle(Manual-pts)	**3.72**	43.15
Ours	6.82	**29.74**

Table 2. Error Resolution Ratio

Method	Error Resolution Ratio (ERR, %)	
	Lattice House	Exhibit Hall
SIFT [33] + BFM [22]	46.83	5.9
SuperGlue [3] + SuperPoint [2]	17.32	1.7
Oracle(Manual-pts)	**0.34**	1.42
Ours	0.63	**0.98**

Table 3. Root Mean Square Error

Method	Root Mean Square Error (RMSE, %)
	Lattice House
SIFT [33] + BFM [22]	69.81
SuperGlue [3] + SuperPoint [2]	20.12
Oracle(Manual-pts)	**0.31**
Ours	1.11

internal reference and the camera's external reference. For Exhibit Hall, we use Zhang's calibration to calibrate the camera.

Lattice House is a virtual dataset. We build a $200\,m^2$ simulation scene. We set the camera at a height of $3\,m$. The focal length of the sensor is $16\,mm$, and the image resolution is 1920×1080. To meet the Manhattan World hypothesis, we cover the walls, ground, and roof with a mesh texture.

Exhibit Hall is a new scene shot by us in a collaborator's workspace with the iPhone 13 Pro. The camera height is about $2.5\,m$, the image resolution is 4032×3024, the scene size is $100\,m^2$, and there is a glass frame in the scene to provide orthogonal line segments on the façade.

4.2   Comparison with Baselines

We present the results of RPE, ERR, and RMSE in Tables 1, 2 and 3, respectively, with "Manual-pts" denoting the manually labeled 2D point correspondence. In Table 1, we report the reprojection error using the pixel measure. In Table 2, the error resolution is defined as RPE/min (H,W), min (H,W) is the image resolution. For Tables 1, 2 and 3, we observe the following (1) None of the baselines except Oracle can predict a reasonable camera pose on both datasets; (2) Our method outperforms all baselines except Oracle in all three metrics; (3) In Lattice House, our method's performance is slightly worse than Oracle, in Exhibit Hall, our method is better than Oracle. Due to the higher resolution of the Exhibit Hall in comparison to the Lattice House, manually labeling feature points tends to result in a higher error. Conversely, lower resolution helps reduce this error. Additionally, real scenes often exhibit higher levels of noise, which further contributes to decreased accuracy in manual feature point annotation.

Table 4. Euler angle and translation

	Lattice House@1	Lattice House@2	Lattice House@3
α	3.156°	2.165°	2.629°
β	0.194°	1.565°	0.419°
γ	1.533°	0.54°	**0.121°**
x	220 mm	**10 mm**	440 mm
y	50 mm	80 mm	70 mm
z	504 mm	650 mm	357 mm

(a) projection results of our method

(b) 3D point projection of ground-truth

(c) Matching results of SFM method

Fig. 4. Reproject of Exhibit Hall.

Our camera positional errors on the 6-dof are listed in Table 4. We decompose the rotation matrix into α, β and γ, and the translation estimate into x, y, and z, and compare them with Ground Truth. The results are shown in Table

IV, and the following results are obtained: the rotation error in all three directions is less than 4°, and the maximum translation error is 0.650 m. To verify that the calibration results of this accuracy are applicable for some large parallax indoor scene applications, we performed human mapping on a multi-target, multi-camera tracking system. By drawing polar lines, we can easily map the same person under multiple cameras.

In addition to this, we make some subjective evaluations based on our experience: we project the 3D points onto the 2D image using absolute external parameters in Fig. 4, as (a) shows the projection effect, (b) shows we also plotted the real position of the 2D points for comparison. For comparison, as (c) shows, we use the standard SFM method to detect and match feature points for the current scene. From the results, the accuracy and reliability of feature point matching in the current environment are extremely low. Therefore, in indoor scenes with large parallaxes, avoiding mismatching in (c) is the main reason for the good performance of our calibration method.

5 Conclusion

In this paper, we address the problem of multi-camera calibration in wide-baseline scenes by leveraging an indoor 3D model. We propose a method that utilizes the orthogonal information present in indoor environments to detect vanishing points and estimate camera poses. We evaluate the effectiveness of our method using datasets from various camera networks, including both virtual and real scenes. Our method achieves comparable results to SFM methods that rely on manually labeled feature points. Furthermore, our approach is suitable for indoor scenes with orthogonal information, allowing us to overcome the challenges posed by wide baselines and large parallaxes.

References

1. Agarwal, S., Mierle, K., Others: Ceres solver. www.ceres-solver.org
2. Antunes, M., Barreto, J.P.: A global approach for the detection of vanishing points and mutually orthogonal vanishing directions. In: Proceedings of the IEEE Conference on Computer Vision and Pattern Recognition (CVPR) (2013)
3. Arth, C., Pirchheim, C., Ventura, J., Schmalstieg, D., Lepetit, V.: Instant outdoor localization and slam initialization from 2.5d maps. IEEE Trans. Visual. Comput. Graph. 21(11), 1309–1318 (2015). https://doi.org/10.1109/TVCG.2015.2459772
4. Bao, S.Y., Savarese, S.: Semantic structure from motion. In: CVPR 2011, pp. 2025–2032 (2011). https://doi.org/10.1109/CVPR.2011.5995462
5. Calonder, M., Lepetit, V., Strecha, C., Fua, P.: Brief: binary robust independent elementary features. In: Daniilidis, K., Maragos, P., Paragios, N. (eds.) Computer Vision - ECCV 2010, pp. 778–792 (2010)
6. Coughlan, J., Yuille, A.: Manhattan world: compass direction from a single image by Bayesian inference. In: Proceedings of the Seventh IEEE International Conference on Computer Vision, vol. 2, pp. 941–947(1999). https://doi.org/10.1109/ICCV.1999.790349
7. Dame, A., Prisacariu, V.A., Ren, C.Y., Reid, I.: Dense reconstruction using 3d object shape priors. In: 2013 IEEE Conference on Computer Vision and Pattern Recognition, pp. 1288–1295 (2013). https://doi.org/10.1109/CVPR.2013.170

8. DeTone, D., Malisiewicz, T., Rabinovich, A.: Superpoint: self-supervised interest point detection and description. In: 2018 IEEE/CVF Conference on Computer Vision and Pattern Recognition Workshops (CVPRW), pp. 337–33712 (2018). https://doi.org/10.1109/CVPRW.2018.00060

9. DeTone, D., Malisiewicz, T., Rabinovich, A.: Superpoint: self-supervised interest point detection and description. In: 2018 IEEE/CVF Conference on Computer Vision and Pattern Recognition Workshops (CVPRW), pp. 337–33712 (2018). https://doi.org/10.1109/CVPRW.2018.00060

10. Dusmanu, M., Rocco, I., Pajdla, T., Pollefeys, M., Sattler, T.: D2-net: a trainable CNN for joint description and detection of local features. In: 2019 IEEE/CVF Conference on Computer Vision and Pattern Recognition (CVPR) (2019)

11. Jakubović, A., Velagić, J.: Image feature matching and object detection using brute-force matchers. In: 2018 International Symposium ELMAR, pp. 83–86 (2018). https://doi.org/10.23919/ELMAR.2018.8534641

12. Kendall, A., Grimes, M.K., Cipolla, R.: Convolutional networks for real-time 6-dof camera relocalization. arXiv preprint arXiv:1505.07427 (2015)

13. Laskar, Z., Melekhov, I., Kalia, S., Kannala, J.: Camera relocalization by computing pairwise relative poses using convolutional neural network. In: 2017 IEEE International Conference on Computer Vision Workshops (ICCVW), pp. 920–929 (2017). https://doi.org/10.1109/ICCVW.2017.113

14. Li, H., Zhao, J., Bazin, J.C., Liu, Y.H.: Quasi-globally optimal and near/true real-time vanishing point estimation in manhattan world. IEEE Trans. Pattern Anal. Mach. Intell. **44**(3), 1503–1518 (2022). https://doi.org/10.1109/TPAMI.2020.3023183

15. Lowe, D.G.: Distinctive image features from scale-invariant keypoints. Int. J. Comput. Vision **60**(2), 91–110 (2004)

16. Lu, X., Yaoy, J., Li, H., Liu, Y., Zhang, X.: 2-line exhaustive searching for real-time vanishing point estimation in Manhattan world. In: 2017 IEEE Winter Conference on Applications of Computer Vision (WACV), pp. 345–353 (2017). https://doi.org/10.1109/WACV.2017.45

17. Melekhov, I., Ylioinas, J., Kannala, J., Rahtu, E.: Image-based localization using hourglass networks. IEEE Computer Society (2017)

18. Naseer, T., Burgard, W.: Deep regression for monocular camera-based 6-dof global localization in outdoor environments. In: 2017 IEEE/RSJ International Conference on Intelligent Robots and Systems (IROS), pp. 1525–1530 (2017). https://doi.org/10.1109/IROS.2017.8205957

19. Rublee, E., Rabaud, V., Konolige, K., Bradski, G.: Orb: an efficient alternative to sift or surf. In: 2011 International Conference on Computer Vision, pp. 2564–2571 (2011). https://doi.org/10.1109/ICCV.2011.6126544

20. Yang, T.Y., Nguyen, D.K., Heijnen, H., Balntas, V.: Ur2kid: Unifying retrieval, keypoint detection, and keypoint description without local correspondence supervision (2020)

21. Yi, K.M., Trulls, E., Lepetit, V., Fua, P.: LIFT: learned invariant feature transform. In: Leibe, B., Matas, J., Sebe, N., Welling, M. (eds.) ECCV 2016. LNCS, vol. 9910, pp. 467–483. Springer, Cham (2016). https://doi.org/10.1007/978-3-319-46466-4_28

22. Zhang, Z.: Flexible camera calibration by viewing a plane from unknown orientations. In: Proceedings of the Seventh IEEE International Conference on Computer Vision, vol. 1, pp. 666–673 (1999). https://doi.org/10.1109/ICCV.1999.791289

A Real-Time and Globally Consistent Meshing Reconstruction Without GPU

Yubao Chen[✉], Xiujie Wang, Jiajia Wang, Dongchen Wang, Hao Zhou, and Jianhua Zhang

School of Computer Science and Engineering, Tianjin University of Technology, Tianjin, China
cybao292261@163.com

Abstract. Real-time 3D reconstruction is vital for various applications, such as human-robot interaction, virtual reality, and environment perception. The prevalence of low power devices and the rapid advancement of human-robot interaction techniques have resulted in the widespread use of RGB-D sensors for 3D reconstruction. However, high computational complexity and high fidelity make it challenging to perform dense reconstruction in real-time on low-power devices. In this paper, we propose a 3D reconstruction system that runs in real-time without GPU. Our system has three key novelties. The first one is the Single Instruction Multiple Data (SIMD) to speed up feature extraction. The second one is a depth image completion strategy to fill holes in the depth image. The last one is a sparse Robin-Hood voxel hashing algorithm to generate a consistent 3D model from key frames. Real world benchmark shows that our system can run on mobile devices at speeds of up to 30 fps in certain situations. TUM-RGBD dataset is conducted for depth image completion and feature extraction acceleration. On average, compared to ORBSLAM2 and ORBSLAM3, the feature extraction module is 1–2 times faster. We also evaluate our algorithm on the ICL-NUIM dataset which provides the ground truth of surface reconstruction and outperform FlashFusion's performance while delivering competitive results against the state-of-the-art BundleFusion.

Keywords: SLAM · Mesh Reconstruction · Depth Optimization · Feature Acceleration · SIMD · Robin-Hood Hashing

1 Introduction

Real-time 3D reconstruction is a challenging problem in recent years. With the advent of Microsoft Kinect and other consumer-grade RGB-D sensors, depth camera has made great strides in dense reconstruction and Simultaneous Localization And Mapping(SLAM). Dense method is playing an increasingly important role in solving some human-robot interaction and environment perception problems in robotics, due to the decreasing cost of sensors and the large-scale use of GPU devices in high-performance computing.

© The Author(s), under exclusive license to Springer Nature Singapore Pte Ltd. 2023
H. Yang et al. (Eds.): ICIRA 2023, LNAI 14268, pp. 39–51, 2023.
https://doi.org/10.1007/978-981-99-6486-4_4

Early environmental representation such as the pioneering work KinectFusion [12] uses full-body voxels. This approach requires prior knowledge of the scene scale and the selection of a suitable voxel size. It covered the entire scene with each small voxel. Scene reconstruction is limited to a fixed-sized area, only suitable for indoor reconstruction, and cannot be used for outdoor large-scale reconstruction. Worse still, this representation method required massive memory consumption and computational complexity. To ensure the real-time performance of the entire algorithm, it depends on the powerful computing capabilities of GPUs, which greatly reduces the possibility of performing reconstruction tasks on mobile devices. In order to reconstruct larger scenes, the voxel hashing [13] algorithm completely rewrite the model representation method, making real-time dense reconstruction possible in a CPU-only environment. Later, the InfiniTAM [7] emerges, which uses an improved voxel hashing method to store surface information of the scene. The state-of-the-art BundleFusion [3] uses voxel hashing and two high-end GPUs to achieve real-time and high-precision dense reconstruction. Nevertheless, these algorithms are either limited by scene scale or require powerful GPU computing. Theoretically, only the voxel region observable in the current viewpoint needs to be updated. Therefore, we still use the voxel hashing implemented in [9]. However, we uses a more efficient robin-hood hashing scheme to map the 3D points to an integer. The robin-hood hashing scheme only uses bit and logical operations, which is more efficient than the one in [13], including three multiplication operations.

In addition, feature extraction has always been a time-consuming process in SLAM. In recent years, as hardware computing power has continued to increase, algorithms have run faster on the latest computers without any improvements, than on older computers years ago. It can be imagined that if some of the features of modern computers were applied to previous algorithms, the increase in algorithm speed would be quite significant. Therefore, we considered using Intel's SIMD instruction set, which has the characteristics of fast, single-instruction multiple-data parallelism. From the perspective of feature extraction modules, our feature extraction algorithm implemented with Intel SIMD is on average 1–2 times faster than the one implemented in ORBSLAM2 [11] and ORBSLAM3 [2] (see Table 1).

In this paper, we propose a real-time dense 3D reconstruction system running without GPU. We test our method on ICL-NUIM [6] dataset and outperform FlashFusion [5]. We also compare with the state-of-the-art BundleFusion [3] in different scenarios and the result is competitive. Overall, the main contributions in this paper are summarized as follows:

- We propose a real-time globally consistent dense 3D reconstruction system that can run on the CPU computation of portable devices. Geometry and texture are rendered at high frame rates with fine detail.
- In the traditional SLAM algorithm, feature extraction is a time-consuming process. We use the SIMD instruction set to speed up the feature extraction process and further reduce the computing time.
- Aiming at the situation that the depth camera will have some missing and noise when collecting depth information, we use depth image completion and denoising strategy to improve the integrity and accuracy of the model.

- We adopt a method based on the voxel hashing algorithm to fuse keyframes into the global model. This method can not only improve the speed of meshing reconstruction but also save a lot of running memory usage. After the online reconstruction, we also have offline reconstruction to perform global optimization to get a more refined global consistent model. More importantly, we use a more efficient robin-hood voxel hashing to reduce hash collision and improve the speed of reconstruction.

2   Related Works

The use of consumer-grade depth cameras has gained popularity and sparked interest among researchers for 3D reconstruction. Dense 3D reconstruction has become prevalent in academia and industry, leading to the development of impressive products. In this article, we provide a concise overview of notable works in this field due to space constraints.

Previously, there have been algorithms such as KinectFusion [12] that require only a low-cost, portable depth camera to reconstruct complex indoor scenes. The algorithm integrates the depth data from the RGB-D sensor into a global implicit surface model (TSDF model) in real-time and optimizes the camera pose by using Iterative Closest Point (ICP) [1] algorithm. However, this approach has a few limitations, including the use of a dense volume representation that requires significant memory resources. Additionally, the algorithm is only suitable for reconstructing relatively small spaces, as accumulated errors can cause drift phenomena when reconstructing larger buildings.

For scene scale, Kintinuous [17] uses GPU-based circular buffer tricks to efficiently scale volume fusion of dense depth maps to operate on large spaces. [20] represents the SDF in an octree to speed up in-door scene reconstruction. InfiniTAM [7] proposes a more efficient voxel hashing algorithm to reconstruct larger and more accurate scenes. BundleFusion [3] uses two GPUs to achieve real-time reconstruction of large scale models on PC by introducing voxel hashing [13] to break through the limitations of TSDF fusion.

For the pose accuracy, the BundleFusion [3] uses the powerful computing power of the GPU to search all the previous image frames to achieve high-precision pose while another GPU is responsible for the back-end high-precision reconstruction. The FlashFusion [5] utilizes loop closure detection to achieve globally consistent pose estimation. Recently, the ReFusion [14] leverages color information encoded in the TSDF stored in voxel hashing to estimate the pose of the sensor. Mobile3DScanner [19] proposes a novel visual-inertial ICP approach for real-time accurate 6DoF pose estimation. ROSEFusion [21], without additional hardware assistance, only relies on depth information to solve the pose by stochastic optimization under fast movement, and finally realize real-time high-precision 3D reconstruction. ElasticFusion [18] adopts a surfel-based method to achieve dense mapping, combining model-to-model local loop closure with larger-scale global loop closure.

The previous method did not have obvious advantages in terms of reconstruction speed or hardware configuration. Compared to the previous method, our system does not use additional powerful computing power, such as the GPU, and only uses the CPU by using SIMD and robin-hood voxel hashing to achieve fast, efficient and high-precision 3D reconstruction.

3   Methodology

3.1   System Overview

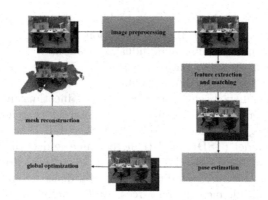

Fig. 1. The framework of our approach.

The overview of system is shown in Fig. 1, which mainly includes data preprocessing, feature extraction and matching, pose estimation, global optimization, and mesh reconstruction. Given the RGB-D image data, we first perform data preprocessing on the original image, including depth map complementation and denoising. The filtered image goes to the next step for feature extraction and matching. In the feature extraction module, we use SIMD technique to accelerate it. After that, we perform the pose estimation and LM optimization. In the last step, we integrate RGB-D keyframes and pose information into the mesh model.

3.2   Depth Image Optimization

Due to the perspective of the depth camera, there will be some depth loss and noise when collecting depth image data. It is of importance to fill and denoise the depth image before mapping. The processing mechanism for sparse depth images is to apply morphological operations to cover smaller pixel values with larger pixel values. In order to get more reliable depth information from the depth camera, we rewrite the previous method in [10] in C++ and only consider depth information within the range of 0.1 to 10.0 m.

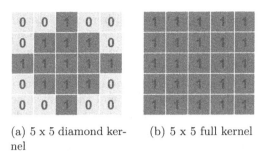

(a) 5 x 5 diamond ker-   (b) 5 x 5 full kernel
nel

Fig. 2. The comparison of different kernels.

In order to fill the null value closest to the valid pixel value, the key is to design the kernel shape such that the most likely pixels with the same depth value are filled, therefore, a 5×5 diamond kernel in Fig. 2a is used in this step.

After the first expansion operation, there are still some small holes. Because these areas have no effective depth value. Considering the structure of the object, it is found that the adjacent depths can be connected to form the edge of the object after expansion. Therefore, in this step, a 5×5 full kernel in Fig. 2b is used to perform the closing operation, connecting the adjacent depth values, and filling the small holes.

After the previous steps, there are still some small to medium sized holes in the depth map that are not filled. To patch these holes, we first compute an empty pixel mask, followed by a 7×7 full-kernel dilation operation. The operation will only fill in the empty pixels, while keeping the previously computed valid pixels unchanged.

The expansion operation in the previous steps will introduce some noise. In order to remove these noise, we use Bilateral Filter to eliminate the introduced noise. Bilateral filter adds pixel value weights on the basis of Gaussian filter, which means that not only distance factors must be considered, the influence of pixel value differences should also be considered. The closer the pixel values are, the greater the weight.

We refer the readers to ref. [10] for more detailed information about the theoretical explanation.

3.3   Feature Extraction and Matching Using SIMD

For a new frame, the current frame needs to perform feature matching with its previous frame, and feature extraction is required before matching. We use the ORB [15] feature followed ORBSLAM2 [11]. In SLAM, feature extraction is a time-consuming process, so we use the SIMD(Single Instruction Multiple Data) to parallelize the process of ORB feature extraction to shorten the extraction time. Compared with ORBSLAM2 [11] and ORBSLAM3 [2], the feature extraction method we implemented is about 1–2 times faster on average than them while ensuring feature consistency. For details, see Sect. 4.1. We input the raw image into an eight-layer image pyramid with a scale factor of 1.2 between each layer, and then extract features for each layer of the image separately.

In the Oriented FAST keypoint extraction stage, we use the SIMD to speed up the process of FAST corner extraction. The FAST feature detection algorithm is based on the gray value of the image around the feature point. If there are enough pixels around the candidate point and the gray value of the candidate point is significantly different, the candidate point is identified as a feature point. After extracting the FAST key points, we use the gray-scale centroid method to calculate the direction of the keypoints.

In the stage of calculating descriptors, Gaussian Filters are applied to each layer of image to remove some high-frequency signals. It will make the later calculated BRIEF descriptors more robust. Finally, we apply the quadtree algorithm to the FAST keypoints and corresponding BRIEF descriptors extracted from each layer. This can homogenize the feature points and avoid excessive concentration of these feature points. This makes it easier to perform pose estimation in Sect. 3.4.

In the feature matching stage, the Hamming distance is used as a metric to evaluate the similarity of two feature points. For the 256-bit BRIEF feature descriptor, a bitwise XOR operation is performed on each binary bit. We then calculate the calculated value for each bit and sum the results. Since there is no close dependency between each bit in the process of each bit calculation, we execute the _mm_popcnt_u64 instruction (Intel SIMD instruction) four times to complete the Hamming distance calculation of the 256-bit BRIEF descriptor. After the calculation, by giving a similarity threshold, such as 90%, if it is higher than this threshold, the two descriptors are considered to be successfully matched. Since there are many mismatches in the preliminary matching results, we further use the RANSAC algorithm to eliminate them to get more reliable point pairs.

3.4   Robust Localization and Optimization

Our system optimizes all keyframe poses in the optimization thread. The pose estimation plays an important role in SLAM. The pose estimation aligns the current frame to previous frame. If current frame is recognized as keyframe, the current keyframe matches all previous keyframes in keyframe database. The camera's pose transformation matrix T contains a position vector t and a rotation matrix R, formulated by

$$T = \begin{bmatrix} R & t \\ 0^T & 1 \end{bmatrix} \tag{1}$$

For two matched images named F_i and F_j and the corresponding matching feature points are p_i and p_j, the error between two images formulated by

$$e_{ij} = p_i - T_{ij}p_j \tag{2}$$

We minimize the reprojection error of previously matched image feature relationships formulated by

$$E = \min_{T_{ij}} \sum_{k=1}^{N} e_{ij}^T e_{ij} \tag{3}$$

where N is the number of features. Then we calculate the Jacobian matrix J of the error function e.

$$J = \frac{\partial e}{\partial T} \tag{4}$$

We use the Levenberg-Marquardt algorithm to solve the least squares problem.

$$(H + uI)\delta = g \tag{5}$$

where $H = J^T J$, $g = -J^T e$ and u is a parameter that can increase the robustness of the algorithm. The update rule for parameter u is as follows:

$$\begin{aligned} u = \max(1/3, 1 - (2\rho - 1)^3), v = 2.0, \quad &if \quad \rho > 0 \\ u = uv, v = 2v, \quad &otherwise \end{aligned} \tag{6}$$

The initial values of u_0 and v_0 are $u_0 = \max(H_{diag})$, $v_0 = 2.0$ respectively, where H_{diag} is the diagonal matrix of H. ρ is the ratio of the error function increment to the first-order term of Taylor's formula, which means the confidence of the real increment and the actual increment.

$$\rho = \frac{e(x + \delta_x) - e(x)}{J\delta_x} \tag{7}$$

So we have $\delta = (H + uI)^{-1}g$ according to the linear Eq. (5). Finally we update the pose $T = T + \delta$.

3.5   Online Meshing Reconstruction

Early environmental representation used full-body voxels. This approach required prior knowledge of the scene's size and the selection of a suitable voxel size. It covered the entire scene with each small voxel, which exposed a problem. Scene reconstruction is limited to a fixed-sized area, only suitable for indoor reconstruction, and cannot be used for outdoor large-scale reconstruction. Worse still, this representation method required massive memory consumption and computational complexity. Theoretically, only the voxel region visible in the current viewpoint needs to be updated. However, this approach updates all voxels globally, leading to another problem. To ensure the real-time performance of the entire algorithm, it depends on the powerful computing capabilities of GPUs, which greatly reduces the possibility of performing reconstruction tasks on mobile devices.

In our approach, we use Truncated Signed Distance Function (TSDF) to represent the model of the environment. We briefly review its algorithm description. The basic idea of the algorithm is to use a three-dimensional voxel grid to represent the entire environment, which is divided into many small voxel grids of equal size. And each voxel contains an SDF function value, which represents the distance of point in space to the nearest surface. In addition, each voxel also contains a weight to represent the reliability of the SDF function value at the current position, as well as a color value representing the color of environment coming from the pixel of rgb image back-projected to the current position. At each fusion stage, the weight will be used to update the current voxel using a weighted average method. The purpose is to prevent outliers affect the effect of the model. The rules of voxel update can be expressed as:

$$TSDF_i(x) = \frac{W_{i-1}(x)TSDF_{i-1}(x) + w_i(x)tsdf_i(x)}{W_{i-1}(x) + w_i(x)}$$

$$W_i(x) = W_{i-1}(x) + w_i(x)$$

(8)

where $tsdf_i(x)$ and $w_i(x)$ represent the TSDF value and weight of the current frame, respectively.

Each depth keyframe is incrementally integrated into the global voxel model using its corresponding camera pose provided by Sect. 3.4. At this time, all TSDF data need to be updated, regardless of whether the voxels under the current camera view can be seen or not. Under the current camera perspective, the number of unobservable voxel blocks is much more than the number of voxel blocks that can be observed. It's a huge challenge for memory, therefore, we adopt the voxel hashing [13] algorithm. The hash function used in the [13] is shown bellow:

$$hash(x, y, z) = x * p_1 \oplus y * p_2 \oplus z * p_3$$

(9)

where p_1, p_2 and p_3 are three large prime numbers. $p_1 = 73856093$, $p_2 = 19349669$, $p_3 = 83492791$.

However, Eq. (9) requires a lot of arithmetic power due to multiplication and is prone to hash conflicts compared to the hash function we use below. Therefore, we use the robin-hood[1] hash scheme which uses only bitwise and logical operations and thus requires less arithmetic power than Eq. (9) and further reduces hash conflict rate by applying the idea of avalanche effect in the field of cryptography. Voxel Hashing only allocates voxel on the scene surface measured by the camera, instead of allocating voxel in the whole space, so the memory consumption is greatly reduced. This algorithm breaks through the constraints of the space range and also improves the speed of voxel retrieval.

4   Experiments

To verify the feasibility of our method, we evaluate our algorithm on different datasets. In Sect. 4.1, we test the speed of our feature extraction method. We use SIMD comparing with the method in ORBSLAM2 and ORBSLAM3 on the TUM-RGBD dataset and achieve a faster speed. In Sect. 4.2, we compare the

---

[1] https://github.com/martinus/unordered_dense.

effects with the state-of-the-art BundleFusion in some scenarios and get some competitive results. Finally, in Sect. 4.3, since the ICL-NUIM dataset provides the ground truth of surface reconstruction, we conduct a comparison experiment on the reconstruction accuracy error with some previous representative algorithms on the ICL-NUIM dataset.

4.1 Comparison of Feature Extraction Time Consuming

Table 1. The comparison of speed per frame between ours and ORBSLAM on TUM-RGBD dataset

	Ours	ORBSLAM2	ORBSLAM3
freiburg3_long_office	**7.6 ms**	10.9 ms	11.7 ms
freiburg3_structure_texture	**6.8 ms**	12.1 ms	13.3 ms
freiburg3_structure_notexture	**3.8 ms**	8.9 ms	6.2 ms
freiburg2_desk	**8.7 ms**	12.7 ms	13.7 ms
freiburg1_room	**9.4 ms**	11.7 ms	13.3 ms

In order to further verify the acceleration effect of our feature extraction algorithm implemented by SIMD, we test our method on five scenarios of the real world TUM-RGBD [16] dataset (freiburg3_long_office, freiburg3_structure_texture, freiburg3_structure_notexture, freiburg2_desk and freiburg1_room). From the results in Table 1, our method has a definite speed advantage over ORBSLAM2 and ORBSLAM3. In some texture-rich scenes (e.g. freiburg1_room, freiburg2_desk, freiburg3_long_office and freiburg3_structure_texture), our method does not show much speed advantage over ORBSLAM2 and ORBSLAM3 due to the relatively large number of features extracted. The likely reason for this is that OpenCV is built with SIMD enabled. But in terms of overall results, our algorithm still has the speed advantage. In some scenes lacking texture information (e.g. freiburg3_structure_notexture), the feature extraction speed of ORBSLAM2 and ORBSLAM3 implemented with OpenCV can be maintained within 10 ms, while our algorithm achieves an amazing average of 3.8 ms.

In general, compared to ORBSLAM2 while ensuring feature consistency, the ORB feature extraction speed of our algorithm implemented by SIMD is 1–2 times faster than the method in ORBSLAM2. SIMD technique shows significant advantages in accelerating feature extraction.

4.2 Surface Reconstruction

To validate our proposed method, in Fig. 3, we compare with the state-of-the-art BundleFusion in different scenarios including apartment and office. BundleFusion simultaneously uses two high-end GPUs to integrate each frame into the model

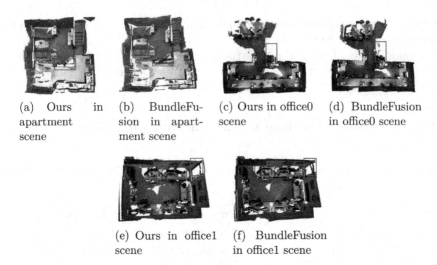

(a) Ours in apartment scene   (b) BundleFusion in apartment scene   (c) Ours in office0 scene   (d) BundleFusion in office0 scene

(e) Ours in office1 scene   (f) BundleFusion in office1 scene

Fig. 3. Different Scene Comparison Between Ours and BundleFusion.

to achieve real-time global consistent reconstruction, one of which performs pose estimation and the other for incremental mesh reconstruction. In contrast, our algorithm only relies on the CPU to fuse keyframes into the model in real time, which can achieve results that are competitive with BundleFusion.

Due to technical difficulties, we only evaluate the results of this from a qualitative point of view. In the apartment scene, the reconstruction effect marked by the red box in Fig. 3a is significantly better than that of the counterpart of the red box in Fig. 3b. The overall reconstruction results of the two images are comparable, but our method requires less computational power support (CPU only). In the office scenario, the BundleFusion algorithm does not do well to reconstruct corners in the red boxes in Fig. 3d. On the contrary, our algorithm (Fig. 3c) recovers small details well (see the red boxes in Fig. 3e and Fig. 3f for the same analogy). However, the reconstruction in the blue box of Fig. 3e has double shadow phenomenon. One possible reason is the accumulated error of pose estimation.

4.3   Accuracy of Surface Reconstruction

We evaluate the reconstruction accuracy of our proposed method on the ICL-NUIM dataset. We compare the maps of four reconstructed scenes with the ground-truth maps provided by ICL-NUIM dataset to obtain the average error distance. As shown in Table 2, the first four rows of the table are the algorithms running on the GPU, and the last four rows of the table are the algorithms running on the CPU. From the data point of view, BundleFusion achieves very high-precision real-time dense reconstruction on the GPU. And on the CPU, our algorithm is ahead of FlashFusion in some scenarios such as kt0 and kt3, and slightly behind FlashFusion in scene kt2. In some scenarios such as kt0, kt2 and

Table 2. The comparison of surface reconstruction error on ICL-NUIM dataset

	kt0	kt1	kt2	kt3
Kintinuous (GPU)	0.011 m	0.008 m	0.009 m	0.150 m
ElasticFusion (GPU)	0.007 m	0.007 m	0.008 m	0.028 m
InfiniTAM (GPU)	0.013 m	0.011 m	**0.001 m**	0.028 m
BundleFusion (GPU)	**0.005 m**	**0.006 m**	0.007 m	**0.008 m**
DVO SLAM[8] (CPU)	0.032 m	0.061 m	0.119 m	0.053 m
RGB-D SLAM[4] (CPU)	0.044 m	0.032 m	0.031 m	0.167 m
FlashFusion (CPU)	0.008 m	**0.008 m**	**0.010 m**	0.013 m
Ours (CPU)	**0.006 m**	0.013 m	0.011 m	**0.011 m**

kt3, the reconstruction accuracy of our CPU-only algorithm can compete with the state-of-the-art BundleFusion.

5   Conclusion

In this paper, we propose a real-time incremental mesh reconstruction algorithm based on the robin-hood voxel hashing method, utilizing CPU processing power. This approach can perform real-time large scene reconstruction and provide accurate pose and model information. To address missing depth, we implement a depth map completion strategy to fill holes in the model. We also take advantage of SIMD to speed up feature extraction. In comparison to existing real-time reconstruction algorithms, our method can run in real-time on the CPU with linear memory consumption. Moving forward, we plan to optimize the depth map completion strategy to further improve the robustness and accuracy of our real-time mesh reconstruction system.

References

1. Besl, P., McKay, N.D.: A method for registration of 3-d shapes. IEEE Trans. Pattern Anal. Mach. Intell. **14**(2), 239–256 (1992). https://doi.org/10.1109/34. 121791
2. Campos, C., Elvira, R., Rodríguez, J.J.G., Montiel, J.M.M., Tardós, J.D.: Orb-slam3: an accurate open-source library for visual, visual-inertial, and multimap slam. IEEE Trans. Robot. **37**(6), 1874–1890 (2021). https://doi.org/10.1109/TRO. 2021.3075644
3. Dai, A., Nießner, M., Zollöfer, M., Izadi, S., Theobalt, C.: Bundlefusion: real-time globally consistent 3d reconstruction using on-the-fly surface re-integration. In: ACM Transactions on Graphics 2017 (TOG) (2017)
4. Endres, F., Hess, J., Sturm, J., Cremers, D., Burgard, W.: 3-d mapping with an rgb-d camera. IEEE Trans. Rob. **30**(1), 177–187 (2014). https://doi.org/10.1109/ TRO.2013.2279412

5. Han, L., Fang, L.: Flashfusion: real-time globally consistent dense 3d reconstruction using CPU computing. In: Robotics: Science and Systems XIV (2018)
6. Handa, A., Whelan, T., McDonald, J., Davison, A.J.: A benchmark for rgb-d visual odometry, 3d reconstruction and slam. In: 2014 IEEE International Conference on Robotics and Automation (ICRA), pp. 1524–1531 (2014). https://doi.org/10.1109/ICRA.2014.6907054
7. Kähler, O., Prisacariu, V.A., Ren, C.Y., Sun, X., Torr, P.H.S., Murray, D.W.: Very high frame rate volumetric integration of depth images on mobile device. In: Proceedings International Symposium on Mixed and Augmented Reality 2015, IEEE Transactions on Visualization and Computer Graphics, vol. 22, no. 11 (2015)
8. Kerl, C., Sturm, J., Cremers, D.: Dense visual slam for rgb-d cameras. In: 2013 IEEE/RSJ International Conference on Intelligent Robots and Systems, pp. 2100–2106 (2013). https://doi.org/10.1109/IROS.2013.6696650
9. Klingensmith, M., Dryanovski, I., Srinivasa, S.S., Xiao, J.: Chisel: real time large scale 3d reconstruction onboard a mobile device using spatially hashed signed distance fields. In: Robotics: Science and Systems (2015)
10. Ku, J., Harakeh, A., Waslander, S.L.: In defense of classical image processing: fast depth completion on the CPU. In: 2018 15th Conference on Computer and Robot Vision (CRV), pp. 16–22. IEEE (2018)
11. Mur-Artal, R., Tardós, J.D.: ORB-SLAM2: an open-source SLAM system for monocular, stereo and RGB-D cameras. IEEE Trans. Rob. **33**(5), 1255–1262 (2017). https://doi.org/10.1109/TRO.2017.2705103
12. Newcombe, R.A., et al.: Kinectfusion: real-time dense surface mapping and tracking. In: 2011 10th IEEE International Symposium on Mixed and Augmented Reality, pp. 127–136 (2011). https://doi.org/10.1109/ISMAR.2011.6092378
13. Nießner, M., Zollhöfer, M., Izadi, S., Stamminger, M.: Real-time 3d reconstruction at scale using voxel hashing. Int. Conf. Comput. Graph. Interact. Techniq. (2013)
14. Palazzolo, E., Behley, J., Lottes, P., Giguère, P., Stachniss, C.: Refusion: 3d reconstruction in dynamic environments for rgb-d cameras exploiting residuals. In: 2019 IEEE/RSJ International Conference on Intelligent Robots and Systems (IROS), pp. 7855–7862 (2019). https://doi.org/10.1109/IROS40897.2019.8967590
15. Rublee, E., Rabaud, V., Konolige, K., Bradski, G.: Orb: an efficient alternative to sift or surf. In: 2011 International Conference on Computer Vision, pp. 2564–2571 (2011). https://doi.org/10.1109/ICCV.2011.6126544
16. Sturm, J., Engelhard, N., Endres, F., Burgard, W., Cremers, D.: A benchmark for the evaluation of rgb-d slam systems. In: Proceedings of the International Conference on Intelligent Robot Systems (IROS) (2012)
17. Whelan, T., Johannsson, H., Kaess, M., Leonard, J.J., McDonald, J.: Robust real-time visual odometry for dense rgb-d mapping. In: 2013 IEEE International Conference on Robotics and Automation, pp. 5724–5731 (2013). https://doi.org/10.1109/ICRA.2013.6631400
18. Whelan, T., Leutenegger, S., Salas-Moreno, R.F., Glocker, B., Davison, A.J.: Elasticfusion: dense slam without a pose graph. In: Robotics: Science and Systems (2015)
19. Xiang, X., et al.: Mobile3dscanner: an online 3d scanner for high-quality object reconstruction with a mobile device. IEEE Trans. Visual Comput. Graph. **27**(11), 4245–4255 (2021). https://doi.org/10.1109/TVCG.2021.3106491

20. Zeng, M., Zhao, F., Zheng, J., Liu, X.: Octree-based fusion for realtime 3d reconstruction. Graph. Model. **75**, 126–136 (2013). https://doi.org/10.1016/j.gmod.2012.09.002
21. Zhang, J., Zhu, C., Zheng, L., Xu, K.: Rosefusion: random optimization for online dense reconstruction under fast camera motion. ACM Trans. Graph. (SIGGRAPH 2021) **40**(4) (2021)

All-in-One Image Dehazing Based on Attention Mechanism

Qingyue Dai, Tong Cui$^{(\boxtimes)}$, Meng Zhang, Xinyi Zhao, and Binbin Hou

College of Artificial Intelligence, Shenyang Aerospace University,
Shenyang 110136, China
ct61ct61@126.com

Abstract. The objective of image dehazing is to restore the clear content from a hazy image. However, different parts of the same image pose varying degrees of difficulty for recovery. Existing image dehazing networks treat channel and pixel features equally, making it challenging to handle images with non-uniform haze distribution and weighted channels. To address this limitation, we propose a feature attention module for all-in-one image dehazing. The feature attention module comprises channel attention and pixel attention, offering enhanced flexibility in processing different types of information. Specifically, we perform stitching between adjacent layers in the channel dimension during feature extraction. Subsequently, we apply channel attention and pixel attention on the stitching layer with a large channel dimension. To preserve detailed texture features and minimize information loss from the attention mechanism, we use summation operations between the feature layer obtained after each attention operation and the input layer. Our model prioritizes attention to the dense haze region while maintaining overall brightness. Extensive experiments demonstrate that our method surpasses state-of-the-art dehazing techniques in terms of performance, requiring fewer parameters and FLOPs.

Keywords: Image Dehazing · All-in-one · channel attention · pixel attention

1 Introduction

Due to the presence of haze, outdoor images often suffer from low contrast and limited visibility, which significantly hampers the performance of advanced computer vision tasks such as object detection and recognition. Therefore, image dehazing has garnered increasing attention as it aims to recover clear images from hazy inputs. According to the physical scattering model [25], the hazing process is usually represented as:

$$I(x) = t(x)J(x) + (1 - t(x))A \tag{1}$$

Supported by Liaoning Education Department General Project Foundation (LJKZ0231, LJKZZ20220033); Huaian Natural Science Research Plan Project Foundation (HAB202083).

where I(x) is the observed haze image and J(x) is the scene brightness to be recovered. There are two key parameters:A is the global atmospheric light, t (x) is the transmittance, and t(x) is defined as:

$$t(x) = e^{-\beta d(x)} \tag{2}$$

where β is the atmospheric scattering coefficient and d(x) is the distance between the object and the camera. In single image dehazing, given I, the target is estimated J.

Estimating clean images from a single haze image input is an ill-posed problem. Earlier approaches [1,8,9,11–13] attempted to estimate the transmittance by a physical prior and then recover the image by a scattering model. However, these physical priors were not always reliable, leading to inaccurate transmission estimates and unsatisfactory defogging results. With the advancement of deep learning, many convolutional neural network (CNN) based methods [3,4,6,14,23] have been proposed to overcome the drawbacks of using physical priors. They are more efficient and superior to traditional prior-based algorithms. Despite the significant progress achieved by learning-based methods, several factors hinder their performance, and the results are still suboptimal. These factors include inaccurate transmittance estimation and the lack of end-to-end learning to capture the intrinsic relationship between the transmittance map, atmospheric light, and dehazed images. The disjoint optimization may also affect the overall defogging results.

To address these limitations, a method for joint optimization of the entire dehazing network was proposed in the literature [14]. This approach involves embedding the transmission map and atmospheric light into a single formula using a linear transformation and employing a lightweight CNN to recover clear images. The atmospheric scattering model is reformulated to directly minimize the pixel domain reconstruction error. In this paper, we propose an all-in-one image dehazing network based on the attention mechanism to further improve the performance. Considering the uneven distribution of haze in real scenes, our network extracts features with different weight information for different channels to handle this non-uniform distribution. We design our attention block based on the idea in FFA [10]. Specifically, when extracting features, the adjacent layers are stitched in the channel dimension, and the results are then processed through channel attention and pixel attention consecutively. This approach enables our network to effectively handle different features and pixels, fully exploit the learning capability of the network, and improve the generalization ability of the dehazing network while ensuring its lightweight nature.

In conclusion, our proposed all-in-one image dehazing network based on the attention mechanism addresses the limitations of existing methods. By leveraging the attention mechanism, our network effectively handles the uneven distribution of haze and makes efficient use of the limited network capacity. We demonstrate the superior performance of our approach through comprehensive experiments, showcasing improved generalization ability and lightweight characteristics compared to existing state-of-the-art methods.

2   Related Work

2.1   Single Image Dehazing

Priori-based methods: Priori-based haze removal methods utilize the statistical properties of a clean image to estimate the transmission map and use a scattering model for haze removal [1,8,9,11–13]. For instance, Tan [12] proposed a method that maximizes the local contrast of a hazy image. He et al. [11] achieved impressive results using a dark channel prior (DCP) which assumes near-zero values for each channel. Zhu et al. [13] introduced color attenuation prior by estimating scene depth. Fattal [9] utilized a color line prior based on the one-dimensional distribution of small image block pixels in RGB space. Berman et al. [1] developed a defogging algorithm based on approximating fog-free image colors with several hundred different colors. While effective for image defogging, these hand-crafted priors have limited applicability to diverse blurred images.

Learning-based methods: Learning-based methods for haze removal have gained popularity due to the availability of large-scale paired data and powerful convolutional neural networks. MSCNN [16] trained a CNN to estimate the haze input's transmission map in a coarse-to-fine manner. Cai et al. [2] proposed an end-to-end network for generating transmittance estimates. Zhang and Patel [4] incorporated a physical scattering model into the network, allowing for joint estimation of transmittance, atmospheric light, and dehazed images. Ren et al. [18] introduced a gated fusion network that utilizes a derived input from the original fog image. Qu et al. [20] treated dehazing as an image-to-image translation problem and proposed an enhanced pix2pix network. These methods have demonstrated excellent dehazing results.

However, when applied to real non-uniform haze images, equally weighted attention to each pixel can be computationally expensive and impractical for advanced vision tasks. To address this, we propose an attention-based integrated dehazing network that maximizes neural network performance while minimizing computational resources.

2.2   Attentional Mechanisms

The attention mechanism enhances the performance and generalization of neural networks by allowing them to focus on relevant parts of the input data. It enables the networks to automatically learn and emphasize important information.

The channel attention mechanism improves the representation capability of neural networks in the channel dimension. It adjusts the importance of each channel by learning channel weights. This mechanism captures the correlation and importance between channels, resulting in an attention-adjusted feature map. Pixel attention adjusts the attention to different pixel regions by learning the importance weights of each pixel in an image. It adaptsively adjusts weights based on image content, improving the performance of image dehazing networks.

In our approach, we apply both channel attention and pixel attention sequentially to fully exploit the learning capability of the network. This improves the generalization ability of the dehazing network while keeping it lightweight.

2.3 Perceived Loss

Perceptual loss is a crucial method in computer vision and image processing that quantifies the difference between generated and real images. It involves using a pretrained convolutional neural network (CNN) model to extract image features and measure the semantic similarity between the predicted and real images. Perceptual loss consists of two steps: feature extraction and distance calculation.

In feature extraction, popular pretrained CNN models like VGG-16 and ResNet are used to extract high-level features from images. These models have been trained on large image datasets and can effectively capture semantic information. The predicted and real images are inputted into the CNN model to obtain their respective high-level feature representations.

For distance calculation, the Euclidean distance or cosine similarity is often used to measure the dissimilarity or similarity between the generated and real image features. The Euclidean distance quantifies geometric differences, while cosine similarity measures angular similarities. These metrics determine the disparity between the generated and real images, forming the basis of the perceptual loss function.

Perceptual loss is widely applied in tasks like image defogging and super-resolution. Compared to traditional pixel-based loss functions such as mean square error, perceptual loss focuses more on the high-level semantic information of images. This emphasis enhances the visual quality and perceptual consistency of the predicted images. Therefore, we combine perceptual loss with pixel-level loss functions to further improve the performance of the dehazing model.

3 Our Approach

3.1 Overall Network Structure

This section presents a detailed approach of our proposed lightweight defogging network based on passband attention and pixel attention. Figure 1 illustrates the overall structure of our network.

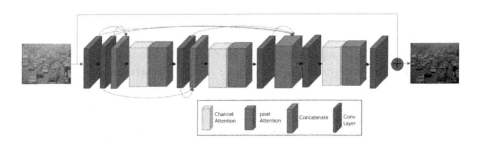

Fig. 1. Overall network structure.

In this study, we propose a novel approach for image dehazing. Firstly, we adopt a feature map channel stitching strategy inspired by AODNet to capture semantic and visual features at different levels effectively. By fusing features from different layers, our method combines low-level detail features with high-level semantic features, improving the model's robustness to scale changes.

Secondly, we introduce a passband attention module that dynamically adjusts the importance of image features on different frequency passbands. Using an attention mechanism, this module learns passband weights and selectively fuses features from different frequency passbands. This enhances the model's ability to perceive details at various frequencies and mitigates dehazing blur and artifacts.

Finally, we incorporate a pixel attention module to enhance image detail and texture recovery. This module selectively emphasizes important details while reducing the impact of unimportant regions. By introducing pixel attention, our network excels at restoring image details and structure.

Our network is trained end-to-end using an integrated loss function that combines perceptual loss and pixel-level loss. This striking a balance between visual quality and detail recovery. The training process utilizes the Adam optimizer, and techniques such as batch normalization and residual concatenation are employed to accelerate convergence.

Experimental results demonstrate that our lightweight dehazing network performs excellently in complex scenes. Compared to traditional methods, our approach offers advantages in terms of computational resources and model complexity. Moreover, our network shows potential for real-time implementation on mobile devices, providing an efficient solution for real-world dehazing applications.

3.2   Multi-scale Attention Mechanism

This section presents a detailed approach to our proposed channel attention mechanism and pixel attention mechanism in the dehazing network. These two attention mechanisms aim to improve the network's ability to focus on and capture important features in the haze images, thus improving the quality of the dehazing results and preserving the details of the images.

In the channel attention module, we first perform multi-scale feature extraction on the input haze images. By using convolution kernels of different sizes or pooling operations, we can obtain feature representations at different scales. This allows capturing different scale variations of detail and global information in the image. For each feature map extracted at each scale, we apply the channel attention computation separately. The purpose of the channel attention computation is to learn the importance weight of each feature channel to control the degree of contribution of different channels to the dehazing task. By using a global average pooling operation and a series of convolutional layers, we can generate the attention weights for each feature channel. After computing the attention weights of the channels at each scale, we weight the feature maps at different scales according to the corresponding weights for fusion. This allows the network to pay more attention to the feature channels that are more important for the dehazing task and to combine the information from multiple scales effectively (Figs. 2 and 3).

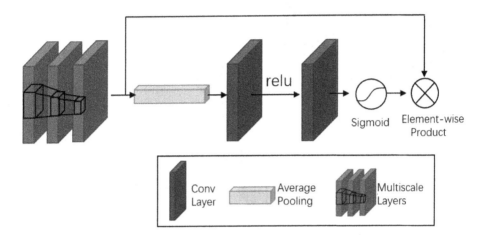

Fig. 2. Multi-scale channel attention.

Similar to the multi-scale channel attention for the feature maps extracted at each scale, we apply pixel attention computation separately. The purpose of pixel attention computation is to learn the importance weights of each pixel location to control the degree of contribution of different locations to the defogging task. By using a series of convolutional layers and activation functions, we can generate the attention weights for each pixel location. After computing the pixel attention weights at each scale, we weight the feature maps at different scales according to the corresponding weights and fuse them. This allows the network to focus more on important image regions and enhance the details and structure of the image, thus improving the effect of dehazing and the clarity of the image.

Both our multi-scale channel attention mechanism and pixel attention mechanism are implemented by learning to obtain the corresponding attention weights. Experimental results show that both the channel attention mechanism and the pixel attention mechanism in our proposed defogging network achieve significant performance improvements in various complex scenarios. Compared with traditional dehazing methods, our method has significant advantages in the capture of important features and the retention of image details, which effectively improves the dehazing effect and image quality.

3.3   Loss Function

To optimize the training process of the network, a perceptual loss function and a pixel-level loss function are used to guide the optimization of the network. Perceptual loss measures the quality of the dehazed image by calculating the feature differences between the dehazed image and the clear image. We use a

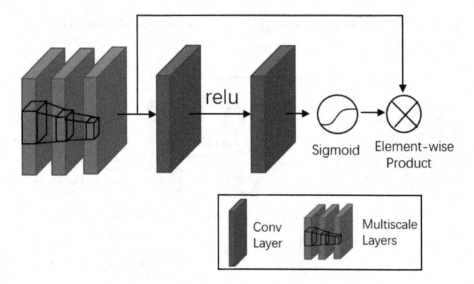

Fig. 3. Multi-scale pixel attention.

pre-trained deep learning model as the basis of perceptual loss to extract the differences between the dehazed image and the real image in the high-level feature space. On the other hand, L1 loss is a commonly used pixel-level difference metric to measure the pixel-level difference between the dehazed image and the real image. l1 loss can effectively drive the dehazed image to be consistent with the real image at the pixel level, which helps to preserve the detail and structure of the image. To better balance the tradeoff between perceptual loss and L1 loss, we introduce a weighting factor for weighting the combination of the two loss functions. By adjusting the value of the weighting factor, we have the flexibility to control the degree of contribution of perceptual loss and L1 loss in the overall loss function. A higher perceptual loss weight will focus more on the visual quality and realism of the defogged image, while a higher L1 loss weight will focus more on the detail retention and pixel-level consistency of the defogged image.

$$L = \gamma 1 * L1 + \gamma 2 * Lper \qquad (3)$$

We validate the effectiveness of the method by conducting experimental evaluations on multiple datasets. The experimental results show that the defogging model with a combination of perceptual loss and L1 loss weighting is able to achieve better results than a single loss function in defogging, with better visual quality and detail retention.

4   Experiment

Since the proposed algorithm is a lightweight network, we compare our haze removal network not only with DehazeNet [2], AOD-Net [14], FFA [10] and other haze removal networks, but also with the classical method DCP [11], which has a much smaller number of parameters. Among the compared methods, DCP focuses on hand-crafted features for haze removal, while the other methods are based on convolutional neural networks. We retrain the original (published) implementations of these methods and test them on a public dataset to obtain their haze removal results.

4.1   Experiment Setup

We evaluated our fog removal network qualitatively and quantitatively on a synthetic dataset and a real dataset, respectively.

Train Details: Our dehazing model is implemented with PyTorch library and trained on one NVIDIA GeForce RTX3090 GPU. Our model is trained for 60 epochs on the RESIDE dataset, 20 epochs on the NH-HAZE dataset.

4.2   Experimental Results and Analysis

Fig. 4. Our method was compared with four other methods on synthetic datasets.

In our experiments, we assess the performance of our proposed defogging algorithm on both synthetic and real datasets. We compare it with four commonly used defogging algorithms, namely DehaeNet [2], DCP [11], FFANet [10], and AODNet [14].

To begin with, we compare the predicted image results of each algorithm on the synthetic dataset. This dataset is created by adding haze to real images,

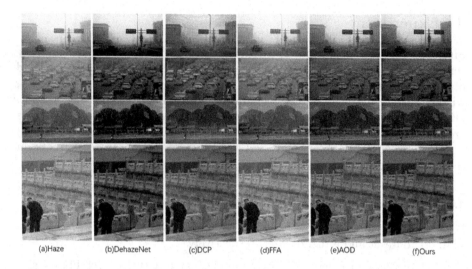

(a)Haze   (b)DehazeNet   (c)DCP   (d)FFA   (e)AOD   (f)Ours

Fig. 5. Our method is compared with the other four methods on real data sets.

allowing us to accurately determine the true defogging outcomes. By visually comparing the predicted images with the real defogged images, we can evaluate how effectively the algorithms restore image details and remove haze. As shown in Fig. 4, DehaeNet [2], DCP [11] and AODNet [14] are visually significantly different from ground truth (Gt). While FFA [10] outperforms our method in certain textures, its model complexity is significantly different from ours, Further experiments were performed to confirm our conclusions. The overall ability of our algorithm to produce clear, detailed, and realistic defogged images on the synthetic dataset demonstrates its strong defogging performance in a simulated environment (Table 1).

Table 1. Quantitative comparisons between our network and compared methods.

Images	Method	DehazeNet	DCP	FFANet	AOD	Ours
1	PSNR	20.13	11.04	33.25	17.26	20.54
	SSIM	0.886	0.728	0.964	0.851	0.965
2	PSNR	18.49	10.84	32.51	19.21	19.35
	SSIM	0.902	0.741	0.321	0.874	0.913
3	PSNR	21.65	10.58	35.22	20.36	22.69
	SSIM	0.889	0.639	0.975	0.883	0.860
4	PSNR	20.5	11.05	33.35	19.88	22.93
	SSIM	0.912	0.722	0.98	0.872	0.932

We quantitatively evaluate the results on the synthetic dataset using two widely used evaluation metrics: structural similarity metric (SSIM) and peak signal-to-noise ratio (PSNR). SSIM measures the structural similarity between the predicted image and the true dehazed image, with values ranging from 0 to 1, where higher values indicate greater similarity. PSNR measures the peak signal-to-noise ratio between the predicted image and the real defogged image, with larger values indicating smaller differences. Comparing our algorithm with the four others, we find that our algorithm achieves SSIM and PSNR scores second only to FFANet on the synthetic dataset. This suggests that our algorithm performs well in preserving structural information and reducing image noise.

Furthermore, we evaluate the quality of the predicted images on the real dataset despite the absence of reference dehazed images. We assess the algorithm's performance by visually examining the sharpness and level of detail restoration in the predicted images. Our algorithm effectively reduces haze and restores image details on the real dataset, producing high-quality images that outperform other algorithms significantly. The results are shown in Fig. 5.

The proposed All-in-one defogging network has several advantages in terms of efficiency. Firstly, it has low computational complexity due to its simplified model structure and operations, reducing parameters and computational effort. This enables efficient defogging with limited computational resources. Secondly, the lightweight defogging network provides fast inference speed, quickly generating clear images in a relatively short time. It also requires fewer parameters and storage space, conserving storage resources and facilitating deployment and transmission. Lastly, the lightweight defogging network is adaptable and general, achieving good results across various scenarios and datasets in multiple defogging tasks. Overall, the efficiency of lightweight defogging networks makes them well-suited for real-time defogging and embedded applications, offering an important solution in resource-constrained environments (Table 2).

Table 2. Comparison results of the number of parameters and calculation volume.

Methods	Efficiency	
	Params (K)	FLOPs (GMac)
DehazeNet	8.305	0.396
DCP	–	–
FFANet	4456	220.6
AOD	1.761	0.089
Ours	2.086	0.997

In summary, our integrated lightweight defogging network algorithm based on a multiscale attention mechanism demonstrates superior performance on both synthetic and real datasets. By comparing with four comparative algorithms, including DehaeNet [2], DCP [11], FFANet [10], and AODNet [14], we demonstrate the advantages of our algorithm in terms of quality and detail retention of the defogged images. These experimental results verify the effectiveness and practicality of our proposed algorithm in image defogging tasks, and provide useful references and guidance for solving image defogging problems in practical applications.

5 Conclusion

In this paper, we propose an integrated defogging network based on multiscale channel attention and multiscale pixel attention to enhance the visual quality and detail retention ability of haze images. The multi-scale channel attention mechanism enables the network to better focus on features at different scales, enhancing the clarity and naturalness of the defogging results. The multi-scale pixel attention mechanism effectively enhances image details and structure, resulting in more detailed and realistic defogging outcomes. Furthermore, we introduce a perceptual loss function to guide the training of the network. This loss function measures the perceptual difference between the generated image and the real clear image, thereby enhancing the visual quality of the defogging results. Experimental results demonstrate that the perceptual loss has a significant positive impact on network optimization, producing generated images that are more realistic, clearer, and closely resemble the real clear images.

Although our integrated defogging network achieves significant performance improvements in various metrics, there are still some challenges and room for improvement. Future work can further explore the optimization and improvement of the network structure to improve the generalization ability of the network in complex scenes. In addition, the introduction of more prior knowledge and constraints can be considered to further improve the quality and realism of the defogging results.

References

1. Berman, D., Avidan, S.: Non-local image dehazing. In: Proceedings of the IEEE Conference on Computer Vision and Pattern Recognition, pp. 1674–1682 (2016)
2. Cai, B., et al.: Dehazenet: an end-to-end system for single image haze removal. IEEE Trans. Image Process. **25**(11), 5187–5198 (2016)
3. Ren, W., et al.: Gated fusion network for single image dehazing. In: Proceedings of the IEEE Conference on Computer Vision and Pattern Recognition, pp. 3253–3261 (2018)
4. Zhang, H., Patel, V.M.: Densely connected pyramid dehazing network. In: Proceedings of the IEEE Conference on Computer Vision and Pattern Recognition, pp. 3194–3203 (2018)
5. Chen, D., et al.: Gated context aggregation network for image dehazing and deraining. In: 2019 IEEE Winter Conference on Applications of Computer Vision (WACV), pp. 1375–1383. IEEE (2019)
6. Dong, J., Pan, J.: Physics-based feature dehazing networks. In: Vedaldi, A., Bischof, H., Brox, T., Frahm, J.-M. (eds.) ECCV 2020. LNCS, vol. 12375, pp. 188–204. Springer, Cham (2020). https://doi.org/10.1007/978-3-030-58577-8_12

7. Cui, T., Tian, J., Wang, E., Tang, Y.: Single image dehazing by latent region Segmentation based transmission estimation and weighted L1-norm regularization. IET Image Process **11**(2), 145–154 (2016)
8. Fattal, R.: Single image dehazing. ACM Trans. Graph. **27**(3), 1–9 (2008)
9. Fattal, R.: Dehazing using color-lines. ACM Trans. Graph. **34**(1), 1–14 (2014)
10. Qin, X., et al.: FFA-Net: feature fusion attention network for single image dehazing. Proc. AAAI Conf. Artif. Intelli. **34**(7), 11908–11915 (2020)
11. He, K., Sun, J., Tang, X.: Single image haze removal using dark channel prior. IEEE Trans. Pattern Anal. Mach. Intell. **33**(12), 2341–2353 (2010)
12. Tan, R.T.: Visibility in bad weather from a single image. In: 2008 IEEE Conference on Computer Vision and Pattern Recognition, pp. 1–8. IEEE (2008)
13. Zhu, Q., Mai, J., Shao, L.: A fast single image haze removal algorithm using color attenuation prior. IEEE Trans. Image Process. **24**(11), 3522–3533 (2015)
14. Li, B., et al.: Aod-net: all-in-one dehazing network. In: Proceedings of the IEEE International Conference on Computer Vision, pp. 4770–4778 (2017)
15. Isola, P., Zhu, J.-Y., Zhou, T., Efros, A.A.: Image-to-image translation with conditional adversarial networks. In: CVPR, pp. 1125–1134 (2017)
16. Ren, W., Liu, S., Zhang, H., Pan, J., Cao, X., Yang, M.-H.: Single image dehazing via multi-scale convolutional neural networks. In: Leibe, B., Matas, J., Sebe, N., Welling, M. (eds.) ECCV 2016. LNCS, vol. 9906, pp. 154–169. Springer, Cham (2016). https://doi.org/10.1007/978-3-319-46475-6_10
17. Li, B., et al.: End-to-end united video dehazing and detection. In: Proceedings of the AAAI Conference on Artificial Intelligence, vol. 32, no. 1 (2018)
18. Ren, W., et al.: Gated fusion network for single image dehazing. In: Proceedings of the IEEE Conference on Computer Vision and Pattern Recognition, pp. 3253–3261 (2018)
19. Li, R., et al.: Task-oriented network for image dehazing. IEEE Trans. Image Process. **29**, 6523–6534 (2020)
20. Qu, Y., et al.: Enhanced pix2pix dehazing network. In: Proceedings of the IEEE/CVF Conference on Computer Vision and Pattern Recognition, pp. 8160–8168 (2019)
21. Simonyan, K., Zisserman, A.: Very deep convolutional networks for large-scale image recognition. arXiv preprint arXiv:1409.1556 (2014)
22. Li, B., et al.: RESIDE: A Benchmark for Single Image Dehazing. arXiv e-prints (2017)
23. Liu, Y., et al.: Learning deep priors for image dehazing. In: Proceedings of the IEEE/CVF International Conference on Computer Vision, pp. 2492–2500 (2019)
24. McCartney, E.J.: Optics of the Atmosphere: Scattering by Molecules and Particles. New York (1976)
25. Narasimhan, S.G., Nayar, S.K.: Vision and the atmosphere. Int. J. Comput. Vision **48**(3), 233 (2002)

Reliable AI on Machine Human Reactions

A Feature Fusion Network for Skeleton-Based Gesture Recognition

Xiaowen You[1], Qing Gao[2(✉)], Hongwei Gao[1], and Zhaojie Ju[3(✉)]

[1] School of Automation and Electrical Engineering, Shenyang Ligong University,
Shenyang 110159, China
[2] School of Electronics and Communication Engineering, Sun Yat-Sen University,
Shenzhen 518107, China
`gaoqing.ieee@gmail.com`
[3] School of Computing, University of Portsmouth, Portsmouth PO13HE, UK
`Zhaojie.Ju@port.ac.uk`

Abstract. With the development of the times, the requirements for human-computer interaction methods have gradually increased, and naturalness and comfort are constantly pursued on the basis of traditional precision. Gesture is one of the innate ways of human communication, which is highly intuitive and can be employed as an effective means of natural human-computer interaction. In this paper, dynamic gestures are investigated based on the 3D skeletal information of gestures, and different cropping boxes are placed at generate global and local datasets respectively according to whether they depend on the motion trajectory of the gesture. By analyzing the geometric features of skeletal sequences, a dual-stream 3D CNN (Double_C3D) framework is proposed for fusion at the feature level, which relies on 3D heat map video streams and uses the video streams as the input to the network. Finally, the Double_C3D framework was evaluated on the SHREC dynamic gesture recognition dataset and the JHMBD dynamic behavior recognition dataset with an accuracy of 91.72% and 70.54%, respectively.

Keywords: 3D Skeleton · Pseudo Heat Map · 3D CNN

1 Introduction

Gestures are a unique form of expression for humans, possessing characteristics such as naturalness, ease of understanding, and universality. They have great potential in the field of human-computer interaction (HCI). With the development of technology, HCI needs to be richer, more operative and more in line with natural human interaction,

☆ The authors would like to acknowledge the support from the National Natural Science Foundation of China (62006204, 52075530), the Guangdong Basic and Applied Basic Research Foundation (2022A1515011431), and Shenzhen Science and Technology Program (RCBS20210609104516043, JSGG20210802154004014). This work is also partially supported by the AiBle project co-financed by the European Regional Development Fund.

H. Yang et al. (Eds.): ICIRA 2023, LNAI 14268, pp. 67–78, 2023.
https://doi.org/10.1007/978-981-99-6486-4_6

while gestures are universal and not restricted by factors such as professional knowledge [1–3], users only need to do some simple gestures to interact with the machine, which greatly improves the convenience of interaction between humans and machines. However, gesture recognition also faces great challenges, such as changes in skin tone among different races, lighting changes for non-skin tone, dynamic background changes or multiple people making gestures at once.

The existing research has explored various modalities for feature representation, such as RGB frames [4, 5], optical flow [6], deep flow [7], audio waves [8], or human body skeletons [9–12]. Among these modalities, skeleton-based methods have received increasing attention in recent years for gesture recognition tasks [10, 13] due to their focus on motion characteristics and stronger adaptability to complex backgrounds. Graph convolutional network (GCN) [14, 15] has been part of the most popular methods in all skeleton-based gesture recognition tasks. GCN uses raw skeleton features such as joint coordinates or bond lengths to construct spatial-temporal graphs. There is evidence from experiments [16–18] that representations from different modalities, such as RGB, optical flow, and skeleton, are complementary, and effective combinations of these modalities can lead to improving performance in gesture recognition. However, GCN operates on irregular skeleton graphs, which make it difficult to integrate with features from other modalities. In convolutional neural networks, 2-dimensional convolutional operations are mainly applied to spatial image processing, and 3-dimensional convolution is to take the temporal dimension into account on top of the spatial dimension, which is more flexible and has become the mainstream method for gesture recognition [19–21]. In addition, from a data standpoint, it is equally important to consider the global motion trajectory for different gestures. For instance, when classifying gestures such as "swiping left" and "swiping right", the overall motion trajectory of the gesture is more critical than the gesture itself, which requires that the skeleton sequence should include global motion information. Based on the above factors, the Double_C3D framework is proposed in this paper. Unlike the research method that directly uses skeletal joint coordinates, this paper combines skeletal modalities with RGB modalities by transforming skeletal information into a two-dimensional pseudo-heatmap. Then heat maps with different time steps are stacked along the time dimension to form a 3D heat map video stream, and finally a 3D convolutional neural network is used to recognize gestures.

Compared to research methods that directly use RGB image input, the skeleton modality avoids the influences of factors such as complex backgrounds, changes in lighting conditions, occlusion problems, and skin tone on gesture recognition. Furthermore, in order to extract more gesture global trajectory characteristics, this paper is based on a complete gesture sequence, forming a global data source into the network. However, since the global data source only focuses on the motion trajectory, a local data source is introduced to focus on the changes of the gesture itself, and then the global and local data sources are fused with features to improve the generalization ability of Double_C3D. Finally, gesture recognition performance is further improved by using the depth information in the nodes to represent the dimensions of the nodes in the pseudo-heat map without increasing the computational complexity. To verify the effectiveness of Double_C3D, it was tested on 14-class benchmarks of the SHREC dataset [22] and JHMBD datasets [23], and the accuracy rate reached 91.72% and 70.54%, respectively.

The paper is structured according to the following structure: In Sect. 2, the related work of RGB-based and skeleton-based gesture recognition methods is introduced, respectively. In Sect. 3, details on how to generate heat map video streams and network architecture is described. The experimental results and discussion are provided in Sect. 4. Finally, the paper is outlined in Sect. 5.

2 Related Work

RGB-Based Gesture Recognition Methods. In the field of gesture recognition, the common type of dataset is image data. These data are usually obtained using a regular RGB camera. It is able to capture the natural color and texture of the gesture, which can provide more realistic image features for gesture analysis and recognition. However, RGB cameras cannot directly acquire gesture poses information, and before feature extraction, gesture segmentation of the image is required, and the quality of the segmented features is closely related to the segmentation algorithm. Köpüklü [24] et al. implemented real-time gesture detection using C3D and ResNet-101 as detector and classifier, and achieved accuracy rates of 83% and 94% on the nvGesture dataset and EgoGesture dataset, respectively. Dhingra [25] et al. constructed a three-dimensional residual attention network (Res3ATN) for gesture recognition, based on stacked multiple attentional fastness, generating different features on each attentional fastness. Since the segmented RGB images are susceptible to image background variability, racial color differences, shadows and other illumination variations, Dadashzadeh [26] et al. proposed an HGR-Net that uses a fully convolutional residual network to segment the gesture from the image in the first stage and constructs a dual-stream CNN to fuse the features of the input RGB image and the segmented map in the second stage with an accuracy of 93% on the OUHANDS dataset. However, most of the existing methods suffer from large model size and slow execution speed. In this paper, a shallow 3D CNN is chosen to improve the execution speed and enable better learning of spatio-temporal features in videos.

Skeleton-Based Gesture Recognition Methods. Depth cameras can directly acquire skeletal information of gesture movements [27], eliminating to some extent the challenges posed by RGB images. In addition, the skeletal joint spot feature is robust to changes in the tester's body size and sensor location compared to the RGB image feature. The position of the skeletal joints can be obtained in the depth map of each viewpoint of the captured gesture, the effect of changes in skeletal joint features is insensitive with respect to the camera viewpoint, and the orientation features of the skeletal joints are also robust to differences in human gesture shape. Choutas [28] et al. aggregated heat maps along the temporal dimension into video streams with color coding, and this novel segment-level use of shallow CNNs achieved 67.9% accuracy on the JHMBD dataset. Although the rules are created manually, they are prone to information loss during the aggregation process, resulting in poor recognition performance. To avoid hand-crafted rules, Shi [29] et al. proposed a new decouple spatial-temporal attention network (DSTA-Net) for skeleton-based gesture recognition, which is entirely based on self-attentive mechanisms and does not use structure-related RNNs, CNNs or GCNs, which is suitable for datasets with few nodes and video frames and has limited generalization capability. In this paper, it is proposed to stack 3D pseudo-heatmaps along the time dimension to form 3D video streams, in which all information is retained and the storage space of 3D pseudo-heatmaps is independent of the number of nodes, with good scalability.

3   Double_C3D Method

3.1   Overview

In this paper, skeleton-based geometric features [30, 31] are chosen as the object of study, and an overview of Double_C3D is depicted in Fig. 1. Since the original skeletal information provided by the dataset is rather messy, the original information is first arranged and regularized, and these coordinate points are arranged into a number of meta matrices, each of which has a size of K*C, where K denotes the number of joints and C denotes the dimension of coordinates. Then a meta matrix represents one frame of skeletal joint data, and the number of meta matrices is the number of frames of a gesture sequence, which varies depending on the duration of the gesture.

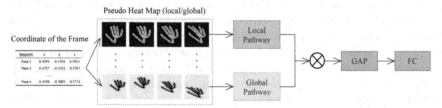

Fig. 1. The overview of the method. Firstly, the coordinate triples are pre_processed and saved as (x, y, z). Then the local pseudo-heat map sources and global pseudo-heat map sources are stacked along the time dimension. Finally, the gestures are classified using a dual-path network. "GAP" denotes global average pooling and "FC" denotes fully connected layer.

In order to reduce redundant elements and improve the image quality of the pseudo-heatmap, inspired by PoseConv3D [32], two types of crop boxes - a global crop box (see Fig. 2a) and a local crop box (see Fig. 2b) - are used to form a global data source and a local data source, respectively.

To improve the running speed, the pseudo-heat map is sampled with a fixed time step, and the remaining frames are discarded after extracting T frames. For gesture sequences with less than T frames, the last frame is used to fill them, so that all gesture sequences have no less than T frames. Lastly, all frames are stacked along the time dimension to form a 3D heat map volume, which are fed into the Double-C3D network for gesture classification.

3.2   Generate 3D Heat Map Volumes

In this experiment, 2D pseudo-heat maps are generated using joint triad coordinates, and the sizes of the joints are represented by the depth value z. However, if the depth

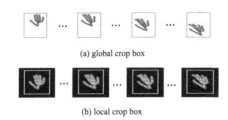

(a) global crop box

(b) local crop box

Fig. 2. Crop box. To reduce the space size, the crop box is used to crop all the T Frames. The global crop box (red box in Fig. a) contains the full motion trajectory of the gesture, while the local crop box (gold box in Fig. b) shows the motion details more specifically.

values are used directly in the pseudo-heat map to represent the sizes of the nodes, two problems arise. On the one hand, in the same gesture sequence, some pseudo-heat maps do not show the joint points, and some pseudo-heat maps have too large joint points, making the ratio of joint points to fingers out of proportion, resulting in extreme cases. On the other hand, in different gesture sequences, certain gestures, such as pinching and shaking, have clear images of the pseudo-heat map after cropping, which are easy for the network to extract features; however, certain gestures, such as swipe left and swipe right, have blurred images after cropping, and K nodes are stacked together, which are likely to result in gestures that are not easily distinguishable. So, a mapping relationship is set:

$$depth = \begin{cases} \alpha * (M - z_i), z_i \leq M \\ \alpha * (z_i - M), z_i > M \end{cases} \quad (1)$$

where depth denotes the new depth value and M denotes the average number of depth values in a gesture sequence, z_i representing the depth values in a given frame, α is to balance the depth values.

Based on the motion trajectory of the gesture, two dataset types were generated using a crop box---a global dataset and a local dataset. In the global dataset, a complete gesture sequence is used as a unit to find the largest crop box containing the motion trajectory, and the box is used to crop all of that gesture sequence, which ensures the integrity of all motion trajectory information in a gesture sequence. In the local dataset, on a frame-by-frame basis, the crop box encloses the full gesture and is used to crop that gesture, thus ensuring that the joints and fingers are clearly visible. The size of the pseudo-heat map after cropping is the same whether it is globally cropped or locally cropped. Finally, T frames are sampled for all frames with fixed time steps and the remaining frames are discarded, and the T-frame pseudo-heat maps are stacked along the time dimension to form pseudo-heat maps volumes, whose size is T*H*W.

3.3 3D-CNN for Skeleton-Based Gesture Recognition

The Double_C3D network structure is shown in Fig. 3a, and its underlying architecture is C3D [33].

Dynamic gestures are composed of consecutive frames of gesture images. 2D convolutional neural networks only consider the internal information of single frames and

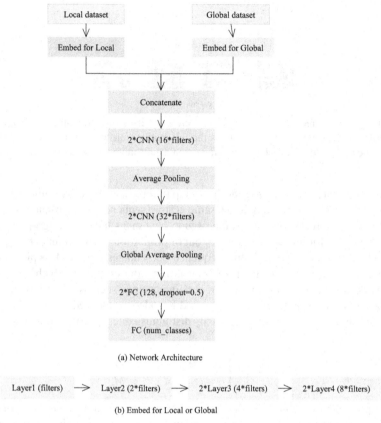

(a) Network Architecture

Layer1 (filters) $\longrightarrow$ Layer2 (2*filters) $\longrightarrow$ 2*Layer3 (4*filters) $\longrightarrow$ 2*Layer4 (8*filters)

(b) Embed for Local or Global

Fig. 3. The network architecture of Double_C3D. (a) Embed is symmetric, and change the size of the model by changing the value of the filter, "FC" denotes Fully Connected Layer. (b) "Layer" denotes one 3D CNN layer and one average pooling layer.

cannot extract the temporal information of consecutive frames. In contrast, 3D convolutional neural network can better model temporal information through 3D convolution and 3D pooling operation, which is more suitable for spatial-temporal feature learning and can improve the recognition effect of dynamic gestures. But, the large number of parameters in 3D CNN increases the computational cost and puts higher demands on computer hardware equipment.

To address this issue, two modifications were made to the C3D structure: (1) reducing the number of channels on top of C3D because the spatial resolution of 3D heat map video streams is not as large as RGB video streams; (2) since 3D heat map video streaming is already an intermediate level feature for gesture recognition, the number of network layers is reduced based on C3D. With these two improvements, the network parameters can be significantly reduced and the operating speed can be increased.

As a whole, the Double_C3D framework is a dual-stream 3D CNN where the local and global paths are symmetric (see Fig. 3b) with the same channel width, network depth and input spatial resolution, processing local and global information respectively. The input of the local path is the local information of the gesture to obtain the representation information of the video frame. The global information is input to the global path to obtain the motion information of the video frame. Feature fusion is performed by bi-directional lateral connection after the respective information is obtained for both paths. Finally, the fused information is fed into the classification network and the fully connected layer to classify the gestures.

4 Experiments

4.1 Datasets

SHREC'2017. The SHREC'2017 dataset contains 14 gestures, each performed 1 and 10 times by 28 participants in two ways (using one finger and the whole hand), generating a total of 2800 video sequences with sequence lengths ranging from 20 to 50 frames, so it has two benchmarks: 14 gestures for coarse classification and 28 gestures for fine-grained classification. The dataset was split into 1,960 training sequences and 840 test sequences in a 7:3 ratio. The dataset provides depth images with a pixel resolution of 640*480 and coordinates of 22 joints. The dataset provides binary and ternary coordinates of 22 joints, and 3-dimensional spatial coordinates are used in this experiment.

JHMBD. The JHMBD dataset is derived from the HMBD51 dataset and contains 928 video samples from 21 gesture categories, each sample includes the start and end time of the behavior, and each sample includes 14–40 frames. In each frame, the person performing the gesture is labeled with 2D joint position, scale, viewpoint, segmentation, puppet mask, and puppet flow.

4.2 Implementation Details

To show the generalizability of the experimental approach, the same configuration was used for all experiments. The input video is sampled uniformly at 32 frames, and then each frame is cropped using the center crop. The network uses a two-branch fusion structure. Explore how performance varies with different model sizes by varying the filter values. For training, the initial learning rate is 0.004 and is divided by 10 in 60 and 100 epochs, for a total of 150 epochs. The batch size is 16 and the weight decay is 0.0005. Stochastic gradient descent (SGD) with Nesterov momentum (0.9) is used as the optimizer and cross entropy as the loss function.

4.3 Comparison with Previous Methods

The gesture recognition results for the SHREC dataset are shown in Table 1, and the filter values of 64, 32, 16 are selected for the experiments, respectively.

Double_C3D achieves the best performance on the SHREC dataset when the filter value is 16, with an accuracy of 91.72%. This is because the scale of the SHREC dataset is small, and the smaller the value of the filter, the smaller the parameters of the 3D CNN, and the amount of data in the dataset and network framework reaches a relatively balanced state.

Table 1. Results on SHREC.

Method	Accuracy
Dynamic hand [9]	88.2%
Key-frame CNN [22]	82.9%
3 Cent [11]	77.9%
CNN + LSTM [19]	89.8%
Parallel CNN [21]	91.3%
MFA-Net [12]	91.3%
Double_C3D(filters = 64)	85.45%
Double_C3D(filters = 32)	91.19%
Double_C3D(filters = 16)	**91.72%**

In addition, training and testing are also performed in the JHMBD dataset. In the experiment, the network input size remains at 32*56*56, and the number of total network parameters is adjusted by modifying the value of the filter.

Table 2. Results on JHMBD.

Method	Accuracy
Chanined Net [17]	56.8%
EHPI [34]	65.5%
PoTion [28]	67.9%
Double_C3D(filters = 64)	67.61%
Double_C3D(filters = 32)	68.18%
Double_C3D(filters = 16)	**70.54%**

As shown in Table 2, Double_C3D achieves the best performance when filters = 16, but it is much lower than the results in the SHREC dataset. This is because the JHMBD dataset contains only 2D skeleton information and the small length of each video stream makes the number of dataset parameters small. However, compared with Chained Net [17], EHPI [34], and PoTion [28] methods, the experimental method of fusing features of global and local information helps to improve the recognition performance.

4.4 Ablation Studies

Center Cropping. Since the motion trajectory of the gestures in the dataset can vary significantly, center cropping is chosen to use a smaller resolution and to preserve the complete joint information. To verify the effectiveness of center cropping, a set of comparative experiments is conducted when filters = 64, and the results as shown in Table 3. Using center cropping can better help data pre-processing, and the accuracy rate improved from 77.50% without center cropping to 85.45% with center cropping, an improvement of 7.95%.

Table 3. Results with and without central cropping on SHREC.

Method	Accuracy
Double_C3D (without center crop)	77.50%
Double_C3D (with center crop)	**85.45%**

Local Pathway or Global Pathway. From the results of the single-path test in Table 4, it can be seen that using only local motion information to extract features does not produce satisfactory performance, and the accuracy is only 63.33% at filters = 16. However, there is a significant improvement in accuracy when only global motion information is used to extract features, and the accuracy of global paths is higher than that of local paths when the filter values are 64,32,16, respectively.

In addition, it can be seen from Table 4 that with the decrease in the value of the filter, whether it is a local pathway and a global pathway, the accuracy rate increases. This is due to the fact that the amount of data in the dataset and the number of parameters in the network architecture gradually tend to balance as the filtering value decreases. So, when filters = 16, the optimal performance of local and global paths is achieved.

Moreover, the results after the fusion show that when the filter value is 64, 32, and 16, respectively, the accuracy of the use of dual -flow feature fusion network structure is increased than using only the single -flow path, which shows that the integration of local characteristics and global characteristics can be improved classification performance.

Table 4. Results of Ablation on SHREC.

Method	Accuracy
Double_C3D (filters = 64, only local pathway)	59.00%
Double_C3D (filters = 64, only global pathway)	84.40%
Double_C3D (filters = 64, local pathway & global pathway)	85.45%
Double_C3D (filters = 32, only local pathway)	61.55%
Double_C3D (filters = 32, only global pathway)	91.07%
Double_C3D (filters = 32, local pathway & global pathway)	91.19%
Double_C3D (filters = 16, only local pathway)	63.33%
Double_C3D (filters = 16, only global pathway)	91.54%
Double_C3D (filters = 16, local pathway & global pathway)	**91.72%**

5 Conclusion

By analyzing the geometric features of skeletal sequences, we propose a skeleton-based gesture recognition method, which takes a 3-dimensional pseudo-heat map video stream as input and effectively combines local features with global features. Although Double_C3D uses a small number of network layers, it achieves an accuracy of 91.72% and 70.54% on the SHREC dataset and the JHMBD dataset, respectively.

In order to further improve the performance of Double_C3D, the following aspects are considered in the next step of work:

- Although the effectiveness of Double_C3D has been verified on the SHREC dataset and the JHMBD dataset, it still needs to be tested on a large-scale dataset.
- More features, such as depth flow or depth HHA features, are fused into the network to further improve the recognition performance.
- Exploring other convolutional neural networks, such as GCN, can better capture the spatial and temporal information of skeletal sequence data.

References

1. Oudah, M., Al-Naji, A. and Chahl, J.: Hand gesture recognition based on computer vision: a review of techniques. J. Imaging **6**(8), 73 (2020)
2. Gao, Q., Chen, Y., Ju, Z., et al.: Dynamic hand gesture recognition based on 3D hand pose estimation for human-robot interaction. IEEE Sens. J. **22**(18), 17421–17430 (2021)
3. Yu, J., Gao, H., Zhou, D., Liu, J., Gao, Q., Ju, Z.: Deep temporal model-based identity-aware hand detection for space human-robot interaction. IEEE Trans. Cybern. **52**(12), 13738–13751 (2022). https://doi.org/10.1109/TCYB.2021.3114031
4. Kolkur, S., Kalbande, D., Shimpi, P., et al.: Human skin detection using RGB, HSV and YCbCr color models. arXiv preprint arXiv:1708.02694 (2017)
5. Wu, Z., Xiong, C., Jiang, Y.G., et al.: Liteeval: A coarse-to-fine framework for resource efficient video recognition. Adv. Neural Inform. Process. Syst. **32** (2019)
6. Hongchao, S., Hu, Y., Guoqing, Z., et al.: Behavior Identification based on Improved Two-Stream Convolutional Networks and Faster RCNN. In: 2021 33rd Chinese Control and Decision Conference (CCDC). IEEE, pp. 1771–1776 (2021)
7. Wang, P., Li, W., Ogunbona, P., et al.: RGB-D-based human motion recognition with deep learning: a survey. Comput. Vis. Image Underst. **171**, 118–139 (2018)
8. Xiao, F., Lee, Y.J., Grauman, K., et al.: Audiovisual slowfast networks for video recognition. arXiv preprint arXiv:2001.08740 (2020)
9. De Smedt, Q., Wannous, H., Vandeborre, J.P.: Skeleton-based dynamic hand gesture recognition. In: Proceedings of the IEEE Conference on Computer Vision and Pattern Recognition Workshops, pp. 1–9 (2016)
10. Cai, J., Jiang, N., Han, X., et al.: JOLO-GCN: mining joint-centered light-weight information for skeleton-based action recognition. In: Proceedings of the IEEE/CVF winter conference on applications of computer vision, pp. 2735–2744 (2021)
11. Caputo, F.M., Prebianca, P., Carcangiu, A., et al.: A 3 cent recognizer: simple and effective retrieval and classification of mid-air gestures from single 3D traces. In: STAG, pp. 9–15 (2017)
12. Chen, X., Wang, G., Guo, H., et al.: Mfa-net: Motion feature augmented network for dynamic hand gesture recognition from skeletal data. Sensors **19**(2), 239 (2019)

13. Li, M., Chen, S., Chen, X., et al.: Actional-structural graph convolutional networks for skeleton-based action recognition. In: Proceedings of the IEEE/CVF Conference on Computer Vision and Pattern Recognition, pp. 3595–3603 (2019)
14. Si, C., Chen, W., Wang, W., et al.: An attention enhanced graph convolutional lstm network for skeleton-based action recognition. In: Proceedings of the IEEE/CVF Conference on Computer Vision and Pattern Recognition, pp. 1227–1236 (2019)
15. Yang, H., Yan, D., Zhang, L., et al.: Feedback graph convolutional network for skeleton-based action recognition. IEEE Trans. Image Process. **31**, 164–175 (2021)
16. Deng, Z., Gao, Q., Ju, Z., et al.: Skeleton-based multifeatures and multistream network for real-time action recognition. IEEE Sens. J. **23**(7), 7397–7409 (2023)
17. Zolfaghari, M., Oliveira, G.L., Sedaghat, N., et al.: Chained multi-stream networks exploiting pose, motion, and appearance for action classification and detection. In: Proceedings of the IEEE International Conference on Computer Vision, pp. 2904–2913 (2017)
18. Baradel, F., Wolf, C., Mille, J.: Human action recognition: pose-based attention draws focus to hands. In: Proceedings of the IEEE International Conference on Computer Vision Workshops, pp. 604–613 (2017)
19. Nunez, J.C., Cabido, R., Pantrigo, J.J., et al.: Convolutional neural networks and long short-term memory for skeleton-based human activity and hand gesture recognition. Pattern Recogn. **76**, 80–94 (2018)
20. Yu, J., Gao, H., Chen, Y., Zhou, D., Liu, J., Ju, Z.: Adaptive spatiotemporal representation learning for skeleton-based human action recognition. IEEE Trans. Cogn. Develop. Syst. **14**(4), 1654–1665 (2022). https://doi.org/10.1109/TCDS.2021.3131253
21. Devineau, G., Xi, W., Moutarde, F., et al.: Convolutional neural networks for multivariate time series classification using both inter-and intra-channel parallel convolutions. In: Reconnaissance des Formes, Image, Apprentissage et Perception (RFIAP'2018) (2018)
22. De Smedt, Q., Wannous, H., Vandeborre, J.P., et al.: Shrec'17 track: 3d hand gesture recognition using a depth and skeletal dataset. In: 3DOR-10th Eurographics Workshop on 3D Object Retrieval, pp. 1–6 (2017)
23. Jhuang, H., Gall, J., Zuffi, S., et al.: Towards understanding action recognition. In: Proceedings of the IEEE International Conference on Computer Vision, pp. 3192–3199 (2017)
24. Köpüklü, O., Gunduz, A., Kose, N., Rigoll, G.: 2019 Real-time hand gesture detection and classification using convolutional neural networks. In: 2019 14th IEEE International Conference on Automatic Face & Gesture Recognition (FG IEEE 2019), pp. 1–8 (2019)
25. Dhingra, N., Kunz, A.: Res3atn-deep 3D residual attention network for hand gesture recognition in videos. In: 2019 International Conference on 3D Vision (3DV). IEEE, pp. 491–501 (2019)
26. Dadashzadeh, A., et al.: HGR-Net: a fusion network for hand gesture segmentation and recognition. IET Comput. Vision **13**(8), 700–707 (2019)
27. Chen, Y., Ding, Z., Chen, Y. L., et al.: Rapid recognition of dynamic hand gestures using leap motion. In: 2015 IEEE International Conference on Information and Automation. IEEE, 2015: 1419–1424
28. Choutas, V., Weinzaepfel, P., Revaud, J., et al.: Potion: pose motion representation for action recognition. In: Proceedings of the IEEE Conference on Computer Vision and Pattern Recognition, pp. 7024–7033 (2018)
29. Shi, L., Zhang, Y., Cheng, J., et al.: Decoupled spatial-temporal attention network for skeleton-based action recognition. arXiv preprint arXiv:2007.03263 (2020)
30. Zhang, S., Yang, Y., Xiao, J., et al.: Fusing geometric features for skeleton-based action recognition using multilayer LSTM networks. IEEE Trans. Multimedia **20**(9), 2330–2343 (2018)

31. Zhang, S., Liu, X., Xiao, J.: On geometric features for skeleton-based action recognition using multilayer LSTM networks. In: 2017 IEEE Winter Conference on Applications of Computer Vision (WACV). IEEE, pp.148–157 (2017)
32. Duan, H., Zhao, Y., Chen, K., et al.: Revisiting skeleton-based action recognition. In: Proceedings of the IEEE/CVF Conference on Computer Vision and Pattern Recognition, pp. 2969–2978 (2022)
33. Tran, D., Bourdev, L., Fergus, R., et al.: Learning spatiotemporal features with 3D convolutional networks. In: Proceedings of the IEEE International Conference on Computer Vision, pp. 4489–4497 (2015)
34. Ludl, D., Gulde, T., Curio, C.: Simple yet efficient real-time pose-based action recognition. In: 2019 IEEE Intelligent Transportation Systems Conference (ITSC). IEEE, pp. 581–588 (2019)

Dynamic Hand Gesture Recognition Based on Multi-skeletal Features for Sign Language Recognition System

Bohong Wu, Zhiwen Deng, and Qing Gao[✉]

School of Electronics and Communication Engineering,
Shenzhen Campus of Sun Yat-Sen University, Shenzhen 518107, China
gaoqing.ieee@gmail.com

Abstract. The action recognition system based on deep learning has achieved great success in recent years. By this, the dynamic hand gesture recognition development provides the possibility for new human-computer interaction methods. However, most existing hand gesture recognition feature extraction models are difficult to balance the accuracy and speed of recognition. To improve the performance of the hand gesture recognition model, this paper analyzes the hand skeleton sequence, proposes Multi-skeletal Features (MSF), and constructs a dynamic hand gesture feature extraction model based on the MSF. The MSF includes the distance of the hand skeleton points and the angle of the skeleton connections, which can effectively reduce the angle of view and distance noise in the expression of skeleton features. The model has superior performance on the SHREC dataset and can achieve an accuracy of 96.43% in 14 gesture classifications. At the same time, we combine our method with a hand pose estimator to design a real-time sign language recognition (SLR) system.

Keywords: Deep Learning · Dynamic Hand Gesture Recognition · SLR

1 Introduction

Nowadays, all kinds of common contact interactions (such as keyboards, mice, etc.) have certain shortcomings. As a very intuitive way of communication, hand gestures are the most proficient body language we use. In social communication, we often use various gestures to express all kinds of information. Dynamic gesture recognition can transform gesture communication into a way to interact with computers, opening up the possibility of new contactless interactions.

The vision-based gesture recognition methods include video-based gesture recognition and skeleton-based gesture recognition. The video-based dynamic hand gesture recognition method judges the type of gesture by analyzing and processing the image or video of hand movement and extracting feature information. It often uses 3D convolutional networks [1] for feature extraction. This method requires high computational power and large storage capacity to process a large amount of image or video data, but

H. Yang et al. (Eds.): ICIRA 2023, LNAI 14268, pp. 79–91, 2023.
https://doi.org/10.1007/978-981-99-6486-4_7

it can be greatly affected by the change of ambient light intensity. The skeleton-based dynamic gesture recognition method [14, 15] is based on the changes in the human skeleton and captures the changes in hand skeleton posture in the process of movement to carry out gesture recognition. This method mainly uses sensor devices (such as depth cameras) or hand pose estimation to obtain human skeleton information, with a small amount of calculation and high recognition accuracy, which is suitable for gesture tracking and gesture recognition, or other fields.

However, skeletal information cannot comprehensively represent the characteristics of gesture movements. In actual recognition processes, due to the difference in distance and the relative angle between the hand and the camera, there is noise caused by different perspectives and distances. Moreover, even for the same gesture, due to the different personal habits of the subject, the relative angle, amplitude, and details of finger rotation of the hand during movement are different. Therefore, it's difficult to extract useful feature information from it. That makes it difficult to balancing the accuracy and running speed of the network.

To solve the problems above, we use a 1D CNN to simplify the model to ensure the real-time performance of the system. To eliminate noise from multi-view and different distances, we designed skeleton length and skeleton connection angle features to achieve comprehensive feature representation. At the same time, we also use the different time strides of Cartesian spatial coordinates of skeletons in the network structure to solve the interference caused by different sampling. To realize the convenient application of dynamic gesture recognition in human-computer interaction systems, we have designed a relatively complete sign language gesture recognition (SLR) system, which includes hand detection, skeleton detection, and gesture recognition modules. And we collected a dataset related to Chinese sign language, and trained network models on SHREC [13] and the self-collected dataset.

The main contributions and innovations of this paper are summarized as follows: (1) Based on 1D CNN, new skeleton-related features and a new network (MSF-Net) are proposed. (2) A dataset containing 8 Chinese sign language classes is collected, and a real-time dynamic hand gesture recognition system is designed. (3) The proposed method achieves good performance on the SHREC dataset. The proposed SLR system with the MSF-Net can realize real-time and accurate SLR recognition.

The remainder of this paper is organized as follows. Section 2 produces the related work. Section 3 produces the proposed dynamic hand gesture recognition method based on multi-skeletal features. Section 4 shows the SLR system. Section 5 shows the experiment results and analysis. Conclusion and future work are introduced in Sect. 6.

2   Related Work

In recent years, with the continuous development of deep learning, various algorithms based on deep learning methods have demonstrated their superior performance in the field of computer vision. Therefore, this method is also widely used in the task of gesture recognition. The related works about video-based and skeleton-based dynamic hand gesture recognition are shown as follows.

2.1 Video-Based Dynamic Hand Gesture Recognition

In video-based gesture recognition methods, the convolution method is often used for feature extraction.

For dynamic gestures, 2D convolution will lose the timing information of dynamic gestures, while 3D convolution can extract the corresponding features from adjacent frames of the input video. Therefore, most video-based dynamic gesture recognition methods use 3D CNN based methods.

Z. Hu [2] introduced 3D convolution in gesture recognition tasks, realizing advanced performance in human behavior recognition tasks. However, 3D convolution has high redundancy in the actual feature extraction process. To reduce resource consumption, Z. Chen [3] proposed a convolutional LSTM network to reduce the number of model parameters. Long Short-term Memory (LSTM) is a variant of cyclic recurrent neural networks. In this kind of gesture recognition method based on 3D CNN and LSTM, the video sequence is first decomposed into equal time steps, and RGB images or depth images of each time step are extracted, then 3D CNN is used to extract features of each time step, and the extracted features are input into LSTM network for time series modeling, to capture time sequence information in the video, Finally, the features input by LSTM are input into the classifier for gesture recognition, and finally the gesture category labels are output. On this basis, X. Zhang [4] proposed a method that combines attention mechanisms with LSTM to achieve higher performance on ChaLearn's IsoGD [5] gesture dataset.

Although this type of method has strong robustness, due to its high demand for computing resources, high computational complexity, and the need for a large amount of annotated data for training in the neural network training process, the learning ability of the network is limited, and it cannot achieve good recognition results.

2.2 Skeleton-Based Dynamic Hand Gesture Recognition

The skeleton-based dynamic gesture recognition method [20–22] first detects the skeleton points in the input video and image, and then uses the trained network model to extract the features of the obtained skeleton point sequence.

This method can directly extract time series of skeleton joints, model the action time sequence between joints, and better characterize the dynamics of gestures. Since the feature extraction model does not require direct convolution operations on images or videos, it greatly reduces the computational complexity. For skeleton time sequences, 1D convolution can also be used for processing, which can further reduce the computational complexity of the model. At the same time, the requirement for data volume during the model training process is fewer. Usually, just collecting fewer video sequences can obtain sufficient skeleton data for training, reducing the cost of making a dataset.

The gesture recognition method based on GCN (Graph Convolutionary Networks) is a skeleton-based gesture recognition method. S. Yan [6] tried to design a GCN-based gesture recognition method for the first time and named it ST-GCN. That is, all key points of the hand are constructed into a graph, and GCN is used to model the dynamic patterns therein to achieve classification and prediction. This method received great attention after it was proposed. On this basis, W. Jingyao [7] proposed gesture recognition and matching methods combining ST-GCN and Mask R-CNN. Reference [8] proposed ResGCN, which follows the bottleneck structure of ResNet [9], increasing model capacity while reducing the number of model parameters.

Y. Fan [10] analyzed the characteristics of skeleton sequences and proposed a double feature double motion network (DD-Net) for skeleton-based action recognition. DD-Net uses 1D convolution to process skeleton point data, which can achieve fast running speed while ensuring good accuracy. Its input is 3D or 2D skeleton data, and the corresponding action classification is the output.

However, such skeleton-based gesture recognition methods also have some short-comings. This method first needs to estimate human skeleton points from RGB or depth images, which is difficult to obtain. And then, the quality of the obtained skeleton points has a great impact on the accuracy of the model, which will affect the model's performance. Also, the inability of skeleton coordinate data to accurately represent various motion features of the hand. This article introduces the skeleton joint distance and joint connection angles, which eliminate the noise generated by the perspective and distance, improving the recognition performance of the network.

3 Dynamic Hand Gesture Recognition Based on Multi-skeleton Features

3.1 Multi-skeletal Features

The JCD [10] feature effectively reduces the noise generated by the overall rotation of the hand, allowing the model constructed by DD-Net [10] to achieve a relatively high recognition rate with fewer parameters. However, when the hand is moving away or close to the camera, due to changes in object distance, the JCD features of the skeleton point will change accordingly, which means bringing in new noise.

When the hand only moves away or close, the angles of the hand-skeleton connections do not change. Therefore, a new feature, Joint Connection Angle (JCA), is introduced into the network. To minimize the computational complexity, only the joint connections of five fingers (a total of 16 vectors) are used for JCA feature calculation. Its definition is shown in Fig. 1:

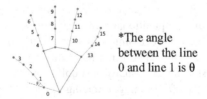

*The angle between the line 0 and line 1 is θ

Fig. 1. JCA Definition

$$JCA_{i,j}^n = angle(i,j) = arccos\left(\frac{\vec{i}\,\vec{j}}{\left|\vec{i}\right|\left|\vec{j}\right|}\right)\{i \neq j\} \tag{1}$$

$$JCA^n = \begin{bmatrix} JCA^n_{2,1} \\ \vdots & \ddots \\ JCA^n_{5,1} & \cdots & JCA^n_{5,4} \end{bmatrix}, n \in \{1, 2, \cdots, N\} \tag{2}$$

For K joint connection vectors, the length of the corresponding joint line angle vector is:

$$L_{JCA} = \binom{K}{2} \tag{3}$$

Combine JCA features with JCD features and Cartesian coordinate features to form Multi-skeletal Feature (MSF), which together serve as the input of gesture recognition network.

3.2 Network Structure

The network has a total of 4 inputs. JCA inputs do not involve temporal differential operations. So, the network structure of JCA feature inputs in the embedding layer adopts the same structure as JCD feature inputs 9. The structure of network input about the entire multi-skeletal feature is shown in Fig. 2.

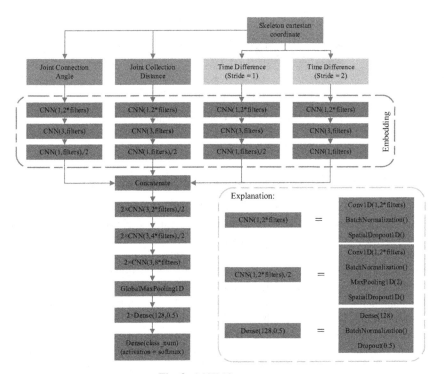

Fig. 2. MSF-Net structure

The network uses multi-class classification cross-entropy loss function, the convolution layer uses LeakyReLU activation function, and the output layer uses softmax activation function. At the same time, Batch Normalization [11] is also used within the model, making it easier and more stable to train the deep network model.

4 Sign Language Recognition System

4.1 Frame Structure

We use Mediapipe Hands [12] as the implementation method for hand tracking and skeleton prediction. The entire gesture interaction system mainly includes four parts: data collection, data processing, feature extraction, and recognition result output. The data collection part obtains hand video images through a camera; In the data processing stage, processing the image by simple color transformation and filtering. And use Mediapipe for hand detection and prediction of skeleton coordinates. Then there is the feature extraction section, which uses the skeleton coordinates as input. The predicted coordinates are used for feature extraction and recognition in the MSF-Net network. Finally, output the recognition results and corresponding real-time images of skeleton in the form of a window. The whole structure is shown in Fig. 3.

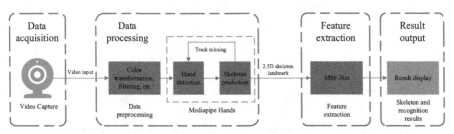

Fig. 3. Structure of sign language recognition system

4.2 Implementing a Sign Language Recognition System with Mediapipe

When using OpenCV to obtain cameras, due to the default format of the real-time image read being BGR format, and the image is mirrored and flipped relative to the general front camera, it is necessary to first perform horizontal flipping and format transformation on the obtained image, and then combine it with Mediapipe for skeleton prediction. When the hand is not recognized in the image, the Mediapipe detection output is None. It can only continue running when the detection output isn't None.

The hand landmark detection model in Mediapipe Hands outputs a matrix of size for single-frame image detection, which represents the number of joint points and represents the data dimension. Due to the need to obtain real-time video timing information during the actual operation of the system, a Numpy variable with a column needs to be created to store the output data of Mediapipe. After each image is detected, the detected results are added to the end of the variable to ensure real-time updates. Meanwhile, since subsequent sign language action detection only requires sign language actions over a while, its length needs to be controlled, always retaining only the last 50 frames of data. When Mediapipe detects multiple hands simultaneously, it does not cause a change in the output format. For example, when detecting two hands, a matrix of size is output instead of a one-dimensional vector of length. Therefore, when detecting multiple hands, a DD-Net network with the same structure can also be used for recognition.

Due to the default input frame length of the DD Net network being 32, it is necessary to standardize the frame length of the skeleton coordinate data outputted from Mediapipe and transform the input data of any frame length to 32 frame lengths. If the input data frame length is, the corresponding scaling coefficient is, and the obtained 3D coordinate data are standardized by subtracting the mean of the corresponding dimensions.

$$\begin{cases} X_{i,j} = X_{i,j} - mean(X), \\ Y_{i,j} = Y_{i,j} - mean(Y), \ i \in \{1, 2, \cdots 32\}, j \in \{1, 2, \cdots 21\} \\ Z_{i,j} = Z_{i,j} - mean(Z), \end{cases} \quad (4)$$

After standardization is completed, the corresponding JCD feature matrix and JCA feature matrix are calculated, and then the coordinate data, JCD features, and JCA features are fed into the trained DD Net network for recognition.

4.3 SLR Dataset

The SHREC dataset [13] only contains simple hand movements, and for the system to recognize sign language actions, it is necessary to first have a dataset containing sign language action information. There is a slight difference between sign language and simple gesture actions. Sign language uses gestures to measure actions, and gestures include sign language. Since all types of sign language datasets in China use sign languages from other countries, and the number of sign language datasets in China is relatively small and mostly contains body language, a self-collected dataset is used in this research.

Table 1. Classification of self-collected dataset

Order	Gesture	Type
1	Ni	single-handed
2	Hao	single-handed
3	Zai Jian	single-handed
4	Hen	single-handed
5	Ming Tian	single-handed
6	Jian	bimanual
7	Zao Shang	single-handed
8	Xie Xie	single-handed

This data collection was captured using a monocular camera. The data collection subjects included 8 Chinese sign language actions with different sign language meanings provided by 16 individuals, totaling 136 valid video samples. The sign language meanings and corresponding serial numbers included are shown in Table 1.

To ensure the richness of the data in the dataset, different lighting conditions, backgrounds, and angles were selected for shooting sign language actions. At the same time, for sign language movements that only use one hand, separate shots were taken for the left and right hands.

Since the more samples collected is not the better, to avoid overfitting and underfitting, the collected samples need to be screened to ensure that screened samples can represent the characteristic gestures corresponding to the specific sign language; The screened samples should avoid similarity and repetition with each other; The selected sample set can represent the corresponding motion state of a specific sign language; There are no obvious errors in the selected samples (such as hands exceeding video boundaries, gesture errors, etc.).

Due to the limited self-collected video data, to improve the generalization performance of the model, it is necessary to enhance the data. In this project, two main methods are used: geometric transformation and temporal sampling.

Firstly, a single video is mirrored, scaled to different proportions, and rotated at different angles. Then, Mediapipe is used to process the transformed video and output the coordinates of the corresponding skeleton, resulting in a total of 1180 sets of skeleton coordinate data with different frame lengths. Then, these data were sampled at equal intervals with a step size of 2, resulting in a total of 2000 sets of skeleton coordinate samples with frame lengths ranging from 30 frames to 70 frames.

From the obtained skeleton coordinate samples, a total of 1120 sets were randomly selected as the training set, and then 480 sets were randomly selected from the remaining samples as the testing set. The training and testing sets have a total of 1600 sets of samples. The ratio of sample size between the training and testing sets is 7:3.

5   Experiment Results and Analysis

5.1   Ablation Experiments on SHREC

SHREC [13] is a 3D gesture recognition dataset from Online-DHG, which contains 14 kinds of gestures, mainly divided into Coarse gestures and Fine gestures. In this experiment, we used the Windows 11 system and code with Python on Anaconda's environment. The results obtained from training on the SHREC dataset are as Fig. 6 (epochs = 600, batch size = 490, learn rate = 1.7×10^{-3}).

The results of ablation experiments using the DD-Net model and the MSF-Net model on the SHREC dataset are shown in Table 2 and Fig. 4.

With the same filter, the number of MSF-Net parameters is slightly more than DD-Net, and the training time is longer, but the recognition accuracy can be improved significantly. For the 64 filters MSF-Net, the recognition rate increased by 2.74% (compared to the research results of Fan Yang et al., an increase of 1.83%). Meanwhile, for MSF-Net with 16 filters, still has an accuracy of nearly 94% even with a parameter count of no more than 0.2M. Overall, MSF-Net has better performance.

Table 2. Ablation Experiments on SHREC Datasets

Network	Dimension	Parameters	Accuracy	Training time
DD-Net(filter = 64)	2D	1.816M	92.02%	51 m 4 s
	3D	1.821M	93.69%	54 m 26 s
DD-Net(filter = 32)	2D	0.496M	91.43%	17 m 49 s
	3D	0.499M	92.86%	19 m 50 s
DD-Net(filter = 16)	2D	0.152M	89.17%	12 m 43 s
	3D	0.154M	90.95%	14 m 57 s
MSF-Net(filter = 64)	2D	1.885M	94.52%	107 m 41 s
	3D	1.891M	96.43%	121 m 13 s
MSF-Net(filter = 32)	2D	0.518M	95.12%	59 m 51 s
	3D	0.521M	95.24%	62 m 43 s
MSF-Net(filter = 16)	2D	0.160M	93.69%	52 m 42 s
	3D	0.161M	94.40%	56 m 52 s

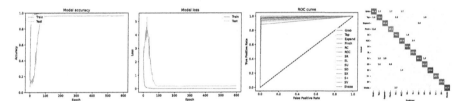

Fig. 4. Training results on the SHREC dataset. (3D skeleton, from left to right: accuracy curve, loss curve, ROC curve, and Confusion matrix)

5.2 Comparative Experiments on SHREC

The comparison of various methods on the SHREC dataset is shown in the Table 3.

It can be seen from Table 3 that MSF-Net not only has a relatively fewer number of parameters, but also performs well on the SHREC dataset. This indicates that MSF-Net has a good ability to extract features and can recognize various dynamic gesture actions accurately.

5.3 Application Experiments on Self-collected Dataset

By using 2D and 3D skeleton coordinates, the results obtained from training on the SHREC dataset are as Fig. 5 (epochs = 600, batch size = 1960):

Table 3. Comparative experiments on SHREC Datasets

Network	Parameters	Accuracy
Depth CNN + LSTM [16]	-	85.5%
Key-frame CNN [13]	7.92M	82.9%
STA-Res-TCN [18]	5–6M	93.6%
SRU-SPD [19]	-	86.31%
SRU-HOS-NET [17]	-	94.4%
MSF-Net(filter = 64)	1.891M	96.4%
MSF-Net(filter = 32)	0.521M	95.2%
MSF-Net(filter = 16)	0.161M	94.4%

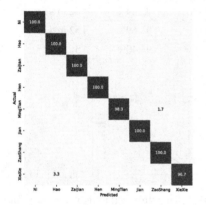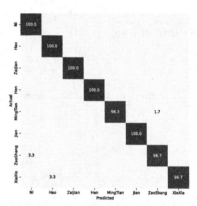

Fig. 5. Confusion matrix of training on the self-collected dataset (8 hand actions, left: 2D skeleton, right: 3D skeleton)

The model trained by MSF-Net on a self-collected dataset can achieve accuracy close to 99%. In addition to the superior performance of the network, the main reasons are twofold. Firstly, the selected 8 gesture action features are obvious; The second reason is that the self-collected dataset has a small number of data samples, and the subtle differences between each sample are small.

The result of dynamic gesture recognition in the SLR system is shown in Fig. 6.

Fig. 6. Classification results of Chinese sign language

6 Conclusion and Future Work

As a challenging task in computer vision, it's difficult to achieve both high recognition accuracy and good real-time performance in a sign language recognition system. The skeleton-based gesture recognition studied in this topic uses the coordinates of the skeleton to extract features on the one-dimensional convolutional neural network, which has a relatively simple structure. At the same time, MSF was proposed, which can achieve an accuracy of 96.43% on 14 gesture classifications in the SHREC dataset. Besides, to achieve the function of system sign language recognition, this project used a self-collected sign language action dataset to train the MSF-Net and achieved high recognition accuracy on a total of 8 sign language actions.

Although Mediapipe's Palm Detector Model has achieved good performance, the model will result in poor detection performance in poor environments. Finding a better hand detection model can achieve better detection results. And the self-collected sign language dataset mentioned in Sect. 4 has fewer samples and contains limited sign language action categories. In the future, we will enrich the sign language action categories of the dataset.

Acknowledgement. This work was supported in part by the National Natural Science Foundation of China (62006204), the Guangdong Basic and Applied Basic Research Foundation (2022A1515011431), and Shenzhen Science and Technology Program (RCBS20210609104516043, JSGG20210802154004014).

References

1. Tran, D., Bourdev, L., Fergus, R., Torresani, L., Paluri, M.: Learning spatiotemporal features with 3D convolutional networks. In: IEEE International Conference on Computer Vision, pp. 4489–4497 (2015)
2. Hu, Z., Hu, Y., Liu, J., et al.: 3D separable convolutional neural network for dynamic hand gesture recognition. Neurocomputing **318**, 151–161 (2018)

3. Xingjian, S.H I., Chen, Z., Wang, H., et al.: Convolutional LSTM network: a machine learning approach for precipitation nowcasting. In: Advances in neural information processing systems, pp. 802–810 (2015)
4. Zhang, X., Tie, Y., Qi, L.: Dynamic gesture recognition based on 3D separable convolutional LSTM networks. In: 2020 IEEE 11th International Conference on Software Engineering and Service Science (ICSESS), Beijing, China, pp. 180–183 (2020). https://doi.org/10.1109/ICS ESS49938.2020.9237672
5. Wan, J., et al.: ChaLearn looking at people: IsoGD and ConGD large-scale RGB-D ges-ture recognition. IEEE Trans. Cybern. **52**(5), 3422–3433 (2022). https://doi.org/10.1109/TCYB. 2020.3012092
6. Yan, S., Xiong, Y.J., Lin, D.H.: Spatial temporal graph convolutional networks for skeleton-based action recognition. In: Proceeding of the National Conference on Artificial Intelligence (2018)
7. Jingyao, W., Naigong, Y., Firdaous, E.: Gesture recognition matching based on dynamic skeleton. In: 2021 33rd Chinese Control and Decision Conference (CCDC), Kunming, China, 2021, pp. 1680–1685 (2021). https://doi.org/10.1109/CCDC52312.2021.9601572
8. Song, Y.-F., Zhang, Z., Shan, C., Wang, L.: Stronger faster and more explainable: a graph convolutional baseline for skeleton-based action recognition. In: Proceedings of ACM International Conference on Multimedia, pp. 1625–1633 (2020)
9. He, K., Zhang, X., Ren, S., Sun, J.: Deep residual learning for image recognition. In: Proceedings of the IEEE Conference on Computer Vision and Pattern Recognition, pp. 770–778 (2016)
10. Yang, F., et al.: Make skeleton-based action recognition model smaller, faster and better. arXiv:1907.09658 (2020)
11. Ioffe, S., Szegedy, C.: Batch normalization: accelerating deep network training by reducing internal covariate shift. In: International Conference on Machine Learning, pp. 448–456 (2015)
12. Zhang, F., Bazarevsky, V., Vakunov, A., et al.: Mediapipe hands: on-device real-time hand tracking arXiv:2006.10214 (2020)
13. Smedt, Q-D., Wannous, H., Vandeborre, J-P., Guerry, J., Saux, B-L., Filliat, D.: Shrec 2017 track: 3d hand gesture recognition using a depth and skeletal dataset. In: 10th Eurographics Workshop on 3D Object Retrieval (2017)
14. Shotton, J., et al.: Real-time human pose recognition in parts from single depth images. Commu. ACM **56**(1), 116–124 (2011)
15. Ohn-Bar, E., Trivedi, M.M., Katz, I.: Joint angles similarities and HMM for skeleton-based gesture recognition. IEEE Trans. Multimedia **16**(1), 37–48 (2014)
16. Lai, K., Yanushkevich, S.N.: CNN+RNN Depth and skeleton based dynamic hand gesture recognition. In: 2018 24th International Conference on Pattern Recognition (ICPR), Beijing, China, pp. 3451–3456 (2018). https://doi.org/10.1109/ICPR.2018.8545718
17. Nguyen, X.S., Brun, L., Lézoray, O., Bougleux, S.: Learning recurrent high-order statistics for skeleton-based hand gesture recognition. In: 2020 25th International Conference on Pattern Recognition (ICPR), Milan, Italy, pp. 975–982 (2021). https://doi.org/10.1109/ICPR48806. 2021.9412036
18. Hou, J., Wang, G., Chen, X., Xue, J.-H., Zhu, R., Yang, H.: Spatial-temporal attention res-tcn for skeleton-based dynamic hand gesture recognition. In: Leal-Taixé, L., Roth, S. (eds.) ECCV 2018. LNCS, pp. 273–286. Springer, Cham (2019). https://doi.org/10.1007/978-3-030-11024-6_18
19. Chakraborty, R., et al.: A statistical recurrent model on the manifold of symmetric positive definite matrices. In: Advances in Neural Information Processing Systems, NeurIPS, vol. 31, pp. 8897–8908 (2018)

20. Deng, Z., Gao, Q., Ju, Z., Yu, X.: Skeleton-based multifeatures and multistream network for real-time action recognition. IEEE S. J. **23**(7), 7397–7409 (2023). https://doi.org/10.1109/JSEN.2023.3246133

21. Gao, Q., Liu, J., Ju, Z., Zhang, X.: Dual-Hand detection for human-robot interaction by a parallel network based on hand detection and body pose estimation. IEEE Trans. Industr. Electron. **66**(12), 9663–9672 (2019). https://doi.org/10.1109/TIE.2019.2898624

22. Gao, Q., Chen, Y., Ju, Z., Yi, L.: Dynamic hand gesture recognition based on 3D hand pose estimation for human–robot interaction. IEEE Sens. J. **22**(18), 17421–17430 (2022). https://doi.org/10.1109/JSEN.2021.3059685

An Amended Time-Scaling Algorithm for Kino-Dynamic Trajectories

Sen Xu and Ye Ding[✉]

School of Mechanical Engineering,State Key Laboratory of Mechanical System and Vibration, Shanghai Jiao Tong University, Shanghai 200240, China
y.ding@sjtu.edu.cn

Abstract. This paper presents a computational geometry-based implementation of the time scaling algorithm, with a linear-time complexity. The proposed method involves sampling N points along a robot's motion path and scaling their speed profiles to meet the kino-dynamic constraints at those points. The method consists of two steps. First, it decomposes the original problem into $N - 1$ 2-D subproblems, and describes the feasible domain of each subproblem using a closure that does not have redundant constraints. The algorithm considers both linear and quadratic radical constraints, and the feasible domain of every subproblem is the intersection of the discretized constraints from forward, backward and central difference schemes. Second, it solves the original problem by recursively updating the domain of the subproblems twice in two oppressive directions, and guarantees optimality when constraints of every subproblem are peaked ones. Numerical experiments show that this method can not only provide the same solution as the original forward-backward algorithm in peaked-constraint cases with similar time complexity, but also be used to handle general kinodynamic trajectories with a sparse sampling strategy.

Keywords: Time Scaling · Kino-dynamic Trajectory Generation

1 Introduction

Path-velocity decomposition is a common methodology used to address trajectory generation problems, particularly for robots with high degrees of freedom [3, 8, 15]. This approach was first introduced by [2]. It scales the parameter derivative on the sampled points of the given twice-differentiable smooth path to minimize the execution time under kinodynamic constraints. This approach has been successfully used not only in quasi-static cases [5, 7] but also in dynamic cases [14, 15]. [8] proposed a general framework for humanoid motion generation consisting of three parts: path generation, feasible set computation, and time-scaling. He verified the effectiveness of this method by solving a dynamic motion on a pendulum and some quasi-static motions on the humanoid. [3] also used the time-scaling method to accelerate the quasi-static motion of HRP4. The advantage

H. Yang et al. (Eds.): ICIRA 2023, LNAI 14268, pp. 92–103, 2023.
https://doi.org/10.1007/978-981-99-6486-4_8

of this technique is that it discusses the time optimality along a given 1D path under almost all the constraints above, rather than searching for the trajectory in the whole state space, although it will sacrifice global optimality as a price. Thus, the formulated optimization problem would be easier (often convex with linear constraints) and lower dimensional. However, discussion on dynamic cases is still limited. To decrease or eliminate constraint violations, especially dynamic ones, on the unsampled points along the path, strategies combining dense sampling with limit shrinking are often used. The denser the grids are sampled, the closer to time optimality the solution is, which will yield bang-bang control laws and constraint saturation on the sampled points [3]. Therefore, as side effects, frequent mutation of acceleration from one extreme to another might occur, and the computation time for the higher dimensional time-scaling problem and smooth speed curve interpolation will also increase. For dynamic trajectory time scaling, the selection of grids requires further discussion.

Two mainstream methods efficiently solve the discretized version of the original problem. The first is numerical integration, which originated from the bang-bang control law [1,13,14]. Pham proposed the Time-Optimal Path Parameterization Algorithm with a complete dynamic singularity [13] solution and a methodology to generate truly dynamic motion [14]. Barnett and Gosselin [1] used the bisection algorithm to locate the acceleration switching points along the path, so that forward and backward integration needs to be performed only once. However, repeated numerical integration is needed to find the next switch point in the bisection step. Also, the kino-dynamic constraints are approximated by interpolation in that process, meaning that dense sampling is needed. The second method is convex optimization [6,9,10]. The problem formulation usually has two versions: linear program [9] and second-order cone program. For the latter formulation, specific structures could be exploited to improve the computation efficiency [6,10]. Focusing on the sparse structure of the linear constraint matrix and the objective function's Hessian, Lipp and Boyd [10] developed Minimum-Time Speed Optimization Subroutines (MTSOS) to accelerate the Newton iteration of the barrier method in the interior point method framework. By introducing a specific difference scheme using only two variables that could convert the original constraints into peak constraints, [6] proposed a forward-backward (FB) algorithm that manages to solve the optimization problem in $NlogN$ time complexity in the linear-constraint case based on the theory of order and lattice.

This paper reformulates the speed planning problem for robots with high degrees of freedom, drawing inspiration from Consolini et al.'s forward-backward algorithm [6] and Hauser's constraint simplification technique [8]. The solution is presented from a computational geometry perspective to address kino-dynamic speed planning problems. The feasible domain of each 2-D subproblem is described by a closure whose edges are the active constraints. The left vertex of each edge is also stored, and redundant constraints are eliminated during the closure construction process. Subproblems can be solved by accessing the points along the edges, rather than solving the intersection of two piecewise functions using the fix-point method. The original problem is solved by sequentially solving each subproblem and updating the domain of the adjacent one. Additionally, this paper presents a case study showing that sparse sampling can give a more robust speed profile, with acceptable sacrifice of time optimality.

This paper is organized as follows. In Sect. 2, we gives the general formulation of the discretized version of the speed planning problem. Section 3 decomposes the original problem and describes how to construct the feasible domain with active constraints, and the solving process is given in Sect. 4. Section 5 presents the numerical results, including a bipedal dynamically walking case. The conclusions are summarized in Sect. 6.

2   Problem Formulation

Let $x \in \mathbb{R}^p$ be the generalized coordinate that describes the configuration of a robot with p degrees of freedom. Then, the curve $x(s) : \mathbb{R} \mapsto \mathbb{R}^p, s \in [s_1, s_N]$ represents the motion path of the robot. Let a differentiable monotone increasing function $s(t) : \mathbb{R} \mapsto \mathbb{R}, t > 0$ represent the path parameter as a function of time t. Then, $x(s(t))$ can be a trajectory. By viewing $\dot{s}$ as a function of s and noting that $\dot{s}_s^2 := \frac{\mathrm{d}\dot{s}^2}{\mathrm{d}s} = 2\dot{s}_s\dot{s} = 2\ddot{s}$, we obtain

$$\dot{x} = x_s\dot{s}, \ddot{x} = \tfrac{1}{2}x_s\dot{s}_s^2 + x_{ss}\dot{s}^2 \tag{1}$$

where $(*)_s$, $(*)_{ss}$ denote the operator $\frac{\mathrm{d}(*)}{\mathrm{d}s}$, $\frac{\mathrm{d}^2(*)}{\mathrm{d}s^2}$ respectively. The actuator torque τ and external wrench w can be represented as a linear function of $\dot{s}_s^2, \dot{s}^2$ using the robot dynamic equation as follows

$$\begin{bmatrix} w \\ \tau \end{bmatrix} = M(x)\ddot{x} + c(x, \dot{x}) + g(x)$$

$$= a(s)\dot{s}_s^2 + b(s)\dot{s}^2 + g(s), \tag{2}$$

$$a(s) = \tfrac{1}{2}Mx_s, \quad b(s) = Mx_{ss} + c(x, x_s)$$

where $M(x), c(x, \dot{x}), g(x)$ denote the mass matrix, generalized Coriolis and gravity terms respectively.

The ith actuated joint torque can be modeled as follows according to the equivalent circuit model of a DC motor

$$|\tau_i + k_i\dot{x}_i| \le \tau_i^U, \ |\tau_i| \le \tau_i^U \tag{3}$$

In cases involving humanoid locomotion, the contact wrench w must lie within the linearized contact wrench cone [3], introducing the linear constraint $Aw \le 0$. All the constraints above including the velocity and acceleration ones have the same form and can be written as follows,

$$D(s) \begin{bmatrix} \dot{s}_s^2 & \dot{s}^2 & \dot{s} & 1 \end{bmatrix}^T \le 0 \tag{4}$$

where $D(s) \in \mathbb{R}^{M \times 4}$ and M is the total number of the constraints at that point.

Let N sampled points $s_1, s_2, \ldots, s_N$ uniformly splitting $[s_1, s_N]$ into $N - 1$ intervals with Δs. In interval $[s_i, s_{i+1}](i = 1, \ldots, N - 1)$, the constraints in (4) are validated at $s_i, s_{i+1}, \bar{s}_i = \frac{s_i + s_{i+1}}{2}$ to obtain a robust evaluation when Δs is not small. Using the finite difference approximation $\dot{s}_s^2 \approx \frac{\dot{s}_{i+1}^2 - \dot{s}_i^2}{\Delta s}$, all the time dependent variables is converted to path parameter dependent ones. Therefore, the constraints evaluated at those three points in interval $[s_i, s_{i+1}]$ can be written as follows

$$
\begin{aligned}
&\boldsymbol{D}(s_i) \left[\tfrac{\Delta \nu_i}{\Delta s} \; \nu_i \; \sqrt{\nu_i} \; 1 \right]^T \leq 0, \\
&\boldsymbol{D}(s_{i+1}) \left[\tfrac{\Delta \nu_i}{\Delta s} \; \nu_i \; \sqrt{\nu_{i+1}} \; 1 \right]^T \leq 0, \\
&\boldsymbol{D}(\bar{s}_i) \left[\tfrac{\Delta \nu_i}{\Delta s} \; \bar{\nu}_i \; \sqrt{\nu_i} \; 1 \right]^T \leq 0, \\
&\boldsymbol{D}(\bar{s}_i) \left[\tfrac{\Delta \nu_i}{\Delta s} \; \bar{\nu}_i \; \sqrt{\nu_{i+1}} \; 1 \right]^T \leq 0
\end{aligned}
\tag{5}
$$

where $\nu_i = \dot{s}_i^2, \Delta \nu_i = \nu_{i+1} - \nu_i, \bar{\nu}_i = \frac{\nu_{i+1} + \nu_i}{2}$. At $\bar{s}_i$, $\ddot{s}_i^2$ and $\dot{s}_i$ are approximated by $\bar{\nu}_i$ and $\max\{\sqrt{\nu_i}, \sqrt{\nu_{i+1}}\}$ respectively. Those approximations can give a conservative evaluation of the original constraints. Estimating the time of every interval by the average parameter speed, the optimal time-scaling problem can be formulated as follows

$$
\min_{\boldsymbol{\nu}} T(\boldsymbol{\nu}) = \sum_{i=1}^{N-1} \frac{2\Delta s}{\sqrt{\nu_i} + \sqrt{\nu_{i+1}}} \tag{6a}
$$

$$
s.t. \; \nu_i > 0, \tag{6b}
$$

$$
\boldsymbol{E}_i \left[\nu_{i+1} \; \nu_i \; \sqrt{\nu_{i+1}} \; \sqrt{\nu_i} \; 1 \right]^T \leq \boldsymbol{0} \tag{6c}
$$

where $\boldsymbol{E}_i$ is the matrix form of (5).

3 Subproblem Decomposition and Simplification

No doubt that Problem 6 can be solved by general nonlinear optimization methods like SQP or interior-points method to obtain a local minima, but a more efficient method with linear time complexity can be used to find a solution near the global minimum by exploiting the special structure of this problem.

To simplify Problem 6, redundant constraints need to be eliminated. Note that every constraint contains no more than two adjacent components of $\boldsymbol{\nu}$ and their square roots. Some intuitive geometric methods in a 2D plane can be used for this purpose. For any two ν_i, ν_{i+1}, the constraints associated with them form a closure noted as C_i in the first quadrant of the plane spanned by them. Noting that a convex closure can be expressed by its vertices and edges arranged in polar angle ascending order, the closure can also be expressed by its edges indexed by j with their left vertices, i.e. $(\boldsymbol{e}_{ij}, \boldsymbol{v}_{ij})$, arranged in the polar angle ascending order of their secants, as shown in Fig. 1a. Using the following three linear constraints where $(*)./(*)$ means element-wise division of two equal size vectors, an initial closure without redundant constraints can be given.

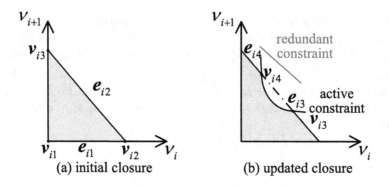

Fig. 1. The illustration of the closure construction and updating process.

$$\nu_i > 0, \ \nu_{i+1} > 0,$$

$$\frac{\nu_{i+1} + \nu_i}{2} \leq \left(\min \left(\dot{x}_{\lim}./ \left| \frac{d\boldsymbol{x}}{ds} \right|_{\bar{i}} \right) \right)^2 \tag{7}$$

Afterwards, the dynamic constraints can be checked to see if they are redundant or not and then added to C_i one by one while maintaining their secants' ascending polar angle order, as shown in Fig. 1. Although the rows of $\boldsymbol{E}_i$ in Problem 6 might number in the hundreds due to the conservative constraint evaluation in Eq. 5, the number of edges in C_i will be about 10 and it will only vary slightly during the procedure, meaning that the time it takes to solve all the closures is $O(N)$.

4   Solution Algorithm via Updating the Domain of the Subproblem

To solve Problem 6, the forward-backward algorithm splits it into N − 1 2D subproblems [6] as follows

$$\min_{\boldsymbol{\nu}_{i:i+1}} T(\boldsymbol{\nu}_{i:i+1}) = \frac{2\Delta s}{\sqrt{\nu_i} + \sqrt{\nu_{i+1}}} \tag{8}$$

$$s.t. \ \boldsymbol{\nu}_{i:i+1} \in C_i$$

Then, it solves every subproblem in turn and uses its solution to update the domain of the next subproblem from C_1 to C_{N-1}. After that, the process is repeated from C_{N-1} to C_1 and the solution of the original problem will be obtained. Using the closure represented as a set of edges and left vertices discussed in Sect. 3, that iteration process can be implemented by locally updating $\boldsymbol{\nu}_{i:i+1}$, C_i, C_{i+1}, as shown in Fig. 2, and the pseudocode is demonstrated in Algorithm 1. In Fig. 2a, $\nu_{i+1} \leq \nu_{i+1}^*$ is redundant, while $\nu_i \leq \nu_i^*$ is the active one. The minimum is found at vertex $\boldsymbol{v}_{ij}$, so $\nu_{i+1} \leq v_{ij}^{i+1}$ will be active in the

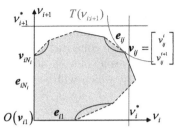

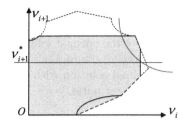

(a) The closure C_i before forward phase.   (b) The closure C_i before backward phase.

Fig. 2. A illustration of the closure C_i and its variation in Algorithm 1.

Algorithm 1: Forward-backward algorithm for Problem 6

Data: $\dot{x}_i$, C_i, $\dot{x}_{\lim}$, $i = 1, \ldots, N-1$

Result: ν^*

// initialize ν^*

1 **for** $i = 1$ to N **do**

2      $\nu_i^* = \left(\min \left(\dot{x}_{\lim} \cdot / \left| \frac{dx}{ds} \right|_i \right) \right)^2$;

3 **end**

// Forward phase

4 **for** $i = 1$ to $N-1$ **do**

5   Update C_i with constraints $\nu_i \leq \nu_i^*$, $\nu_{i+1} \leq \nu_{i+1}^*$;

6   Update $\nu_{i:i+1}^*$ by solving the ith subproblem with updated C_i;

7 **end**

// Backward phase

8 **for** $i = N-1$ to 1 **do**

9   Update C_i with constraints $\nu_{i+1} \leq \nu_{i+1}^*$;

10   Update $\nu_{i:i+1}^*$ by solving the ith subproblem with updated C_i;

11 **end**

12 **return** ν^*

---

backward phase in Fig. 2b. With the knowledge of edges and vertices of C_i, the optimal solution of the subproblems can be easily found by searching along C_i's boundary. Besides, the constraints of C_i will be peaked ones after the forward phase, and the solution of the subproblems can only be found at C_i's vertices, as illustrated in Fig. 2. Also, considering that C_i's edge number is limited, the time complexity of Algorithm 1, consisting of 3 for-loops, is still $O(N)$.

The optimality of the solution given by this algorithm is guaranteed only when all the constraints of C_i form peaked constraints, and the proof can be found in [12]. Another advantage of the peaked constraints is that it takes few steps to find the optimal solutions of the subproblems using the fixed point solver without knowledge of their feasible domain. To construct the peaked constraints purposely, the original FB algorithm changes the difference rule, which may overestimate the feasible domain of (ν_i, ν_{i+1}). When the constraints are no longer peaked ones, however, not only can optimality not be guaranteed, but also the efficient fixed point solver does not work. To make a tradeoff among the optimality, efficiency and robustness for online trajectory planning, the proposed algorithm uses the optimal solution of every subproblem to construct the peaked approximations of its original feasible domain, and gives a solution adjacent to the true optimal solution with similar time complexity, which will be validated in the experiment parts.

5   Experimental Result

The results of two groups of experiments are demonstrated in this section. The first one compares the result with the original FB algorithm, while the second one shows its application in dynamic trajectories with a sparse sampling strategy.

5.1   Comparison with the Original FB-Algorithm

In this part, we implement the proposed algorithm and the FB algorithm (Alg1 + Alg2) [6] with MATLAB.

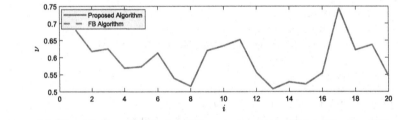

(a) The solution ν given by different algorithms ($M = 20$, $N = 20$).

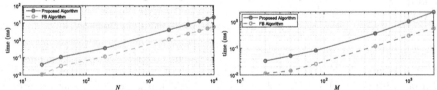

(b) The execution time of the two algorithms as N grows ($M = 20$).

(c) The execution time of the two algorithms as M grows ($N = 20$).

Fig. 3. The comparison between the proposed algorithm and the original FB algorithm.

To test the feasibility of this method for online planning, the implementation of the proposed method in MATLAB is converted to C++ by the *codegen* toolbox. The dimension of Problem 6 can be described by two parameters: the dimension of ν denoted as N, and the row number of E_i denoted as M.

To compare the performance with the original FB algorithm, the test problem is constructed with N groups of M linear peaked constraints, and the result is

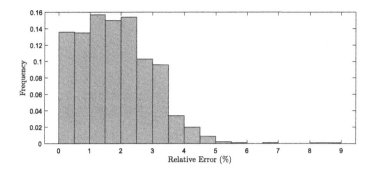

Fig. 4. The histogram of the relative error.

shown in Fig. 3. When the constraints are peaked, the proposed algorithm gives the same solution as the original FB algorithm. The execution time of the two algorithms grows almost linearly as N or M grows. Although the extra effort of the proposed algorithm to construct the closure of every subproblem makes it a little slower than the original FB algorithm, their execution times are in the same order of magnitude. The performance of the proposed algorithm is similar to another implementation of the FB algorithm (Alg1 + Alg3) [6] for linear constraints, which eliminates the redundant constraints and sorts the active ones.

For general cases, the original FB algorithm cannot work, and the interior point method implemented with the $fmincon$ function of the $Optimization$ toolbox is introduced as a comparison. One thousand randomly generated problems, where N varies from 10 to 100 and M varies from 20 to 70, are solved by those two algorithms, and the solutions given by the interior point are regarded as the true optimal solution. The result is shown in Fig. 4, where the relative error is described as $|T(\nu) - T(\nu^*)|/T(\nu^*)$. Here, ν is solved by the proposed algorithm and ν^* represents the optimal solution. The median is 1.73%, and the relative error of 99.4% of samples is within 5%. The difference of the solutions given by the two algorithms is demonstrated in Fig. 5.

5.2 Application in Dynamic Trajectory Generation

In this part, we use the proposed to generate the dynamic walking trajectory of a humanoid. The experimental subject is a simplified JAXON [4] with 15 actuated joints, and the motion paths are given by B-spline interpolation. The proposed algorithm is introduced to decelerate the path segments that violate the kino-dynamic constraints and accelerate some conservative path segments. The effect can be visualized through the trajectory of the center of pressure (CoP) of the contact sole surface. The value of $\nu(s)$ at unsampled points is estimated by a B-spline curve, whose control points are used to bound the speed profile, and $s(t)$ is obtained by numerical integration.

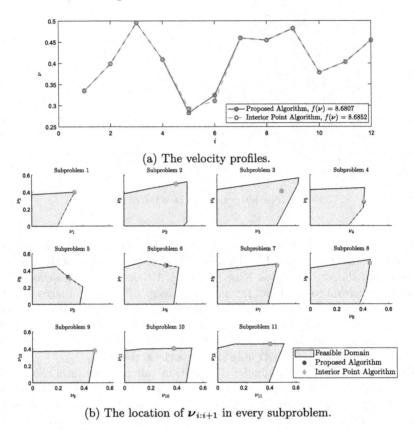

(a) The velocity profiles.

(b) The location of $\nu_{i:i+1}$ in every subproblem.

Fig. 5. The solutions given the proposed algorithm and the interior point algorithm, where $f(\nu) = T(\nu)/(2\Delta s)$. ($M = 50$, $N = 12$)

7 walking paradigms are manually given with variant step lengths, directions, and terrains to validate the feasibility of the proposed algorithm, as shown in Fig. 6. The sampling number N varies from 10 to 1000, and the trajectories of the CoP are shown in Fig. 7. The CoP trajectories, after time scaling, shrink inward towards the sole, and the variation of the speed profile $\nu(s)$ of one paradigm is shown in Fig. 8. As N grows, $T(\nu)$ decreases by about 5%, but spikes appear and exceed the sole boundary. This can be explained from the perspective of numerical integration. The formulation of constraint 5 makes $\ddot{s}$ at $(s_i, \dot{s}_i)$ located in the cross set of the motion cones [11] defined at $(s_i, \dot{s}_i)$, $(s_{i+1}, \dot{s}_{i+1})$ and $(\bar{s}_i, \sqrt{\bar{\nu}_i})$, forcing the line segment connecting them down the time optimal path-parameter curve, as shown in Fig. 9. This effect will be evident when N is small with the introduction of constraints at $s = \bar{s}_i$, shown in Fig. 8. It can naturally give a safety margin for the speed profile interpolation.

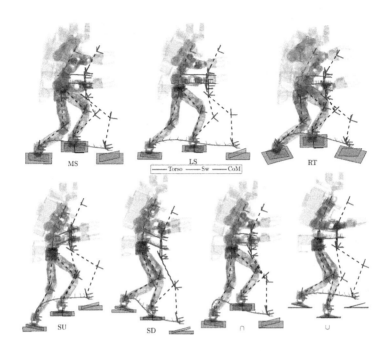

Fig. 6. The whole trajectories for the 7 walking paradigms.

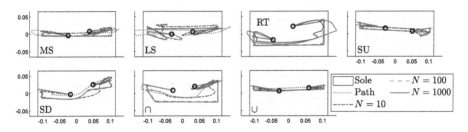

Fig. 7. CoP trajectories in SS phase after the time scaling solved by the proposed algorithm with different grid size N for the 7 paradigms.

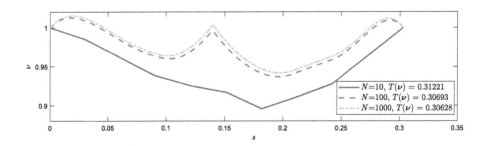

Fig. 8. The variation of the speed profile $\nu(s)$ of the MS paradigm.

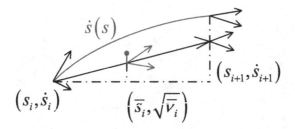

Fig. 9. The deviation of the discretized solution (the black line segment) w.r.t. the time optimal path-parameter curve $\dot{s}(s)$ (the red curve) in the $(s, \dot{s})$ plane. To show that $\ddot{s}$ at $(s_i, \dot{s}_i)$ is located in the cross set of the motion cones defined at $(s_i, \dot{s}_i)$, $(s_{i+1}, \dot{s}_{i+1})$ and $(\bar{s}_i, \sqrt{\bar{\nu}_i})$, the motion cone defined at $(\bar{s}_i, \sqrt{\bar{\nu}_i})$ is moved down to $(\bar{s}_i, \dot{s}_i)$.

6   Conclusion

This paper proposes a linear-time complexity algorithm compatible with more general constraint types for the time-scaling problem. First, it divides the original problem into several 2D subproblems and constructs their feasible domains using the forward, backward, and central difference schemes. Then, the peaked approximations of those domains based on their optimal solutions are solved in the forward phase. Finally, the solution can be obtained after the backward phase. It can handle more general constraint types while having a similar execution time compared to the original FB algorithm.

Due to the robust peaked approximation of the feasible domain for every subproblem, the solution given by the proposed algorithm will be a lower bound of the time optimal path-parameter curve $\dot{s}(s)$, and the gap between can be controlled by the grid size N. A large grid size can narrow the gap, but will increase the risk of the curve interpolated from the given discretized solution violating constraints. Numerical experiments show that the proposed algorithm, with a sparse grid size such as $N = 10$, is an economical and capable method to generate dynamic walking trajectories for a biped. Further efforts are needed to integrate this method into high-level optimization problems to generate more types of efficient locomotion.

References

1. Barnett, E., Gosselin, C.: A bisection algorithm for time-optimal trajectory planning along fully specified paths. IEEE Trans. Rob. **37**(1), 131–145 (2021). https://doi.org/10.1109/TRO.2020.3010632
2. Bobrow, J.: Optimal robot plant planning using the minimum-time criterion. IEEE J. Robot. Autom. **4**(4), 443–450 (1988). https://doi.org/10.1109/56.811
3. Caron, S., Pham, Q., Nakamura, Y.: Stability of surface contacts for humanoid robots: closed-form formulae of the contact wrench cone for rectangular support areas. In: 2015 IEEE International Conference on Robotics and Automation (ICRA), pp. 5107–5112 (2015). https://doi.org/10.1109/ICRA.2015.7139910

4. Caron, S.: JAXON humanoid robot. https://github.com/robot-descriptions/jaxon_description

5. Chen, Y., Dong, W., Ding, Y.: An efficient method for collision-free and jerk-constrained trajectory generation with sparse desired way-points for a flying robot. Sci. China Technol. Sci. **64**(8), 1719–1731 (2021). https://doi.org/10.1007/s11431-021-1836-7

6. Consolini, L., Locatelli, M., Minari, A., Nagy, A., Vajk, I.: Optimal time-complexity speed planning for robot manipulators. IEEE Trans. Rob. **35**(3), 790–797 (2019). https://doi.org/10.1109/TRO.2019.2899212

7. Fang, T., Ding, Y.: A sampling-based motion planning method for active visual measurement with an industrial robot. Robot. Comput.-Integr. Manuf. **76**, 102322 (2022). https://doi.org/10.1016/j.rcim.2022.102322

8. Hauser, K.: Fast interpolation and time-optimization with contact. The International Journal of Robotics Research 33(9), 1231–1250 (2014,8). DOI: 10.1177/0278364914527855

9. Heng, M.: Smooth and time-optimal trajectory generation for high speed machine tools (2008)

10. Lipp, T., Boyd, S.: Minimum-time speed optimisation over a fixed path. Int. J. Control **87**(6), 1297–1311 (2014). https://doi.org/10.1080/00207179.2013.875224

11. Lynch, K.M., Park, F.C.: Modern Robotics: Mechanics, Planning, and Control. Planning, and Control. Cambridge Univeristy Press, Cambridge, UK, Mechanics (2017)

12. Nagy, A.: Optimization Methods for Time-Optimal Path Tracking in Robotics. Ph.D. thesis, Budapest University of Technology and Economics (Sep 2019)

13. Pham, Q.C.: A general, fast, and robust implementation of the time-optimal path parameterization algorithm. IEEE Trans. Rob. **30**(6), 1533–1540 (2014). https://doi.org/10.1109/TRO.2014.2351113

14. Pham, Q.C., Caron, S., Lertkultanon, P., Nakamura, Y.: Admissible velocity propagation: beyond quasi-static path planning for high-dimensional robots. Int. J. Robot. Res. **36**(1), 44–67 (2017). https://doi.org/10.1177/0278364916675419

15. Pham, Q.C., Nakamura, Y.: Time-optimal path parameterization for critically dynamic motions of humanoid robots. In: 2012 12th IEEE-RAS International Conference on Humanoid Robots (Humanoids 2012), pp. 165–170. IEEE, Osaka, Japan (2012). https://doi.org/10.1109/HUMANOIDS.2012.6651515

Adapted Mapping Estimator in Visual Servoing Control for Model-Free Robotics Manipulator

Jun Tian[1](✉), Xungao Zhong[2,3](✉), Jiaguo Luo[2,3], and Xiafu Peng[1]

[1] School of Aerospace Engineering, Xiamen University, Xiamen 361005, China
tianjun256@163.com
[2] School of Electrical Engineering and Automation, Xiamen University of Technology,
Xiamen 361024, China
zhongxungao@163.com
[3] Xiamen Key Laboratory of Frontier Electric Power Equipment and Intelligent Control,
Xiamen 361024, China

Abstract. This paper presents a model-free approach to visual servoing control of a robotic manipulator operated in unknown environments. A mapping estimator with the learning network is applied to visual servoing control of model-free robotic manipulator, which can online estimate the vision-motor relationship in a stochastic environment without knowledge of noise statistics. The dynamic mapping identification problems are solved by incorporating the improved Kalman filtering (KF) and network learning techniques, moreover, an observation correlation updating method is used to estimate the variance of the noises via online learning. Various grasping positioning experiments are conducted to verify the proposed approach by using an eye-in-hand robotic manipulator without calibration.

Keywords: Robot manipulation · Visual servoing · Mapping estimator · Model-free robotics system

1 Introduction

Visual-based feedback control is one promising solution for robots to operate in unstructured environments through image features [1–3]. There are many successful implementation of visual feedback control in robots, such as a position-based visual servoing (PBVS) [4] and image-based visual servoing (IBVS) methods are popular tracked [5]. In PBVS, the task is defined in the Cartesian space and the systems retrieve the 3D information about the scene by using the geometric model. Then the pose of the target was estimated with respect to the robotics coordinate system [6, 7]. Thus, this servoing system is inevitably associated with the robotic hand-eye calibration. In consequence, the PBVS is more sensitive to the calibration errors and the image features may disappear from the field of view (FOV) of camera [8, 9]. In contrast, the IBVS method regulates the robot dynamic behavior by using image features from its visual sensor [10–13]. This method does not require the 3D reconstruction of target, but requires the camera calibration and the image depth information. IBVS more suitable for preventing the image feature from leaving the FOV. However, it cannot keep the robot movement insider its workspace, particularly when a large displacement of positioning is required.

© The Author(s), under exclusive license to Springer Nature Singapore Pte Ltd. 2023
H. Yang et al. (Eds.): ICIRA 2023, LNAI 14268, pp. 104–114, 2023.
https://doi.org/10.1007/978-981-99-6486-4_9

It is clear that the robotics calibration model and the image depth information should be provided for mentioned visual servoing (VS) methods for computing the dynamic mapping between the vision space and the robot workspace. Thus, to overcome the difficulties regarding in mapping calculation, we propose a new VS method with mapping estimator, which is treated as a stochastic state estimation problem.

The Kalman filter (KF) is one of the best linear state estimators, and its filtering gain is evaluated from the Gaussian white noise statistics of plant. As the noises are unknown in most real-world applications, the optimality of Kalman filter is never guaranteed. Therefore, some colored noise handling solutions have been presented, such as the dimension extension of Kalman filter [14, 15], LMS-based adaptive filtering [16], adaptive Wiener filtering [17], and others such neural network techniques [18, 19]. However, most of these filtering approaches require the noise variance parameters that are difficult to be derived in most situations.

This paper proposes a model-free approach to visual servoing control of a robotic manipulator operated in unknown noise variance environments. The visual-motor mapping and online estimation are conducted using adaptive Kalman filter with network learning techniques, in which the Kalman filtering model is built by adopting an equivalent observation equation for universal non-Gaussian noise. An observation correlation updating method is used to estimate the variance of the measurement noise via online learning. The network learning adjusts the network weights and enables the noise variances to be dynamically estimated.

The proposed mapping estimator does not require systems calibration and the depth information, and the 2D image measurements are directly used to estimate the desired movement of the robotic manipulator. The grasping positioning tasks are performed by reducing the image error between a set of current and desired image features in the image plane, providing highly flexibility for robot to operate in unknown environments. Extensive experiments are conducted on challenging tasks to verify the significant performance of the proposed approach.

2   The Problem Descriptions

The visual servoing control should firstly estimate a mapping matrix $J(k)$ to describes the dynamic differential relationship between the visual space S and the robotic workspace P, and then construct a controller to derive the end-effector moving $U(k)$ needed to minimize the errors of the image features $F(k)$.

We consider a model-free system without the hand-eye calibration, let $J(k) = \frac{\partial F(k)}{\partial U(k)} \in R^{r \times l}$ be the robot visual-motor mapping matrix. It then be formulated as the state estimation problem with KF techniques, in which the system state vector formed by concatenations of the row and the column elements of $J(t)$, i.e. $J(k) \subset R^{r \times l} \rightarrow X(k) \subset R^n$, $n = r \cdot l$. Assume that the state and observation equations of a robotic system are as follows:

$$X(k) = \varphi X(k-1) + \Gamma \xi(k) \tag{1}$$

$$Z(k) = hX(k) + \upsilon(k) \tag{2}$$

where $Z(k) \in R^m$ is the observation vector, $\varphi \in R^{n \times n}$ and $h \in R^{m \times n}$ are the state transformation and state observation matrix, respectively.

Assume that the system processing noise $\xi(k) \in R^n$ and observation noise $\upsilon(k) \in R^m$ are the random Gaussian white noise sequences with zero mean, and the covariance matrices that are designated by Q_ξ and R_υ respectively. According to the KF equations [20], the system state estimation is based on the following recurrence equations:

$$\hat{X}(k/k-1) = \varphi \hat{X}(k-1/k-1) \tag{3}$$

$$\hat{X}(k/k) = \hat{X}(k/k-1) + K(k/k)(Z(k/k) - C\hat{X}(k/k-1)) \tag{4}$$

$$K(k/k) = P(k/k-1)h^T (hP(k/k-1)h^T + R_\upsilon)^{-1} \tag{5}$$

$$P(k/k-1) = \varphi P(k/k)\varphi^T + Q_\xi \tag{6}$$

$$P(k/k) = (E - K(k)h)P(k/k-1) \tag{7}$$

The mapping online estimation value can be recovered from the system state, i.e. $\hat{X}(k/k) \subset R^n \rightarrow \hat{J}(k) \subset R^{r \times l}$. Since the observation noise of sensors is not the standard Gaussian white noise sequences, the noise variances are very difficult to be determined. Therefore, the observation Eq. (2) needs to be adjusted, and the noises variances Q_ξ and R_υ should be online estimated before using KF in our visual servoing control system.

3   The Mapping Estimator with Online Learning

Considering the universal non-Gaussian noise model is stationary that can be generated by passing a white noise through a filter:

$$\upsilon(k) = \lambda \upsilon(k - 1) + \eta(k-1) \tag{8}$$

where λ is the transition coefficient and $\eta(k)$ is the random white noise sequences with zero mean and the covariances R_η.

Based on Eqs. (1), (2) and (8), we can derive the observation vector:

$$\begin{aligned} Z(k + 1) &= hX(k + 1) + \upsilon(k + 1) \\ &= (h\varphi - \lambda h)X(k) + \lambda Z(k) + h\xi(k) + \eta(k) \end{aligned} \tag{9}$$

Equation (9) is considered as equivalent observation equation, and can be deformed to:

$$\underbrace{(Z(k + 1) - \lambda Z(k))}_{Z^*(k)} = \underbrace{(h\varphi - \lambda h)}_{h^*} X(k) + \underbrace{h\Gamma\xi(k) + \eta(k)}_{\upsilon^*(k)} \tag{10}$$

The variance of the observation noise $\upsilon^*(k)$ is computed as:

$$\begin{aligned} R_{\upsilon^*}(k) &= E\left\{(h\Gamma\xi(k) + \eta(k))(h\Gamma\xi(k) + \eta(k))^T\right\} \\ &= h\Gamma Q_\xi(k)(h\Gamma)^T + R_\eta(k) \end{aligned} \tag{11}$$

Then, an observation correlations approach is conducted for online estimation of Q_ξ and R_η in Eq. (11).

According to Eq. (2) and Eq. (10), we have:

$$Z^*(k) = h^*\varphi^i X(k-i) + h^*\Gamma\xi(k) + \upsilon^*(k) \tag{12}$$

Assume that $X(k)$ and $\upsilon^*(k)$ are not correlated, the random series $\{Z^*(k)\}$ is stationary and ergodic. Then the auto-correlation function $C_{z^*}(i)$ of new observation series $\{Z^*(k)\}$ can be derived as follows:

$$\begin{aligned} C_{Z^*}(i) &= E\left[Z^*(k)Z^{*T}(k-i)\right] \\ &= E\left\{\left[h^*\varphi^i X(k-i) + h^*\Gamma\xi(k) + \upsilon^*(k)\right] \times \left[h^*X(k-i) + \upsilon^*(k-i)\right]\right\} \\ &= h^*\varphi^i \varepsilon_X h^{*T} + h\Gamma Q_\xi (h\Gamma)^T + R_\eta, i \geq 1 \end{aligned} \tag{13}$$

where $\varepsilon_X = E\left[X(k)X(k)^T\right]$. However, $C_{Z^*}(i)$ cannot be computed as Q_ξ and R_η are unknown.

Figure 1 shows an online single layer network learning used to estimate the $C_{Z^*}(i)$ simultaneously. Let the input vector of the network be:

$$X(i) = \left(h^*\varphi^i \varepsilon_X h^{*T}, (h\Gamma)^T, I\right)^T \tag{14}$$

According to Eq. (13), the network output for the i-th training sample is given by:

$$C_{Z^*}(i) = W^T X(i) \tag{15}$$

where W is the network's weight vector shown below:

$$W = \left(I, h\Gamma Q_\xi, R_\eta\right)^T \tag{16}$$

After $Z^*(0),\dots,Z^*(k)$ have been obtained, we can get the estimate of the auto-correlation function $C_{Z^*}(i)$ below:

$$\begin{aligned} \hat{C}_{Z^*}(i) &= \frac{1}{k+1}\sum_{m=i}^{k} Z(m)Z^T(m-i) \\ &= \frac{1}{k+1}\left(k\hat{C}_{k-1}(i) + Z(k)Z^T(k-i)\right), 1 \leq i \leq k, k \geq 1 \end{aligned} \tag{17}$$

It is obvious that (17) is updated sequentially and $\hat{C}_{Z^*}(i)$ can be estimated online from the previous and new measurements. The network training updates the weights W to minimum the error between $C_{Z^*}(i)$ and $\hat{C}_{Z^*}(i)$, with the training cost function below:

$$E = \frac{1}{k}\sum_{i=1}^{k}\left|\hat{C}_{Z^*}(i) - C_{Z^*}(i)\right|^2 \tag{18}$$

The weight vector is updated according to:

$$W(j+1) = W(j) + \frac{\gamma}{k}\sum_{i=1}^{k}\left(\hat{C}_{z^*}(i) - W^T X(i)\right)X(i) \tag{19}$$

where j and γ are the time instant and the learning rate, respectively.

Thus, we can obtain the noises variances Q_ξ and R_η from weights W. The non-Gaussian noise Kalman filtering structure with the online learning algorithm which called mapping estimator is shown in the Fig. 1.

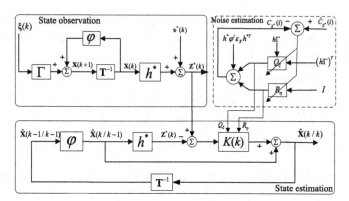

Fig. 1. The structure of mapping estimator based on KF and the learning network, in which the network is used to estimate the variance of the noises.

4 Model-free Robotics Visual Servoing Base on Mapping Estimator

This section gives a model-free visual servoing scheme base on the mapping estimator. The image error function in image plane is defined as follows:

$$e_F(k) = F(k) - F^d \tag{20}$$

where $F(k)=(f_1(k), ..., f_n(k)) \in R^n$ and $F^d=\left(f_1^d, ..., f_n^d\right) \in R^n$ are the n-D current image features and desired, respectively. As the desired features F^d are constant, the derivation of error function (20) is:

$$\dot{e}_F(k) = \frac{d}{dk}\left(F(k) - F^d\right) = \dot{F}(k) \tag{21}$$

For a discretionary manipulation task, the association of the time change of the image feature $F(k)$ with the robot's motion $U(k)$ is done by [8]:

$$\dot{F}(k)=J(k)U(k) \tag{22}$$

Substituting (22) into (21), we have:

$$\dot{e}_F(k) = J(k)U(k) \tag{23}$$

where $U(k)=\left(V(k)\ W(k)\right)^{\mathbf{T}}$ is the robotic control variable, in which $V(k)$ and $W(k)$ are linear and angular velocity of the end-effector, respectively.

There is nonzero constant ρ to make the following equation:

$$\dot{e}_F(k) = -\rho e_F(k) \tag{24}$$

Then substituting (24) into (23), we have the control law:

$$U(k) = -\rho J^+(k) e_F(k) \tag{25}$$

where ρ is the control rate, and $J^+(k)$ is the inverse mapping matrix as follows:

$$J^+(k) = J(k)^T \left(J(k) J(k)^T \right)^{-1} \tag{26}$$

where the mapping matrix $J(k)$ is estimated by mapping estimator shown in Fig. 2.

The steps of the model-free visual servoing are detailed below:

1) Given the desired feature F^d, control rate ρ, mapping matrix $J(0)$, and initial state vector $J(0) \rightarrow X(0/0)$.
2) At the k time, updating the system state $X(k)$ for time k by Eq. (1), and then calculate the observation vector $Z^*(k)$ by Eq. (10).
3) The state estimate $\hat{X}(k/k)$ at k time can be obtained by using the mapping estimator shown in Fig. 1.
4) To conduct mapping estimation $\hat{X}(k/k) \rightarrow \hat{J}(k)$.
5) To control the robot motion by Eq. (25).
6) $k \leftarrow k + 1$, go to Step 2).

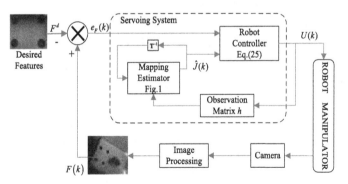

Fig. 2. The schema of model-free robotics visual servoing

5   Results and Discussions

For simplicity but without loss of generality, the system state transformation matrix and the noises drive matrix in state Eq. (1) are given by $\Gamma = \varphi = I$. Let the observation vector $Z(k) = \Delta F(k) = J(k) U(k)$, and the observation matrix in Eq. (2) is

$$h=\begin{pmatrix} U(k) & & 0 \\ & \ddots & \\ 0 & & U(k) \end{pmatrix}$$. The observation noise model is described by the filter (8) λ=0.5.

Thus, the new equivalent observation equation can be obtained by using (10). The noise variances are estimated simultaneously by the observation correlation-based algorithm with a learning network mentioned in Fig. 1.

The real experiment has been carried out by an eye-in-hand robot in our lab, which is shown in Fig. 3. The task is to control the manipulator from an arbitrary initial pose to the desired grasping pose by using the proposed model-free visual servoing with close feedback of image features. The center points of small circular disks on the object board are used as image feature. The control rate ρ in Eq. (25) is selected as 0.25.

In test 1, the initial pose of the robot is far from the desired pose, and the test results are shown in Fig. 4. In test 2, the initial features and desired features are located for the initial pose of the robot relative to the desired pose is rotation combined with translation positioning, the test results are shown in Fig. 5.

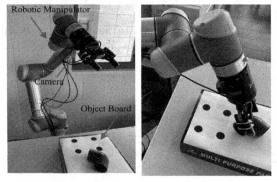

Fig. 3. The eye-in-hand robot system without any calibration parameters, the robot current pose and desired pose.

The FOV of the camera is 640×480 pixels in above two groups of positioning tests. The initial and the desired feature points are set as close as possible to the edge of the FOV. It can be seen from Fig. 4 (a) and Fig. 5 (a) that the motion trajectories of image features are smooth and stable within the FOV, and there are no feature points deviate from the image plane. On the other hand, it can be seen from Fig. 4 (b) and Fig. 5 (b) that the end-effector had the stabile motion without retreat and vibration in the process of the robot positioning. The robot trajectories in Cartesian space are almost the straight line from initial pose to the desired pose, with no conflict among the robot joints.

Figure 6 shows image errors for two tests, in which the error of the feature points uniformly converges, and the positioning steady-state error is within 10 pixels. It is clear that the model-free visual serving controller can provide high positioning precision.

In the following tests, we verify the performance of the mapping estimator and the traditional KF method in Eq. (3) to Eq. (7). Two kinds of estimation approaches are applied to the model-free visual servoing controller. We chose the Gaussian distribution

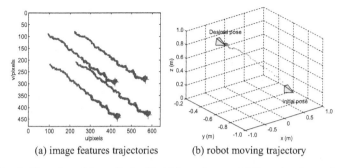

(a) image features trajectories   (b) robot moving trajectory

Fig. 4. Experimental results for Test 1 by using model-free visual servoing.

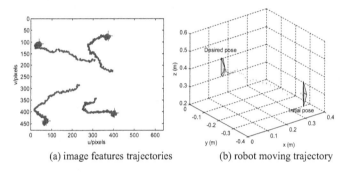

(a) image features trajectories   (b) robot moving trajectory

Fig. 5. Experimental results for Test 2 by using model-free visual servoing.

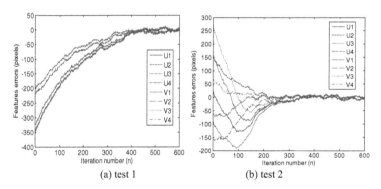

(a) test 1   (b) test 2

Fig. 6. The image errors during testing

white noise with zero mean. The system noise variance is $Q_\xi = 0.02$ and the observation noise variance is $R_\upsilon = 0.15$ for the KF method. The mapping estimator uses the proposed approach and the learning network to estimate the variance of the noise online. The robot motion from initial pose to the desired pose has large range moving and a rotation of X and Z axis.

Figure 7 shows the results of mapping estimator using in model-free visual servoing and Fig. 8 shows the results of the traditional KF method. Comparing Fig. 7 (a) with Fig. 8 (a), it can be seen that the image feature trajectories by using our estimator are smoother, short and stable than the feature trajectories by the KF method. From Fig. 7 (b) and Fig. 8 (b), we can see that the robot trajectories in Cartesian space by using proposed estimator is stable without oscillation, while the KF estimation method has large motion oscillation, retreat and serious detour in the same tasks. As can be seen from Fig. 9 the steady-state positioning error for our estimator is smaller than the KF method.

To sum up, the model-free visual servoing with the mapping estimator has eliminated the requirement for the system calibration and target modeling. Also, it has the capability of online estimating the visual-moto mapping in a stochastic environment without the knowledge of noise statistics, and the performances of the robotics is improved greatly.

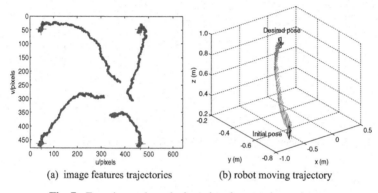

(a) image features trajectories   (b) robot moving trajectory

Fig. 7. Experimental results by using the mapping estimator.

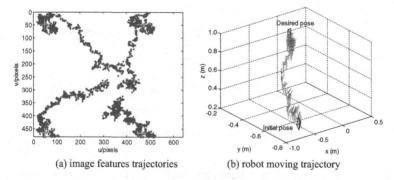

(a) image features trajectories   (b) robot moving trajectory

Fig. 8. Experimental results by using the KF method.

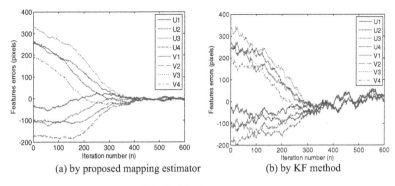

(a) by proposed mapping estimator   (b) by KF method

Fig. 9. The image errors

6 Conclusion

In this work, a mapping estimator and a model-free robotic visual servoing scheme have been investigated for robotic grasping manipulation. The proposed mapping estimator can be used in the visual servo system without the need of calibration and the image depth information. Moreover, the mapping identification problems were solved by incorporating KF and network learning techniques. The proposed approach is able to online estimate the vision-motor differential relationship in unknown environments without noise statistical information. Various experiments were conducted by using both the KF and our methods. The results clearly show that the proposed visual servoing with mapping estimator approach outperform the traditional approach in terms of the trajectories of the image features and robot movement in the Cartesian space.

Acknowledgments. This work was supported in part by the National Natural Science Foundation of China under Grant (NO. 61703356), in part by the Natural Science Foundation of Fujian Province under Grant (NO. 2022J011256), in part by the Innovation Foundation of Xiamen under Grant (NO. 3502Z20206071).

References

1. Said, H.B., Marie, R., Stéphant, J., Labbani-Igbida, O.: Skeleton-based visual servoing in unknown environments. IEEE/ASME Trans. Mechatron. **23**(6), 2750–2761 (2018)
2. Mao, H., Xiao, J.: Real-time conflict resolution of task-constrained manipulator motion in unforeseen dynamic environments. IEEE Trans. Rob. **35**(5), 1276–1283 (2019)
3. Yang, C., Peng, G., Li, Y., Cui, R., Cheng, L., Li, Z.: Neural networks enhanced adaptive admittance control of optimized robot–environment interaction. IEEE Trans. Cybern. **49**(7), 2568–2579 (2019)
4. Josip, M., Mirjana, B., Mojmil, C.: Comparison of uncalibrated model-free visual servoing methods for small-amplitude movements: a simulation study. Int. Jour. Adv. Robot. Syst. **108**(11), 1–16 (2014)
5. Farrokh, J.S., Deng, L., Wilson, W.J.: Comparison of basic visual servoing methods. IEEE/ASME Trans. Mechatron. **16**(5), 967–983 (2011)

6. Chaumette, F., Hutchinson, S.: Visual servo control. part I: basic approaches. IEEE Robot. Autom. Mag. **13**(4), 82–90 (2006)
7. Jiang, P., Cheng, Y., Wang, X., Feng, Z.: Unfalsified visual servoing for simultaneous object recognition and pose tracking. IEEE Trans. Cybern. **46**(12), 3032–3046 (2016)
8. Chaumette, F., Hutchinson, S.: Visual servo control. part II: Advanced approaches. IEEE Robo. Auto. Maga. **14**(1), 109–118 (2007)
9. Do-Hwan, P., Jeong-Hoon, K., In-Joong, H.: Novel position-based visual servoing approach to robust global stability under field-of-view constraint. IEEE Trans. Ind. Electron. **59**(12), 4735–4752 (2012)
10. Keshmiri, M., Xie, W.: Image-based visual servoing using an optimized trajectory planning technique. IEEE/ASME Trans. Mech. **22**(1), 359–370 (2017)
11. Shi, H., Sun, G., Wang, Y., Hwang, K.S.: Adaptive image-based visual servoing with temporary loss of the visual signal. IEEE Trans. Ind. Infor. **15**(4), 1956–1965 (2019)
12. Liang, X., Wang, H., Liu, Y., You, B., Liu, Z., Chen, W.: Calibration-free image-based trajectory tracking control of mobile robots with an overhead camera. IEEE Trans. Autom. Sci. Eng. **17**(2), 933–946 (2020)
13. Xie, H., Lynch, A.F., Low, K.H., Mao, S.: Adaptive output-feedback image-based visual servoing for quadrotor unmanned aerial vehicles. IEEE Trans. Control Syst. Technol. **28**(3), 1034–1041 (2020)
14. Gibson, J.D., Koo, B., Gray, S.D.: Filtering of colored noise for speech enhancement and coding. IEEE Trans. Signal Process. **39**(8), 1732–1742 (1991)
15. Alanis, A.Y., Sanchez, E.N., Loukianov, A.G., Perez-Cisneros, M.A.: Real-time discrete neural block control using sliding modes for electric induction motors. IEEE Trans. Control Syst. Technol. **18**(1), 11–21 (2010)
16. Soni, T., Rao, B.D., Zeidler, J.R., Ku, W.H.: Enhancement of images using the 2-D LMS adaptive algorithm. In: Proceedings of IEEE International Conference on Acoustic Speech and Signal Processing, pp. 3029–3032. IEEE, Toronto, ON, Canada (1991)
17. Stephanakis, I.M., Kollias, S.D.: Wavelet-based approach to adaptive wiener filtering of images in the presence of colored noise. Opt. Eng. **39**(5), 1353–1363 (2000)
18. Khanesar, M.A., Kayacan, E., Teshnehlab, M., Kaynak, O.: Extended Kalman filter based learning algorithm for type-2 fuzzy logic systems and its experimental evaluation. IEEE Trans. Ind. Electron. **59**(11), 4443–4455 (2012)
19. Zhan, R., Wan, J.: Neural network-aided adaptive unscented Kalman filter for nonlinear state estimation. IEEE Signal Process. Lett. **13**(7), 445–448 (2006)
20. Kalman, R.E.: A new approach to linear filtering and prediction problems. Trans. ASME-J. Basic Eng. **82**(1), 34–45 (1960)

FairShare: An Incentive-Based Fairness-Aware Data Sharing Framework for Federated Learning

Liyuan Liu[1], Ying Kong[2], Gaolei Li[3], and Meng Han[4(✉)]

[1] Saint Joseph's University, Philadelphia, PA, USA
lliu@sju.edu
[2] Zhejiang Electronic Information Product Inspection and Research Institute, Hangzhou, China
[3] Shanghai Jiaotong University, Shanghai, China
gaolei_li@sjtu.edu.cn
[4] Zhejiang University, Hangzhou, China
mhan@zju.edu.cn

Abstract. Federated learning protects sensitive data during AI model training, enabling collaboration without sharing raw data. Ensuring fairness and addressing un-shared decisions are crucial for reliable federated learning. This study introduces "FairShare", an incentive mechanism enhancing reliability in applications like financial fraud detection and chatbot customer service. FairShare has two stages: stage one uses the Vickrey-Clarke-Groves (VCG) auction to estimate clients' true costs, ensuring truthfulness, individual rationality, and computational efficiency. Stage two employs the Shapley Value method to allocate fair payments, promoting high-quality data usage. FairShare encourages clients to balance local datasets, reducing bias and increasing reliability. Theoretical proofs and experiments demonstrate FairShare's effectiveness in ensuring fairness and protecting data privacy, leading to reliable outcomes. Experiments confirm the VCG-based mechanism's truthfulness and Shapley Value's fairness in payment allocation. In conclusion, FairShare addresses fairness challenges and fosters reliability in federated learning, facilitating dependable human-machine interactions. Implementing FairShare can enhance sensitive data protection, promote fairness, and improve reliability in human-machine interactions, supporting federated learning adoption across sectors.

Keywords: incentive mechanism · federated learning · shapley value · fairness · reliability

1 Introduction

The advancement of artificial intelligence (AI) has transformed information into knowledge, continuously reshaping the world. AI is expected to grow in the coming years, bringing significant benefits and value to businesses. However, data

H. Yang et al. (Eds.): ICIRA 2023, LNAI 14268, pp. 115–126, 2023.
https://doi.org/10.1007/978-981-99-6486-4_10

privacy remains a critical challenge that could potentially hinder AI development and impact its reliability in human-machine interactions. Companies seeking to expand their market share rely on customer data and its secure, efficient utilization (2019). Ensuring AI reliability is essential for maintaining customer trust and protecting sensitive information. In response to data privacy concerns and compliance with data protection regulations such as Europe's General Data Protection Regulation (GDPR) (2017), federated learning was proposed. Federated learning aims to safeguard sensitive data during AI model training, enhancing the reliability of AI systems. Edge devices (e.g., mobile phones, tablets) or different organizations can collaboratively train an AI model using their data on the edge, upload local models to a server, and update the global model. This approach not only addresses data privacy issues but also fosters trust and reliability in human-machine interactions, such as chatbot customer service, financial fraud detection, and personalized content recommendations.

Federated learning offers a range of applications such as disease prediction from wearables, credit risk assessment across organizations, pedestrian behavior adaptation in self-driving environments, and smart grid energy optimization (2019). It allows decentralized model training, safeguarding sensitive edge data. However, federated learning faces challenges like fairness, bias (2019), and competition among organizations with common interests (2020). For example, in open banking (2017), financial institutions may be reluctant to share data without fair rewards, as they are also competitors. Additionally, biased training data, such as imbalanced datasets, can lead to low recall and negatively impact prediction quality, affecting AI reliability in human-machine interactions. Therefore, designing a fairness-aware incentive mechanism is crucial to motivate participants to contribute high-quality local data to federated learning.

We propose FairShare, a fairness-aware incentive mechanism for federated learning, integrating monetary and non-monetary incentives unlike previous research (2015; 2015). The federation aggregates local models, reminds clients to check dataset bias, encourages truthful cost claims, and assigns fair payments. FairShare has two stages: the first uses a service-based mechanism to incentivize clients to claim truthful costs and earn credits. The second stage utilizes a monetary-based mechanism, leveraging costs from the first stage and the Shapley Value to determine client payments. This approach fosters fairness and motivates high-quality data use, enhancing AI reliability in human-machine interactions. Section 3 further elaborates on the scheme. Our contributions focus on improving human-machine interaction reliability and fairness:

(1) We introduced "FairShare" to encourage federated learning participation, honest cost claims, and fair payments, improving human-machine interaction reliability through collaboration.

(2) FairShare includes monetary and non-monetary incentives. Stage one employs the VCG auction for truthful cost estimation and local data protection, enhancing human-machine interaction reliability.

(3) Stage two uses a Shapley Value-based method for fair payment determination, encouraging clients to use high-quality data in local models, improving AI

reliability in human-machine interactions.

(4) FairShare reduces training bias by urging clients to balance local datasets, thereby improving interaction reliability.

(5) FairShare bolsters data privacy in federated learning, maintains trust, lowers breach risks, and promotes AI reliability.

2   Related Work

Fairness is a critical challenge in federated learning, particularly for reliable human-machine AI interactions (2021). The fairness and privacy-enhancing technologies are crucial for addressing privacy concerns in the context of federated learning (2023). Limited research exists on fairness-aware incentive mechanisms. Tu *et al.* provided a comprehensive review of economic and game theoretic approaches for incentivizing data owners' participation in federated learning training (2022). Yu *et al.* proposed the "Federated Learning Incentivizer" to maximize utility and minimize inequality (2020). Qi *et al.* introduced a blockchain-based federated learning approach with a reputation mechanism (2022). Salazar *et al.* presented a reinforcement learning-based demand response model for efficient consumer demand management. Fairness-aware incentive mechanisms in federated learning are an open research question. Privacy concerns complicate matters, as clients withholding information make cost determination and data protection challenging. We propose a VCG-based incentive mechanism (2020) and recommend addressing local dataset biases to improve human-machine AI interaction reliability.

The VCG mechanism, promoting social welfare maximization (2020; 2019), enhances AI reliability and is used in federated learning research. Wu *et al.* introduced a long-term online VCG auction mechanism for federated learning, addressing the challenges of precise strategy derivation and successive correlation between rounds (2022). Li *et al.* incorporated VCG in offloading games for mobile edge computing (2018b) and mobile crowdsensing, attracting participants (2018a). Zhou *et al.* proposed a VCG-based crowdsensing framework, implementing edge computing and recommending deep learning algorithms like CNNs to filter false information, demonstrating high robustness (2018). The VCG mechanism ensures social cost minimization but not fairness. We propose using VCG for truthful cost disclosure and Shapley Value calculations to maintain fairness and promote high-quality data, enhancing AI reliability. The Shapley Value, introduced in 1951, addresses payment fairness in coalitions (1953). Recent studies apply it to interpret black-box machine learning models. Rozemberczki *et al.* discussesed the applications of the Shapley value, a cooperative game theory concept, in various machine learning domains, including feature selection, explainability, multi-agent reinforcement learning, ensemble pruning, and data valuation (2022). Since 2019, federated learning research has used Shapley Value for model interpretation or profit allocation. Wang estimated feature importance for vertical federated learning (2019). Yang *et al.* presented an incentive mechanism for Federated Learning based on an enhanced Shapley value method, which considers multiple influence factors as weights in measuring income distribution (2022).

Training dataset bias greatly impacts federated learning fairness, often under-representing marginalized groups, affecting AI reliability (2019). In healthcare, algorithms trained on majority populations can create inaccurate results for minority groups, exacerbating disparities (2022). Biases in facial analysis AI systems against demographic subgroups have been highlighted (2022). The potential for principles of human and animal intelligence to improve AI performance and reduce bias has been explored (2022). It's vital to develop a bias-reducing global model, with clients identifying local dataset biases. We suggest a federation strategy for reducing the bias in federated learning.

3   The FairShare Scheme

The FairShare Scheme encompasses two distinct phases, as depicted in Fig. 1. This scheme focuses on AI reliability for human-machine interaction, particularly in the context of federated learning. The FairShare Scheme has two phases. Phase

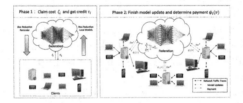

Fig. 1. Overview of FairShare Scheme

one uses the VCG auction for two goals: (1) motivating clients to reveal true costs, ζ_i, for federated learning tasks, and (2) accounting for potential bias in client request distribution. Selected clients participate in task j within a reward budget, $\mathbb{B}$. This auction incentivizes cost disclosure and provides a reward credit, τ_i, for future service requests.

In the second phase, the federation model updating process is executed through federated learning. This decentralized approach assigns tasks to clients, enabling them to generate, store, and process local models without sharing their local data. Clients only exchange intermediate updates with the federation, maintaining data privacy. The federated learning process aims to minimize the global model's objective function, as shown in Eq. 1, where N represents the number of clients, ρ_i denotes each client's relative impact, with two natural settings: $\rho_i = \frac{1}{n}$ or $\rho_i = \frac{n_i}{n}$. $\mathbb{F}_i$ symbolizes the ith client's local objective function, $\rho_i \geq 0$, and $\sum_i \rho_i = 1$ (2020).

$$\min_{\varpi} \sum_{i=1}^{N} \rho_i \mathbb{F}_i(\varpi) \tag{1}$$

The Federated Averaging algorithm is used within the federation to combine client updates and generate a new global model (2018). Clients first compute the average gradient using local data and the current model through SGD. They then update their local models with a specific learning rate and federation, followed by a weighted aggregation to obtain a new global model. After the federated learning task, Shapley value theory determines a payment, $\psi_i(v)$, ensuring fairness, motivating participation, and guaranteeing just payment relative to contributions. Details are provided in Sect. 4.

4   The Formulation of FairShare

In Phase 1, the Vickrey-Clarke-Groves (VCG) model is employed to conduct an auction. The process of implementing a service-based incentive mechanism can be outlined as follows:
(1)The federation, holding a bias-reducing global model, assigns learning tasks to clients and manages a credit budget.
(2) Clients receive tasks and a bias check reminder, urging local data bias assessment. They report costs and bid for credit to participate.
(3) The VCG model selects winning bids. Post-auction, rewards are given, and earned credits are available for future services.

When each client i receives a federated learning task k, they first estimate their cost ζ_i for task k, which includes factors such as computational consumption, bias reduction strategy, and power consumption. Subsequently, client i determines their bid credit price τ_i. The federation employs the VCG mechanism to select the winners to complete task k, ensuring that the sum of the winners' bid credit prices remains within the federation's budget, as illustrated in Eq. 2. W_s represents the set of winners.

$$\sum_{i \in W_s} \tau_i \leq \mathbb{B} \qquad (2)$$

VCG mechanisms have been proven to exhibit truthfulness and individual rationality (2007). According to the VCG algorithm, each winner's credit payment τ_i is calculated as the difference between the total cost for others when client i is not participating and the total cost for others when client i joins. This can be defined as:

$$\tau_i = \sum_{j \neq i} \zeta_j(W^{-i}) - \sum_{j \neq i} \zeta_j(W^i) \qquad (3)$$

The utility of each client is maximized during the auction process. Utility can be defined as:

$$U_i = \begin{cases} \tau_i - \zeta_i, & \text{if i is a winner.} \\ 0, & \text{otherwise.} \end{cases} \qquad (4)$$

In Phase 2, the Shapley value is employed to determine the monetary payment ρ_i for the winning client i, ensuring fairness in the data sharing and exchange process. The monetary-based incentive mechanism process can be described as follows:

(1) Given that the truthful cost ζ_i was reported by client i in Phase 1, the federation collects the ζ_i from each client.

(2) The payment for each client ρ_i is calculated using Shapley value.

We first present the desirable properties for Phase 1 of the FairShare framework:

(1) Truthfulness: In an auction mechanism, it is truthful for every client i to report the true cost ζ_{true}. The client's utility U_i will not be improved if they report a cost different from their true value, denoted as ζ_{false}.

(2) Individual Rationality: When bidding the true cost ζ_{true}, each client will have a non-negative utility, $U_i \geq 0$, $\forall i \in U$.

(3) Computational Efficiency: The incentive mechanism is considered computationally efficient if the outcome can be computed in polynomial time.

According to previous research (2016; 2016; 2017), we present the following definitions:

Definition 1. *Monotonicity* *The client winners' selection process is monotone if the winner selected with bid credit score γ_s and S still wins with any γ_s' and S', given that $\gamma_s \geq \gamma_s'$ and $S \leq S'$.*

Definition 2. *Critical payment* *A critical payment of credit τ_{ci} exists for the winning client i who claims their bid credit score γ_s individually. Client i will win if $\gamma_s' \leq \tau_{ci}$; otherwise, they will lose.*

Theorem 1. *An auction mechanism is truthful if and only if it satisfies monotonicity and the existence of a critical payment.*

We now present the desirable properties of Phase 2. A value function, denoted as ψ, represents each possible characteristic function of a cooperative game in Shapley value. $\psi_i(v)$ is the computed value of client i in the federated learning process with characteristic function v. The Shapley value has four desirable properties of fairness (2005; 2017):

(1) Efficiency: The total gain is distributed, i.e., $\sum_{i \in N} \psi_i(v) = v(N)$.

(2) Symmetric: If two clients have the same contribution, their payment should be equal. If i and j are such that $v(S \cup i) = v(S \cup j)$ for every coalition S not containing i and j, then $\psi_i(v) = \psi_j(v)$.

(3) Dummy: If the client is a dummy player, their payment should be 0. Theoretically, if i satisfies the condition v(S) = v(S∪i) for every coalition S that does not contain i, then $\psi_i(v) = 0$.

(4) Additivity: Given characteristic functions u and v, $\psi(u+v) = \psi(u) + \psi(v)$, illustrating that when two coalition games with gain functions u and v are combined, the distributed gains correspond to the individual gains derived from u and the gains derived from v.

The detailed Shapley value formulation can be found in (1953; 2017). Furthermore, a unique function exists to calculate the payment that satisfies the desirable properties of Phase 2, as demonstrated by Theorem 5. The proof of this theorem can be found in 4. This section first illustrates the proofs of designed properties: truthfulness, individual rationality, and computation efficiency in Phase 1.

Theorem 2. *Our proposed skill verification system is truthful.*

Proof. Regarding the definition 1, definition 2, and theorem 1, this theorem can be proven.

Theorem 3. *Our proposed Phase 1 auction is individually rational.*

Proof. For each client, i, there exists a critical cost ζ_{ci} which equals their credit payment τ_i. A client's utility will be non-negative when i is selected as a winner, and there must have $\zeta_i \leq \zeta_{ci}$. Otherwise, the utility of the client will be 0. Theorem 3 can be proven because individual rationality is guaranteed.

Theorem 4. *Our proposed Phase 1 auction is computation efficiency.*

Proof. The time complexity of algorithms is O(n), which indicates the implementation time complexity of our proposed Phase 1 is adequate.

We then prove the Theorem 5 to show that in phase 2, there exists a unique function to compute the Shapley value and to satisfy the four desirable properties.

Theorem 5. *A unique function ψ satisfies the efficiency, symmetric, dummy players, and additivity of the Shapley Value.*

Proof. Based on the previous materials (2005), we now present the proof of Theorem 5. There exists a special characteristic function denotes to π_V and a set $V \subset N$, then for all $W \subset N$, there exist a function $\pi_V(W)$, if set $V \subset W$:

$$\pi_V(W) = \begin{cases} 1 \text{ if } V \subset W \\ 0 \text{ otherwise} \end{cases} \tag{5}$$

Then We can apply desirable properties (Efficiency, Symmetric and dummy player) with Eq. 5. Then we can get the three equations as follows: From axiom 1, we can get Eq. 6.

$$\sum_{i \in N} \psi_i(\pi_V) = \pi_V(N) = 1 \tag{6}$$

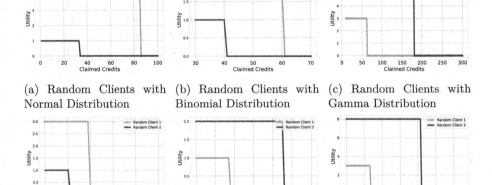

(a) Random Clients with Normal Distribution

(b) Random Clients with Binomial Distribution

(c) Random Clients with Gamma Distribution

(d) Random Clients with Poisson Distribution

(e) Random Clients with Chi-square Distribution

(f) Random Clients with Exponential Distribution

Fig. 2. Random clients with different payment distributions

From axiom 2, if we have two clients, $i, j \in S$, then we can get Eq. 7.

$$\psi_i(\pi_V) = \psi_j(\pi_V) \tag{7}$$

From axiom 3, if a client $i \notin S$, then we can get Eq. 8.

$$\psi_i(\pi_V) = 0 \tag{8}$$

From Eq. 6, for all $i \in S$, we can get $\psi_i(\pi_V) = \frac{1}{|V|}$. Therefore, when we apply a similar analysis to a characteristic function with an arbitrary number λ, $\lambda \pi_V$, we get Eq. 9.

$$\psi_i(\lambda \pi_V) = \begin{cases} \frac{\lambda}{|V|} & \text{if} i \in V. \\ 0 & \text{otherwise.} \end{cases} \tag{9}$$

Regarding 5, we can notice that for any characteristic function v, there exists $v = \sum_{V \in N} \lambda_V \pi_V$, which represents the unique weighted sum of several characteristic functions. Then after we apply axiom 4, we can get the Eq. 10 shown below:

$$\psi_i(v) = \sum \frac{\lambda_V}{|V|}, V \subset N, i \in V \tag{10}$$

In addition, if the arbitrary number λ_V is negative, Eq. 10 still works because regarding the additivity, the minus of Shapley value will also be satisfying the equation below, u, v, and u-v are characteristic functions:

$$\psi(u - v) = \psi(u) - \psi(v) \tag{11}$$

Then it is not difficult to show that Eq. 10 and λ_V should satisfy the four axioms. Then for any characteristic function v, there exists $v = \sum \lambda_V \pi_V$ if there exists a constant λ_V where $V \subset N$. For all $W \subset N$, when $\lambda_\varnothing = 0$, there exists:

$$\lambda_W = v(W) - \sum \lambda_V, V \subset W, V \neq W. \tag{12}$$

Then we found each λ_W is defined in terms of λ_V as shows below:

$$\sum_{V \subset N} \lambda_V \pi_V(W) = \lambda_W + \sum_{V \subset W, V \neq W} \lambda_V = \sum_{V \subset W} \lambda_V = v(W) \tag{13}$$

Therefore, it can be prove that $v = \sum_{V \subset N} \lambda_V \pi_V$. In order to show the unicity of the function, we assume there are two sets of constants λ_V and λ'_V. Therefore, there exists the Equation shown below:

$$v(W) = \sum_{V \subset N} \lambda_V \pi_{V(W)} = \sum_{V \subset N} \lambda'_V \pi_{V(W)} \tag{14}$$

Therefore, we then show that $\lambda_V = \lambda'V$ for all V. If W is the singleton set i in Eq. 14, then all $p_U(V, W)$ vanish except for $V = i$. Because $\lambda i = \lambda'_i$ for all clients. Let S be an arbitrary coalition, then $\lambda_V = \lambda'_V$ for $V \subset S$. Then all terms will be canceled except the term with $V = S$ leaving $\lambda_S = \lambda'_S$ when $W = S$.

5   Experiments Results

We tested Phase 1 of FairShare for truthfulness, focusing on clients' marginal contribution claims, ζ_i. With clients' strategies kept secret, we simulated their contributions across six distributions with 50 and 100 clients each. For Normal distribution, claimed contributions ranged from 1 to 100. Poisson had an expected interval of 100, Gamma had a shape of 2 and scale of 50, and Exponential's scale was 50. Chi-square's degree of freedom was 100, while Binomial's parameters were 100 and 0.5 for n and p. As shown in Fig. 2a-2f, clients must truthfully claim contributions and request credits, or gain no utility.

In Phase 2, our primary goal was to demonstrate that the Shapley value is a fair payment method compared to equal payment, reversed first price, and reversed second price. We selected 20 random clients from each distribution, and the results are displayed in Fig. 3a-3f. These figures indicate that the Shapley value is the fairest payment method across distributions compared to other traditional payment methods. However, the second price does not perform well in some distributions, particularly for data with larger scales.

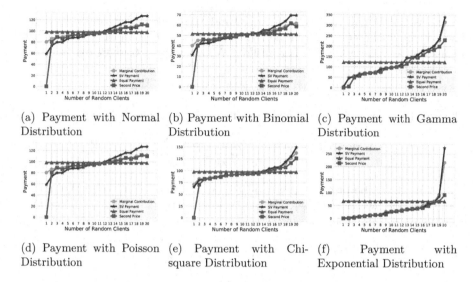

(a) Payment with Normal Distribution

(b) Payment with Binomial Distribution

(c) Payment with Gamma Distribution

(d) Payment with Poisson Distribution

(e) Payment with Chi-square Distribution

(f)   Payment   with Exponential Distribution

Fig. 3. Payment distributions

6   Conclusion

This study proposed an incentive mechanism, "FairShare", which combines monetary incentives and non-monetary incentives in the federated learning environment. The two phases mechanism can ensure fairness when the federation distributes the payments and protects data privacy. Phase 1 employed VCG algorithm to ask the clients to claim their contributions truthfully, individual rationality, and computational efficiency. Phase 2 used Shapley value to maintain fairness and encourage clients to use their high-quality data to train the local model. We can prove that FairShare is an incentive mechanism that can significantly solve the fairness challenges in federated learning with the experiment results.

References

Brodsky, L., Oakes, L.: Data Sharing and Open Banking. McKinsey & Company (2017)

Crnoja, I.: Machine learning and data privacy: contradiction or partnership? (2019). https://www.digitalistmag.com/digital-economy/2019/05/21/machine-learning-data-privacy-contradiction-or-partnership-06198537/

Duan, Z., Yan, M., Cai, Z., Wang, X., Han, M., Li, Y.: Truthful incentive mechanisms for social cost minimization in mobile crowdsourcing systems. Sensors **16**(4), 481 (2016)

Ferguson, T.: (2005). https://www.math.ucla.edu/tom/Game_Theory/

Goyal, A., Bengio, Y.: Inductive biases for deep learning of higher-level cognition. Proc. Royal Soc. A **478**(2266), 20210,068 (2022)

Hard, A., et al.: Federated learning for mobile keyboard prediction (2018). arXiv preprint arXiv:1811.03604

Jaimes, L.G., Vergara-Laurens, I.J., Raij, A.: A survey of incentive techniques for mobile crowd sensing. IEEE Internet Things J. **2**(5), 370–380 (2015)

Kairouz, P., et al.: Advances and open problems in federated learning (2019). arXiv preprint arXiv:1912.04977

Kostick-Quenet, K.M., et al.: Mitigating racial bias in machine learning. J. Law, Med. Ethics **50**(1), 92–100 (2022)

Li, J., Cai, Z., Wang, J., Han, M., Li, Y.: Truthful incentive mechanisms for geographical position conflicting mobile crowdsensing systems. IEEE Trans. Comput. Soc. Syst. **5**(2), 324–334 (2018)

Li, L., Quek, T.Q., Ren, J., Yang, H.H., Chen, Z., Zhang, Y.: An incentive-aware job offloading control framework for mobile edge computing (2018b). arXiv preprint arXiv:1812.05743

Li, T.: Federated learning: challenges, methods, and future directions (2019). https://blog.ml.cmu.edu/2019/11/12/federated-learning-challenges-methods-and-future-directions/

Li, T., Sahu, A.K., Talwalkar, A., Smith, V.: Federated learning: challenges, methods, and future directions. IEEE Signal Process. Mag. **37**(3), 50–60 (2020)

Liu, L., Han, M., Zhou, Y., Parizi, R.M., Korayem, M.: Blockchain-based certification for education, employment, and skill with incentive mechanism. Blockchain cybersecurity, trust and privacy, pp. 269–290 (2020)

Liyuan, L., Meng, H., Yiyun, Z., Reza, P.: E2 c-chain: a two-stage incentive education employment and skill certification blockchain. In: 2019 IEEE International Conference on Blockchain (Blockchain), pp 140–147. IEEE (2019)

Mosaiyebzadeh, F., et al.: Privacy-enhancing technologies in federated learning for the internet of healthcare things: a survey. Electronics **12**(12), 2703 (2023)

Nisan, N., Roughgarden, T., Tardos, E., Vazirani, V.V.: Algorithmic Game Theory. Cambridge University Press, Cambridge (2007)

Qi, J., Lin, F., Chen, Z., Tang, C., Jia, R., Li, M.: High-quality model aggregation for blockchain-based federated learning via reputation-motivated task participation. IEEE Internet Things J. **9**(19), 18,378–18,391 (2022)

Rozemberczki, B., et al.: The shapley value in machine learning (2022). arXiv preprint arXiv:2202.05594

Shapley, L.S.: A value for n-person games. Contrib. Theory Games **2**(28), 307–317 (1953)

Singh, R., Majumdar, P., Mittal, S., Vatsa, M.: Anatomizing bias in facial analysis. Proc. AAAI Conf. Artif. Intell. **36**, 12351–12358 (2022)

Tu, X., Zhu, K., Luong, N.C., Niyato, D., Zhang, Y., Li, J.: Incentive mechanisms for federated learning: from economic and game theoretic perspective. IEEE Transactions on Cognitive Communications and Networking (2022)

Voigt, P., von dem Bussche, A.: The EU General Data Protection Regulation (GDPR). Springer, Cham (2017). https://doi.org/10.1007/978-3-319-57959-7

Wang, G.: Interpret federated learning with shapley values (2019). arXiv preprint arXiv:1905.04519

Wang, J., Tang, J., Yang, D., Wang, E., Xue, G.: Quality-aware and fine-grained incentive mechanisms for mobile crowdsensing. In: 2016 IEEE 36th International Conference on Distributed Computing Systems (ICDCS), pp. 354–363. IEEE (2016)

Wu, L., Guo, S., Liu, Y., Hong, Z., Zhan, Y., Xu, W.: Sustainable federated learning with long-term online vcg auction mechanism. In: 2022 IEEE 42nd International Conference on Distributed Computing Systems (ICDCS), pp 895–905. IEEE (2022)

Xu, J., Rao, Z., Xu, L., Yang, D., Li, T.: Mobile crowd sensing via online communities: Incentive mechanisms for multiple cooperative tasks. In: 2017 IEEE 14th International Conference on Mobile Ad Hoc and Sensor Systems (MASS), pp. 171–179. IEEE (2017)

Yang, S., Wu, F., Tang, S., Gao, X., Yang, B., Chen, G.: On designing data quality-aware truth estimation and surplus sharing method for mobile crowdsensing. IEEE J. Sel. Areas Commun. **35**(4), 832–847 (2017)

Yang, X., Tan, W., Peng, C., Xiang, S., Niu, K.: Federated learning incentive mechanism design via enhanced shapley value method. Wireless Commun. Mobile Comput.2022 (2022)

Yu, H., et al.: A fairness-aware incentive scheme for federated learning. In: Proceedings of the AAAI/ACM Conference on AI, Ethics, and Society, pp 393–399 (2020)

Zhan, Y., Zhang, J., Hong, Z., Wu, L., Li, P., Guo, S.: A survey of incentive mechanism design for federated learning. IEEE Trans. Emerg. Top. Comput. **10**(2), 1035–1044 (2021)

Zhang, X., et al.: Incentives for mobile crowd sensing: a survey. IEEE Commun. Surv. Tutorials **18**(1), 54–67 (2015)

Zhou, Z., Liao, H., Gu, B., Huq, K.M.S., Mumtaz, S., Rodriguez, J.: Robust mobile crowd sensing: when deep learning meets edge computing. IEEE Netw. **32**(4), 54–60 (2018)

Combating Label Ambiguity with Smooth Learning for Facial Expression Recognition

Yifan Chen[1], Zide Liu[2], Xuna Wang[2], Shengnan Xue[3], Jiahui Yu[3], and Zhaojie Ju[1(✉)]

[1] School of Computing, University of Portsmouth, Portsmouth PO13HE, UK
zhaojie.ju@port.ac.uk
[2] School of Automation and Electrical Engineering, Shenyang Ligong University, Shenyang 110000, China
[3] Zhejiang Univeristy, Hangzhou 310027, China
{3210105824,jiahui.yu}@zju.edu.cn

Abstract. Accurately learning facial expression recognition (FER) features using convolutional neural networks (CNNs) is a non-trivial task because of the presence of significant intra-class variability and inter-class similarity as well as the ambiguity of the expressions themselves. Deep metric learning (DML) methods, such as joint central loss and softmax loss optimization, have been adopted by many FER methods to improve the discriminative power of expression recognition models. However, equal supervision of all features with DML methods may include irrelevant features, which ultimately reduces the generalization ability of the learning algorithm. We propose the Attentive Cascaded Network (ACD) method to enhance the discriminative power by adaptively selecting a subset of important feature elements. The proposed ACD integrates multiple feature extractors with smooth center loss to extract to discriminative features. The estimated weights adapt to the sparse representation of central loss to selectively achieve intra-class compactness and inter-class separation of relevant information in the embedding space. The proposed ACD approach is superior compared to state-of-the-art methods.

Keywords: Deep Metric Learning · Ambiguous Expressions · Facial Expression Recognition

1 Introduction

In the past few years, facial expression recognition has attracted increasing attention in the field of human-computer interaction [5,13,21,25]. Facial expressions

The authors would like to acknowledge the support from the National Natural Science Foundation of China (52075530), the AiBle project co-financed by the European Regional Development Fund, and the Zhejiang Provincial Natural Science Foundation of China (LQ23F030001).

can be seen as reflecting a person's mental activity and mental state. With the rapid growth in the field of human-computer interaction, scientists have conducted a great deal of research to develop systems and robots that can automatically sense human feelings and states [24]. The ultimate goal is to sense human emotional states and interact with the user in the most natural way possible. This is a very complex and demanding task, as performing expression recognition in real-world conditions is not easy and straightforward. Facial expression recognition is significant in human-computer interaction. Although facial expression recognition has been studied and developed for many years, achieving accurate facial expression recognition is still challenging.

One of the main challenges of facial expression recognition is the labeling ambiguity problem. There are two reasons: one is the ambiguity of the expression itself, where some expressions are similar and difficult to distinguish. The other is the labeling ambiguity caused by different people, resulting in inconsistent labeling. For example, "happy" and "surprise" are similar and hard to distinguish. Moreover, the model may learn unuseful facial expression features instead of helpful information resulting in insufficient accuracy. Developing robust facial recognition systems is still a challenging task. Three elements primarily affect FER tasks based on deep learning techniques: data, models, and labels [2]. Researchers have made significant advances in models and data, but they need to pay more attention to labels. Xu et al. [22] suggested a Graph Laplacian Label Enhancement (GLLE) recover distribution from logical labels. However, the algorithm's rigid feature space topology assumptions make it unsuitable for big field datasets.

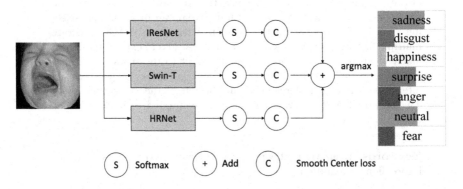

Fig. 1. They have different lateral connections (with or without skip connections), feature extract methods, and resolution streams (gradually decreasing or staying the same). Alternative architectures could be able to pick up different functionalities. We are ensembling these three backbones in the coarse net to get reliable prediction results and avoid over-fitting.

To solve this problem, we propose a cascade network to obtain more reliable features in different ways as shown in Fig. 1. Specifically, we train multiple models based on various architectures and improve the whole performance using an ensemble. Finally, Joint optimization using softmax and smooth center loss.

The main contributions of our work can be summarized as follows:

- We propose the cascaded networks to address the label ambiguity problem in facial expression recognition.
- We propose the smooth center loss selectively achieves intra-class compactness and inter-class separation for the relevant information in the embedding space. Smooth center loss is jointly optimized with softmax loss and can be trained.

2 Related Work

Facial expression recognition is an important research topic in the field of computer vision and human-computer interaction. The earliest expression recognition methods were based on hand-crafted features [1,27]. Recently, deep learning methods have significantly advanced the development of facial expression recognition [26]. Some works [6,23] regard multi-branch networks to capture global and local features. A hybrid architecture combining CNN and Transformer has achieved state-of-the-art performance in several benchmarks to improve recognition generalization. Recently, several researchers [5,21] proposed extracting discriminative features through an attention mechanism, which was robust to occlusions.

Deep Metric Learning (DML) approaches constrain the embedding space to obtain well-discriminated deep features. Identity-aware convolutional neural network can simultaneously distinguish expression-related and identity-related features [18]. They employed contrast loss on depth features to combine features with similar labels and separate features with different labels. Similarly, Liu et al. [15] proposed the (N+M)-tuplet clusters loss function. By constructing a set of N-positive samples and a set of M-negative samples, the negative samples are encouraged to move away from the center of positive samples while the positive samples cluster around their respective centers. This integration improves intra-class compactness by leveraging the k-nearest neighbor algorithm for the local clustering of deep features. Furthermore, Farzaneh and Qi [8] proposed the discriminative distribution uncertainty loss, which in the case of class imbalance of the forward propagation process, regulates the Euclidean distance between the classes in the embedding space of the samples.

3 Methodology

This section briefly reviews the necessary preliminaries related to our work. We then introduce the two building blocks of our proposed Attentive Cascaded Network (ACN): the smooth center loss and the cascaded network. Finally, we discuss how ACN is trained and optimized.

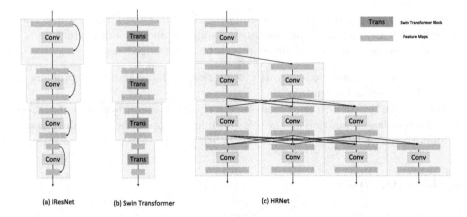

Fig. 2. An illustration of our collaborative methodology. Each backbone network's feature logits are extracted independently, and the softmax function generates the per-class confidential scores. The argmax function is used to generate the ultimate result after adding the scores.

3.1   Cascaded Network

Prior studies split expressions into seven basic categories to cover emotions common to humans. However, these seven categories of expressions are very similar, especially negative ones. Particularly, four negative expressions-anger, contempt, fear, and sadness-have comparable facial muscle motions. In contrast to positive sentiments, negative ones are more challenging to accurately forecast. The majority of in-the-wild facial expression datasets, on the other hand, are gathered from the Internet, where people typically share pleasant life experiences. Negative emotions are difficult to obtain in real scenarios, making the existing FER training dataset unbalanced regarding category distribution.

Specifically, we use two branches to predict positive expressions (happy, surprised, normal) and negative labels (anger, disgust, fear, and sadness). In this way, the low-frequency negative samples are combined in the negative samples, making the training dataset more balanced.

As shown in Fig. 2. We use the model ensemble strategy to our coarse net in order to further increase the robustness of our framework. The backbone networks are specifically HRNet, Swin-S, and IResNet-152. These architectures differ significantly from one another, as seen in Fig. 3, and each one extracts distinctive features. Pooling or path merging layers are used by IResNet (a) and Swin Transformer (b) to reduce the spatial resolution of feature maps, which lowers processing costs and broadens the perceptual field. To gain rich semantic features, HRNet (c) continues to be the high-resolution representation and exchanges features across resolutions. Unlike the other models, which employ the conventional convolution method, model (b) uses the attention mechanism with shifted windows to study relationships with other locations. (c) uses more connections between different resolutions to extract rich semantic features. These different architectural designs can help different models learn different features and prevent the whole framework from overfitting to some noisy features.

3.2   Smooth Central Loss

Center loss, a widely used Deep Metric Learning technique, assesses how similar the deep features are to the class centers that correspond to them. The goal of center loss is to reduce the sum of squares between deep features and their corresponding class centers within each cluster, mathematically represented as shown below. Specifically, given a training minibatch of m samples,

$$\mathcal{L}_C = \frac{1}{2n} \sum_{i=1}^{n} \sum_{j=1}^{m} \|x_{ij} - c_{y_ij}\|_2^2 \tag{1}$$

where the center loss penalizes the Euclidean distance between a depth feature and its corresponding class center in the embedding space. The depth features are made to cluster at the class centers.

Not all elements in a feature vector are useful for classification. Therefore, we select only a subset of elements in the deep feature vector to help discriminate. Our goal is to filter out irrelevant features during the classification process, and we assign weights to the Euclidean distance in each dimension in Eq. 3 and develop a smooth central loss method as follows:

$$\mathcal{L}_{SC} = \frac{1}{2n} \sum_{i=1}^{n} \sum_{j=1}^{m} \alpha_{ij} \otimes \|x_{ij} - c_{y_ij}\|_2^2 \tag{2}$$

where $\otimes$ indicates element-wise multiplication and denotes the weight of the deep feature along the dimension in the embedding space. It should be noted that $\mathcal{L}_{SC}$ and $\mathcal{L}_C$ are the same if $\alpha_{ij} = 1$.

4   Experimental Settings and Results

In this section, we first present two publicly available FER datasets, the in-the-lab dataset ck+ [16] and the Real World Affective Facial Database (RAF-DB) [10]. Then, we conducted validation experiments on these two widely used facial expression recognition (FER) datasets to demonstrate the superior performance of our proposed Attentive Cascaded Network (ACN). Finally, we evaluated our method on the publicly available FER dataset compared to two baselines and various state-of-the-art methods.

4.1   Datasets

RAF-DB: The RAF-DB contains 12,271 training images and 3,068 images. It is a facial image obtained by crowdsourcing techniques and contains happy, sad, surprised, angry, fearful, disgusted, and neutral expressions. The dataset are acquired in an unconstrained setting offering a broad diversity across pose, gender, age, demography, and image quality.

CK+: A total of 123 individual subjects are represented by 593 video sequences in the Extended Cohn-Kanade (CK+) dataset. One of the seven expression classes-anger, contempt, disgust, fear, pleasure, sorrow, and surprise are assigned to 327 of these movies. Most facial expression classification methods employ the CK+ database, which is largely recognized as the most frequently used laboratory-controlled facial expression classification database available.

4.2 Implementation Details

Our experiments use the standard convolutional neural network (CNN) ResNet-18 as the backbone architecture. Before performing the expression recognition task, we pre-trained ResNet-18 on Imagenet, a face dataset containing 12 subtrees with 5247 synsets and 3.2 million images. We employ a typical Stochastic Gradient Descent (SGD) optimizer with weight decay of 5×10^{-4} and momentum of 0.9. We add new elements to the supplied photographs instantly by removing arbitrary crops. We utilize the supplied image's middle crop for testing. Crops with dimensions of 224× 224 are taken from input photos with dimensions of 256× 256.

We train ResNet-18 on the public dataset for 80 epochs with an initial learning rate of 0.01, decaying by a factor of 10 every 20 periods. The batch size is set to 128 for both datasets. The hyper-parameters α and λ are empirically set to 0.5 and 0.01, respectively. Our experiments use the PyTorch deep learning framework on an NVIDIA 1080Ti GPU with 8GB of V-RAM.

4.3 Recognition Results

Table 1 displays the results for RAF-DB, while Table 2 presents the results for CK+. Notably, the test set of RAF-DB is characterized by an unbalanced distribution. As a result, we provide average accuracy, computed as the mean of the diagonal values in the confusion matrix, and the standard accuracy, which encompasses all classes in RAF-DB.

Table 1. Performance of different methods on RAF-DB

Method	Accurancy
Gate-OSA [14]	86.32
gaCNN [12]	85.07
LDL-ALSG [6]	85.53
PAT-ResNet [4]	84.19
NAL [9]	84.22
Center Loss [11]	82.86
PAT-VGG [4]	83.83
ACD	**86.42**

Table 2. Performance of different methods on CK+

Method	Accurancy
FN2EN [7]	96.80
Center Loss [3]	92.26
DRADAP [17]	90.63
IL-CNN [3]	94.35
IDFERM [15]	98.35
Block-FerNet [20]	98.41
DeepEmotion [19]	90.63
ACD	**99.12**

As can be seen from Table 1, our ACN method outperforms the baseline method and other state-of-the-art methods, achieving 86.42% recognition accuracy on RAF-DB. In addition, the improvement of ACN over the two baseline methods is greater than the improvement of center loss over softmax loss. In other words, ACN significantly enhances the generalization ability of the model.

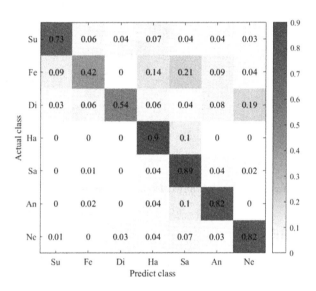

Fig. 3. The ACD framework in this paper: the diagonal line is the proportion of correctly identified and the non-diagonal line is the proportion of confused.

As shown in the Fig. 3 and Fig. 4, the confusion matrices obtained by the baseline approach and our proposed ACN framework are shown on the two FER datasets to analyze each category's recognition accuracy visually. Compared with softmax loss, ACN improves the recognition accuracy of all categories except surprise in the RAF-DB test set. The overall performance of ACN on RAF-DB is better because the recognition accuracy for surprise, fear, and disgust is significantly higher than that of central loss. We note that ACN outperforms the baseline approach on CK+ except for the anger category, while the recognition accuracy for the sadness and disgust categories is significantly higher than both baselines. Overall, ACN outperformed the baseline method for all classes in both RAF-DB and CK+.

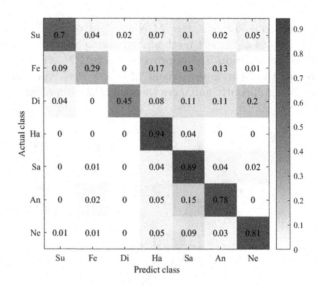

Fig. 4. The confusion matrix obtained from the baseline method (softmax loss)

5 Conclusions

This paper proposes an enhanced robustness approach called Attentive Cascaded Network (ACN). Our hybrid system uses smoothed central loss to enable the model to learn discriminative features that can distinguish between similar expressions. In addition, a cascaded network is proposed to address the label ambiguity problem. Our experimental results show that ACD outperforms other state-of-the-art methods on two publicly available FER datasets, namely RAF-DB and CK+.

ACD can easily be applied to other network models to solve other classification tasks and increase feature discrimination. In the future, we can extend the model to gesture and hand gesture recognition.

References

1. Amos, B., et al.: OpenFace: a general-purpose face recognition library with mobile applications. CMU School Comput. Sci. **6**(2) (2016)
2. Bagherinezhad, H., Horton, M., Rastegari, M., Farhadi, A.: Label refinery: improving ImageNet classification through label progression. arXiv preprint arXiv:1805.02641 (2018)
3. Cai, J., et al.: Island loss for learning discriminative features in facial expression recognition. In: 2018 13th IEEE International Conference on Automatic Face & Gesture Recognition (FG 2018), pp. 302–309. IEEE (2018)
4. Cai, J., Meng, Z., Khan, A.S., Li, Z., O'Reilly, J., Tong, Y.: Probabilistic attribute tree in convolutional neural networks for facial expression recognition. arXiv preprint arXiv:1812.07067 (2018)

5. Chen, C., Crivelli, C., Garrod, O.G., Schyns, P.G., Fernández-Dols, J.M., Jack, R.E.: Distinct facial expressions represent pain and pleasure across cultures. Proc. Natl. Acad. Sci. **115**(43), E10013–E10021 (2018)
6. Chen, S., Wang, J., Chen, Y., Shi, Z., Geng, X., Rui, Y.: Label distribution learning on auxiliary label space graphs for facial expression recognition. In: Proceedings of the IEEE/CVF Conference on Computer Vision and Pattern Recognition, pp. 13984–13993 (2020)
7. Ding, H., Zhou, S.K., Chellappa, R.: FaceNet2ExpNet: regularizing a deep face recognition net for expression recognition. In: 2017 12th IEEE International Conference on Automatic Face & Gesture Recognition (FG 2017), pp. 118–126. IEEE (2017)
8. Florea, C., Florea, L., Badea, M.S., Vertan, C., Racoviteanu, A.: Annealed label transfer for face expression recognition. In: BMVC, p. 104 (2019)
9. Goldberger, J., Ben-Reuven, E.: Training deep neural-networks using a noise adaptation layer (2016)
10. Li, S., Deng, W.: Reliable crowdsourcing and deep locality-preserving learning for unconstrained facial expression recognition. IEEE Trans. Image Process. **28**(1), 356–370 (2018)
11. Li, S., Deng, W., Du, J.: Reliable crowdsourcing and deep locality-preserving learning for expression recognition in the wild. In: Proceedings of the IEEE Conference on Computer Vision and Pattern Recognition, pp. 2852–2861 (2017)
12. Li, Y., Zeng, J., Shan, S., Chen, X.: Occlusion aware facial expression recognition using CNN with attention mechanism. IEEE Trans. Image Process. **28**(5), 2439–2450 (2018)
13. Lin, Z., et al.: CAiRE: an empathetic neural chatbot. arXiv preprint arXiv:1907.12108 (2019)
14. Liu, H., Cai, H., Lin, Q., Li, X., Xiao, H.: Adaptive multilayer perceptual attention network for facial expression recognition. IEEE Trans. Circuits Syst. Video Technol. **32**(9), 6253–6266 (2022). https://doi.org/10.1109/TCSVT.2022.3165321
15. Liu, X., Kumar, B.V., Jia, P., You, J.: Hard negative generation for identity-disentangled facial expression recognition. Pattern Recogn. **88**, 1–12 (2019)
16. Lucey, P., Cohn, J.F., Kanade, T., Saragih, J., Ambadar, Z., Matthews, I.: The extended Cohn-Kanade dataset (CK+): a complete dataset for action unit and emotion-specified expression. In: 2010 IEEE Computer Society Conference on Computer Vision and Pattern Recognition-Workshops, pp. 94–101. IEEE (2010)
17. Mandal, M., Verma, M., Mathur, S., Vipparthi, S.K., Murala, S., Kumar, D.K.: Regional adaptive affinitive patterns (RADAP) with logical operators for facial expression recognition. IET Image Proc. **13**(5), 850–861 (2019)
18. Meng, Z., Liu, P., Cai, J., Han, S., Tong, Y.: Identity-aware convolutional neural network for facial expression recognition. In: 2017 12th IEEE International Conference on Automatic Face & Gesture Recognition (FG 2017), pp. 558–565. IEEE (2017)
19. Minaee, S., Minaei, M., Abdolrashidi, A.: Deep-Emotion: facial expression recognition using attentional convolutional network. Sensors **21**(9), 3046 (2021)
20. Tang, Y., Zhang, X., Hu, X., Wang, S., Wang, H.: Facial expression recognition using frequency neural network. IEEE Trans. Image Process. **30**, 444–457 (2020)
21. Wells, L.J., Gillespie, S.M., Rotshtein, P.: Identification of emotional facial expressions: effects of expression, intensity, and sex on eye gaze. PLoS ONE **11**(12), e0168307 (2016)
22. Xu, N., Liu, Y.P., Geng, X.: Label enhancement for label distribution learning. IEEE Trans. Knowl. Data Eng. (2019)

23. Xu, N., Shu, J., Liu, Y.P., Geng, X.: Variational label enhancement. In: International Conference on Machine Learning, pp. 10597–10606. PMLR (2020)
24. Yu, J., Gao, H., Chen, Y., Zhou, D., Liu, J., Ju, Z.: Deep object detector with attentional spatiotemporal LSTM for space human-robot interaction. IEEE Trans. Hum.-Mach. Syst. **52**(4), 784–793 (2022)
25. Yu, J., Gao, H., Sun, J., Zhou, D., Ju, Z.: Spatial cognition-driven deep learning for car detection in unmanned aerial vehicle imagery. IEEE Trans. Cogn. Dev. Syst. **14**(4), 1574–1583 (2021)
26. Yu, J., Xu, Y., Chen, H., Ju, Z.: Versatile graph neural networks toward intuitive human activity understanding. IEEE Trans. Neural Netw. Learn. Syst. (2022)
27. Zhang, K., Zhang, Z., Li, Z., Qiao, Y.: Joint face detection and alignment using multitask cascaded convolutional networks. IEEE Signal Process. Lett. **23**(10), 1499–1503 (2016)

EMG Denoising Based on CEEMDAN-PE-WT Algorithm

Guoyan Sun and Kairu Li[✉]

Shenyang University of Technology, Liaoning 110870, China
Kairu.Li@sut.edu.cn

Abstract. Raw Surface Electromyography (sEMG) generally contains baseline noise, random noise, power line interference and other noises. The performance of signal denoising is a prerequisite for sEMG feature extraction and recognition. However, traditional filtering methods may sacrifice some effective sEMG signals during denoising process. For improving the denoising effect and eliminate the modal aliasing problem in the Empirical Mode Decomposition (EMD) decomposition process, this paper proposes a hybrid denoising algorithm based on complete ensemble empirical mode decomposition with Adaptive Noise (CEEMDAN) and permutation entropy (PE) combined with wavelet threshold (WT). Firstly, CEEMDAN decomposition is performed on raw sEMG signals to calculate the PE value of each Intrinsic Mode Functions (IMF). Then, high-frequency (H-F) IMF components dominated by random noise is identified and wavelet threshold denoising is applied. Results show that EMG signals denoised by the proposed CEEMDAN-PE-WT algorithm perform a higher signal-to-noise ratio (SNR) and lower root mean square error (RMSE) compared with WT, EMD and CEEMDAN denoising methods.

Keywords: sEMG signal denoising · CEEMDAN · Wavelet Threshold · PE

1 Introduction

Electromyography (EMG) refers to the measurement of electrical signals which isgenerated by muscle contraction and it can reflect the strength of muscle contraction. It is widely applied in various fields and disciplines such as medicine, rehabilitation and sports science. The surface electromyography (sEMG) collected by electrodes can reflect the activity of neuromuscular cells to a certain extent [1]. They are non-invasive and have applications in prosthetics, rehabilitation, gesture recognition, rehabilitation robots and exoskeletons [2, 3]. Like other physiological measurements, EMG records are contaminated with different types of noises, such as baseline noise, motion artifacts and many other types of noises [4]. Therefore, identifying real EMG signals remains an important task.

Denoising remains challenging because no significant distortion of EMG signal should be ensured during denosing processing. Nonlinear and adaptive filtering techniques minimize noise while sacrificing some EMG signals [5]. Due to its better time-frequency performance, wavelet analysis is also used to minimize the impact of EMG signal noise [6]. Another method used for processing non-stationary signals is EMD. EMD decomposes the signal into Intrinsic Mode Functions (IMFs) and a residue [7, 8]. Zhang et al. [9] Executed a research study on the denoising of EMG signals, and the results showed that EMD denoising technology performed better than traditional filtering techniques. EMD has the advantages of data-driven adaptability, being able to analyze nonlinear and non-stationary signals, and not being constrained by the Heisenberg uncertainty principle [11]. However, the IMFs obtained by Huang's EMD based on Sifting algorithm [12] exhibit Mode Mixing [10]. The occurrence of modal aliasing not only leads to false time-frequency distribution, but also makes the IMFs lose its physical significance. There have been numerous studies conducted both domestically and internationally on the elimination or suppression of modal aliasing, and varying degrees of effectiveness have been achieved. Ensemble Empirical Mode Decomposition (EEMD) is an advanced variant of EMD that incorporates Gaussian white noise during the decomposition process. By averaging the results obtained from multiple decompositions, EEMD produces a final outcome for signal decomposition that has a lower susceptibility to plagiarism detection. [13–15], but the IMF generated by EEMD often contains residual noise. Torres et al. proposed a CEEMDAN method. [16] This method eliminates residual noise and is widely used, but when used alone for denoising, Useful information will also be removed. Bandt and Pompe proposed a method for detecting the randomness of time series in a research study [17], which enables quantitative estimation of random noise in signals. By utilizing the value of PE, the method identifies the IMFs that require denoising, thereby reducing computational complexity and computation time. This paper proposes a CEEMDAN-PE-WT denoising algorithm to address the problem of modal aliasing and signal loss caused by CEEMDAN denoising in sEMG signal denoising. Section 2 introduces the proposed algorithm. Experiment settings are demonstrated in Sect. 3. The Sect. 4 briefly discusses experiment results and then ends with a summary in Sect. 5.

2   CEEMDAN-PE-WT Denoising Algorithm

2.1   Framework

In this study, the CEEMDAN-PE-WT algorithm was utilized for denoising the sEMG signals. Firstly, the raw signals were decomposed into IMFs using the CEEMDAN algorithm. The PE algorithm was utilized to partition the IMFs into H-F and low-frequency (L-F) parts. The high-frequency IMFs were denoised using the WT method, while the L-F IMFs were directly rid of baseline drift noise. Eventually, the signal was reconstructed by combining the denoised H-F IMFs and the untreated L-F IMFs. Figure 1 illustrates the denoising workflow in this study, and the principles of each algorithm are explained in the following text.

2.2   Decomposition of Raw sEMG Signal

Let $E_k(\cdot)$ be the k-th intrinsic mode function obtained after performing Empirical Mode Decomposition (EMD). The k-th intrinsic mode function obtained from CEEMDAN

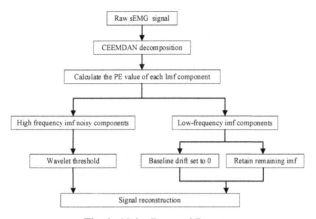

Fig. 1. Noise Removal Process

decomposition is denoted as IMF. We define v^j as a Gaussian white noise signal that follows a standard normal distribution. The index j represents the number of times white noise is added, ranging from 1 to N. The parameter ε represents the standard deviation of the white noise, while $y(n)$ represents the signal to be decomposed. The steps involved in the CEEMDAN decomposition are as follows:

(1) We introduce Gaussian white noise, into the raw signal to obtain a new signal, where q = 1,2. EMD decomposition is performed on the new signal $y(n)+(-1)^q \varepsilon v^j(t)$ obtain the IMF_1:

$$E\left(y(t) + (-1)^q \varepsilon v^j(t)\right) = IMF_1^j(t) + r^j \tag{1}$$

(2) The first intrinsic mode function (IMF) of CEEMDAN decomposition is obtained by taking the overall average of the N generated mode components:

$$IMF_1 = \frac{1}{N} \sum_{j=1}^{N} IMF_k^j(t) = \overline{IMF_1} \tag{2}$$

(3) the residual signal is calculated when k = 1:

$$r_1(t) = x(t) - IMF_1 \tag{3}$$

(4) Gaussian white noise $(-1)^q \varepsilon v^j(t)$ is added to the residual signal $r_1(t)$, and the new signal is used as the carrier for EMD decomposition to obtain the first modal component D_1, thus the second eigenmode component of CEEMDAN decomposition can be obtained, and the second-order IMF component can be obtained:

$$IMF_2 = \frac{1}{N} \sum_{j=1}^{N} D_1^j(t) \tag{4}$$

(5) Determine the residual by subtracting the second modal component from the original signal:

$$r_2(t) = r_1(t) - IMF_2 \tag{5}$$

(6) These steps are repeated until the extreme of the residual signal has no more than 2 value points. At this point, the CEEMDAN algorithm terminates and a total of K intrinsic mode functions are obtained, along with the final residual value, At this point, the raw deformation time series can be expressed as:

$$x(t) = \sum_{i=1}^{k} IMF_k + r_k(t) \tag{6}$$

In this paper, CEEMDAN method is used to add a certain amount of Gaussian white noise to the raw sEMG signal, and then EMD decomposition is carried out. Due to the introduction of noise, the frequency range of each IMF is expanded, thereby avoiding the problem of sEMG signal mode aliasing. When using the CEEMDAN algorithm alone for denoising, in order to preserve the essential information contained in sEMG signals to the greatest extent possible, we have combined the CEEMDAN algorithm with the PE-WT algorithm.

2.3 Division of IMF Component

PE is a nonlinear method used to detect the complexity (randomness) or dynamical transitions in time series [18]. It provides a quantitative assessment of the presence of random noise in the signal. The basic principle of the algorithm is as follows, Firstly, the given time series $\{x(i), i = 1, 2, \cdots, n\}$ is reconstructed in phase space to obtain the corresponding phase space matrix.

$$\begin{bmatrix} x(1) \ x(1+\tau) \ \cdots \ x(1+(m-1)\tau) \\ \vdots \quad \vdots \quad \cdots \quad \vdots \\ x(j) \ x(j+\tau) \ \cdots \ x(j+(m-1)\tau) \\ \vdots \quad \vdots \quad \cdots \quad \vdots \\ x(k) \ x(k+\tau) \ \cdots \ x(k+(m-1)\tau) \end{bmatrix} \tag{7}$$

In Equation: The parameter m refers to the embedding dimension, which represents the number of components used to reconstruct the phase space. The parameter t represents the time delay, indicating the time lag between consecutive components in the reconstruction, $j = 1, 2, \cdots, k$. For each row vector of the reconstruction matrix, a set of symbol sequences can be obtained: $S(g) = (j_1, j_2, \cdots, j_m)$, where: $j_1, j_2, \cdots, j_m$, represents column index indicating the location of the new component. $g = 1, 2, \cdots, L$, and $L \leq m!$. Calculate the probability P_g $(g = 1, 2, \cdots, L)$ of each sequence, there is $\sum_{g=1}^{l} P_g = 1$. The PE of deformed time series x(t) is defined as:

$$H_p(m) = -\sum_{g=1}^{l} P_g \ln P_g \tag{8}$$

where: $0 \leq H_{P(m)} \leq \ln(m!)$ A Subsection Sample. When $P_g = 1/m!$, $H_{P(m)}$ eaches the maximum value $\ln(m!)$. The larger the value of $H_{P(m)}$, the more random noise in the signal. After consulting the data, m generally takes a value between 3 and 7, and t is generally greater than or equal to 1 [19]. When calculating the PE, choose 4 for m and 1 for t. By calculating the PE value, we can select H-F IMF components for WT.

2.4   WT for High-Frequency IMF Denoising

WT is a multi-scale signal analysis method, and its excellent denoising effect [20] is very popular. The basic principle of WT denoising is to perform a wavelet transform on the raw signal to obtain wavelet decomposition coefficients C_j:

$$C_j = W(s(t)) \tag{9}$$

in Equation: In wavelet transform, $w(s(t))$ represents the wavelet coefficients, and j represents the level of wavelet decomposition. We can set a threshold value λ, and when the wavelet coefficient is $\leq \lambda$, we consider it to be influenced by noise and thus it needs to be excluded. On the other hand, when the wavelet coefficient is $> \lambda$, we consider it unaffected by noise, and therefore it needs to be retained. The denoised signal can be obtained by reconstructing the wavelet coefficients. WT includes hard thresholding and soft thresholding methods, the hard thresholding function is:

$$\hat{C}_j = \begin{cases} C_j, |C_j| > \lambda \\ 0, |C_j| \leq \lambda \end{cases} \tag{10}$$

The soft thresholding function is as follows:

$$\hat{C}_j = \begin{cases} \text{sgn}(C_j)(|C_j| - \lambda), |C_j| > \lambda \\ 0, \qquad\qquad |C_j| \leq \lambda \end{cases} \tag{11}$$

By calculating the PE value of all the IMFs. The H-F IMFs were decomposed into four layers using the sym8 wavelet basis function, and the Minimax threshold method (minimaxi) soft threshold was used, achieving ideal denoising results.

3   Experiment

Figure 2 Demonstrates the experiment setting. An sEMG device is employed to acquire double channels of the arm signals and transmit them to the computer via Bluetooth. The raw sEMG signals can be processed, demonstrated and saved by users through the interface.

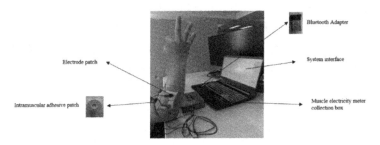

Fig. 2. sEMG signal acquisition system

3.1 Participants

Four able-bodied male and female subjects (20 to 30 years old) participated in this study. BMI of the participants in the experiment are shown in Table 1. Each subject was provided with a detailed explanation of the experimental procedure and was required to sign an informed consent form prior to the experiment.

Table 1. BMI Table

Subjects	Gender	Age	Height/cm	Weight/kg	BMI
1	male	25	175	70	22.85
2	male	26	177	75	23.93
3	female	25	165	55	20.20
4	female	26	168	55	19.48

3.2 Experiment Design

Before the experiment, subjects' forearm skin was cleaned with alcohol cotton to reduce impedance interference between the skin and the electrode. Intramuscular adhesive was used to adhere the electrode patch to the skin. The subjects were asked to relax on their seats for 2–3 min to achieve optimal physical and mental relaxation. Five kinds of gestures were chosen for the experiment: OK hand (OH), hand open (HO), hand closure (HC), wrist inward flip (WF), and wrist enstrophe (WE) (see Fig. 3.). Patch 1 channel and patch 2 channel were applied to the positions of the radial and ulnar wrist flexor muscles, respectively, with a sampling frequency of 2k. In this experiment, four healthy subjects underwent the experiment, and each subject completed four movements. The duration of each action in the experiment is 10 s. To prevent interference caused by continuous testing of muscle fatigue, muscle relaxation should be performed between two movements, with a minimum interval of 3 min of rest time between each experiment.

Fig. 3. Samples of dynamic gestures OK hand (OH), hand open (HO), hand closure (HC), wrist inward flip (WF), and wrist enstrophe (WE)

4   Results

A group of representative sEMG signals generated by the flexor carpi radialis muscle in the grip state is selected. sEMG signal CEEMDAN is decomposed and the decomposition results are shown in Fig. 4. The original deformed time series is decomposed into 14 IMF components.

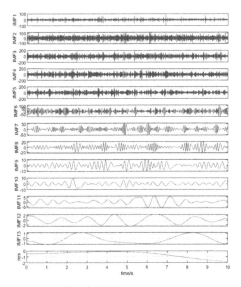

Fig. 4. IMF components

In order to divide the IMG components corresponding to the high and low frequencies, the PE value calculation and analysis are performed on the decomposed IMFs, and then the data is reconstructed. In PE calculation, τ is taken as 1. According to the experiment, the embedding dimension m is selected as 4. When m $= 4$, $\tau = 1$, and the PE value line diagram of IMF component is shown in Fig. 5.

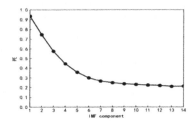

Fig. 5. Arrangement entropy values of various IMF components

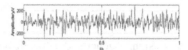

Fig. 6. Raw sEMG signal

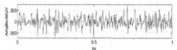

Fig. 7. sEMG Wavelet threshold denoising

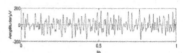

Fig. 8. sEMG EMD denoising

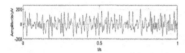

Fig. 9. sEMG CEEMDAN denoising

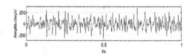

Fig. 10. sEMG CEEDAN-PE-WT denoising

By using the PE value, it is possible to determine that the first five are H-F IMFs, while the remaining nine are L-F IMFs. The sEMG noise is mainly in the H-F range, so the WT denoising is performed on the H-F IMFs. Baseline drift is a slowly changing ultra-L-F interference signal, the baseline drift signal is decomposed into L-F IMFs. Its frequency can be estimated by the zero-crossing rate (ZCR) of the IMFs (the number of zero-crossing points per unit time) [21]. Since the frequency of the baseline drift is lower than 5 Hz, by setting the threshold to 5, the ZCR of the L-F IMFs, the IMFs whose ZCR is less than the threshold 5 is regarded as the baseline drift signal, and can be directly eliminated to realize the correction of the baseline drift. In this paper, by calculating the ZCR, the ZCR of the last three IMFs is lower than 5, which is the baseline drift component, which is directly eliminated, and the remaining L-F IMFs are retained.

Finally, the denoised sEMG signal is obtained by combining the wavelet denoised signals of the first five IMFs with the L-F preserved signals. Figure 6, 7, 8, 9 and 10 respectively show the results of raw signal, wavelet threshold denoising, EMD denoising, CEEMDAN denoising, and CEEMDAN-PE-WT denoising within 1 s.

In Equation, X_i is the raw sEMG signal collected; Y_i is a sEMG signal that has been denoised; N is the sample data of sEMG signal; This experimental study introduces SNR and RMSE as standards to evaluate the effectiveness of denoising. After denoising the collected sEMG signal, the higher the SNR value, the better the denoising effect.

RMSE is utilized to quantify the extent of disparity between the denoised signal and the raw signal. The lower the value, The higher the degree of match between the signals before and after denoising.

$$RMSE = \sqrt{\frac{\sum_{i=1}^{n}(Y_i - X_i)^2}{n}} \tag{12}$$

$$SNR = 10\lg\left[\frac{\sum\limits_{i=1}^{n}(Y_i)^2}{\sum\limits_{i=1}^{n}(Y_i - X_i)^2}\right] \tag{13}$$

Table 2. The average value of various evaluation indicators

Evaluation indicators	Wavelet threshold	EMD	CEEMDAN	CEEMDAN-PE-WT
SNR	11.849	8.298	9.743	13.81
RMSE	76.786	69.442	64.459	60.813

Table 2 presents the performance indices by various denoising methods. As shown in Table 2, based on the comprehensive denoising indicators of SNR and RMSE, by comparing the denoising effects of the real WT method, EMD method, CEEMDAN method, and CEEMDAN-PE-WT method, the CEEMDAN-PE-WT algorithm has the highest SNR and the lowest RMSE, indicating that the CEEMDAN-PE-WT denoising algorithm has better signal-to-noise separation effect.

5 Summary

This paper proposes CEEMDAN-PE-WT for sEMG denoising. The PE is used to determine the high-frequency IMFs that needs WT de-noising, the ZCR of the L-F IMFs are used to determine the baseline drift signal that needs to be eliminated, and finally the IMFs are reconstructed. The denoising results of sEMG signals demonstrate that CEEMDAN-PE-WT performs high SNR which balance the denoising performance and effective signals.

Acknowledgments. We appreciate all the participants in the experiment. This work is supported by the National Natural Science Foundation of China (Grant No. 62003222), the Natural Science Foundation of Liaoning (Grant No. 2022-MS-267) and the Research Fund of Liaoning Provincial Department of Education (Grant No. LQGD2020018).

References

1. Loss, J.F., Cantergi, D., Krumholz, F.M., Torre, M.L., Candotti, C.T.: Evaluating the Electromyographical signal during symmetrical load lifting. In: Applications of EMG in Clinical and Sports Medicine. IntechOpen (2012)
2. Al-Dhief, F.T., et al.: A survey of voice pathology surveillance systems based on internet of things and machine learning algorithms. IEEE Access. **8**, 64514–64533 (2020)
3. Mutlag, A., et al.: MAFC: Multi-agent fog computing model for healthcare critical tasks management. Sensors. **20**, 1853 (2020)

4. Lu, G., et al.: Removing ECG noise from surface EMG signals using adaptive filtering. Neurosci. Lett. **462**, 14–19 (2009)
5. Scarpiniti, M., Comminiello, D., Parisi, R., Uncini, A.: Nonlinear spline adaptive filtering. Signal Process. **93**, 772–783 (2013)
6. Grujić, T., Kuzmanić, A.: Denoising of surface EMG signals: a comparision of wavelet and classical digital filtering procedures. Tech. Health Care **12**, 130–135 (2004)
7. Huang, N.E., Shen, S.S.: World Scientific (Firm) eds: Hilbert-Huang transform and its applications. World Scientific Pub. Co, Singapore ; Hakensack, N.J (2014)
8. Flandrin, P., Rilling, G., Gonçalves, P.: Empirical mode decomposition as a filterbank. IEEE Signal Proc Lett. Signal Process. Lett. **11**, 112–114 (2004)
9. Huang, N., et al.: The empirical mode decomposition and the Hilbert spectrum for nonlinear and non-stationary time series analysis. Proc. Royal Soc. London. Ser. A: Math. Phys. Eng. Sci. **454**, 903–995 (1998)
10. Zhao, X.-Y., Fang, Y.-M., Wang, Z.-G., Zhai, Z.: EEMD De-noising adaptively in raman spectroscopy. Guang pu xue yu guang pu fen xi = Guang pu. **33**, 3255–3258 (2013)
11. Singh, D.S., Zhao, Q.: Pseudo-fault signal assisted EMD for fault detection and isolation in rotating machines. Mech. Syst. Signal Process. **81**, 202–218 (2016)
12. Lei, Y., He, Z., Zi, Y.: Application of the EEMD method to rotor fault diagnosis of rotating machinery. Mech. Syst. Signal Process. **23**, 1327–1338 (2009)
13. Guo, W., Tse, P.: An enhanced empirical mode decomposition method for blind component separation of a single-channel vibration signal mixture. J. Vib. Control **22**, 2603–2618 (2015)
14. Colominas, M., Schlotthauer, G., Torres, M.E., Flandrin, P.: Noise-assisted EMD methods in action. Adv. Adapt. Data Anal. **4**, 1250025 (2012)
15. Torres, M.E., Colominas, M.A., Schlotthauer, G., Flandrin, P.: A complete ensemble empirical mode decomposition with adaptive noise. In: 2011 IEEE International Conference on Acoustics, Speech and Signal Processing (ICASSP), pp. 4144–4147 (2011)
16. Bandt, C., Pompe, B.: Permutation Entropy: a natural complexity measure for time series. Phys. Rev. Lett. **88**, 174102 (2002)
17. Zunino, L., Soriano, M.C., Fischer, I., Rosso, O.A., Mirasso, C.R.: Permutation-information-theory approach to unveil delay dynamics from time-series analysis. Phys. Rev. E **82**, 046212 (2010)
18. Yan, R., Liu, Y., Gao, R.X.: Permutation entropy: a nonlinear statistical measure for status characterization of rotary machines. Mech. Syst. Signal Process. **29**, 474–484 (2012)
19. To, A.C., Moore, J.R., Glaser, S.D.: Wavelet denoising techniques with applications to experimental geophysical data. Signal Process. **89**, 144–160 (2009)
20. Cetinkaya, H., Kizilhan, A., Vertiy, A., Demirci, S., Yigit, E., Ozdemir, C.: The millimeter-wave imaging of concealed objects, pp. 228–231 (2011)
21. Qiu, JH., Qi, J., Wang, Nn., Denisov, A.: Passive Millimeter-wave imaging technology for concealed contraband detection. In: Sidorenko, A. (ed.) Functional Nanostructures and Metamaterials for Superconducting Spintronics. NanoScience and Technology, pp. 129–159. Springer, Cham (2018). https://doi.org/10.1007/978-3-319-90481-8_7

AS-TransUnet: Combining ASPP and Transformer for Semantic Segmentation

Jinshuo Wang[1], Dongxu Gao[2], Xuna Wang[1], Hongwei Gao[1], and Zhaojie Ju[2(✉)]

[1] School of Automation and Electrical Engineering, Shenyang Ligong University, Shenyang 110159, China
[2] School of Computing, University of Portsmouth, Portsmouth PO13HE, UK
{dongxu.gao,Zhaojie.Ju}@port.ac.uk

Abstract. Semantic segmentation is a task to classify each pixel in an image. Most recent semantic segmentation methods adopt full convolutional network FCN. FCN uses a fully convolutional network with encoding and decoder architecture. Encoders are used for feature extraction, and the decoder uses encoder-encoded features as input to decode the final segmentation prediction results. However, the convolutional kernel of feature extraction is not too large, so the model can only use local information to understand the input image, limiting the initial receptive field of the model. In addition, semantic segmentation tasks also need details in addition to semantic information, such as contextual information. To solve the above problems, we innovatively introduced the space pyramid structure (ASPP) into TransUnet, a model based on Transformers and U-Net, which is called AS-TransUnet. The spatial pyramid module can obtain more receptive fields to obtain multi-scale information. In addition, we add an attention module to the decoder to help the model learn relevant features. To verify the performance and efficiency of the model, we conducted experiments on two common data sets and compared them with the latest model. Experimental results show the superiority of this model.

Keywords: FCN · TransUnet · ASPP

1 Introduction

Over the past few years, deep convolutional networks (CNN) have performed above the state of the art in many visual recognition tasks [16, 19–21, 24] such as [3, 4]. Although CNNS has been around for a long time [5], its success has been limited due to the size of the training set available and the size of the network considered. Breakthroughs by Krizevsky et al. [3] are because a large network with 8 layers and millions of parameters is supervised and trained on the ImageNet data set with 1 million training images. Since then, larger and deeper networks have been trained [7]. Ciresan et al. [6] Train the network in a sliding window setting by providing a local area (patch) around each pixel to predict the category label of that pixel as input. 2015 [1] builds on a more elegant architecture, the so-called "complete convolutional network" [5]. The objective of semantic segmentation is to assign a label to each pixel of the input image, which is

H. Yang et al. (Eds.): ICIRA 2023, LNAI 14268, pp. 147–158, 2023.
https://doi.org/10.1007/978-981-99-6486-4_13

the object classification task at the pixel level. The algorithm model is used to predict and classify the pixels of the input image and generate semantic labels. The proposal of FCN provides a classical scheme for semantic segmentation. Most of the structures based on FCN follow the encoder-decoder framework. In the encoder, CNN is used for feature extraction, which gradually reduces the resolution of the feature map and makes the feature map rich in semantic information. Then CNN in decoder uses an encoder encoding feature as input to decode the final segmentation prediction result. In essence, CNN's method has a huge problem, that is, when the image is input to the network at the initial stage- since the convolution kernel of CNN is not too large, the model can only use local information to understand the input image, which inevitably affects the discriminability of the features extracted by the encoder. This is a flaw that cannot be escaped by using CNN. Therefore, PSPNet [8], Deeplab [9–12] series, and a series of methods based on the self-attention mechanism (Non-Local [21], DANet [13], CCNet [14], etc.) have been proposed to obtain local, multi-scale and even global context. Another example is that the semantic segmentation framework has an unsatisfactory effect on the edges of objects, so Gated-SCNN [15] and other methods focus on solving these problems. Some plug-and-play modules based on the self-attention mechanism are inserted between the encoder and the decoder to obtain the global context so that the model can understand the image from a global perspective and improve the features. However, if the model acquires the wrong characteristics at the beginning, it is doubtful whether it can be corrected by using the global context later.

To overcome these difficulties, some researchers focus on the improvement of the FCN encoder and decoder. The transformer was first proposed by [22] and applied to machine translation. The great progress made by Transformer in NLP has successfully driven its development in other fields, and many studies have attempted to apply Transformer to computer vision tasks. In addition to the above models that completely rely on Transformer, there are also CNN and Transformer combination models, DETR [26] attaches Transformers inside the detection head for object detection, and LSTR [25] uses Transformers for lane shape prediction. Recently, the Vision Transformer (VIT) [27] achieved state-of-the-art for ImageNet classification by directly applying Transformers with global self-attention to full-size images. This provides direct inspiration for developing Transformer based encoder designs in semantic segmentation models. TransUNet [2] builds on the very successful VIT, which adopts a network architecture of CNN-Transformer and uses high-resolution features extracted from the CNN network and global context information encoded by the Transformer model to achieve accurate feature positioning and has achieved excellent results in the field of medical images. Although, this model combining the CNN model and Transformer solves the disadvantages of using CNN or Transformer alone and solves some problems in the field of medical images. However, for other semantic segmentation tasks, such as automatic driving, due to the large data set and multiple categories of data, therefore, When using the TransUNet model, shallow and deep information is not enough for images with rich feature details and high resolution, and the extraction of detail information is also limited.

To solve this problem, we propose an efficient and robust model called AS-TransUNet. Specifically, we improved the structure of the TransUnet encoder and introduced the spatial pyramid structure (ASPP) [10] into the feature extraction of TransUnet, so that the model can obtain more receptive fields of different scales, extract more feature information of more scales, and improve the segmentation performance of the model. Specifically, our contribution is to:

1. We innovatively introduce the ASPP block after CNN of the encoder to extract features of more scales and more details, to improve the segmentation effect of the model.
2. We added an attention block (CBAM) [23] to the decoder, which helps the model learn relevant features. Although some researchers prefer to add more attention mechanisms to the model. But we found that increasing the location of attention blocks is more important than the number. In this article, we only add a CBAM block to the end of the decoder.

2 Related work

TransUNet [2] is the first to introduce Transformer into medical image segmentation and has achieved excellent results. The transformer treats the input as a one-dimensional sequence, making the feature map much smaller than the original image reducing segmentation accuracy. To solve this problem, TransUNet combines CNN and Transformer in encoding, where CNN extracts and retains feature maps of higher resolution. Features of different levels extracted are connected with the decoding process through skip connection to help the decoder achieve more accurate segmentation. Transformer makes the model more focused on capturing long-range spatial relationships. However, although Transformer overcomes the inherent limitations of convolution operation, for huge data with a large number of categories and rich feature details and high resolution, feature information of different scales is limited, and some key details are easy to be lost. To solve this problem, we choose to add the space pyramid module to CNN to help the model extract and integrate multi-scale features, retain more detailed information, and improve the segmentation accuracy and robustness of the model.

2.1 Atrous Spatial Pyramid Pooling (ASPP)

Atrous Spatial Pyramid Pooling (ASPP) was first proposed by Chen et al. [10]. Its main idea is to extract multi-scale features of images by Dilated Convolution at different scales. Then, Spatial Pyramid Pooling is carried out to obtain global image representation. ASPP contains empty convolution with sampling rates of 6, 12, and 18, convolution with 1×1 and an average pooling layer. Empty convolution with different sampling rates is used in parallel to obtain receptive fields of different scales to extract multi-scale features of input feature graphs. Then four different scale feature maps are combined to get a feature map with more detailed global information. We added an ASPP block into the feature extraction process of TransUNet [2] to extract richer multi-scale features for the encoding input of subsequent encoders.

2.2   Combining Attention Mechanism Cascaded Upsampler

TransUNet [2] contains a cascading upsampler (CUP) which consists of multiple upsampling steps to decode hidden features to output the final segmentation mask. After the feature sequence is obtained by the encoder, the feature sequence is first reshaped, and the feature map after reshaping is fused with the features of the corresponding layer extracted by CNN through skip connection and up-sampling. In this way, CUP and the hybrid encoder together form a U-shaped architecture, enabling feature aggregation at different resolution levels, and finally restoring the feature map to a full-resolution segmentation mask. We introduced attention mechanisms in the decoding process to improve model performance. Although this is a common way to improve model performance, we believe that the location of attention mechanisms needs careful consideration. Blindly adding more attention mechanisms may increase the complexity of the model and reduce the model's prediction. Subsequent ablation experiments verified our method.

3   Method

In this Section, we will introduce the AS-TransUnet model structure and algorithm principle. Then explain each section in detail. In Sect. 3.1, we first introduce how to use the features extracted by CNN, then obtain more abundant multi-scale features through the ASPP module, and embed them into the converter to decompose the feature representation of image blocks for coding. Then, in Sect. 3.2, we elaborate on the overall framework of the TransUNet model used. Finally, in Sect. 3.3 we will look at how to add an attention module to the decoder.

3.1   CNN and ASPP as Feature Extraction

Give the model an image $X \in R^{H \times W \times C}$ the spatial resolution is H × W and the number of channels is C. The purpose of semantic segmentation is to predict the same pixel-level label graph with size H × W. A common method is to directly train CNN (such as UNet [28] and DeepLab [12]), firstly extract the representation of advanced features of the image (we call it encoding process), and then restore it to the full spatial resolution (we call it decoding). Different from other methods at present, the method in this paper uses ASPP combined with TransUnet to extract richer multi-scale information from the features extracted by CNN after ASPP, which is converted into patch blocks as input of Transformers encoder after fusion. Transformers include a self-attention mechanism. Firstly, feature extraction is carried out by the CNN network module. Given that the width, height, and number of channels of an image are 224 × 224 × 3 respectively, we first change it into 112 × 112 × 64 by subsampling through convolution. Then GroupNorm and ReLU get a 56 × 56 × 64 feature map, Then, three blocks are used to change the width and height of the channel into 56 × 56 × 256, 28 × 28 × 512 and 14 × 14 × 1024 in turn. The output of these three blocks is used for jumping connection with the features of the corresponding size in the up-sampling process. Then we feed the extracted features into the ASPP module. The Atrous Spatial Pyramid Pooling (ASPP) structure can extract multi-scale features from the feature map extracted by the CNN

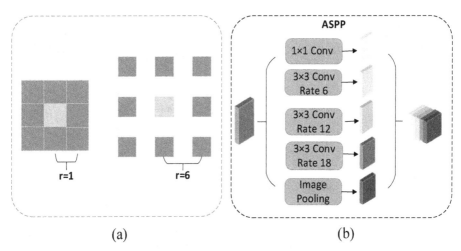

Fig. 1. (a) Atrous convolution kernels with different sampling rates;(b) Structure of Atrous Spatial Pyramid Pooling (ASPP)

network by using the hollow convolution of different sampling rates [10]. The expression is shown as follows:

$$y[i] = \sum_{k} x[i + rk]\omega[k] \tag{1}$$

where x and y are input and output feature graphs respectively; w is the convolution kernel; k: is the size of the convolution kernel; r is the sampling rate.

The formula for calculating the receptive field of vacuous convolution is shown in (2). When the sampling rate r is 1, vacuous convolution is a common convolution operation. As shown in Fig. 1 (a). It is the convolution kernel when the sampling rate is 1 and 6 respectively.

$$RF_{i+1} = RF_i + [k + (k-1) \times (r-1)] \times \sum_{i=1}^{n} S_i \tag{2}$$

where k is the convolution kernel of empty convolution; RF_i, RF_{i+1} are the receptive fields of the current layer and the previous layer respectively. r is the expansion rate; S is the step size. Atrous Spatial Pyramid Pooling structure as shown in Fig. 1 (b). ASPP module through the parallel using different sampling rates of the hollow convolution for different scales of the receptive field, Thus, multi-scale features of the input feature map are extracted, and then four feature maps of different scales are combined to obtain a feature map with more detailed global information [10].

We serialize the obtained features because we need to input them into Transformers for downsampling. We reshape the input X into a sequence of flattened 2D blocks $\left\{ X \; \mathbb{R}^{P^2 \cdot C} | i = 1, .., N \right\}$ for tokenization, where each block has a size of $P \times P$, and $N = \frac{HW}{P^2}$ is the number of image blocks (i.e., the input sequence length). Then, the

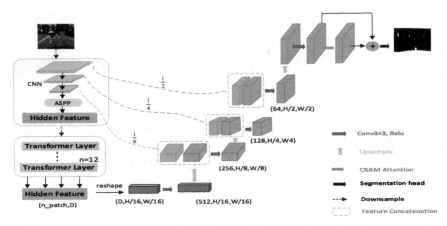

Fig. 2. Overview of the framework. The AS-TransUNet model consists of three main modules: skip connection, encoder, and decoder. The encoder consists of CNN, ASPP Bottleneck, and Transformer. The decoder consists of upsampling, 3×3 convolution, and CBAM block.

obtained vector blocks are embedded. We use a trainable linear projection to map the vectorized block X_P to a latent D-dimensional embedding space. Specific position embeddings that retain positional information are learned and used for encoding. The process is shown below:

$$Z_0 = \left[X_p^1 E; X_p^2 E; \cdots ; X_p^N E \right] + E_{pos} \tag{3}$$

where $E \in \mathbb{R}^{(P^2 \times C) \times D}$ is the patch embedding projection, and E_{pos} denotes the position embedding.

Then, We feed these patches into the Transformer for encoding. The Transformer encoder consists of L layers of Multihead Self-Attention (MSA) and Multi-Layer Perceptron (MLP) blocks (Eq. (4), (5)). Therefore the output of the $\ell - th$ layer can be written as follows:

$$z_{\ell'} = MSA(LN(z_{\ell-1})) + z_{\ell-1} \tag{4}$$

$$z_\ell = MLP(LN(z_{\ell'})) + z_{\ell'} \tag{5}$$

where $LN(\cdot)$ denotes the layer normalization operator and z_ℓ is the encoded image representation.

3.2 Structure of AS-TransUNet

Our proposed AS-TransUNet model consists of an encoder, skip connection, and decoder (Fig. 2). Below we will introduce the specific structure of these three parts. The encoder in the model first performs feature extraction using a CNN network. After adding the ASPP module to the CNN network, we obtain shallow feature maps through the CNN and then input these to the ASPP to extract features of different scales. The ASPP uses dilated convolutions with dilation rates of 6, 12, and 18 to obtain feature maps of different receptive fields, thus obtaining multi-scale feature information. The deep feature map obtained by fusing the multi-scale information is used to embed positional information and transform it into patch blocks that can be input to the Transformer for encoding. For the decoder, we also use the cascade upsampling module proposed by TransUNet to decode hidden features and output the final segmentation mask. We first reshape the hidden feature sequence z_L $\mathbb{R}^{\frac{HW}{P^2} \times D}$ from the encoder into $\frac{H}{P} \times \frac{W}{P} \times D$ and then use the cascade upsampling module (CUP) to transform the feature map from $\frac{H}{P} \times \frac{W}{P}$ to $H \times W$ at full resolution. CUP forms a U-shaped architecture with the encoder through skip connections, and feature aggregation is achieved through different resolution levels enabled by the skip connections, resulting in accurate segmentation results.

3.3 Attention Block

In a convolutional neural network, different channels usually represent different features. The role of the channel attention block is to assign weights to the feature maps of each channel. We choose to add the CBAM (Convolutional Block Attention Module) [23] block in the model. The CBAM block is a type of attention mechanism module that combines spatial and channel attention. The module's channel attention block (CAM) has an unchanged channel dimension and a compressed spatial dimension. The module focuses on meaningful information in the input image; the spatial attention block (SAM) has an unchanged spatial dimension and a compressed channel dimension. The module focuses on the location information of the target. Compared with the SE attention block that only focuses on the attention mechanism of the channel, the CBAM module can achieve better results.

Although adding attention mechanisms is a common way to improve model performance, the location of attention mechanisms needs to be carefully considered. Blindly adding more attention mechanisms may reduce the model's predictions. We believe that only adding a CBAM block in the last layer of the decoder can achieve better results than adding a CBAM block in each layer of the decoder. The subsequent ablation experiments have verified our hypothesis.

4 Experiments

To evaluate the effectiveness of the AS-TransUnet, we carry out comprehensive experiments on the Cityscapes dataset [35], and the CamVid dataset [36]. Experimental results demonstrate that AS-TransUnet achieves state-of-the-art performance on Cityscapes and CamVid. In the following subsections, we first introduce the datasets and implementation details, then we report our results Comparison with State-of-the-arts. Finally, we perform a series of ablation experiments on the CamVid dataset.

4.1 Datasets and Implementation Details

Datasets. We used two publicly available datasets: Cityscapes [35], and CamVid [36]. Cityscapes is tasked with urban segmentation. Only the 5,000 finely annotated images are used in our experiments and are divided into 2,975/500/1,525 images for training, validation, and testing, respectively. CamVid is one of the datasets focusing on semantic segmentation for autonomous driving scenarios. It is composed of 701 densely annotated images with the size of 720 × 960 from five video sequences.

Implementation Details. To ensure the fairness of the model comparison, the resolution sizes of the input images of the two datasets are adjusted to 512 × 512 and, 256 × 256 respectively. All experiments use an Nvidia Quadro P5000 GPU with 16 GB of memory. According to the characteristics of our model, we trained 200 epochs. For the Cityscapes dataset, we set the batch size to 6; and for the CamVid dataset, we set the batch size to 8. Additionally, we adopt a CosineAnnealing learning rate decay schedule and employ SGD as the optimizer, the momentum is 0.9 and the learning rate is 0.01. We use Mean IoU (mIOU, the mean of class-wise intersection over union) as the evaluation metric.

Table 1. Comparison with state-of-the-art on Cityscapes (test).

Method	Encoder	mIoU
DeepLab-v2 [9]	ResNet-101	70.4
OCNet [29]	ResNet-101	80.1
PSANet [30]	ResNet-101	80.1
DenseASPP [31]	DenseNet-161	80.6
PSPNet [8]	ResNet-101	78.4
CCNet [14]	ResNet-101	81.9
Axial-DeepLab [32]	AxiaiResNet-XL	79.9
OCRNet [22]	ResNet-101	81.1
SETR [17]	ViT-Large	81.6
SegFormer [18]	MiT-B5	83.1
Ours	R50-VIT-B-16	**83.5**

4.2 Comparison with State-of-the-Arts

We now compare our results with existing approaches on the CamVid [36], and Cityscapes [35] datasets.

Cityscapes. Table 1 shows the comparative results on the test set of Cityscapes respectively. Most methods [8, 9, 14, 22, 29, 30], adopt the same backbone as ResNet-101, and the others [31, 32] utilize stronger backbones. The [17, 18] adopt a backbone network similar to our approach. We can see that our model AS-TransUnet yields 83.5% mIoU, as compared superior to currently popular baselines, and other methods based on CNN combined with transformer. Figure 3 shows qualitative results on Cityscapes, AS-TransUnet provides better detail and smoother predictions than the currently popular baselines.

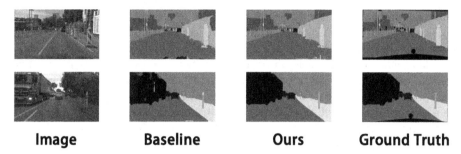

| Image | Baseline | Ours | Ground Truth |

Fig. 3. Visualization results of AS-TransUnet on Cityscapes test set.

Table 2. Comparison with state-of-the-art on CamVid (test).

Method	Encoder	mIoU
PSPNet [8]	ResNet-50	69.1
Dilate8 [33]	Dilate	65.3
SegNet [34]	VGG16	60.1
DenseDecoder [37]	ResNeXt-101	70.9
BiSeNet [38]	ResNet-18	68.7
CCNet [14]	ResNet-101	79.1
Ours	R50-VIT-B-16	**79.6**

CamVid. To validate the segmentation performance of AS-TransUnet, we conducted experiments on the CamVid dataset, which is one of the datasets focusing on semantic segmentation for autonomous driving scenarios. We follow the standard protocol proposed in Segnet [34] to split the dataset into 367 training, 101 validation, and 233 test images. For a fair comparison, we only report single-scale evaluation scores. As can be seen in Table 2, we achieve a mIoU of 79.6%, outperforming all other methods by a large margin.

4.3 Ablation Study

We conduct ablation experiments on the AS-TransUNet model using the CamVid dataset to discuss the impact of different factors on model performance. Specifically, it includes (1) ASPP block; (2) Attention block.

ASPP Block. In this study, we evaluated the impact of adding an ASPP block to the model encoder on model accuracy and segmentation performance. We add the ASPP module after CNN feature extraction. The experimental results in Table 3 show that the accuracy and segmentation performance of the model is improved after adding the ASPP module.

Attention Block. We analyzed and discussed the location and number of attention blocks used in our model. Currently, many researchers tend to add more attention blocks in the networks, which may not give a performance boost to the model. We believe that adding attention blocks helps the model learn features. However, after adding more attention blocks, the number of parameters of the model will increase, and the risk of overfitting will also increase and it leads to the reduction of model accuracy. So we ran a series of comparative experiments. Table 4 shows the results of our comparative experiments, where setting I means adding CBAM blocks at the end of each layer of the decoder; setting II means that only one CBAM block is added at the end of the last layer. The experimental results in Table 4 show that the first configuration fails to improve performance and has a negative impact. While only adding the CBAM block to the last layer of the decoder is more beneficial to improve segmentation accuracy.

Table 3. Influence of ASPP block on segmentation accuracy.

Method	OA	mIoU
TransUnet	87.3	71.8
TransUnet + ASPP	91.3	79.4
TransUnet + Attention	88.1	73.6

Table 4. Influence of attention blocks location on segmentation accuracy.

Method	OA	mIoU
TransUnet	87.3	71.8
TransUnet + ASPP	91.3	79.4
TransUnet + ASPP + I	89.6	79.0
TransUnet + ASPP + II	92.5	79.6

5 Conclusion

In this paper, we innovatively propose an AS-TransUNet model. By introducing the ASPP module, the model can capture richer multi-scale features and retain more detailed information, thereby improving the segmentation accuracy and robustness of the model. In addition, We add an attention module to the decoder to help the model learn relevant features and recover more detailed information. Experimental results on two public datasets show that our proposed AS-TransUNet outperforms the SOTA models.

Acknowledgment. The authors would like to acknowledge the support from the National Natural Science Foundation of China (52075530).

References

1. Long, J., Shelhamer, E. and Darrell, T.: Fully convolutional networks for semantic segmentation In: CVPR, pp. 3431–3440 (2015)
2. Chen, J., et al.: TransUNet: Transformers Make Strong Encoders for Medical Image Segmentation. arXiv:2102.04306 (2021)
3. Krizhevsky, A., Sutskever, I., Hinton, G.E.: Imagenet classification with deep convolutional neural networks. In: NIPS, pp. 1106–1114 (2012)
4. Girshick, R., Donahue, J., Darrell, T., Malik, J.: Rich Feature Hierarchies for Accurate Object Detection and Semantic Segmentation. In: 2014 IEEE Conference on Computer Vision and Pattern Recognition, Columbus, OH, USA, 2014, pp. 580–587 (2014)
5. LeCun, Y., et al.: Backpropagation applied to handwritten zip code recognition. Neural Comput. 1(4), 541–551 (1989)
6. Ciresan, D.C., Gambardella, L.M., Giusti, A., Schmidhuber, J.: Deep neural networks segment neuronal membranes in electron microscopy images. In: NIPS, pp. 2852–2860 (2012)
7. Simonyan, K., Zisserman, A.: Very deep convolutional networks for large-scale image recognition (2014), arXiv:1409.1556
8. Zhao, H., Shi, J., Qi, X., Wang, X., Jia, J.: 2017 Pyramid scene parsing network. In: CVPR, pp. 28881–2890
9. Chen, L.C., Papandreou, G., Kokkinos, I., Murphy, K., Yuille, A.L.: DeepLab: semantic image segmentation with deep convolutional nets, atrous convolution, and fully connected CRFs. IEEE Trans. Pattern Analysis Mach. Intell. 40(4), 834–848 (2017)
10. Chen, L.C., Papandreou, G., Schroff, F., Adam, H.: Rethinking atrous convolution for semantic image segmentation. arXiv:1706.05587 (2017)
11. Chen, L.C., Zhu, Y., Papandreou, G., Schroff, F., Adam, H.: Encoder-decoder with atrous separable convolution for semantic image segmentation. In: ECCV (2018)
12. Chen, L.C., Papandreou, G., Kokkinos, I., Murphy, K., Yuille, A.L.: "Deeplab: Semantic image segmentation with deep convolutional nets, atrous convolution, and fully connected CRFs. IEEETPAMI 40(4), 834–848 (2018)
13. Fu, J., Liu, J., Tian, H., Fang, Z., Lu, H.: Dual attention network for scene segmentation. In: CVPR (2019)
14. Huang, Z., Wang, X., Huang, L., Huang, C., Wei, Y., Liu, W.: Ccnet: Criss-cross attention for semantic segmentation. In: ICCV (2019)
15. Takikawa, T., Acuna, D., Jampani, V., Fidler, S.: Gated-SCNN: gated shape CNNs for semantic segmentation. In: 2019 IEEE/CVF International Conference on Computer Vision (ICCV), Seoul, Korea (South), pp. 5228–5237 (2019)
16. Yu, J., Gao, H., Chen, Y., Zhou, D., Liu, J., Ju, Z.: Deep object detector with attentional spatiotemporal LSTM for space human-robot interaction. IEEE Trans. Hum.-Mach. Syst. 52(4), 784–793 (2022). https://doi.org/10.1109/THMS.2022.3144951
17. Zheng, S. et al.: Rethinking semantic segmentation from a sequence-to-sequence perspective with transformers. In: CVPR (2021)
18. Xie, E., Wang, W., Yu, Z., et al.: SegFormer: simple and efficient design for semantic segmentation with transformers. Adv. Neural Inform. Process. Syst. 34 (2021)
19. Li, X., et al.: Improving Semantic Segmentation via Decoupled Body and Edge Supervision. In: Vedaldi, A., Bischof, H., Brox, T., Frahm, J.-M. (eds.) ECCV 2020. LNCS, vol. 12362, pp. 435–452. Springer, Cham (2020). https://doi.org/10.1007/978-3-030-58520-4_26
20. Yuan, Y., Xie, J., Chen, X., Wang, J.: SegFix: Model-Agnostic Boundary Refinement for Segmentation. In: Vedaldi, A., Bischof, H., Brox, T., Frahm, J.-M. (eds.) ECCV 2020. LNCS, vol. 12357, pp. 489–506. Springer, Cham (2020). https://doi.org/10.1007/978-3-030-58610-2_29

21. Wang, X., Girshick, R., Gupta, A., He, K.: Non-local neural networks. In: Proceedings of the IEEE Conference on Computer Vision and Pattern Recognition, pp. 7794–7803 (2018)
22. Vaswani, A., et al.: Attention is all you need. Adv. Neural Inform. Process. Syst., **30**. Curran Associates (2017)
23. Woo, S., Park, J., Lee, JY., Kweon, I.S.: CBAM: Convolutional Block Attention Module. In: Ferrari, V., Hebert, M., Sminchisescu, C., Weiss, Y. (eds) Computer Vision – ECCV 2018. ECCV 2018. Lecture Notes in Computer Science(), vol 11211. Springer, Cham. TPAMI, vol. 40, no. 4, pp. 834–848 (2018).
24. Yu, J., Gao, H., Sun, J., Zhou, D., Ju, Z.: Spatial cognition-driven deep learning for car detection in unmanned aerial vehicle imagery. IEEE Trans. Cogn. Develop. Syst. **14**(4), 1574–1583 (2022). https://doi.org/10.1109/TCDS.2021.3124764
25. Liu, R., Yuan, Z., Liu, T., Xiong, Z.: End-to-end lane shape prediction with transformers. In: WACV (2020)
26. Carion, N., Massa, F., Synnaeve, G., Usunier, N., Kirillov, A., Zagoruyko, S.: End-to-end object detection with transformers. In: ECCV (2020)
27. Dosovitskiy, A., et al.: An image is worth 16x16 words: transformers for image recognition at scale. In: ICLR (2021)
28. Ronneberger, O., Fischer, P., Brox, T.: U-net: Convolutional networks for biomedical image segmentation. In: Navab, N., Hornegger, J., Wells, W.M., Frangi, A.F. (eds) MICCAI 2015. LNCS, vol. 9351, pp. 234–241. Springer, Cham (2015). https://doi.org/10.1007/978-3-319-24574-4_28
29. Yuan, Y. and Wang, J.O.: Ocnet: Object context network for scene parsing. arXiv (2018)
30. Zhao, H., et al.: Psanet: Point-wise spatial attention network for scene parsing. In: ECCV, pp. 270–286 (2018)
31. Yang, M., Yu, K., Zhang, C., Li, Z., Yang, K.: Denseaspp for semantic segmentation in street scenes. In: CVPR, pp. 3684–3692 (2018)
32. Wang, H., Zhu, Y., Green, B., Adam, H., Yuille, A., Chen, LC.: Axial-DeepLab: Stand-Alone Axial-Attention for Panoptic Segmentation. In: Vedaldi, A., Bischof, H., Brox, T., Frahm, JM. (eds.) Computer Vision – ECCV 2020. ECCV 2020. LNCS, vol 12349. Springer, Cham (2020). https://doi.org/10.1007/978-3-030-58548-8_7
33. Yu, F., Koltun, V.: Multi-scale context aggregation by dilated convolutions ICLR (2016)
34. Badrinarayanan, V., Kendall, A., Cipolla, R.: Segnet: a deep convolutional encoder-decoder architecture for image segmentation. IEEE TPAMI. **39**(12), 2481–2495 (2017)
35. Cordts, M., et al.: The cityscapes dataset for semantic urban scene understanding. In: CVPR, pp. 3213–3223 (2106)
36. Brostow, G.J., Shotton, J., Fauqueur, J., Cipolla, R.: Segmentation and recognition using structure from motion point clouds. In: ECCV, pp. 44–57 (2008)
37. Bilinski, P., Prisacariu, V.: Dense decoder shortcut connections for single-pass semantic segmentation. In: CVPR, pp. 6596–6605 (2018)
38. Yu, C., Wang, J., Peng, C., Gao, C., Yu, G., Sang, N.: Bisenet: bilateral segmentation network for real-time semantic segmentation. In: ECCV (2018)

Trajectory Planning of Aerial Manipulators Based on Inertial Decomposition

Xuan Zhang[1,2,3], Liying Yang[1,2](✉), Guangyu Zhang[1,2], Siliang Li[1,2], and Yuqing He[1,2]

[1] State Key Laboratory of Robotics, Shenyang Institute of Automation, Chinese Academy of Sciences, Shenyang 110016, China
yangliying@sia.cn

[2] Institutes for Robotics and Intelligent Manufacturing, Chinese Academy of Sciences, Shenyang 110169, China

[3] University of Chinese Academy of Sciences, Beijing 100049, China

Abstract. Aerial manipulator poses a challenging trajectory planning problem because of the dynamical coupling between the quadrotor and the robotic arms. Aiming at the system trajectory planning problems of the center of mass(CoM) offset after the dynamic swing of manipulator, this paper proposes a trajectory planning method based on inertial decomposition. Meanwhile, in the proposed method, the dynamic constraints of the quadrotor are also taken into account to ensure the pitch angle and angular velocity of quadrotors are suitable and feasible. A geometry controller is used to ensure accurate tracking of the planned trajectory. Simulations are carried out to verify the proposed method.

Keywords: Aerial manipulator · Center of mass offset · Trajectory planning · Dynamic constraints · Inertial decomposition

1 Introduction

Flying vehicle equipped with a robotic manipulator, which is also called aerial manipulators [1], attracts people's strong interest due to the versatility of the tasks they are able to perform [2, 3]. Although it becomes complex because of the dynamical coupling between the two system, many researchers still try to use aerial manipulators to achieve task operations, such as transportation [4, 5], collection [6–8], surveillance [9], etc. In all the applications mentioned above, the simultaneous motion of quadrotor and manipulator is essential. Causes the center of mass offset, which affects the trajectory tracking accuracy of quadrotor. For the dynamic strong coupling characteristics of the aerial manipulator system, there are many problems with trajectory tracking control caused by center of mass shift.

This work was supported by National key research and development program (2022YFC3005104), National Natural Science Foundation of China (92248303), Shenyang Science and Technology Plan (21-108-9-18), Shenyang Science and Technology Bureau (RC210477), Youth Innovation Promotion Association of the Chinese Academy of Sciences (Y2022065).

H. Yang et al. (Eds.): ICIRA 2023, LNAI 14268, pp. 159–169, 2023.
https://doi.org/10.1007/978-981-99-6486-4_14

In recent years, researchers mainly focused on solving the parameter uncertainty and external disturbance problems of robots to improve tracking accuracy, such as fuzzy dynamic sliding mode control based on hierarchical improved algorithm [10], integral sliding film control based on extended state observer [11], sliding mode control based on disturbance observer [12], model predictive control based on center of mass offset compensation [13], etc. In [14], a multi-rotor hybrid matrix-based estimation method is proposed to compensate for the position drift caused by the center of gravity offset. In [15], the center of gravity position of the robot is estimated based on a neural network and combined with an adaptive weighted data fusion algorithm to obtain the final center of gravity position, which is then controlled by a reverse dynamics module. Existing methods for estimating centroid shift parameters based on data-driven modelling have hysteresis in real-time control problems. This paper solves the problem of center of mass offset of aerial manipulator system from the perspective of trajectory planning.

As it is well known that the accuracy of model-based control methods is closely related to the accuracy of the established model. There is extremely strong coupling in the aerial manipulator system we used. In order to improve control accuracy, the controller used needs to adapt to changes in the system model in real time. This leads to poor implementation effectiveness and serious lag in the system. Therefore, it has been proposed to address these issues from a planning perspective. The trajectory planning method for these problems is necessary to avoid overall flight performance degradation.

Towards the problems mentioned above, the main contributions of this article can be summarized as follows: Firstly, for the disturbance caused by moving manipulator on the dynamic of quadrotor, a flight dynamic model of the aerial manipulator base on variable inertial parameters is proposed. Secondly, a robust geometric controller is designed which is composed of a disturbance compensator of the torque and the dynamic constraints of drones are also considered and derived. Thirdly, to achieve passable and aggressive maneuvers in complex environments, a trajectory optimizer that considers the quadrotor's dynamics constraints is constructed. Lastly, we implement this planning and control algorithm on the aerial manipulator in simulations to verify the feasibility and validity of proposed methods.

This paper is organized as follows: In Sect. 2, the dynamic model of aerial manipulator is presented, which uses the variable inertia parameters to describe the coupling effect. The control method is proposed in Sect. 3. Based on this, the trajectory of quadrotor is derived and analyzed in Sect. 4. Subsequently, the simulations and results are given in Sect. 5. Finally, Sect. 6 summarizes this article and presents possible extensions in future works.

2 Dynamics

In this section, the kinematic relations that reflect the kinematic coupling between the quadrotor and the manipulator are introduced. Then the dynamics of aerial manipulator is presented, in which the center of mass offset term is used to describe the dynamical coupling relationship between quadrotor and manipulator.

2.1 Coordinates Transformation

The goal of this section is to provide a coordinate system that can describe the state of the quadrotor and manipulator. The aerial manipulator presented in this paper is composed of a quadrotor and a single-degree-of-freedom robotic arm. As shown in Fig. 1, O_I represents the NED inertial coordinate frame. O_b represents the body frame of the quadrotor. O_m represents the body frame of the manipulator, which is constructed based on standard DH parameters. The origins of the coordinate system O_b and O_m are both located at the center of mass of their respective rigid bodies. And we suppose that the point S is the CoM of the whole system, which is changing with the movement of the manipulator.

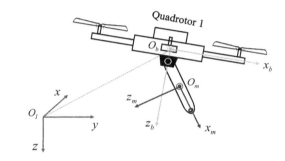

Fig. 1. Illustration of aerial manipulator and related frames.

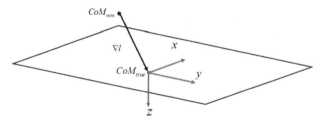

Fig. 2. Schematic diagram of CoM offset.

2.2 Dynamics

In this section, a variable inertia parameter approach is used to describe the dynamics model of the aerial manipulator. As we know, with the movement of the robot arm, the center of mass of the aerial manipulator changes. We can use the definition of the center of mass to obtain a model of its dynamics.

Under these basis frames motioned above, the basic equations of motion of the quadrotor, which is not equipped with robotic arm, can be expressed as:

$$T = \begin{bmatrix} \cos(\theta) & \sin(\theta) & 0 & a_x \\ 0 & 0 & 1 & a_y \\ \sin(\theta) & -\cos(\theta) & 0 & a_z \\ 0 & 0 & 0 & 1 \end{bmatrix} \tag{1}$$

According to the definition of center of mass, the Kinetic equations of quadrotor under the influence of manipulator can be expressed as:

$$m\dot{v} = mge_3 - fRe_3 - mR(\Omega \times (\Omega \times r_c) + \dot{\Omega} \times r_c + 2\Omega \times \dot{r}_c + \ddot{r}_c) \tag{2}$$

$$(J + J_m)\dot{\Omega} + \Omega \times (J + J_m)\Omega = M - \dot{J}_m\Omega + m(r_c \times R^{-1}(ge_3 - \dot{v})) - \frac{m^2}{m_{man}}r_c \times \ddot{r}_c$$
$$- \frac{m^2}{m_{man}}\Omega \times (r_c \times \dot{r}_c)\frac{1}{n} \tag{3}$$

where m is the total mass of the whole system and m_{man} is the mass of the manipulator. $\Omega \in \mathbb{R}^3$ is the angular velocity in the body-fixed frame. r_c is the vector from point CoM_{nom} to point CoM_{true} as shown in Fig. 2. f is the thrust of the quadrotor, which is the sum of the four propellers. $R \in SO(3)$ is the rotation matrix from the body-fixed frame to the inertial frame J, J_m are the inertia matrix of the quadrotor and manipulator.

$$\dot{p}_g = v \tag{4}$$

$$m\dot{v} = mge_3 - f_gRe_3 \tag{5}$$

$$\dot{R} = R\hat{\Omega} \tag{6}$$

$$J_g\dot{\Omega} + \Omega \times J_g\Omega = M_g \tag{7}$$

3 Control

In this section, the separated control strategy is used to design the geometric controller as shown in Fig. 3. Then considering the safety and speed of the quadrotor, the dynamic constraints are derived to guarantee the aerial manipulator system gets suitable and feasible pitch angle and angular velocity.

3.1 Geometric Controller

The nonlinear controller associated with the thrust magnitude and the moment vector can be given as:

$$f = (k_p e_p + k_v e_v + mge_3 - m\ddot{p}_d) \cdot Re_3 \tag{8}$$

$$M = -k_R e_R - k_\Omega e_\Omega + \Omega \times J\Omega - J(\hat{\Omega} R^T R_c \Omega_c - R^T R_c \dot{\Omega}_c) \tag{9}$$

where e_p is the position error and e_v is the velocity error. $e_R \in \mathbb{R}^3$ is the attitude tracking error. $e_\Omega \in \mathbb{R}^3$ is the angular velocity tracking error k_p, k_v, k_R, k_Ω are constants.

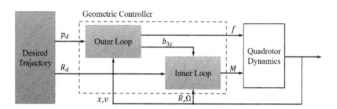

Fig. 3. Controller structure.

3.2 Dynamic Constraints

The dynamic constraints of quadrotor are the most important factors limiting trajectory planning. The orientation $R = [b_1; b_2; b_3]$ can be written as an algebraic function of four differentially flat outputs [16], called:

$$\sigma = [p_x, p_y, p_z, \varphi]^T \tag{10}$$

where $p = [p_x, p_y, p_z]$ is the coordinate of quadrotor CoM and φ is yaw angle. Instead of studying all details of derivation $R(\sigma)$, it can be given by:

$$R(\sigma) = [b_1(\sigma); b_2(\sigma); b_3(\sigma)] \tag{11}$$

The body attitude $R(\sigma)$ of the quadrotor can be denoted as:

$$b_1 := \frac{s}{AB} \tag{12}$$

$$b_2 := \frac{k}{B} \tag{13}$$

$$b_3 = \frac{t}{A} \tag{14}$$

where $A, B \in \mathbb{R}, s, k, t \in \mathbb{R}^3$.

All of them are functions of differentially flat outputs σ, which can be expressed as follow:

$$A := \sqrt{\ddot{p}_x^2 + \ddot{p}_y^2 + (\ddot{p}_x + g)^2} \tag{15}$$

$$B := \sqrt{(\ddot{p}_x + g)^2 + (\ddot{p}_x \sin\varphi - \ddot{p}_y \cos\varphi)^2} \tag{16}$$

$$s := \begin{bmatrix} (\ddot{p}_z + g)^2 \cos\varphi + \ddot{p}_y^2 \cos\varphi - \ddot{p}_x \ddot{p}_y \sin\varphi \\ (\ddot{p}_z + g)^2 \sin\varphi + \ddot{p}_x^2 \sin\varphi - \ddot{p}_x \ddot{p}_y \cos\varphi \\ -(\ddot{p}_z + g)(\ddot{p}_x \cos\varphi + \ddot{p}_y \sin\varphi) \end{bmatrix} \tag{17}$$

$$k := \begin{bmatrix} -(\ddot{p}_z + g) \sin\varphi \\ (\ddot{p}_z + g) \cos\varphi \\ \ddot{p}_x \sin\varphi - \ddot{p}_y \cos\varphi \end{bmatrix} \tag{18}$$

$$t := \begin{bmatrix} \ddot{p}_x \\ \ddot{p}_y \\ \ddot{p}_z + g \end{bmatrix} \tag{19}$$

The results in this section show that by choosing the appropriate period and radius, we can set the desired pitch angle at any angle within the quadrotor flight capability.

According to this, we can determine specific parameters of the trajectory during binary star like flight to ensure the simulation work.

4   Trajectory Planning

The method proposed in this work establish a trajectory that considering CoM offset of the whole system in advance, which can provide a stable base for the motion of the manipulator. There are still some requirements that the planned trajectory should guarantee. To ensure a steady and safe flight, it should be noted that, the trajectory of a quadrotor should meet its own dynamic constraints.

4.1   Trajectory of Manipulator

We assume that the joint angle of the manipulator changes in a sinusoidal manner. It can be defined as:

$$q = \frac{\pi \sin(\omega_q t)}{4} + \frac{\pi}{2} \tag{20}$$

The first order derivative can be expressed as:

$$\dot{q} = \frac{\pi \omega_q}{4} \cos(\omega_q t) \tag{21}$$

4.2 Trajectory of Quadrotor

In the case of circular motion, we choose the trajectory form of the quadrotor as:

$$\begin{cases} p_x = r\sin(\varphi) \\ p_y = r\cos(\varphi) \\ p_z = c \end{cases} \tag{22}$$

$$\varphi = \omega t \tag{23}$$

where ω is the yaw rate and r is the rotation radius of the quadrotor. And c is the flight altitude of the quadrotor, which can be set as a constant value.

The velocity of the quadrotor can be expressed as:

$$\begin{cases} \dot{p}_x = r\omega\cos(\varphi) \\ \dot{p}_y = -r\omega\sin(\varphi) \\ \dot{p}_z = 0 \end{cases} \tag{24}$$

And the acceleration of the quadrotor can be expressed as:

$$\begin{cases} \ddot{p}_x = -r\omega^2\sin(\varphi) \\ \ddot{p}_y = -r\omega^2\cos(\varphi) \\ \ddot{p}_z = 0 \end{cases} \tag{25}$$

To ensure that the quadrotor can maintain circular motion within the flight capability of the quadrotor, we need to consider the quadrotor dynamics constraints mentioned in Sect. 3. The pitch angle is defined as the angle between the x-axis in the body-fixed frame and the z-axis in the inertial reference frame. For the convenience of calculations, we define an unit vector $z_0 = [0; 0; 1][0; 0; 1]$ alone the direction of $\overrightarrow{e}_3$. Then there is a relationship between the two vector and pitch angle, which has the following conditions to be satisfied:

$$b_1 \cdot z_0 = |b_1||z_0|\cos\theta \tag{26}$$

where θ is the pitch angle.

By combining (4–7) and (22–26), finally we get the relationship between the rotation radius r and velocity of yaw ω of the quadrotor. It can be given as:

$$r^2\omega^4 = \frac{g^2}{\tan^2\theta} \tag{27}$$

The results in this section show that by choosing the appropriate period and radius, we can set the desired pitch angle at any angle within the quadrotor flight capability. But equation is the trajectory of the quadrotor that does not take into account effect of the CoM shift due to manipulator movement.

To describe the influence of the CoM offset, the trajectory of the quadrotor can be expressed as:

$$L = [0.5l\cos(q); 0; 0.5l\sin(q)] \tag{28}$$

$$p\prime = \frac{p * m - L * m_{man} - a * m_{man}}{m} \tag{29}$$

$p\prime$ is the is the final flight trajectory of the quadrotor, which can avoid the effects of quadrotor movement.

5 Simulation Result

In this section, in order to verify the proposed controller and trajectory planning method, a great deal of simulation in MATLAB has been applied. And the results and analysis will be given in this section.

5.1 Simulation Conditions

The simulations are conducted in MATLAB R2020b. The solver use ode23 algorithm and the fixed-step size is set to be 0.01s.

The relevant parameters of the aerial manipulator used in our simulation are shown in Table 1. It contains relevant parameters of quadrotor and manipulator.

Table 1. Aerial manipulator parameters.

Description	Parameter
Mass of quadrotor	$m_q = 22.461kg$
Mass of manipulator	$m_{man} = 5kg$
Mass of whole system	$m = 22.461kg$
Length of single-joint manipulator	$l = 1m$
Inertia on X axis(Quadrotor)	$I_{xx} = 4.624kg \cdot m^2$
Inertia on Y axis(Quadrotor)	$I_{yy} = 7.081kg \cdot m^2$
Inertia on Z axis(Quadrotor)	$I_{zz} = 10.061kg \cdot m^2$
Inertia on X axis(Manipulator)	$I_{xx}^{man} = 0.7kg \cdot m^2$
Inertia on Y axis(Manipulator)	$I_{yy}^{man} = 0.8kg \cdot m^2$
Inertia on Z axis(Manipulator)	$I_{zz}^{man} = 0.9kg \cdot m^2$
Position of manipulator in body frame of quadrotor	$a = [0; 0; 0.1]m$

The pitch angle of quadrotor θ was selected as 15 degrees. To ensure the posture requirements, other relevant parameters of the trajectory used in the simulation are chosen as follows:

$$r = 1.2\,m;\, \omega = 1.4317\text{rad/s}; c = 5\,m.$$

Then the continuous-time function of the quadrotor trajectory can be given as:

$$p_d(t) = [1.2\sin(1.4317t); -1.2\cos(1.4317t); -5],$$

$$b_{1d}(t) = [\sin(1.4317t); \cos(1.4317t); 0].$$

The controller parameters are chosen as follows:

$$k_x = 124.8689, \ k_v = 43.6754, \ k_R = 7.94, \ k_\Omega = 2.35.$$

The joint angle of the manipulator can be given as:

$$q = \frac{\pi \sin(3t)}{4} + \frac{\pi}{2}.$$

5.2 Simulation Results

The diagram of the flight path is shown in Fig. 4. We can see from the picture that the quadrotor flies along a circular trajectory.

In simulation experiments, the desired pinch angle was set as 15°. The quadrotor follows separate trajectories that take into account the offset of the CoM and the conventional trajectory. Compare the angle between the x-axis and the horizontal plane of the quadrotor in two cases mentioned above.

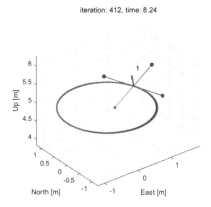

Fig. 4. Diagram of the flight path

From Fig. 5, it can be clearly seen that the angle between x-axis and the horizontal plane trajectory considering the CoM offset is closer to the desired value. By quantitative analysis, the error of the green curve is 4.322° and the error of the green curve is 2.143°. The trajectory planning method used reduces the error by 50.13%.

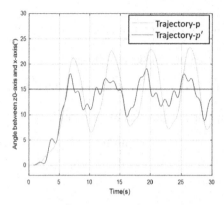

Fig. 5. Angle between x-axis and the horizontal plane.

6 Conclusion and Future Work

To solve the trajectory planning problem of aerial manipulators, we propose a trajectory planning method based on inertial decoupling the dynamic constraints of the quadrotor were also considered to ensure stable flight of the quadrotor. And the geometric controllers with high control accuracy are used in the quadrotor control. Finally, the simulation results demonstrate the high stability and accuracy of our method.

In future work, we will focus on two main areas: firstly, an attempt to investigate a trajectory planning method that takes into account more reasonable constraints; secondly, Secondly, an online trajectory generation approach will be used in trajectory planning to improve the flexibility of the system.

References

1. Ruggiero, F., Lippiello, V., Ollero, A.: Aerial manipulation: a literature review. IEEE Robot. Autom. Lett. **3**(3), 1957–1964 (2018)
2. Kondak, K., et al.: Aerial manipulation robot composed of an autonomous helicopter and a 7 degrees of freedom industrial manipulator. In: 2014 IEEE international conference on robotics and automation (ICRA), pp. 2107–2112. IEEE, Hong Kong (2014)
3. Cataldi, E., et al.: Impedance control of an aerial-manipulator: preliminary results. In: 2016 IEEE/RSJ International Conference on Intelligent Robots and Systems (IROS), pp. 3848–3853. IEEE, Daejeon (2016)
4. Lee, H., Kim, H., Kim, H.J.: Path planning and control of multiple aerial manipulators for a cooperative transportation. In: 2015 IEEE/RSJ International Conference on Intelligent Robots and Systems (IROS), pp. 2386–2391. IEEE, Hamburg (2015)
5. Lindsey, Q., Mellinger, D., Kumar, V.: Construction of cubic structures with quadrotor teams. Proc. Robot. Sci. Syst. **7**(7), 986–995 (2011)
6. Willmann, J., Augugliaro, F., Cadalbert, T., D'Andrea, R., Gramazio, F., Kohler, M.: Aerial robotic construction towards a new field of architectural research. Int. J. Archit. Comput. **10**(3), 439–459 (2012)
7. Kim, S., Choi, S., Kim, H.J.: Aerial manipulation using a quadrotor with a two DOF robotic arm. In: 2013 IEEE/RSJ International Conference on Intelligent Robots and Systems, pp. 4990–4995. IEEE Robotics and Automation Society, Chicago (2013)

8. Yoshikawa, T., Zheng, X.Z.: Coordinated dynamic hybrid position/force control for multiple robot manipulators handling one constrained object. Int. J. Robot. Res. **12**(3), 219–230 (1993)
9. Zhan, W., Chen, Y., Wang, Y., Chao, F., Shen, Q.: Robust control for autonomous surveillance with unmanned aerial manipulator. In: Jansen, T., Jensen, R., Parthaláin, N.M., Lin, C.-M. (eds.) UKCI 2021. AISC, vol. 1409, pp. 215–226. Springer, Cham (2021). https://doi.org/10. 1007/978-3-030-87094-2_19
10. Hwang, C.L., Yang, C.C., Hung, J.Y.: Path tracking of an autonomous ground vehicle with different payloads by hierarchical improved fuzzy dynamic sliding-mode control. IEEE Trans. Fuzzy Syst. **26**(2), 899–914 (2017)
11. Yang, H., Wang, S., Zuo, Z.: Trajectory tracking for a wheeled mobile robot with an omnidirectional wheel on uneven ground. IET Control Theory Appl. **14**(7), 921–929 (2020)
12. Huang, J., Ri, S., Fukuda, T., Wang, Y.: A disturbance observer based sliding mode control for a class of underactuated robotic system with mismatched uncertainties. IEEE Trans Autom. Control **64**(6), 2480–2487 (2018)
13. Shahbazzadeh, M., Sadati, S.J., Minagar, S.: Trajectory tracking control for mobile robots considering position of mass center. Optimal Control Appl. Methods **42**(6), 1542–1555 (2021). https://doi.org/10.1002/oca.2744
14. Fresk, E., Wuthier, D., Nikolakopoulos, G.: Generalized center of gravity compensation for multirotors with application to aerial manipulation. In: 2017 IEEE/RSJ International Conference on Intelligent Robots and Systems (IROS), pp. 4424–4429. IEEE, Vancouver (2017)
15. Zhang, J., Yang, L., Shen, G.: New hybrid adaptive control approach for aircraft with centre of gravity variation. IET Control Theory Appl. **6**(14), 2179–2187 (2012)
16. Yang, S., He, B., Wang, Z., Xu, C., Gao, F.: Whole-body real-time motion planning for multicopters. In: 2021 IEEE International Conference on Robotics and Automation (ICRA), pp. 9197–9203. IEEE, Xi'an (2021)
17. Zhang, X., et al.: Trajectory planning of quadrotors flight like binary star. In: 2022 12th International Conference on CYBER Technology in Automation, Control, and Intelligent Systems (CYBER), pp. 935–940. IEEE, Changbai Mountain (2022)

Wearable Sensors and Robots

The Application of Hybrid Dynamic Recurrent Fuzzy Neural Network in Lower Limb Rehabilitation Function Evaluation

Yujia Liao[1], Quan Liu[1], Jie Zuo[1], Wei Meng[1(✉)], and Qingsong Ai[1,2]

[1] Artificial Intelligence & Rehabilitation Robotics Laboratory, School of Information Engineering, Wuhan University of Technology, Wuhan 430070, China
weimeng@whut.edu.cn
[2] School of Artificial Intelligence, Hubei University, Wuhan 430062, China
http://ai.hubu.edu.cn/

Abstract. To enhance the human-robot interaction ability of a lower-limb rehabilitation robot for stroke patients, it is crucial to accurately quantify the rehabilitation status. This paper proposes an adaptive rehabilitation assessment approach based on a Takagi-Sugeno (T-S) fuzzy neural network aided by a multi-signal acquisition platform. By extracting five kinematic data and electromyographic (EMG) data of clinical rehabilitation training, the method obtains the lower limb characteristic parameters of patients to simulate the rehabilitation evaluation process. The multi-factor line regression method evaluates the impact of maximum joint activity, free acceleration, angular acceleration, average velocity, jerk, and EMG signal data on the evaluation results. The mapping between rehabilitation feature metrics and recovery conditions is initially estimated using a T-S fuzzy neural network. The paper then proposes a hybrid optimization learning method for the above network, which includes particle swarm optimization (PSO) and recursive least squares estimator (RLSE). PSO modifies the function parameters used to calculate the membership degree to optimize the fitness of fuzzy rules. However, the PSO algorithm can easily trap into local optima, so the freedom coefficient that calculates the consequent of fuzzy rules is further corrected based on RLSE. The iterative learning of the T-S fuzzy neural network is completed using gradient descent. Finally, the proposed approach is compared for convergence efficiency with two intelligent algorithms, and the results demonstrate the proposed network's excellent convergence performance and high model accuracy (RMSE = 2.336×10^{-3}), which is essential for lower-limb rehabilitation.

Keywords: Fuzzy Neural Network · T-S Model · Rehabilitation Assessment · Hybrid Evolutionary Programming

© The Author(s), under exclusive license to Springer Nature Singapore Pte Ltd. 2023
H. Yang et al. (Eds.): ICIRA 2023, LNAI 14268, pp. 173–184, 2023.
https://doi.org/10.1007/978-981-99-6486-4_15

1   Introduction

Stroke is a cerebrovascular disease that is characterized by hemiplegia, which seriously endangers people's physical and mental health [1]. The results of the China National Stroke Screening Survey (CNSSS) showed that stroke prevalence was 2.06% in adults aged $\geq$ 40 [2]. With China's population aging, the huge challenge facing modern medicine is evident. China currently needs to rehabilitate nearly 2 million stroke patients, who typically have defects in motor function, each year [3]. Weakness in the lower limb is the most common form of stroke among the elderly [4]. Physical therapy is often delivered by physical therapists in a traditional way as a rehabilitative strategy for patients. For instance, Constraint-Induced Movement Therapy (CIMT) advocates for strengthening the use of the affected limb with the assistance of therapists, while restraining the healthy side to intensify the spontaneous use of the affected limb [5]. In supine auxiliary leg lifting training, therapists encourage the spontaneous use of the affected leg and keep the range of motion of the injured articulatio coxae in focus for judging the recovery. Unlike CIMT, Mirror Therapy (MT) takes advantage of optical illusion and enables the patient to visually sense the motion of the healthy limb, thereby directly contributing to the recovery of the affected side [6]. As can be seen from the definitions, these therapies can be broadly grouped as task-based rehabilitation because patients are often coached to continue practicing the task until it is perfected. However, the personal care of medical staff is still indispensable for these therapies.

Although task-based rehabilitation has been practiced for a long time, conducting physiotherapy tests to investigate the clinical features in some cases can be onerous. Consequently, doubts have been raised within the scientific and public community in recent years regarding the efficiency of traditional rehabilitation evaluations. Therefore, it is crucial to propose an approach for objectively and quantitatively evaluating the motor function status of stroke patients during the rehabilitation process. Previous studies have focused on developing performance-based regression models to determine data-driven capacity relevance. For instance, Hendriks [7] established the validity of using inertial measurement units (IMUs) data to investigate how gait performance relates to gait capacity over the course of gait training sessions conducted on separate days. While the proposed algorithm performed a univariate linear regression analysis for the number of steps and walking time as a function of capacity for each subtask, only 84% of gait bouts were under stride detection and corresponded to actual precision. Bijalwan [8] advanced a novel automated system designed for detecting and recognizing upper extremity exercises using an RGB-Depth camera. A dataset with ten human upper limb rehabilitation exercises was collected from twenty-five subjects. By combining the use of three various classifiers, namely CNN, CNN-LSTM, and CNN-GRU, the classification of different human activities was reported to have an average testing accuracy of 99%. Although these works further argue the potential of data-driven intelligent software for the establishment and practice of rehabilitation evaluation, none of them focused precisely on the valid values of measurement used to gain on the fuzzy and precision functions of complex systems effectively. As the kinematic data follow the characteristics of quantitatively measured quality, the high level of abstraction becomes a bottleneck of model design, and development costs are increased.

On the one hand, neural networks (NN) are capable of non-linear mappings and adaptive learning, while fuzzy logic (FL) can handle highly non-linear and indeterminate systems. Chu [9] developed a modified fuzzy neural network (FNN) for estimating uncertain functions in non-linear systems. The FNN has better generalization capability and stability is ensured using Lyapunov analysis. The FNN, composed of many simple and highly interconnected processing elements, cleverly incorporates expert experience into the complex training process of NN and benefits from the advantages of FL and NN. However, the study only analyzed the network structure of fuzzy neural networks, lacking the selection and setting of parameters and the optimization of training efficiency, a significant challenge arises when trying to balance system complexity and required accuracy.

To address the above problems, this study presents a clinical rehabilitation assessment model for the lower limb using the T-S fuzzy neural network. The network is trained using rehabilitation data collected from sensors and professional evaluations by therapists. To enhance accuracy and convergence speed, a hybrid parameter optimization algorithm is proposed to adaptively adjust network parameters. The paper is organized as follows: Sect. 2 describes the network structure utilized for rehabilitation assessment. In Sect. 3, the parameter optimization process is detailed. Section 4 presents the experimental background and results. Finally, Sect. 5 includes a discussion of the findings and the research contributions.

2   Fuzzy Neural Network Structure

2.1   Fuzzy System Based on Takagi-Sugeno Model

Takagi and Sugeno first proposed T-S model [10], which is generally composed of several fuzzy rules. In general, a fuzzy system has M inputs and one output, given as follows [11].

$$R^i : \text{IF } x_1 \text{ is } A_1^i \text{ and } x_2 \text{ is } A_2^i \text{ and } ... \text{ and } x_n \text{ is } A_n^i$$
$$\text{THEN } y_i = p_0^i + p_0^i x_1 + ... + p_n^i x_n \tag{1}$$

where p_j^i are free parameters corresponding to the output of the fuzzy system, A_j^i are fuzzy sets. Denote input as $\boldsymbol{\xi} = [x_1, x_2, ..., x_n]^{\text{T}}$, where x_j is the jth base variable, y_i is the output calculated according to rule R^i. Gaussian-type membership grade function is used to give the calculation of output membership rules with singleton fuzzifier. The fitness function for each rule and the Gauss membership grade function definition can be expressed as follows:

$$\omega_i = \prod_{j=1}^{n} \mu_j^i(x_j) \tag{2}$$

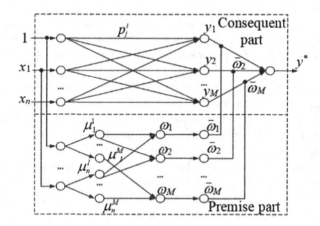

Fig. 1. Fuzzy neural network structure based on Takagi-Sugeo model

$$\mu(x) = \text{gaussmf}(x, \delta, c) = e^{\frac{-(x-c)^2}{2\delta^2}} \tag{3}$$

where c and δ are the center and width of membership function. The overall expected value is represented as a weighted mean, expressed as:

$$y^* = \frac{\sum_{i=1}^{M} \omega^i y^i}{\sum_{i=1}^{M} \omega^i} = \sum_{i=1}^{M} \lambda^i \times (p_0^i + p_1^i x_1 + \dots + p_n^i x_n) \tag{4}$$

$$\lambda^i = \frac{\omega^i}{\sum_{i=1}^{M} \omega^i} \tag{5}$$

2.2   Design of Fuzzy Neural Network

The diagram for the FNN shown in Fig. 1 can be designed. The network can be divided by premise part and consequent part.

Premise Part. The premise part of the neural network consists of four layers. The first layer is the input layer, which plays the role of transmitting the input value $\xi = [x_1, x_2, ..., x_n]^T$ to the next layer. The second layer calculates the membership grade function of each input component belonging to the fuzzy set of linguistic variable according to (3). In the third layer, the fitness of each rule is calculated via (2). For a given input, the fitness value of the linguistic variable that matches the input is higher, while linguistic variables that are far away from the input point get a lower fitness value. This is similar to a local approximation neural network, where inputs closer to the training points have a larger influence on the network's output, while inputs further away have a smaller influence. The fourth layer is used to realize normalization calculation, expressed as (5).

Consequent Part. For general multiple-output networks, the consequent part typically consists of several parallel subnets with the same structure. However, this study only includes one subnet.

The structure of subnet is to adopt standard FNN. Each node in the input layer feed its output to each of twelve hidden-layer nodes, which in turn feed twelve output nodes. y^* is weighted sum of the consequent of each rule with single-dimension attribute, and the weight coefficient is expressed as the normalized fitness of the corresponding fuzzy rule, namely the connection weight of the antecedent network to the consequent network.

3   Dynamic Optimization Algorithm

The above FNN learning algorithm proceeds as follows, the parameters for optimizing consist of center (c) and width (δ) of the membership grade function, as well as the consequent parameters (p_j^i).

3.1   PSO Algorithm

The concept of particle swarm optimization (PSO) is inspired by the study of foraging behavior in birds. By promoting cooperation and information sharing among individuals in a group, the optimal solution can be achieved [12]. The key to membership grade remodelling lies in the center c and width δ of the membership function. The update of the PSO algorithm is governed by the following equations:

$$c_j^i(k+1) = c_j^i(k) + Vc_j^i(k) \tag{6}$$

$$\delta_j^i(k+1) = \delta_j^i(k) + V\delta_j^i(k) \tag{7}$$

Velocities of particles are expressed as follows,

$$\begin{aligned} V_j^i(k+1) =& \omega \times V_j^i(k) + c_1 \times r_1 \times (pbest_j^i(k) - X_j^i(k)) \\ &+ c_2 \times r_2 \times (gbest(k) - X_j^i(k)) \end{aligned} \tag{8}$$

where k is to indicate the kth iteration, X_j^i refers to center c_j^i and width δ_j^i, and V_j^i is the velocity of the ith particle. $\{c_1, c_2\}$ are interpreted individual as learning factors and global learning factors respectively, and $\{r_1, r_2\}$ are random number distributed in [0, 1] to increase the search randomness.

3.2   RLSE Algorithm

The ordinary least squares estimator (LSE) is a commonly used method for function fitting [13]. The recursive least squares estimator (RLSE) utilizes a recursive algorithm for the least squares method, simplifying computations and allowing for iterative solutions to the problem [14].

The least squares problem can be defined as follows in matrix notation,

$$Ap = f(\xi) \tag{9}$$

where A is an $n \times m$ matrix, $p = [p_1, p_2, ..., p_m]^T$ is undetermined coefficient vector and $f(\xi)$ is the output vector of the system. The following results can be given by the iterative algorithm.

$$\mathbf{k}(n) = \frac{\lambda^{-1}\mathbf{P_{In}}(n-1)\mathbf{u}(n)}{1 + \lambda^{-1}\mathbf{u}^T(n)\mathbf{P_{In}}(n-1)\mathbf{u}(n)} \tag{10}$$

$$\zeta(n) = \mathbf{d}(n) - \mathbf{p}^T(n-1)\mathbf{u}(n) \tag{11}$$

$$\mathbf{p}(n) = \mathbf{p}(n-1) + \mathbf{k}(n)\zeta^*(n) \tag{12}$$

$$\mathbf{P_{In}}(n) = \lambda^{-1}\mathbf{P_{In}}(n-1) - \lambda^{-1}\mathbf{k}(n)\mathbf{u}^T(n)\mathbf{P_{In}}(n-1) \tag{13}$$

where n is to indicate the nth iteration, $\mathbf{u}(n)$ and $\mathbf{d}(n)$ are extended sub-columns of matrix A and expected output y respectively [15].

3.3   Hybrid Algorithm Optimization

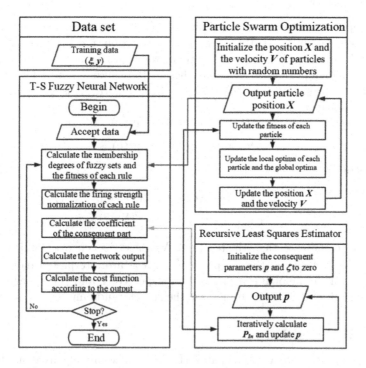

Fig. 2. PSO-RLSE hybrid algorithm optimization process

The parameter learning process of PSO-RLSE hybrid optimization is illustrated in Fig. 2.

In this study, the root mean square error (RMSE) is used as the cost function in the parameter correction process. Specifically, since this study only involves one output node, RMSE can be expressed as:

$$\text{RMSE} = \sqrt{(y - y^*)^2} \tag{14}$$

where y_i and y_i^* represent expected output and actual output respectively. The optimization process is described in steps as follows.

Step1: Generate input data pairs with training set.

Step2: Initialize particle swarm and RLSE parameters.

Step3: Calculate the membership grade function of each input component of each sample data corresponding to hidden layers with (3).

Step4: Calculate the fitness of fuzzy rules of each hidden layer according to (2).

Step5: Calculate the consequent network output and the weighted normalized output on the basis of RLSE.

Step6: Calculate cost function value given in (14) from expected output and actual output. Update the best particle and the PSO fitness of each sampl-e particle.

Step7: Update the consequent network parameter p according to (10) - (13). U-pdate c and δ for calculating Gauss membership grade function with (6)-(7), and check whether the particle position is out of range.

Step8: Go back to Step3 until the iterative training is completed.

4   Experimental Procedures

4.1   Materials and Experimental Method

The data collection experiment was conducted at the Lower Limb Rehabilitation Robot Engineering Experiment of Wuhan University of Technology, under the guidance of clinical professionals with rich experience in stroke patient rehabilitation research. This study recruited 20 healthy adults (mean age ± standard deviation: 34.9 ± 9.83 years old) and 15 stroke patients (mean age ± standard deviation: 52.73 ± 3.87 years old) to participate in the experiment. All subjects volunteered and provided written informed consent. They were instructed to undergo a Brunnstrom II-VI simulation of lower limb motor dysfunction in stroke patients, and data was collected on the maximum joint activity, free acceleration, angular acceleration, average velocity, jerk, and EMG signals. A total of 350 valid samples were selected and used to create a dataset consisting of tuples in the form $(\boldsymbol{\xi}, \boldsymbol{y})$, where $\boldsymbol{\xi}$ represents the set of clinical test samples and $\boldsymbol{y}$ represents the normalized clinical evaluation index. To obtain effective parameter estimates for the corresponding FNN, the maximum likelihood estimation method was applied to the dataset.

The study utilized the Delsys Trigno^{TM} wireless electromyography (EMG) analysis system, IMU array, and a computer to establish a comprehensive platform for capturing motion and physiological signals in lower limb scenarios. The

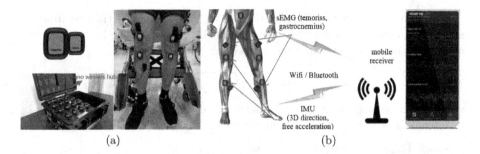

(a)   (b)

Fig. 3. The principle and structure of data acquisition (a) wearable sensors nodes (b) motion measurement scenario

Table 1. Sensor Performance Specification

Sampling Frequency	60 Hz
Induction Axis	3 axes
Tilt Azimuth (Static)	0.5o, 1.0o 1σ RMS
Tilt Azimuth (Dynamic)	1.0o, 2.0o 1σ RMS

Delsys Trigno^{TM} wireless electromyography (EMG) acquisition system is composed of the Trigno wireless base station, EMG Flex sensors, and computer control software, forming a comprehensive solution for EMG data collection. The sEMG signals were captured from the rectus femoris (RF) and gastrocnemius (GM) muscles on both sides of the lower limbs, with a sampling frequency of 2000 Hz. IMU array (Xsens DOT, Xsens Technologies, Netherlands) includes accelerometer, gyroscope sensor and magnetic sensor. The sensor can be tied to the limbs and torso of the human body for motion measurement. Attitude parameters is logged and then communication through Bluetooth 5.0 at 60 Hz. Table 1 gives that the main performance specifications parameter of sensor. The principle and structure of data acquisition experiment is shown in Fig. 3.

To verify the generalization ability and dynamic optimization efficiency of the proposed algorithm in the presence, this study conducted simulation research based on Matlab platform. The free parameters of the premise network to be optimized form a two-dimensional matrix with dimension 12×6, while the consequent part form a two-dimensional matrix with dimension 7×12 (the matrix row vector includes a constant coefficient term and six variable coefficient terms corresponding to the input terms). The model parameters of the PSO algorithm for optimizing the antecedent network were selected as $\omega = 0.5$, $c_1 = 2$, $c_2 = 2$, and the consequent network were selected as $\delta = 0.004$, $\lambda = 0.98$. The particle velocity is limited to the range $[0, 2]$. The RMSE in (14) is used as the cost function of the above two algorithms.

Control experiments are designed to compare and analyze the training effects of the proposed algorithm. The proposed FNN algorithm is compared with the improved Backpropagation (BP) algorithm and the T-S network algorithm optimized based on BP algorithm respectively. The improved BP algorithm adaptively adjusts the learning rate by adding momentum term, which can be expressed as.

$$\Delta y(t) = \eta \times err \times x + \alpha \times \Delta y(t-1) \tag{15}$$

where η is the learning rate, and α is the momentum term, which reflects the impact of experience before the current time and play a damping role for time t. The parameters in this article were selected as $\eta = 0.001$, $\alpha = 0.5$. The T-S network algorithm optimized based on BP algorithm uses the above BP algorithm to optimize the network parameters.

4.2   Experimental Result

The normalized evaluation results of the two evaluation algorithms mentioned above, as well as those of the proposed PSO-RLSE hybrid optimization algorithm, are presented in Fig. 4, Fig. 6 and Fig. 7. The figures illustrate the training results of the last iteration for the first 100 samples. To facilitate a clear comparison of the evaluation effects, each different type of output was assigned a unique style, with the sample numbers plotted on the x-axis and the normalized expected score plotted on the y-axis.

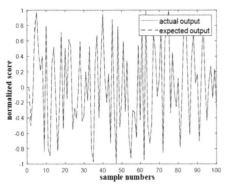
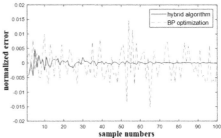

Fig. 4. Evaluation score of T-S network algorithm based on PSO-RLSE hybrid algorithm and physician's FMA score deviation analysis chart.

Fig. 5. Evaluation score of T-S network algorithm based on BP optimization and physician's FMA score deviation analysis chart.

Table 2. Performance Comparison.

Optimization Algorithm	Sample Size	Training Time (sec)	RMSE Mean
improved BP	350	0.09776	0.09872
T-S (BP)	350	0.01746	0.02148
T-S (PSO-RLSE)	350	3.237	2.336×10^{-3}

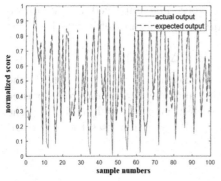

Fig. 6. Evaluation score of improved BP algorithm and physician's FMA score deviation analysis chart.

Fig. 7. Evaluation score of T-S network algorithm based on BP optimization and physician's FMA score deviation analysis chart.

The results show that the learning curves generated by the improved BP algorithm are overall inferior to those of the T-S fuzzy model. When using the BP algorithm, the network output exhibits a certain degree of error before reaching the peak of the actual value, whereas the T-S model almost perfectly matches the expected output value. This suggests that the T-S fuzzy neural network possesses excellent ability to reflect the dynamic evolution process of assessments.

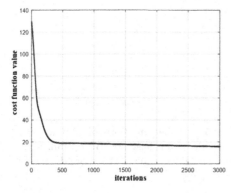

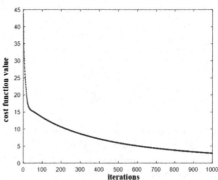

Fig. 8. Error iteration curve by the improved BP algorithm.

Fig. 9. The iteration curve of estimation error using the T-S fuzzy model-based algorithm.

In order to compare the parameter optimization performance of the hybrid algorithm and the BP algorithm, their RMSE values are presented in Fig. 5. The BP network suffers from weak generalization ability and local minimization problem, which results in clear oscillations in the learning curve. The performance of the proposed hybrid algorithm is better, with the integrated error curve showing improvement after the tenth group of samples. To evaluate the overall convergence speed, the RMSE estimation error of all samples is averaged at each iteration. The gradient descent of the proposed PSO-RLSE and the BP algorithm is illustrated in Fig. 8 and Fig. 9, respectively, and the former shows a faster convergence speed. The comparison results of algorithm performance are summarized in Table 2, indicating that the proposed PSO-RLSE hybrid optimization algorithm achieves better approximation accuracy than the single optimization algorithm. However, using two methods to optimize the parameters of the premise and consequent parts increases both the computational complexity and training time.

5 Conclusion

This paper proposes a fuzzy neural network structure based on a multisensor system that can track changes in overall motion parameters for adaptive evaluation of lower limb movement function. The advantage of the movement data acquisition system based on IMUs is its high flexibility in sample collection, which makes it suitable for long-term clinical rehabilitation monitoring as well as home use. The FNN provides personalized rehabilitation evaluation functions for patients based on the degree of task completion, thereby improving patient motivation in follow-up rehabilitation training and avoiding the inefficiency caused by redundant or improper training decisions.

PSO-RLSE is used to iteratively optimize the membership function parameters and objective weights of the FNN consequent part. Experimental results show that the PSO algorithm is easy to implement and can converge quickly but is prone to local optimal values and lacks mathematical theory support. RLSE can more accurately find the global optimal solution but has a slower convergence speed. In the T-S fuzzy model, the large dimension of the optimization space also increases computation time. This paper proposes combining two different intelligent algorithms to form a hybrid optimization algorithm, which improves the approximation accuracy of the fuzzy neural network. The superiority and feasibility of using artificial neural networks to enhance critical evaluation in rehabilitation of stroke patients with hemiplegia is explained.

Acknowledgements. This work is supported by the National Natural Science Foundation of China under Grant 52275029 and 52075398.

References

1. Xu, Rui, et al.: Lower-Limb motor assessment with corticomuscular coherence of multiple muscles during ankle dorsiflexion after stroke. IEEE Trans. Neural Syst. Rehabil. Eng. **31**, 160–168 (2022)

2. Yi, X., et al.: Prevalence and risk factors of high-risk population for stroke: a population-based cross-sectional survey in southwestern China. Front. Neurol. 13 (2022)
3. Bai, J., Song, A., Li, H.: Design and analysis of cloud upper limb rehabilitation system based on motion tracking for post-stroke patients. Appl. Sci. 9(8), 16–20 (2019)
4. Aimoto, K., et al.: Gait improvement in stroke patients by gait exercise assist robot training is related to trunk verticality. J. Phys. Therapy Sci. 34(11), 715–719 (2022)
5. Roberts, H., et al.: Constraint induced movement therapy camp for children with hemiplegic cerebral palsy augmented by use of an exoskeleton to play games in virtual reality. Phys. Occupational Therapy Pediatr. 41(2), 150–165 (2020)
6. Tharani, G., et al.: Effects of mirror therapy vs modified constraint induced movement therapy on upper extremity in subacute stroke patients. Bangladesh J. Med. Sci. 20(2), 323–329 (2021)
7. Hendriks, M.M.S., et al.: Using sensor technology to measure gait capacity and gait performance in rehabilitation inpatients with neurological disorders. Sensors 22(21), 83–87 (2022)
8. Bijalwan, V., et al.: HDL-PSR: modelling spatio-temporal features using hybrid deep learning approach for post-stroke rehabilitation. Neural Process. Lett. 1–20 (2022)
9. Chu, Y., et al.: Modified recurrent fuzzy neural network sliding mode control for nonlinear systems. Front. Neurol. (2021)
10. Li, J.: Research on robot motion control based on variable structure fuzzy neural network based on TS model. IOP Conf. Ser.: Earth Environ. Sci. 440(3) (2020)
11. Kwon, W., Jin, Y., Lee, S.M.: PI-type event-triggered H∞ filter for networked TS fuzzy systems using affine matched membership function approach. Appl. Math. Comput. 38(5) (2020)
12. Li, Z.: Intelligent electrical engineering automation on account of particle swarm optimization (PSO) algorithm. J. Phys.: Conf. Ser. 2355(1) (2022)
13. Ivanov, O., Lymar, O.V.: The asymptotic normality for the least squares estimator of parameters in a two dimensional sinusoidal model of observations. Theory Prob. Math. Stat. 100, 107–131 (2020)
14. Wen, S., et al.: Real-time estimation of time-dependent imposed heat flux in graded index media by KF-RLSE algorithm. Appl. Thermal Eng. 150, 1–10 (2019)
15. Chen, J., Gong, Z.: Collaborative software engineering model dependent on deep recursive least squares. Mobile Inf. Syst. (2022)

A Strain Gauge Based FMG Sensor for sEMG-FMG Dual Modal Measurement of Muscle Activity Associated with Hand Gestures

Yifan Tang[1], Jiayi Wang[1], Peiji Chen[1], Wenyang Li[1], Haokang Xu[1], Shunta Togo[1,2], Hiroshi Yokoi[1,2], and Yinlai Jiang[1,2(✉)]

[1] Department of Mechanical Engineering and Intelligent Systems, The University of Electro-Communications, Tokyo, Japan
jiang.yinlai@uec.ac.jp
[2] Center for Neuroscience and Biomedical Engineering, The University of Electro-Communications, Tokyo, Japan

Abstract. To improve the daily living independence of people with limb impairments, researchers are developing various prosthetic limbs. This study aims to design a dual-modality sensor integrating surface electromyography (sEMG) and force myography (FMG) to measure muscle activities for forearm and hand motion recognition. sEMG records electrical signals from muscle contractions, while FMG measures muscle mechanical deformation during contraction. Combining these two models compensates for individual limitations and increases overall performance. An integrated design of the FMG and sEMG measurement units enables simultaneous measurement while keeping the sensor compact. Using strain gauges to sense FMG instead of traditional force-sensitive resistors can enhance signal stability and sensitivity. The dual-modality sensor combines sEMG and FMG advantages to offer accurate and reliable hand gesture recognition. Experimental results show a 91.8% classification accuracy for recognizing 22 forearm and hand motions using the dual-modal sensor. This technology offers an effective means of controlling prosthetic limbs, improving life quality for individuals with limb impairments, and has potential applications in biomedical engineering, rehabilitation, and robotics.

Keywords: sEMG · FMG · Strain gauges · Dual-mode sensor · Forearm-hand movement recognition

This research was supported in part by JSPS KAKENHI grant numbers JP23H00166, JP23H03785, JP22K04025, a project commissioned by JSPS and NSFC under the Japan-China Scientific Cooperation Program, and JKA through its promotion funds from KEIRIN RACE.

H. Yang et al. (Eds.): ICIRA 2023, LNAI 14268, pp. 185–194, 2023.
https://doi.org/10.1007/978-981-99-6486-4_16

1   Introduction

Approximately 1 billion people worldwide are affected by physical, mental, or intellectual disabilities, with limb disabilities accounting for the highest proportion at 45.0% [10]. To improve their self-care abilities in daily life, researchers are developing various prostheses. To achieve active control of the prostheses, it is often necessary to measure the user's muscle activities. Surface electromyography (sEMG) is currently a widely used non-invasive measurement technique for controlling prostheses [17], which determines muscle states by recording the bioelectric signals generated by muscle fiber contractions and relaxations [5].

However, sEMG has limitations, such as signal quality being easily affected by skin characteristics, relative motion, and biopotential interference [8], as well as sensitivity to external electromagnetic interference and other noise sources [18]. Therefore, researchers are developing other sensing technologies such as Mechanomyography (MMG) and Force myography (FMG) to compensate for the interference-prone drawbacks of sEMG and assist in measuring muscle contractions.

MMG is a method of analyzing muscle activity by measuring the mechanical signals in the form of low-frequency vibrations or sounds generated by muscle contractions [6]. Compared to EMG signals, MMG is not affected by changes in skin impedance or sensor failure. Accelerometers were among the first methods used to measure MMG but are susceptible to motion artifacts [3]. Consequently, capacitive microphone sensors have become the mainstream choice, improving resistance to ambient noise and low-frequency response by placing the microphone in a conical acoustic chamber [7]. Optical measurement techniques have also been applied to MMG detection. Bansal et al. developed a flexible wearable photoelectric sensor that detects muscle contractions by measuring the amount of incident light scattered back from skeletal muscle tissue [1]. Sharma et al. used near-infrared photoelectric sensors to indirectly detect skin surface displacement caused by muscle contractions [14]. However, optical sensors are inevitably affected by ambient light and sweat. Clearly, near-infrared sensors may exhibit significant errors under natural light conditions, and sweat on the skin surface can cause refraction and reflection of light intended for irradiating skeletal muscles, interfering with sensor readings. Therefore, photoelectricity is not a suitable method for controlling prosthetics or for people in motion.

FMG is another method for detecting muscle activity, which detects muscle activity by measuring changes in skin tension caused by the increased cross-sectional area of the limb during muscle contraction [16]. The advantage of FMG is that it is not affected by external electrical noise and sweat, and it has high stability over time, as muscle fatigue does not affect the strength of the FMG signal. We believe that FMG is an excellent method for assisting in the measurement of muscle contractions.

Most of the current force myography sensors use force-sensitive resistors (FSR) sensors [4,12]. FSRs are made of conductive polymers, which change their resistance when force is applied to their surfaces. The main advantage of this sensor is its extremely low cost, but typically, applying an FSR sensor directly to the skin presents obvious problems due to the unstable and uncertain contact between the sensor and the user's skin. The force applied to the sensor does not fully equal the change in resistance, so it cannot linearly characterize the degree of muscle contraction. Moreover, when pressure changes rapidly, the FSRs cannot change their resistance fast enough, exhibiting time-lag behavior and producing unstable results [13].

Therefore, to avoid the problems associated with FSR sensors and reduce the size and thickness of the sensor, we propose another FMG measurement method. We intend to replace FSR with strain gauges, known for their high accuracy and sensitivity, for use in FMG sensors. As an auxiliary sensor for sEMG, we will measure and force signals from the same location where sEMG is measured. Studies have shown that multimodal signals from the same location can be helpful for recognizing hand gestures [9].

2 Materials and Methods

In this study, we designed a dual-modal sensor armband that combines sEMG sensors and strain gauge based FMG sensors. We aim to employ machine learning techniques to classify and recognize the acquired forearm EMG and FMG data, identifying various gestures that may be required for controlling a prosthetic hand.

2.1 Strain Gauges Based FMG Measurement Unit

When an external force is applied to a material, the material of length L undergoes a deformation amount of ΔL. L, and ΔL at this time is defined as the strain ϵ. By attaching the strain gauge to the object to be measured, the measurement When the object is deformed, the strain gauge is also deformed. A metal strain gauge with a resistance value of R generates strain. The cross-sectional area and length change as a result. As a result, the value of electrical resistance changes. Under this strain, If the amount of change in resistance is ΔR, the relationship between the generated strain ϵ is expressed by:

$$\varepsilon = \frac{\Delta L}{L} = \frac{\Delta R/R}{K} \tag{1}$$

The coefficient K is an intrinsic proportionality constant of the strain gauge, called the gauge factor.

Since the resistance change of the strain gauge is a small value, it is difficult to measure the resistance change directly. As shown in Fig. 1b, it is necessary to use a Wheatstone bridge circuit to convert the resistance change into a voltage. When R = R1 = R2 = R3 = R4, and $\Delta R \approx R$, the change in output voltage Δe is represented by:

$$\Delta e = \frac{\Delta R}{4R}E = \frac{E}{4}K\varepsilon \tag{2}$$

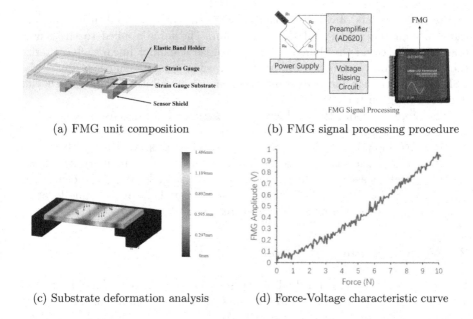

(a) FMG unit composition

(b) FMG signal processing procedure

(c) Substrate deformation analysis

(d) Force-Voltage characteristic curve

Fig. 1. FMG Unit

Based on the theory mentioned above, we designed an FMG-based measurement unit consisting of four components: strain gauge, strain gauge substrate, strap fixture, and measurement circuit(see Fig. 1a). To minimize the sensor size, we used an ultra-small strain gauge (EFLX-02-11-6FC1LT, Tokyo Keiki Research Institute Co., Ltd.) with dimensions of 1.8 mm x 1.2 mm and fixed it to an 18 mm x 12 mm strain gauge substrate. We chose the baking plate as the strain gauge substrate because simulations and experiments showed that the Young's modulus of this type of baking plate allows the strain gauge's measuring range to reach its maximum under preset conditions. When the muscle contracts, the strap exerts a downward force on the baking plate through the strap fixture, causing the baking plate to deform. The strain gauge fixed to the baking plate changes its resistance value under the influence of the deformation.

The strap fixture interacts with the force generated by muscle contraction, achieving the functions of fixing the sensor assembly on the arm and applying the force generated by muscle contraction to the strain gauge substrate. As shown in the Fig. 1c, when the pressure applied to the strain gauge substrate reaches 10N, the deformation of the strain gauge substrate is approximately 1.48mm.

We connected the strain gauge to a 120-ohm Wheatstone bridge, which consists of three high-precision resistors RG1608P-121-B-T5 (Susumu, Japan). Due to the small changes in voltage across the Wheatstone bridge, the signal needs to be amplified by the AD620 (Analog Devices, USA) with a gain of approximately 52dB after passing through the bridge, so that the output voltage can be detected by a A/D converter(see Fig. 1b)

2.2 sEMG Unit

We employed dry electrodes developed by TOGO et al. [15]., which utilize carbon-doped silicone as the electrode material. This type of electrode utilizes carbon-doped silicone as the electrode material, which is more suitable for long-term measurements compared to traditional Ag/AgCl wet electrodes. It can also function properly under conditions involving sweat.

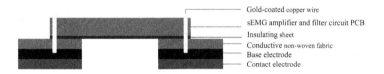

Fig. 2. sEMG unit composition

The sEMG signals were acquired through differential electrodes and fed into a precision instrumentation amplifier (AD620, Analog Devices, USA) with a gain set at 40 dB. Subsequently, the signals underwent filtering via a 50 Hz notch filter and a 1 to 1000 Hz bandwidth band-pass filter, followed by further amplification using an operational amplifier, resulting in an output voltage range of 0 to 5 V.

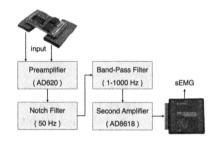

Fig. 3. sEMG signal processing procedure

2.3 Dual-Modal Sensor Design

To achieve simultaneous measurement of the sEMG signal at the same location, we positioned the FMG measurement unit above the sEMG measurement unit(see Fig. 4a). This is a significant advantage of FMG sensors over other types of sensors: they do not require direct contact with the skin.

To prevent interference between signal measurement units, we designed a sensor shield(see Fig. 4c). The design of this sensor shield maintains a gap of approximately 2 mm between the sEMG measurement unit and the strain gauge

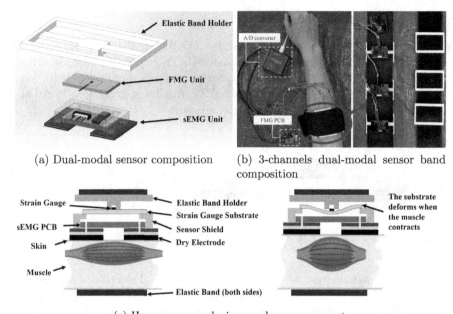

(a) Dual-modal sensor composition

(b) 3-channels dual-modal sensor band composition

(c) How sensor works in muscle measurement

Fig. 4. Dual-modal sensor design

substrate, avoiding contact between the strain gauge substrate and the EMG sensor PCB due to muscle bulging, thus reducing interference with strain gauge measurement. The sensor shield also serves to fix the sEMG measurement unit. Both the strap fixture and the sensor shield are made of PLA material and manufactured with a 3D printer.

The dual-modal sensor has a total thickness of 10 mm (FMG measurement part 4 mm, sensor shield 4 mm, dry electrode 2 mm). The voltage collected by the sensor is uniformly sent to an 8-channel 24-bit resolution ADC(AIO-160802AY-USB, CONTEC Co., Ltd.) with a sampling frequency of 1000 Hz(see Fig. 4b).

3   Experiment

3.1   Hand Gestures

We selected hand movements that are similar to those in existing research and are helpful for prosthetic design, in order to compare the performance of our sensor with existing studies [11]. Based on the top 10 most frequently used grasping actions in daily life as identified by Bullock et al. [2], we included an additional 8 forearm-hand actions and 4 finger actions in the experiment, resulting in a total of 22 forearm-hand actions. The names of the respective actions are shown in Fig. 5.

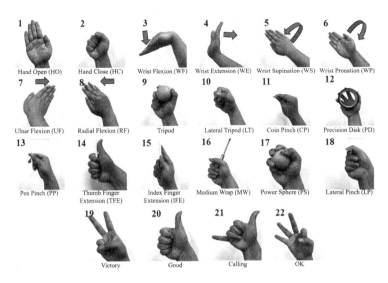

Fig. 5. 22 hand gestures

3.2   Experiment Movements

We recruited 9 healthy participants (labeled S1 to S9). All participants were right-handed, and they wore the elastic band on their right forearms. During the measurement process, the reference electrode was ensured to have close contact with the participant's skin. The bimodal sensor was positioned over the flexor digitorum superficialis, flexor carpi ulnaris, and extensor carpi radialislongus, as these locations have been proven to yield effective signal acquisition in previous research. By adjusting the strap fixture, the sensor position could be tailored to each participant's muscle location. During the experiment, participants sat with their elbows on a table. In order to correct for initial errors, a 10-second posture 0 (Relax) was collected as baseline data for each trial. Upon hearing the command, participants maintained the testing posture for three seconds, followed by a two-second relaxation, and repeated this twice.

4   Results

Four recognition methods were adopted to evaluate the classification accuracy (CA). As shown in Table 1 and Fig. 6, the recognition accuracy was 64.1% when using only the sEMG signal in the SVM classifier. The recognition accuracy was 60.0% when using only the FMG signal. The recognition accuracy reached 83.5% when both sEMG and FMG signals were used, an improvement of 19.4% compared to using only the sEMG sensor. Similar tendency was also observed in the results of KNN and RFC. Generally, the recognition accuracy of CNN was higher than the traditional machine learning methods. The recognition accuracy

Table 1. Classification results

Classifier	Modality	Subject									all	average
		s1	s2	s3	s4	s5	s6	s7	s8	s9		
SVM	sEMG	61.80%	57.90%	53.00%	62.6%	68.60%	61.10%	69.20%	66.20%	69.80%	64.14%	63.36%
	FMG	58.40%	61.40%	47.90%	61.40%	71.20%	66.20%	62.50%	56.00%	66.50%	59.97%	61.28%
	Hybrid	87.60%	81.40%	76.30%	86.40%	93.20%	85.60%	90.60%	76.50%	86.00%	83.46%	84.84%
KNN	sEMG	61.20%	59.20%	56.40%	61.10%	67.20%	59.20%	68.10%	63.20%	68.60%	63.19%	62.69%
	FMG	60.10%	59.80%	54.00%	62.10%	68.40%	56.20%	56.40%	53.00%	63.30%	59.47%	59.26%
	Hybrid	85.30%	79.00%	74.70%	85.10%	92.40%	81.40%	91.20%	72.70%	82.20%	80.81%	82.67%
RFC	sEMG	62.00%	58.40%	57.20%	62.50%	66.70%	60.10%	67.20%	65.90%	68.40%	64.27%	63.16%
	FMG	54.90%	58.40%	42.10%	68.90%	67.80%	65.40%	59.80%	62.50%	65.90%	58.90%	60.71%
	Hybrid	84.60%	58.40%	81.80%	85.80%	92.50%	86.30%	90.90%	84.40%	87.40%	81.00%	86.64%
CNN	sEMG	78.46%	76.21%	72.20%	79.10%	89.20%	82.60%	84.50%	74.30%	81.20%	81.63%	79.75%
	FMG	68.61%	66.25%	65.40%	71.00%	76.10%	71.20%	71.10%	68.10%	72.80%	70.01%	70.06%
	Hybrid	89.94%	88.46%	85.21%	88.90%	95.20%	91.80%	94.30%	91.20%	92.90%	91.79%	90.88%

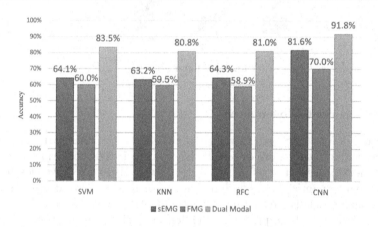

Fig. 6. Classification accuracy of four classifiers

was 81.6% when using sEMG signal only, 70.0% when using FMG signal only, and 91.8% when both sEMG and FMG signals were used.

These results indicated that CNNs had a significant advantage in forearm gesture recognition compared to the other methods and the recognition accuracy of our dual-modal sensor were higher than that of using a single sensor alone under any classifier, demonstrating that FMG signals were an excellent supplementary signal for sEMG signals. When using a CNN, the recognition accuracy of the sEMG-FMG bimodal sensor reached 91.8%, achieving high recognition accuracy among the 22 forearm-hand gestures.

5   Conclusions

A strain gauge-based FMG measurement unit has been designed to form a novel dual-modal sensor structure that incorporates both sEMG and FMG. This sensor structure provides high recognition accuracy for forearm-hand gesture recognition, offering substantial implications for gesture recognition and control in practical applications. Through our innovative design of the sensor structure, we have successfully managed to sense the force exerted by muscles mainly in a direction perpendicular to the sensor. This design contributes to a reduction in sensor volume, offering a practical solution to spatial constraints in real-world applications.

Further research will focus on refining both the sensor design and signal processing methods to enhance the performance of hand gesture recognition. It is expected that the recognition accuracy and real-time performance will be further improved. This technology has the potential to play an important role in areas such as bio-medicine, rehabilitation, prosthetic, and robotics. Furthermore, by monitoring muscle signals, this technology can also be used for rehabilitation training and assessment, providing physical therapists with more information about a patient's recovery progress.

References

1. Bansal, A.K., Hou, S., Kulyk, O., Bowman, E.M., Samuel, I.D.W.: Wearable organic optoelectronic sensors for medicine. Adv. Mater. **27**(46), 7638–7644 (2015). https://doi.org/10.1002/adma.201403560
2. Bullock, I.M., Zheng, J.Z., De La Rosa, S., Guertler, C., Dollar, A.M.: Grasp frequency and usage in daily household and machine shop tasks. IEEE Trans. Haptics **6**(3), 296–308 (2013). https://doi.org/10.1109/TOH.2013.6
3. Cescon, C., Farina, D., Gobbo, M., Merletti, R., Orizio, C.: Effect of accelerometer location on mechanomyogram variables during voluntary, constant-force contractions in three human muscles. Med. Biol. Eng. Comput. **42**(1), 121–127 (2004). https://doi.org/10.1007/BF02351021
4. Esposito, D., et al.: A piezoresistive sensor to measure muscle contraction and mechanomyography. Sensors **18**(8), 2553 (2018). https://doi.org/10.3390/s18082553, number: 8 Publisher: Multidisciplinary Digital Publishing Institute
5. Farina, D., et al.: The extraction of neural information from the surface EMG for the control of upper-limb prostheses: emerging avenues and challenges. IEEE Trans. Neural Syst. Rehabil. Eng.: Publication IEEE Eng. Med. Biol. Soc. **22**(4), 797–809 (2014). https://doi.org/10.1109/TNSRE.2014.2305111
6. Frangioni, J.V., Kwan-Gett, T.S., Dobrunz, L.E., McMahon, T.A.: The mechanism of low-frequency sound production in muscle. Biophys. J . **51**(5), 775–783 (1987). https://doi.org/10.1016/S0006-3495(87)83404-5
7. Guo, W., Sheng, X., Liu, H., Zhu, X.: Mechanomyography assisted myoeletric sensing for upper-extremity prostheses: a hybrid approach. IEEE Sens. J. **17**(10), 3100–3108 (2017). https://doi.org/10.1109/JSEN.2017.2679806, conference Name: IEEE Sensors Journal
8. Hargrove, L., Englehart, K., Hudgins, B.: The effect of electrode displacements on pattern recognition based myoelectric control. In: 2006 International Conference of the IEEE Engineering in Medicine and Biology Society, pp. 2203–2206. IEEE (2006). https://doi.org/10.1109/IEMBS.2006.260681
9. Jiang, S., Gao, Q., Liu, H., Shull, P.B.: A novel, co-located EMG-FMG-sensing wearable armband for hand gesture recognition. Sens. Actuators, A **301**, 111738 (2020). https://doi.org/10.1016/j.sna.2019.111738

10. Organization, W.H., Bank, W.: World Report on Disability. World Health Organization (2011)
11. Raurale, S.A., McAllister, J., Del Rincon, J.M.: Real-time embedded EMG signal analysis for wrist-hand pose identification. IEEE Trans. Signal Process. **68**, 2713–2723 (2020). https://doi.org/10.1109/TSP.2020.2985299
12. Rehman, M.U., Shah, K., Haq, I.U., Iqbal, S., Ismail, M.A., Selimefendigil, F.: Assessment of low-density force myography armband for classification of upper limb gestures. Sensors **23**(5), 2716 (2023). https://doi.org/10.3390/s23052716, number: 5 Publisher: Multidisciplinary Digital Publishing Institute
13. Schofield, J.S., Evans, K.R., Hebert, J.S., Marasco, P.D., Carey, J.P.: The effect of biomechanical variables on force sensitive resistor error: implications for calibration and improved accuracy. J. Biomech. **49**(5), 786–792 (2016). https://doi.org/10.1016/j.jbiomech.2016.01.022
14. Sharma, N., Prakash, A., Sharma, S.: An optoelectronic muscle contraction sensor for prosthetic hand application. Rev. Sci. Instrum. **94**(3), 035009 (2023). https://doi.org/10.1063/5.0130394
15. Togo, S., Murai, Y., Jiang, Y., Yokoi, H.: Development of an sEMG sensor composed of two-layered conductive silicone with different carbon concentrations. Sci. Rep. **9**(1), 13996 (2019). https://doi.org/10.1038/s41598-019-50112-4
16. Wininger, M.: Pressure signature of forearm as predictor of grip force. J. Rehabil. Res. Dev. **45**(6), 883–892 (2008). https://doi.org/10.1682/JRRD.2007.11.0187
17. Young, A.J., Smith, L.H., Rouse, E.J., Hargrove, L.J.: Classification of simultaneous movements using surface EMG pattern recognition. IEEE Trans. Biomed. Eng. **60**(5), 1250–1258 (2013). https://doi.org/10.1109/TBME.2012.2232293
18. Zazula, D., Karlsson, S., Doncarli, C.: Advanced signal processing techniques. In: Electromyography, pp. 259–304. John Wiley & Sons, Ltd (2004). https://doi.org/10.1002/0471678384.ch10

Enable Intuitive and Immersive Teleoperation: Design, Modeling and Control of a Novel Wearable Exoskeleton

Ruohan Wang[1], Xi Cui[1], Honghao Lv[1], Guangyao Zhang[1], Haiteng Wu[2], and Geng Yang[1,2(✉)]

[1] State Key Laboratory of Fluid Power and Mechatronic Systems, School of Mechanical Engineering, Zhejiang University, Hangzhou, China
gengyang@zju.edu.cn
[2] Key Laboratory of Intelligent Robot for Operation and Maintenance of Zhejiang Province, Hangzhou Shenhao Technology, Hangzhou, China

Abstract. Haptic devices with human motion capture function enable natural and flexible teleoperation within unstructured environment. As one of the typical types among haptic devices, wearable exoskeleton allows intuitive and immersive teleoperation. For such a portable device, weight and motion compatibility have a great influence on the potential control performance. This paper presents the development of WIE, the wearable intelligent equipment, a 5-DOF portable exoskeleton that is lightweight and accessible. The mechanism of WIE is designed to suit the majority of human using the adjustable links. Kinematic analysis of it shows a high motion compatibility with human upper limb in the workspace. Furthermore, an incremental motion mapping method is adopted in the joint space to control the slave robot. The pick-and-place experiment is conducted to evaluate the performance of WIE as well as the remote-control strategy. The results indicate that the robot manipulator presents a good following behavior according to the human motions captured by WIE.

Keywords: Wearable Exoskeleton · Teleoperation · Mechanism · Motion Mapping

1 Introduction

The last several decades have witnessed a booming development of robotics, relieving people from some repetitive, dangerous, and cumbersome tasks. Despite the technological advancements in the field of autonomous robots, fully autonomous control is still confronted with enormous challenges, especially in the dynamic and unstructured environment. Therefore, teleoperated robots with human-in-loop functions are the most beneficial and practical solutions in some scenarios such as space exploration, explosive ordnance disposal, nuclear waste management, etc. Teleoperation, where master operators control slave robots remotely, gives an alternative solution to semi-autonomous robots [1].

© The Author(s), under exclusive license to Springer Nature Singapore Pte Ltd. 2023
H. Yang et al. (Eds.): ICIRA 2023, LNAI 14268, pp. 195–205, 2023.
https://doi.org/10.1007/978-981-99-6486-4_17

The major objective of teleoperation is to telepresence the human operator in the remote site of the robot [2]. The operator should manipulate robot and perceive the remote surroundings as if the robot is an avatar of the user. In such a content, one of the most essential parts in teleoperation is the haptic devices, which aim to capture the human's intension of motion and even provide force sensation to the operator. Generally, haptic devices can be categorized into two types, grounded devices and wearable devices, according to the way that linked to the operator. For the grounded devices, the bases of them are usually put on the ground, fixed to the wall, or put on the desktop. Devices, such as Phantom [3] and Omega [4], have been used widely for telemedicine. Although they are of high-precision and can provide compelling force feedback during human-machine interaction, the workspace of these devices is usually very limited, leading to intuitiveness decrease especially when dual-arm teleoperation is needed. In addition, the users are restricted in confined spaces during the operation. For the wearable devices, their bases are located on the operators' body part, such as waist [5] and back [6]. These wearable devices are usually lightweight and portable, allowing operators to move around during the operation [7]. However, the waist attached wearable method also generate the control commands for the slave robot in cartesian space, which has the same working principle as grounded devices. Anthropomorphic robots' control requires more information than only the end-effector pose. Hence, to fulfill the promise of intuitive and immersive teleoperation, exoskeleton is one of the promising types in wearable devices.

Exoskeleton used for teleoperation is different from those for motion assistance and rehabilitation to some extends [8]. Exoskeleton devices can capture the position of other parts of human body, not only the end-effector. In spite of complexity, exoskeleton contact users with several points, providing large workspace considerably equivalent to human arms. Nevertheless, most exoskeletons adopt motors as the joint driver. The transmission structure, the motors with reduction gearbox, as well as battery of high-capacity make the system heavier, which poses problems for long time use. In this paper, we present the development of a novel wearable intelligent equipment (WIE), a 5-DOF fully portable exoskeleton featuring lightweight.

The reminder of this article is organized as follows. The overall mechanical design of the WIE is introduced based on the arm kinesiology analysis in Sect. 2. In addition, the kinematic analysis of both the novel WIE and human upper limb is given in Sect. 2 to evaluate the rationality of WIE's mechanical structure. Then the robot teleoperation method is described in Sect. 3 based on the WIE's joint information. Section 4 presents the process of the teleoperation experiment using the WIE, and validates the robot remote control strategy. The conclusions are summarized in Sect. 5.

2 Exoskeleton System Architecture

2.1 Analysis of Arm Kinesiology

One of the prominent characteristics of the exoskeleton in teleoperation is the wearability, which enables the device to naturally adapt to the operator's upper limb movement. As a human-robot interface facility between the operator and the robot, exoskeleton is attached to several points of operators' body, captures the human movement and sends commands to the remote side. To certain extend, the wearing experience will influence

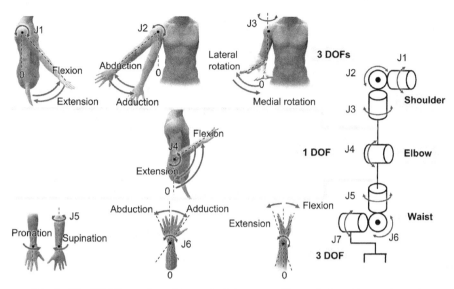

Fig. 1. The 7 DOFs motion of human's right arm and its equivalent kinematic model.

the effectiveness of teleoperation. Hence, it is essential to establish a comprehensive analysis of human arm biomechanics before mechanical structure construction.

According to anatomy, the upper limb of human can be divided into six main parts: shoulder, elbow, wrist, upper arm, forearm and palm. The first three parts are responsible for the degree of freedom (DOF), while the last three parts control the maximum reachable space. Several studies describe the upper limb as a 7 DOFs rotational kinematic system for human biomechanics simplification [9, 10]. As shown in Fig. 1, these 7 DOFs can be further divided into three joint types, including glenohumeral joint with 3 DOFs, elbow joint with 1 DOF and wrist joint with 3 DOFs. The motion range of each joint given in Fig. 1 is based on the normal male subject studied in research [11]. Also, the length of upper arm and forearm is another crucial parameter related to exoskeleton design. Table 1 indicates the human dimensions of Chinese adults according to GB/T 10000–1998 [12].

Table 1. Human dimensions of Chinese adults according to GB/T 10000–1998.

Items	Male (From 18 to 60 years old)					Female (From 18 to 55 years old)				
	5%	10%	50%	90%	99%	5%	10%	50%	90%	99%
Height/ mm	1583	1604	1678	1754	1814	1484	1503	1570	1640	1697
Weight/ kg	48	50	59	71	83	42	44	52	63	74
Upper arm Length/ mm	289	294	313	333	349	262	267	284	303	319
Forearm Length/ mm	216	220	237	253	268	193	198	213	229	242

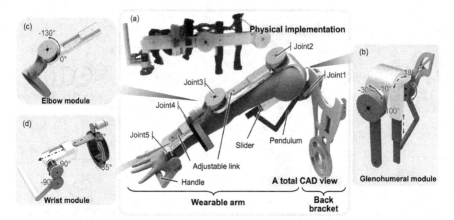

Fig. 2. The structure overview of WIE, a novel wearable exoskeleton: (a) A total CAD view and physical implementation of the single arm, (b) Detailed view of glenohumeral module, (c) De-tailed view of elbow module, (d) Detailed view of wrist module

2.2 Mechanical Design of Exoskeleton

As a master device that closely attached to the human arm, exoskeleton should be ergonomic, mechanical transparent, common to most people and safe in usage. Based on the arm kinesiology described above, WIE is designed to have certain kinematics compatibility with human. Considering the most common human activities of daily living, the 5-DOFs exoskeleton, featuring light weight, is sufficient to keep the workspace of human upper limb. The whole structure of WIE is illustrated in Fig. 2.

WIE is a series mechanism, of which the back bracket and the wearable arm are the two main components. The back bracket, served as the base of the exoskeleton, is used for wearing and control board settling. There are 5 actuated DOFs on the wearable arm from the shoulder to the wrist, including 2-DOFs shoulder joint, 1-DOF elbow joint and 2-DOFs wrist joint. To avoid the injuries caused by mismatched joint rotational axes between human and exoskeleton, the size of exoskeleton is designed based on Table 1. Aiming to cover the vast majority of human workspace, the link lengths between joints 1 and 2, joints 2 and 3, and joints 4 and 5 can be adjusted into several sizes, which allows exoskeleton to give adequate alignment with different operators' upper limb. All the links utilize elastic nylon bands to tie to the human body, preventing the offset between the exoskeleton and human arms. For the modular design, each joint can be regarded as an independent driving unit, which employs the active mechanism for connection. The total wearable arm can be separated into three sub-modules, i.e., glenohumeral module, elbow module and wrist module. The following gives detailed descriptions of each sub-module.

The human's shoulder joint is a typical spherical joint with all the rotation axes pass through one point within the human body, which poses challenges to the construction of glenohumeral module. In addition, in the teleoperation scenario, the master and slave device are required to have similar kinematic configurations to improve the intuitiveness. Hence, the glenohumeral module of WIE retains two DOFs (flexion/extension and abduction/adduction) to match the motion of the slave manipulator (Kinova Jaco2). As shown in Fig. 2(b), the flexion and extension movements are realized using the pendulum slider mechanism, where the scalable slider allows the axis of the exoskeleton to align with the axis of the operator at that rotational direction. The abduction and adduction motions adopt direct motor (RMD-L-7015) drive manner, where the rotation angle of joint can be directly obtained by the motor. The elbow module, given in Fig. 2(c), deploys the identical method and motor as the abduction/adduction motions of the glenohumeral module.

Similar to the shoulder mechanism, the spherical wrist joints can help to decouple the motion of position and orientation, control them independently. For lightweight design and mechanism simplification, two DOFs (pronation/supination and flexion/extension) are used at the wrist module. The rotation axis of the forearm is located inside the human body. Consequently, to achieve the alignment with the pronation and supination rotational axis of the human arm, a circular rotational mechanism using a rolling bearing is designed with an internal diameter of 90mm, as depicted in Fig. 2(d). Column motors (RoboMaster M2006 P36) with a speed reducer is located parallel to the axis of rotation, driving the circular ring through a spur gear set (with 33:125 gear ratio). The same motor is also adopted at the flexion and extension motion in the wrist module. It captures the movement by the motion of the handle through a spur gear set (with 1:1 gear ratio).

2.3 Kinematic Analysis

In order to explore the rationality of the structural design and realize position tracking of the slave manipulator, the kinematics modeling and analysis are required.

Glenohumeral Module Analysis. Different from conventional manipulators using rotational or translational joints, WIE adopts the pendulum slider mechanism at the glenohumeral module. To simplify the kinematic model of the exoskeleton, the analysis on this mechanism at Joint1 will be carried out separately.

The Fig. 3 illustrates mathematical model of the pendulum slider mechanism. In Fig. 3(a), the mechanism is at the initial state where the angle of Joint1 is denoted as zero. The Jointv1 is a virtual joint that is located at the center of flexion/extension rotation movement. Link-1 is connected to Link-3 through a slider denoted as Link-2. The distance L_{AB} between the rotation center A and B is considered as a constant during the motion. L_{ABx} and L_{ABy} are the horizontal and vertical distance between A and B, respectively. Furthermore, L_{AD} and R also remain constant for they are the length of Link-1 and Link-3. When Jointv1 rotates, we desire to find the relationship between shoulder flexion angle θ_B and measured Joint1 angle θ_A. According to the geometric relationship shown in Fig. 3(b), θ_B can be expressed as follows:

$$\theta_B = \beta_1 + \phi_1 - \phi_2 \tag{1}$$

$$\phi_1 = cos^{-1}(\frac{L_{AB} - L_{AD}cos((90° - \theta_A + \alpha_0))}{\sqrt{L_{AB}^2 + L_{AD}^2 - 2L_{AB}L_{AD}cos(90° - \theta_A + \alpha_0)}}) \tag{2}$$

$$\phi_2 = cos^{-1}(\frac{R}{\sqrt{L_{AB}^2 + L_{AD}^2 - 2L_{AB}L_{AD}cos(90° - \theta_A + \alpha_0)}}) \tag{3}$$

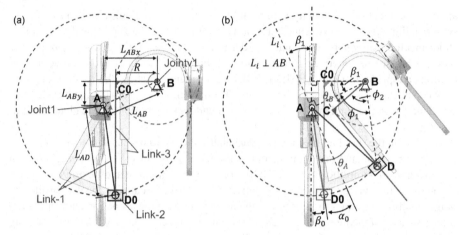

Fig. 3. The mathematical model of the pendulum slider mechanism at the glenohumeral module: (a) The mechanism is at its initial state, (b) The mechanism is at the state where there is a flexion motion.

Kinematic Analysis and Evaluation. To evaluate the kinematic performance of WIE, the workspace needs to be compared between WIE and human upper limb. After the analysis of pendulum slider mechanism, the relationship between Joint1 and Jointv1 can be obtained using formula (1)-(3). Hence, the virtual joint denoted as Jointv1 is used in the forward kinematic analysis of WIE. In addition, WIE adopts the adjustable links, where the length of upper arm ranges from 305 mm to 355 mm and the length of forearm ranges from 225mm to 255mm. The forward kinematics models of WIE and human upper arm are established using the modified Denavit-Hartenberg (MDH), as shown in Fig. 4(a)(b), respectively. The MDH parameters of WIE and human upper limb are shown in Table 2, where 50% male parameters (i.e., 313mm upper arm length and 237mm forearm length) in Table 1 is used for analysis. Based on the MDH table, Monte Carlo method is applied to estimate the workspace, which is one of the critical evaluations of an exoskeleton. The workspace of WIE is shown in Fig. 4(c), and the comparison between WIE and human upper limb is shown in Fig. 4(d), which indicates that the workspace of WIE can cover the vast majority of the human upper limb.

3   Control System

3.1   Exoskeleton Control System

The control system for WIE is implemented on a STM32 F4 micro-controller, which is distributed to the exoskeleton. Each joint on WIE deploys the motor, which can be regarded as a node mounted on the controller area network. To the lower level, the micro-controller adopts field-oriented control method to control the current of motor driver. To the upper level, the micro-controller communicates with the personal computer (PC) through universal asynchronous receiver/transmitter (UART). The PC is the upper

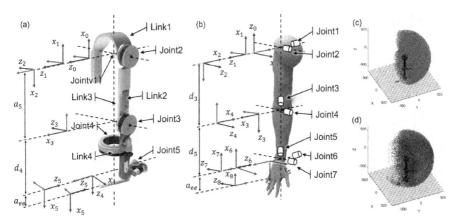

Fig. 4. The forward kinematic model of WIE and human upper limb using MDH modeling method: (a) The mathematic model of WIE, (b) The mathematic model of human upper limb, (c) The workspace of WIE, (d) The workspace of comparison between WIE(red) and human upper limb(blue). (Color figure online)

Table 2. The MDH table of WIE and human upper limb.

Joint	WIE					Human upper limb				
	α_{i-1}	a_{i-1}	d_i	θ_i	Range of θ_i	α_{i-1}	a_{i-1}	d_i	θ_i	Range of θ_i
1	0	0	0	θ_1	$-10° \sim 180°$	$\pi/2$	0	0	θ_1	$0° \sim 180°$
2	$-\pi/2$	0	0	θ_2	$-30° \sim 100°$	$\pi/2$	0	0	θ_2	$-60° \sim 170°$
3	0	a_2	0	θ_3	$-130° \sim 0°$	$\pi/2$	0	d_3	θ_3	$-70° \sim 90°$
4	$\pi/2$	0	d_4	θ_4	$-85° \sim 85°$	$\pi/2$	0	0	θ_4	$0° \sim 135°$
5	$\pi/2$	0	0	θ_5	$-90° \sim 90°$	$\pi/2$	0	d_5	θ_5	$-90° \sim 90°$
6	0	a_{ee_w}	0	0	0	$\pi/2$	0	0	θ_6	$-70° \sim 80°$
7	---					$\pi/2$	0	0	θ_7	$-20° \sim 30°$
8	---					0	a_{ee_h}	0	0	0

computer integrated with the robotic operating system (ROS), which includes various functions such as inverse kinematics computing, path planning, controller designing, etc. Moreover, a visual interaction interface is designed based on MATLAB software to send the data from micro-controller to ROS.

3.2 Motion Mapping and Robot Control

In a teleoperation system with motion capture function, the information including the joint position of master and slave devices is exchanged between the operator and robot. To improve the intuitiveness and immersion for the operator, WIE is designed isomorphic to robotic arm, which keeps them to be kinematically consistent. Hence, the information can be done in the joint space with a possible scaling.

The slave device is an in-house developed robot with dual arm (Kinova Jaco2). Since WIE and robot manipulator have isomorphic mechanism, the mapping method is established in the joint space from WIE to robot arm as follows:

$$q_{rd} = S_{trans}q_{WIE} + q_o \tag{4}$$

where q_{rd} and q_{WIE} represents the desired joint angle vector of the robot and the current joint angle vector of WIE respectively. q_o is the offset vector that shows the joint angle difference between WIE and robot at the initial state. S_{trans} is a diagonal matrix that determines the mapping factor of each joint. The robot adopts joint velocity control method with the desired joint position using the PID controller given as follows:

$$\dot{q}_{rd} = k_p e + k_i \int edt + k_d \frac{de}{dt} \tag{5}$$

where e represents the error between the current and desired robot joint position. $\dot{q}_{rd}$ is desired robot joint velocity. k_p, k_i and k_d are the parameters to enable the robot to take a quick and stable response through the PID controller.

4   Experiments and Results

4.1   Experimental Setup

The Fig. 5 illustrates the experimental setup for evaluating WIE and robot teleoperation methods.

The master device WIE is connected to the slave robot through local area network and sends the control commands at a rate of 100Hz. The controller of the robot is an industrial computer based on ROS, which publishes the robot current states and subscribes desired joint angles from topics sent by WIE. The visual interaction interface is on the PC of WIE side, responsible for docking of WIE's underlying driver and ROS platform. Through the customize application programming interface, the visual interaction interface can obtain the joint angle, speed, and torque information, which can be visualized on the upper computer and be published in a ROS-based message format. In addition, the gripper control commands are obtained through UART serial port and published to the robot. The robot desired velocity is generated by the desired joint position given by WIE and sent to the robot manipulator at a rate of 100Hz.

4.2   Robot Teleoperation Tasks and Results

To access the teleoperation function of WIE, we only use three joints at the end of WIE for performance evaluation. In this task, the operator is required to control the slave robot to grasp a bottle on the table, move randomly in the WIE workspace and put it back to the desktop. Figure 6 shows the movement of human arm and robot manipulator during the task. At the initial position, the human and the robot are in the similar position with the

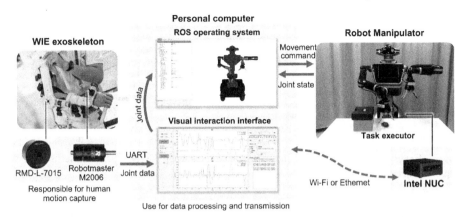

Fig. 5. The experimental setup for teleoperation verification. The encoders built in the motors capture the human's motion and send the data to the micro-controller, which communicates with PC through UART. A visual interaction interface is designed and can send data to ROS, which controls the robot motion.

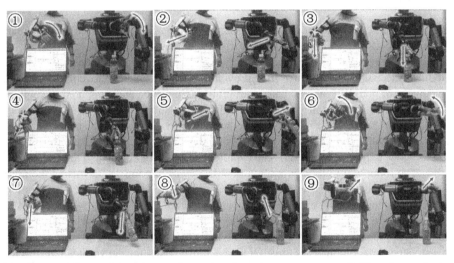

Fig. 6. Image flows of the teleoperation task, where the operator wears WIE and controls the robot to grasp the bottle, move randomly and put it back.

position offset recorded at the start time. Then, the human control WIE to move the robot to the target place using the motion mapping method introduced above. The S_{trans} in formula (4) is an identity matrix, meaning that the movement on the i_{th} joint of WIE will cause the same movement on the i_{th} joint of robot manipulator. The operator presses the button on the handle to close the gripper to grasp the bottle. After the random motion in the workspace, the bottle is placed back to the desktop. Figure 7 gives the corresponding joint angles change of both WIE and robot during that task. The green curve represents the change of WIE joint angles, and the blue curve represents the change of robot joint

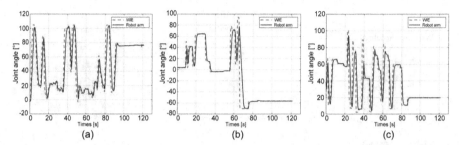

Fig. 7. Experimental result of WIE and robot joint angles when the robot performs tasks according to the teleoperation commands.

angles. Note that there exists a certain delay smaller than 100ms. This delay is caused by the response speed of PD controller as well as the limited maximum robot joint velocity, which is up to 48°/s.

5   Conclusion

In this work, a novel wearable exoskeleton named WIE was designed based on the human upper limb kinesiology and robot arm structure to achieve intuitive and immersive teleoperation. The pendulum slider mechanism was creatively adopted at the glenohumeral module's mechanical design of WIE to provide two DOFs shoulder movement. Forward kinematics of both WIE and human upper limb was analyzed and compared, giving the rationality in accordance of workspace. Additionally, an incremental motion mapping strategy was devised in the joint space to control the robot remotely. The novel wearable exoskeleton with its teleoperation strategy is validated using the Kinova Jaco2 arms. The results showed the developed WIE can capture the motion of human and teleoperate the robot. The robot will follow the motion of WIE device in a low latency using the joint mapping method. Overall, the system showed an intuitive and immersive teleoperation due to the direct mapping on the joint space.

The current research is focused on the mechanical design of exoskeleton and the motion mapping method in joint space. The force feedback from the slave robot is not investigated. In addition, only three DOFs have been used for the verification of teleoperation. In future work, dual master-slave isomorphic exoskeletons will be designed and constructed to fill more flexible tasks. Furthermore, haptic feedback function will be integrated to achieve immersive teleoperation.

Acknowledgment. This work was supported in part by the National Natural Science Foundation of China (No. 51975513), the Natural Science Foundation of Zhejiang Province, China (No. LR20E050003), the Major Research Plan of National Natural Science Foundation of China (No. 51890884), the Major Research Plan of Ningbo Innovation 2025. (Grant No. 2020Z022), the Bellwethers Research and Development Plan of Zhejiang Province (No. 2023C01045).

References

1. Lv, H., et al.: GuLiM: a hybrid momion mapping technique for teleoperation of medical assistive robot in combating the COVID-19 pandemic. IEEE Trans. Med. Robot. Bionics **4**(1), 106–117 (2022)
2. Mallwitz, M., Will, N., Teiwes, J., Kirchner, E.A.: The CAPIO active upper body exoskeleton and its application for teleoperation. In: Proceedings of the 13th Symposium on Advanced Space Technologies in Robotics and Automation. ESA/Estec Symposium on Advanced Space Technologies in Robotics and Automation (ASTRA-2015) (2015)
3. Silva, A.J., Ramirez, O.A.D., Vega, V.P., Oliver, J.P.O.: PHANToM OMNI haptic device: kinematic and manipulability. In: Proceedings of the Electronics, Robotics and Automotive Mechanics Conference, pp. 22–25 (2009)
4. Aggravi, M., Estima, D.A.L., Krupa, A., Misra, S., Pacchierotti, C.: Haptic teleoperation of flexible needles combining 3D ultrasound guidance and needle tip force feedback. IEEE Robot. Autom. Lett. **6**(3), 4859–4866 (2021)
5. Mo, Y., Song, A., Qin, H.: A lightweight accessible wearable robotic interface for bimanual haptic manipulations. IEEE Trans. Haptics **15**(1), 85–90 (2022)
6. Falck, F., Larppichet, K., Kormushev, P.: DE VITO: a dual-arm, high degree-of-freedom, lightweight, inexpensive, passive upper-limb exoskeleton for robot teleoperation. Towards Auton. Robot. Syst., pp. 78–89 (2019)
7. Yang, G., et al.: Keep healthcare workers safe: application of teleoperated robot in isolation ward for COVID-19 prevention and control. Chinese J. Mech. Eng., 33(1) (2020)
8. Gull, M.A., et al.: A 4-DOF upper limb exoskeleton for physical assistance: design, modeling, control and performance evaluation. Appl. Sci., 11(13) (2021)
9. Holzbaur, K.R.S., Murray, W.M., Delp, S.L.: A model of the upper extremity for simulating musculoskeletal surgery and analyzing neuromuscular control. Ann. Biomed. Eng. **33**(6), 829–840 (2005)
10. Roderick, S., Liszka, M., Carignan, C.: Design of an arm exoskeleton with scapula motion for shoulder rehabilitation. In: Proceedings of the 12th International Conference on Advanced Robotics, 18–20 July (2005)
11. Qianxiang Zhou, Y., Jin, Z.L.: The Measurement and analysis of Chinese adults' range of motion joint. In: Duffy, V.G. (ed.) HCII 2021. LNCS, vol. 12777, pp. 163–177. Springer, Cham (2021). https://doi.org/10.1007/978-3-030-77817-0_14
12. Human dimensions of Chinese adults, China, S.A.O. (1988)

Design and Fabrication of an Artificial Skin Integrated with Soft Ultrasonic Waveguides for Finger Joint Motion Detection

Medhanit Alemu, Yuan Lin, and Peter Shull[✉]

School of Mechanical Engineering, Shanghai Jiao Tong University, Shanghai 201100, China
{medhanit,lin_yuan,pshull}@sjtu.edu.cn

Abstract. Soft sensors have garnered substantial attention in robotics due to their ability to measure significant deformations and adapt to different surface textures. Soft and stretchable sensors, with their ability to undergo deformations, have been utilized to measure the movements of human body parts, such as finger joint movements. However, there is still a need to develop soft sensors that are transparent, stretchable, lightweight, and easy to wear on human hands. This paper proposes the design and fabrication of soft, transparent, and stretchable artificial skin integrated with ultrasonic waveguides for finger joint movement detection. The artificial skin and ultrasonic waveguides were manufactured using Ecoflex™ 00–31 and Ecoflex™ 00–45 Near Clear™ silicone elastomers. Thin silver-plated copper wires with 0.1 mm diameter were used to connect the transducers in the waveguides to the electrical system. The wires were encapsulated within an additional elastomer layer, resulting in an overall thickness of approximately 500 μm. The system was configured and integrated, and its validity was verified through static hand gesture experiments. The experiment involved a subject wearing the ultrasonic waveguide-integrated artificial skin and performing six static hand gestures designed for the study. Results indicate that the output signals had distinct differences with different finger positions highlighting the system's reliability and suitability for hand motion detection. To the best of our knowledge, the device introduced in this paper is the first to use soft ultrasonic waveguide based sensing skin to detect finger joint motion. This study offers a promising solution to the challenges of developing soft sensors that are biocompatible with human hands for wearable devices, potentially offering comfortable and convenient wear for users.

Keywords: Artificial skin · Ultrasonic waveguides · Finger joint movement detection

This work was supported by the National Natural Science Foundation of China under Grant 52250610217.

H. Yang et al. (Eds.): ICIRA 2023, LNAI 14268, pp. 206–218, 2023.
https://doi.org/10.1007/978-981-99-6486-4_18

1   Introduction

Soft sensors have many potential benefits including biocompatibility, adaptability, and effective and safe interactions with humans and objects as compared with conventional sensors crafted from rigid materials which may not be adequate to measure significant deformations because of their inability to adapt to different surface textures [1–3]. In addition, rigid sensors are often bulky and may create user discomfort when in contact with the skin. Instead, soft sensors with stretchable capabilities along with flexibility can resolve these issues using simpler structures. Such sensors can be fabricated from relatively inexpensive materials and offer high reliability and accuracy. Generally, soft sensors can be made from various materials, including but not limited to elastomers, polymers, and hydrogels. Elastomers like silicone rubber are commonly used due to their elasticity and flexibility. Polymers, such as polyurethane and polydimethylsiloxane (PDMS), are also popular due to their ability to be easily molded into different shapes and biocompatibility. Hydrogels, such as polyacrylamide and alginate, are also frequently used due to their high-water content and biocompatibility [4].

Stretchable soft sensors can be employed to capture movements of various parts of the human body, such as the wrists, elbows, and knees, due to their ability to undergo stretchable deformations. Several types of soft wearable sensors have been reported in the literature, depending on the materials used in their construction [5,6]. Theoretically, using soft materials offers an intriguing chance to develop new wearable systems that adapt and adjust to the user's morphology and motions without impeding them, resulting in comfortable wearable devices. Nevertheless, soft sensors are still developing, as evidenced by the scarcity of widely used commercial products used for their fabrication. It is still unclear which soft sensing technique is the most suitable for strain or curvature measurement. So far, the proposed soft sensing technologies faced subpar intrinsic performance or scaling capabilities [2,7].

Different types of soft sensors with varying levels of performance have been proposed. Soft piezoresistive strain sensors are made of soft polymers loaded with conductive particles but suffer from creep and hysteresis [8]. Although soft capacitive sensors typically have excellent linearity and minimal hysteresis, they generally have low sensitivity [2]. Soft, optical waveguides with high stretchability and low optical loss have also been developed [9,10]. However, although highly promising, they can have poor linearity [11] and are also relatively heavy. A filmy stretchable strain sensor with three layers was developed using carbon conductive grease as the resistance electrode layer in the middle and soft elastomer as the two sealing layers [12]. Even though these sensors demonstrate high functionality, there is variability in the properties with repeated use. Approaches relying on graphene [13] and carbon nanotubes [14] have shown excellent sensitivity but require advanced fabrication methods. Recent advancements have demonstrated the capacity of these soft ultrasonic waveguides to perform decoupled measurement of strain and contact location by guiding ultrasonic acoustic waves within the soft polymer waveguide [7]. Due to their fabrication using an unmodified elastomer, these waveguides possess a softer nature and exhibit reduced hysteresis than comparable piezoresistive and capacitive particle-loaded composites. Moreover, these sensors offer the advantage of simplified manufacturing processes and eliminate the possibility of leakage.

Given that hands play a crucial role in human interaction with the surrounding environment by recognizing, grasping, and manipulating objects, it is of significant practical importance to develop soft sensors capable of detecting hand movements [15]. In this regard, there have been several noteworthy research publications related to sensing skins with soft sensors for hand motion detection and estimation [16–20]. A sensing skin that measures finger abduction/adduction was developed by Kyongkwan et al. [16]; however, it was relatively bulky. Commercial elastomer VHB and conductive bond were used to create a transparent, very thin artificial skin to make the sensing skin lighter and thinner [20]. However, since VHB elastomer exhibits excessive viscoelasticity, it could lead to user discomfort or self-adhesion. Other significant studies have utilized the elastomer Ecoflex as a substrate material owing to its exceptional stretchability [17–19]. However, the Ecoflex substrate is milky white in color after curing, which makes it challenging to attain the objective of being transparent. In [18], a wearable soft artificial skin was developed using the elastomer Ecoflex and liquid metal by incorporating microchannels into the elastomer base to inject conductive materials. However, a common drawback of these production methods is that they typically require a certain thickness of elastomer base to create channels, thereby restricting the reduction of overall sensor thickness. Therefore, reducing the overall weight of soft sensing gloves is challenging, and the manufacturing procedures are relatively intricate. Although previous studies have shown great potential for applying soft sensors for hand motion detection, developing ideal soft sensors with features such as being transparent, stretchable, lightweight, and easily worn on human hands remains challenging due to the limited availability of fabrication materials and complex manufacturing processes. An ideal artificial skin should be transparent, highly stretchable, lightweight, and thin.

This study presents a solution to the aforementioned challenges by introducing the design and fabrication of a soft, transparent, and stretchable artificial skin integrated with soft ultrasonic waveguides for finger joint movement detection. The artificial skin and the ultrasonic waveguides are designed and fabricated. For the system integration, electronic configuration and system assembly are performed. Finally, experimental validation is performed, and results are discussed. This work is the first to integrate soft ultrasonic waveguides with artificial skin to be used as stretchable sensing skins for hand motion detection. The primary contribution of this study involves the utilization of soft ultrasonic waveguides to create a sensing skin that is transparent, soft, lightweight, and possesses remarkable stretchability. These combined factors contribute significantly to enhancing the wearability of the developed system. Moreover, the artificial skin covers the dorsal part of the hand, while leaving the fingertips uncovered, thereby minimizing any impediment to the user's dexterity. This novel sensing skin has the potential for effective hand motion detection.

2   Design and Fabrication

The system design and fabrication phase includes artificial skin manufacturing, hand frame manufacturing, and soft ultrasonic waveguide manufacturing.

2.1   Artificial Skin and Hand Frame

The preparation procedure for the artificial skin is as follows. The plate for the spin coater (KW-4C, Beijing Saidecase Electronics Co., Ltd, China) is designed on the user interface of a laser cutter and cut using the laser cutting machine (GD Han's Yueming Laser Group Co., Ltd, China) (Fig. 1). The plate used is acrylic material with a thickness of 0.1 mm. The dimension of the plate design is chosen based on the average human hand size, which is 16 cm by 9 cm in length and breadth, respectively [21]. The length is shorter than the average hand length because the artificial skin does not cover the whole finger since only the metacarpophalangeal(MCP) joints of the fingers are the targets for this study. Next, the chosen elastomer is mixed, degassed then poured onto the plate, and the spin coater is used to spread the elastomer throughout the plate with specified parameters to get the desired skin thickness. The parameters used for the elastomer Ecoflex^{TM} 00–31 Near Clear^{TM} are Speed: 200 round per minute (rpm), Acceleration: 500, and Time: 30 s (s). Then it is degassed again and cured on a hot plate at 60 °C for approximately 25 min. After curing, it is unmolded and removed from the plate.

Fig. 1. Design and fabrication process of the artificial skin manufacturing plate.

The material for the artificial skin should be chosen carefully to make it soft, lightweight, transparent, and compatible with the human hand. Four elastomers from the Ecoflex series were tested for the artificial skin, including Ecoflex^{TM} 00–10, Dragon Skin^{TM} FX- Pro^{TM}, Ecoflex^{TM} 00–31 Near Clear^{TM}, and Ecoflex^{TM} 00–45 Near Clear^{TM}. Ecoflex^{TM} 00–10 and Dragon Skin^{TM} FX Pro^{TM} have good softness and stretchability properties but are translucent and not as transparent as the Ecoflex^{TM} Near Clear^{TM} series. The Ecoflex^{TM} 00–45 Near Clear^{TM} (Table 1) exhibits transparency; however, upon curing, it tends to possess a slightly increased hardness and thickness compared to Ecoflex^{TM} 00–31 Near Clear^{TM}. At last, the Ecoflex^{TM} 00–31 Near Clear^{TM} (Table 1) was chosen for the artificial skin manufacturing because it is transparent, soft, thin, and stretchy enough to make it comfortable to be worn directly on the hand and suitable for any hand size. The thickness of the fabricated artificial skin was measured to be around 200 μm.

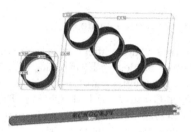

Fig. 2. Hand frame design.

Since the artificial skin covers only the dorsal part of the hand, a hand frame is designed to fix the artificial skin with the hand (Fig. 2). The hand frame consists of finger rings and a wristband. The hand frame is 3D printed using a soft and transparent Thermoplastic Polyurethane (TPU) material (30° soft glue) by Wenext company. The finger rings are highly stretchable, being easily adapted for different hand sizes. A Velcro material is attached to the opposite ends of the wristband to fit the artificial skin for different hand sizes.

2.2   Soft Ultrasonic Waveguide

The soft ultrasonic waveguides were designed to meet the following design requirements for this project. 1) The piezoelectric transducer (AM1.2 × 1.2 × 1.7D-1F, Tokin, Japan) should be fully embedded within the waveguide. 2) The soft ultrasonic waveguides should be long enough to cover the finger joint and, at the same time, short enough to guarantee tolerably low acoustic losses. 3) The soft ultrasonic waveguides should be soft, lightweight, and transparent.

The soft ultrasonic waveguide manufacturing process follows a previously proposed procedure [22]. Molds were fabricated using a stereolithographic 3D printer (Objet 30, Stratasys, USA). The waveguide manufacturing steps are as follows: 1) Spray a release agent (Mann, Ease Release 200, USA) onto the mold; 2) Mix and degas the chosen elastomer; 3) Manually place and align the transducer on the designated platform within the waveguide; 4) Pour the degassed elastomer into the mold and leave it to cure in the oven at 50°C for approximately 40 min; 5) Demold and clean the manufactured ultrasonic waveguide.

Choosing the appropriate material for the soft ultrasonic waveguide is crucial to ensure the waveguide's high accuracy and sensitivity to minor joint movements. Since one of our design requirements is for the soft ultrasonic waveguides to be transparent, we only tested the two materials in Ecoflex™ Near Clear™ series (Table 1). The Ecoflex™ Near Clear™ series has a water-clear translucent color. When cured, it is transparent, which is in harmony with our design

Table 1. Properties description of the materials in Ecoflex^{TM} Near Clear^{TM} series.

Ecoflex^{TM} Near Clear^{TM} Series	Mixed Viscosity	Specific Gravity (g/cc)	Specific Volume (cu.in.-/lb.)	Pot Life	Cure Time	Shore Hardness	Tensile Strength	100% Modulus	Elongation at Break %	Die Tear Strength	Shrinkage
Ecoflex^{TM} 00–31 Near Clear^{TM}	3,000 cps	1.07	26.0	40 min	4 h	00–31	200 psi	10 psi	900%	38 pli	<.001 in./in.
Ecoflex^{TM} 00–45 Near Clear^{TM}	2,000 cps	1.06	26.2	45 min	4 h	00–45	315 psi	12 psi	980%	50 pli	<.001 in./in.

requirements. Furthermore, the Ecoflex^{TM} 00–45 Near Clear^{TM} has an excellent signal property with a stronger echo signal and less noise when compared to the Ecoflex^{TM} 00–31 Near Clear^{TM}. Hence, the Ecoflex^{TM} 00–45 Near Clear^{TM} silicone elastomer is chosen for manufacturing the waveguide.

3 Electronic Configuration and System Assembly

The overall system is composed of five soft ultrasonic waveguides, one multiplexer (CD74HC4067, Texas Instruments, USA), one MAX14808 acoustic pulser evaluation board (Maxim Integrated Products, USA), an Analog Digilent 2 digital oscilloscope (AD2, Digilent, USA), power supplies, and a PC. Each ultrasonic waveguide is sequentially excited by the MAX14808 acoustic pulser evaluation board, with the excitation pulse timing controlled via the AD2 digital output channels. Once the transmitted acoustic wave is reflected back, the transducers act as receivers, receiving the echo waves, and the signal is captured using one of AD2's oscilloscope channels. To enable the simultaneous collection of data from all five sensors using a single oscilloscope channel in AD2, we utilize a multiplexer to expand the number of available input channels. This is necessary because there are only two oscilloscope channels available in AD2. The multiplexer is also controlled by digital signals through the AD2 digital output channels.

The system assembly process comprises four main stages: artificial skin manufacturing, wire embedding, hand frame attachment, and waveguide integration (Fig. 3). The ultrasonic waveguides are positioned on the MCP joint, on top of the artificial skin covering the dorsal part of the hand. The free end of the waveguides is attached to each finger ring of the hand frame using a soft, thin, and translucent two-sided tape (YZ202 0316, TianTian Factory, China).

Different wiring methods were tested to connect the transducer wires on the other end of the waveguides to micro coaxial cables (IPEX 1st generation, Xinlisheng Hardware Electronics Co., China), which transmit electrical signals to and from the MAX14808 acoustic pulser evaluation board. Two ink materials were tested to print the wire on the artificial skin using the DB100 multifunctional electronics printer (Shanghai MiFang Electronic Technology Co., Ltd.,

China). First is BASE-CD01, a silver paste prepared by mixing silver powder and resin filler. This material is suitable for dispensing and screen-printing processes and is widely used in conductive lines, flexible switches, shielding circuits, and other scenarios. However, when printed on the soft artificial skin, the adhesion was not very good, and it fell off after curing, so this material could not be used for our application. The second one is BASE-CGI1which is a Ga/In Alloy liquid metal material. Compared to other conductive materials, it has high density and conductivity and is suitable for preparing flexible and stretchable wires on elastic substrates. This material also has good tensile properties than BASE-CD01; however, the manufacturing process is relatively complex.

In contrast to silver paste, liquid metal doesn't cure and remains fluid after printing, so it requires to be encapsulated by another layer of polymer. Encapsulating the printed liquid metal wire with another layer of Ecoflex elastomer using an adjustable film applicator (KTQ-II1, Guangzhou Xinyi Laboratory Equipment Co., Ltd, China) can be challenging due to its fluidity. It may result in a disconnected line, causing an interruption in the electrical flow. Another challenge of working with liquid metals is achieving a specific wire thickness, as the material's fluidity and peculiar properties can make it difficult to control the parameters accurately. As reported by other researchers [18, 23, 24], the best way to use liquid metals for wiring is to embed microchannels within the elastomer-based artificial skin and fill the microchannels with liquid metal. Nevertheless, this manufacturing process is complex relative to the purpose of serving simple wiring in our case, as it requires dexterity and extra care. Additionally, the manual manufacturing process may not be precise enough to prevent liquid metal from leaking. Therefore, this material was also not used for our application.

Fig. 3. The system assembly process.

Finally, thin silver-plated copper wires (Kunshan Lvchuang Electronic Technology Co., Ltd., China) with a diameter of 0.1 mm were chosen for connecting the wires of the transducers on the waveguides to the micro coaxial cables. Once the artificial skin is fabricated, the thin silver-plated copper wires are placed on top of the artificial skin with the same double-sided tape mentioned above. Next, the Ecoflex™ 00–31 Near Clear™ elastomer is poured on top of the wired artificial skin and coated evenly using the adjustable film applicator to embed the wires, leaving a small portion out on both ends for electrical connection with the rest of the system. Finally, it is cured on a hot plate at 60 °C for about 25 min. The overall thickness of the wire-embedded artificial skin is around 500 μm. The ends of the embedded wires closer to the fingers are soldered to the transducers on the waveguides, and the other ends closer to the wrist are soldered to the micro coaxial cables. This choice of wiring reduced the manufacturing complexity while also keeping the thickness of the wire-embedded artificial skin relatively thin. Finally, the artificial skin is attached to the finger rings and wristband of the hand frame using super glue (deli, SUPER GLUE No.7146, China). The finger rings fix one side of the artificial skin to the user's fingers, and the wristband with the Velcro attached is used to fix the other side of the artificial skin to the user's wrist.

4   System Performance

4.1   Operating Principle of Soft Ultrasonic Waveguides

The transducer within the ultrasonic waveguide is excited using MAX14808 acoustic pulser evaluation board by an acoustic pulse train generated by a series of 4 consecutive square pulse waves with a frequency of 980 kHz and a voltage of 15 V [22]. This generates acoustic waves within the waveguide. Once the waves reach the other end, they get reflected back, and the transducer, which now acts as a receiver, receives the reflected echo signals and finally outputs a voltage. The imaging method used in this case is called "pulse-echo" because the same transducer is used to generate the acoustic pulse train and to measure the reflected acoustic wave [25]. The distance between the transducer and the waveguide's end increases upon stretching the waveguide, changing the Time of Flight (TOF) of the acoustic waves. The TOF is the time interval between the generation of the acoustic pulse train and the echo signal's main peak. The waveguide's length can be estimated by measuring this time interval.

4.2   Signal Processing

The AD2 oscilloscope channel captures analog voltage signals data during a 1040 µs long window, divided into five 208 µs long windows for each waveguide on the MCP joints. The sampling frequency used is $1/15 * 10^8$ Hz. The data is collected on a PC by a Python program which filters the signal in real-time using the Chebyshev bandpass filter, 8th order, 500 KHz–3 MHz. The data is appended row-wise to a CSV file. The echo signal's peak can be obtained through signal enveloping by performing Hilbert transform. Then the signal's TOF can be obtained by subtracting the time of generation of the acoustic pulse train from the time of the echo signal's main peak. Each of the five different colors on the sample filtered signal (Fig. 4) represents the signal from each waveguide on the five fingers' MCP joints. The first wave packet in each window is noise from reflected signals at the transducer-elastomer interface, and the second wave packet is the first received echo which is our target.

4.3   Application for Hand Motion Detection

The integrated sensing system has a total weight of about 12 g and an area of about 140 cm^2, resulting in a pressure of approximately 8 Pa towards the dorsal

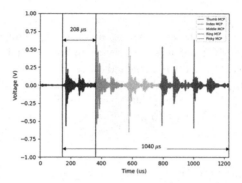

Fig. 4. Filtered analog signal collected by the oscilloscope channel of the AD2.

part of the hand. Owing to the excellent stretchability of the soft artificial skin and ultrasonic waveguides, the developed system can be used to detect large deformations such as finger joint movements. A static hand gesture experiment was conducted to demonstrate the system's capability of detecting static finger joint positions. The experiment involved a subject wearing the ultrasonic waveguide-integrated artificial skin and performing static hand gestures (Fig. 5).

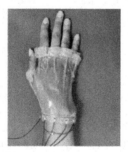

Fig. 5. The ultrasonic waveguide-integrated artificial skin worn on a human hand.

A series of gestures were designed and performed, first extending all five fingers, then flexing each finger from the thumb to the pinky finger one by one, and finally flexing all fingers to make a fist (Fig. 6a). The subject was requested to perform each gesture for 4 s, and we measured the MCP joints of the five fingers. The changes in the received echo signals and the corresponding TOF when subjected to different hand gestures can be real-time observed through a Python program (Fig. 6b and 6c). The experiment was repeated ten times for each gesture, and the performance of the integrated sensor system did not change significantly, implying excellent repeatability. All the signals were stable, and their distinct differences under different finger positions highlighted the system's reliability and suitability for hand motion detection.

When performing the first gesture, all the MCP joints on the five fingers are extended, keeping all the ultrasonic waveguides unstretched. Therefore, the echo signals received from all five ultrasonic waveguides are stronger and have higher amplitude. However, when performing the second gesture, the thumb MCP joint is flexed, stretching the ultrasonic waveguide attached to that joint. Hence, the

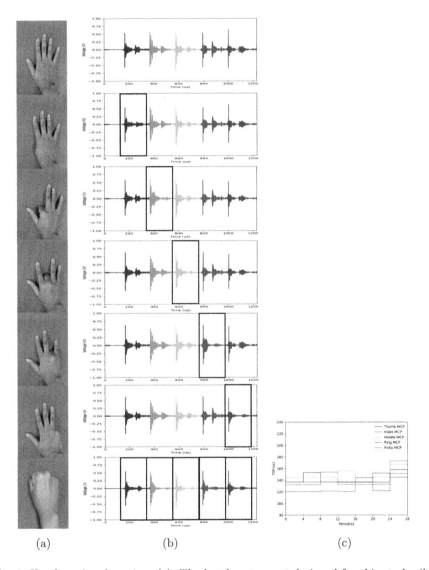

(a)   (b)   (c)

Fig. 6. Hand motion detection. (a): The hand gesture set designed for this study. (b): The corresponding output signals of the hand gestures in (a). (c): The TOF plot for each gesture while performing the gesture within 4 s with a total period of 24 s for performing the whole gesture set.

signal from the ultrasonic waveguide attached to the thumb finger has increased TOF and reduced amplitude, while the signals received from the other waveguides attached to the rest of the fingers remained similar to the first gesture. The output signal for the remaining gestures can be explained in a similar manner (Fig. 6a and 6b). The outcomes observed during the execution of the last fist gesture reveal the system's capability to detect motion across multiple finger joints, distinguishing it from the other gestures which solely involve single finger joint motion.

The increase in the TOF may not be easily seen from Fig. 6b but is clearly displayed in Fig. 6c. When there is no flexion of the MCP joint on any of the fingers, the TOF values of the ultrasonic waveguide remain at a low level, nearly 135–145 μs. When the MCP joint of any finger flexes, the length of the ultrasonic waveguide extends, resulting in an increase in the TOF values up to nearly 155–160 μs. If the MCP joint of any finger returns to the extension state, the TOF values drop back to the low level again (Fig. 6c). Throughout the experiment, each gesture's highest and lowest TOF levels remain in a certain narrow range, indicating that the developed system has excellent repeatability, which is an essential characteristic for practical applications.

From the TOF plot (Fig. 6c), we saw a noticeable increase in TOF whenever joint flexion occurs in any of the fingers' MCP joints. This implies that the TOF is a fundamental feature of the ultrasonic waveguides that can be used to detect different static finger joint positions. In future work, more advanced gestures can be recognized using this sensor system by applying machine learning algorithms.

5   Conclusion

This paper presents the design and fabrication of an artificial skin integrated with soft ultrasonic waveguides. The work involved designing and fabricating the artificial skin, hand frame, and soft ultrasonic waveguides and integrating them into a functional system. Hand gesture experiments were conducted to validate the system's performance and suitability for hand motion detection. The experiment results indicate the excellent reliability and repeatability of the proposed system. The features of the soft ultrasonic waveguides are more to be explored, and it provides a promising prospect for hand gesture recognition applications.

Acknowledgements. The authors would like to thank the National Natural Science Foundation of China under Grant 52250610217.

References

1. Roberts, P., Zadan, M., Majidi, C.: Soft tactile sensing skins for robotics. Curr. Robot. Rep. 2(4), 343–354 (2021)
2. Souri, H., et al.: Wearable and stretchable strain sensors: materials, sensing mechanisms, and applications. Adv. Intell. Syst. 2(8), 2000039 (2020)

3. Perera, Y.S., Ratnaweera, D., Dasanayaka, C.H., Abeykoon, C.: The role of artificial intelligence-driven soft sensors in advanced sustainable process industries: a
critical review. Eng. Appl. Artif. Intell. **121**, 105988 (2023)
4. Bahram, M., Mohseni, N., Moghtader, M.: An introduction to hydrogels and some
recent applications. InTech. (2016)
5. Pantelopoulos, A., Bourbakis, N.G.: A survey on wearable sensor-based systems for
health monitoring and prognosis. IEEE Trans. Syst. Man Cybern. Part C (Appl.
Rev.) **40**, 1–12 (2010)
6. Poh, M., Swenson, N.C., Picard, R.W.: A wearable sensor for unobtrusive, long-
term assessment of electrodermal activity. IEEE Trans. Biomed. Eng. **57**, 1243–
1252 (2010)
7. Chossat, J., Shull, P.B.: Soft acoustic waveguides for strain, deformation, localization, and twist measurements. IEEE Sens. J. **21**(1), 222–230 (2021)
8. Duan, L., D'hooge, D.R., Cardon, L.: Recent progress on flexible and stretchable
piezoresistive strain sensors: From design to application. Progr. Mater. Sci. **114**,
100617 (2020)
9. To, C., Hellebrekers, T.L., Park, Y.: Highly stretchable optical sensors for pressure,
strain, and curvature measurement. In: 2015 IEEE/RSJ International Conference
on Intelligent Robots and Systems (IROS), pp. 5898–5903 (2015)
10. Zhao, H., O'Brien, K., Li, S., Shepherd, R.F.: Optoelectronically innervated soft
prosthetic hand via stretchable optical waveguides. Sci. Robot. **1**(1), eaai7529
(2016)
11. Leber, A., Cholst, B., Sandt, J., Vogel, N., Kolle, M.: Stretchable thermoplastic
elastomer optical fibers for sensing of extreme deformations. Adv. Func. Mater.
29(5), 1802629 (2019)
12. Li, L., Jiang, S., Tao, Y., Shull, P.B., Gu, G.: Fabrication and testing of a filmy
"feelingless" stretchable strain sensor. In: 2017 IEEE/SICE International Symposium on System Integration (SII), pp. 362–367 (2017)
13. Shi, G., et al.: Highly sensitive, wearable, durable strain sensors and stretchable
conductors using graphene/silicon rubber composites. Adv. Func. Mater. **26**(42),
7614–7625 (2016)
14. Tang, Z., et al.: Highly stretchable core-sheath fibers via wet-spinning for wearable
strain sensors. ACS Appl. Mater. Interfaces **10**(7), 6624–6635 (2018)
15. Jiang, S., Kang, P., Song, X., Lo, B., Shull, P.B.: Emerging wearable interfaces
and algorithms for hand gesture recognition: a survey. IEEE Rev. Biomed. Eng.
15, 85–102 (2021)
16. Ro, K., Kim, S., Park, W., Bae, J.: Development of a wearable soft sensor system
for measuring finger motions. In: 2016 16th International Conference on Control,
Automation and Systems (ICCAS), pp. 549–554 (2016)
17. Hammond, F.L., Mengüç, Y., Wood, R.J.: Toward a modular soft sensor-
embedded glove for human hand motion and tactile pressure measurement. In: 2014
IEEE/RSJ International Conference on Intelligent Robots and Systems(IROS), pp.
4000–4007 (2014)
18. Chossat, J.B., Yiwei, T., Duchaine, V., Park, Y.L.: Wearable soft artificial skin for
hand motion detection with embedded microfluidic strain sensing. In: 2015 IEEE
International Conference on Robotics and Automation (ICRA), pp. 2568–2573
(2015)
19. Xu, Y., et al.: The boom in 3D-printed sensor technology. Sensors **17**(5), 1166
(2017)

20. Bartlett, M.D., Markvicka, E.J., Majidi, C.: Rapid fabrication of soft, multilayered electronics for wearable biomonitoring. Adv. Func. Mater. **26**(46), 8496–8504 (2016)
21. Charmode, S., Kadlimatti, H.S., Pujari, D.: Correlation of human height with hand dimensions: a study in young population of central India. Int. J. Hum. Anat. **1**(3), 36–44 (2019)
22. Lin, Y., Shull, P.B., Chossat, J.-B.: Design of a wearable real-time hand motion tracking system using an array of soft polymer acoustic waveguides. Soft Robotics (2023)
23. Park, Y.-L., Chen, B.-R., Wood, R.J.: Design and fabrication of soft artificial skin using embedded microchannels and liquid conductors. IEEE Sens. J. **12**(8), 2711–2718 (2012)
24. Chossat, J.-B., Park, Y.-L., Wood, R.J., Duchaine, V.: A soft strain sensor based on ionic and metal liquids. IEEE Sens. J. **13**(9), 3405–3414 (2013)
25. Papadakis, E.P.: Ultrasonic phase velocity by the pulse-echo-overlap method incorporating diffraction phase corrections. J. Acoust. Soc. Am. **42**(5), 1045–1051 (1967)

Noncontact Heart Rate Variability Monitoring Based on FMCW Radar

Xiangyu Han and Tao Liu[✉]

Zhejiang University, Hangzhou 310058, People's Republic of China
liutao@zju.edu.cn

Abstract. Noncontact vital sign monitoring based on radar has attracted great interest in many fields. Heart rate variability(HRV), which measures the fluctuation of heartbeat intervals, has been considered an important indicator for general health evaluation. In this paper, we proposed a new algorithm for HRV monitoring using frequency-modulated-continuous-wave (FMCW) radar. We calculate the acceleration of the reflected signal to enhance the heartbeat and suppress the impact of respiration. Finally, a joint optimization algorithm is used to segment the acceleration signal and the time interval of each heartbeat can be extracted for analyzing HRV. Experimental results over 10 participants show the potential of the proposed algorithm for noncontact HRV estimation with high accuracy. The results indicate the possibility for the algorithm to be employed in emotion recognition, sleep, and heart disease monitoring.

Keywords: FMCW · HRV · Wireless signal

1 Introduction

Heart rate variability (HRV) describes the variation in the time interval between successive heartbeats. In recent years, research on HRV has attracted lots of interest. Extracting HRV accurately plays an important role in the diagnosis of cardiovascular diseases [1,2], assessment of mental stress [3], and monitoring of sleep [4]. Electrocardiography (ECG) and photoplethysmography (PPG) are the mainstream monitoring method for HRV [5]. However, they both have many limitations in practice as contact measurement methods. For example, their lead wires will hinder the user's physical movement.

In the past 50 years, contactless physiological monitoring has developed rapidly [6,7], largely overcoming the disadvantages of contact equipment such as electrocardiographs. Monitoring based on millimeter-wave radar is considered a promising non-contact physiological monitoring method, which can penetrate

Supported in part by the National Natural Science Foundation of China (NSFC) under Award 52175033 and Award U21A20120, in part by the Zhejiang Provincial Natural Science Foundation under Award LZ20E050002.

non-metallic obstacles to capture physiological signals of the human body [8]. In addition, radiofrequency (RF) signal isn't easily affected by temperature change or environmental thermal noise compared with methods based on the infrared thermal imaging [9] and can avoid insufficient image resolution, blind areas, and potential privacy problems compared with vision-based monitoring methods [10].

However, measuring the time interval between successive heartbeats and analyzing HRV remains a significant challenge due to the weak amplitude of heartbeat signal and interferences from respiration, trunk movement, and various noise. Most of the existing research in this field focuses on monitoring respiration rate and heartbeat rate [11–14]. Few of them study the extraction of HRV characteristics.

2   Algorithm

For an FMCW radar, each transmitting antenna sends a linear frequency modulated pulse (a chirp) at a time. The instantaneous frequency f_t can be described as

$$f_t = f_0 + St, \tag{1}$$

where f_0 is the initial frequency. S is the slope of frequency over time, which is a constant. Figure 1a and Fig. 1b shows an FMCW pulse with time in time domain and frequency domain respectively. The phase of the FMCW pulse signal φ_t can be obtained from (1) by

$$\varphi_t = \int_0^t f_\tau d\tau = f_0 t + \frac{1}{2} St^2. \tag{2}$$

So the mathematical expression of the impulse is denoted as

$$S_T(t) = A_T e^{j2\pi \left(f_0 t + \frac{1}{2} St^2\right)}. \tag{3}$$

where A_T is the transmitting power. When the impulse is reflected by the human wall at distance R, the reflected signal $S_R(t)$ can be expressed as

$$S_R(t) = A_R e^{j2\pi \left(f_0(t-\tau) + \frac{1}{2} S(t-\tau)^2\right)}. \tag{4}$$

where A_R is the amplitude of the received signal. τ stands for the round-trip delay and can be denoted as

$$\tau = \frac{2R}{c}. \tag{5}$$

where c is the speed of light. The output of the mixer is an intermediate frequency (IF) signal which can be expressed as the convolution of the reflected signal and a replica of the transmitted signal

$$S_{IF}(t) = S_T(t) S_R^*(t) \tag{6}$$

$$S_{IF}(t) = A e^{j2\pi \left(S \frac{2R}{c} t + \frac{2R}{\lambda}\right)}. \tag{7}$$

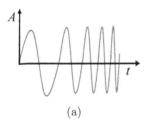 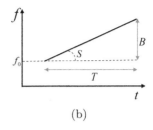

(a)   (b)

Fig. 1. The waveform of an FMCW pulse in the (a) time and the (b) frequency domain.

where λ stands for the wavelength of the impulse and can be calculated by $\lambda = \frac{c}{f_0}$ It's clear from (7) that the frequency f and phase φ of the IF signal are proportional to the distance between the chest wall and antenna and can be shown as

$$f = S\frac{2R}{c} \qquad (8)$$

and

$$\varphi = \frac{4\pi R}{\lambda}. \qquad (9)$$

For each chirp, the IF signal is digitized by Analog-to-Digital Converter (ADC), producing N samples, referred to as fast time. The components of different frequencies in the output of the mixer can be separated by Fast Fourier Transform (FFT). The component reflected by the human chest wall can be selected by (8) if the distance between the chest wall and antenna is known, from the phase of which the movement waveform of chest wall can be obtained. Donate the chest wall motion signal as $R(n)$. Figure 2-(a) shows an example of $R(n)$, in which breathing is more pronounced than heartbeats.

Although it is convenient to extract the heartbeat signal using a bandpass filter, some details of the heartbeat signal can be filtered out because the heartbeat is not sinusoidal motion, which is undesirable for performing HRV analysis. Considering the amplitude of vibration caused by heartbeat in $R(n)$ is small but intense compared with the inhale-exhale motion which is slow and smooth. The acceleration $a(n)$ of $R(n)$ is calculated through (10) to suppress the respiration signal and strengthen the heartbeat signal. Where T_s is the sampling interval referred to as slow time.

$$a(n) = \frac{R(n+1) + R(n-1) - 2R(n)}{(T_s)^2} \qquad (10)$$

Figure 2-(b) shows the acceleration of the example shown in Fig. 2-(a). ECG signal sampled synchronously is shown in Fig. 2-(c). It is clear that the heartbeat signal is emphasized and the breathing motion is dampened.

Note that while the periodicity of the heartbeat signal can be observed in the acceleration, it is still difficult to pick out each heartbeat cycle by zero-crossing detection or peak detection because the heartbeat in acceleration is not a simple

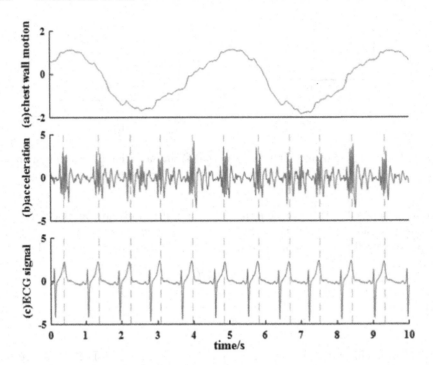

Fig. 2. An example of chest wall motion signal $R(n)$ (a), corresponding acceleration signal (b) and ECG sampled synchronously (all of them are normalized) (c)

sinusoidal signal like respiration waveform. So short-time mean power P_L is used to smooth the acceleration waveform. P_L can be calculated by (11).

$$P_L = \frac{1}{2L+1} \sum_{n=-L}^{L} |a(n)|^2 \tag{11}$$

where L is half the length of the time window. The length of the time window in this paper is 0.4 s after trying. Figure 3 shows the acceleration signal before and after smoothing. The heartbeat signal is sinusoidal after smoothed so it can be segmented easily. However, the heartbeat signal after smoothing still can't meet the accuracy requirements for HRV measurement.

In this paper, a new idea of segmentation through "template" is adopted [15], which is directly based on the acceleration signal. Although the waveform of a single heartbeat is very complex in acceleration, they are very similar in a short period. If a template (donated as μ) of a single heartbeat can be found, then it can be used to segment the acceleration signal and determine the location of the cut-off points (donated as S) between each heartbeat. The solving process can be described as the following joint optimization problem.

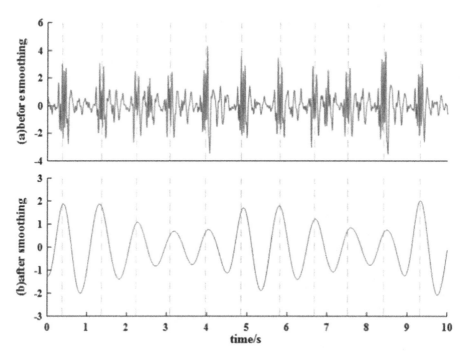

Fig. 3. The acceleration signal (a) before and (b) after smoothed. (all of them are normalized)

$$\arg\min_{S,\mu} \sum_{s_{i-1},s_i \in S} \left\| a\left(s_{i-1}+1:s_i\right) - \omega\left(\boldsymbol{\mu}, s_i - s_{i-1}\right) \right\|^2 \tag{12}$$

where $S = \left\{ s_1\ s_2\ s_3 \cdots \right\}$. Each element in the set represents a subscript of the cut-off point in the acceleration signal. $a\left(s_{i-1}+1:s_i\right)$ is the sequence consisting of the $(s_{i-1}+1)$-th to the s_i-th elements of acceleration. $\omega(\mu,p)$ donates changing the length of the template $\boldsymbol{\mu}$ into p elements by cubic spline interpolation. The goal of the algorithm is to find the optimal segmentation S and template $\boldsymbol{\mu}$ that minimize the sum of the square differences between each subsection and template as shown in (12).

Instead of estimating the segmentation S and the template $\boldsymbol{\mu}$ simultaneously, the algorithm alternates between updating the segmentation and template, while fixing the other. During each iteration, the algorithm updates the segmentation given the current template through (13), then updates the template given the new segmentation through (14).

$$S^{l+1} = \arg\min_{S} Var(S) \tag{13}$$

$$\mu^{l+1} = \arg\min_{\mu} Var(S) \tag{14}$$

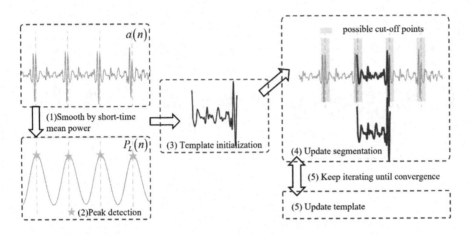

Fig. 4. The schematic diagram of the algorithm

where
$$Var(s) = \sum_{s_{i-1}, s_i \in S} \|a\left(s_{i-1} + 1 : s_i\right) - \omega\left(\boldsymbol{\mu}, s_i - s_{i-1}\right)\|^2. \qquad (15)$$

The script in the upper right corner indicates the number of iterations. The complete algorithm for extracting the time interval of successive heartbeats can be described as follows. Figure 4 shows the schematic diagram of the algorithm.

1) Calculate the second-order differential of the chest wall motion signal to obtain acceleration $a(n)$.
2) Smooth the acceleration signal through short-time average power $P_L(n)$
3) Estimate the cut-off points between every two heartbeats through peak detection based on the smoothed heartbeat signal, so S^0 is obtained.
4) Initialize the template of a single heartbeat acceleration based on S^0 to obtain T^0
5) Start the iteration
   Explore S^{l+1} based on $\boldsymbol{\mu}^l$
   Calculate $\boldsymbol{\mu}^{l+1}$ based on S^{l+1}
6) Finish the iteration until convergence.

3   Experiments

Figure 5 shows the experimental setup for indoor lab testing and evaluation. The FMCW radar sensor is fixed 60 cm above the mattress by a camera support. To measure the interbeat interval (IBI) of each heartbeat, ECG monitoring is used. A total of 10 electrodes, including 4 attached to the extremities and 6 attached to the chest, are pasted on the body of the monitored subject in a way of Wilson lead. II lead data was selected to extract IBIs. 10 human subjects were recruited for the experiments. The study was approved by the Medical Ethics Committee

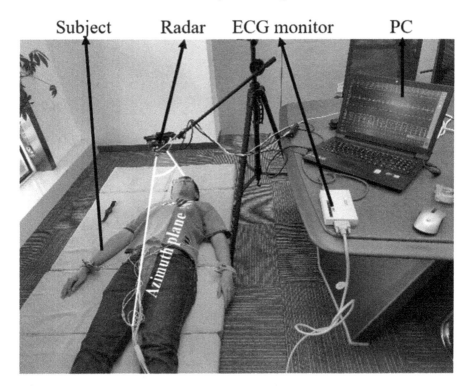

Fig. 5. Indoor experimental setup for HRV estimation

of Zhejiang Hospital (Approval Letter NO: AF/SC-06/04.2). The subjects were asked to lay down on the mattress, keep their torso still but breathe normally. During the experiment, several sets of results with a length of 15 s were collected for each subject. Five sets of data for each subject were retained after removing the poor-quality fragments. The data were exported and processed by MATLAB.

4   Results and Discussion

For 10 subjects, we obtained a total of 50 sets of data, containing 971 heartbeats. Figure 6 shows all IBIs measurement results. The scatter is plotted for each heartbeat using IBI extracted from ECG as the horizontal axis and IBI extracted from radar as the vertical axis.

The HRV features can be further obtained from IBIs. We use the three most widely used time-domain metrics to evaluate the HRV. MEAN is the average value of IBIs, which can be calculated by (16).

$$MEAN = \frac{\sum_{n=1}^{N} IBI(n)}{N} \tag{16}$$

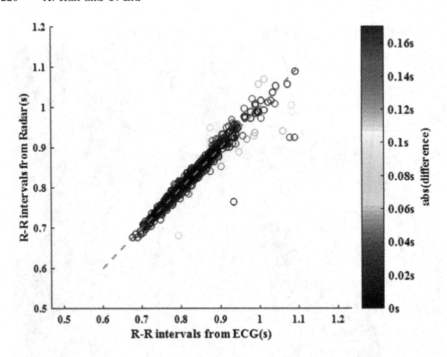

Fig. 6. The scatterplot of IBI measurement results from ECG and radar

The standard deviation of normal to normal (SDNN) measures the standard deviation of all IBIs and can be calculated by (17).

$$SDNN = \sqrt{\frac{\sum_{n=1}^{N}(IBI(n) - MEAN)^2}{N}} \tag{17}$$

The root square of successive differences (RMSSD) measures the successive IBI changes and can be calculated as (18).

$$RMSSD = \sqrt{\frac{\sum_{n=2}^{N}(IBI(n) - IBI(n-1))^2}{N-1}} \tag{18}$$

The above 3 metrics are calculated for each set of sampling data and the results are drawn in scatter with the same form as Fig. 6. Figure 7a shows the estimation results of MEAN. It can be seen that our algorithm can estimate MEAN accurately. The RMSE of MEAN in all 50 sets of data is 2.14 ms. Figure 7b and Fig. 7c show the estimation results of SDNN and RMSSD, respectively. The RMSE of SDNN in all 50 sets of data is 4.00 ms and 7.29 ms for RMSSD.

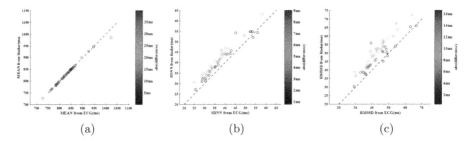

(a)   (b)   (c)

Fig. 7. The scatterplot of (a) MEAN (b) SDNN and (c) RMSSD estimates from ECG and radar

5 Discussion

In this article, we proposed an algorithm to extract IBIs and calculate HRV metrics. The method of enhancing heartbeat signals by second-order difference has been adopted in previous work [16], showing a good ability to suppress the harmonics of breath and the potential for HRV monitoring. However, this algorithm has not been validated in a large number of experiments. The stochastic resonance algorithm [17] can't accurately measure the time interval of each heartbeat. Although it can estimate SDNN with a relative error less than 6.53% through the average heart rate within 3 s, the estimation effect for some HRV characteristics, such as pNN50, is not ideal. Our method can measure the IBIs accurately with RMSE of 15.2 ms. Compared with the heartbeat extraction algorithm based on decomposition [18], which realized that the RMSE of MEAN, SDNN, and RMSSD were 4.65 ms, 10.31 ms, and 9.18 ms respectively, Our algorithm achieves higher accuracy. The RMSE are correspondingly 2.14 ms, 4.00 ms, and 7.29 ms. Experimental results show that it can achieve the HRV measurement accuracy of millisecond level. Since our actual sampling frequency is 100 Hz, so we think the above accuracy is satisfactory.

6 Conclusion

We proposed an algorithm for HRV monitoring in this article. Firstly, it extracts the echo signal of the heart. The acceleration of the chest wall motion signal is calculated to suppress respiration and strengthen the heartbeat. Then the acceleration is smoothed by short-time average power, from which the cut-off points are estimated. Finally, IBIs are extracted by a joint optimization algorithm and HRV features are estimated. Experimental results show that this algorithm can achieve good measurement accuracy in a laboratory environment, but the measurement effect is not ideal in a complex real scenario or long-time monitoring scenario. In an environment that is not suitable for ECG and PPG measurement, the measurement method based on RF technology can provide a new idea for the measurement and analysis of HRV.

References

1. Silveri, G., et al.: Identification of ischemic heart disease by using machine learning technique based on parameters measuring heart rate variability. In: 2020 28th European Signal Processing Conference (EUSIPCO), pp. 1309–1312. IEEE (2021)
2. Kirtana, R., Lokeswari, Y.: An IoT based remote HRV monitoring system for hypertensive patients. In: 2017 International Conference on Computer, Communication and Signal Processing (ICCCSP), pp. 1–6. IEEE (2017)
3. Gandhi, S., Baghini, M.S., Mukherji, S.: Mental stress assessment-a comparison between HRV based and respiration based techniques. In: 2015 Computing in Cardiology Conference (CinC), pp. 1029–1032. IEEE (2015)
4. Szypulska, M., Piotrowski, Z.: Prediction of fatigue and sleep onset using HRV analysis. In: Proceedings of the 19th International Conference Mixed Design of Integrated Circuits and Systems-MIXDES 2012, pp. 543–546. IEEE (2012)
5. Faust, O., et al.: Heart rate variability for medical decision support systems: a review. Comput. Biol. Med. **145**, 105407 (2022)
6. Brüser, C., Antink, C.H., Wartzek, T., Walter, M., Leonhardt, S.: Ambient and unobtrusive cardiorespiratory monitoring techniques. IEEE Rev. Biomed. Eng. **8**, 30–43 (2015)
7. Wang, P., et al.: Research progress in millimeter wave radar-based non-contact sleep monitoring-a review. In: 2021 13th International Symposium on Antennas, Propagation and EM Theory (ISAPE), pp. 1–3. IEEE (2021)
8. Hu, W., Zhao, Z., Wang, Y., Zhang, H., Lin, F.: Noncontact accurate measurement of cardiopulmonary activity using a compact quadrature doppler radar sensor. IEEE Trans. Biomed. Eng. **61**(3), 725–735 (2013)
9. Al-Naji, A., Gibson, K., Lee, S.H., Chahl, J.: Monitoring of cardiorespiratory signal: principles of remote measurements and review of methods. IEEE Access **5**, 15776–15790 (2017)
10. Wang, G., Gu, C., Inoue, T., Li, C.: A hybrid FMCW-interferometry radar for indoor precise positioning and versatile life activity monitoring. IEEE Trans. Microw. Theory Tech. **62**(11), 2812–2822 (2014)
11. Zhai, Q., Han, X., Han, Y., Yi, J., Wang, S., Liu, T.: A contactless on-bed radar system for human respiration monitoring. IEEE Trans. Instrum. Meas. **71**, 1–10 (2022)
12. Wiesner, A.: A multifrequency interferometric CW radar for vital signs detection. In: 2009 IEEE Radar Conference, pp. 1–4. IEEE (2009)
13. Rathna, G., Meshineni, D.: Analysis of FM CW-radar signals to extract vital-sign information. In: 2021 IEEE International Conference on Electronics, Computing and Communication Technologies (CONECCT), pp. 1–6. IEEE (2021)
14. Zhu, Z., Yang, D., Zhao, R., Liang, B.: Vital sign signal extraction method based on permutation entropy and EMD algorithm for ultra-wideband radar. In: 2019 3rd International Conference on Electronic Information Technology and Computer Engineering (EITCE), pp. 1268–1273. IEEE (2019)
15. Zhao, M., Adib, F., Katabi, D.: Emotion recognition using wireless signals. In: Proceedings of the 22nd Annual International Conference on Mobile Computing and Networking, pp. 95–108 (2016)
16. Xiong, Y., Peng, Z., Gu, C., Li, S., Wang, D., Zhang, W.: Differential enhancement method for robust and accurate heart rate monitoring via microwave vital sign sensing. IEEE Trans. Instrum. Meas. **69**(9), 7108–7118 (2020)

17. Lv, W., Zhao, Y., Zhang, W., Liu, W., Hu, A., Miao, J.: Remote measurement of short-term heart rate with narrow beam millimeter wave radar. IEEE Access **9**, 165049–165058 (2021)
18. Wang, F., Zeng, X., Wu, C., Wang, B., Liu, K.R.: Radio frequency based heart rate variability monitoring. In: ICASSP 2021-2021 IEEE International Conference on Acoustics, Speech and Signal Processing (ICASSP), pp. 8007–8011. IEEE (2021)

A Diving Glove with Inertial Sensors for Underwater Gesture Recognition

Qi Tang[1,2], Jingeng Mai[1,2,4(✉)], Tiantong Wang[1,2], and Qining Wang[1,2,3,4]

[1] Department of Advanced Manufacturing and Robotics, College of Engineering, Peking University, Beijing 100871, China
jingengmai@pku.edu.cn
[2] Beijing Engineering Research Center of Intelligent Rehabilitation Engineering, Peking University, Beijing 100871, China
[3] Medical Robotics Laboratory, University of Health and Rehabilitation Sciences, Qingdao 266071, China
[4] Institute for Artificial Intelligence, Peking University, Beijing 100871, China

Abstract. Underwater gesture recognition has emerged as a popular research area for achieving efficient and secure underwater human-human interaction and human-robot collaboration. Previous research primarily relied on visual methods, which face challenges related to low visibility and motion blur in underwater environments. In this paper, we introduce a diving glove embedded with inertial sensors for underwater gesture recognition. The Nearest Centroid (NC), Random Forest (RF) and Support Vector Machine (SVM) classifiers are used in our diving glove. To demonstrate the underwater gesture recognition performance, we conducted a two-stage underwater experiment with ten underwater gestures. For the same user, The average recognition accuracies of the NC, RF and SVM classifiers are 97.5%±5.4%, 98.6%±0.6% and 99.2%±0.3%, respectively. For new users, the average recognition accuracies of the NC, RF and SVM classifiers are 86.4%±2.18%, 88.6%±7.4% and 96.5%±0.31%, respectively. The study suggests that the diving glove with inertial sensors is a feasible solution for underwater gesture recognition.

Keywords: diving glove · underwater gesture recognition · inertial sensors · machine learning

1 Introduction

Underwater gesture recognition has gradually become an important research field due to the popularity of diving sports and the demand for underwater human-machine collaboration. Hand gestures are the primary method for underwater communication for recreational scuba divers, and are also in general use by professional divers [1]. Divers can express information underwater to surface personnel, other divers, or underwater robots through hand gestures, including diving

This work was supported by National Natural Science Foundation of China under Grant 91948302.

direction, danger alerts, underwater organisms and environmental factors. However, in complex and harsh underwater environments, the gesture receiver may experience occlusion or loss of visual contact with the sender, which can result in reduced efficiency of underwater tasks, as well as increased risks to the diver's safety. In addition, divers' gestures can be used to control autonomous underwater vehicles [2], which is important to provide efficient underwater human-robot interaction. Intelligent underwater gesture recognition system can be used in both of the above underwater situations, enabling safe and efficient human-human interaction as well as human-robot collaboration.

In the land environment, there have been a variety of innovative approaches to capture gesture information [3–5]. For example, a flexible iontronic capacitive sensing array is placed on the wrist to recognize gestures by detecting pressure changes. Additionally, self-powered triboelectric smart glove, which exhibit high sensitivity and a rapid response time, have been used in combination with deep learning algorithms to recognize and translate sign language. Although gesture recognition technology is well established on land, it becomes difficult in the underwater environment, as a consequence of the physical properties of water [6].

In the underwater environment, previous research primarily used visual methods [7,8]. This approach faces challenges related to low visibility and motion blur in underwater environments. Although algorithms for robust underwater gesture recognition have been proposed to improve these issues, they cannot fundamentally solve the problem of underwater visual sensing [9]. The Diving glove is a good platform for embedding sensors for underwater gesture recognition. Some researchers have placed capacitive sensors on gloves for gesture recognition, whitch are not affected by dark environments [10]. But capacitive sensors are disrupted by water pressure and require calibration before each use. This can reduce the efficiency of completing underwater tasks. Inertial sensors are robust for capturing motion and posture information. When waterproofed, they can overcome various types of interference in the underwater environment. Some researchers have already used inertial sensors for real-time monitoring of underwater activities [11], but there are no reports of their usage for underwater gesture recognition.

In this study, we propose a diving glove embedded with inertial sensors to address the challenges of the underwater environment. Our diving glove was embedded with inertial sensors in seven locations to capture the user's gesture information. Data collection and processing were achieved by embedding circuits inside the diving glove. We conducted a two-stage experiment and thoroughly evaluated the underwater gesture recognition performance of the diving glove. Three machine learning algorithms were used for offline analysis and online recognition, and their performance differences were compared. Additionally, we investigated the underwater gesture recognition generalization ability of the diving glove for new users.

2 Method

2.1 System Overview

The diving glove designed in this study consists of seven inertial sensors, a multiplexer (MUX), a microcontroller unit (MCU), a communication module, a voltage conversion module and a waterproof box. The appearance of the diving glove and the placement of each component are shown in Fig. 1(a). Seven inertial sensors are embedded in the fingertips, dorsum and wrist of the diving glove respectively. The MCU and MUX are placed on the dorsum. The communication module and voltage conversion module are placed inside the waterproof box. The waterproof box is made of aluminum alloy, fixed on the wrist, and reinforced with a strap with velcro.

The inertial sensor used in this study is a 9-axis inertial sensor that can output attitude information, including acceleration, angular velocity, and Euler angles. The MCU used in this study is the STM32F407VGT6 (STMicroelectronics), which is equipped with a 32-bit high-performance ARM Cortex-M4 processor, used for signal acquisition, data processing and gesture recognition. The inertial sensors, MCU and MUX are all waterproofed with silicone.

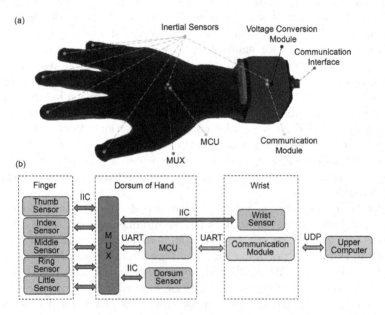

Fig. 1. (a) The appearance of the diving glove and the placement of each component. (b) Signal acquisition system of the diving glove.

The signal acquisition system of the diving glove is shown in Fig. 1(b). When the diver uses underwater gestures, the inertial sensors capture and output the hand's attitude information at a frequency of 100 Hz. To reduce the I/O consumption of the MCU, the seven inertial sensors send sensing data to the MUX via the IIC protocol. The MUX sends the fused data to the MCU via the UART protocol. The MCU sends the raw data or real-time recognition results to the communication module via the UART protocol. The converted data is sent to the upper computer via the UDP protocol. The upper computer is used to record the raw data and recognition results.

2.2   Experimental Procedure

Seven healthy subjects (6 males, 1 female) with an age of 25.2 ± 2.3 years participated in the study. All subjects were provided informed written consents. We selected ten basic underwater gestures, as illustrated in Fig. 2, to evaluate the recognition performance of the diving glove. These gestures include "OK", "Stop", "Level-off", "Ascend", "Descend", "3 min to stay safe", "Follow me", "Turn around", "Share air" and "Lack of air".

Fig. 2. Ten basic underwater gestures.

The experiment was conducted at the swimming pool of Peking University. After wearing the diving glove, the subjects performed underwater gestures in the swimming pool, and the surface personnel operated the upper computer to record the experimental data.

We conducted a two-stage experiment to evaluate the underwater gesture recognition performance of the diving glove. The first stage was an offline experiment with four subjects. Each subject sequentially performed ten underwater gestures. They held each gesture for ten seconds, followed by a five-second rest, and then executed the next gesture until all ten gestures were performed. We trained machine learning classifiers using their data separately and conducted offline analysis to evaluate the diving glove's recognition performance on the same object. Their underwater gesture data was also combined into a single dataset to train online machine learning classifiers deployed in the MCU of the diving glove for the second stage. The second stage was an online experiment with three new subjects. They wore the diving glove with the online machine learning classifier to evaluate its online recognition performance and generalization ability to new users. The experimental procedure was the same as the first stage.

2.3 Recognition Framework

The underwater gesture recognition framework is shown in Fig. 3. The raw data of acceleration, angular velocity, and Euler angles are output by seven inertial sensors. Only the Euler angle data is used, as it can uniquely determine the orientation of a fixed rotating rigid body. Additionally, the diving glove should not be sensitive to the orientation in the horizontal plane, so we only use the original data of the pitch angle and roll angle of the Euler angles.

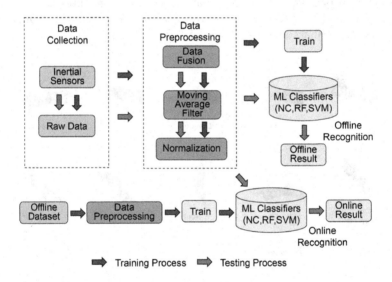

Fig. 3. Recognition framework.

In the data preprocessing stage, the sensor raw data is fused into a 14-dimensional feature vector containing 7 pitch angles and 7 roll angles. Due to the signal being sampled at 100 Hz, a moving average filter (MAF) with a buffer size of 20 ms was implemented to eliminate noise signals. Additionally, since the pitch angles range from $-\pi/2$ to $\pi/2$ and the roll angles range from $-\pi$ to π, to eliminate the difference in data range, during the preprocessing stage, the data was normalized to be within the range of -1 to 1:

$$\theta_{pitch}^{scale} = \frac{2 * \theta_{pitch}}{\pi} \tag{1}$$

$$\theta_{roll}^{scale} = \frac{\theta_{roll}}{\pi} \tag{2}$$

where θ_{pitch} and θ_{roll} are the original pitch angle and roll angle output by the inertial sensor, and θ_{pitch}^{scale} and θ_{roll}^{scale} are the normalized values.

In the offline recognition framework, the normalized data samples were randomly shuffled and divided into a training set (90% of the data) and a testing set (10% of the data). In the online recognition framework, the data sets collected from offline experiments were merged together to train the online machine learning classifier.

Due to the limitations of MCU computing power and storage space, we need to choose machine learning algorithms with fewer parameters and lower computational requirements. In this study, three classic machine learning algorithms were used to train the classifiers, which are Nearest Centroid (NC), Random Forest (RF) and Support Vector Machine (SVM). The classifiers trained using these three algorithms can all be deployed on the MCU for online recognition.

Nearest Centroid is a simple algorithm for classification [12], where the centroid of each class can be obtained by taking the average of the features of all samples in that class:

$$m_c = \frac{\sum_{y_i=c} x_i}{N_c} \tag{3}$$

where m_c is the calculated mean vector of class c, x_i is the feature vector of the sample, y_i is the class label corresponding to x_i, and N_c is the number of data samples in class c.

In the test stage, a test sample was classified to the class with the smallest Euclidean distance between the feature vector and the class mean vector:

$$y = \arg \min_c \|x - m_c\|^2 \tag{4}$$

where x is the feature vector of the sample to be classified, m_c is the centroid of class c, and $\|\cdot\|$ is the Euclidean distance.

Random Forest is an ensemble algorithm based on decision trees as the base learners [13]. Each decision tree produces a classification result. Random Forest selects the class that appears the most frequently as the final classification result:

$$y = \mathrm{mode}\, T_1(x), T_2(x), \ldots, T_m(x) \tag{5}$$

where $T_i(x)$ is the classification result of the decision tree with the index i, mode selects the most frequently occurring class.

During the construction of each tree, the samples used are obtained by randomly sampling with replacement from the training set. Additionally, when splitting nodes during tree construction, the best split is selected from a randomly selected subset of size k of the features. The parameter k controls the degree of randomness. In general, $k = log_2 d$ where d is the number of features. In this study, $d = 14$, so we set $k = 3$. The random forest we trained consisted of 100 decision trees, with a maximum depth of 3 and a minimum number of samples per leaf of 5.

Support Vector Machine finds the optimal separating hyperplane in the feature space that maximizes the margin between the positive and negative samples in the training set [14]. Its decision function is

$$f(\boldsymbol{x}) = sgn\left(\sum_{i \in SV} \alpha_i y_i K(\boldsymbol{x}_i, \boldsymbol{x}) + b\right) \tag{6}$$

where α_i is the Lagrange multiplier of the support vector machine, and b is the bias term. α_i and b are obtained from the optimization problem during the training process. $\boldsymbol{x}_i$ is the support vector. $\boldsymbol{x}$ is the feature vector of the sample to be classified. SV is the set of support vectors. K is the kernel function that maps the data to a higher dimensional space for linear classification. In this study, a Gaussian kernel function was adopted:

$$K(\boldsymbol{x}_i, \boldsymbol{x}) = exp(-\frac{\|\boldsymbol{x}_i - \boldsymbol{x}\|^2}{2\sigma^2}) \tag{7}$$

where σ is the standard deviation of the Gaussian kernel function.

The basic form of SVM is for binary classification. In our study, we used the One-VS-One (OVO) method to implement multi-class SVM. For each pair (i, j) of the k classes, a binary classifier is trained to separate the samples belonging to class i and those belonging to class j. In this study, 45 binary SVM classifiers were trained. These binary SVM classifiers vote to select the final classification result.

3   Results

3.1   Offline Results

For the offline experiment, the time-domain waveforms of the normalized pitch angle θ_{pitch}^{scale} and roll angle θ_{roll}^{scale} of each inertial sensor are shown in Fig. 4. Each hand part corresponds to one pitch angle and one roll angle. When the subject maintains a gesture, the signals in each channel are relatively stable. When the subject switches from one gesture to another, the signals in each channel show significant changes.

The underwater gesture data from 4 subjects were separately trained as NC, RF, and SVM classifiers. These three classifiers were used to recognize the test sets from the same subject. The offline recognition accuracy of underwater gestures is shown in Fig. 5. The recognition accuracies of NC classifiers for the 4 subjects were 94.3%, 99.8%, 99.5% and 96.2%, with an average accuracy of 97.5%±5.4%. The recognition accuracies of RF classifiers for the 4 subjects were 99.5%, 98.6%, 98.2% and 98.0%, with an average accuracy of 98.6%±0.6%. The recognition accuracies of SVM classifiers for the 4 subjects was 99.5%, 99.2%, 99.5% and 98.6%, with an average accuracy of 99.2%±0.3%. The three machine learning classifiers demonstrated excellent classification abilities for the test sets from the same subject.

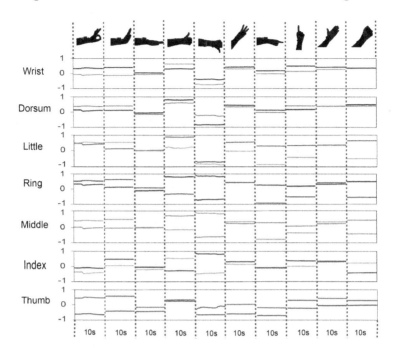

Fig. 4. The time-domain waveforms of the normalized pitch angle and roll angle of each inertial sensor.

3.2 Online Results

For the online experiment, three new subjects tested the diving glove with online machine learning classifiers. Figure 6 shows the recognition accuracy of the three online machine learning classifiers for the three new subjects. The NC classifier had a recognition accuracy less than 90% for all three subjects, with an average accuracy of 86.4% ± 2.18%. The RF classifier had recognition accuracy greater than 90% for two subjects, but for subject 6, the recognition accuracy was only 78.5%, resulting in an average accuracy of 88.6% ± 7.4%. The SVM classifier had recognition accuracy greater than 96% for all three subjects, resulting in an average accuracy of 96.5% ± 0.31%. Among the three classifiers, SVM had the most superior and stable average online recognition results.

We also constructed confusion matrices shown in Fig. 7 to evaluate the online recognition performance of the classifiers. The labels for each row of the confusion matrix represent the ground truth, while the labels for each column represent the gestures predicted by the classifier. The diagonal elements represent the percentage of correctly classified samples, while the off-diagonal elements represent the percentage of incorrectly classified samples. For each classifier and gesture, the confusion matrix was computed by taking the average recognition results of the three subjects.

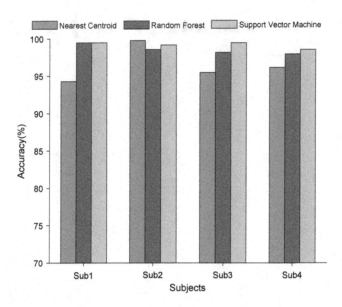

Fig. 5. The offline recognition accuracy of underwater gestures for 4 subjects. The offline data of each subject is separately trained as Nearest Centroid, Random Forest and Support Vector Machine classifiers, and these classifiers are used to recognize the test sets from the same subject.

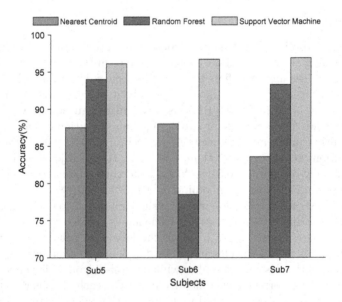

Fig. 6. The online recognition accuracy for 3 new subjects using the three online machine learning classifiers

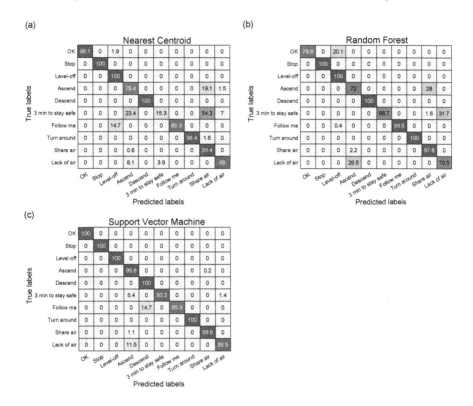

Fig. 7. The online recognition results of 3 subjects are combined and presented separately in the confusion matrix (%) of: (a) Nearest Centroid, (b) Random Forest and (c) Support Vector Machine.

The confusion matrix using the NC classifier is shown in Fig. 7(a). The recognition accuracies of "OK", "Stop", "Level-off", "Ascend", "Descend", "3 min to stay safe", "Follow me", "Turn around", "Share air" and "Lack of air" are 98.1%, 100%, 100%, 79.4%, 100%, 15.3%, 85.3%, 98.4%, 99.4% and 88%, respectively. The confusion matrix using the RF classifier is shown in Fig. 7(b). The recognition accuracies of "OK", "Stop", "Level-off", "Ascend", "Descend", "3 min to stay safe", "Follow me", "Turn around", "Share air" and "Lack of air" are 79.9%, 100%, 100%, 72%, 100%, 66.7%, 99.6%, 100%, 97,8% and 70.5%, respectively. The confusion matrix using the SVM classifier is shown in Fig. 7(c). The recognition accuracies of "OK", "Stop", "Level-off", "Ascend", "Descend", "3 min to stay safe", "Follow me", "Turn around", "Share air" and "Lack of air" are 100%, 100%, 100%, 99.8%, 100%, 93.2%, 85.3%, 100%, 98.9% and 88.5%, respectively.

4   Discussion

The purpose of the experiment is to evaluate the underwater gesture recognition ability of the diving glove we designed, and to compare three classic machine learning classifiers, including the NC classifier, RF classifier and SVM classifier.

We selected ten typical underwater gestures as target gestures. As shown in the time-domain waveform of the ten underwater gestures, there are significant differences in the sensor data of different channels for different gestures, and the sensor data for the same gesture is relatively stable. This indicates that simple classifiers can be used to accomplish the underwater hand gesture recognition task.

For the offline experiment, three machine learning classifiers were separately trained and tested on each subject. The experimental results showed that when the training set and testing set were from the same subject, all three classifiers exhibited excellent performance. The average recognition accuracies of the NC, RF and SVM classifiers are $97.5\% \pm 5.4\%$, $98.6\% \pm 0.6\%$ and $99.2\% \pm 0.3\%$.

For the online experiment, all three machine learning classifiers were able to perform online recognition on three new subjects, but their accuracy rates showed varying degrees of decline. The average recognition accuracies of the NC, RF and SVM classifiers decreased to $86.4\% \pm 2.18\%$, $88.6\% \pm 7.4\%$ and $96.5\% \pm 0.31\%$, respectively. From the confusion matrix, it can be observed that the NC classifier had difficulty recognizing the gestures "3 min to stay safe", "Ascend", "Follow me", and "Lack of air", with recognition accuracies of 15.3%, 79.4%, 85.3%, and 88%, respectively. The RF classifier had lower recognition accuracies for the gestures "3 min to stay safe", "Lack of air", "Ascend" and "OK", with accuracies of 66.7%, 70.5%, 72%, and 79.9%, respectively. Especially for the "3 min to stay safe" gesture, 54.3% of the samples were misclassified as "Share air" by the NC classifier, and 31.7% were misclassified as "Lack of air" by the RF classifier. The SVM classifier, which used a Gaussian kernel function, achieved recognition accuracies greater than 85% for all ten gestures, with accuracies greater than 95% for seven gestures, demonstrating excellent generalization performance for new users.

We speculate that there are three reasons for the misclassifications of the diving glove on new users. Firstly, the different hand sizes of each subject may result in variations in the inertial sensor data of the same gesture. Secondly, the underwater gestures made by the subjects may not be completely standardized due to the lack of long-term training. Thirdly, some gestures have a high degree of similarity, which could lead to confusion between them.

5   Conclusion

In this study, we proposed a diving glove embedded with inertial sensors for underwater gesture recognition. The results showed that our diving glove could achieve real-time underwater gesture recognition. We used three machine learning classifiers (NC, RF, and SVM) and compared their performance in recognizing underwater gestures of both the same and new users. We found that all three classifiers exhibited excellent performance when the training set and testing set were from the same subject. However, the accuracy rates of the three classifiers varied when new users used the diving glove. The SVM classifier achieved an average recognition accuracy of 96.5% ± 0.31% for new users, demonstrating superior generalization ability compared to the NC and RF classifiers. In the future, we plan to expand the target gesture set to include international standard diving gesture sets and underwater robot control gesture sets, including both static and dynamic gestures. We will also optimize the number and location of the inertial sensors in the diving glove to reduce the number of sensors while maintaining high recognition accuracy.

References

1. Bevan, J.: The Professional Diver's Handbook, 2nd edn. Submex, London (2005). https://doi.org/10.3723/175605407783359992
2. Bandeira, G.M., Carmo, M., Ximenes, B., Kelner, J.: Using gesture-based interfaces to control robots. In: Kurosu, M. (ed.) HCI 2015. LNCS, vol. 9170, pp. 3–12. Springer, Cham (2015). https://doi.org/10.1007/978-3-319-20916-6_1
3. Molchanov, P., Gupta, S., Kim, K., Kautz, J.: Hand gesture recognition with 3D convolutional neural networks. In: Proceedings of the IEEE Conference on Computer Vision and Pattern Recognition Workshops, Boston, MA, USA, pp. 1–7. IEEE (2015). https://doi.org/10.1109/CVPRW.2015.7301342
4. Wang, T., Zhao, Y., Wang, Q.: A flexible iontronic capacitive sensing array for hand gesture recognition using deep convolutional neural networks. Soft Rob. (2022). https://doi.org/10.1089/soro.2021.0209
5. Zhou, Z., et al.: Sign-to-speech translation using machine-learning-assisted stretchable sensor arrays. Nat. Electron. 3(9), 571–578 (2020). https://doi.org/10.1038/s41928-020-0428-6
6. Huy, D.Q., Sadjoli, N., Azam, A.B., Elhadidi, B., Cai, Y., Seet, G.: Object perception in underwater environments: a survey on sensors and sensing methodologies. Ocean Eng. 267, 113202 (2023). https://doi.org/10.1016/j.oceaneng.2022.113202
7. Zahn, M.: Development of an underwater hand gesture recognition system. In: Global Oceans 2020: Singapore-US Gulf Coast, Biloxi, MS, USA, pp. 1–8. IEEE (2020). https://doi.org/10.1109/IEEECONF38699.2020.9389313
8. Codd-Downey, R., Jenkin, M.: Human robot interaction using diver hand signals. In: 2019 14th ACM/IEEE International Conference on Human-Robot Interaction (HRI), Daegu, Korea (South), pp. 550–551. IEEE (2019). https://doi.org/10.1109/HRI.2019.8673133
9. Chavez, A.G., Ranieri, A., Chiarella, D., Birk, A.: Underwater vision-based gesture recognition: a robustness validation for safe human-robot interaction. IEEE Robot. Autom. Mag. 28(3), 67–78 (2021). https://doi.org/10.1109/MRA.2021.3075560
10. Antillon, D.W.O., Walker, C.R., Rosset, S., Anderson, I.A.: Glove-based hand gesture recognition for diver communication. IEEE Trans. Neural Netw. Learn. Syst. (2022). https://doi.org/10.1109/TNNLS.2022.3161682
11. Wu, X., Zhou, Z., Wang, Q.: Real-time kinematics measurement of human lower-limb underwater motions based on inertial units. In: 2021 27th International Conference on Mechatronics and Machine Vision in Practice (M2VIP), Shanghai, China, pp. 715–720. IEEE (2021). https://doi.org/10.1109/M2VIP49856.2021.9665010

12. Webb, A.R., Copsey, K.D.: Statistical Pattern Recognition, 3rd edn. Wiley, Hoboken (2011). https://doi.org/10.1002/9781119952954
13. Breiman, L.: Random forests. Mach. Learn. **45**, 5–32 (2001). https://doi.org/10.1023/A:1010933404324
14. Vapnik, V.: The Nature of Statistical Learning Theory, 2nd edn. Springer, Heidelberg (1999). https://doi.org/10.1007/978-1-4757-3264-1

Low-hysteresis Flexible Strain Sensors Based on Liquid Metal for Human-Robot Interaction

Tianyun Dong, Yi Chen, Juntao Wang, and Hui You$^{(\boxtimes)}$

Guangxi Key Laboratory of Manufacturing System and Advanced Manufacturing Technology, School of Mechanical Engineering, Guangxi University, Nanning 530004, China
hyou@gxu.edu.cn

Abstract. Flexible strain sensors have aroused great interest in the fields of human-machine interaction, human motion detection, and wearable devices. However, developing flexible strain sensors with low hysteresis, large strain range, fast response time, and excellent dynamic and static stability remains a challenge. In this paper, we prepared three types of flexible strain sensors: wave-shaped, triangle-shaped, and line-shaped by injecting liquid metal (EGaIn) into the silicon elastomer (Ecoflex) microchannel. Then, the performance of the three types of flexible strain sensors was tested. The results show that these sensors can withstand more than 150% strain and have extremely low hysteresis. Among these sensors, the triangle-shaped strain sensor exhibits a negligible hysteresis of 0.049% and the line-shaped strain sensor has the most obvious hysteresis of 1.406%, followed by the wave-shaped strain sensor with a hysteresis of 0.146%. However, the line-shaped strain sensor has the highest sensitivity with the value about 1.2, while the wavy-shaped and triangle-shaped strain sensors have a lower value of 0.95 and 0.83, respectively. In addition, the three types of sensors simultaneously exhibit many excellent performance characteristics such as excellent dynamic and static stability, long durability, and fast response time. To demonstrate the capability of the sensors in practical application, we used the triangle-shaped strain sensor to detect the bending motion of the robot finger. The results indicate that the developed flexible strain sensors are expected to be used for human-robot interaction.

Keywords: Flexible strain sensor · Liquid metal · Hysteresis · Human-robot interaction

1 Introduction

In recent years, strain sensors based on flexible and stretchable materials have received increasing attention due to their high strain detection range ($>50\%$) [1], which is much higher than that of conventional metal coil strain sensors ($<5\%$) [2]. Therefore, flexible strain sensor can be applied in many fields such as human-machine interaction, human motion detection, health detection, and soft robotics. Currently, flexible strain sensors based on elastomer substrates using metal nanowires [3, 4], carbon nanotubes [5–8], carbon black [9, 10] or graphene [11, 12] as conductive materials have been extensively reported. These strain sensors demonstrated excellent performance such as high sensitivity and long durability. Li et al. [7] proposed a fabrication method for a flexible strain sensor based on multi-walled carbon nanotubes/polydimethylsiloxane (MWCNTs/PDMS) microspheres, which can achieve high sensitivity about 7.22 and high durability over 500 stretch and release cycles. However, the delamination between the elastomer substrate and conductive material is frequently observed in these sensors [13], which severely limits the performance. The main reason is that the mismatch in Young's modulus between the elastomer substrate and conductive material. Moreover, the conductive path recovery is incomplete due to friction between the elastomer substrate and the conductive material in the process of stretching/releasing [14], which will result in large hysteresis and seriously affect the practical application of the sensors.

To solve these problems, fluid-type flexible strain sensors have been proposed [1, 2, 13–23], which use conducting liquid materials as the sensing element and encapsulate them into microchannels of elastomer substrate. There will be no delamination observed between the conductive material and the elastomer substrate due to the use of liquid conductors. Therefore, they can easily reach 100% strain without deterioration of performance. In addition, the resistance change of these fluid-type flexible strain sensors is caused by the geometrical change of microchannel, so the problem of the incomplete recovery of conducting paths was circumvented. Hence, these sensors have low hysteresis and can precisely detect strain signals. Yoon et al. [20] developed a flexible strain sensor with [BMIM][Ntf2] and [BMIM][Ac] ionic liquid mixtures embedded into the polydimethylsiloxane (PDMS) substrate exhibiting low hysteresis with the value about 1.89%. Choi et al. [14] proposed a highly stretchable, low-cost ionic-liquid-based wavy strain sensor by using an extremely cost-effective ionic liquid of ethylene glycol/sodium chloride. The ILBW sensors exhibited a low degree of hysteresis about 0.15% at 250% strain. However, the ionic liquid has some disadvantages such as low conductivity, low vapor pressure, and toxicity, which severely limit its application. Another type of conductive liquid that is liquid metal has increasing attention, especially eutectic gallium-indium (EGaIn). EGaIn has high surface energy, high conductivity, and low toxicity and can maintain liquid state at room temperature. Therefore, it is highly suitable for the manufacture of flexible sensors.

In this paper, combined with the advantages of low Young's modulus and high stretchability of Ecofelx and low toxicity and high conductivity of EGaIn, we simultaneously prepared wave-shaped, triangle-shaped and line-shaped strain sensors by encapsulating EGaIn into the microchannel of Ecoflex. Then the performance of the three types of sensors were investigated. The results show that the three types of sensors exhibit excellent dynamic and static stability, long durability, and fast response time (184ms). In addition, the hysteresis of the wavy-shaped, triangle-shaped, and line-shaped strain sensors are 0.146%, 0.049%, and 1.406%, respectively. Finally, due to these sensors having good performance, the triangle-shaped strain sensors were used to detect the bending motion of the robot finger.

2 Working mechanism of sensors

The sensing mechanism of fluid-type flexible resistance strain sensors can described in Eq. (1) [17].

$$\Delta R = R - R_0 = \rho \left(\frac{L + \Delta L}{(w + \Delta w)(h + \Delta h)} - \frac{L}{wh} \right) \tag{1}$$

where R and R_0 are the resistances of the microchannel stretched by ΔL and not stretched, respectively. ρ is the electrical resistivity of EGaIn. L is the length of the microchannel, and w and h are the width and height of the cross-section of the microchannel, respectively. When the sensor is stretched by an external tension, the length of the microchannel increases and the cross-sectional area of the microchannel decreases, as shown in Fig. 1. Therefore, the resistance increases. When the external tension is removed, the sensor microchannel will return to its original dimensions and the resistance will return to its initial value.

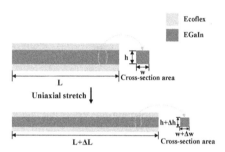

Fig. 1. Schematic illustration of the geometrical deformation of fluid-type flexible strain sensors before and after stretching.

3 Preparation

The three types of sensors were fabricated by embedding EGaIn into the microchannel of Ecoflex silicon elastomer. Ecoflex is composed of part A and part B. The cross-section area of the sensor microchannel is 800 μm(width) × 800 μm(height) and the specific fabrication process is shown in Fig. 2. First, polylactic acid (PLA) molds with and without patterns were made by 3D printing. Second, the part A and part B of the Ecoflex silicon elastomer were evenly mixed at a weight ratio of 1:1 and poured into the PLA molds with and without patterns after degassing. Then, the filled mold with pattern was put into a drying oven and heated at 45 °C for approximately 10min. After the liquid silicone elastomer was completely cured, the patterned silicon elastomer was carefully peeled from the mold with pattern. The liquid silicone elastomer in the mold without pattern remained in a half-cured state at room temperature. Two parts of silicon elastomer was bonded to together. Next, EGaIn was injected into the microchannel using two syringes. One is used to inject EGaIn and the other is used to extract the trapped air in the microchannel. Finally, two copper wires were inserted through the two holes left during injection, and then two injection holes were sealed using sealant to prevent EGaIn from leaking out.

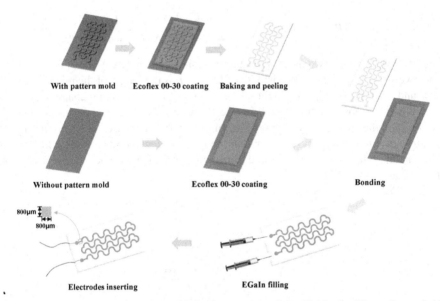

Fig. 2. Schematic illustration of the fabrication process of the highly flexible and stretchable sensor.

4   Results and discussion

We fabricated wave-shaped, triangle-shaped, and line-shaped strain sensors by injecting EGaIn into the Ecoflex microchannel. Figure 3 shows photographs of the three types of sensors at 0% and 150% strains, respectively.

The hysteresis of the strain sensor is a key feature, reflecting the degree of inconsistency in input-output characteristic curves during positive and negative movements of the sensor. The hysteresis can be calculated by the following Eq. (2).

$$\gamma_{max} = \frac{\Delta H_{max}}{Y_{FS}} \times 100\% \tag{2}$$

where ΔH_{max} is the maximum hysteresis difference of the sensor in the full-scale range, and Y_{FS} is the full-scale range of the sensor output. To characterize the hysteresis of the three types of strain sensors, they were stretched to 150% strain at the speed of 50mm/min and released back to the original state at the same speed. Figure 4(a), (b), and (c) show the experimental results of wave-shaped, triangle-shaped, and line-shaped strain sensors, respectively. As can be seen from the Fig. 4(a), (b), and (c), these sensors have extremely low hysteresis. The maximum hysteresis difference between loading

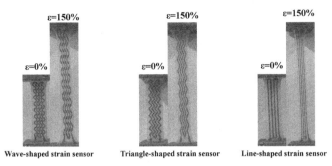

Fig. 3. Photographs of wave-shaped, triangle-shaped, and line-shaped strain sensors at 0% and 150% strains.

and unloading curves for the three types of sensors are 0.002, 0.0006, and 0.0044, respectively. The hysteresis of these sensors was calculated by Eq. (2). The results show that the triangle-shaped sensor exhibits negligible hysteresis of the value about 0.049%, while the line-shaped sensor exhibits the most obvious hysteresis of 1.406%, followed by the wavy microchannel sensor with the hysteresis of 0.141%. The hysteresis of the wave-shaped and triangle-shaped strain sensors is considerably lower than previous reports, e.g., Liu et al. [17] developed a strain sensor based on EGaIn and Ecoflex that exhibits 1.14% hysteresis at 178% strain. In addition, we conducted step-by-step tests, as shown in Fig. 4(d). Firstly, the sensors were stretched in six steps at a speed of 50 mm/min with the same strain applied during each step, until they reached 100% strain. And the sensors were held for 20 s after each stretching step. Then, they were released, the releasing procedure was the same as during the stretching. It can be seen from Fig. 4(d) that the relative resistance of line-shaped strain sensor has the maximum value at 100% strain, while the triangle-shaped strain sensor has the minimum value. The sensitivity of wavy-shaped, triangle-shaped, and line-shaped strain sensors are 0.95, 0.83, and 1.2, respectively, as calculated by following Eq. (3).

$$GF = \frac{\Delta R/R_0}{\varepsilon} \tag{3}$$

where R_0 is the initial resistance at 0% strain. ΔR_0 is the change of resistance when sensor is stretched. These results indicate that there was a compromise between sensitivity and hysteresis. The main reason is that the elongation ratio of the wavy-shaped and triangle-shaped microchannel is less than that of the line-shaped microchannel under the same strain.

In addition to hysteresis and sensitivity, we investigated other properties of these sensors. We measured the resistance changes of the three types of sensors at 30%, 60% and 90% strains, and repeated them five times at each strain, as shown in Fig. 5(a), (b), and (c). It can be seen that the relative resistance of the three sensors is periodic variations with strain cycling, and the peak of the relative resistance remains roughly constant in 5 cycles under each strain. The curves reveal that the sensors have excellent ability to respond to different strains.

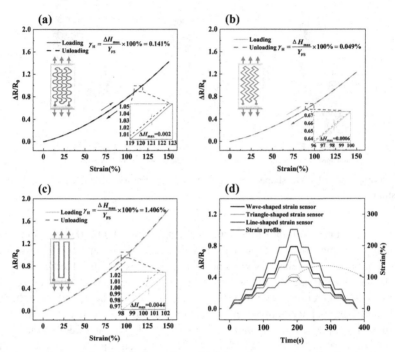

Fig. 4. Comparison of the electrical responses between the wave-shaped, triangle-shaped, and line-shaped strain sensors. (a) Hysteresis curve of the wave-shaped strain sensor. (b) Hysteresis curve of the triangle-shaped strain sensor. (d) Hysteresis curve of the line-shaped strain sensor. (d) Plot of the relative changes in the resistance of the wave-shaped, triangle-shaped, and line-shaped strain sensors under step-by-step tests.

Figure 5(d), (e), and (f) shows that the relative resistance changes of the three types of sensors were stretched to 50% strain and held for 10min, and then back to 0% strain. It can be seen that the resistance of the sensors gradually increases to the maximum value with the increase of strain, and the relative resistance of the three types of sensors remains stable with maintaining strain at 50%. When the sensors were released, the resistance of these sensors gradually returns to the original state with the decrease of the strain, indicating that the sensors have excellent stability.

The response time of sensor is also very important. To evaluate the response time of the three types of sensors, they were stretched to 2% strain at the speed of 500mm/min and maintained for 3s. Then they were released to the initial state at the same speed as the stretching speed, as shown in Fig. 5(g), (h), and (i). The result show that recovery time of wave-shaped, triangle-shaped, and line-shaped strain sensors are 184ms, 245ms, and 245ms, respectively, and their response time are all 184ms. These sensors exhibit faster response time and recovery time compared to previous reports, e.g., Soomro et al. [18] fabricated a strain sensor using composite of glycerol and potassium chloride and Ecoflex with a response time of 800ms and a recovery time of 900ms. The results indicate that these sensors have extremely fast response and recovery time. Which provides great potential for real-time monitoring of motion.

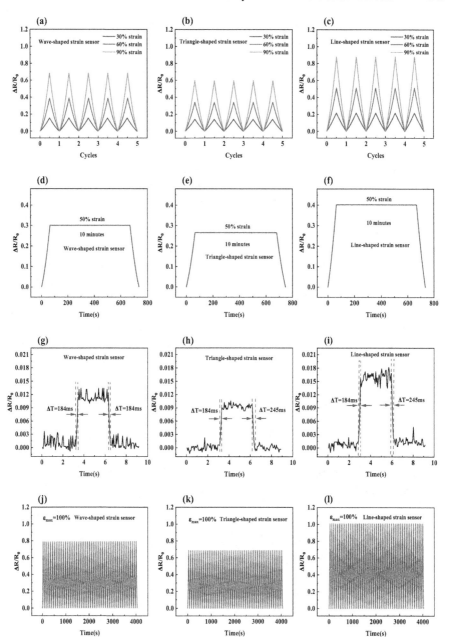

Fig. 5. The performance of the wave-shaped, triangle-shaped, and line-shaped strain sensors. (a, b, c) Dynamic responses of the three types of strain sensors to different strains (30%, 60% and 90%). (d, e, f) The three types of strain sensors response at 50% strain for 10 min. (g, h, i) The response time and recovery time of the three types of sensors. (j, k, l) the relative change in the resistance of the three types of strain sensors being subjected to 50 stretching/releasing cycles with up to 100% strain.

Figure 5(j), (k), and (l) show the repeatability of the three types of sensors. A total of 50 times of stretching and releasing cycles were applied to these strain sensors with a maximum strain of 100%. The initial value and peak value of the relative resistance of the three types of sensors have basically no change in 50 cycles, indicating that the sensors excellent stability and durability in continuous dynamic loading.

5 Applications

Due to the excellent properties of our sensors, we mounted the triangle-shaped strain sensor on the robot finger using tape to detect the bending motion of the robot finger, as shown in Fig. 6. We found that the sensor can accurately detect the bending motion of the robot finger at different angles. We conducted five bending-holding-straightening cycles at two different bending angles, respectively. In the initial state, the robot finger was in a straight position, and the resistance of the sensor maintained roughly constant. In the small-angle and large-angle bending cycles, the sensor exhibited clear periodic changes in resistance. The resistance rapidly increased with the joint bending, and returned to its original value when the joint was entirely relaxed. In addition, when the robot finger was held in a bent position, the resistance of the sensor also remained basically stable. On the other hand, we observed that the resistance variation amplitude was significantly greater in large-angle bending compared to small-angle bending. And the resistance peak value of the sensor remained remarkably close during five cycles of bending. These results indicate that the sensor has a strong potential for human-robot interaction.

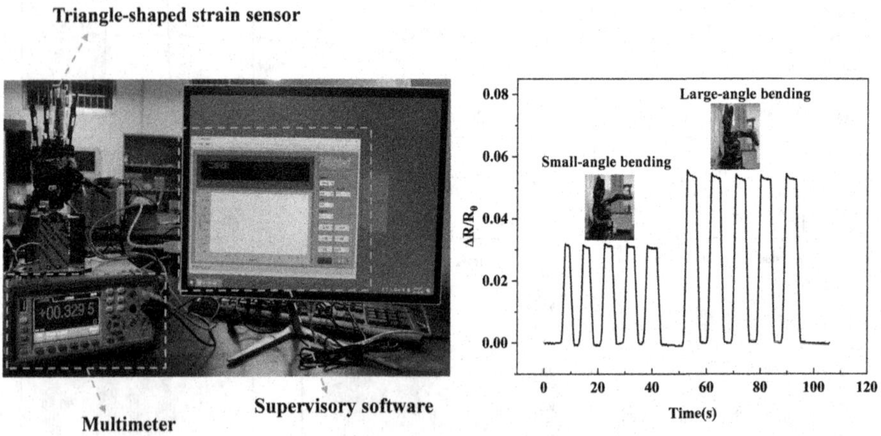

Fig. 6. Application of the triangle-shaped strain sensor on robot finger.

6 Conclusions

In this paper, we fabricated three types of flexible strain sensors: wavy-shaped, triangle-shaped, and line-shaped. Through a series of performance tests on these sensors, we found that all sensors have low hysteresis, long durability, fast response time (184ms), good static and dynamic performance, and the ability to withstand more than 150% strain. Moreover, we found that the triangle-shaped strain sensor has lower hysteresis (0.049%) than the wavy-shaped (0.146%) and triangle-shaped (1.406%) strain sensors. However, the line-shaped strain sensor has higher sensitivity (1.2) than the wavy-shaped (0.95) and triangle-shaped (0.83) strain sensors. Finally, we successfully utilized the triangle-shaped sensor to accurately detect the bending motion of the robot finger at different angles. In the future, we will investigate the causes for the different hysteresis performance of the three types of sensors and explore methods to improve their sensitivity. We will create more immersive human-robot interaction applications.

Acknowledgements. The authors thank the support from: (1) the Base and Talent Special Project of Guangxi Science and Technology Plan Project (Gui Ke AD23026285; (2) the Basic Ability Promotion Project for Yong Teachers in Guangxi (2023KY0013); (3) the Scientific Research Start-up Foundation of Guangxi University (A3010051026).

References

1. Shi, C., Zhao, Y., Zhu, P., Xiao, J., Nie, G.: Highly stretchable and rehealable wearable strain sensor based on dynamic covalent thermoset and liquid metal. Smart Mater. Struct. **30**, 105001 (2021)
2. Wang, S.L., Xu, X., Han, Z., Li, H., Wang, Q., Yao, B.: Highly stretchable liquid-metal based strain sensor with high sensitivity for human activity monitoring. Mater. Lett. **308**, 131277 (2022)
3. Yang, Z., et al.: Ultra-sensitive flexible sandwich structural strain sensors based on a silver nanowire supported PDMS/PVDF electrospun membrane substrate. J. Mater. Chem. C. **9**, 2752–2762 (2021)
4. Zhang, L., et al.: High performance flexible strain sensors based on silver nanowires/thermoplastic polyurethane composites for wearable devices. Appl. Compos. Mater. **29**, 1621–1636 (2022)
5. Bai, D., Liu, F., Xie, D., Lv, F., Shen, L., Tian, Z.: 3D printing of flexible strain sensor based on MWCNTs/flexible resin composite. Nanotechnology **34**, 045701 (2023)
6. Chen, J., Zhu, Y., Jiang, W.: A stretchable and transparent strain sensor based on sandwich-like PDMS/CNTs/PDMS composite containing an ultrathin conductive CNT layer. Compos. Sci. Technol. **186**, 107938 (2020)
7. Li, T., et al.: A flexible strain sensor based on CNTs/PDMS microspheres for human motion detection. Sens. Actuators, A **306**, 111959 (2020)
8. Dong, T., Gu, Y., Liu, T., Pecht, M.: Resistive and capacitive strain sensors based on customized compliant electrode: comparison and their wearable applications. Sens. Actuators, A **326**, 112720 (2021)
9. Hu, M., et al.: High-performance strain sensors based on bilayer carbon black/PDMS hybrids. Adv. Composites Hybrid Materials **4**(3), 514–520 (2021). https://doi.org/10.1007/s42114-021-00226-z
10. Lian, H., et al.: Three-dimensional printed carbon Black/PDMS composite flexible strain sensor for human motion monitoring. Micromachines. **13**, 1247 (2022)
11. Del Bosque, A., Sánchez-Romate, X.F., Gómez, A., Sánchez, M., Ureña, A.: Highly stretchable strain sensors based on graphene nanoplatelet-doped ecoflex for biomedical purposes. Sens. Actuators, A **353**, 114249 (2023)

12. Zhang, X.M., Yang, X.L., Wang, K.Y.: Conductive graphene/polydimethylsiloxane nanocomposites for flexible strain sensors. J. Mater. Sci. Mater. Electron. **30**(21), 19319–19324 (2019). https://doi.org/10.1007/s10854-019-02292-y

13. Wang, Y., Gong, S., Wang, S.J., Simon, G.P., Cheng, W.: Volume-invariant ionic liquid microbands as highly durable wearable biomedical sensors. Mater. Horiz. **3**, 208–213 (2016)

14. Choi, D.Y., et al.: Highly stretchable, hysteresis-free ionic liquid-based strain sensor for precise human motion monitoring. ACS Appl. Mater. Interfaces **9**, 1770–1780 (2017)

15. Kim, S., et al.: Stretchable and wearable polymeric heaters and strain sensors fabricated using liquid metals. Sens. Actuators, A **355**, 114317 (2023)

16. Kim, S., Yoo, B., Miller, M., Bowen, D., Pines, D.J., Daniels, K.M.: EGaIn-Silicone-based highly stretchable and flexible strain sensor for real-time two joint robotic motion monitoring. Sens. Actuators, A **342**, 113659 (2022)

17. Liu, J., Lei, B., Jiang, W., Han, J., Zhang, H., Liu, H.: A novel intrinsically strain sensor for large strain detection. Sens. Actuators, A **332**, 113081 (2021)

18. Soomro, A.M., Khalid, M.A.U., Shah, I., Kim, S. wan, Kim, Y.S., Choi, K.H.: Highly stable soft strain sensor based on Gly-KCl filled sinusoidal fluidic channel for wearable and waterproof robotic applications. Smart Mater. Struct. **29**, 025011 (2020)

19. Wu, Y., et al.: Liquid metal fiber composed of a tubular channel as a high-performance strain sensor. J. Mater. Chem. C. **5**, 12483–12491 (2017)

20. Yoon, S.G., Koo, H.-J., Chang, S.T.: Highly Stretchable and Transparent Microfluidic Strain Sensors for Monitoring Human Body Motions. ACS Appl. Mater. Interfaces **7**, 27562–27570 (2015)

21. Zhang, H., Lowe, A., Kalra, A., Yu, Y.: A flexible strain sensor based on embedded ionic liquid. Sensors **21**, 5760 (2021)

22. Zhang, Q., et al.: Highly stretchable and sensitive strain sensor based on liquid metal composite for wearable sign language communication device. Smart Mater. Struct. **30**, 115005 (2021)

23. Zhou, Y., et al.: Asymmetric structure based flexible strain sensor for simultaneous detection of various human joint motions. ACS Appl. Electron. Mater. **1**, 1866–1872 (2019)

A Clinic-Oriented Ground Reaction Force Prediction Method in Gait

Xiangzhi Liu[1], Zexia He[1], Meimei Han[3], Ningtao Cheng[2], and Tao Liu[1(✉)]

[1] School of Mechanical Engineering, Zhejiang University,
Hangzhou 310058, Zhejiang, China
liutao@zju.edu.cn
[2] School of Medicine, Zhejiang University, Hangzhou 310058, Zhejiang, China
[3] Zhejiang FuZhi Technology and Innovation Co., Ltd.,
Hangzhou 310058, Zhejiang, China

Abstract. Gait is a feature set to describe the human walking state, so it is one of the important methods for doctors to diagnose, evaluate, and judge the rehabilitation process of patients with neurological diseases in clinic. However, at present, doctors often rely on scales to evaluate patients' gait performance, which are often biased by patients' self-perception and doctors' subjective experience. With the development of MEMS technology, wearable sensors have gradually been applied in clinic practice, but most of wearable sensors in clinic are still limited to the acquisition of kinematics data, and seldom involves dynamic evaluation, which makes the lack of multifaceted evaluation. In view of the above problems, the method proposed in this paper realizes ground reaction force prediction by simplifying the human dynamics walking model and multiple nonlinear regression model based on inertial measurement units (IMUs) attached on shanks. The proposed method has been verified on 6 healthy subjects and 8 stroke patients, and the mean accuracy for all subjects is controlled within 7.4%, which has good clinical application value.

Keywords: Clinical application · Gait Analysis · Ground Force Prediction · IMU-Based Analysis

1 Introduction

Gait is a characteristic description of a person's characteristic way of walking. Many neurological diseases often lead to a deterioration in human motor control

Supported in part by the NSFC Grant No. 52175033 and No. U21A20120, in part by the Key Research and Development Program of Zhejiang under awards 2023C03196, 2022C03103, and 2021C03051, and in part by Zhejiang Provincial Natural Science Foundation of China under Grant LZ20E050002.
This study was approved by the Medical Ethics Committee of School of Biomedical Engineering and Instrument Science, Zhejiang University(Project identification code:2021-39).

ability, manifested as abnormal gait during exercise [1]. Stroke patients [2] often exhibit a hemiplegic gait, showing significantly weaker motor control of the hemiplegic side than the healthy side. Therefore, the range of motion and speed of the limbs on the hemiplegic side are significantly lower than those on the healthy side, and there is additional lateral displacement on the hemiplegic side. Parkinson's patients [3] often show freezing gait and flustered gait, that is, difficulty starting, flustering steps, and difficulty stopping. Therefore, gait analysis is often used by doctors to evaluate the condition of patients with neurological diseases. As early as 1991, Ewa et al. [4] evaluated 50 patients with acute stroke through Scandinavian Neurological Stroke Scale, and verified the high reliability of gait analysis in the classification and long-term monitoring of stroke patients. Yi et al. [5] combined the UPDRS (Unified Parkinson's Disease Rating Scale) and gait movement data to quantitatively evaluate the gait performance of Parkinson's patients, and realized the automatic scoring of Parkinson's patients through a nonlinear regression model.

With the development of MEMS technology and data processing algorithms, gait analysis systems based on wearable sensors are becoming more and more common, such as smart wearable bracelets and watches [6], which have been widely used in daily motion detection. Moreover, with more quantitative and objective than traditional scale evaluation method, the clinical application of wearable systems is gradually accepted by the doctors. Xiangzhi et al. [7] realized the prediction of the posture angle of the thigh through the data of the shank IMUs and established a comprehensive evaluation system for the lower limb gait, which is used to compare the gait difference of stroke patients and healthy subjects. Martina et al. [8] designed a wearable system consisting of three inertial sensors that can be used for monitoring the freezing of gait (FoG) in the daily life of Parkinson's patients, and conducted experiments on 48 Parkinson's patients for up to seven days. The experimental results show that the daily monitoring results are consistent with the clinical scores and have future application prospects.

At present, the gait analysis used in clinic is more limited to the kinematics analysis, and the research on the dynamics analysis is still relatively rare. In fact, the gait abnormalities caused by many neurological diseases have a more direct relationship with the ground reaction force. For example, the mean value of the second peak of the vertical ground reaction force is significantly decreased due to the decreased performance of the ankle plantar flexors in patients with Parkinson's disease [9]. Therefore, some scholars also analyze the gait dynamics of patients with neurological diseases. Veeraragavan et al. [10] used vertical ground reaction force (VGRF) to diagnose and assess the severity of early and intermediate PD. Gait features extracted and selected from VGRF are used as training features for an artificial neural network (ANN) model, which achieves up to 97.4% PD diagnostic accuracy. Su et al. [11] decomposed the ground reaction force into components of different frequencies through wavelet transform to form a frequency feature set of ground reaction force. And the correlation between the force components with the same frequency of different limbs is used to characterize the gait symmetry of Parkinson's patients. The results show that the proposed gait symmetry evaluation method can effectively distinguish the difference between Parkinson's disease patients and healthy subjects.

However, the commonly used gait dynamics analysis system is limited to force-measuring shoes and force-measuring insoles, which are expensive and heavy, especially for patients with weak motor ability, Therefore, the movement interference from sensors is large, which will inevitably distort the patient's natural gait. Aimed at this problem, many scholars have begun to combine human dynamics models with deep learning methods to indirectly measure ground reaction force, which not only realizes the analysis of human gait dynamics but also meets the requirements of light wear and small movement interference. Hossain et al. [12] designed a prediction method for unilateral hip, knee, and ankle joint moments and three-dimensional ground reaction forces based on three IMU motion data worn on the thigh, shank, and foot. And the method is applied to the dynamic estimation of daily activities such as running on a treadmill, walking on flat ground, and climbing stairs. The results demonstrate the possibility of indirect measurement of ground reaction force, replacing traditional laboratory-based measurements. Shahabpoor et al. [13] proposed a vertical ground reaction force prediction method using only one IMU, and verified that the 7th cervical vertebrae is one of the best locations for the sensor. Applies the method to indoor and outdoor ground reaction force prediction, with a 4–8% peak-to-peak normalized root mean square error (RMSE).

In view of the current indirect measurement of ground reaction force mostly for healthy subjects, this paper proposes a clinically oriented IMU-based ground reaction force prediction method. The method only needs two IMUs placed on the shank, with the force excitation model, motion feature extraction, and force calculation model. The method was validated on 6 healthy subjects and 8 stroke patients, with the mean accuracy less than 7.4%.

2   Materials and Methods

2.1   Overview of Experiments

As shown in Table 1, a total of 6 healthy subjects and 8 stroke patients were recruited to participate in the gait experiment. In order to ensure the safety of the experiment and the accuracy of ground reaction force measurements, all subjects were required wo walk independent without additional walking aids. Each subject was asked to walk in a straight line (along the landmark line) for 10m, back and forth three times. Stay still for 5 s before starting and after stopping each time as static correction data, which is used to correct the error caused by the IMU wearing offset.

The experimental data acquisition system consists of kinematics acquisition equipment and force acquisition equipment. The kinematics collection device is Fuzhi^{TM}-gait, which collects three-axis acceleration, three-axis angular velocity, and three-axis magnetometer data in real time. The maximum acquisition frequency of the IMU is as high as 100 Hz. In order to minimize the impact of the

Table 1. Subjects' information.

Subjects	Age	Height	Weight
Patients	65 ± 12	1.67 ± 0.11	64 ± 6
Healthy Subjects	24 ± 6	1.71 ± 0.03	67 ± 3

external magnetic field on the IMU data acquisition, we chose the experimental environment in the rehabilitation corridor of the hospital, which is very open around and there are no other electrical equipment. The ground reaction force collection device mainly uses the force-sensing shoes, consisting of two commercial SRI force sensors (M3705C, Sunrise Instruments, Inc., Shanghai, China) for each shoes, and also applied in other researches [14–16]. The force-sensing shoe consists of two force sensors placed on the toe and sole respectively, which can collect three-dimensional force and three-dimensional moment in real time.

As shown in Fig. 1, motion data collected directly on the shank was used for gait event detection and raw data segmentation (also used in [17,18]). Then, according to the gait cycle, with the input of shank motion data, the thigh prediction model, which is developed in past research [7], can output the thigh posture data with an average error of less than 5°. The directly measured shank kinematics data and estimated thigh posture data are input into the force incentive model, which can provide incentive force and will be expanded in detail in next section. The shank, thigh kinematics data and incentive force will be input to gait feature selection and used for force calculation model. The calculated ground reaction force is compared with that directly measured by the force sensor, and the root mean square error (RMSE), percent Error (RMSE divided by Gravity), and R-value (linear correlation coefficient between predicted and measured ground reaction forces) is calculated as an indicator of the accuracy of the prediction system.

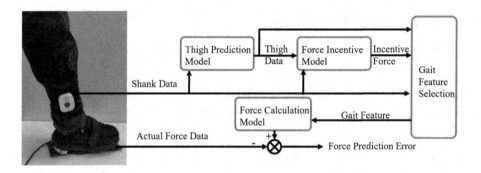

Fig. 1. Experimental block diagram.

2.2   Force Incentive Model

As shown in Fig. 2, a complete gait cycle can be divided into single stance phase and double stance phase. In the single stance phase, only one side of the limb is in contact with the ground, while the other side is off the ground, so the ground reaction force on one side often reaches its peak, while the ground reaction force on the other side is zero. The double stance phase is much more complicated than the single stance stage. At this time, both limbs are in contact with the ground, and the ground reaction force of one limb will gradually decrease, and the ground reaction force will be transferred to the other limb. Due to the different states of the limbs on both sides in single stance phase and double stance phase, this also leads to the difference in the calculation method of the ground reaction force in the two states.

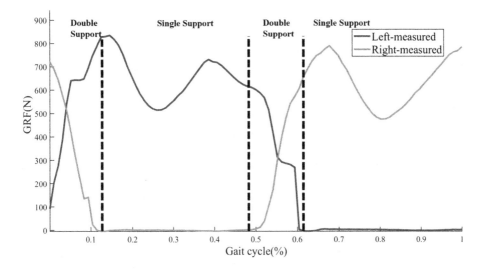

Fig. 2. Time division of ground reaction force within a single gait cycle.

We used human anatomy data from previous studies [19] to indirectly calculate the mass, length, and center of each limb mass from the subject's height and mass. In order to reduce the cost of kinematic calculations, we simplified the human body into a skeleton model with four limbs and three rotating joints. The mass of the shanks in the model is the sum of the actual human shanks and foot. The mass of the upper body is concentrated in the human hip joint.

For the single stance phase, only one side of the limb touches the ground at this time. We can calculate directly by Eq. (1).

$$F_y = M * a_y = \begin{bmatrix} m_{shank} & m_{shank} & m_{thigh} & m_{thigh} & m_{upper} \end{bmatrix} \begin{bmatrix} a_{y\_left\_shank} \\ a_{y\_right\_shank} \\ a_{y\_left\_thigh} \\ a_{y\_right\_thigh} \\ a_{y\_upper} \end{bmatrix} \quad (1)$$

where F_x is the component of the ground reaction force in the horizontal direction (friction force) and F_y is the vertical component, which we pay attention to. M_{xy} is the torque exerted by the ground on the human body in gait. M is the mass matrix, which is the mass of each limb of the simplified walking model. a_y is the acceleration of each limb in the vertical direction, which can be calculated from the directly obtained shank acceleration and the indirect obtained thigh attitude angle, shank length, and thigh length. F_x and M_{xy} can be directly calculated using the moments of inertia for each limb, angular acceleration, and horizontal acceleration, but are not the focus of our study.

For the double stance phase, since both limbs touch the ground at the same time, the distribution of ground reaction force on both limbs cannot be directly calculated from kinematic data. We designed a multiple nonlinear regression model, by inputting the ground reaction force data of healthy subjects (because the ground reaction force of healthy subjects is more regular than that of patients, it is beneficial to regress the ideal model), and directly regress each parameter of the model. By Eq. (2), we can calculate the real-time input signal x of the regression model.

$$x = \sqrt{L_{thigh}^2 + L_{shank}^2 + 2L_{thigh}L_{shank}\cos(\theta_{thigh} - \theta_{shank})} \quad (2)$$

where L_{thigh} and L_{shank} are the thigh and shank lengths of the human body, respectively. θ_{thigh} and θ_{shank} are the posture angles (angles with vertical) of the thigh and shank.

$$F_{y\_left} = F_{y\_mean} * norm(\alpha_1 x(\alpha_2 - \frac{\alpha_3}{1 + e^{-\alpha_4 \dot{x}}}) + \alpha_5 \max(0.2, x) + \alpha_6 \sin(c)) \quad (3)$$

where F_{y_left} is the ground reaction force of the left leg during the double stance phase. Similarly, the ground reaction force of the right leg can be calculated using the same regression method. F_{y_mean} is the mean value of ground reaction force during a single stance period. $norm()$ is a normalization function, which limits the value range from 0 to 1. α_i is a series of undetermined parameters of the regression model, which need to be calculated by regression method. $sin(c)$ is a fixed sine function and c is the ratio of the current gait item to the gait cycle, the purpose is to smooth the change curve of the double stance period.

2.3   Feature Selection and Force Calculation Model

The above-mentioned force incentive model has achieved a technological breakthrough from kinematics acquisition to dynamics estimation through the dual-track calculation method of Newtonian mechanics and regression model. However, the force incentive model is based on the actual measured ground reaction force of healthy subjects, which is poorly adaptable to the abnormal gait of the patient. This situation has also been mentioned in previous studies [20,21]. Therefore, in order to expand the scope of application, we designed a force calculation model to compensate for the pathological gait neglected in the force incentive model. The force calculation model is shown in Eq. (4).

$$F_{prediciton\_left} = \beta_1 F_{y\_left} + (1 - \beta_1)(e^{-\frac{F_{y\_left}}{\beta_2}} - 1) + 0.1\cos(\beta_3 + c) \qquad (4)$$

where $F_{prediction\_left}$ is the final left limb estimated ground reaction force, $beta_i$ is the undetermined coefficient of the force calculation model, and their calculation methods will be expanded in detail later.

In Eq. (4), the left half reflects the weight of the normal gait. When β_1 is equal to 1, the calculation model and the force excitation model are basically the same. The right half reflects the weight of the subject's abnormal gait. Through the change of β_2, it can simulate the lagging and leading situations of the ground reaction force change in the abnormal gait. Regarding the calculation of β_i, we designed a cubic support vector machine regression method and used cross-validation to prevent the model from overfitting. In order to improve the regression accuracy of the model, we perform feature calculation and selection on the shank motion data, thigh motion data, and incentive force. Combined with the external performance of the actual pathological gait and normal gait, we selected the motion range of thigh, the motion range of shank, the difference between the incentive force and the *sin* function, the abnormally number of the high change rate and the low change rate of incentive force, stride length, double stance period duration, and gait cycle as model feature.

3   Results

In order to show the difference in ground reaction force changes between healthy subjects and patients more specifically, we selected the actual measured force and estimated force of a healthy subject (subject3) and a patient (subject10) in a complete gait cycle.

As shown in Fig. 3, the upper part shows the ground reaction force prediction results of healthy subject, and the lower part shows the ground reaction force prediction results of pathological gait. The solid blue and red lines are the predicted forces of the left and right limb, respectively, and the dotted blue and red lines are the directly measured forces of the left and right limb, respectively. The gait cycle begins with the last left heel strike and ends with the current left heel strike.

As shown in Fig. 4, we take the actual measured force as the abscissa value, and the predicted force as the ordinate value. Ideally, the predicted force is exactly the same as the actual measured force. At this time, the force coordinates

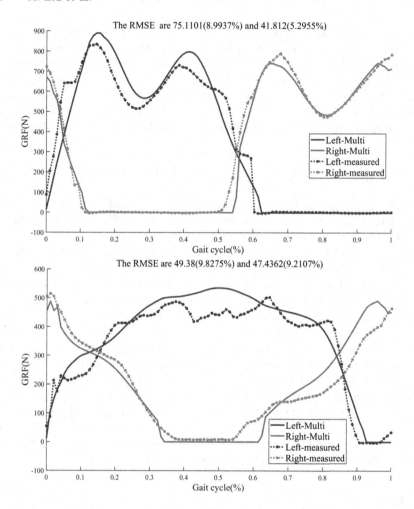

Fig. 3. Prediction of ground reaction force in healthy subjects and patients.

of different gait items should be distributed on the straight line $y = x$ (drawn in black). The farther the coordinate is from the black line, the larger the prediction deviation of the gait item is.

In the Table 2, we list ground reaction force predictions for all subjects and present them in terms of RMSE and R-value. In order to better compare the error between subjects of different weights, we also calculated the relative error of the ground reaction force, which is to divide the RMSE by the gravity of the subject and the mean accuracy for all subjects is controlled within 7.4%, which has good clinical application value.

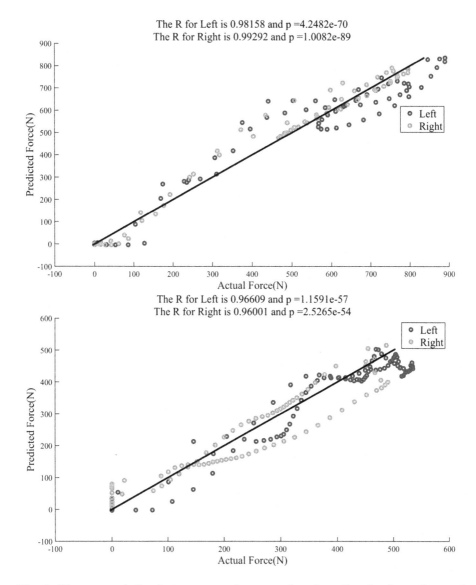

Fig. 4. Linear correlation between actual measured and predicted values of ground reaction force.

4   Discussion

As shown in Fig. 3 and Fig. 4, the ground reaction force of healthy subjects have obvious characteristics, and the force of the left and right limbs has two peaks. And because healthy subjects walk coherently and have strong limb support, the single stance period is longer than the double stance period. The change curves of left and right limbs are similar, and the symmetry is great. Pathological gait is

Table 2. The ground reaction force prediction results of all subjects.

Subjects	RMSE (%) for left	RMSE (%) for right	R for left	R for right
Subject1	35.2 (6.4%)	31.2 (5.8%)	0.99	0.99
Subject2	80.2 (9.3%)	41.9 (5.8%)	0.98	0.99
Subject3	65.0 (7.8%)	38.3 (4.8%)	0.98	0.99
Subject4	57.3 (9.4%)	38.9 (6.4%)	0.98	0.99
Subject5	43.6 (9.3%)	40.9 (8.7%)	0.98	0.98
Subject6	43.1 (7.0%)	47.7 (7.7%)	0.99	0.99
Subject7	74.7 (8.1%)	99.5 (10.7%)	0.98	0.97
Subject8	54.7 (8.7%)	43.9 (6.9%)	0.98	0.98
Subject9	33.4 (4.8%)	67.4 (8.5%)	0.99	0.98
Subject10	49.4 (9.8%)	47.4 (9.2%)	0.97	0.96
Subject11	58.0 (8.3%)	42.2 (5.9%)	0.99	0.99
Subject12	28.6 (5.8%)	32.5 (6.9%)	0.99	0.99
Subject13	35.9 (6.7%)	32.7 (5.9%)	0.98	0.99
Subject14	62.6 (6.7%)	51.0 (5.0%)	0.98	0.99

much more complicated than that of healthy subjects, with poor regularity and even no double-peak curve of normal gait. Because stroke patients often have a hemiplegic gait, that is, the motor control ability of one side is much weaker than that of the other side, so the variation of force for both sides is large and the symmetry is poor. In addition, due to the poor walking balance of stroke patients, it is often difficult to maintain a single stance period for a long time, so the time of the double stance period is much longer.

As shown in the Table 2, the proposed method is robust to both healthy subjects and stroke patients. This has a relatively objective application value for actual clinical scenarios. First of all, this system is only composed of two IMUs placed on the shank. It is easy to wear, light in weight, small in size, and will not interfere with the patient's natural gait. Secondly, the accuracy of this method can be controlled within 10% even for pathological gaits with poor regularity, which has high scientific research value and can aids physicians in dynamic assessment of patient gait. Finally, this method only needs the motion data of the last complete gait cycle to predict the force, which has strong real-time performance and can be used in combination with actual rehabilitation walking aids.

This method also has the following deficiencies. First of all, the sample size of this method is not rich enough for the clinical point of view (although compared with previous studies, the number of subjects is quite considerable), whether the method can be fully adapted to each patient remains to be verified. Second, common neurological diseases include not only stroke, but also other diseases such as Parkinson's disease. However, this method has only been verified on stroke patients so far, and its adaptability to other diseases needs further verification. Finally, the healthy subjects recruited in this experiment were too young, and age is also an important factor affecting gait, which will also have an additional impact on the results of force comparisons between healthy subjects and patients.

References

1. Perry, J., Davids, J.R., et al.: Gait analysis: normal and pathological function. J. Pediatr. Orthop. **12**(6), 815 (1992)
2. Richards, C.L., Malouin, F., Dean, C.: Gait in stroke: assessment and rehabilitation. Clin. Geriatr. Med. **15**(4), 833–856 (1999)
3. Morris, M.E., Huxham, F., McGinley, J., Dodd, K., Iansek, R.: The biomechanics and motor control of gait in Parkinson disease. Clin. Biomech. **16**(6), 459–470 (2001)
4. Lindenstrøm, E., Boysen, G., Waage Christiansen, L., Würtzen Nielsen, P., et al.: Reliability of Scandinavian neurological stroke scale. Cerebrovasc. Dis. **1**(2), 103–107 (1991)
5. Han, Y., et al.: Automatic assessments of Parkinsonian gait with wearable sensors for human assistive systems. Sensors **23**(4), 2104 (2023)
6. Xu, W., Shen, Y., Zhang, Y., Bergmann, N., Hu, W.: Gait-watch: a context-aware authentication system for smart watch based on gait recognition, pp. 59–70 (2017)
7. Liu, X., Zhou, B., Zhang, B., Liu, T.: A potential-real-time thigh orientation prediction method based on two shanks-mounted IMUs and its clinical application. IEEE Trans. Autom. Sci. Eng. (2022)
8. Mancini, M., et al.: Measuring freezing of gait during daily-life: an open-source, wearable sensors approach. J. Neuroeng. Rehabil. **18**, 1–13 (2021)
9. Sharifmoradi, K., Farahpour, N.: An assessment of gait spatiotemporal and GRF of Parkinson patients. Health Reh **1**(1), 1–6 (2016)
10. Veeraragavan, S., Gopalai, A.A., Gouwanda, D., Ahmad, S.A.: Parkinson's disease diagnosis and severity assessment using ground reaction forces and neural networks. Front. Physiol. **11**, 587057 (2020)
11. Su, B., Song, R., Guo, L., Yen, C.-W.: Characterizing gait asymmetry via frequency sub-band components of the ground reaction force. Biomed. Signal Process. Control **18**, 56–60 (2015)
12. Hossain, M.S.B., Guo, Z., Choi, H.: Estimation of lower extremity joint moments and 3D ground reaction forces using IMU sensors in multiple walking conditions: A deep learning approach. IEEE J. Biomed. Health Inform. (2023)
13. Shahabpoor, E., Pavic, A.: Estimation of vertical walking ground reaction force in real-life environments using single IMU sensor. J. Biomech. **79**, 181–190 (2018)
14. Li, T., Chen, F., Zhao, Z., Pei, Q., Tan, Y., Zhou, Z.: Hybrid data-driven optimization design of a layered six-dimensional FBG force/moment sensor with gravity self-compensation for orthopedic surgery robot. IEEE Trans. Industr. Electron. (2022)
15. Azocar, A.F., Mooney, L.M., Hargrove, L.J., Rouse, E.J.: Design and characterization of an open-source robotic leg prosthesis, pp. 111–118 (2018)
16. Gabert, L., Lenzi, T.: Instrumented pyramid adapter for amputee gait analysis and powered prosthesis control. IEEE Sens. J. **19**(18), 8272–8282 (2019)

17. Wang, L., Sun, Y., Li, Q., Liu, T., Yi, J.: IMU-based gait normalcy index calculation for clinical evaluation of impaired gait. IEEE J. Biomed. Health Inform. **25**(1), 3–12 (2020)
18. Wang, L., Sun, Y., Li, Q., Liu, T., Yi, J.: Two shank-mounted IMUs-based gait analysis and classification for neurological disease patients. IEEE Robot. Autom. Lett. **5**(2), 1970–1976 (2020)
19. De Leva, P.: Adjustments to Zatsiorsky-Seluyanov's segment inertia parameters. J. Biomech. **29**(9), 1223–1230 (1996)
20. Karatsidis, A., Bellusci, G., Schepers, H.M., De Zee, M., Andersen, M.S., Veltink, P.H.: Estimation of ground reaction forces and moments during gait using only inertial motion capture. Sensors **17**(1), 75 (2016)
21. Shahabpoor, E., Pavic, A., Brownjohn, J.M., Billings, S.A., Guo, L.-Z., Bocian, M.: Real-life measurement of tri-axial walking ground reaction forces using optimal network of wearable inertial measurement units. IEEE Trans. Neural Syst. Rehabil. Eng. **26**(6), 1243–1253 (2018)

Development of a Novel Plantar Pressure Insole and Inertial Sensor System for Daily Activity Classification and Fall Detection

Bingfei Fan[1,2], Fugang Yi[1,2], Shuo Yang[1,2], Mingyu Du[1,2], and Shibo Cai[1,2(✉)]

[1] The Key Laboratory of Special Purpose Equipment and Advanced Processing Technology, Ministry of Education and Zhejiang Province, Hangzhou, China
ccc@zjut.edu.cn
[2] College of Mechanical Engineering, Zhejiang University of Technology, Hangzhou 310014, China

Abstract. Quantifying human daily activities can provide relevant monitoring information about physical activities and fall risk, and wearable sensors are promising devices for activity monitoring in daily life scenarios. This paper designed a novel plantar pressure insole and inertial sensor system and presented classification algorithms for activity classification and fall detection. We designed each plantar pressure insole with eight thin uniaxial load cells placed in the key area of a foot. Twenty healthy young adults performed selected activities in the laboratory while wearing the plantar pressure shoes and six inertial measurement units (IMUs) on their feet, shanks, and thighs of both sides. We adopted the convolutional neural network (CNN), ensemble learning, and support vector machine (SVM) methods for activity classification, and the input data were inertial data, pressure data, and both data. We adopted CNN, RNN (recurrent neural network), LSTM (long short-term memory), and CNN-LSTM method for fall detection, and compared results before and after the Dempster-Shafer evidence theory. Results show that for activity classification, CNN with both inertial and plantar pressure data got the best accuracy of 97.1%. For fall detection, the accuracy of RNN, CNN, LSTM, and CNN-LSTM were 93.77%, 95.85%, 96.16%, and 97.76%, respectively. LSTM got comparable accuracy as CNN-LSTM but with much less latency. The presented wearable system and algorithms show good feasibility in activity classification and fall detection, which could serve as a foundation for physical activity monitoring and fall alert systems for elderly people.

Keywords: Inertial Sensor · Pressure insole · Daily activity classification · Fall Detection · Machine learning

1 Introduction

Daily physical activities, such as standing, walking, sitting, squatting, etc., are the cornerstones of a healthy life. Keeping appropriate activities in daily life is associated with numerous health benefits for both women and men [1, 2]. Quantifying human physical

© The Author(s), under exclusive license to Springer Nature Singapore Pte Ltd. 2023
H. Yang et al. (Eds.): ICIRA 2023, LNAI 14268, pp. 265–278, 2023.
https://doi.org/10.1007/978-981-99-6486-4_23

activities provide objective indications for patients' or elderly's condition monitoring [3]. Besides, fall is one of the most dangerous physical activities in daily life. Detecting falls can send emergency alerts for immediate help in time, and thus can avoid secondary injury [4, 5]. Consequently, physical activity classification and fall detection are significant for health monitoring and fall alerting for elderly people.

Wearable sensing technology is becoming increasingly popular in activity classifications [6, 7]. For their advantage of small size, lightweight, easy to wear, and available in daily life scenarios. Among wearable devices, the inertial sensor (IMU) is a frequently used motion analysis device [8]. It includes an accelerometer, a gyroscope, and a magnetometer, which can directly measure the acceleration and angular velocity and can also obtain the IMU orientation through a sensor fusion algorithm [9, 10]. However, inertial sensors can only measure the kinematic information. Kinetics, including ground reaction force, and center of pressure also provides useful information for activity classification [11, 12]. Force sensor is required for kinetics analysis. Flexible force-sensing resistor (FSR) is a commonly used sensing unit for plantar pressure collecting [13, 14]. However, FSRs exhibit a non-linearity, lower accuracy, and less durable compared to load cells [15, 16]. Another alternative force sensor is a miniature six-dimensional force sensor. Liu Tao et al. [17]designed a wearable force-sensing shoe for gait kinetics analysis by adding a six-dimensional force sensor to the sole to estimate the center of pressure and ground reaction force during walking. However, introducing two force sensors outside the shoe affected the comfort, and also increase the cost. Hence, an insole with an accurate, durable, linearity force sensing unit is still desired. Additionally, previous studies have shown that combination of inertial sensors and foot planter sensors is promising in measuring both kinematic and kinetics for human movement analysis [18], including daily activities classification and fall detection.

To identify various activities based on measured inertial and foot pressure data, a classification algorithm is required. Recently, the machine learning model has been widely used in human movement analysis. Zexia He et al. [13] proposed deep-recurrent neural networks (RNNs) for real-time intended knee joint motion prediction. Tian Tan et al. [19] proposed a subject-independent CNN model with a single shank-worn IMU data for vertical average loading rate estimation. Lei Wang et al. developed an SVM-based classifier to classify the four types of gait patterns for neurological disease patients [20]. Compared with traditional rule-based classification [3, 6]. Machine learning approaches can learn from the data and do not rely on complex rules. Previous studies show machine learning models have promising results in classification. For a newly developed system, a proper machine-learning model is in demand.

The purpose of this paper is to design a wearable sensing system, including a novel durable sensing pressure insole, and inertial sensors, and then to establish a machine learning model to classifier daily activities and detect fall events. We hypothesized that the developed system and established algorithms can classify activities of daily living (ADLs) and fall events in daily life scenarios.

2   Wearable Sensor System Design

2.1   Plantar Pressure Sensor Design

To increase the durability of the pressure insole, we selected a mini uniaxial load cell as the basic sensor unit (Model 1059, Arizon Technology, Chang Zhou, China). Its size is 15 mm × 9 mm. The full-scale range is 200 N and the voltage is 5 V. Each sensor can only sense a small area. Thus, multiple sensors are required to sense the foot plantar pressure. The sensor unit should be placed in an area where the pressure change during walking is obvious and easy to measure. We placed 8 sensor units according to the heat map of foot pressure distribution of the right foot during normal walking [21]. Specifically, we placed 8 sensor units at the first phalanx, the fifth metatarsal, the third metatarsal, the first metatarsal, outside of midfoot, inside of midfoot, inside of the heel, and back of the heel (Fig. 1a).

To make a suitable insole to hold and fix eight sensor units, we first made an insole mold through 3D printing with resin material. The hole for placing the sensor was a through-hole, which can better measure the pressure of the foot. Then, a soft silicone insole was manufactured using Ecoflex silicone (Smooth-On, USA), and the sensor unit was secured in the hole of the silicone insole and was kept vertical to the ground. Thus, obtaining a soft and deformable multi-point foot pressure insole (Fig. 1b).

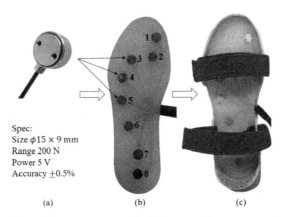

Spec:
Size φ15 × 9 mm
Range 200 N
Power 5 V
Accuracy ±0.5%

(a)   (b)   (c)

Fig. 1. The designed wearable sensor system, including two plantar pressure insoles in two customized shoes. (a) Load cell. (b) Pressure insole, each insole contains 8 load cells. (c) Sensing shoe

We also designed a shoe and made it through polyurethane 3D printing (Fig. 1c), thus, the designed insole can be fixed in the shoe without slippage. The polyurethane material has the advantages of being light-weight, having good abrasion resistance, and comfort. In addition, to enhance the bending performance and decrease the weight of the sole during walking, hollow processing was also performed between the midsole and the outsole. Finally, we designed a data collecting unit with MCU (STM32F103) and AD converter (CS5530) to collect and process the pressure data. The sampling rate was set as 50 Hz.

2.2 Inertial Sensing and System Integration

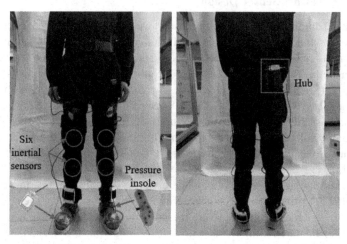

Fig. 2. The overview of the designed wearable sensor system integrated foot plantar pressure sensor and inertial sensors

The inertial sensor is a highly modularized sensor that can be easily integrated into a wearable system. Six inertial sensors (HWT901B-CAN, wit-motion Intelligent Technology, Shenzhen, China) were used to collect the inertial data of the lower limb. Each IMU consists of a tri-axis accelerometer, gyroscope, and magnetometer. The sampling rate was 100 Hz. Six IMUs were placed on the foot instep, shank, and thigh of both sides. A hub was designed to connect all the IMUs through the CAN bus. The hub was also connected to plantar pressure sensors. Thus, both IMU and plantar pressure sensors were integrated into one system (Fig. 2). The hub will record all inertial data and plantar pressure data into SD card for off-line analysis. Additionally, the sensor data will also be transmitted to the host PC for real-time monitoring through a Bluetooth module.

3 Classification Algorithms

3.1 Activity Classification Algorithm

An activity classification algorithm was developed to recognize daily activities using foot pressure data and accelerometer data. For the algorithm, foot pressure data from each sensor was considered a separate feature, thus, both feet resulted in a sixteen-dimensional feature array. Six three-dimensional accelerometers resulted in an eighteen-dimensional feature array. Each channel's data was scaled and normalized from 0 to 1 by using the minimum and maximum values from each respective trial. In our wearable system, we used different classifiers with different characteristics and complexities to assess the classification performance and then choose an appropriate algorithm. The candidate algorithms included ensemble learning, support vector machine (SVM), and convolutional neural network (CNN).

SVM is a machine learning method based on statistical learning, which is effective in statistical classification and regression analysis of nonlinear features [20]. Unlike the machine learning method of SVM, ensemble learning can organically combine a variety of different classifiers, and finally obtain a unified model, to obtain more accurate and stable results.

For the above machine learning methods, researchers have proposed many feature extraction and processing approaches and achieved relatively high recognition accuracy on some data sets. However, there are still some problems when manually selecting the feature. First, when identifying sitting and squatting, the data characteristics of them are very similar. It is hard to differentiate the features of the two motions. Second, feature extraction depends on the dataset. The features extracted from one dataset are not necessarily applicable to another dataset, redesigning the feature is complex. Finally, computing complex features can lead to extensive delay. To solve the above problems and improve the accuracy and real-time performance of the classification algorithm, we use the convolutional neural network (CNN) to automatically mine and learn the latent features of the data to distinguish various activities. CNN model can omit the steps of feature selection and extraction, processes the input sensor information, and then output the classification results directly.

3.2 Fall Detection Algorithm

For fall detection, we compared several machine learning algorithms, including RNN, LSTM, and CNN-LSTM, then, to find the best algorithm. RNN is a recently developed neural network suitable for time series data classification. In theory, the output of the current node of the RNN is based on the previous time series data, but actually, the RNN can only briefly remember the previous time series data because of the problems of gradient explosion and gradient disappearance. To solve these problems, Long Short-Term Memory Network (LSTM) was designed, which successfully solves the problem of gradient disappearance and explosion by using a special gate structure. At the same time, it is determined whether to update the memory pool by comparing the information of the current time node with the information in the memory pool, which ensures the efficient utilization of the time series data before the current node.

This paper designed a fall prediction model based on LSTM. It mainly consists of three parts: (1) Input layer: The input data is the data from the accelerometer and the plantar pressure insole, and the time window function is used to select the appropriate data to construct the motion information matrix. (2) Nonlinear layer: After the input layer, the nonlinear operation is performed on the data through the ReLU activation function, so that the neural network model can mine the hidden features of the motion information matrix. (3) LSTM layer: To make full use of the motion information, a three-layer LSTM model is designed. (4) Softmax classifier: This layer classifies and identifies the output of the LSTM network, and decides whether it is a fall through the output probability data. The training strategy of the LSTM network is the same as the CNN-based activity classification method.

A CNN-LSTM model is a combination of CNN layers that extract the feature from input data and LSTM layers to provide sequence prediction. These networks are used in a variety of problems such as activity recognition, image description, video description, etc. We used the combined model CNN-LSTM for fall detection, and the convolution dimension of the CNN network in the CNN and CNN-LSTM networks is thirty-four. The remaining parameters are the same as the LSTM used in this paper.

4 Experimental Validation

To validate the developed wearable sensor system and the proposed classification algorithms, we performed three experiments, including load cell calibration, daily activity classification, and fall detection. In the daily activity classification experiment, we compared the accuracy of activity classification of SVM, ensemble learning, and CNN, and also compared the accuracy before and after sensor fusion. In the fall detection experiment, we compared the accuracy of RNN, CNN, LSTM, and CNN-LSTM models, and also compared the accuracy before and after sensor fusion.

4.1 Validation of Pressure Insole

The pressure sensor needs to be calibrated and tested to obtain the relationship between the output voltage and the applied pressure. We used a vertical push-pull force gauge (HANDPI, Wenzhou, China) to provide stable and accurate pressure. The accuracy of this instrument was ±0.5%. When performing the calibration, we put the pressure sensor on the force point of the push-pull gauge, then, increased the applied pressure from small to large. Then, read and recorded the output of the developed pressure sensor module. The sampling frequency of the foot pressure module was 50 Hz. We collected foot pressure data from one insole that integrated 8 sensor units during normal walking.

4.2 Activity Classification

The purpose of this experiment was to differentiate daily activities, such as standing still, sitting/standing, squatting/standing, walking, jumping, descending, and ascending stairs. This paper used the developed wearable sensor system to collect data, including to pressure insole and 6 inertial sensors attached to the thigh, shank, and foot instep of both sides. The sampling frequency was 50 Hz.

20 healthy participants were recruited (age 23 ± 2 years, weight 70 ± 12 kg, height 1.75 ± 0.05 m, foot length 25 ± 1 cm). Each participant was asked to perform 8 normal activities, including standing still, sitting down/standing up, squatting/standing up, walking on flat ground, turning in place, jumping, going downstairs, and going upstairs (Fig. 3). Standing still and walking on flat ground lasted 30 s. sitting down/standing up, squatting/standing up, turning in place, and jumping were repeated six times, each time lasting 5 s. Walking up and down stairs was repeated three times, each time lasting 10 s. The average period of all the activities was 30 s. The time window function was used to intercept the data with obvious cycles for analysis. Accuracy, Precision, recall, and

F1-score were used to analyze the performance of the proposed system and they are defined as follows:

$$Accuracy = \frac{TP + TN}{TP + TN + FP + FN} \quad Precision = \frac{TP}{TP + FP}$$

$$Recall = \frac{TP}{TP + FN} \quad F_1 Score = 2 * \frac{Precision \times Recall}{Precision + Recall}$$

where TP is the true positive, FP is the false positive, and FN is the false negative.

Fig. 3. Experiments scenario for activity classification, (a) Standing still, (b) Walking (4 km/h), (c) Jumping in place, (d) Sitting down/standing up, (e) Squatting/Standing up, (f) Turning around in place, (g) Going up the stairs, (h) Go down the stairs

4.3   Fall Detection

The recruited 20 healthy participants also performed fall detection experiments. All fall experiments were performed on soft pads to ensure the safety of the subjects. Each subject performed 6 falling behaviors, including falling forward, falling backward, falling to the left, falling to the right, sliding to the ground along the wall, and vertical syncope fall in a standing state. Each falling action lasted about 5 s. Besides, the normal behavior includes 8 daily activities, which were the same as the actions in activity classification experiments. The fall behavior experiment is shown in Fig. 4. We also calculated accuracy to evaluate the performance of the presented model.

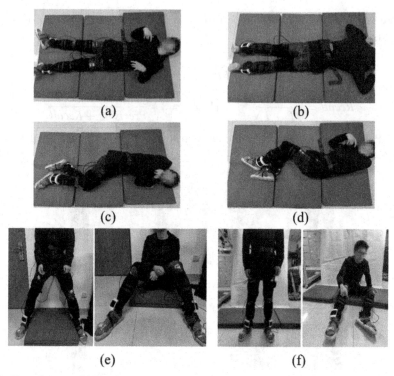

Fig. 4. Experiments of falling behavior. (a) Falling backward, (b) Falling forward, (c) Falling on the left side, (d) Falling on the right side, (e) Falling down the wall to the ground, (f) Falling vertically to the point of paralysis

5   Results and Discussion

5.1   Validation of Pressure Insole

In the process of pressure sensor calibration, the relationship between the exerted pressure and the output of the AD converter from each sensor unit is shown in Fig. 5.

It can be seen that the sensor output is approximately proportional to the pressure exerted on the sensor unit. The eight pressure sensors are fitted by the equation $y = ax+b$, where, x is the exerted pressure; y is the output of the sensor module; a and b are the parameters to be fitted. The fitted coefficients are listed in Table 1.

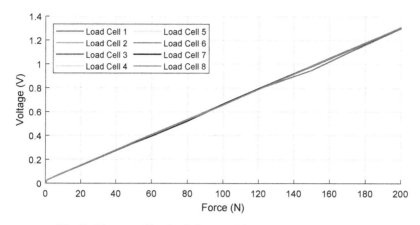

Fig. 5. Diagram of load cell force and the output of AD converter

Table 1. The calibrated coefficients of each sensor unit in one pressure insole

coefficients	Sensor 1	Sensor 2	Sensor 3	Sensor 4	Sensor 5	Sensor 6	Sensor 7	Sensor 8
a	0.21	0.21	0.21	0.21	0.21	0.21	0.21	0.21
b	61.50	65.69	62.52	60.97	63.80	62.99	57.91	61.22

A typical pressure data of the whole insole during normal walking is shown in Fig. 6. It can be seen that at the time of the heel strike, only the heel area had a pressure value, which increased from zero to maximum. When the foot was flat, the plantar pressure in the phalangeal area, metatarsal area, and mid-foot area was increased from zero to the peak value. The pressure in the heel area increases to the peak and then gradually decreases. After the heel off, the pressure in the phalangeal area continued to increase, and the pressure in the metatarsal area and the midfoot area increased to the maximum value and then gradually decrease. The pressure in the heel area gradually decreased. After the toe-off, there was no pressure in the metatarsal area, midfoot area, and heel area, and the pressure in the phalangeal area decreased from the maximum value to 0. The results demonstrated the effectiveness of the designed pressure insole.

5.2 Activity Classification

The activity classification accuracies of the convolutional neural network, ensemble learning, and support vector machine are presented in Fig. 7. It can be seen that the average accuracy of the convolutional neural network algorithm is better than that of ensemble learning and support vector machine. Results also contain accuracy when using only inertial data, only plantar pressure data, and combined data. Accuracy, precision, recall, and F1 Score were also calculated to better compare the classification accuracy under the conditions of single sensor data and combined data (Table 2). The results

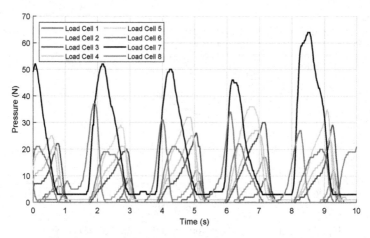

Fig. 6. Data curve of 8 sensors during walking in one foot

are based on the CNN model. Experimental results show that using accelerometer data achieved better accuracy than using foot pressure data. The accuracy after multi-sensor data fusion is higher than that of single-sensor data.

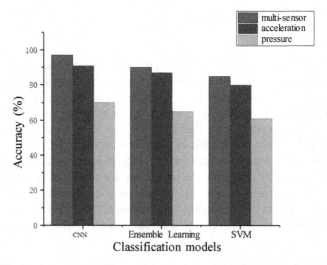

Fig. 7. Accuracy of different classification models in gait recognition.

Figure 8 presents the classification accuracy of each specific activity under different combinations of sensor data. It can be seen that for any activity, the accuracy of multi-sensor fusion is higher than that of using the single-sensor data. Interestingly, the accuracy of using accelerometer data in squatting/standing and sitting/standing is very different. This is probably due to the characteristics of the acceleration in these two activities being quite similar, which makes the classifier hard to distinguish.

Table 2. Activity classification accuracy of CNN when using single-sensor data and multi-sensor data fusion

Indicators	Pressure data	Accelerometer data	Multi-sensor data fusion
Accuracy	0.711	0.913	0.971
Precision	0.763	0.907	0.969
Recall	0.741	0.894	0.963
F_1 Score	0.740	0.901	0.967
Latency (ms)	2.7	3.5	5.8

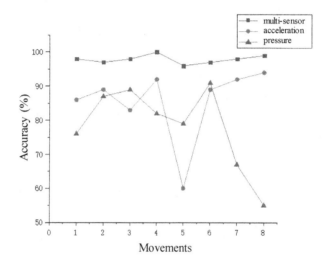

Fig. 8. Accuracy of each action sequence under different sensor information combinations

5.3 Fall Detection

For fall detection, the accuracy of the LSTM, RNN, CNN, and CNN-LSTM model are shown in Fig. 9. The results also include before and after Multi-modal data fusion. The confusion matrix of each model after Multi-modal data fusion is presented in Fig. 10. The detailed performance comparison of the selected four fall prediction models after Multi-modal data fusion is listed in Table 3, including the Acc, Rec, and Pre indicators of each model.

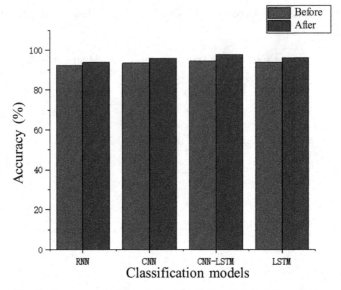

Fig. 9. Accuracy of different classification models in fall prediction

Table 3. Performance comparison of fall prediction models after fusion

Model	Acc	Rec	Pre	Latency (ms)
RNN	93.77%	90.13%	92.54%	**1.56**
CNN	95.85%	91.56%	92.58%	5.573
CNN-LSTM	**97.76%**	**92.85%**	**93.54%**	26.646
LSTM	96.16%	92.78%	93.32%	2.893

Experimental results show that the CNN-LSTM model achieved the highest accuracy. However, the latency of CNN-LSTM is much larger than LSTM. Thus, LSTM model-based fall prediction algorithms are the relatively most efficient algorithm.

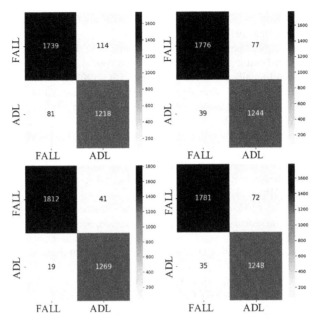

Fig. 10. Confusion matrix of LSTM, RNN, CNN, and CNN-LSTM models after multi-modal data fusion

6 Conclusion

In conclusion, we developed a lower limb wearable sensor system integrated with novel plantar pressure shoes and inertial sensors for human activity classification and fall detection. Experimental results demonstrated that plantar pressure can measure plantar pressure accurately. CNN model with multi-sensor data got the highest accuracy in activity classification, and the LSTM model is the most efficient algorithm in fall detection. The results of this study could enable more precise foot plantar pressure sensing for human physical activity classification and fall detection outside the lab.

Acknowledgment. This work was supported in part by the Natural Science Foundation of Zhejiang province under Grant Q23E050077; in part by the Key Research and Development Program of Zhejiang province under Grant 2023C03159.

References

1. Ekelund, U., et al.: Does physical activity attenuate, or even eliminate, the detrimental association of sitting time with mortality? A harmonised meta-analysis of data from more than 1 million men and women. The Lancet **388**(10051), 1302–1310 (2016)
2. Vogel, T., Brechat, P.-H., Leprêtre, P.-M., Kaltenbach, G., Berthel, M., Lonsdorfer, J.: Health benefits of physical activity in older patients: a review. Int. J. Clin. Pract. **63**(2), 303–320 (2009)

3. Liu, J., Sohn, J., Kim, S., Classification of daily activities for the elderly using wearable sensors. J. Healthc. Eng. **2017** (2017)

4. Harari, Y., Shawen, N., Mummidisetty, C.K., Albert, M.V., Kording, K.P., Jayaraman, A.: A smartphone-based online system for fall detection with alert notifications and contextual information of real-life falls. J. Neuroeng. Rehabil. **18**(1) (2021)

5. Pannurat, N., Thiemjarus, S., Nantajeewarawat, E.: Automatic fall monitoring: a review. Sensors **14**(7), 12900–12936 (2014)

6. el Achkar, C.M., Lenoble-Hoskovec, C., Paraschiv-Ionescu, A., Major, K., Buela, C., Aminian, K.: Instrumented shoes for activity classification in the elderly. Gait Posture **44**, 12–17 (2016)

7. Song, M., Kim, J.: An Ambulatory Gait Monitoring System with Activity Classification and Gait Parameter Calculation Based on a Single Foot Inertial Sensor. IEEE Trans. Biomed. Eng. **65**(4), 885–893 (2018)

8. Fan, B., Li, Q., Liu, T.: How magnetic disturbance influences the attitude and heading in magnetic and inertial sensor-based orientation estimation. Sensors **18**(1), 76 (2018)

9. Fan, B., Li, Q., Liu, T.: Improving the accuracy of wearable sensor orientation using a two-step complementary filter with state machine-based adaptive strategy. Measur. Sci. Technol. **29**(11), 115104 (2022)

10. Madgwick, S.O.H., Wilson, S., Turk, R., Burridge, J., Kapatos, C., Vaidyanathan, R.: An Extended Complementary Filter for Full-Body MARG Orientation Estimation. IEEE-ASME Transactions on Mechatronics **25**(4), 2054–2064 (2020)

11. Ren, D., Aubert-Kato, N., Anzai, E., Ohta, Y., Tripette, J.: Random forest algorithms for recognizing daily life activities using plantar pressure information: a smart-shoe study. Peerj **8** (2020)

12. Subramaniam, S., Majumder, S., Faisal, A.I., Deen, M.J., Insole-based systems for health monitoring: current solutions and research challenges. Sensors **22**(2) (2022)

13. Huang, Y., et al.: Real-Time Intended Knee Joint Motion Prediction by Deep-Recurrent Neural Networks. IEEE Sens. J. **19**(23), 11503–11509 (2019)

14. He, Z., Liu, T., Yi, J.: A wearable sensing and training system: Towards gait rehabilitation for elderly patients with knee osteoarthritis. IEEE Sens. J. **19**(14), 5936–5945 (2019)

15. Matute, A., Paredes-Madrid, L., Gutierrez, E., Parra Vargas, C.A.: In characterization of drift and hysteresis errors in force sensing resistors considering their piezocapacitive effect. In: 16th IEEE Sensors Conference, Glasgow, Scotland, Oct 29-Nov 01, 2017; Glasgow, SCOTLAND, pp. 489–491 (2017)

16. Saadeh, M.Y., Carambat, T.D., Arrieta, A.M.: In evaluating and modeling force sensing resistors for low force applications. In: ASME Conference on Smart Materials, Adaptive Structures and Intelligent Systems (SMASIS 2017), Snowbird, UT, Sep 18–20 (2017)

17. Li, G., Liu, T., Yi, J., Wang, H., Li, J., Inoue, Y.: The lower limbs kinematics analysis by wearable sensor shoes. IEEE Sens. J. **16**(8), 2627–2638 (2016)

18. Refai, M.I.M., Beijnum, B.F.V., Buurke, J.H., Veltink, P.H.: Gait and dynamic balance sensing using wearable foot sensors. IEEE Trans. Neural Syst. Rehabil. Eng. **27**(2), 218–227 (2019)

19. Tan, T., Strout, Z.A., Shull, P.B.: Accurate impact loading rate estimation during running via a subject-independent convolutional neural network model and optimal IMU placement. IEEE J. Biomed. Health Inform. **25**(4), 1215–1222 (2021)

20. Wang, L., Sun, Y., Li, Q., Liu, T., Yi, J.: Two shank-mounted IMUs-based gait analysis and classification for neurological disease patients. IEEE Robot. Autom. Lett. **5**(2), 1970–1976 (2020)

21. Hessert, M.J., Vyas, M., Leach, J., Hu, K., Lipsitz, L. A. Novak, V.: Foot pressure distribution during walking in young and old adults. BMC Geriatrics **5**(1), 8 (2005)

Visual–Inertial Sensor Fusion and OpenSim Based Body Pose Estimation

Tong Li[1](✉), Juntao Wang[2], Yi Chen[2], and Tianyun Dong[2](✉)

[1] National University of Singapore, Singapore 117583, Singapore
zjulitong@zju.edu.cn
[2] Guangxi Key Laboratory of Manufacturing System and Advanced Manufacturing Technology,
School of Mechanical Engineering, Guangxi University, Nanning 530004, China
dty@gxu.edu.cn

Abstract. Body pose estimation is crucial for many human motion-related applications. Stable and low-cost methods for body pose estimation are highly desirable for daily life usage. In this paper, we propose a sensor fusion method for upper body pose estimation. A monocular camera and several IMU-marker sensor modules are integrated to achieve a visual-inertial sensor system. ArUco markers are attached to the IMUs to remove the usage of magnetometers. The raw IMU data are firstly corrected with pre-calibrated intrinsic parameters and then fused with the marker poses detected from the images via an extended Kalman filter. The driftless sensor orientation and marker trajectory are then imported into the OpenSim software to compute body states using the inverse kinematics approach. Experiments were conducted on human subjects to validate the effectiveness of the method. Movements used in the Fugl-Meyer assessment procedure are adopted during the experiments. The estimation results are compared with the joint states from the optical motion capture system showing good accuracy. The proposed method shows the potential to be applied in clinical assessment to reduce the efforts of professional physicians.

Keywords: Pose Estimation · Visual-Inertial · Rehabilitation

1 Introduction

Upper body pose estimation is useful for many application scenarios such as rehabilitation [1], virtual-reality games [2], industry [3], etc. However, different scenarios may have different requirements on cost, accuracy, and usability. For example, sensor systems for rehabilitation training should be simple to set up and accurate for evaluation. Traditional optical motion capture (OMC) systems for human motion analysis are only suitable for lab-based use as they are too expensive to afford for common community applications [4]. Low-cost systems are highly desirable to be widely applied in daily-life rehabilitation and assistance.

Inertial measurement units (IMUs) have been extensively studied for human motion analysis as they are cheap, small, and require little power [5, 6]. Body pose can be

© The Author(s), under exclusive license to Springer Nature Singapore Pte Ltd. 2023
H. Yang et al. (Eds.): ICIRA 2023, LNAI 14268, pp. 279–285, 2023.
https://doi.org/10.1007/978-981-99-6486-4_24

computed from the orientations of the IMUs which are obtained from the sensor fusion of raw data including accelerations, angular velocities, and magnetic strength. However, several issues such as magnetic distortion and drifting exist, resulting in lower accuracy in purely IMU-based systems [7–9]. Besides, due to the movements of soft tissue such as muscles and skin, known as the soft tissue artifact issue, the body poses computed from the IMU orientations are not reliable during large movements [10, 11].

In this paper, we present a sensor system based on a monocular camera and multiple IMU sensors to achieve reliable upper-body pose estimation. The sensor system does not rely on magnetometers for orientation estimation, thus, making it immune to magnetic distortion. The calibration technique and estimation procedure are detailed for measuring arm movements. The experimental testing validates the effectiveness of the proposed sensor system and the sensor fusion algorithms.

The paper is organized as follows. The methods for calibration and sensor fusion are presented in Sect. 2. Experimental testing and results are included in Sect. 3, followed by Sect. 4, where the conclusions and discussions are conducted.

2   Materials and Methods

2.1 Sensor System

To capture the upper body pose, we designed a sensor system with four sensor modules as shown in Fig. 1. A large sensor module is placed on the chest facing forward, with another module on the upper arm at the middle of the humerus. The third module is attached to the forearm close to the wrist joint. The last module is attached to the back of the hand. The modules all consist of a 6-axis IMU (3-axis accelerations and 3-axis angular velocities) and an ArUco marker [12].

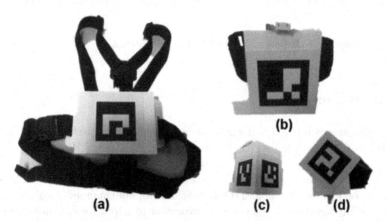

Fig. 1. The sensor system worn on the body. (a–d) are the modules worn on the chest, upper arm, forearm, and hand, respectively.

2.2 Sensor Calibration

To use the low-cost IMUs for high-precision pose estimation, the sensor modules are first calibrated carefully. For the accelerometer, the raw acceleration outputs (a_r) contains errors from noise, drifting, and axis alignment errors. Thus, they are usually corrected as follows to compute the unbiased acceleration (a_c) [13].

$$a_c = A \times S \times (a_r + b_a) \tag{1}$$

where $A = \begin{bmatrix} 1 & a_{12} & a_{13} \\ 0 & 1 & a_{23} \\ 0 & 0 & 1 \end{bmatrix}$ is matrix to correct the axis alignment error, $S = \begin{bmatrix} s_{11} & 0 & 0 \\ 0 & s_{22} & 0 \\ 0 & 0 & s_{33} \end{bmatrix}$ is the diagonal matrix to correct the magnitude error, and $b_a \in \mathbb{R}^3$ is the bias error due to manufacturing error.

The transform between the ArUco marker and IMU sensor is then calibrated firstly with a series of quasi-static poses. The relative rotational transform ($^Q R_S$) can be solved with the regular least square error approach

$$^Q R_S, {}^G R_C = \underset{^Q R_S, {}^G R_C}{\mathrm{argmin}} \int \left(\| ^Q R_S{}^T \cdot {}^C R_Q{}^T \cdot {}^G R_C{}^T \cdot {}^G g - a_c \|^2 \right) \tag{2}$$

where $^G g$ is the gravitation vector, a_c is the corrected IMU accelerations, $^G R_C$ is the constant orientation of the camera and $^C R_Q$ is marker pose detected from images. The projected gravitation acceleration coincides with the measured acceleration as in Fig. 2.

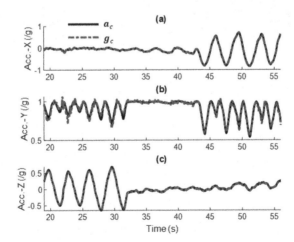

Fig. 2. The acceleration during the calibration stage. The projected gravitation acceleration (g_c) and measured acceleration (a_c) are plotted in red and black lines. (Color figure online)

The translational transform between the marker and IMU can also be solved with a dynamic movement from a similar least square error method.

2.3 Sensor Orientation

The orientation of the sensor module can be estimated by fusing the IMU data and marker poses from vision. An extended Kalman filter (EKF) is used to calculate the sensor orientation iteratively.

The orientation of the IMU $^G q^S$ can be computed by integrating the angular velocity with the equation below.

$$^G q^S_{k|k-1} = {}^G q^S_{k-1|k-1} + \frac{1}{2}{}^G q^S_{k-1|k-1} \otimes [\, 0 \ {}^S \omega_k \,] \Delta_t \tag{3}$$

The EKF to correct the orientation is formulated by setting the acceleration and marker poses as the observations.

2.4 Body Pose Estimation

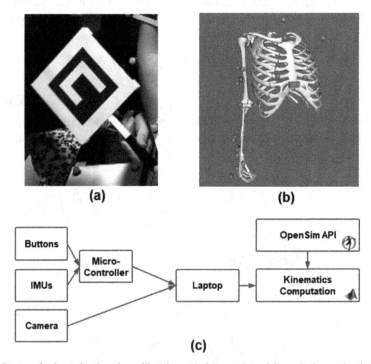

Fig. 3. System for bony landmarks calibration. (a) the wand used for pointing to landmarks. (b) the OpenSim model for computation. (c) the signal connection and data flow in the system.

The sensor modules are attached to the body segments manually. Thus their pose in the segment frame needs to be calibrated. We adopt a similar approach as [14] using a marker wand to calibrate the bony landmarks. The wand is similar to the sensor modules with an ArUco marker and a built-in IMU to achieve accurate pose estimation, in comparison to the purely vision-based method. An additional button is used as an indicator for the calibration procedure (Fig. 3). The button is pressed when calibrating a certain landmark and released when moving to another landmark. This enables automatic processes in the post-analysis and future practical use.

An upper body model built in OpenSim was modified for the kinematics computation, including the inverse kinematic using OMC trajectory data and IMU data. The IMU pose in the segment frame can be computed using the landmark locations. Then the sensor-to-segment poses are updated in the OpenSim model file. The inverse kinematics process can then be conducted to compute the joint angles from the estimated IMU orientations and locations of the markers.

3 Experiments and Results

Experiments were conducted to validate the proposed method. A subject sat before the camera with an experimenter and conducted the calibration procedure. The subject then performed standard movements in the Fugl-Meyer assessment protocol [15]. The collected data are then processed following the procedure in Fig. 4.

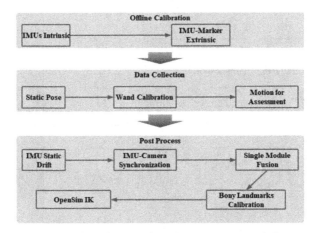

Fig. 4. The flowchart of the data process procedure.

The calibration of landmarks is shown in Fig. 5. The calibration intervals are identified based on the button states. Then, the pose of the marker plate is used to compute the location of the wand tip as the location of the bony landmarks. Once all the landmarks are calibrated, an inverse kinematics (IK) process is performed. Then the location of the sensor modules in the segment frame can be computed and set in the model file as shown in Fig. 5.

The results of the IK process using the IMU poses are shown in Fig. 6. In general, the body states solved from the sensor data coincide well with the ground truth, which is obtained from the OMC trajectory data. When only using orientation data, the translational movements of the torso (t-x, t-y, t-z) cannot be estimated while the rotational

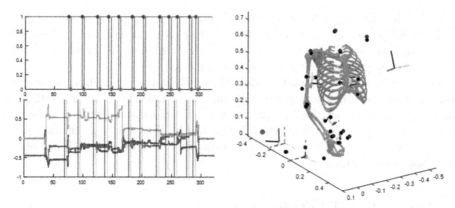

Fig. 5. Results of calibration of landmarks.

movements and joint angles agree with those using all the pose data of sensor modules. The major differences observed from the profiles are at the peaks with errors of around 3 ~ 5°. Besides, the wrist-hand angle also presents an observable error. This is probably due to the small size of the hand and the markers on the hand.

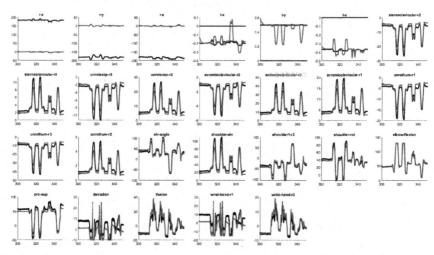

Fig. 6. Results of the IK process using the sensor data. The data from the OMC system is shown in black lines. Results using only sensor orientation and both sensor orientation and marker position are plotted in blue and red lines. (Color figure online)

4   Conclusion

In this work, we present a visual-inertial fusion-based sensor system for the capture of upper body movements. The sensor system is integrated with the popular human movement analysis software OpenSim. The calibration and inverse kinematics procedure are detailed and the methods are experimentally validated. Estimation results during the performance of the Fugl-Meyer assessment movements are close to the ground truth captured by the OMC system, verifying the effectiveness of the proposed sensor system and methods. Future work may be conducted to examine the accuracy of whole-body movements. Further clinical analysis of the estimation results is also desirable.

Acknowledgment. The authors thank the support from (1) the Base and Talent Special Project of Guangxi Science and Technology Plan Project (Gui Ke AD23026285); (2) the Basic Ability Promotion Project for Yong Teachers in Guangxi (2023KY0013).

References

1. Dean, C., Mackey, F.: Motor assessment scale scores as a measure of rehabilitation outcome following stroke. Aust. J. Physiother. **38**, 31–35 (1992)
2. Domínguez-Téllez, P., Moral-Muñoz, J.A., Salazar, A., Casado-Fernández, E., Lucena-Antón, D.: Game-based virtual reality interventions to improve upper limb motor function and quality of life after stroke: systematic review and meta-analysis. Games Health J. **9**, 1–10 (2020)
3. Menolotto, M., Komaris, D.S., Tedesco, S., O'Flynn, B., Walsh, M.: Motion capture technology in industrial applications: a systematic review. Sensors **20** (2020)
4. Eichelberger, P., et al.: Analysis of accuracy in optical motion capture - a protocol for laboratory setup evaluation. J. Biomech. **49**, 2085–2088 (2016)
5. Li, T., Wang, L., Yi, J., Li, Q., Liu, T.: Reconstructing walking dynamics from two shank-mounted inertial measurement units. IEEE/ASME Trans. Mechatron. **26**, 3040–3050 (2021)
6. Nazarahari, M., Rouhani, H.: 40 years of sensor fusion for orientation tracking via magnetic and inertial measurement units: methods, lessons learned, and future challenges. Inf. Fusion **68**, 67–84 (2021)
7. Picerno, P.: 25 years of lower limb joint kinematics by using inertial and magnetic sensors: a review of methodological approaches. Gait Posture **51**, 239–246 (2017)
8. Picerno, P., et al.: Upper limb joint kinematics using wearable magnetic and inertial measurement units: an anatomical calibration procedure based on bony landmark identification. Sci. Rep. **9**, 1–10 (2019)
9. Li, T., Wu, X., Dong, H., Yu, H.: Estimation of upper limb kinematics with a magnetometer-free egocentric visual-inertial system. In: Proceedings of the IEEE International Conference on Robotics and Automation, pp. 1668–1674 (2022)
10. Barre, A., Thiran, J.P., Jolles, B.M., Theumann, N., Aminian, K.: Soft tissue artifact assessment during treadmill walking in subjects with total knee arthroplasty. IEEE Trans. Biomed. Eng. **60**, 3131–3140 (2013)
11. Fiorentino, N.M., Atkins, P.R., Kutschke, M.J., Goebel, J.M., Foreman, K.B., Anderson, A.E.: Soft tissue artifact causes significant errors in the calculation of joint angles and range of motion at the hip. Gait Posture **55**, 184–190 (2017)
12. Li, T., Yu, H.: Upper body pose estimation using a visual-inertial sensor system with automatic sensor-to-segment calibration. IEEE Sens. J., 1–11 (2023)
13. Tedaldi, D., Pretto, A., Menegatti, E.: A robust and easy to implement method for IMU calibration without external equipments. In: IEEE International Conference on Robotics and Automation, pp. 3042–3049. IEEE (2014)
14. Mallat, R., Bonnet, V., Khalil, M.A., Mohammed, S.: Upper limbs kinematics estimation using affordable visual-inertial sensors. IEEE Trans. Autom. Sci. Eng. **19**, 1–11 (2022)
15. Gladstone, D.J., Danells, C.J., Black, S.E.: The Fugl-Meyer assessment of motor recovery after stroke: a critical review of its measurement properties. Neurorehabil. Neural Repair **16**, 232–240 (2002)

A Rotary-Cage Valve (RCV) for Variable Damper in Prosthetic Knee

Wu Fan[1], Zhe Dai[1], Wenyu Li[1], Xiufeng Zhang[2], João Paulo Ferreira[3], and Tao Liu[1](✉)

[1] State Key Laboratory of Fluid Power and Mechatronic Systems, School of Mechanical Engineering, Zhejiang University, Hangzhou 310027, China
{zjufanwu,liutao}@zju.edu.cn
[2] National Research Center for Rehabilitation Technical Aids, Beijing 100176, China
zhangxiufeng@nrcrta.cn
[3] Institute of Superior of Engineering of Coimbra, Quinta da Nora, 3030-199 Coimbra, Portugal
ferreira@mail.isec.pt

Abstract. The hydraulic microprocessor-controlled prosthetic knee is a widely used replacement for the human knee. As a typical damper component, the rotary-cage valve (RCV) can effectively decouple the pressure difference and the actuation force, thereby increasing the energy efficiency. We design and analyze a RCV for prosthetic knee and demonstrate how it fulfill the gait features. We also build its pressure-flow-angle model (PFA) to describe its force-velocity characteristics with different inner cage angles. Through experiments, the numerical model of PFA is specified and the PFA-based control strategy is constructed for pressure control. We built a passive actuation platform to test the RCV and compare it with a BLDC motor. The trajectory tracking and impact experiments were conducted, and the results show that RCV can be controlled to profile specific trajectories with high energy efficiency. Meanwhile, RCV provides considerable compliance and backdrivability for the joint.

Keywords: Prosthesis · Actuation · Control algorithm

1 Introduction

There are more than 30 million limb amputees among the world [1]. For transfemoral amputees, the prosthetic knee is an effective replacement for standing, walking, and even walking up and down stairs. An intelligent prosthetic knee joint can considerably refine the user's living quality. The microprocessor-controlled prosthetic knee is popular among amputees because it can adjust

This work was supported in part by the National Natural Science Foundation of China under Grant No. U1913601, No. 51775485, No. 52175033 and No. U21A20120; the Zhejiang Provincial Natural Science Foundation of China under Grant No. LZ20E050002; funded by Open Foundation of the State Key Laboratory of Fluid Power and Mechatronic Systems under Grant GZKF-202101.

H. Yang et al. (Eds.): ICIRA 2023, LNAI 14268, pp. 286–297, 2023.
https://doi.org/10.1007/978-981-99-6486-4_25

the damping of the knee joint on flexion and extension directions respectively according to the gait event detected in real time [13]. Generally, knee prostheses can be divided into three categories: passive, semi-active and active [14]. This research mainly focuses on the semi-active microprocessor-controlled knee joints, especially the well-known C-Leg, a widely studied knee prosthesis manufactured by the German company Otto Bock [15], as shown in Fig. 1(a). Besides, there are many research about the performance comparison between several typical variable-damping products, such as the Össur Rheo Knee [10], Orion, Plié2.0, etc. [21].

There are several typical ways to generate variable damping force: mechanical friction, motor damping, magnetorheological fluid (MRF) [8], and hydraulic throttling [16]. In [19], Ioannis et al. have designed a spring loaded, screw driven clutch to regulate the physical damping through friction. The mechanism has limited responding speed and is hard to be miniaturized. The DC motor damping strategy proposed in [20] is more suitable for system for low sampling frequency. Beside, if brushless DC motor is used, the controlling of BLDC motor at passive state and the reduction of cogging torque are challenging [12]. The MR fluid has fast responding speed [3], while its feasibility is restricted by the potential particle settling and the decline of viscosity under a high temperature [5]. The hydraulic throttling valve has compact size and relatively high responding speed, besides, it has a wide range of resistance, which is from nearly zero to completely blocked.

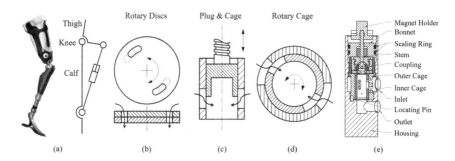

Fig. 1. (a) Photo of a typical product of hydraulic prosthetic knee, C-Leg, and its two-bar linkage diagram. (b)–(d) Three different types of valve trims. (e) The section of the proposed RCV.

1.1   Hydraulic Damper in Passive Actuation

From the perspective of compliance and shock resistance, hydraulic dampers perform much better than motor systems without elastic elements. Generally, for electric actuators, external rotor motors and high ratio reducers are used to gain high torque. Meanwhile, the output speed is restricted, and more seriously, the backdrive inertia of the rotor enlarges quadratically relative to the gear ratio. Such actuators with large inertia lack compliance with the environment. There is a trade-off between the high reduction ratio and compliance. When suffering an impact, the intrinsic damping characteristics of a hydraulic throttle valve can effectively absorb the energy. And the valve orifice can be adjusted in real time to control the resistance for multiple functions [21].

From the perspective of energy consumption, the hydraulic damper is more efficient. In wheels or lifting machines, stable continuous rotation is needed, however, legged robots' joints need to implement frequent starts and stops, which causes very low energy efficiency. For Industrial arms, there are many gravity compensation methods to reduce the load of actuators [2], but most of the methods can not be used in legged robots. When the motor system is actuated passively, it is hard to regenerate the energy when speed is not enough, while hydraulic valves only consume a little energy to adjust the orifice.

Among Hydraulic dampers, there are many different hydraulic circuits to realize different functions [21]. Different kinds of valve trims are used to regulate the damper resistance. Cao et al. [4] have used a butterfly-shaped rotary disc valve to regulate the damping on flexion and extension directions. As shown in Fig. 1(b), the two discs need to fit with each other tightly to avoid leakage through the gap. When there is a large pressure drop from one side to the other side, the friction between two discs is inevitable, which could bring extra load to the motor through the stem, leading to low efficiency. For the plug & cage valve shown in Fig. 1(c), the plug is controlled by the screw rod precisely on the vertical direction. The plug also suffers axial force caused by the pressure difference between upper and lower surfaces, which makes the energy consumption increase and the precision lose. For the rotary-cage valve shown in Fig. 1(d), the inner cage is nested in the outer cage, and the inner cage rotates to adjust the orifice. As long as the surface roughness, the radial tolerance and the concentricity are well guaranteed, there will be no extra torque applied on the inner cage actuator, and the efficiency is increased. The coupling shown in Fig. 1(e) is used to achieve transmission without constraint.

2   Characteristics of the Rotary-Cage Valve

Before delving into the controlling of the throttling valve, the characteristics of the rotary-cage valve should be analyzed and tested to quantize the relation between the pressure drop and the flow rate. The 3D models of the inner cage and the outer cage are shown in Fig. 2(a). The orifices are formed by the overlap of the intersection of the holes on inner cage and outer cage. The inner cage spins to change the shape and area of the orifices. There are three sets of orifices around the cylindrical surface, and the flatten drawing of them is shown in Fig. 2(b). There are two symmetric cashew-like orifices set vertically so that the two overlapped areas compensate with each other to tolerant axial position error between inner cage and outer cage.

As shown in Fig. 2(c), the orifice area is not linear with the angle of the inner cage. This trim characteristics is more like an modified equal percentage valve.

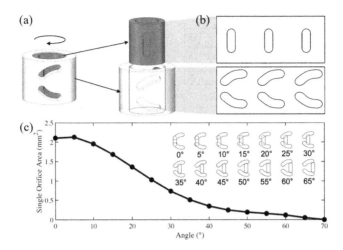

Fig. 2. (a) The 3D model of the disassembled inner cage and outer cage. (b) The developed drawing of the cylindrical surface of inner cage and outer cage. (c) The diagram and the curve of the orifice area as the angle of the inner cage changes.

As is known from experience, vales with the equal percentage characteristics are usually used in processes where large changes in pressure drop are expected, which is eminently suitable for the robotic knee joints. As the angle of inner cage increases, the area of the orifice decreases slowly at 0°–15° and 40°–70°, which makes the resistance can be controlled more smoothly and reduces the precision requirement of the servo actuators.

In the classical orifice plate situation, the mass flow rate is directly proportional to the square root of the pressure differential across the orifice [7]. However, this cashew-like trim can not be simply modeled like that. To express the pressure-flow-angle (PFA) numerical relationship, we propose a undetermined coefficients model to describe the characteristics of the valve,

$$Q = K_v(\alpha)\Delta P^{m(\alpha)}, \tag{1}$$

where

Q is the mass flow rate (expressed in [kg/s]),

ΔP is the pressure loss (expressed in [kPa]),

α is the angle of the inner cage (expressed in [°]).

$K_v(\alpha)$ is the flow coefficient, $m(\alpha)$ is the power of ΔP, they are polynomials whose degrees and coefficients are determined by the fitting effect.

The data of flow rate and pressure loss were collected in a series of experiment. The experiments were done at 25 °C, and we use the #46 hydraulic oil, whose kinematic viscosity is 120 mm^2/s at 25 °C and the density is 850 kg/m^3. The raw data are shown in Fig. 3. The experiments were conducted in three flow groups, and the wide range of the pressure and flow rate can guarantee the precision of the modeling. The results of the polynomial curve fitting of $K_v(\alpha)$ and $m(\alpha)$ are expressed as follows.

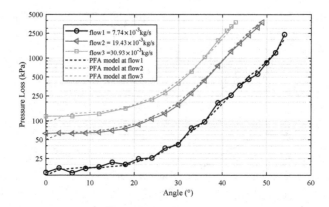

Fig. 3. The pressure loss of the rotary-cage valve at different angle of the inner cage. The red, blue, and black elements represent three different flow rate. The y axis of the graph is plotted as a logarithmic coordinates. The solid lines and markers are the experimental data, and the dashed lines are the results of PFA model expressed in (1). (Color figure online)

$$K_v(\alpha) = -5.08 \times 10^{-11}\alpha^5 + 7.69 \times 10^{-9}\alpha^4 - 3.98 \times 10^{-7}\alpha^3$$
$$+ 7.686 \times 10^{-6}\alpha^2 - 5.303 \times 10^{-5}\alpha + 1.203 \times 10^{-3} \tag{2}$$
$$m(\alpha) = -3.507 \times 10^{-3}\alpha + 0.7132$$

3   Experiments of Passive Actuation

For most prosthetic knee, the peak torque and power density of the knee actuators is a significant indicator of agility and the stability of supporting. The compliance is also an important property to interact with the environment. At the meantime, energy consumption is always tested to evaluate the efficiency of the actuators.

3.1   Modeling and Control

For most prosthetic knee joint, the transmission from the linear movement of the cylinder to the rotary movement of the joint is realized by two-bar linkage. To test the performance of the rotary-cage valve for force controlling and trajectory tracking, we designed and fabricated a passive actuation test platform to implement experiments of a hydraulic damper or a BLDC motor respectively. The actuation can The platform's diagram and its physical information are shown in Fig. 4. The hydraulic cylinder can be substituted with a BLDC motor at axis A. The platform can be driven by either RCV or BLDC, or both can coexist at the same time. The arm rotates relative to axis A, the gravity actuates the joint actively, and the hydraulic damper is actuated passively. The dynamics of this system is modeled as follows.

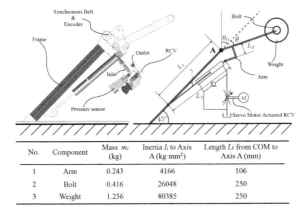

No.	Component	Mass m_i (kg)	Inertia I_i to Axis A (kg·mm²)	Length L_i from COM to Axis A (mm)
1	Arm	0.243	4166	106
2	Bolt	0.416	26048	250
3	Weight	1.256	80385	250

Fig. 4. The section drawing, a schematic diagram of the experiment platform and the physical parameters of the rotary components.

$$
\begin{cases}
I\ddot{\theta} = \displaystyle\sum_{i=1}^{n} m_i L_i \sin\left(\theta + \theta_0\right)g - T \\[2mm]
T = L_1 \sin\gamma F_{push} \\[2mm]
\sin\gamma = L_2 \sin\left(\dfrac{\pi}{2} - \theta\right)/L_3 \\[2mm]
L_3 = \sqrt{L_1^2 + L_2^2 - 2L_1 L_2 \cos\left(\dfrac{\pi}{2} - \theta\right)}
\end{cases}
\tag{3}
$$

where I is the sum of all the rotary parts, T is the torque applied by the cylinder, F_{push} is the linear force of the cylinder. All the other symbols are defined in Fig. 4. We choose a part of a sinusoidal curve for the actuators to track, and the selected curve is:

$$
\theta(t) = \frac{\pi}{6} - \frac{\pi}{6}\cos\left(\frac{\pi}{2}t\right) \ , \ t \in [0, 2]
\tag{4}
$$

Different from electromagnetic actuators, the force generated by the valve depends on the flow rate and the area of the orifice. We design a feedback controller integrating a PFA model solver to derived the real-time angle of the inner cage. In Eq. (1) and (2) constructs a transcendental equation, which has no analytical solution. Combining (1) and (2), we can find that the flow rate Q decreases monotonically as α increases when $\alpha \in [16, 58]$. Therefore, we use the bisection method to solve out the wanted α when desired pressure and flow is given. To avoid infinite loop, the iteration stops at the 8th step to get a sufficiently accurate result within the resolution of the valve actuator. The algorithm is shown in Fig. 5.

With a precise solution of the PFA model in finite time, a PID controller based on the PFA solver is designed and tuned to track the desired trajectory in (4). The control diagram is shown below. θ is the angle of the joint, T is the

---

Algorithm 1. PFA model solver

Require: Desired Pressure loss ΔP_d, real-time flow rate Q_r
Ensure: The value of α that satisfy equation (1)
 1: Set the lower bound α_{min} and the upper bound α_{max}
 2: **for** number of training iterations $(n = 8)$ **do**
 3:     $\alpha_{tmp} = (\alpha_{max} + \alpha_{min})/2$
 4:     $Q_{tmp}(\alpha_{tmp}) = K_v(\alpha_{tmp})\Delta P_d^{m(\alpha_{tmp})}$
 5:     **if** $Q_{tmp} < Q_r$ **then**
 6:         $\alpha_{max} = \alpha_{tmp}$
 7:     **else**
 8:         $\alpha_{min} = \alpha_{tmp}$
 9:     **end if**
10: **end for**
11: **return** α_{tmp}

---

torque of the joint applied by the cylinder, P is the pressure difference of the RCV, *alpha* is the angle of the inner cage, Q is the flow rate through RCV. For all these symbols, the subscript X_d represents desired nominal value, and the subscript X_r represents real data observed by sensors. K_p, K_i, K_d are the proportional, integral, and derivative coefficients respectively.

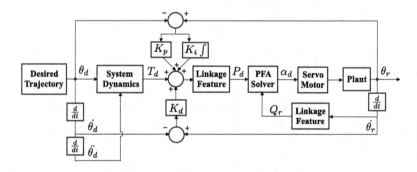

Fig. 5. A diagram of the control strategy.

3.2   Real-Time Control Experiment of RCV and BLDC

We added two barbell pieces at the end of arm and fixed them with a bolt and nut. Firstly, we controlled the valve to block the orifice and maintained its height at the initial position $(\theta = 0)$. Then the servo motor started to actuate the RCV according to the control strategy shown in Fig. 4. As shown in Fig. 6(d), the arm accelerated, decelerated and stopped at the position where $\theta = 60$ in 2 s. For the BLDC motor, we used Tmotor AK10-9, a high-torque BLDC motor, whose rated torque is 25 Nm and reduction ratio is 9:1, and the motor can be controlled in torque model or position mode with a traditional PID controller.

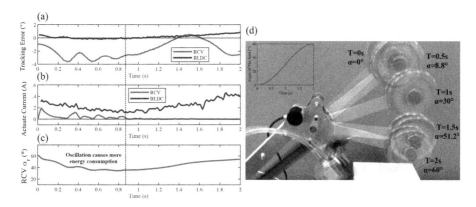

Fig. 6. (a) The tracking error of RCV adn BLDC. (b) The current of actuators, RCV's servo motor and BLDC. (c) The angle of RCV's inner cage. (d) The trajectory and key frames of the passive actuated joint.

During the experiment, multiple sensing data were collected, including actuator current, battery voltage, angle of the joint, angle of the RCV, and the pressure in the cylinder. The Tracking error and current of RCV and BLDC are shown in Fig. 6. We can see that the passive hydraulic actuator based on RCV can track the trajectory well, but the precision is not good as the brushless DC motor. In the first second, the servo motor's oscillation is mainly due to the modeling error of the PFA model and the limited speed of the servo motor. The frequent shifting cause relatively higher current as shown in Fig. 6. However, RCV is definitely more energy-saving than BLDC. The oscillation decays when α is smaller, where the PFA model has sufficient accuracy, at the meantime, the current of RCV becomes very low when the RCV works stably. We can see that even if the BLDC is doing negative work, it consume energy, which makes it much more energy-consuming than RCV.

3.3   Impact Experiment

To evaluate and compare the compliance of these two means of passive actuation, we design a experiment to get the impact force. When the arm is nealy stop at the end of the trajectory, it impact on the load cell, and the load sensor recorded the force data transformed from the kinetic energy. For RCV, the control program continued until the time reached the end. For the BLDC motor, the impact is detected through the reading of the load cell. Once the impact is detected, the program disable the motor torque at that time. The trajectory stops at the impact point as shown in Fig. 7(a).

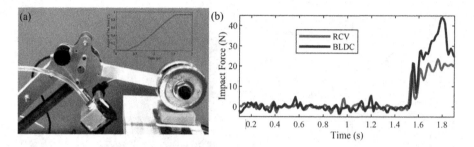

Fig. 7. (a) The trajectory of RCV's impact experiment. (b) The impact force comparison between RCV and BLDC.

We collected the force data of the impact instant, and the comparison between RCV and motor is shown in Fig. 7(b). We can see that the peak force of BLDC is much greater than that of RCV, and the force fall back to the weight of barbell immediately. This phenomenon verify that the motor system has larger inertia, which reduce the compliance and the backdrivability. On the contrast, the transmission medium of the RCV is fluid, whose inertia is very low, and the unique equal percentage characteristics of the trim can avoid hydraulic shock.

3.4   Gait Characteristics

We invited a well-trained subject who had a right-leg transfemoral amputation three years age, to generate natural prosthetic gait wearing a prosthetic knee product. The testing protocol was approved by Medical Ethics Committee of School of Biomedical Engineering and Instrument Science at Zhejiang University (Project identification code: 2021-39. Data were collected with a 12-camera motion capture system (Vicon Motion Systems Ltd. Uk), and a force platform (OR-65, AMTI, USA). The moment of the knee joint is calculated from the lower-limb kinematics, ground reaction force, and segmental inertial characteristics using the Newton-Euler method mentioned in [17] Chapter 7. We conducted the experiment of trajectory tracking, in which the BLDC provides joint torque that simulates the real walking state, including inertial forces, gravity and mechanical limits of the knee joint. The torque profile is shown in Fig. 8(b). At the same time, RCV is controlled to tracking the target curve of the knee joint, as shown in Fig. 8(a). The tracking result is shown in Fig. 8(a). The result shows that the tracking error is within $4°$.

From Fig. 8(a), we can see that the knee joint has no flexion at stance phase, which is significantly different from a normal gait of a health leg. That is because the prosthetic knee is a passive component, which can not provide positive power to extend again from the flexion at stance phase. At the fully extended position, the linkage has a mechanical limit to avoid overextension. The gait is divided into 7 stages according to [9]. At the early stance phase, the flexion nearly blocked to provide a safe support. At the terminal stance, the valve starts to open gradually and allows flexion to prepare for pre-swing. At initial swing, the valve is controlled to adjust the resistance to let the shank swing to a given maximum swing flexion angle, which is a parameter that can be adjusted individually for the user to provide sufficient toe clearance and avoid stumbling. At mid-swing, the knee starts to extend, and the swing extension resistance is preset by the user to get a proper extension speed to keep symmetric with the sound side.

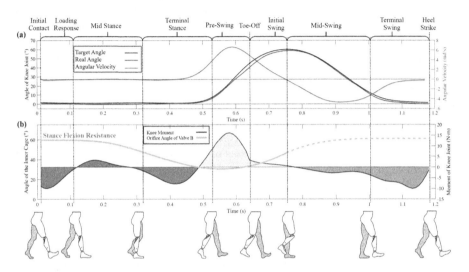

Fig. 8. The prosthetic knee gait and the position tracking of RCV. (a) The angle θ of the prosthetic knee joint from the fully extended position and its angular velocity in a gait cycle. The blue curve is the resulting trajectory of the joint under RCV's control. The gait events are labeled and the whole gait cycle is divided into 7 gait stages. The corresponding lower-limb diagrams are shown at the bottom. (b) The moment of knee joint in a gait cycle and the real-time trajectory of inner cage angle of the valve. The blue zones represent the torque contributed by mechanical limit. The gray zone represents the torque provided by the block effect of the valve. The cyanine zone balance the swing flexion resistance torque provided by the valve, and the magenta zone is the swing extension force torque. (Color figure online)

4   Discussion

In this paper, we propose a rotary-cage valves (RCVs) to adjust the resistance in the flexion direction in real-time. As a semi-active component, it only consumes energy when the valve is actuated to change the angle of the inner cage, but the orifice can generate considerable range of resistance force, even totally blocked. Compared to other passive actuator, the RCV has relative high response speed, very low energy consumption, and very compact size. We propose a PFA model to describe the numerical relationship between pressure difference, flow rate and the angle of the valve. The PFA model's undetermined polynomials were fitted by experimental data. To validate the extensive usage of the RCV in prosthetic knee, we designed and built a platform to explore the trajectory tracking control of the valve and its compliance to impact. The tracking error data show in Fig. 6 indicates that the RCV's precision for trajectory tracking is limited. Compared with the BLDC motor, the force generated by the RCV depends on the velocity, especially when the orifice is small. Due to the low density of hydraulic oil, the hydraulic actuators have relatively low inertia, which makes the compliance greater, and interacts more friendly to the environment. The low impact force and high energy efficiency is also validated through the trajectory tracking experiments. The natural knee gait trajectory is also tested in the experiment.

In other words, the RCV is a highly efficient compact passive force generator, which can be needed in prosthesis field. There are many researches focusing on increasing the energy efficiency of prosthesis and building the prosthetic joint more compactly [6,11,18]. Electromagnetic actuator need energy to maintain force, higher load makes the heat effect consume energy quadratically relative to the current [22]. The RCV is a rare means of passive actuation that combine the feature of high efficiency and high power density. The features make it suitable for legged system scenario.

5   Conclusions

The rotary-cage valve (RCV) can adjust the resistance of the knee joint in real-time to tracking the knee curve of human gait. The PFA model shows that RCV can provide a wide range of force by adjusting the angle of the inner cage. Experiments were conducted to verify that RCV has high efficiency and proper compliance while actuated passively. These features make it suitable for prosthetic knee joint.

References

1. Alcaide-Aguirre, R.E., Morgenroth, D.C., Ferris, D.P.: Motor control and learning with lower-limb myoelectric control in amputees. J. Rehabil. Res. Dev. 50(5), 687–698 (2013)
2. Arakelian, V.: Gravity compensation in robotics. Adv. Robot. 30(2), 79–96 (2016)
3. Bellmann, M., Köhler, T.M., Schmalz, T.: Comparative biomechanical evaluation of two technologically different microprocessor-controlled prosthetic knee joints in safety-relevant daily-life situations. Biomed. Eng./Biomed. Tech. 64(4), 407–420 (2019)
4. Cao, W., Yu, H., Chen, W., Meng, Q., Chen, C.: Design and evaluation of a novel microprocessor-controlled prosthetic knee. IEEE Access 7, 178553–178562 (2019). https://doi.org/10.1109/ACCESS.2019.2957823
5. Chen, S., Huang, J., Jian, K., Ding, J.: Analysis of influence of temperature on magnetorheological fluid and transmission performance. Adv. Mater. Sci. Eng. 2015 (2015)
6. Fan, W., et al.: A passive hydraulic auxiliary system designed for increasing legged robot payload and efficiency. In: 2021 IEEE International Conference on Robotics and Automation (ICRA), pp. 3097–3103 (2021)

7. Idelchik, I.E.: Handbook of Hydraulic Resistance. Washington (1986)
8. Imaduddin, F., Mazlan, S.A., Zamzuri, H.: A design and modelling review of rotary magnetorheological damper. Mater. Design **51**, 575–591 (2013). https://doi.org/10.1016/j.matdes.2013.04.042, www.sciencedirect.com/science/article/pii/S0261306913003658
9. Jacquelin Perry, M.: Gait Analysis: Normal and Pathological Function. SLACK, New Jersey (2010)
10. Johansson, J.L., Sherrill, D.M., Riley, P.O., Bonato, P., Herr, H.: A clinical comparison of variable-damping and mechanically passive prosthetic knee devices. Am. J. Phys. Med. Rehabil. **84**(8), 563–575 (2005)
11. Li, T., Li, Q., Liu, T., Yi, J.: How to carry loads economically: analysis based on a predictive biped model. J. Biomech. Eng. **142**(4), 041005 (2020)
12. Li, T., Slemon, G.: Reduction of cogging torque in permanent magnet motors. IEEE Trans. Magn. **24**(6), 2901–2903 (1988). https://doi.org/10.1109/20.92282
13. Maqbool, H.F., et al.: Real-time gait event detection for lower limb amputees using a single wearable sensor. In: 2016 38th Annual International Conference of the IEEE Engineering in Medicine and Biology Society (EMBC), pp. 5067–5070 (2016). https://doi.org/10.1109/EMBC.2016.7591866
14. Martinez-Villalpando, E.C., Herr, H.: Agonist-antagonist active knee prosthesis: a preliminary study in level-ground walking. J. Rehabil. Res. Dev. **46**(3), 361–373 (2009)
15. Ottobock: C-leg above knee prosthetic leg (2020). https://www.ottobockus.com/prosthetics/lower-limb-prosthetics/solution-overview/c-leg-above-knee-system/
16. Palmer, M.L., Bisbee III, C.R.: Computer controlled prosthetic knee device (2010)
17. Robertson, D.G.E., Caldwell, G.E., Hamill, J., Kamen, G., Whittlesey, S.: Research Methods in Biomechanics. Human Kinetics (2013)
18. Collins, S.: Efficient bipedal robots based on passive-dynamic walkers. Science **307**, 1082–1085 (2005)
19. Sarakoglou, I., Tsagarakis, N.G., Caldwell, D.G.: Development of a hybrid actuator with controllable mechanical damping. In: 2014 IEEE International Conference on Robotics and Automation (ICRA), pp. 1078–1083 (2014). https://doi.org/10.1109/ICRA.2014.6906988
20. Srikanth, M.B., Vasudevan, H., Muniyandi, M.: DC motor damping: a strategy to increase passive stiffness of haptic devices. In: Ferre, M. (ed.) EuroHaptics 2008. LNCS, vol. 5024, pp. 53–62. Springer, Heidelberg (2008). https://doi.org/10.1007/978-3-540-69057-3_6
21. Thiele, J., Westebbe, B., Bellmann, M., Kraft, M.: Designs and performance of microprocessor-controlled knee joints. Biomed. Tech./Biomed. Eng. **59**(1), 65–77 (2014)
22. Urata, J., Hirose, T., Namiki, Y., Nakanishi, Y., Mizuuchi, I., Inaba, M.: Thermal control of electrical motors for high-power humanoid robots. In: IEEE/RSJ International Conference on Intelligent Robots & Systems, pp. 2047–2052 (2008)

Flexible Sensors Used for Lower Assisting Exoskeleton

Yang Xiao[1,2], Chunjie Chen[1,2(✉)], and Yao Liu[1,2]

[1] Shenzhen Institute of Advanced Technology, Chinese Academy of Sciences,
Shenzhen 518055, China
cj.chen@siat.ac.cn

[2] Guangdong Provincial Key Laboratory of Robotics and Intelligent System, Shenzhen Institute
of Advanced Technology, Chinese Academy of Sciences, Shenzhen 518055, China

Abstract. In recent years, with the aging of the social population, exoskeleton robots have a wide range of application prospects in rehabilitation assistance, walking assistance, and physical expansion. However, the sensors developed for traditional robots currently have problems such as poor wearability, poor biocompatibility, and poor adaptability. To realize human-machine motion coordination assistance with multiple degrees of freedom and multiple motion states more effectively, and improve the flexibility, real-time performance, and reliability of the interaction between the wearer and the exoskeleton, it is necessary to design a set of flexible sensing systems to monitor the wearer's motion status. It provides intelligent sensing technology support for adaptive control of exoskeleton in complex environments. This paper proposes a new flexible stretchable capacitive sensor and introduces its selection and manufacturing process. In the following experiments, three different slopes in the static experiment and dynamic experiment were used to test its performance and explore the accuracy and stability of its angle measurement.

Keywords: Flexible sensor · Joint angle · Capacitance sensor · Pattern recognition

1 Introduction

Traditionally, IMUs have been the standard for measuring joint angles in wearable devices such as exoskeletons. However, flexible and stretchable sensors made from conductive polymers or piezoresistive materials have shown great potential as an alternative due to their unique properties.

One of the primary advantages of using these sensors over traditional IMUs is their flexibility and conformability to the skin, which makes them more comfortable to wear during movement. This is especially important for applications where the sensor needs to be worn for long periods, such as in rehabilitation or sports training.

Another benefit of flexible sensors is that they provide a continuous stream of data, allowing for real-time monitoring of joint movement. By contrast, IMUs typically sample at discrete intervals, which can result in inaccurate measurements or missed movements.

H. Yang et al. (Eds.): ICIRA 2023, LNAI 14268, pp. 298–309, 2023.
https://doi.org/10.1007/978-981-99-6486-4_26

Calibration and initialization are another key issue with IMUs, which can be time-consuming and error-prone. In contrast, flexible sensors do not require calibration or initialization, making them easier to use and maintain. Additionally, flexible sensors are less sensitive to external factors such as magnetic interference, which can affect the accuracy of IMUs in certain environments.

Moreover, flexible sensors can be integrated into soft and wearable exoskeletons, which can support and augment human movements. They can provide accurate information on joint angles and movements, enabling the exoskeleton to adjust its assistive strategy accordingly. This can help reduce fatigue and improve the performance of the wearer.

Overall, the flexibility, continuous data output, ease of use, and robustness of flexible and stretchable sensors make them a promising alternative to IMUs for measuring joint angles. Therefore, a flexible stretchable capacitance sensor is proposed in this paper, and its reliability is verified by dynamic testing experiments under different slopes.

2 Methods

2.1 Experimental Equipment and System

Introduction to Flexible Sensor. The flexible sensor in the measurement principle is mainly divided into the piezoelectric sensor, resistance sensor, and capacitive sensor, because the capacitive sensor in only tensile conditions of the reliability is better than the other two, in different temperature and humidity reliability is higher, and capacitive sensor processing technology is simpler and easier to realize. Therefore, this paper will introduce a capacitive tension sensor.

The mechanical properties of flexible stretchable conductive materials, such as Young's modulus and maximum tensile length, are mainly affected by the elastic substrate. The stretchable elastomer can eliminate the applied stress well and protect the metal filler from damage. Therefore, the elastic base of the flexible sensor is one of the key factors to determine the performance of the sensor. Elastomers can be divided into chemically crosslinked elastomers and physically crosslinked elastomers according to the interaction between adjacent chains in an elastic network. In chemically crosslinked elastomers, polymers are connected through covalent bonds to form polymer networks. The strong interaction generated by chemical covalent bonds makes chemically crosslinked elastomers have good mechanical properties and thermal stability. Another physically crosslinked elastomer is different from the above in that it is a polymer chain connected by a weaker interaction, such as poly (Styrene-butadiene-styrene) (SBS) and hydrogenated poly (Styrene-butadiene-styrene) (SEBS), so the material properties can be optimized by adjusting the proportion of the parts in the block copolymer. Due to weak bond interactions, physically crosslinked elastomers are more machinable and easier to reshape by heating or pressurizing. The sensor described in this paper uses physically crosslinked elastomer SEBS. This new thermoplastic elastomer does not contain unsaturated double bonds, has good stability, oxidation resistance, and aging resistance, but also has plasticity, high elasticity, and other excellent mechanical properties, so it is very suitable for different use scenarios and not easy to damage.

To fabricate a stretchable strain sensor, a single layer of 1H, 1H, and 2H evaporated clean silicon wafers were first prepared, and 2H Perfluorooctyl trichlorosilane was removed from the layer at the end of preparation. SEBS was diluted in toluene with a weight concentration of 15% and manually dripped onto the wafers. Subsequently, SEBS was cured at 25 °C for 24 h to prepare the SEBS coating with a thickness of 100 m. A 25 nm thick gold film was deposited by a magnetron sputtering system (JS4S-75G, China). After the mask was peeled off at the end of the sputtering process, the stretchable gold film electrode was obtained. The large-area flexible sensor is made on a mold with a certain shape, and then the stretchable electrode is cut into appropriate slices. Using the self-adhesive properties of SEBS, two stretchable electrodes are connected from back to back to form a capacitance sensor. The copper wire is then connected to both ends of the sensor. Finally, the sensor is encapsulated through the SEBS layer and encapsulation film to maintain its insulation and robustness.

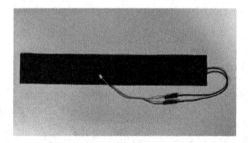

Fig. 1. The flexible stretchable capacitive sensor used in this paper

Data Acquisition System. The data acquisition system also includes a 555 timer circuit board and a USB-A WIFI wireless receiver module for connecting to the computer. The acquisition system uses a 555 timer to convert the capacitance variation of the deformation sensor into the frequency variation, and then the capacitance of the sensor can be accurately obtained by measuring the frequency. The frequency data received by the data receiving and processing unit is sent to the WIFI wireless transmission module after unpacking, conversion, packaging, and other operations. The human-computer interaction interface receives the data wirelessly sent by the WIFI in real time and can draw the capacitance change waveform diagram of the flexible sensor in real time (Fig. 2).

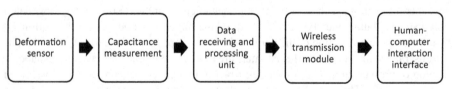

Fig. 2. Test system flow of flexible deformation sensor

To test the performance of the flexible sensor, an optical motion capture system will be used in the experiment to obtain the angle change of the human joint on the sagittal plane. The accuracy of the sensor can be judged by comparing the signals measured by the system with those measured by the sensor. The optical motion capture system used in this experiment is Vicon optical motion capture system produced by Oxford Metrics Limited. The system uses 14 infrared cameras to capture the infrared reflection spot pasted on the human body and obtains the motion state and joint angle of the human lower limb through the position change track of the reflection spot.

2.2 Experimental Procedure

The flexible sensor used in this paper is mainly used to measure the angle of the knee joint of the lower limb during human movement, which needs to be used in combination with the special flexible sheath. The two ends of the flexible sensor are stitched on the flexible sheath, to ensure more accurate positioning when wearing. At the same time, the sensor can be stretched at any point in the process of the lower limb movement after wearing, and no slack will appear.

While the subjects wore the flexible sensing system, to obtain the real motion of human lower limbs, the optical motion capture system was used. PlugInGait LowerBody Ai mode was selected according to the built-in model of the software, in which 16 infrared reflective markers were pasted on the lower limbs of the subjects, and the corresponding positions were as follows: Pelvis (4): left and right anterior superior iliac spine, left and right posterior superior iliac spine; Lower limbs (12, 6 in each side): thigh, knee joint, calf, ankle joint, heel, and toe. Before pasting marks, some body parameters of the subject should be measured, including lower limb length, knee width, ankle width, and subject height and weight. The specific position of the infrared reflection spot and the arrangement of the flexible stretchable sensor is shown in Fig. 3.

Fig. 3. The locations of 16 infrared reflectance spots were marked. The left knee sheath was a tension sensor that had been arranged

The Theoretical Basis of the Sensor. Usually, the external surface of the knee joint is considered to be circular, so it can be seen that under such conditions, the amount of stretch can be calculated according to the knee joint model:

$$\Delta x = \Delta L = \Delta\alpha \times r \tag{1}$$

$$\alpha = \frac{\theta\pi}{180°} \tag{2}$$

According to Eq. (2), it can be deduced from the above formula that, the stretching quantity Δx is directly proportional to the angle change quantity $\Delta\theta$.

In general, the capacitance of a sensor can be expressed as:

$$C = \varepsilon_0\varepsilon_r \frac{Lw}{d} \tag{3}$$

Assuming that the material constituting the dielectric layer between parallel plates of the sensor is isotropic, the variation of the length, width, and thickness of the dielectric layer during the stretching process can be expressed as:

$$\begin{aligned} \Delta w &= -v\varepsilon w \\ \Delta d &= -v\varepsilon d \\ \Delta L &= \varepsilon L \end{aligned} \tag{4}$$

It can be obtained from Eqs. (3) and (4):

$$\Delta C = C - C_0 = \varepsilon_0\varepsilon_r\left(\frac{(L + \Delta L)(w + \Delta w)}{d + \Delta d} - \frac{Lw}{d}\right) \tag{5}$$

where v represents Poisson's ratio and ε represents strain.

Simplify the above Eqs. (3), (4) and (5), get capacitance expression:

$$\Delta C = \varepsilon C_0 \tag{6}$$

In addition, the relationship between capacitance variation and length variation is as follows:

$$\Delta C = \frac{C_0}{L_0}\Delta L \tag{7}$$

C_0 is the initial capacitance and L_0 is the initial length.

In summary, the capacitance variation of the sensor before and after stretching can be expressed as:

$$\Delta C = \frac{rC_0}{L_0} \times \frac{\Delta\theta\pi}{180°} \tag{8}$$

This formula represents the relationship between capacitance variation and joint angle, which can be used as a theoretical basis for sensor measurement of joint angle. Therefore, we only need to measure the capacitance value of the sensor at $0°$ and $90°$, so that the proportional coefficient between the capacitance change and the angle change can be directly obtained, and then the corresponding angle value of the knee joint can be calculated through the capacitance change.

Static Experiment. The external surface of the knee joint is not a standard circular arc, and the above theoretical basis has some errors, so a new static experiment will be carried out in this paper.

After the subjects put on the flexible sensor and pasted the Marker infrared reflective marker, the optical capture system, and the flexible sensor system were opened to establish the human lower limb model. The subjects then remained upright on the treadmill for 10 s, then began to slowly bend their knees and squat so that the knee angle changed from 0° to 90° as Fig. 4, then returned to the upright position and repeated the process five times. Record experimental data.

Fig. 4. In the static experiment, subjects squat to a position of about 90°

Dynamic Experiment. After the subjects kept upright on the treadmill for 10s, they turned on the treadmill, set the speed at 4.5 km/h, the slope at 0, walked for 100 s, and then rested for 60 s. Repeat the process for 3 groups.

After the subjects kept upright on the treadmill for 10s, they turned on the treadmill, set the speed at 4.5 km/h, the slope at 15°, walked for 100 s, and then rested for 60 s. Repeat the process for 3 groups.

After the subjects kept upright on the treadmill for 10s, they turned on the treadmill, set the speed at 4.5 km/h, the slope at 25°, walked for 100 s, and then rested for 60 s. Repeat the process for 3 groups as you can see in Fig. 5.

A total of three subjects carried out the above dynamic experimental data acquisition, while the optical motion capture system and the flexible sensing system carried out data acquisition simultaneously.

3   Experimental Result

3.1   Static Data Analysis

Firstly, the data of static experiments are analyzed. Figure 1 shows the changes of knee angle and capacitance changes of the flexible sensor at the knee during squatting. As can be seen from Fig. 6a and 6b, during the whole static experiment, the changing trend

Fig. 5. In the dynamic experiment, subjects walked on a 25° treadmill.

of sensor capacitance and angle changing tends to be consistent basically, and there is a certain transformation relationship. The two groups of data were fitted, with the x coordinate as capacitance change (ΔC) and the y coordinate as knee angle (θ). The fitting situation was shown in Fig. 7.

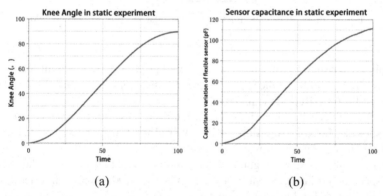

Fig. 6. (a) Graph of knee angle change over time in the static experiment. (b) Time variation diagram of flexible stretchable sensor capacitance in the static experiment.

As can be seen from the figure, the fitting effect of the cubic function relationship is better, and the specific relationship is shown in the following formula:

$$\theta = -1.631 \times 10^{-5}\Delta C^3 + 0.00436\Delta C^2 + 0.5361\Delta C + 0.4134 \qquad (9)$$

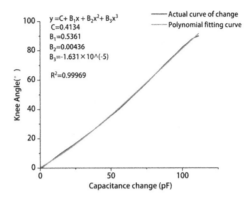

Fig. 7. The blue curve in the figure is the actual corresponding curve of capacitance-angle, while the red curve is the fitting graph of cubic polynomial (Color figure online)

3.2 Dynamic Data Analysis

In the walking experiment, the capacitance variation of the sensor and the angle data of the knee joint on the sagittal plane were collected. A total of 15 groups of data with 5 groups of gait data of each of the three subjects were averaged to make the following Fig. 8.

As can be seen from the above 3 groups of comparison graphs, no matter at which angle, the changing trend of sensor capacitance is in good consistency with the change of knee angle, and the sensor can basically reflect the change of knee angle.

The capacitance data from the experiments of $0°$, $15°$, and $25°$ were substituted into the capacitance-angle relation formula Eq. (9) obtained in the static experiments above. After converting the capacitance value into the angle value, the comparison was made with the angle value measured by Vicon infrared dynamic capture, and the standard deviation of 30 groups of data was calculated, as shown in Fig. 9.

In the three pictures on the left of Fig. 9, the blue line represents the angle measured by Vicon, the red line represents the angle converted from the capacitance measured by the sensor, and the light-colored part is the tolerance band of the corresponding angle value. By comparing the two lines in the figure, it can be seen that the angle value converted from the capacitance value of the sensor is consistent with the actual angle value no matter the actual value or the trend.

However, for the above images, the inconsistency of fitting is mainly reflected in the two peaks. The premature and delayed appearance of the peaks as well as the inconsistent height of the peaks appear. The reason may be that there is a certain wearing error when wearing the sensor on different people, and the sensor will be relaxed after wearing it for a long time.

The figure on the right shows the error angle in each slope experiment. It can be seen that the maximum error is about $6°$ and usually occurs at two wave peaks. The overall error is within the acceptable range and the fitting is generally good.

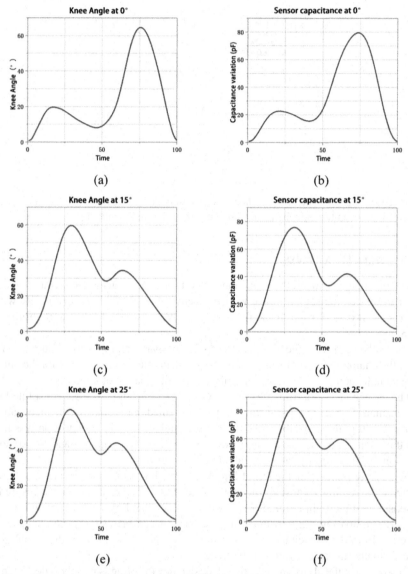

Fig. 8. (a)(c)(e) The three figures on the left respectively show the changes of knee angle when the slope is 0°, 15°, and 25°. (b)(d)(f) The corresponding sensor capacitance changes are shown on the right.

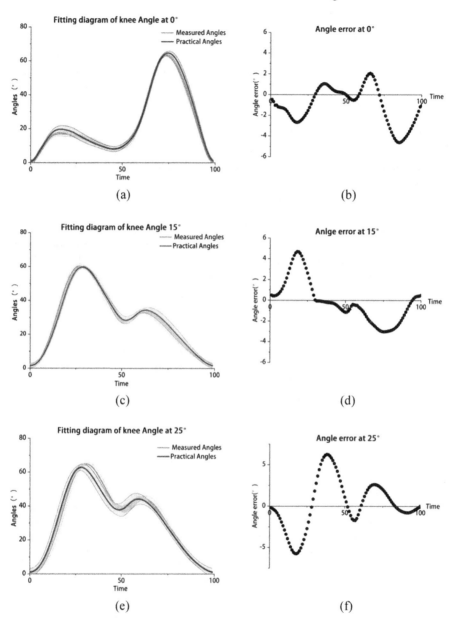

Fig. 9. (a)(c)(e) The three figures on the left are the comparison between the actual angle and the angle converted by the sensor capacitance value when the slope is 0°, 15°, and 25°. (b)(d)(f) The three figures on the left are respectively the error graphs of the angle converted from the actual angle to the sensor capacitance value when the slope is 0°, 15°, and 25°.

4 Conclusion

In this paper, we propose a new flexible stretchable capacitive sensor, discuss the selection of its elastic base and operating mechanism, and briefly describe its manufacturing process. Then we carried out two static and dynamic experiments. In the static experiment, we used the method of continuous sampling recording to fit the function relationship between the sensor capacitance change and the angle of the knee joint. In the dynamic experiment, we selected three different slopes for the experiment. It can be seen from the data that the angle measurement results are relatively ideal and the corresponding judgment of different slopes is relatively accurate, which can be used in terrain recognition in the future.

However, there are still some problems in the application of the sensor, such as loose binding after wearing it for a long time, which will directly lead to inaccurate sensor data measurement. There are also questions about the sensitivity of the sensor because the ankle joint has less angular variation than the knee joint. The negative angle at the hip joint is not measured by the tension sensor, so the placement of the hip joint needs more research. In addition, how to reduce the shape error between different wearers is also a problem worth considering. Finally, the sampling frequency of the flexible tensile sensor needs to be improved.

Acknowledgments. This work was partially supported by the NSFC-Shenzhen Robotics Research Center Project (U2013207), the National Key R\&D Program of China (2022YFC3601704), the Natural Science Foundation of China (62273325, U191320, 62003327), the Natural Science Foundation of Guangdong Province (2019A1515010782), and SIAT-CUHK Joint Laboratory of Robotics and Intelligent Systems.

References

1. Asbeck, A.T., De Rossi, S.M.M., Galiana, I., Ding, Y., Walsh, C.J.: Stronger, smarter, softer: next-generation wearable robots. IEEE Robot. Autom. Mag. **21**(4), 22–33 (2014)
2. Sbernini, L., Pallotti, A., Saggio, G.: Evaluation of a Stretch Sensor for its Inedited Application in Tracking Hand Finger Movements. In: 2016 IEEE International Symposium on Medical Measurements and Applications (MeMeA), pp. 1–6. IEEE (2016)
3. Chander, H., et al.: Wearable stretch sensors for human movement monitoring and fall detection in ergonomics. Int. J. Environ. Res. Public Health **17**(10), 3554 (2020)
4. Huang, B., et al.: Wearable stretch sensors for motion measurement of the wrist joint based on dielectric elastomers. Sensors (Basel) **17**(12), 2708 (2017)
5. Tonazzini, A., Shintake, J., Rognon, C., Ramachandran, V., Mintchev, S., Floreano, D.: Variable stiffness strip with strain sensing for wearable robotics. In: 2018 IEEE International Conference on Soft Robotics (RoboSoft) (2018)
6. Xueping, L., Xiaofeng, Y., Xinlin, Q.: Pressure Sensing Characteristics and Mechanism of a Flexible Capacitive Sensor
7. Jing, S., Hanfei, L., Peizhi, G., Guanglin, L., Zhiyuan, L.: A short review on bio-signals acquisition and feedback via soft and stretchable conductive materials. Mater. Rep. **35**, 5158–5165 (2021)
8. Mengüç, Y., et al.: Wearable soft sensing suit for human gait measurement. Int. J. Rob. Res. **33**(14), 1748–1764 (2014)

9. Moon, D.-H., Kim, D., Hong, Y.-D.: Intention detection using physical sensors and electromyogram for a single leg knee exoskeleton. Sensors **19**(20), 4447 (2019)

10. Vertechy, R., Frisoli, A., Solazzi, M., Dettori, A., Bergamasco, M.: Linear-quadratic-gaussian torque control: application to a flexible joint of a rehabilitation exoskeleton. In: 2010 IEEE International Conference on Robotics and Automation, pp. 223–228. IEEE (2010)

11. Peng, Y., Song, X., Pang, K., Yang, Q., Zhen, X., Zhang, M.: A flexible and stretchable bending sensor based on hydrazine-reduced porous graphene for human motion monitoring. IEEE Sens. J. **20**(21), 12661–12670 (2020)

12. Parsons, E.K.: An experiment demonstrating pointing control on a flexible structure. IEEE Control. Syst. Mag. **9**(3), 79–86 (1989)

13. Attar,I., Altintig, K.S., Bozyel, I., Gokcen, D.: Design of a highly sensitive, flexible and stretchable tactile sensor for electronic skin applications. In: 2019 IEEE International Conference on Flexible and Printable Sensors and Systems (FLEPS), pp. 1–3. IEEE (2019)

14. Chen, W., Li, J., Zhu, S., Zhang, X., Men, Y., Wu, H.: Gait recognition for lower limb exoskeletons based on interactive information fusion. Appl. Bionics Biomech. **2022**, 9933018 (2022)

15. Kim, J., et al.: Reducing the energy cost of walking with low assistance levels through optimized hip flexion assistance from a soft exosuit. Sci. Rep. **12**(1), 1–13 (2022)

16. Ma, L., Shuai, X., Zhu, P., Sun, R.: A highly sensitive flexible pressure sensor based on multiscale structure and silver nanowires. In: 2017 18th International Conference on Electronic Packaging Technology (ICEPT), pp. 1366–1370. IEEE (2017)

17. Atalay, A., et al.: Batch fabrication of customizable silicone-textile composite capacitive strain sensors for human motion tracking. Adv. Mater. Technol. **2**(9), 1700136 (2017)

Highly Compressible and Stretchable Piezoresistive Sensor Based 3D Graphene-Melamine Composite Foam for Gait Motion Detection

Eric Kwame Owusu, Aristide Djoulde, Zhen Jiang$^{(\boxtimes)}$, and Mei Liu$^{(\boxtimes)}$

Shanghai Key Laboratory of Intelligent Manufacturing and Robotics, School of Mechatronic Engineering and Automation, Shanghai University, Shanghai 200444, China
2843546330@qq.com

Abstract. High-performance piezoresistive sensors that are stretchable, compressible, and ultralight have fueled significant interest in gait motion detection. However, developing a highly sensitive, low-cost sensor with ultralow detection and excellent mechanical stability for sensitive body flexion monitoring is a significant challenge. To address the aforementioned challenges, a stretchable and compressible piezoresistive pressure sensor is fabricated by embedding multilayer graphene (Gr) nanoparticles into the porosity of melamine foam (MF). The graphene melamine nanocomposite foam (GMNCF) is prepared by soaking the MF in a dissolved dispersion of Gr. The as-fabricated GMNCF piezoresistive sensors featured sensitivities ranging between, 0.11–8.21 kPa^{-1} in pressure ranges between 0–0.03 kPa, as well as excellent durability over a long period of time (1000 s). The device can effectively detect gait motions such as jogging, walking, running, heel striking, foot flat, and toes-off due to its strong piezoresistive sensing capabilities. Our results showcase the potential application of GMNCF, as a wearable device for monitoring human motions.

Keywords: Graphene · melamine foam · piezoresistive sensor · compressible · gait motion

1 Introduction

Traditional metal and inorganic semiconductor-based resistive sensors have limitations [1], such as low sensitivity or low gauge factors (GFs) [2, 3], as well as a lack of flexibility and stretchability [4]. To overcome these limitations, piezoresistive pressure sensors with multiple functions and improved integration have gained considerable interest, particularly in gait motion detection [5], flexible wearable healthcare devices [6], and human-machine interface (HMI) [7]. According to different sensing mechanisms, a significant number of pressure sensors are currently designed and classified into four main categories: piezoresistive sensors [8], capacitive sensor [9, 10], piezoelectric sensors [11, 12], and triboelectric sensors. Piezoresistive sensors that convert mechanical deformation into electrical resistance change have gained significant attention due to their

© The Author(s), under exclusive license to Springer Nature Singapore Pte Ltd. 2023
H. Yang et al. (Eds.): ICIRA 2023, LNAI 14268, pp. 310–318, 2023.
https://doi.org/10.1007/978-981-99-6486-4_27

simple structure, stability, and high sensitivity [13]. Sensitivity and stretchability are crucial qualities for response signals. However, achieving a balance between sensitivity and stretchability remains a challenge. Therefore, comprehensive research on strain sensors is necessary to achieve the desired qualities [14]. Conductive polymers such us Poly(3,4-ethylenedioxythiophene) (PEDOT): PEDOT, melamine foam, and Polythiophene (PT) been widely employed in the development of 3D pressure sensors [15]. For example, Pang et al. fabricated strain sensors using Pt-coated polymer nanofiber arrays, which exhibited remarkable sensitivity with a minimum detectable pressure of approximately 5 Pa. However, the strain range of these sensors was limited to 5% [16].

On the other hand, melamine foam, a readily available and cost-effective porous elastic material, has emerged as a promising candidate for piezoresistive sensors when used as a conductive porous elastic nanocomposite [17]. It is crucial to select a conductive, porous elastic matrix that effectively addresses the challenges posed by these sensors [18]. The addition of conducting nanofiller in MF offers a suitable solution, as it maintains the original porous structure while providing excellent electrical conductivity [19]. The lightweight nature and hydrophobic properties of carbon-based materials align well with the requirements of wearable sensors. However, the insulating elastic sponge matrix presents a challenge when the conductive filler detaches [20]. Moreover, the use of MF as a substrate helps minimize errors caused by the shedding of conductive materials on insulation [21].

To achieve high sensitivity in piezoresistive sensors, two key elements are necessary: a low initial current and a large current output under specific pressure conditions [22]. To address this limitation, the incorporation of a conductive filler with excellent conductivity becomes essential [23]. Graphene, with its conductive mechanism involving electrons, offers remarkable sensitivity [24]. Additionally, graphene possesses several advantages over silver nanowires (AgNWs), including high electrical conductivity, a large surface area, and mechanical strength, making it an ideal candidate for sensor applications [25]. When incorporated into nanocomposites, graphene enhances the sensor's sensitivity, and stability, while the nanocomposite matrix provides mechanical support and improves compatibility with different environments.

In this study, we propose innovative approach to fabricate a graphene-melamine-based sensor for body motion detection, a straightforward and cost-effective method for fabricating highly compressible and stretchable piezoresistive sensor using soaking techniques. Sensor fabrication consist of incorporating Gr into porous skeleton melamine foam. The fabricated Gr melamine nanocomposite foam (GMNCF) exhibited exceptional sensitivity (between 1.675–150.95 kPa^{-1} in pressure ranges between 0–0.03 kPa) and good working stability. The presented Gr-based sensor demonstrates remarkable performance in human gait motions such as walking, running, heel strike, foot flat, highlighting their possibilities for widespread applications in wearable electronic sensing and body flexion monitoring.

2   Experimental Section

Material. Graphene powder (0.8 nm in thickness and 0.5-5 μm in diameter) were purchased from Nanjing XF-NANO Materials Tech Co., Ltd, China, and were directly used in their original form. Melamine foam were purchased from a commercial store.

Fabrication Method. To adequately incorporate Gr in the MF, direct soaking techniques were used. Figure 1 depicts the GMNCF's schematic fabrication process. MF (2 × 2 × 2 cm³) was washed in ethanol and deionized (DI) water for 15 min (Fig. 1(a-c)). It was squeezed to remove extra liquid before being dried in an oven at 80 °C for 1 h. Following that, 0.5 mL of Gr was poured into a 10 mL DI solution and mechanically agitated for 15 min before soaking cubes of MF in the Gr/DI solution and squeezing off the excess solution (Fig. 1(d)). It was then dried on a hot plate at 50 °C for 8 h. The foam was immersed again in 0.5 mL Gr solution, and the surplus solution was strained out (Fig. 1(e)). The sample was then dried for one hour in a 70°C oven. This method was performed multiple times to obtain the final GMNCF as shown in Fig. 1(g).

Assembling. To connect the piezoresistive pressure sensor, conductive electrodes were attached to both sides of the GMNCF for electric connections as shown in Fig. 1(i).

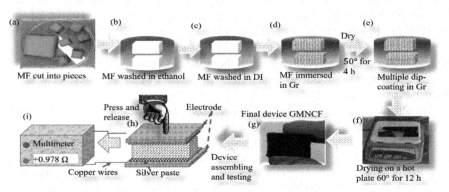

Fig. 1. Schematic illustration of the fabrication steps of GMNCF piezoresistive sensor.

To avoid contact resistance, both sides of the foam were pasted with conductive silver paste before adding the conductive electrode in order to fix it properly without detaching during use or testing.

3   Results and Discussion

Morphology Characterization. Characterization of the sponges' surface morphology was studied using SEM. The resulting GMNCF exhibited an interconnected 3D porous structure with average pores diameter between 100–300 μm, as shown in Fig. 2(a). Figure 2(b) shows two sponges both held by only one leaf without bending, highlighting the lightness of the GMNCF samples. Furthermore, to showcase the homogeneity of the mixture and the linked 3D porous structure, the GMNCF was sliced into two. Photograph in Fig. 2(c) proves well distribution of Gr throughout the MF. These results are a clear indication of the effectiveness of our fabrication methods.

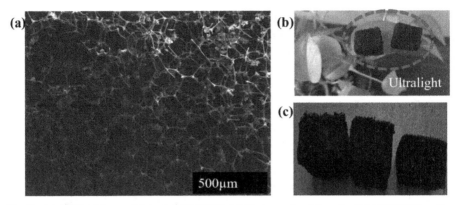

Fig. 2. (a) SEM of the as-fabricated GMNCF. (b) Photograph of the ultralight GMNCF resting on a leaf showing no bending. (c) Photograph of the sectioned GMNCFs.

4 Electrical Characterization

Elastomer/nanomaterial nanocomposites are often sought for their good electrical conductivity to serve as efficient sensing components. To evaluate the conductivity of GMNCF, varying amounts of Gr were used. A voltage (V) of up to 20 V was applied to each conductive GMNCF, and corresponding current (I) was recorded using the experimental setup as shown in Fig. 3(a). Subsequently, device resistance was determined. Figure 3(b) shows current-voltage measurements of GMNCF with different Gr loading amounts. Throughout the trials, several sizes of composite samples were evaluated, producing consistent conductivity statistics. The conductivity of the GMNCF increased significantly with loading percentage of Gr, from 0.003 S/m (0.5g of Gr) to 4.3 S/m (1g of Gr), and 5 S/m (1.1g of Gr).

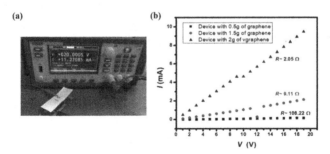

Fig. 3. (a) I-V measurements setup. (b) I-V curve of the as-prepared GMNCF with varying Gr concentrations.

I-V characteristics of the GMNCF were also assessed under compressive forces ranging from 1 N to 30 N, and it was determined that a higher concentration of Gr was necessary to achieve a significant I-V response. Specifically, nanocomposites containing 1.1g of Gr produced a voltage signal of 0.02 V and current of 9 nA as shown in Fig. 4.

The data also revealed that peaks of I and V both increased as the applied force increased, regardless of the filler concentration, as the Gr nanostructures are responsible for voltage generation upon exposure to force. Furthermore, previous research has also reported on these findings.

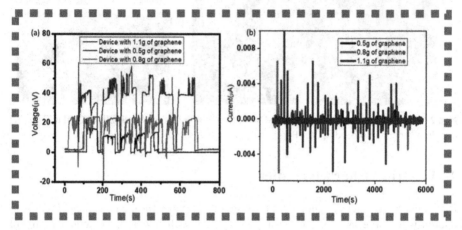

Fig. 4. (a) Output characteristics (a) voltage and (b) current when applying and releasing compressive forces on the sensor using human fingers (black 0.5g, red 0.8g and blue 1.1g of graphene.

5   Piezoresistive Characterization

Piezoresistivity test were taken under various applied pressures using the CellScale compression test machine as illustrated in Fig. 5(a). Copper tape with conductive silver paste was utilized to reduce the electrical resistance at the electrode-GMNCF contacts. Additionally, to prevent distortion or twisting of the sample when clamped by the digital multi-source meter clip, copper wires were soldered to the edges of the copper bands using conductive clippers.

To determine sensitivity of the pressure sensor, we employed the following equation:

$$s = \frac{\Delta R}{\Delta P \times R_0} \tag{1}$$

where P represents the applied pressure, R_0 as the initial resistance and R represent resistance with the applied pressure. The pressure responses for each GPNCS sample were recorded, as shown in Fig. 5(b).

During a continuous dynamic pressing test, sensitivity of the samples was measured. The pressure loads ranged from 1 N to 30 N, and the resulting sensitivities were calculated and reported as shown in Table 1. It clearly shows that sensitivity increases as the mass of incorporated Gr increases. The sponges containing 1.1g of Gr mass loading exhibited the highest average sensitivity (as seen in the green curve in Fig. 5(b)). This leads to

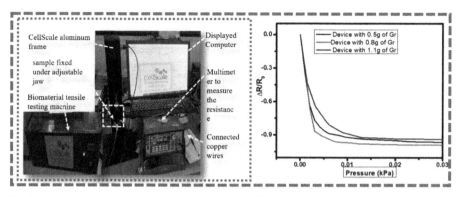

Fig. 5. (a) Pressure response resistance plot for the GMF piezoresistive pressure sensors with 0.5g (black curve), 0.8g (red curve), and 1.1g (green curve) of Gr.(Color figure online)

more contact points between Gr sheets and the foam matrix, resulting in better interfacial bonding.

The improved interfacial bonding enhances the transfer of mechanical or thermal energy from the foam to the Gr sheets, which increases the sensitivity of the composite foam to external stimuli. Furthermore, the high aspect ratio of Gr allows it to form a percolating network within the foam. A percolating network is a connected structure that enables efficient transport of charge or heat throughout the material. The formation of a percolating network of graphene within the foam enhances the foam's electrical and thermal conductivity, which increases its sensitivity to electrical and thermal stimuli.

Table 1. Sensitivities

Gr concentration	Pressure (N)	S (kPa^{-1})
0.5g	0–30	0.07–3.46
0.8g	0–30	0.12–6.60
1.1g	0–30	0.11–8.21

6 Application on Human Gait Motion Detection

Durability and working stability are crucial factors in evaluating performance of piezoresistive sensors in practical applications. Applications of GMNCF piezoresistive sensors for human gait motion detection are illustrated in Fig. 6. The sensors are found to have excellent responsiveness and working stability in monitoring human motion, including jumping, squatting, walking, and tumbling. For instance, during jumping (Fig. 6(a)), the sensors exhibited alternating I signals due to the immediately changed resistance when the feet fell on the ground. On the other hand, when the feet jump up, the sensors exhibit suddenly weakened V signals due to the instantly increased resistance caused by the release compression strain. Additionally, the GMNCF piezoresistive sensors have great potential in detecting unexpected emergencies for special wearers. The output I become non-obvious and remain unchanged at a low I values after a sudden tumble (Fig. 6(d)), indicating that the wearer could not move without assistance. Hence, remote alarms need to be sent to the preset emergency contact for timely first aid. The excellent performance of GMNCF piezoresistive sensors demonstrates their potential in various applications such as wearable electronics, artificial intelligence, human-computer interaction, and soft robotics.

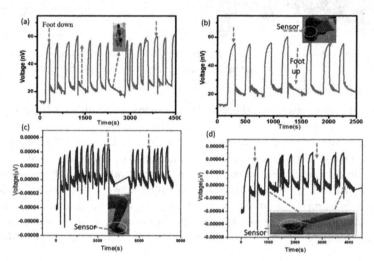

Fig. 6. Human motion detection of the GPNCF piezoresistive sensors in response to (a) jumping, (b) walking, (c) squatting and (d) tumbling.

7   Conclusion

In conclusion, by soaking MF in a Gr solution, stretchable, compressible and flexible piezoresistive pressure sensor with ultrasensitive, and a wide working range was successfully prepared via an effective and low-cost production method. The interconnected conductive network of the Gr on the 3D MF skeleton provides the electrical resistance changes of the sensor under external stimulation. The sensor featured sensitivities between 0.11–8.21 kPa^{-1} in pressure ranges between 0–0.03 kPa, and excellent durability over a long period of time (1000 s). This is owing to the network architecture of the 3D MF skeleton and the higher current variation output of the Gr under strain. The developed sensor is capable of monitoring wide range of human gait motions, such as walking, heel striking, foot flat, and toes-off. The sensor's sensing performance and reproducibility were determined using a series of static and dynamic compressive strain response tests. GMNCF sensors proved to be suitable for human motion detection and personalized health monitoring applications.

References

1. Zhang, Z., Si, T.: Controllable assembly of silver nanoparticles based on the coffee-ring effect for high-sensitivity flexible strain gauges. Sens. Actuators, A **264**, 188–194 (2017)
2. Lee, Y.H., et al.: High-performance hybrid photovoltaics with efficient interfacial contacts between vertically aligned ZnO nanowire arrays and organic semiconductors. ACS omega **4**(6), 9996–10002. https://doi.org/10.1021/acsomega.9b00778 Available: http://eur opepmc.org/abstract/MED/31460092, https://europepmc.org/articles/PMC6648691, https://europepmc.org/articles/PMC6648691?pdf=render Accessed Jun 2019
3. Liu, H., et al.: Electrically conductive strain sensing polyurethane nanocomposites with synergistic carbon nanotubes and graphene bifillers. Nanoscale **8**(26), 12977–12989 (2016). https://doi.org/10.1039/C6NR02216B
4. Romarís, L.H.,et al.: Multifunctional electromechanical and thermoelectric polyaniline–poly(vinyl acetate) latex composites for wearable devices. J. Mater. Chem. C **6**(31), 8502–8512 (2018). https://doi.org/10.1039/C8TC02327A
5. Cai, B., et al.: Compressible piezoresistive pressure sensor based on Ag nanowires wrapped conductive carbonized melamine foam. Appl. Phys. A **128**(1), 6 (2021)
6. Fragkogiannis, C., Koutsioukis, A., Georgakilas, V.: Highly elastic melamine graphene/MWNT hybrid sponge for sensor applications. Molecules **27**(11), 3530 (2022)
7. Canavese, G., Stassi, S., Stralla, M., Bignardi, C., Pirri, C.F.: Stretchable and conformable metal–polymer piezoresistive hybrid system. Sens. Actuators, A **186**(2), 191–197 (2012)
8. Ge, G., et al.: A flexible pressure sensor based on rGO/polyaniline wrapped sponge with tunable sensitivity for human motion detection. Nanoscale **10**(21), 10033–10040 (2018). https://doi.org/10.1039/C8NR02813C
9. Liu, Q., Chen, J., Li, Y., Shi, G.: "High-performance strain sensors with fish-scale-like graphene-sensing layers for full-range detection of human motions", (in eng). ACS Nano **10**(8), 7901 (2016)
10. Kurup, L.A., Cole, C.M., Arthur, J.N., Yambem, S.D.: Graphene porous foams for capacitive pressure sensing. ACS Appl. Nano Mater. **5**(2), 2973–2983 (2022)
11. Lu, P., Wu, X., Guo, W., Zeng, X.C.: Strain-dependent electronic and magnetic properties of MoS2 monolayer, bilayer, nanoribbons and nanotubes. Phys. Chem. Chem. Phys. **14**(37), 13035–13040 (2012). https://doi.org/10.1039/C2CP42181J
12. Li, B., et al.: Tribological behaviour of acrylonitrile-butadiene rubber under thermal oxidation ageing. Polym. Testing **93**(2), 106954 (2021)
13. Georgopoulou, Clemens, F.: Piezoresistive elastomer-based composite strain sensors and their applications. ACS Appl. Electron. Mater. **2**(7), 1826–1842 (2020)
14. Cheng, L., Wang, R., Hao, X., Liu, G.: Design of flexible pressure sensor based on conical microstructure PDMS-bilayer graphene. Sensors **21**(1), 289 (2021)
15. Ding, Y., Xu, T., Onyilagha, O., Fong, H., Zhu, Z.: "Recent advances in flexible and wearable pressure sensors based on piezoresistive 3D monolithic conductive sponges", (in eng). ACS Appl. Mater. Interfaces **11**(7), 6685–6704 (2019)
16. Pang, Z.P., et al.: Induction of human neuronal cells by defined transcription factors. Nature **476**(7359), 220–223 (2011)
17. Zhou, J., Yu, H., Xu, X., Han, F., Lubineau, G.: Ultrasensitive, stretchable strain sensors based on fragmented carbon nanotube papers. ACS Appl. Mater. Interfaces **9**(5), 4835–4842 (2017)
18. Iglio, R., Mariani, S., Robbiano, V., Strambini, L., Barillaro, G.: "Flexible polydimethylsiloxane foams decorated with multiwalled carbon nanotubes enable unprecedented detection of ultralow strain and pressure coupled with a large working range", (in eng). ACS Appl. Mater. Interfaces **10**(16), 13877–13885 (2018)

19. Zhou, S., et al.: Strength-toughness combination in nickel matrix composites reinforced by hybrid graphene nanoplatelets-titanium diboride. Carbon 201, 1137–1148 (2023)

20. Krishnan, S.K., Singh, E., Singh, P., Meyyappan, M., Nalwa, H.S.: A review on graphene-based nanocomposites for electrochemical and fluorescent biosensors. RSC Adv. 9(16), 8778–8881 (2019). https://doi.org/10.1039/C8RA09577A

21. Kim, E., et al.: Solvent-responsive polymernanocapsules with controlled permeability: encapsulation and release of a fluorescent dye by swelling and deswelling. Chem. Commun. 12, 1472–1474 (2009). https://doi.org/10.1039/B823110A

22. Wang, J., et al.: Synergistic effect of well-defined dual sites boosting the oxygen reduction reaction. Energy Environ. Sci. 11(12), 3375–3379 (2018). https://doi.org/10.1039/C8EE02656D

23. Ha, M., Lim, S., Ko, H.: Wearable and flexible sensors for user-interactive health-monitoring devices. J. Mater. Chem. B 6(24), 4043–4064 (2018). https://doi.org/10.1039/C8TB01063C

24. Ho, D.H., Sun, Q., Kim, S.Y., Han, J.T., Kim, D.H., Cho, J.H.: "Stretchable and multimodal all graphene electronic skin", (in eng). Adv. Mater. 28(13), 2601–2608 (2016)

25. Liu, H., et al.: Lightweight conductive graphene/thermoplastic polyurethane foams with ultra-high compressibility for piezoresistive sensing. J. Mater. Chem. C 5(1), 73–83 (2017). https://doi.org/10.1039/C6TC03713E

Wearable Robots for Assistance, Augmentation and Rehabilitation of Human Movements

Research on Fuzzy Iterative Learning Control of Pneumatic Artificial Muscle

Huiru Duan[1] , Shenglong Xie[1,2(✉)] , Zijing Liu[1] , and Yanjian Wan[1]

[1] School of Mechanical and Electrical Engineering, China Jiliang University, Hangzhou 310018, Zhejiang, China
`xieshenglong68@163.com`

[2] Anhui Engineering Laboratory for Intelligent Applications and Security of Industrial Internet, Anhui University of Technology, Ma'anshan, Anhui 243032, People's Republic of China

Abstract. In order to achieve high-precision and rapid trajectory tracking control of pneumatic artificial muscle, a fuzzy iterative learning control scheme is proposed. Firstly, based on the traditional iterative control method, an iterative learning control model of pneumatic artificial muscle is established to solve the problem that it is difficult to establish an accurate mathematical model of the pneumatic system. Then, based on the Zadeh inference method, the fuzzy control law of the control system is established, introducing fuzzy control to compensate for iterative learning control and reduce the system error. Finally, the trajectory tracking control of pneumatic artificial muscle is implemented by using iterative learning control and fuzzy iterative learning control respectively. The experimental results show that both iterative learning control and fuzzy iterative learning control can track the desired curve well and maintain convergence, and iterative learning control converges 11.94% faster than fuzzy iterative learning control, but the error fluctuation amplitude of fuzzy iterative learning control is 41.18% smaller than that of iterative learning control, and the stability is better, so that the pneumatic artificial muscle has good performance in trajectory tracking control.

Keywords: Pneumatic Artificial Muscle · Fuzzy Control · Iterative Learning Control · Fuzzy Iterative Learning Control · Trajectory Tracking Control

1 Introduction

In recent years, pneumatic artificial muscle, as a new type of actuator, has been widely used in surgery, rehabilitation, bionics, rescue and other fields [1] due to its light weight, large output force and good flexibility [2]. However, due to the nonlinear, time-varying, and difficult-to-determine control parameters of pneumatic artificial muscle during operation, it is difficult to achieve rapid and accurate trajectory tracking control.

To solve this problem, extensive research has been conducted both domestically and internationally. Based on the three-element model, Karnjanaparichat [3] introduced variable structure controller on the basis of feedback linearization to study the trajectory tracking control of pneumatic artificial muscle. Liang [4] proposed a nonlinear control strategy for pneumatic artificial muscle based on the three-element model. Hui [5]

H. Yang et al. (Eds.): ICIRA 2023, LNAI 14268, pp. 321–330, 2023.
https://doi.org/10.1007/978-981-99-6486-4_28

first applied the Kriging optimal linear unbiased estimation method to model the pressure/length hysteresis of McKibben muscles, and proposed a new Kriging prediction model (KPM) based on mathematical functions. However, due to the compressibility of gas and the flexibility of pneumatic artificial muscle, it is difficult to establish an accurate mathematical model of the pneumatic artificial muscle motion control system [6, 7], which leads to poor control accuracy in the above methods. Therefore, scholars attempted to use the PID control algorithm [8] combined with feedforward hysteresis compensation to achieve motion control of the pneumatic muscle [9]. Lin [10] established a hysteresis model of pneumatic artificial muscle using the Prandtl-Ishlinski model, and applied PID control and sliding mode control to track the trajectory. Liu [11] applied feedforward compensation based on a modified Prandtl-Ishlinskii model, using traditional PID to control bionic joints synergistically driven by spring and pneumatic muscle. Minh [12] established a hysteresis model based on the Maxwell-slip method for feedforward compensation, and used PI controller to control the pressure. Xu [13] proposed a hysteresis model based on a hybrid Gaussian model, and verified the effectiveness of the inverse model by designing a feedforward hysteresis compensator for trajectory tracking experiments. However, due to the feedforward combined with the feedback control strategy, the above problem has the following problems: since the disturbance information is unknown or unmeasurable, it cannot be compensated by the feedforward controller in the algorithm; and the closed-loop compensation of the feedback controller will bring about a hysteresis in the control [14]. In comparison, iterative learning control can simply and quickly control nonlinear strongly coupled dynamic systems with high uncertainty [15] and track a given desired trajectory with high accuracy without relying on an accurate mathematical model of the system [16]. Therefore, it has been widely used in the control field [17]. However, due to the interference of random noise, nonlinearity of the control system, and non-repeatability of actual trajectories, iterative learning control as an open-loop control architecture does not have relevant feedback and parameter identification mechanisms to deal with these problems [18]. Therefore, it is necessary to combine feedback, robustness, or adaptive control frameworks to achieve the desired control effect.

Therefore, aiming at the problem of poor trajectory tracking control of pneumatic artificial muscle due to the complexity of the control system and time-varying parameters, this paper proposes a fuzzy iterative learning control method for pneumatic artificial muscle by integrating fuzzy controller and iterative learning control. Firstly, ordinary PID is used as the learning law to establish iterative learning control. Then, the fuzzy rules are formulated through Zadeh inference method to establish fuzzy PID control law and construct a fuzzy controller. Finally, the fuzzy iterative learning control is obtained by adding the fuzzy controller to the iterative control. The trajectory tracking control of pneumatic muscle is compared and studied using the two control algorithms, and relevant conclusions are drawn.

2 Theoretical Modeling

2.1 Iterative Learning Control

Pneumatic artificial muscle has characteristics such as nonlinearity and hysteresis. In this section, the iterative learning control method is mainly used to track the controlled object with repetitive motion properties without requiring an accurate mathematical model of the controlled object. The input signal is continuously modified by the learning law of iterative learning control, and the desired curve and the output curve will gradually converge and finally reach stability.

The combined learning law used in this paper refers to the PID-type learning law proposed by Arimoto et al.

$$u_{k+1}(t) = u_k(t) + \Gamma \dot{e}_k(t) + Le_k(t) + \psi \int_0^t e_k(\tau)d\tau, \tag{1}$$

$$e_k(t) = y_d(t) - y_k(t), \tag{2}$$

Γ, L and ψ are learning gain matrices, $u_k(t)$ is the result of the previous iteration, $e_k(t)$ is the error. $y_d(t)$ is the desired output and $y_k(t)$ is the actual output.

From Eq. (2), it can be simplified to obtain

$$u_{k+1}(t) = u_k(t) + U(e_k(t), t), \tag{3}$$

In each iteration of running, the input signal $u_{k+1}(t)$ is the last output $u_k(t)$ added to the learning law. $u_k(t)$ is the previous operation experience in the iterative learning, and each iteration is a correction on the existing basis. If $u_k(t)$ is removed, the previous control experience before this will not be effective. The learning law is a function of the error and can be viewed as the kth iteration, where $u_k(t)$ added $U(e_k(t), t)$ correction compensation to obtain $u_{k+1}(t)$. The input $u_k(t)$ of each iteration calls the output of the last iteration in the control signal memory for computation.

Reference [1] and combined with Eqs. (1) and (3) to construct the pneumatic artificial muscle iterative learning control model, as shown in Fig. 2. Considering the actual situation of pneumatic transmission, D has no effect in PID control, and the parameters of the PID controller in the Simulink model are $k_p = 1000$, $k_i = 100$, and $k_d = 0$ respectively.

2.2 Fuzzy Controller

In order to improve the dynamic performance of the system, a fuzzy controller is introduced. The fuzzy controller represents fuzzy rules using fuzzy sets based on the knowledge of fuzzy mathematics. Then, the fuzzy sets and rules are utilized through a knowledge-based expert system to perform fuzzy inference based on the response situation. Subsequently, defuzzification and fuzzy inverse transformation are performed to optimize the PID controller parameters using the fuzzy rules in the knowledge database. This results in the best-fit PID parameters for equipment, leading to better control effects. The fuzzy parameter tuning model (see Fig. 3) is derived from the above theory.

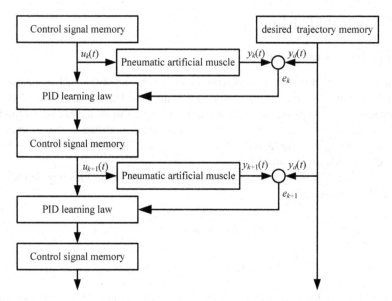

Fig. 1. Iterative learning block diagram.

Referring to the fuzzy parameter tuning model, the error E and error rate of change EC are chosen as input terms, and $\triangle K_p$, $\triangle K_i$, and $\triangle K_d$ are selected as output terms. Seven fuzzy values are adopted for input and output terms, which are Negative Big (NB), Negative Middle (NM), Negative Small (NS), Zero (Z), Positive Small (PS), Positive Middle (PM), and Positive Big (PB). Among them, NB adopts zmf (z-shaped) function, PB adopts smf (s-shaped) function, and the others use trimf (triangular) function. The input universes are $[-3,3]$, and the universes of $\triangle K_p$, $\triangle K_i$, and $\triangle K_d$ are $[-0.3,0.3]$, $[-0.06,0.06]$, and $[-3,3]$, respectively.

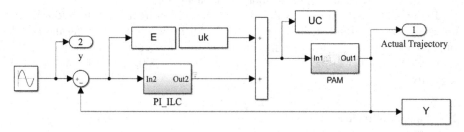

Fig. 2. Iterative learning control of pneumatic artificial muscle trajectory tracking model.

According to references [19, 20], the control rules are as follows:

(1) When E is large and EC is small, increasing K_p can reduce the error. To avoid instantaneous increase of the error E resulting in differential saturation and beyond the control range, K_d is set to a moderate level. To prevent large overshoot and integral saturation, K_i has no effect, that is, $K_i = 0$.

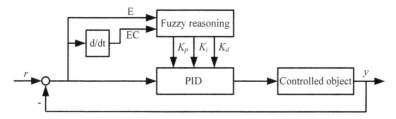

Fig. 3. Fuzzy control parameter tuning model.

(2) When E and EC are of medium size, in order to reduce overshoot, K_p should be small, K_i should be appropriate, and K_d should be moderately set to affect the system response speed.

(3) When the error E is small, in order to maintain system stability, K_p and K_i should be increased. To avoid oscillation near the setpoint, a large K_d is used for small EC, and a small K_d is used for large EC.

(4) When the error rate of change EC is large, in order to avoid system oscillation, K_i and K_d should be reduced.

(5) When E × EC is positive, it means that the actual output deviates from the desired trajectory. If E is large, increasing K_p and reducing K_i can reduce the error. If E is small, reducing K_p and increasing K_i can enhance stability.

(6) When E × EC is negative, it means that the actual output is tending towards the desired trajectory. If E is large, reducing K_p and K_i can reduce the error. If E is small, reducing K_p and increasing K_i can enhance stability.

Based on the above analysis, a fuzzy control rule table is established for the movement control system of pneumatic artificial muscle using the Zadeh inference method (Tables 1, 2 and 3).

Table 1. The fuzzy rule table of $\triangle K_p$.

EC\E	NB	NM	NS	Z	PS	PM	PB
NB	PB	PB	PM	PM	PS	PS	Z
NM	PB	PB	PM	PM	PS	Z	Z
NS	PM	PM	PM	PS	Z	NS	NM
Z	PM	PS	PS	Z	NS	NM	NM
PS	PS	PS	Z	NS	NS	NM	NM
PM	PS	Z	NS	NM	NM	NM	NB
PB	Z	NS	NS	NM	NM	NB	NB

Table 2. The fuzzy rule table of $\triangle K_i$.

EC\E	NB	NM	NS	Z	PS	PM	PB
NB	NB	NB	NB	NM	NM	Z	Z
NM	NB	NB	NM	NM	NS	Z	Z
NS	NM	NM	NS	NS	Z	PS	PS
Z	NM	NS	NS	Z	PS	PS	PM
PS	NS	NS	Z	PS	PS	PM	PM
PM	Z	Z	PS	PB	PM	PB	PB
PB	Z	Z	PS	PM	PB	PB	PB

Table 3. The fuzzy rule table of $\triangle K_d$.

EC\E	NB	NM	NS	Z	PS	PM	PB
NB	PS	PS	Z	Z	Z	PB	PB
NM	NS	NS	NS	NS	Z	PS	PM
NS	NB	NB	NM	NS	Z	PS	PM
Z	NB	NM	NM	NS	Z	PS	PM
PS	NB	NM	NS	NS	Z	PS	PS
PM	NM	NS	NS	NS	Z	PS	PS
PB	PS	Z	Z	Z	Z	PB	PB

2.3 Fuzzy Iterative Learning Control

Iterative control does not have self-learning and adaptive ability, and the control action is not refined, with low steady-state accuracy. A fuzzy controller can be added to iterative learning control to make up for its shortcomings. Therefore, this article proposes fuzzy iterative learning control.

The idea of the fuzzy iterative learning control scheme: change the affiliation function by iteratively following the system state, make corrections and improve the fuzzy rules, then get the adaptive parameters by fuzzy reasoning, and make simple compensation according to the input and output of the system, so that the whole pneumatic artificial muscle control system has better control accuracy and robustness. The fuzzy iterative learning control block diagram is obtained from the above theory (see Fig. 4).

On the basis of the theory of iterative control of pneumatic artificial muscle in Sect. 2.1, this section optimizes the learning law and replaces the PID controller in the iterative learning control of Sect. 2.1 with the fuzzy controller obtained in Sect. 2.2, and compensation is also performed. The fuzzy iterative learning control model is obtained from the above theory (see Fig. 5). $u_k(t)$ is the result of the last iteration, and after modification and compensation, $u_{k+1}(t)$ is obtained.

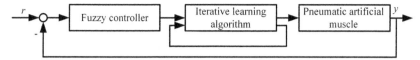

Fig. 4. Fuzzy iterative learning control block diagram.

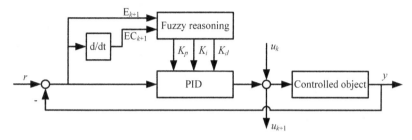

Fig. 5. Fuzzy iterative learning control model.

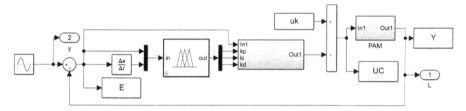

Fig. 6. Fuzzy iterative learning control pneumatic artificial muscle trajectory tracking model.

Based on the fuzzy iterative learning control model (see Fig. 5), the PID law in the iterative learning control is replaced by fuzzy reasoning, and after optimization, the fuzzy iterative learning control pneumatic artificial muscle trajectory tracking model is built (see Fig. 6). The value of the iterative output $u_{k+1}(t)$ is stored in the control signal memory UC, and the next iteration is run, uk is the new learning law after correction.

3 Implementation Analysis

3.1 Iterative Learning Control

The iterative learning control of pneumatic artificial muscle introduced in Sect. 2.1, as shown in the model in Fig. 2, stores the output result of each iteration in the control signal memory UC. When the next iteration is run, the control signal memory UC passes the value of the last iteration result to uk for operation. After several iterations, the output curve can be seen to coincide with the desired curve from the curve of the implementation.

The implementation results are shown in Fig. 7, when the learning law is the traditional PID learning law, and the parameters in the PID controller are set to $k_p = 1000$, $k_i = 100$, and $k_d = 0$, iterative learning control can make the actual output track the

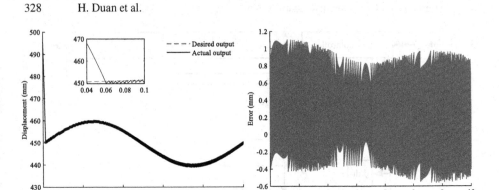

(a) Actual output and desired output curve.   (b) Error curve.

Fig. 7. Iterative control implementation curve of pneumatic artificial muscle.

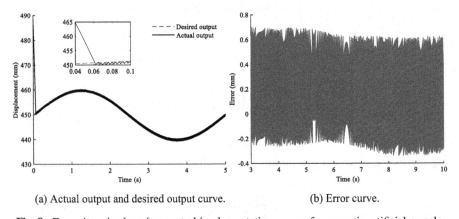

(a) Actual output and desired output curve.   (b) Error curve.

Fig. 8. Fuzzy iterative learning control implementation curve of pneumatic artificial muscle.

desired trajectory curve. The convergence time is T = 0.059 s, and the error amplitude is −0.6 ~ 1.1 mm.

3.2 Fuzzy Iterative Learning Control

The steady-state accuracy of the iterative learning control is not good, so Sect. 2.3 proposes to add a fuzzy controller on the basis of iterative learning control. According to the implementation results (see Fig. 8), the fuzzy iterative learning control can make the actual output track the desired trajectory curve. The convergence time is T = 0.067 s, and the error amplitude is −0.3 ~ 0.7 mm.

3.3 Comparative Analysis

The convergence speed of iterative learning control (see Fig. 7(a)) is 11.94% faster than that of fuzzy iterative learning control (see Fig. 8(a)); however, the error amplitude of fuzzy iterative learning control (see Fig. 8(b)) is 41.18% smaller than that of iterative control (see Fig. 7(b)) (Table 4).

Table 4. Comparison of control methods

Control method	Convergence time (s)	Error amplitude (mm)
Iterative learning control	0.059	−0.6 ~ 1.1
Fuzzy iterative learning control	0.067	−0.3 ~ 0.7

4   Conclusion

In this study, a fuzzy iterative learning control method was proposed for the trajectory tracking control of pneumatic artificial muscle based on the theory of iterative learning control and fuzzy control, and compared with iterative learning control. The experimental results show that the convergence speed of fuzzy iterative learning control in tracking the desired curve is 11.94% faster than that of iterative learning control, and the error amplitude of fuzzy iterative learning control is 41.18% smaller than that of iterative learning control, indicating that fuzzy iterative learning control of pneumatic artificial muscle can effectively achieve fast and high-precision trajectory tracking control.

Acknowledgements. This work is supported by National Natural Science Foundation of China under Grant 52205037, Fundamental Scientific Research Funds for Zhejiang Province under Grant 2022YW43, the open fund of Anhui Engineering Laboratory for Intelligent Applications and Security of Industrial Internet under Grant IASII21–04 and Student Research Program of China Jiliang University under Grant 2022X25008.

References

1. Zhang, D.H., Zhao, X.G., Han, J.D., et al.: Independent force and stiffness control for antagonistic joint driven by pneumatic artificial muscles. Robot **40**(5), 587–596 (2018). https://doi.org/10.13973/j.cnki.robot.180256
2. Xie, S.L., Shao, X., Lu, Y.J., et al.: Comparative research on hysteresis modeling of pneumatic muscle based on neural network. Chin. J. Sens. Actuators **33**(10), 1438–1443 (2020). https://doi.org/10.3969/j.issn.1004-1699.2020.10.010
3. Karnjanaparichat, T., Pongvuthithum, R.: Adaptive tracking control of multi-link robots actuated by pneumatic muscles with additive disturbances. Robotica **35**(11), 1–18 (2016). https://doi.org/10.1017/S0263574716000758
4. Liang, D.K., Sun, N., Wu, Y.M., et al.: Nonlinear control for pneumatic artificial muscle systems with disturbance estimation. Control Theory Appl. **36**(11), 1912–1919 (2019). https://doi.org/10.7641/CTA.2019.90497
5. Hui, Y., Yang, C., Yao, S., et al.: A novel Kriging-median inverse compensator for modeling and compensating asymmetric hysteresis of pneumatic artificial muscle. Smart Mater. Struct. **27**, 115019 (2018). https://doi.org/10.1088/1361-665X/aad758

6. Wang, B.R., Zhang, B., Shen, G.Y., et al.: Modeling and fuzzy control of humanoid elbow driven by cascaded pneumatic muscles. Robot **39**(4), 474–480 (2017). https://doi.org/10. 13973/j.cnki.robot.2017.0474

7. Wang, Q.L., Wang, W., Hao, D.X., et al.: Hysteresis modeling and application of Mckibben pneumatic artificial muscles. Chinese J. Mech. Eng. **55**(21), 73–80 (2019). https://doi.org/10. 3901/JME.2019.21.073

8. Fan, W., Peng, G.Z., Gao, J.Y., et al.: A self-modified fuzzy-PID controller of pneumatic muscle actuator position servo system. Chinese Hydraulics Pneumatics **09**, 30–33 (2003). https://doi.org/10.3969/j.issn.1000-4858.2003.09.014

9. Liang, D.K., Chen, Y.H., Sun, N., et al.: Overview of control methods for pneumatic artificial muscle-actuated robots. Control Decis. **36**(01), 27–41 (2021). https://doi.org/10.13195/ j.kzyjc.2020.0793

10. Lin, C.J., Lin, C.R., Yu, S.K., et al.: Hysteresis modeling and tracking control for a dual pneumatic artificial muscle system using Prandtl-Ishlinskii model. Mechatronics **28**, 35–45 (2015). https://doi.org/10.1016/j.mechatronics.2015.03.006

11. Liu, Y.X., Zang, X.Z., Lin, Z.K., et al.: Position control of a bio-inspired semi-active joint with direct inverse hysteresis modeling and compensation. Adv. Mech. Eng. **8**(11), 1–8 (2016). https://doi.org/10.1177/1687814016677223

12. Minh, T.V., Tjahjowidodo, T., Ramon, H., et al.: Cascade position control of a single pneumatic artificial muscle-mass system with hysteresis compensation. Mechatronics **20**(3), 402–414 (2010). https://doi.org/10.1016/j.mechatronics.2010.03.001

13. Xu, J.H., Xiao, M.B., Ding, Y.: Modeling and compensation of hysteresis for pneumatic artificial muscles based on Gaussian mixture models. Sci. China Technol. Sci. **62**(7), 1094–1102 (2019). https://doi.org/10.1007/s11431-018-9488-1

14. Xie, S.L., Mei, J.P., Liu, H.T., et al.: Hysteresis modeling and trajectory tracking control of the pneumatic muscle actuator using modified Prandtl-Shlinskii model. Mech. Mach. Theor. **120**, 213–224 (2018). https://doi.org/10.1016/j.mechmachtheory.2017.07.016

15. Tao, H.F., Liu, W., Yang, H.Z.: Iterative feedback tuning control and optimization of pneumatic muscle actuators. Inf. Control. **48**(05), 573–579 (2019). https://doi.org/10.13976/j.cnki.xk. 2019.8513

16. Yi, X., Chen, J., Liao, X.D., et al.: Research on trajectory tracking control of manipulator based on adaptive iterative learning. Electric Drive **50**(03), 45–50 (2020). https://doi.org/10. 19457/j.1001-2095.dqcd19353

17. Zhu, P.P., Bu, X.H., Liang, J.Q., et al.: An improved model free adaptive iterative learning control algorithm with data quantization. Control Theor. Appl. **37**(05), 1178–1184 (2020). https://doi.org/10.7641/CTA.2019.90347

18. Peng, X.W., He, Y.G.: Electro-hydraulic proportional servo control based on iterative learning algorithm. Chin. J. Mech. Eng. **54**(20), 271–278 (2018). https://doi.org/10.3901/JME.2018. 20.271

19. Wang, S.Y., Shi, Y., Feng, Z.X.: A method for controlling a loading system based on a fuzzy PID controller. Mech. Sci. Technol. Aerosp. Eng. **30**(01), 166–172 (2011). https://doi.org/10. 13433/j.cnki.1003-8728.2011.01.035

20. Li, F., Chen, Q., Liu, K., et al.: Fuzzy PID control of parallel platform actuated by pneumatic artificial muscle. Robot **43**(02), 140–147 (2021). https://doi.org/10.13973/j.cnki.robot. 200175

Decoding Discrete Gestures Across Different Arm Positions Based on Multimodal Fusion Strategy

Yunzhe Li[1], Zongtian Yin[1], Ting Zhang[2], and Jianjun Meng[1,3(✉)]

[1] School of Mechanical Engineering, Shanghai Jiao Tong University, 800 Dongchuan Road, Shanghai, China
mengjianjunxs008@sjtu.edu.cn
[2] Robotics and Microsystems Center, College of Mechanical and Electrical Engineering, Soochow University, Suzhou, China
[3] State Key Laboratory of Mechanical System and Vibration, Shanghai Jiao Tong University, 800 Dongchuan Road, Shanghai, China

Abstract. Decoding human motion intentions is critical for prosthetic control, where gesture recognition remains a research focus. However, the decoding accuracy of gestures is affected by multiple factors, resulting in poor robustness in practical applications. Variation in arm positions can significantly decrease the accuracy of gesture recognition, negatively impacting the performance of human-machine interfaces (HMIs). We developed a multimodal HMI system that has the potential to improve the robustness of gesture recognition significantly. This multimodal HMI system synchronously acquired surface electromyography (sEMG), A-mode ultrasound, and inertial measurement unit (IMU) signals and has a miniaturized signal processing module to be integrated into a prosthetic hand socket. We conducted an offline experiment on 11 subjects to investigate the discrete recognition of 10 hand gestures across three different arm positions. The results demonstrate that the multimodal fusion approach using the proposed cascaded classifiers has advantages in gesture recognition across different arm positions. The LDA classifier's best recognition accuracy was 97.08% ± 1.90%, outperforming the single modalities significantly.

Keywords: Hand gesture recognition · Arm position variation · Multimodal fusion · Human-machine interface (HMI) · Cascaded classifiers

1 Introduction

The human-machine interface (HMI) bridges the human's nervous system and the peripheral hardware by acquiring physiological signals and decoding movement intentions. A critical and successful application of the HMI is controlling upper limb prostheses

This work was supported by the National Key R&D Program of China (Grant No. 2020YFC207800), and the National Natural Science Foundation of China (Grant No. 52175023).

[1, 2]. Among recent studies on prosthetic control, surface electromyography (sEMG) has garnered the most attention from researchers [1]. Pattern recognition using sEMG has recently become the dominant approach in myoelectric prosthetic control. However, the sEMG interface is still limited in the research lab and seldom used in commercial prosthetic control [3] due to its inadequate spatial resolution [4] and susceptibility to interference from muscle fatigue [5], arm position [6], muscle strength changes [7], skin impedance alterations [8], and other factors.

In recent years, various types of human-machine interfaces have been investigated by detecting muscle activity from multiple modalities for decoding movement intentions. The ultrasound signal has been a prominent research topic in recent years, which can be divided into A-Mode, B-Mode, and M-Mode [9]. Relevant studies have demonstrated that ultrasound is more responsive to the muscles' spatial properties and has advantages in decoding intricate finger movements [10]. However, its temporal resolution is usually worse than sEMG. And there have been recent successful studies on A-mode ultrasound HMI for prosthesis control [11]. In addition, near-infrared spectroscopy (NIRS) [12], and mechanomyography (MMG) [13] are also utilized in HMIs.

In order to improve the decoding performance and ensure the stability of HMIs in practical applications, many studies have explored the feasibility of fusing different types of sensors. Some research has fused several types of multiple signal modalities, such as the fusion of sEMG and NIRS [14], the fusion of sEMG and MMG [15], and the fusion of A-mode ultrasound and sEMG [16]. The findings of these studies indicate a significant enhancement in the decoding accuracy of hand gestures, which is also suggesting that multimodality gives relatively more robust recognition accuracy compared to that of a single type of sensor. Multimodal HMIs have tremendous potential for upper limb prosthetic control since they incorporate richer multiscale signals that reflect muscle characteristics.

In prosthetic control, changes in limb position significantly impact the recognition of discrete gesture patterns [17]. The classification performance is adversely affected when the test and training data are obtained from different limb positions. However, in practical applications, the frequent changes in the user's arm position necessitate a human-machine interface that maintains excellent decoding performance across varying positions. In previous studies, a two-stage classification approach was proposed by a researcher to train classifiers under multiple arm positions [18, 19]. The first stage involved identifying limb positions using accelerometers, followed by pattern recognition of gestures in the second stage. This approach is more effective in mitigating the negative impact of limb positions.

In this study, we have developed a multimodal HMI system that utilizes simultaneous acquisition of sEMG, A-mode ultrasound, and IMU to recognize 10 discrete hand gestures across three arm positions through the multimodal fusion strategy. We conducted experiments on 11 subjects using two different strategies: the approach of a two-stage classification approach using cascaded classifiers and that of a single full-scale classifier. Additionally, we compared several common classifiers, i.e., k-nearest neighbors (KNN), support vector machine (SVM), and linear discriminant classifier (LDA). Using the LDA classifier, the recognition accuracy was 97.08% ± 1.90% and 94.55% ± 2.29% for the two strategies, respectively.

2   Methods

2.1   Multimodal Human-Machine Interface

We have developed customized hardware for the multimodal human-machine interface system, as depicted in Fig. 1. This hardware can simultaneously acquire four channels of A-mode ultrasound and surface electromyography (semg), and one channel of inertial measurement unit (IMU). In addition, the hardware comprises the central signal processing module and the four-channel fusion sensing probes.

The surface side of the fusion probe is shown in Fig. 1(c), consisting of a pair of dry gold-plated copper differential electrodes to acquire the semg signal. The size of a single electrode is 16mm * 6 mm, and the distance between the two differential electrodes is set to 28 mm to alleviate the crosstalk detected from adjacent muscles [20]. The A-mode ultrasound transducer, with a diameter of 12 mm, is positioned at the center between the two semg electrodes to transmit the ultrasound excitation and receive the echo signal. Moreover, the IMU module is securely mounted within the fusion probe's shell, specifically to Channel 1.

The central signal processing module of the multimodal HMI system is connected to the 4-channel fusion probes through shielded signal wires, as shown in Fig. 1(a), and its overall size is 80 mm * 80 mm * 50 mm. The microcontroller (MCU, STM32F7, STMicroelectronics Inc., Switzerland) operated by the FreeRTOS operating system is utilized for the simultaneous processing of four channels of A-ultrasound signals (center frequency of 1 MHz), surface EMG signals (sampling frequency of 1000 Hz), and one channel of triaxial acceleration signals (sampling frequency of 100 Hz), see Fig. 1(d). The MCU performs the analog-to-digital conversion and temporary storage after filtering the raw signals. Then the A-mode ultrasound, semg, and triaxial acceleration signals are transmitted to the computer via high-speed Wi-Fi and Bluetooth modules (ESP8266, Espressif, China, and ATK-HC05, Alientek, China). Customized software on the PC is utilized for receiving, displaying, storing, and analyzing the multimodal signals.

In the experiment, the 4-channel fusion sensing probes are placed on the subjects' flexor carpi radialis (FCR), extensor carpi radialis longus (ECRL), extensor digitorum (ED), and flexor carpi ulnaris (FCU), respectively, as shown in Fig. 1 (e-f). And the muscles are physiologically activated, multimodal signals are acquired during wrist and hand motions. For healthy participants, the semg reference electrodes were placed on the wrist, while for individuals with foream amputation, they were placed on the ulna of the elbow.

2.2   Experimental Protocol

11 healthy subjects, including 8 males and 3 females (average age 22.73 ± 1.56; range: 19–25) participated in this experiment. They were all right-handed and had no history of muscular or joint injury. Before participation, all subjects signed the informed consent. Moreover, the experimental protocol was approved by the SJTU's Institutional Review Board (E2021103).

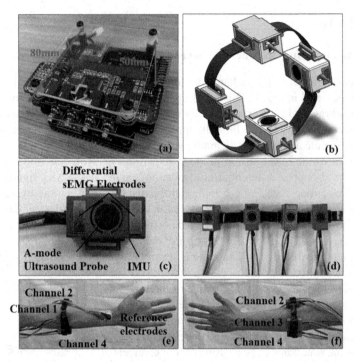

Fig. 1. Implementation of multimodal HMI hardware system: (a) the central signal processing module for the multimodal signals; (b) the 3D model of the four-channel fusion sensing probes; (c) the surface side of the fusion probe; (d) a picture of the wearable four-channel probes of the sEMG/A-mode + 1-channel IMU sensor; placement of fusion sensing probes over the forearm (e) anterior view, (f) posterior view. Channel 1 and Channel 2 are placed on flexor carpi radialis (FCR) and extensor carpi radialis longus (ECRL); Channel 3 and Channel 4 are placed on extensor digitorum (ED) and flexor capri ulnaris (FCU).

During the experiment, the subject was seated in a chair equipped with armrests and wore the 4-channel fusion sensing probes securely, as described in Fig. 2(a) on the left forearm. At the same time, the sEMG reference electrodes were attached to the ipsilateral wrist. As shown in Fig. 2(a), the subject's elbow joint was placed on the left armrest of the chair, and the subject needed to maintain her/his visual fixation on the computer screen throughout the experiment. And the customized software running on the computer would prompt the subject for gestures and display the multimodal signal simultaneously.

Subjects were instructed to perform 10 classes of hand gestures in 3 positions, including fingers abduction (FA), fist (FS), index point (IP), finger pinch (FP), thumb and index finger pinch (TIP), half fist (HF), side pinch (SP), wrist flexion (WF), wrist extension (WE), and wrist radial deviation (WRD). These motions represent the gestures commonly used in daily life. Additionally, the 3 arm positions were vertically upward, horizontally placed, and naturally downward in this experiment.

The experiment was divided into 3 sessions. Each session consisted of a different arm position, and 8 trials were performed under each position. As shown in Fig. 3,

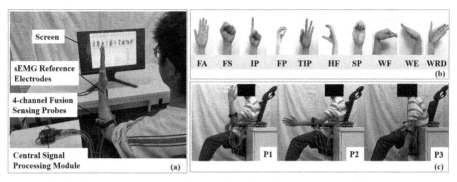

Fig. 2. Experimental setup: (a) the experimental setting; (b) the pre-set motions for hand gestures, including fingers abduction (FA), fist (FS), index point (IP), finger pinch (FP), thumb and index finger pinch (TIP), half fist (HF), side pinch (SP), wrist flexion (WF), wrist extension (WE), and wrist radial deviation (WRD); (c) three arm positions in the experiment, P1 represents the arm in the vertical upward position, P2 represents the horizontal position of the arm, P3 represents the arm's natural downward position.

each gesture was held for 5 s, and each trial consisted of 10 fixed-order gestures, taking 50 s in total. And the subjects were instructed to follow the screen cues to conduct the corresponding gestures. Because the subjects had reaction time when switching motions, only the data in the middle (3 s) was considered stationary signals and kept in the data analysis. There was no rest time between each gesture. Subjects were given a 5 s rest period between each trial and a 1 min break between sessions to prevent muscle fatigue throughout the experiment.

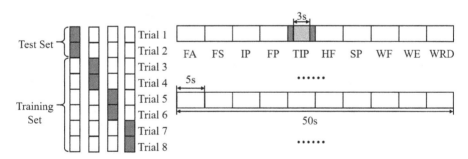

Fig. 3. Experimental protocol in a certain position

2.3 Data Processing and Classification

Data processing of the multimodal signals comprises four stages: preprocessing, data segmentation, feature extraction, and classification. In the preprocessing stage, sEMG signals were sent to a comb filter at 50 Hz and a band-pass filter from 20 to 450 Hz online to eliminate the interference of power line noise and motion artifacts. In addition, a low-pass filter of 2.5 Hz was applied to the triaxial acceleration.

In order to align the data from different sensors, a specific windowing strategy was implemented based on the characteristics of various sensors. The ultrasound probe of each channel needed 12.5 ms to complete the data acquisition, resulting in a frame of 4-channel ultrasound data being obtained every 50 ms. Therefore, the time window step of sEMG was set to 50 ms and the window length to 200 ms with a 150 ms overlap. Similarly, triaxial acceleration was segmented in the same way as sEMG. In data acquisition and processing, each frame of the A-mode ultrasound signals was temporally aligned with the corresponding time windows of the sEMG and IMU signals.

For sEMG signals, time domain statistical features [21] were extracted within a sliding window of 200 ms, including mean absolute value (MAV), root mean square (RMS), waveform length (WL), number of crossing points (ZC), and slope sign changes (SSC). There were four channels of sEMG; thus, sEMG feature dimensions were 20. The waveform characteristics of each frame are acquired for the A-mode ultrasound signals. The signal envelope was obtained according to the discrete Hilbert transform for a frame of ultrasound data [10]. It should be noted that the first 20 points were removed since they represented the echo signals of the probe/skin interface and held no relevance to the muscle. The envelope waveform was processed using a sliding window with a length of 20 points, then the mean and root mean square error (RMSE) within the sliding window were extracted as features. The feature of 4-channel A-mode ultrasound consisted of 72 dimensions. After that, the A-mode ultrasound features were reduced to 20 dimensions using principal component analysis (PCA), and were consistent with the sEMG features. The IMU signal represented by their mean triaxial acceleration values within sliding windows was only used to discriminate the arm position.

This study used a feature fusion strategy to integrate sEMG features and A-mode ultrasound features. Their classification performances using single-modal features and multimodal features were compared. Three classifiers were utilized for training the classification model, namely k-nearest neighbors (KNN), support vector machine (SVM), and linear discriminant analysis (LDA). As shown in Fig. 3, the data obtained from the 8 trials were divided into 4 equal subsets and subjected to 4-fold cross-validation. Specifically, each round of validation involved training using data from 6 trials and testing using the data from the remaining 2 trials. Moreover, an analysis of the classification accuracy was performed for the eleven subjects. It should be noted that arm positions and gestures were two separate factors, and an accurate classification result required gestures in any position to be classified correctly. The classification accuracy (CA) was defined as follows:

$$CA = \frac{Number\ of\ correctly\ recognized\ motions}{Total\ number\ of\ testing\ motions} \times 100\%$$

2.4 Multimodal Fusion Decoding Algorithm

To enhance the accuracy of gesture decoding, we employed a multimodal feature-level fusion approach that leveraged sEMG and A-mode ultrasound features to recognize gesture patterns. Furthermore, in order to validate the advantages of multimodal fusion, we compared the classification results of three conditions: using sEMG features only, ultrasound features only, and a combination of sEMG and ultrasound features.

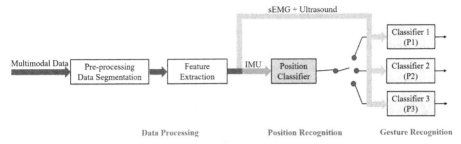

Fig. 4. A multimodal fusion strategy using cascaded classifier approach

Considering that sEMG and ultrasound features varied significantly across different arm positions, which greatly impaired the recognition performance of the classifier, we adopted a cascaded classifier strategy, as shown in Fig. 4. This method separated position recognition and gesture recognition into two cascaded stages. Firstly, three distinct gesture recognition classifiers were trained individually for three different arm positions during the training phase. Then, after the multimodal data were preprocessed, windowed, and feature extracted during the testing phase, the current arm position was determined by classifying the triaxial acceleration feature. Next the corresponding gesture classifier was selected based on the arm position, and the gesture recognition result was obtained based on the input of sEMG and ultrasound features.

Additionally, we employed a single full-scale classifier strategy that simultaneously decoded both arm position and gesture. This approach considered the same gesture performed in different arm positions as distinct categories, resulting in 30 classes for three arm positions and ten gestures. We combined all training data from different arm positions into a comprehensive dataset and trained the full-scale classifier. Ideally, during the testing phase, the input of multimodal data could be decoded simultaneously to determine the current arm position and gesture pattern.

2.5 Statistical Analysis

Paired Wilcoxon signed-rank test was applied to compare the classification accuracy of single-modal sEMG, single-modal ultrasound, and fusion features. Besides, paired t-test was performed to compare the multimodal fusion method's classification accuracy of the cascaded classifier approach and the full-scale classifier approach. The significance level was set to 0.05.

3 Results

3.1 Testing with Single Classifier Approach

Using the data from a single position to train the SVM classification model, the average classification accuracy of 11 subjects on all positions is shown in Fig. 5. Each row represents the position where the test data was collected, and each column represents the position where the training data was collected. It's clear that the diagonal elements represent the case where the training and testing data were from the same position, while the non-diagonal elements represent the case where the training and testing data were from different positions.

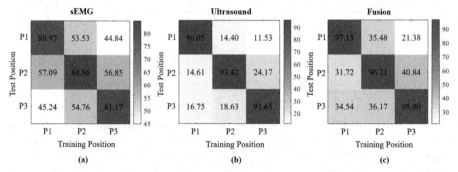

Fig. 5. Confusion matrices for gesture classification (%). Each row represents the position where the test data was collected, and each column represents the position where the training data was collected. (a) using only sEMG features; (b) using only ultrasound features; (c) using fusion features (sEMG + ultrasound).

We compared the classification models trained using single-modal features and fusion features. For both the sEMG and ultrasound features, the classification accuracy of the main diagonal elements (intra-position CA) was significantly higher than that of the non-diagonal elements (inter-position CA). Although the single-modal ultrasound feature achieved higher accuracy in the intra-position CA than the sEMG classifier, its inter-position CA was lower. Furthermore, all the differences mentioned above are statistically significant. The results indicated that arm position changes significantly impact gesture recognition, and ultrasound signals were more sensitive to arm position.

3.2 Testing with Cascaded Classifier Approach

The cascaded classifier approach was applied to classify the 10 different gestures under three arm positions, resulting in 30 distinct classes. Three classifiers, KNN, SVM, and LDA were employed to train the classification model with specific parameter settings: a k-nearest neighbor value of 5 for KNN and a linear kernel function for SVM. The classification accuracy using single-modal sEMG features, single-modal ultrasound features, and multimodal fusion features is shown in Fig. 6. The average classification accuracy and standard error were calculated across the 11 subjects. For the KNN classifier, the CA of sEMG was 75.74% ± 6.42%, that of ultrasound was 93.01% ± 4.27%, and the CA of multimodal fusion was 95.07% ± 3.29%. For the SVM classifier, the CA of sEMG was 79.79% ± 5.31%, that of ultrasound was 93.07% ± 4.03%, and the CA of multimodal fusion was 95.84% ± 2.37%. For the LDA classifier, the CA of sEMG was 80.33% ± 5.24%, that of ultrasound was 94.57% ± 3.59%, and the CA of multimodal fusion was 97.08% ± 1.90%.

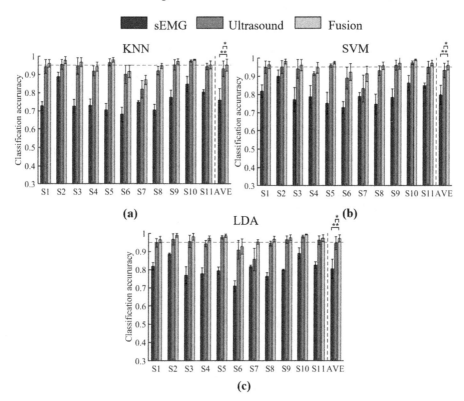

Fig. 6. Comparison of selecting parallel classifiers results among single-modal and multimodal features. (a) KNN classifier, the number of nearest neighbors was set to 5; (b) SVM classifier with a linear kernel function; (c) LDA classifier. Statistical analysis results for different features are shown above the last column, where sign * represents p < 0.05, and sign ** represents p < 0.01.

3.3 Testing with the Full-scale Classifier Approach

We employed a full-scale classification approach to decode 30 arm position and gesture combinations, utilizing KNN, SVM, and LDA classifiers, respectively. And the classification accuracy using single-modal sEMG features, single-modal ultrasound features, and multimodal fusion features is shown in Fig. 7. The average classification accuracy and standard error were calculated across the 11 subjects. For the KNN classifier, the CA of sEMG was 59.53% ± 7.26%, that of ultrasound was 86.45% ± 7.26%, and the CA of multimodal fusion was 92.50% ± 5.04%. For the SVM classifier, the CA of sEMG was 67.31% ± 6.11%, that of ultrasound was 83.85% ± 7.37%, and the CA of multimodal fusion was 92.52% ± 3.63%. For the LDA classifier, the CA of sEMG was 68.09% ± 4.89%, that of ultrasound was 86.08% ± 7.17%, and the CA of multimodal fusion was 94.55% ± 2.29%.

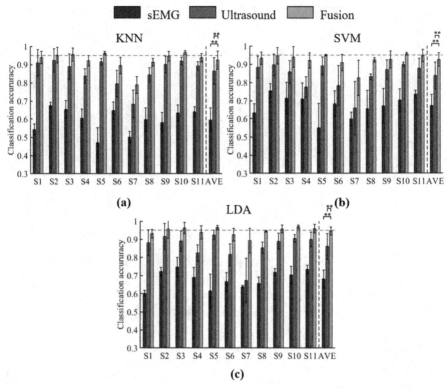

Fig. 7. Comparison of full-scale classifiers results among single-modal and multimodal features. (a) KNN classifier, the number of nearest neighbors was set to 5; (b) SVM classifier with a linear kernel function; (c) LDA classifier. Statistical analysis results for different features are shown above the last column, where sign ** represents p < 0.01.

4   Discussion and Conclusion

Using the paired samples Wilcoxon signed-rank test, we conducted the comparative analysis of CA among 11 subjects for single-modal sEMG, single-modal ultrasound, and fusion features. The significance level was set at p ≤ 0.05. For the method of cascaded classifiers, taking SVM classifier as an example, the results indicated that the CA of the multimodal fusion was significantly higher than that of the single-modal sEMG [z = 2.934, p = 0.00335] and single-modal ultrasound [z = 2.490, p = 0.0128]. And for the method of the full-scale classifiers, the results indicated that the CA of the multimodal fusion was significantly higher than that of the single-modal sEMG [z = 2.934, p = 0.00335] and single-modal ultrasound [z = 2.934, p = 0.00335]. From the comparison results, it can be concluded that multimodal fusion can improve the accuracy of gesture recognition across different arm positions, with a more significant improvement observed for the full-scale classifier approach.

We conducted paired t-tests to compare the multimodal fusion methods' CA of the cascaded classifier approach and the full-scale classifier approach on 11 subjects, with a significance level of $p \leq 0.05$. Taking SVM classifier as an example, the results indicated that the cascaded classifier approach significantly outperformed the full-scale classifier method in the CA of 30 combinations of arm positions and gestures [t = 5.524, p = 0.000253, effect size = 1.665].

In the existing research on multimodal fusion HMIs [14–16], researchers have mostly focused on discrete gesture recognition at a fixed arm position, while overlooking the issue of arm position variation in practical applications. Despite some attempts to mitigate the impact of arm position changes on gesture decoding by incorporating acceleration signals [22, 23], such endeavors mainly rely on off-the-shelf commercial EMG devices, rendering them a gap from practical use in prosthetic control applications.

In this study, we developed a multimodal HMI system that synchronously acquires sEMG, A-mode ultrasound, and IMU data, which holds the potential to be integrated into prosthetic hand socket. The recognition of 10 discrete gestures across 3 arm positions was investigated, and an offline experiment with 11 subjects was conducted. The results demonstrate that the multimodal fusion approach using the cascaded classifiers has advantages in gesture recognition across different arm positions, enhancing the robustness of the HMI. However, this approach may increase the training burden of users to some extent.

In our future work, it is imperative to integrate the multimodal fusion HMI into the prosthetic hand and conduct online experiments on gesture recognition across various arm positions to validate its practical application. Furthermore, to enhance the applicability of gesture recognition and reduce the training burden on subjects, recognizing gestures in non-training positions will be our following research focus. And the application of multimodal fusion methods can also be explored for continuous upper limb movements.

References

1. Zheng, M., Crouch, M.S., Eggleston, M.S.: Surface electromyography as a natural human-machine interface: a review. IEEE Sens. J. **22**, 9198–9214 (2022)
2. Ahmadizadeh, C., Khoshnam, M., Menon, C.: Human machine interfaces in upper-limb prosthesis control: a survey of techniques for preprocessing and processing of biosignals. IEEE Sig. Process. Mag. **38**, 12–22 (2021)
3. Jiang, N., et al.: Bio-robotics research for non-invasive myoelectric neural interfaces for upper-limb prosthetic control: a 10-year perspective review. Nat. Sci. Rev. **10**(5), nwad048 (2023)
4. Farina, D., et al.: The extraction of neural information from the surface EMG for the control of upper-limb prostheses: emerging avenues and challenges. IEEE Trans. Neural Syst. Rehabil. Eng. **22**, 797–809 (2014)
5. Jiang, N., Dosen, S., Muller, K.-R., Farina, D.: Myoelectric control of artificial limbs—is there a need to change focus? IEEE Sig. Process. Mag. **29**, 152–150 (2012)
6. Scheme, E., Englehart, K.: Electromyogram pattern recognition for control of powered upper-limb prostheses: state of the art and challenges for clinical use. J. Rehabil. Res. Dev. **48**(6), 649–659 (2011)

7. Tkach, D., Huang, H., Kuiken, T.A.: Study of stability of time-domain features for electromyographic pattern recognition. J. Neuroeng. Rehabil. **7**, 1–13 (2010)
8. Artemiadis, P.K., Kyriakopoulos, K.J.: An EMG-based robot control scheme robust to time-varying EMG signal features. IEEE Trans. Inf. Technol. Biomed. **14**, 582–588 (2010)
9. Botter, A., Vieira, T.M.M., Loram, I.D., Merletti, R., Hodson-Tole, E.F.: A novel system of electrodes transparent to ultrasound for simultaneous detection of myoelectric activity and B-mode ultrasound images of skeletal muscles. J. Appl. Physiol. **115**, 1203–1214 (2013)
10. Shi, J., Guo, J.-Y., Hu, S.-X., Zheng, Y.-P.: Recognition of finger flexion motion from ultrasound image: a feasibility study. Ultrasound Med. Biol. **38**, 1695–1704 (2012)
11. Yin, Z., et al.: A wearable ultrasound interface for prosthetic hand control. IEEE J. Biomed. Health Inform. **26**, 5384–5393 (2022)
12. Everdell, N.L., Airantzis, D., Kolvya, C., Suzuki, T., Elwell, C.E.: A portable wireless near-infrared spatially resolved spectroscopy system for use on brain and muscle. Med. Eng. Phys. **35**, 1692–1697 (2013)
13. Islam, M.A., Sundaraj, K., Ahmad, R.B., Ahamed, N.U., Ali, M.A.: Mechanomyography sensor development, related signal processing, and applications: a systematic review. IEEE Sens. J. **13**, 2499–2516 (2013)
14. Guo, W., Sheng, X., Liu, H., Zhu, X.: Development of a multi-channel compact-size wireless hybrid sEMG/NIRS sensor system for prosthetic manipulation. IEEE Sens. J. **16**, 447–456 (2015)
15. Guo, W., Sheng, X., Liu, H., Zhu, X.: Mechanomyography assisted myoeletric sensing for upper-extremity prostheses: a hybrid approach. IEEE Sens. J. **17**, 3100–3108 (2017)
16. Xia, W., Zhou, Y., Yang, X., He, K., Liu, H.: Toward portable hybrid surface electromyography/a-mode ultrasound sensing for human–machine interface. IEEE Sens. J. **19**, 5219–5228 (2019)
17. Scheme, E., Fougner, A., Stavdahl, Ø., Chan, A.D.C., Englehart, K.: Examining the adverse effects of limb position on pattern recognition based myoelectric control. In: 2010 Annual International Conference of the IEEE Engineering in Medicine and Biology Society (EMBC), pp. 6337–6340 (2010)
18. Fougner, A., Scheme, E., Chan, A.D.C., Englehart, K., Stavdahl, Ø.: Resolving the limb position effect in myoelectric pattern recognition. IEEE Trans. Neural Syst. Rehabil. Eng. **19**, 644–651 (2011)
19. Geng, Y., Zhou, P., Li, G.: Toward attenuating the impact of arm positions on electromyography pattern-recognition based motion classification in transradial amputees. J. Neuroeng. Rehabil. **9**, 1–11 (2012)
20. Hermens, H.J., Freriks, B., Disselhorst-Klug, C., Rau, G.: Development of recommendations for SEMG sensors and sensor placement procedures. J. Electromyogr. Kinesiol. **10**, 361–374 (2000)
21. Englehart, K., Hudgins, B.: A robust, real-time control scheme for multifunction myoelectric control. IEEE Trans. Biomed. Eng. **50**, 848–854 (2003)
22. Yu, Y., Sheng, X., Guo, W., Zhu, X.: Attenuating the impact of limb position on surface EMG pattern recognition using a mixed-LDA classifier. In: 2017 IEEE International Conference on Robotics and Biomimetics (ROBIO), pp. 1497–1502 (2017)
23. Colli-Alfaro, J.G., Ibrahim, A., Trejos, A.L.: Design of user-independent hand gesture recognition using multilayer perceptron networks and sensor fusion techniques. In: 2019 IEEE 16th International Conference on Rehabilitation Robotics (ICORR), pp. 1103–1108 (2019)

A Brain-Controlled Spherical Robot Based on Augmented Reality (AR)

Minghao Ji⬤, Shang Shi⬤, Mengyang Zhu⬤, Songwei Li⬤, and Jianjun Meng(✉)⬤

Shanghai Jiao Tong University, Shanghai 200240, China
mengjianjunxs008@sjtu.edu.cn

Abstract. Spherical robots have broad application prospects due to their unique structure. This paper introduces a spherical robot that was controlled by an SSVEP-based BCI system. The stimuli of SSVEP were presented by AR, which enabled the subjects to gaze at the stimuli and the robot simultaneously. Offline experiments demonstrated the feasibility of the BCI system using AR stimuli. The average decoding accuracy reached 91.83 ± 9.83% for a 1.5-s decoding time window. An AR scene consisting of a rectangular racetrack with a circumference of 8m was designed to conduct online experiments. The average finishing laps in the brain-controlled group achieved 6.35 ± 1.45 laps in 5 min, with regard to 7.72 ± 1.62 laps in the controller-controlled one. The brain control method proposed in this paper achieved good results and verified the feasibility and stability of the BCI system through experiments. This study still had shortcomings in the decoding effect when subjects switched the gazing stimulus target. There is room for improvement, and it is worth further study.

Keywords: Brain-computer interfaces · AR · SSVEP · Spherical robot

1 Introduction

Spherical robots have gained significant research interest in recent years [1]. Spherical robots are typically mobile robots with spherical shells enclosing internal mechanisms [2]. The spherical shape allows the robot to move easily in any direction [3], and the sealed shell can protect the inner components from harsh working environments [2]. Spherical robots can be controlled by changing the position of the center of mass, generating an angular momentum, or deforming the spherical shell [4]. This paper presents a spherical robot with differential wheels that can move using the first method.

Brain-computer interface (BCI) is an advanced technology that links the human brain with external devices [5]. After years of development, some BCI paradigms have achieved excellent performance that can be used in human-robot interactions like robotic arms [6] and wheelchairs [7]. BCI has several advantages over conventional human-robot interactions, as users do not need physical movements to issue commands. It can enhance the human body's abilities and offer a stimulating experience when used for

---

M. Ji, S. Shi and M. Zhu—denotes the first three authors contribute equally.

© The Author(s), under exclusive license to Springer Nature Singapore Pte Ltd. 2023
H. Yang et al. (Eds.): ICIRA 2023, LNAI 14268, pp. 343–352, 2023.
https://doi.org/10.1007/978-981-99-6486-4_30

entertainment [8]. Among various BCI paradigms, BCI based on steady-state visual evoked potential (SSVEP) has a high information transfer rate and robustness [8]. When the subject gazes at a periodic visual stimulus, EEG signals with the same frequency or its harmonic frequencies can be robustly measured [9].

The BCI paradigm based on steady-state visual evoked potentials relies on periodic visual stimuli, often displayed on a computer monitor [5]. However, this form of presentation has poor interaction, and the integration of augmented reality technology can provide visual stimuli as virtual elements in front of the users, enhancing the immersion of the experience [10]. Currently, the combination of brain-computer interface and augmented reality technology is a major research focus [10–15].

In this study, the designed spherical robot will be controlled by BCI based on SSVEP. The visual stimuli are presented by AR, along with other virtual objects. Combining AR with BCI, robot control presents many challenges. First, the stimuli must be easy to gaze at and should not cover the major visual area. Second, the robot's precise localization must be achieved so that it can interact correctly with the virtual environment. Lastly, the speed and time parameters of the robot are carefully designed to gain better control performance.

2   Materials and Methods

2.1   Subjects

We recruited six healthy subjects (five males and one female, mean age 20 ± 2 years) to participate in the experiment. All subjects had normal or corrected-to-normal vision. The Ethics Committee of Shanghai Jiao Tong University approved the experiment, and all subjects provided informed consent before participation.

2.2   System Design

The components of the system were shown in Fig. 1. The desk computer was used for BCI signal acquisition, BCI signal processing, AR scene generation, and control of the spherical robot. The ZED mini camera, HTC Vive headset, and EEG device were directly connected to the computer.

EEG signals were captured by the EEG cap iRecorder W16 (Shanghai Idea-Interaction Tech., Co., Ltd.). Six electrodes (PO3, POz, PO4, O1, Oz, O2) at the occipital area were used in the project. Meanwhile, according to the international 10–20 system, FCz and CPz electrodes were used as ground and reference, respectively. The sampling frequency was 500 Hz, and a compact wireless amplifier, which was attached to the cap magnetically, transmitted the signal to the USB port on the computer. The collected EEG data were received and decoded by BCI2000 on the computer. Then BCI2000 sent the results to Unity via UDP to control the motion of the spherical robot.

Unity created and displayed the augmented reality scene on the HTC Vive headset. The scene consisted of the following components:

- The real-world environment, which was captured by the ZED mini camera. (The ZED mini camera was attached directly to the front of the HTC Vive headset)

- Virtual objects, such as racetracks, obstacles, etc.
- The stimulus used to elicit SSVEP.

Unity also received the decoding results sent by BCI2000 and converted them to corresponding commands, which were transmitted to the spherical robot and controlled the robot to move forward, turn left, turn right, or stop.

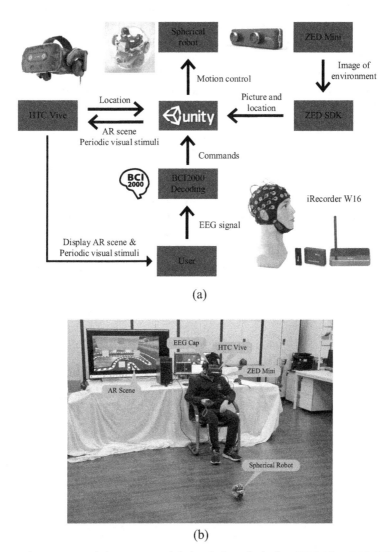

(a)

(b)

Fig. 1. (a) Components of the system and their relations, including HTC Vive, ZED Mini, the spherical robot, etc. (b) Experimental setup of the system. The screen on the left showed the AR scene, which was seen from a first-person perspective.

Subjects wore the EEG cap and the HTC Vive headset simultaneously during the experiment. Subjects could view the AR scene through the HTC Vive headset and could control the spherical robot's movement by gazing at the stimulus.

The spherical robot consisted of a transparent spherical shell and a core inside. The core had a pair of differential wheels at the bottom that made contact with the inner surface of the shell. By changing the speed of the differential wheels, the robot could perform simple planar motions. An HTC Vive Tracker was attached to the top of the core. It could be detected by the computer, which enabled the computer to obtain the exact location and rotation of the spherical robot. The robot operated with an ESP32 microcontroller and could receive commands from the computer via UDP.

The rendering image of the spherical robot was shown in Fig. 2. The structure could be divided into three parts: upper shell, lower shell and inner core. These two hemispherical shells were combined with tape to form a sphere. The inner core consisted of several main parts installed on the bracket. The main control circuit board, battery and two DC motors were assembled to the bracket from top to bottom. Two gear sets were linked to the output shafts of two motors, which meshed with two rubber wheels closely fit to the spherical shell. The main control circuit board received commands from the computer via UDP and made motors rotate at a certain speed. The gear sets were driven, leading to the rubber wheels' rotation. The friction between the rubber wheels and the shell contributed to the motion of the spherical robot. Additionally, two bullseye wheels were set on the pendulous middle surface of two driving devices to maintain the stable structure of the inner core. Therefore, the spherical robot's straight-forward movement and steering motion could be realized by adjusting the rotational speed of two motors.

Fig. 2. Rendering image of the spherical robot.

2.3   Experimental Design

We presented two experimental paradigms to the subjects: offline and online. The offline paradigm consisted of four stimuli (8 Hz, 9 Hz, 10 Hz, 11 Hz), displayed by Unity, to verify the SSVEP accuracy in AR equipment. The online paradigm added the AR racing scene and the spherical robot to the experiment so that the subject could control the robot to finish the whole racetrack by EEG in real-time.

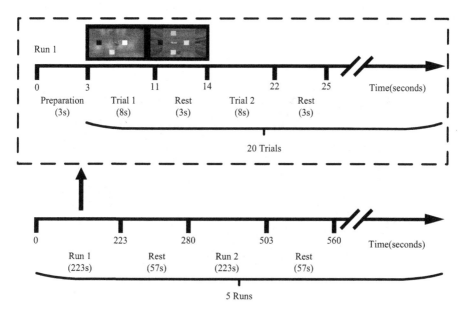

Fig. 3. Offline experiment timeline. Each run contained twenty trials. Each trial randomly chose one of the four stimuli as a target, and each stimuli was presented five times. Subjects were required to gaze at the target stimuli during the trial, and complete five runs in total.

We show the offline experiment timeline in Fig. 3. Each run consisted of twenty trials, randomly assigned to one of the four stimuli by the BCI2000 system for verification of average performance. A single run included a preparation period (3 s), 20 trials (8 s each) with 3s inter-trial interval duration. In the first part (8 s) of one trial, the screen displayed an arrow-shaped cue in the center to inform subjects which stimulus they should focus on. Five runs, in other words, one hundred trials, were implemented for each subject.

The online experiment involved simultaneous decoding by BCI2000 and UDP communication to Unity. Unity constructed an augmented reality scene with a rectangular track and ten archway-shaped checking points, which is shown in Fig. 4. The subjects had to complete the whole racing track in a single run within the specified time by controlling the spherical robot's moving upward or downward and turning left or right by gazing at the corresponding SSVEP stimuli. To be mentioned, the subjects were required to keep the robot inside the racing track by turning and going through every examining point in order because moving off the track and missing point would waste time and reduce the score. The finishing laps were used to evaluate the subjects' performance. To directly analyze the effect of the BCI system, a controller-controlled group was set as a baseline, where the controller means the HTC Vive controller. Six subjects completed the online experiments of four runs, two for the brain-controlled group and two for the controller-controlled one, where the better score of two runs was recorded as the finishing laps for both experimental groups. The battery was full, and the scene location remained basically the same when the online experiments began. The online experiment scene was shown in Fig. 5. Subjects controlled the spherical robot to go through the archway-shaped examining point one by one and finish the whole racetrack by watching the corresponding stimulus.

Fig. 4. The track of the online experiment with ten archway-shaped checking points.

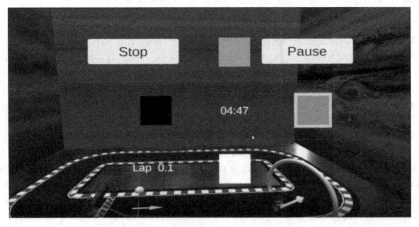

Fig. 5. Online experiment scene on HTC Vive screen.

2.4 Data Analysis Approach

The EEG signal processing procedure was implemented in MATLAB, which was shown in Fig. 6. After being collected by hardware and BCI2000, EEG signals were first filtered from 0.1 Hz to 50 Hz using a zero-phase finite impulse response (FIR) filter and then subtracted to their mean value for normalization. Then Canonical Correlation Analysis (CCA) was computed on a sliding time window of EEG signals. Finally, the decoding results were obtained by comparing the correlations between EEG and reference signals featured by stimulus frequencies and taking the maximum correlation [16].

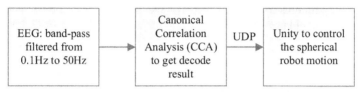

Fig. 6. Data analysis approach.

The decoding results were sent to Unity through UDP during the online experiment. Consequently, subjects could control the spherical robot's motion in real-time.

3 Results and Discussion

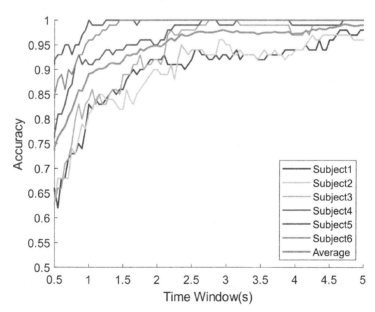

Fig. 7. The relation between the recognition accuracy of six subjects over one hundred trials and EEG data time window.

We completed the offline experiment of 6 subjects, whose data were analyzed through the approach proposed in the former section. Each subject finished 5 runs, in total 100 trials, and achieved a good accuracy, which could be seen in Fig. 7. Note that 6 subjects, on average, acquired an accuracy of over 90% in 100 trials with a 1.5-s-long EEG time window. In addition, accuracy rises to about 95% when the time window is increased to 2 s.

We also used the heatmap tool in MATLAB to draw the confusion matrices of 6 subjects on the basis of 100 trials for 4 stimuli, which was shown in Fig. 8. The vertical axis represented the target stimulus in one trial, whereas the horizontal one referred to the decoding result. The number in one square meant the probability of decoding results in 25 trials for one stimulus so that the squares on the main diagonal of the table should be 1 and the others should be 0. Figure 8 was acquired under a 2-s-long EEG time window, and the result reached a decent level.

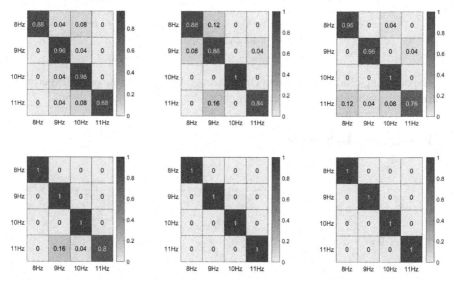

Fig. 8. Confusion matrices (using 2 s time window) of six subjects in twenty-five trials for four target frequencies, respectively, where the vertical axis represents the target frequency, and the horizontal axis refers to the decoding result.

After the offline experiment, we constructed a connection to the spherical robot to control its motion. We designed a rectangular racing track with ten archway-shaped examining points in an AR scene by Unity and sent a controlling message to the spherical robot through UDP. According to the offline experiment result, a 1.5-s-long decoding time window was selected for the online experiment decoding approach, considering both high decoding accuracy and low time delay during the visual transition of switching gaze at the stimulus target when subjects tried to modify the motion direction of the spherical robot. The online experiment result was shown in the following Table 1. Six subjects achieved 6.35 ± 1.45 laps of the brain-controlled group in 5 min, with regard to 7.72 ± 1.62 laps of the controller-controlled one. Although gaps existed between the controlling method of BCI and the HTC Vive controller, the feasibility and stability of the BCI system proposed in this paper were verified through experiments.

Table 1. The online experiment finishing laps in 5 min.

Subjects Id	BCI 1	BCI 2	Controller 1	Controller 2
1	6.1	5.8	7.8	7.3
2	4.3	4.9	7.9	7.6
3	5.4	6.0	6.8	5.8
4	5.6	7.0	6.1	5.2
5	6.5	6.3	7.4	8.8
6	4.7	7.6	8.2	8.9
Average (Max)	6.35 ± 1.45		7.72 ± 1.62	

4   Conclusion

This paper introduced a spherical robot that BCI can control in an AR scene. The robot uses differential wheels to move on the ground and has a stable performance while being controlled by the computer keyboard or AR controllers. We introduced another control method using the SSVEP-based BCI. The stimuli of SSVEP are presented through the HTC Vive headset along with an AR scene. Offline experiments proved the BCI system's feasibility, and subjects could give commands to the spherical robot by gazing at the stimuli. Online experiments verified the BCI system's stability since subjects could finish the mission. This BCI system achieved relatively good results despite the little gap below the controller-controlled method. However, when subjects switched the gazing stimulus target, the decoding performance was not very satisfactory. In addition, subjects also found difficulties in paying attention to the stimulus and the location of the spherical robot simultaneously. There is still room for improvement, and it is worth more effort and further studies.

The future work will contain the enrichment of experiments and deeper research of the performance of this BCI system. More variables may be taken into consideration, such as the size and location of the stimuli. The new experiment paradigm will focus on the effect of the vision switch on the BCI system performance. Subjects will be ordered to gaze at different stimulus targets according to the cues in one trial so that the vision switch period can be further studied.

Acknowledgment. The authors would like to thank the volunteers who participated in the experiments. This work is supported in part by the National Key R&D Program of China (Grant No. 2020YFC207800), the National Natural Science Foundation of China (Grant No. 52175023).

References

1. Crossley, V.A.: A literature review on the design of spherical rolling robots. Pittsburgh, PA, pp. 1–6 (2006)
2. Ylikorpi, T., Suomela, J.: Ball-shaped robots. Climbing and walking robots: towards new applications. IntechOpen (2007)
3. Chase, R., Pandya, A.: A review of active mechanical driving principles of spherical robots. Robotics 1(1), 3–23 (2012)
4. Alexey, B., Alexander, K., Yury, K., Anton, K.: Stabilization of the motion of a spherical robot using feedbacks. Appl. Math. Model. **69**, 583–592 (2019)
5. He, B., Yuan, H., Meng, J., Gao, S.: Brain–computer interfaces. Neural Eng. 131–183 (2020)
6. Meng, J., Zhang, S., Bekyo, A., Olsoe, J., Baxter, B., He, B.: Noninvasive electroencephalogram based control of a robotic arm for reach and grasp tasks. Sci. Rep. **6**(1), 38565 (2016)
7. Long, J., Li, Y., Wang, H., Yu, T., Pan, J., Li, F.: A hybrid brain computer interface to control the direction and speed of a simulated or real wheelchair. IEEE Trans. Neural Syst. Rehabil. Eng. **20**(5), 720–729 (2012)
8. Li, M., He, D., Li, C., Qi, S.: Brain–computer interface speller based on steady-state visual evoked potential: a review focusing on the stimulus paradigm and performance. Brain Sci. **11**(4), 450 (2021)
9. Wang, Y., Wang, R., Gao, X., Hong, B., Gao, S.: A practical VEP-based brain-computer interface. IEEE Trans. Neural Syst. Rehabil. Eng. **14**(2), 234–240 (2006)
10. Ke, Y., Liu, P., An, X., Song, X., Ming, D.: An online SSVEP-BCI system in an optical see-through augmented reality environment. J. Neural Eng. **17**(1), 016066 (2020)
11. Lenhardt, A., Ritter, H.: An augmented-reality based brain-computer interface for robot control. In: Wong, K.W., Mendis, B.S.U., Bouzerdoum, A. (eds.) ICONIP 2010, Part II. LNCS, vol. 6444, pp. 58–65. Springer, Heidelberg (2010). https://doi.org/10.1007/978-3-642-175 34-3_8
12. Kerous, B., Liarokapis, F.: BrainChat-a collaborative augmented reality brain interface for message communication. In: 2017 IEEE International Symposium on Mixed and Augmented Reality (ISMAR-Adjunct), pp. 279–283. IEEE (2017)
13. Chen, X., Huang, X., Wang, Y., Gao, X.: Combination of augmented reality based brain-computer interface and computer vision for high-level control of a robotic arm. IEEE Trans. Neural Syst. Rehabil. Eng. **28**(12), 3140–3147 (2020)
14. Chen, L., et al.: Adaptive asynchronous control system of robotic arm based on augmented reality-assisted brain–computer interface. J. Neural Eng. **18**(6), 066005 (2021)
15. Chen, X., Zhao, B., Wang, Y., Xu, S., Gao, X.: Control of a 7-DOF robotic arm system with an SSVEP-based BCI. Int. J. Neural Syst. **28**(08), 1850018 (2018)
16. Bin, G., Gao, X., Yan, Z., Hong, B., Gao, S.: An online multi-channel SSVEP-based brain–computer interface using a canonical correlation analysis method. J. Neural Eng. **6**(4), 046002 (2009)

Research on Interactive Force Control Method of Upper Limb Exoskeleton Based on Active Intention Recognition

Chengzhi Zhao[1], Yi Cao[1], Xifang Liu[2], and Wendong Wang[1(✉)] ⓘ

[1] School of Mechanical Engineering, Northwestern Polytechnical University, Xi'an 710072, China
wdwang@nwpu.edu.cn
[2] Department of Rehabilitation, Xi'an Honghui Hospital, Xi'an Jiaotong University, Xi'an, Shaanxi, China

Abstract. The paper proposes an upper limb exoskeleton interaction force control method based on active motion intention recognition to address the problems of lack of patient active participation willingness and poor flexibility of the rehabilitation training control method during the middle and late stages of rehabilitation training. Initially, this paper establishes the human-machine interaction force model by analyzing the human-machine interaction dynamics and statics of the upper limb rehabilitation exoskeleton. Moreover, a method for active intention recognition based on interaction force is proposed using a neural network with a radial basis. During the active training process, the adaptive impedance control method based on the interaction force is proposed to increase the range of motion during rehabilitation. The bounded matrix parameter adaptive matrix control method is compared, and experimental results demonstrate that the method proposed in this paper can effectively reduce the human-machine interaction force, improve the flexibility of the exoskeleton robotic arm, and increase the patient's willingness to participate actively.

Keywords: Upper limb rehabilitation exoskeleton · Softness control method · Intent Recognition · RBFNN

1 Introduction

In recent decades, the incidence of upper limb dysfunction due to stroke has been high; as a result, rehabilitation training and motor function remodeling of the upper limb has become essential research areas in medical rehabilitation. Using an upper limb rehabilitation exoskeleton can effectively resolve the issues of low efficiency, poor repeatability, and high cost associated with conventional rehabilitation training. It can obtain accurate training data via various sensors, continuously update and develop scientific and reasonable rehabilitation training methods, improve the deployment of patients' follow-up treatment plans, provide patients with more accurate treatment plans, and enhance the rehabilitation training effects. Most existing upper limb rehabilitation exoskeletons

H. Yang et al. (Eds.): ICIRA 2023, LNAI 14268, pp. 353–364, 2023.
https://doi.org/10.1007/978-981-99-6486-4_31

employ passive training methods, and patients are less involved in the rehabilitation training process. As a result, it is difficult for patients to participate in rehabilitation treatment with high initiative and enthusiasm and to achieve the best rehabilitation effect. For the upper limb exoskeleton robot, active flexibility control [1] is the subject of research by both domestic and international scholars.

Active compliance control is primarily concerned with force control. The force sensor captures the interaction force between the wearer and the exoskeleton robot. It feeds back information about the surrounding environment to maintain the exoskeleton robot's movement within a specific range. The most common approach is to use proportional-integral-derivative (PID) feedback control. For instance, both [2] and [3] utilize this type of joint controller. Although this control method does not require establishing a system model and is comparatively easy to operate, the gain must be adjusted during the control process, which is a disadvantage. The current parameters may add time to the process. Numerous researchers have incorporated elements of PID controllers with advanced control methods, including robust control and adaptive control, as well as intelligent control methods, including neural networks and fuzzy logic. Wu et al. [4] combined PID control with robust and fuzzy logic-based control to assure robustness and reduce tremor effects during exoskeleton tracking.

In contrast to the PID control method, the impedance/conductance control method is a system model-based control technique. This method controls based on position or force feedback, whereas position feedback controllers and feedforward controllers are the most common control methods in exoskeleton systems [5–7]. Kazerooni utilized a method of direct force feedback control to assist the wearer in enhancing upper limb strength. This control method does not diminish the man-machine interaction force. However, it proportionally reduces the force the wearer applies to the load so that it is applied to the exoskeleton robot rather than the wearer [8]. One of the drawbacks of impedance and conductance controls is that they do not compensate for the required parameters over time [9] and may "intervene incorrectly" if the participant regains strength and requires less assistance.

Adaptive control methods can assist with this issue by modifying the undetermined variance of the system's parameters online for the controller based on the current operation. Researchers have addressed bounded external disturbances by integrating adaptive controllers with other controllers, such as robust control techniques. ARMin-V [10] and Kang [11] proposed adaptive robust control methods for robotic exoskeleton systems using adaptive control for an exoskeleton system for upper limb rehabilitation robotics. Sliding mode control (SMC) is a nonlinear, robust strategy that can deal with bounded external disturbances and parameter uncertainties. The high-frequency switching action of sliding mode controllers can result in a jitter in the command output, which can cause attrition or damage to the mechanical system and energy loss in the electrical system. Numerous mathematical smoothing methods can mitigate or eradicate the issue, as mentioned above. In his study, Yun [12] proposed a mathematical smoothing method for sliding mode control to resolve the issue partially.

As the patient's active motor intent increases in the middle and late phases of rehabilitation, the exoskeletal robotic arm must recognize the patient's motor intent to assist the affected limb with active training movements. Using bio signals to control the robotic limb is currently highly challenging. Due to the patient's active motor intent, the movement process generates human-machine interaction, which can be used to determine the patient's motor intent in the middle and late phases of rehabilitation.

This paper's content is based on the force signal collected by the upper limb exoskeleton sensor to devise a softness control method based on the interaction force. This paper seeks to improve human-machine interaction force flexibility. It proposes a human-machine interaction force model based on the upper limb exoskeleton, conducts a static analysis for the model, and designs an adaptive impedance controller based on the above analysis. By optimizing the design of the flexibility control method, the man-machine interaction force is maximized.

2 Man-Machine Interaction Force Model

2.1 Man-Machine Interaction Force Dynamics Modeling

In this study, the 6-degree-of-freedom upper limb exoskeleton robotic arm structure designed in-house is studied, and from the Jacobi matrix $\mathbf{J} = \partial\mathbf{x}/\partial\mathbf{q}$, the position vector of the end position of the exoskeleton in the Cartesian spatial coordinate system is obtained as

$$\dot{\mathbf{x}}(t) = \mathbf{J}(\mathbf{q})\dot{\mathbf{q}} \tag{1}$$

where $x(t) \in \mathbb{R}^3$ is the position vector of the end of the exoskeleton in Cartesian space; $\mathbf{q} \in \mathbb{R}^4$ is the angle vector in joint space; and $\mathbf{J}(\mathbf{q}) \in \mathbb{R}^{3\times4}$ is the Jacobi matrix of the system.

The time derivative of Eq. (1) yields

$$\ddot{\mathbf{x}}(t) = \dot{\mathbf{J}}(\mathbf{q})\dot{\mathbf{q}} + \mathbf{J}(\mathbf{q})\ddot{\mathbf{q}} \tag{2}$$

If $\mathbf{F}(t) \in \mathbb{R}^3$ is used to denote the human-machine interaction force, the human-machine fusion kinetic model of the upper limb rehabilitation exoskeleton robotic arm and the patient's upper limb is

$$\mathbf{M}(\mathbf{q})\ddot{\mathbf{q}} + \mathbf{S}(\mathbf{q}, \dot{\mathbf{q}})\dot{\mathbf{q}} + \mathbf{G}(\mathbf{q}) = \tau + \mathbf{J}(\mathbf{q})\mathbf{F}(t) + \sigma \tag{3}$$

where $\mathbf{M}(\mathbf{q})$, $\mathbf{S}(\mathbf{q}, \dot{\mathbf{q}})$, $\mathbf{G}(\mathbf{q})$ are the equivalent rotational inertia matrix, centripetal and Coriolis force matrices, and gravity term vector of the human-machine fusion model, respectively; τ is the control moment vector; σ is the disturbance term caused by friction and other factors. For the convenience of calculation, we transform the two parts of the human-computer interaction force to the end through the moment transformation.

A pressure sensor was installed on the upper limb exoskeleton robotic arm structure to assess the human-machine interaction force generated during the upper limb rehabilitation exercise. Figure 1 depicts the schematic diagram of human-machine interaction force measurement.

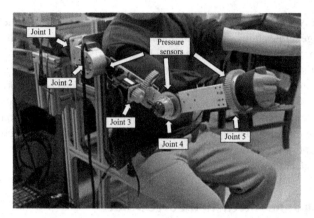

Fig. 1. Man-machine interaction force test chart

2.2 Man-Machine Statics Analysis

The robot plant installed a Guangzhou Sparto S-shaped SBT610T high-precision tension sensor in the connection between the upper and lower parts to measure the interaction force between the human arm and the mechanical arm restraint. As shown in Fig. 2, a support ring (two half-rings snapped together) is installed in the upper arm of the robot arm near the elbow, and four FSR thin-film pressure sensors are installed precisely below, above, and to the left and right of the ring. At the elbow, the pressure sensors installed in positions A, B, C, and D measure the interaction force between the human upper limb and the robot arm in four dimensions. E, F, G, and H depict the installation of four FSR402 thin-film pressure transducers in the wrist portion of the arm and four FSR402 thin-film pressure transducers directly below, above, and to the left and right of the ring. These transducers measure the intensity of interaction between the forearm's wrist and the arm.

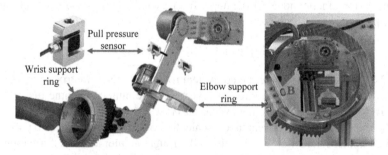

Fig. 2. Interactive force sensor distribution map

Computational methods were used to solve for the HCI forces and moments. The distribution of the human-machine interaction forces during motion in the plumb plane is shown in Fig. 3. In Fig. 3 (a), F_z and F_w denote the binding forces of the human upper limb acting at the elbow support ring of the upper arm and at the wrist support ring, including the main and passive forces, respectively; G_1 and G_2 denote the self-weight components of the human upper limb at the two positions, respectively, with the direction vertical downward; m_1g and m_2g denote the gravitational forces of the upper arm and forearm of the robotic arm concentrated at the elbow and wrist, respectively; l_1 and l_2 denote the lengths of the upper arm and forearm of the robotic arm, respectively; l_1^* and l_2^* denote the distances of the two interactive force contact points from the rotation axis, respectively. q_2 and q_4 denote the angles that the upper arm turns around the Z-*axis* at point O and the forearm turns around the Z-*axis* at point A, respectively. Figure 3 (b) and (c) show the distribution of force measurement points of the elbow support ring and wrist support ring of the upper arm, respectively. F_{zi} and $F_{wi}(i = A, ...H)$ indicate the measured interaction forces at the elbow and wrist force measurement points, respectively.

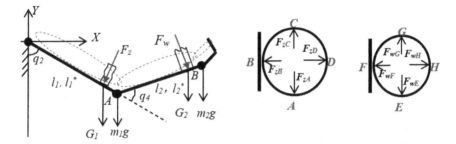

(a) Force Sensor Toroidal Force Point Distribution (b) Elbow support ring (c) Wrist support ring

Fig. 3. Schematic diagram of the human-machine interaction force for motion in the plumb plane

The mechanical arm moves in the plumb plane, that is, it remains $q_1 = q_3 = 0$. The forces on the right and left sides of the mechanical arm from the elbow and wrist of the human upper limb should be zero $F_{zB} = F_{zD} = F_{zF} = F_{zH} = 0$. The passive restraining forces F_{pz} and F_{pw} at the elbow and wrist act mainly at A and E. The relationship between their magnitude and the attitude angle is

$$\begin{cases} F_{pz} = G_1 \sin q_2 \\ F_{pw} = G_2 \sin(q_2 + q_4) \end{cases} \tag{4}$$

Without employing active force, the passive interaction force is measured by a force sensor and backed up in the database. The active interaction force is still determined by subtracting the online-measured interaction force from the inert one. Human upper limbs are delicate bodies, and when the support ring is tilted, the force point is not at the measurement point where the pressure sensor is installed; therefore, the measured interaction force is highly imprecise. Therefore, this paper employs a neural network to determine the active movement intention of the patient.

3 Research on Active Motion Intention Recognition Method

Because the passive interaction forces are not negligible, the upper extremity rehabilita-tion exoskeleton robotic arm system designed in this study makes it highly challenging to determine the patient's motor intent from the signals measured by the force sensors. The interactive forces that a patient can actively apply are very modest. In this section, an approach based on machine learning is used to identify the patient's motion inten-tion using the measurable information of each joint angle position and interaction force information.

3.1 Radial Basis Neural Network Motion Intention Recognition Model

According to the impedance control theory, the contact interaction model between the human upper limb and exoskeleton is generally substituted by the "mass-spring-damper" physical model. This study's upper limb exoskeleton model's equivalent impedance model is

$$\mathbf{F} = M_d(\ddot{\mathbf{x}}_d - \ddot{\mathbf{x}}) + B_d(\dot{\mathbf{x}}_d - \dot{\mathbf{x}}) + K_d(\mathbf{x}_d - \mathbf{x}) \tag{5}$$

where $\mathbf{F}$ is the interaction force between the human body and the end of the exoskeleton robotic arm; x is the actual motion displacement of the end of the robotic arm; $\mathbf{x}_d$ is the target (desired) displacement of the end of the robotic arm; M_d, B_d, K_d are the target mass, target damping and target stiffness, respectively.

In this paper, a simplified mathematical model with damper-spring characteristics is used to describe the dynamic behavior of human-machine interaction at the end of a robotic arm, and the impedance model is

$$-C_H(\mathbf{q}, \dot{\mathbf{q}})\dot{\mathbf{x}} + G_H(\mathbf{q})(\mathbf{x}_{Hd} - \mathbf{x}) = \mathbf{F} \tag{6}$$

where $C_H(\mathbf{q}, \dot{\mathbf{q}})$ and $G_H(\mathbf{q})$ are unknown functions with respect to $\mathbf{q}$ and $\dot{\mathbf{q}}$; $\mathbf{x}_{Hd}$ is the patient's intention to move; and F is the interaction contact force at the end.

The meaning of the human-machine interaction force model is the interaction force exerted by the patient on the robot arm $\mathbf{f}$ because the robot arm ends at $\mathbf{x}$ and the patient intends to go to $\mathbf{x}_{Hd}$ during the motion. The patient's motion intention can be estimated from the measurable information of the joint angles $\mathbf{q}, \dot{\mathbf{q}}$ and the interaction force $\mathbf{F}$ by using machine learning methods as

$$\mathbf{x}_{Hd} = \mathbf{x} + [\mathbf{F} - C_H(\mathbf{q}, \dot{\mathbf{q}})\dot{\mathbf{x}}]/G_H(\mathbf{q}) \tag{7}$$

This functional relationship is clearly unknown, time-varying, and nonlinear, as the virtual impedance of the human upper limb varies during movement.

Radial basis function neural network (RBFNN), as a local approximation network, can handle regular problems that are difficult to resolve, can approximate arbitrary non-linear functions, and has good generalization ability and fast learning and convergence speed. Here, RBFNN is used to estimate the patient's motion intention. Its basic structure can be expressed as

$$\begin{cases} \psi(W, r) = W^T f(r), \ W, f(r) \hat{I} R^p; f(r) = [\varphi_1(r), \varphi_2(r), L, \varphi_p(r)] \\ \varphi_k(r) = \exp[\dfrac{-(r - \mu_k)^T(r - \mu_k)}{2\sigma^2}], \ k = 1, 2, L, p \end{cases} \tag{8}$$

where $\psi(W, r)$ is a continuous function about the input r, $\mathbf{r} \in \Omega_r \subset \mathbb{R}^m$ is the m-*dimensional* input of RBFNN, p is the number of radial base neuron nodes in the hidden layer, $\mu_k = [\mu_{k1}, \mu_{k2}, \cdots, \mu_{km}]^T$ is the centroid, σ is the width of the Gaussian function, and W is the adjustable synaptic weight vector.

We set the input vectors of RBFNN as $\mathbf{r} = [\mathbf{F}^T, \mathbf{q}^T, \dot{\mathbf{q}}^T]^T \in \mathbb{R}^{11}$, $\mathbf{F} = [\mathbf{F}_x, \mathbf{F}_y, \mathbf{F}_z]$ to represent the interaction contact forces in the three axes, and $\mathbf{q} = [q_i]$, $\dot{\mathbf{q}} = [\dot{q}_i]$, $i = 1, 2, 3, 4$ to represent the angles and angular velocity of the four joints. Taking the center point $\mu_k = [F_{xk}^0, F_{yk}^0, F_{zk}^0, q_{1k}^0, q_{2k}^0, q_{3k}^0, q_{4k}^0, \dot{q}_{1k}^0, \dot{q}_{2k}^0, \dot{q}_{3k}^0, \dot{q}_{4k}^0,]^T$, the superscript "0" indicates the average value of the interaction forces measured in various postures without active interaction forces applied, i.e., μ_k indicates the nominal value of the state vector with passive interaction forces only. Then, the mode $\|r - \mu_k\|^2 = (r - \mu_k)^T(r - \mu_k)$ of the vector difference, using the Gaussian kernel function $\varphi(\|r - \mu_k\|^2)$, can be used to estimate the patient's motor intention during training as

$$x_{Hdi} = \overline{W}_i^T \phi_i(r_i) + \varepsilon_i \tag{9}$$

where i is the i component; $\overline{W}$ is the estimate of the ideal weight W; and ε_i is the estimation error.

4 Research on Adaptive Impedance Control Method

4.1 Bounded Matrix Parameter Adaptive Impedance Controller Design

The estimate $\overline{\mathbf{x}}_{Hd}$ representing the patient's active motion intention was estimated above using RBFNN. $\overline{\mathbf{x}}_{Hd}$ is now used instead of $\mathbf{x}_d$ in Eq. (5) to construct a mass-spring-damper virtual impedance model describing the synergistic motion of the human upper limb with the exoskeleton as

$$M_d(\ddot{\overline{\mathbf{x}}}_{Hd} - \ddot{\mathbf{x}}) + B_d(\dot{\overline{\mathbf{x}}}_{Hd} - \dot{\mathbf{x}}) + K_d(\overline{\mathbf{x}}_{Hd} - \mathbf{x}) = \mathbf{F} \tag{10}$$

where $\mathbf{F}$ is the interaction force between the human body and the end of the exoskeleton robot arm; x is the actual motion displacement of the end of the robot arm; $\overline{\mathbf{x}}_{Hd}$ is the target (desired) displacement of the end of the robot arm, M_d, B_d, K_d is the target mass, target damping and target stiffness, respectively.

The design of the adaptive impedance controller(AIC) is to design a model-referenced adaptive control law with Eq. (9) as the target reference model, so that the motion of the actual system shown in Eq. (5) can track the motion of the target reference model. The position error signal $\mathbf{e} = \mathbf{x} - \mathbf{x}_d$ in Cartesian space is constructed from the virtual impedance model to match the error signal $\omega = M_d\ddot{\mathbf{e}} + B_d\dot{\mathbf{e}} + K_d\mathbf{e} - \eta$. The goal of the control of the system is to make $\lim_{t \to 0} \omega(t) = 0$, that is, to enable the system dynamics model to match the impedance model.

Now based on the bounded matrix parameters(BMP), the adaptive impedance controller is designed as

$$\begin{cases} u = -Kz - \sum_{j=1}^{4} \left\{ (\hat{\Xi}_j \phi_j^2)/(\phi_j\|z\| + \sigma_j) \right\} z - \eta \\ \dot{\overline{\Xi}}_j = -a_j\hat{\Xi}_j + \left\{ (b_j\phi_j^2\|z\|^2)/(\phi_j\|z\| + \sigma_j) \right\} \end{cases} \tag{11}$$

where $\hat{\Xi}_j$ is an estimate of the bounded scalar; K is a positive definite matrix; $b_j > 0$, a_j and σ_j are time-varying positive functions and satisfy $\int_0^t a_j(\omega)d\omega = c_j < \infty$, $\int_0^t a_j(\omega)d\omega = c_j < \infty$, $\lim_{t\to\infty} \sigma_j = 0$, and $\int_0^t \sigma_j(\omega)d\omega = d_j < \infty$, respectively.

4.2   RBFNN Online Update Adaptive Impedance Controller Design

The position error signal $\mathbf{e} = \mathbf{x} - \mathbf{x}_d$ in Cartesian space is used, the matching error signal $\omega = M_d\ddot{\mathbf{e}} + B_d\dot{\mathbf{e}} + K_d\mathbf{e} - \eta$ is constructed, and an adaptive impedance controller based on bounded matrix parameters is given. In this section, the angular position error signal $\mathbf{e} = \mathbf{q} - \mathbf{q}_d$ in the joint space is used to construct the matching error expression of the impedance model formally identical to it as

$$\begin{cases} \overline{\omega} = K_\eta\omega = \ddot{\mathbf{e}} + B_m\dot{\mathbf{e}} + K_m\mathbf{e} - K_\eta\eta \\ \overline{\omega} = \ddot{\mathbf{e}} + (\Lambda + \Gamma)\dot{\mathbf{e}} + (\dot{\Lambda} + \Gamma\Lambda)\mathbf{e} - \dot{\eta}_t - \Gamma\eta_t \end{cases} \tag{12}$$

where $K_\eta = W_d^{-1}$; $B_m = M_d^{-1}B_d$, $K_m = M_d^{-1}K_d$; $\Lambda + \Gamma = B_m$; $\dot{\Lambda} + \Gamma\Lambda = K_m$. Let $K_\eta\eta = \dot{\eta}_t + \Gamma\eta_t$. Here, the incremental state variable is denoted as

$$\mathbf{r} = \dot{\mathbf{e}} + \Lambda\mathbf{e} - \eta_t \tag{13}$$

Then the augmentation error is $\overline{\omega} = \dot{\mathbf{r}} + \Gamma\mathbf{r}$.

The kinetic equations of the combined upper limb rehabilitation exoskeleton arm and the patient's upper limb are strongly nonlinear, strongly coupled time-varying system equations. Assuming that the four joint angles $\mathbf{q}$ information can be measured and the angular velocity $\dot{\mathbf{q}}$ information can be estimated, if the state variable $\mathbf{x}_1 = [q_1, q_2, q_3, q_4]^T$, $\mathbf{x}_2 = [\dot{q}_1, \dot{q}_2, \dot{q}_3, \dot{q}_4]^T$ is taken, the kinetic equations of the exoskeleton robotic arm can be written as

$$\begin{cases} \dot{\mathbf{x}}_1 = \mathbf{x}_2 \\ \dot{\mathbf{x}}_2 = M^{-1}[\tau + \mathbf{f} - G - S\mathbf{x}_2] \end{cases} \tag{14}$$

where $\mathbf{f} = \mathbf{J}(\mathbf{q})\mathbf{F}(t)$. Define $\dot{\mathbf{q}}_r$ and $\ddot{\mathbf{q}}_r$ as $\dot{\mathbf{q}}_r = \dot{\mathbf{q}}_d - \Lambda\mathbf{e} - \eta_t$, $\ddot{\mathbf{q}}_r = \ddot{\mathbf{q}}_d - \Lambda\dot{\mathbf{e}} - \dot{\eta}_t$. According to Eq. (12), we define the variables $\mathbf{z}_1, \mathbf{z}_2$ as follows: $\mathbf{z}_1 = \mathbf{x}_1 - \mathbf{q}_d$, $\mathbf{z}_2 = \mathbf{x}_2 - \dot{\mathbf{q}}_r$. For the case of the multi-degree-of-freedom robotic arm in this paper, $\dot{\mathbf{q}}_r \in \mathbb{R}^5$, $\mathbf{z}_1 \in \mathbb{R}^4$, $\mathbf{z}_2 \in \mathbb{R}^4$. The variables are defined as

$$\begin{cases} \dot{V}_1 = \mathbf{z}_1\dot{\mathbf{z}}_1 = \mathbf{z}_1^T(\mathbf{z}_2 - \Lambda\mathbf{z}_1 - \eta_t) \\ \dot{\mathbf{z}}_2 = \dot{\mathbf{r}} = M^{-1}[\tau + \mathbf{f} - G - S\mathbf{x}_2] - \ddot{\mathbf{q}}_r \end{cases} \tag{15}$$

Then, from the above equation, we can deduce

$$\mathbf{z}_2 = \mathbf{r} + \dot{\mathbf{q}}_r - \dot{\mathbf{q}}_r = \mathbf{r} \tag{16}$$

If the Lyapunov function is chosen as $V_2 = V_1 + \frac{1}{2}\mathbf{z}_2^T M\mathbf{z}_2$. Find the time derivative of this function as

$$\begin{cases} \dot{V}_1 = \mathbf{z}_1\dot{\mathbf{z}}_1 = \mathbf{z}_1^T(\mathbf{z}_2 - \Lambda\mathbf{z}_1 - \eta_t) \\ \dot{\mathbf{z}}_2 = \dot{\mathbf{r}} = M^{-1}[\tau + \mathbf{f} - G - S\mathbf{x}_2] - \ddot{\mathbf{q}}_r \end{cases} \tag{17}$$

Considering the above analysis, and based on the addition of the active motion intention online estimation compensation term on the basis of the closed-loop feedback PD control, the adaptive impedance control law using the RBFNN estimation signal to achieve online compensation is designed as

$$\tau = -z_1 - K_2 z_2 + \overline{W}_\tau^T \phi_\tau(Z_\tau) + \overline{W}^T \phi(Z) + \overline{f} \tag{18}$$

where, $\dot{\overline{W}} = -\Upsilon(\phi(Z)z_2 + \theta\overline{W})$ is the update rate of the diagonal position motion intent for neural network estimation compensation, $\dot{\overline{W}} = -\Upsilon_\tau(\phi_\tau(Z_\tau)z_2 + \theta_\tau\overline{W}_\tau)$ is the update rate of the interaction force motion intent for neural network estimation compensation. $\overline{f}$ is the interaction force, $K_2 \in \mathbb{R}^{n*n}$, $\lambda_{\min}(K_2) > 0$, θ and θ_τ are very small positive real numbers, $\Upsilon = \Upsilon^T > 0$, and $\Upsilon_\tau = \Upsilon_\tau^T > 0$. $\overline{W}_\tau^T\phi_\tau(Z_\tau)$ approximates $W_\tau^{*T}\phi_\tau(Z_\tau)$, and $\overline{W}^T\phi(Z)$ approximates $\overline{W}^{*T}\phi(Z)$.

5   Experimental Simulation Verification

The "BMP-AIC mode" refers to the control of the shoulder Joint-2 (denoted by q_2) and elbow Joint-4 (denoted by q_4) using the control quantities formed by the BMP-based AIC. The positive definite matrix parameter $K = [0.5, 2.6]^T$ in the controller, $\hat{\Xi}_j$, is an estimate of Ξ_j. Where f denotes the principal force, which is calculated from the actual measured passive force. The test subjects put on the exoskeleton and performed the casual power-assisted rehabilitation training according to the autonomous movement intention. From the initial position, the upper arm and forearm were lifted forward and upward, q_2 around the maximum angular position $100°$, and q_4 around the maximum angular position $90°$. The moment control signal was recorded, as shown in Fig. 4, and the joint angle change data was recorded, as shown in Fig. 5.

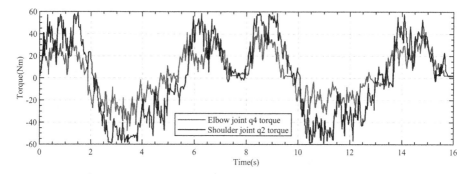

Fig. 4. BMP-AIC mode joint interaction force

The "RBFNN-AIC mode" is a mode that controls the motion of the shoulder Joint-2 (denoted by q_2) and elbow Joint-4 (denoted by q_4) based on the moment control volume formed by the RBFNN online update adaptive impedance controller AIC. The moment controller is formed based on the position difference, velocity difference, measurement

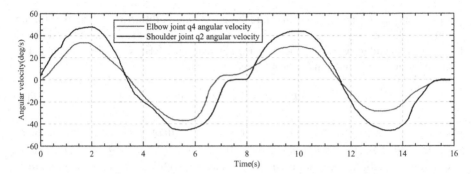

Fig. 5. BMP-AIC mode joint angular velocity

data from the wrist support ring interaction force sensor and the RBFNN online update rate.

The test subjects wore the exoskeleton and performed casual power-assisted rehabilitation training according to the autonomous movement intention. From the initial position, the upper arm and forearm were lifted forward and upward, q_2 around the maximum angular position 100° and q_4 around the maximum angular position 90°. The upward and downward movements were performed three times continuously, and the torque control signal was recorded as shown in Fig. 6. The joint angle change data is recorded with the encoder that comes with the joint actuator, and the two joint angle changes are shown in Fig. 7.

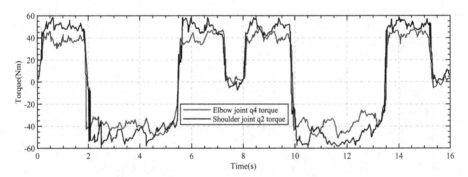

Fig. 6. RBFNN-AIC mode joint torque

The human-machine interaction force control effect of the RBFNN-based adaptive impedance controller is markedly better than that of the BMP-based adaptive impedance control method, as demonstrated by the experimental validation of the two rehabilitation motion control modes described above. The BMP-based adaptive impedance control method does not significantly differentiate force moments during upper limb rehabilitation motion. In contrast, the RBFNN-based controller can significantly differentiate

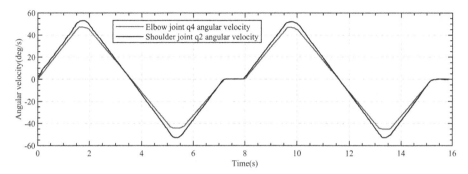

Fig. 7. RBFNN-AIC mode joint angular velocity

the human-machine interaction force information of the upper limb exoskeleton during a complete lifting-dropping motion cycle. The magnitude of the moment oscillation of the BMP controller is significantly greater than that of the RBFNN controller, indicating that the RBFNN-based adaptive impedance control method can effectively optimize the human-machine interaction force moment to achieve a more comfortable and supportive upper limb rehabilitation movement. In future work, we plan to use multi-dimensional force sensors instead of pressure sensors to obtain more accurate human-computer interaction forces.

6 Conclusion

This paper proposes an interactive force control method based on active motion intention recognition to address the issue of inadequate man-machine interaction performance in the upper limb exoskeleton. First, the man-machine interaction model of the upper limb exoskeleton is established. Then the man-machine interaction force is collected by pressure sensors installed in the elbow and wrist joints, based on the man-machine interaction force model, for the controller design. Next, a radial-based neural network-based active motion intention recognition method is developed, and a man-machine interaction force model is established based on this method. Then, an adaptive impedance control scheme based on RBFNN is devised to validate the controller's stability and efficacy. In addition, the conventional BMP-based adaptive impedance control method is intended to be compared to the previously described control scheme. The advantages and disadvantages of the two adaptive impedance control schemes are contrasted using the upper limb rehabilitation movement action to demonstrate that the method proposed in this paper can effectively optimize the man-machine interaction force.

Acknowledgment. This work was supported by the Science and technology plan project of Xi'an city (Grant no. 21XJZZ0079), the Natural Science Foundation of Shaanxi Province (Grant No. 2020JM-131 and 2020KW-058).

References

1. Wang, W., et al.: Research on control method of upper limb exoskeleton based on mixed perception model. Robotica **40**, 3669–3685 (2022)
2. Zhou, L., et al.: Design of a passive lower limb exoskeleton for walking assistance with gravity compensation. Mech. Mach. Theory **150**, 103840 (2020)
3. Wang, W., et al.: Motion intensity modeling and trajectory control of upper limb rehabilitation exoskeleton robot based on multi-modal information. Complex Intell. Syst. **8**, 2091–2103 (2022)
4. Wu, Q., Wang, X., Du, F., Zhu, Q.: Fuzzy sliding mode control of an upper limb exoskeleton for robot-assisted rehabilitation. In: 2015 IEEE International Symposium on Medical Measurements and Applications (MeMeA) Proceedings, pp. 451–456 (2015)
5. Chen, Z., et al.: Gait prediction and variable admittance control for lower limb exoskeleton with measurement delay and extended-state-observer. IEEE Trans. Neural Netw. Learn. Syst., 1–14 (2022)
6. Zhuang, Y., et al.: Voluntary control of an ankle joint exoskeleton by able-bodied individuals and stroke survivors using EMG-based admittance control scheme. IEEE Trans. Biomed. Eng. **68**, 695–705 (2021)
7. Wang, W., et al.: Interval estimation of motion intensity variation using the improved inception-V3 model. IEEE Access **9**, 66017–66031 (2021)
8. Van Engelhoven, L., Kazerooni, H.: Design and intended use of a passive actuation strategy for a shoulder supporting exoskeleton. In: 2019 Wearable Robotics Association Conference (WearRAcon), pp. 7–12 (2019)
9. Miao, Q., Zhang, M., Cao, J.: Xie SQ Reviewing high-level control techniques on robot-assisted upper-limb rehabilitation. Adv. Robot. **32**, 1253–1268 (2018)
10. Just, F., et al.: Online adaptive compensation of the ARMin rehabilitation robot. In: 2016 6th IEEE International Conference on Biomedical Robotics and Biomechatronics (BioRob), pp. 747–752 (2016)
11. Kang, H.-B., Wang, J.-H.: Adaptive robust control of 5 DOF upper-limb exoskeleton robot. Int. J. Control. Autom. Syst. **13**, 733–741 (2015)
12. Yun, D., et al.: Handling subject arm uncertainties for upper limb rehabilitation robot using robust sliding mode control. Int. J. Precis. Eng. Manuf. **17**, 355–362 (2016)

A Feature Extraction Algorithm for Exoskeleton Speech Control System Based on Noisy Environment

Zhenxing Su[1,2], Wenjie Chen[1,2(✉)], Xiantao Sun[1,2], Nana Ding[1], and Yali Zhi[1]

[1] School of Electrical Engineering and Automation, Anhui University, Hefei, China
wjchen@ahu.edu.cn
[2] Anhui Human Machine Integration System and Intelligent Equipment Engineering Laboratory, Anhui University, Hefei, China

Abstract. Exoskeleton devices based on speech systems are often affected by noise in the actual working environment, which reduces the recognition rate of speech systems. In order to reduce the influence of noise on the speech system, this paper proposes using joint features of Mel Frequency Cepstrum Coefficients and Gammatone Frequency Cepstrum Coefficients. Then, an improved Fast Correlation-Based Filtering algorithm is used to perform dimensionality reduction and remove irrelevant and redundant features in the joint features to obtain the optimal feature subset. Finally, the experiments show that the feature recognition effect is greatly improved after dimensionality reduction is performed under a low signal-to-noise ratio.

Keywords: Exoskeleton devices · Feature Extraction · Fast Correlation-Based Filter · Mel Frequency Cepstrum Coefficients · Gammatone Frequency Cepstrum Coefficients

1 Introduction

Powered exoskeleton devices are robotic devices that can enhance human mobility and physical abilities, consisting of a control system and an exoskeleton frame. Powered exoskeletons can assist people with mobility impairments in walking, standing, climbing, and other activities, as well as in heavy-duty operations in industrial production or hazardous environments. In recent years, with the continuous advancement of technology, the performance of powered exoskeleton devices has become increasingly powerful, and their applications have become more and more widespread. In the future, powered exoskeleton devices are expected to become an indispensable part of human life. With the continuous development of artificial intelligence, speech recognition technology has become a reality and has been applied in real life. The advantage of speech recognition technology lies in its low cost and flexibility, making it one of the most convenient ways of human-machine interaction. The use of speech in exoskeleton devices can greatly improve work efficiency and reduce physical burden, and enhance flexibility and applicability. However, in daily life, the existence of noise leads to a sharp decrease in the

© The Author(s), under exclusive license to Springer Nature Singapore Pte Ltd. 2023
H. Yang et al. (Eds.): ICIRA 2023, LNAI 14268, pp. 365–373, 2023.
https://doi.org/10.1007/978-981-99-6486-4_32

recognition rate of speech systems, making it an important issue in current research to improve the recognition rate of speech in noisy environments. Speech feature extraction is an essential link in the process of speech recognition, and the quality of features directly affects the recognition effect of the speech system.

The widely used Mel Frequency Cepstral Coefficients (MFCC) [1, 2] are susceptible to the influence of the external environment, which leads to poor speech recognition. to improve the recognition rate in noisy environments, literature [3, 4] proposed Gamma-tone Frequency Cepstral Coefficients(GFCC) based on gammatone frequency cepstral coefficients. Although the recognition effect is improved, the extracted features are single and cannot completely characterize the complete information of the speech. In [5–7], a hybrid feature based on Mel Frequency Cepstral Coefficients and Gammatone Frequency Cepstral Coefficients is proposed, which improves the speech recognition effect to a certain extent, Although the effect is good but the computational complexity is increased. In this paper, we propose an optimization algorithm to remove irrelevant and redundant features in the hybrid features proposed in the literature [6] by using an improved Fast Correlation Base Filtering algorithm [8] to obtain F-MFGCC features. Finally, we perform training and recognition using a hidden Markov Gaussian hybrid mixture model, and the experiments show that the effect of obtaining F-MFGCC features is better than the hybrid features under low a signal-to-noise ratio.

2 Fast Correlation Based Filter

2.1 Symmetric Uncertainty

Symmetric Uncertainty (SU) represents the correlation between X and Y. The larger the value, the greater the correlation between X and Y. When the value is 0, it means that X and Y are independent of each other. Conversely, a high SU value represents a strong dependence between them, implying that it is possible to infer the other when one of the variables is known. This is expressed by Eq. (1):

$$SU(X, Y) = \frac{2IG(X|Y)}{H(X) + H(Y)} \tag{1}$$

H(X) is denoted as the information entropy of X:

$$H(X) = -\sum_i p(x_i) \log_2 p(x_i) \tag{2}$$

H(X|Y) is the conditional entropy of the variable X with respect to Y:

$$H(X|Y) = -\sum_j p(y_j) \sum_i p(x_i|y_j) \log_2 p(x_iy_j) \tag{3}$$

where IG denotes the mutual information, which can be viewed as the amount of information contained in one random variable about another random variable:

$$IG(X|Y) = H(X) - H(X|Y) = H(Y) - H(Y|X) \tag{4}$$

2.2   Fast Correlation Based Filter Algorithm Process

The fast correlation filtering algorithm is an algorithm used for feature extraction, whose main purpose is to remove irrelevant and redundant features from the feature set to obtain a more accurate feature representation. The basic idea of this algorithm is to measure the correlation between features using the maximum correlation coefficient and symmetric uncertainty. Then, irrelevant and redundant features are removed through a series of filtering operations [9].

- Remove irrelevant features
  Calculate SU(Fi,c) between the feature and the category, set the threshold δ, and add the feature greater than the threshold to the feature subset.
- Remove redundant features
  Let the feature subset be S, where the first element is Fj, and the next element is Fi. Judge the redundancy of i and j. If SU(Fi, Fj) > SU(Fi, Fc), consider Fi as redundant and remove it from S. Continue to judge the next element until the last feature. Then the above process is repeated with the second element in S as Fj until there is no element in S.
  From the above process, the feature selection results of the FCBF algorithm may be affected by the correlation between features. If there is a high correlation between features, the FCBF algorithm may select features with lower correlation but higher redundancy, resulting in less accurate feature selection results. The following solutions are proposed for the above problems.
- Increasing the SU value can improve the correlation between features and reduce the redundancy between features, thus improving the accuracy of feature selection results. Additionally, increasing the SU value can improve the robustness of noisy data and reduce the possibility of selecting features with noise, thus further improving the accuracy of feature selection results.

$$SU(X|Y) = \frac{IG(X;Y)}{\min\{H(X), H(Y)\}} \tag{5}$$

From Eq. (1) and Eq. (5), it can be seen that the value of Eq. (5) is constantly greater than the value of Eq. (1).

- Using the transformed sigmoid function to weight the SU values can make the correlation more accurately reflect the relationship between the features and the target variables, thus increasing the weight of the correlation. Additionally, the nonlinear characteristic of the sigmoid function can make the weighted SU values more flexible. For features with high correlation but also high redundancy, it can reduce their influence on the final feature selection results, enabling the selection of the most representative features more accurately.

The Sigmoid function is a common S function in biology. The Sigmoid function is suitably transformed so that it is defined between (0, 1). Then the SU value is substituted into the function and the result is calculated (Fig. 1).

$$f(x) = \frac{1}{1 + e^{-8*(SU-0.5)}} \tag{6}$$

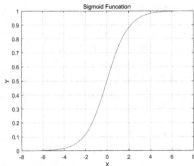

Fig. 1. Sigmoid Function.

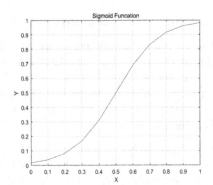

Fig. 2. The Sigmoid function for scaling.

3 Feature Extraction

3.1 Mel Frequency Cepstrum Coefficients

After extensive experiments, it has been shown that the human auditory system does not perceive frequency linearly and is more sensitive to low-frequency signals than high-frequency signals. The Mel filter set was proposed to imitate the human ear's hearing mechanism. It is related to the frequency as in Eq. (7) (Fig. 2).

$$Mel(f) = 2595 * \lg(1 + \frac{f}{700}) \tag{7}$$

3.2 Gammatone Frequency Cepstrum Coefficients

A gammatone filter is a non-uniform overlapping band pass filter that simulates the auditory characteristics of the basilar membrane of the human cochlea. It passes each input signal through a 24-channel gammatone filter.

The impulse response of each filter in the time domain can be expressed as:

$$g(f, t) = at^{n-1}e^{-2\pi/b_{cm}t}\cos(2\pi tf_{cm} + \varphi) \tag{8}$$

α is the amplitude of the filter generally 1, n indicates the order of the filter, fcm indicates the frequency center of the filter, bcm is the attenuation coefficient for calculating the corresponding filter, and φ is the phase shift generally taking the value of 0. ERB is the psychological scale amount of the sound-related channel width at each point along the cochlea. The bandwidth of each filter is calculated as follows:

$$b_m = bERB(f_{cm}) = 24.7(4.37f_{cm}/100 + 1) \tag{9}$$

3.3   The Specific Process of Feature Extraction

MFCC and GFCC are two commonly used features that have been widely used in the fields of speaker recognition and speech recognition. The process of MFCC and GFCC feature extraction is very similar. It can be summarized in six steps: signal pre-emphasis, framing and windowing, finding the power spectrum after Fourier transformation, filtering, taking logarithms, and discrete cosine transformation. The biggest difference is that the two use different filters. The extracted MFCC and GFCC features are substituted into the improved FCBF respectively, and the irrelevant and redundant features in the features are removed to obtain the optimal features for the next experiment. Figure 3 shows the specific calculation process. Figure 4 and Fig. 5 shows the feature distribution.

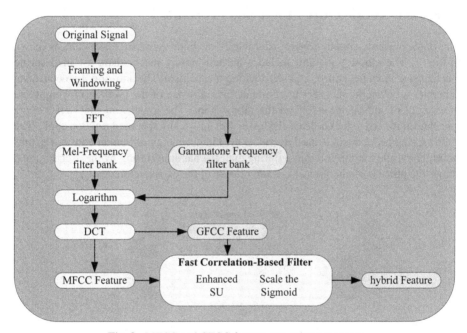

Fig. 3. MFCC and GFCC feature extraction processes

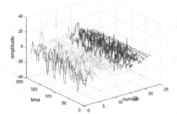

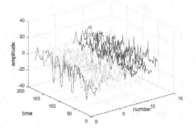

Fig. 4. Unoptimized feature distribution map.

Fig. 5. Optimized feature distribution map.

4 System Architecture Profile and Problems

This paper presents a passive energy-storable elbow joint-assisted exoskeleton, as shown in Fig. 7. The elbow joint unit includes an anti-gravity mechanism, a coiled spring mechanism, and a lower arm unit self-locking mechanism. The anti-gravity mechanism generates a balancing moment to eliminate the influence of the user's arm weight and the weight of the device itself on the elbow joint. The lower arm unit self-locking mechanism is used to lock/release the lower arm unit at any specified rotation angle. The coiled spring mechanism is used to collect the kinetic energy of human body parts, thus avoiding muscle fatigue and injury during material handling/lifting by the user. Figure 6 shows the process of energy storage and release of the exoskeleton device.

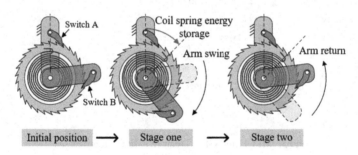

Fig. 6. Exoskeleton energy storage process

However, the passive energy-storable elbow-assisted exoskeleton requires manual storage and release of energy from the actuator in practical use, which suffers from a lack of flexibility. To improve the flexibility and adaptability of the exoskeleton at work, this paper adopts a voice system combined with the exoskeleton device. Through the voice system, the user can control the exoskeleton through verbal commands, achieving a more flexible and natural way of operation. The voice system can also realize the intelligent control of the exoskeleton, automatically adjusting the power-assist mode of the exoskeleton according to the user's needs and environmental changes to improve the adaptability and flexibility of the exoskeleton. This method of the voice system combined with exoskeleton equipment can not only improve the operation convenience

Fig. 7. Exoskeleton devices.   **Fig. 8.** Mechanical structure.

and human-computer interaction of the exoskeleton but also improve the efficiency and safety of the exoskeleton, providing a better solution for the practical application of the exoskeleton.

5 Experimental Results and Analyses

The experimental platform is shown in the Fig. 9. The exoskeleton device uses an ARM microcontroller to collect information through the serial port and control the movement of the exoskeleton device according to different instructions. The experimental data recorded 20 students' speech (half of each gender) in a quiet environment with a sampling frequency of 8 kHz and a duration of about 2 s, including voice commands such as shutdown, self-locking, energy storage, etc. Finally, training and testing results were obtained using the Markov Gaussian mixture model.

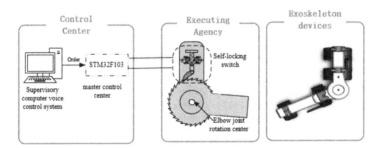

Fig. 9. Experiment schematic

To verify the effectiveness of the proposed feature method in noisy environments, this paper conducted experiments on babble noise and Engine room noise from the Noise-92 database. Clean speech was mixed with additive noise at signal-to-noise ratios of 20 dB, 15 dB, 10 dB, 5 dB, and 0 dB [10].

From the Fig. 10 and Fig. 11, we can see that in a noisy environment, the recognition rate of MFCC decreases sharply as the signal-to-noise ratio of speech decreases. The reason is that MFCC simulates the hearing mechanism of the human ear for frequency, and noise is distributed in all frequency bands of speech, which is destructive to speech and

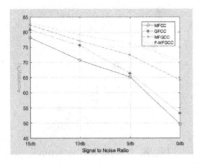 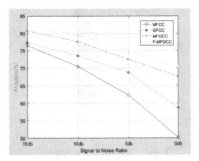

Fig. 10. Recognition rate of different signal to noise ratio under babble noise.

Fig. 11. Recognition rate of different signal-to-noise ratio under Engine room noise.

causes the recognition rate to decrease sharply [11]. On the other hand, the gammatone filter simulates the auditory characteristics of the human cochlear basilar membrane, which reduces the problem of energy leakage and therefore has stronger robustness in noisy environments. The feature parameters based on F-MFGCC are more resistant to noise in a noisy environment, Because speech irrelevant features are removed, and then, redundant features are reduced through these steps, reducing the effect of noise on speech and greatly retaining the original information of speech.

6 Conclusion

Exoskeleton equipment can greatly reduce the physical burden of workers in daily life and improve work efficiency, with a wide range of application prospects. However, noise exists everywhere in daily life, which has a great impact on the speech system. To address this problem, an optimization of MFCC and GFCC hybrid features is proposed to reduce computational complexity on one hand and the impact of noise on speech on the other. Finally, the feasibility of the proposed method is proven by verification.

Acknowledgement. I would like to express my heartfelt thanks and sincere respect to Mr. Wen-jie Chen. He has always encouraged me to continue to learn knowledge with his persistent pursuit of science, practical and realistic work attitude, generous and humble approach and selfless dedication. I also thank the National Natural Science Foundation of China (51975002) for its support.

References

1. Biswas, M., Rahaman, S., Ahmadian, A., et al.: Automatic spoken language identification using MFCC based time series features. Multimed. Tools Appl. **82**, 9565–9595 (2023)
2. Li, Q., et al.: MSP-MFCC: energy-efficient MFCC feature extraction method with mixed-signal processing architecture for wearable speech recognition applications. IEEE Access **8**, 48720–48730 (2020)

3. Shi, X., Yang, H., Zhou, P.: Robust speaker recognition based on improved GFCC. In: IEEE 2016 2nd IEEE International Conference on Computer and Communications (ICCC), Chengdu, China, pp. 1927–1931 (2016)

4. Wang, H., Zhang, C.: The application of Gammatone frequency cepstral coefficients for forensic voice comparison under noisy conditions. Aust. J. Forensic Sci. **52**, 1–16 (2019)

5. Dua, M., Aggarwal, R.K., Biswas, M.: Optimizing integrated features for Hindi automatic speech recognition system. J. Intell. Syst. **29**(1), 959–976 (2018)

6. Dua, M., Aggarwal, R.K., Biswas, M.: Performance evaluation of Hindi speech recognition system using optimized filterbanks. Eng. Sci. Technol. Int. J. **21**(3), 389–398 (2018)

7. Li, Z., Yao, Q., Ma, W.: Matching subsequence music retrieval in a software integration environment. Complexity **2021**, 1–12 (2021)

8. Deng, X., Li, M., Wang, L., et al.: RFCBF: enhance the performance and stability of fast correlation-based filter. Int. J. Comput. Intell. Appl. **21**(02), 2250009 (2022)

9. Zaffar, M., Hashmani, M.A., Savita, K.S., et al.: Role of FCBF feature selection in educational data mining. Mehran Univ. Res. J. Eng. Technol. **39**(4), 772–778 (2020)

10. Muralishankar, R., Ghosh, D., Gurugopinath, S.: A novel modified Mel-DCT filter bank structure with application to voice activity detection. IEEE Signal Process. Lett. **27**, 1240–1244 (2020)

11. Zhao, X., Shao, Y., Wang, D.L.: CASA-based robust speaker identification. IEEE Trans. Audio Speech Lang. Process. **20**(5), 1608–1616 (2012)

Design and Control of a Soft Hip Exoskeleton for Assisting Human Locomotion

Zeshi Sun, Nianfeng Wang$^{(\boxtimes)}$, Jianliang Zhang, Shuhao Xia, and Xianmin Zhang

Guangdong Key Laboratory of Precision Equipment and Manufacturing Technology, School of Mechanical and Automotive Engineering, South China University of Technology, Guangzhou 510640, People's Republic of China
menfwang@scut.edu.cn

Abstract. This paper presents a soft hip exoskeleton (SH-Exo) for healthy people's daily walking, which effectively provides an assisted force for hip extension through an actuation system with flexible Bowden cable. In addition, it is lightweight to satisfy the user's comfort and human-exoskeleton coordination. A control strategy based on Adaptive Hopf Oscillators (AHO) is proposed to achieve gait division and gait phase recognition. In order to achieve the goal of tracking the desired force curve accurately, a control strategy of the PID controller based on feedforward compensation is proposed. The results of the experiment show that the SH-Exo significantly reduces the metabolic cost of walking by an average of 5.3% in the Exo-on condition compared to the Exo-off condition.

Keywords: Hip exoskeleton · Wearable robotics · Walking assistance

1 Introduction

Exoskeleton robots are one of the most challenging and exciting research topics involving neuroscience, biomechanics, robotics automation and other fields [1]. Most exoskeletons [2,3] now use a rigid driving system, which has good robustness and motion accuracy. However, rigid exoskeleton systems have significant limitations in wearability and practicality. Some recent studies have shown that rigid exoskeletons increase the metabolic cost of the human body [4]. Rigid wear exerts additional opposing forces when exoskeletal joints are misaligned or mismatched with biological joints, and more so, rigid links add greater distal inertia on the limb [5,6], disrupting the natural gait kinematics of the body.

Compared with the rigid exoskeletons, soft exoskeletons have advantages such as adaptability, lightweight, and low power consumption. Soft exoskeletons assist joints by applying tension parallel to the muscles through flexible structures. For example, Asbeck et al. developed an exosuit that reduced the wearer's metabolism by 6.4% using a motor-driven Bowden cable actuator [7]. Kim et al. used the same Bowden cable driving system to assist walking and running [8,9], and the experimental results showed that the users' metabolic cost decreased by 9.3% during walking and 4.0% during running.

Control of the soft exoskeletons is more complicated than the rigid exoskeletons. The driving system is susceptible to interference from the flexible wearable structure, which exhibits nonlinearity and time-variability. Many control strategies have been proposed to control soft exoskeletons, such as fuzzy control [10], iterative learning control [11], and adaptive control [12]. Although the feasibility of the above control strategy has been verified, there are still some challenging problems to be solved. The difficulties are mainly focused on the gait recognition of walking in the high-level controller and accurately tracking the assisted force curve in the low-level controller.

This paper develops a soft hip exoskeleton (SH-Exo) for the daily walking of healthy people, which provides an assisted force for hip extension through an actuation system with flexible Bowden cable. A control strategy based on Adaptive Hopf Oscillators (AHO) is proposed to achieve gait division and gait phase recognition. In order to reduce the metabolic energy of human walking, a control strategy of PID controller based on feedforward compensation is proposed, which realizes the accurate tracking of target force trajectory. The control effects of the upper and lower controllers were confirmed in the treadmill experiment. Finally, the assist performance of the SH-Exo is verified by kinematics and metabolism experiments.

2   Exoskeleton Design

2.1   Design Concept

The soft exoskeleton is designed to assist healthy people in hip extension during walking. Some researchers found that the effect should be more prominent in the hip joint than the ankle joint, given the same amount of effort from exoskeletons. Therefore, hip assistance through an powerful soft exoskeleton is a very efficient walking assistance strategy. In walking at a speed of 4.5 km/h, the angle and power of the hip joint [13] are shown in Fig. 1(a), which is easy to find that the hip joint does positive work in the swing phase and the initial phase of the support phase, respectively.

At about 35% of the gait phase, the hip joint passes through the sagittal plane, at which point the hip extension begins to decelerate, and the hip muscles do negative work. At about 55% of the gait phase, the hip joint moves to the maximum extension angle, after which the hip joint enters the swing phase and begins to flexion. It is easy to find that the hip joint does the most positive work during the extension phase from the joint power curve. Therefore, the metabolic cost of human walking is most likely reduced by assisting hip extension during 0% to 35% of the gait phase.

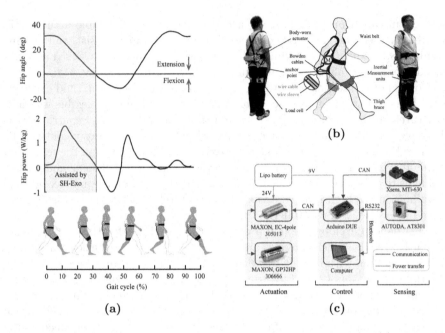

Fig. 1. The design concept and mechanical structures of the SH-Exo. (a) The angle and power of the hip joint. (b) The mechanical structures. (c) The hardware system.

2.2   Mechanical Structures

Based on the design concept described in Sect. 2.1, we designed a soft hip exoskeleton (SH-Exo) that assists in hip extension. The overall structure of the SH-Exo is shown in Fig. 1(b). The driving system transfers the torque output from the motor to the target position by a Bowden cable, referring to the Bowden cable actuator of [9]. The structure does not restrict the range of motion of the lower limbs during daily activities and has good human-exoskeleton coordination.

As shown in Fig. 1(c), the SH-Exo hardware system includes driving, control, and sensing units. The driving unit consists of two actuators to assist the hip joints of each leg. Each actuator consists of a high power ratio motor (#305013, Maxon, Switzerland) connected to a gearbox of ratio 51:1 (#326664, Maxon, Switzerland) and drives a 40-mm radius pulley, which can provide up to 12 Nm of peak torque. Two 1.2 mm diameter Bowden cables are wrapped around the pulley at one end and attached to an anchor point on the thigh brace at the other end. The motor rotates the pulley to contract the Bowden cables, which generates an assist moment in the same direction as the biological moment.

Arduino DUE (Arduino DUE, Ivrea (TO), Italy) is the control unit, sending commands to the driving unit through the CAN bus. The sensing unit consists of two IMUs ((MTi-630, Xsens, Netherlands)) and two load cells (AT8301, AUTODA, China). The IMUs are placed on the front side of the thigh brace, which provides kinematic data on thigh swing. The load cells are connected in series to the anchor point at the end of the driving unit. It is used to provide real-time force data of the driving unit.

In addition, the total weight of the SH-Exo is 3.5 kg, with most of the mass located at the wearer's waist, which facilitates a reduction in the distal mass of the soft exoskeleton [4] and reduces the metabolic cost impact of the load on walking.

3   Control Strategy

3.1   High-Level Controller

As shown in Fig. 2(a), the high-level controller learns the frequency of the low limb motion through the Adaptive Hopf Oscillator (AHO) to achieve gait division and phase recognition. Then the desired force curve is generated by fitting a sinusoidal function in the specified gait phase interval.

Righetti et al. [14] have incorporated the Dynamic Hebbian Learning algorithm into the classical Hopf oscillator to achieve an adaptive Hopf oscillator that can learn external frequency signals. Yan et al. [15] applied adaptive oscillators to gait phase estimation, which feed back the difference between the input signal and the reconstructed signal to drive the dynamics of state variable learning. In this device, the external input signal is the thigh swing angle $\theta(t)$ measured by IMUs, and the dynamic differential equation of AHO can be described as

$$\dot{x}(t) = (\mu - r(t)^2)x(t) + \omega(t)y(t) + \varepsilon F(t) \tag{1}$$

$$\dot{y}(t) = (\mu - r(t)^2)y(t) - \omega(t)x(t) \tag{2}$$

$$\dot{\omega}(t) = \varepsilon F(t)\frac{y(t)}{r(t)} \tag{3}$$

where $r(t) = \sqrt{x(t)^2 + y(t)^2}$ is the amplitude of the AHO. $x(t)$ and $y(t)$ are the right-angle coordinate components of the AHO at time t. μ is the radius of the limit ring of the oscillator, and its value is generally normalized. $\omega(t)$ is the frequency of the output signal of the oscillator. $F(t) = \theta(t) - x(t)$ is the difference between the periodic input signal $\theta(t)$ and the oscillator output signal $x(t)$. ε is the gain coefficient that controls the speed of adaptive learning, and the higher its value, the faster the adaptive speed, but also the more unstable it is.

The current gait phase is obtained by integrating the output signal frequency, and the relevant formula is as follows:

$$\varphi(t) = \sum_{0}^{n} \omega(t)T_c \tag{4}$$

$$P(t) = \frac{\varphi(t)}{2\pi} \times 100\% \tag{5}$$

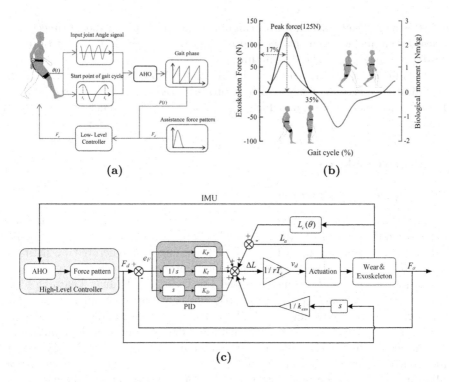

Fig. 2. Control strategy. (a) The AHO-based control scheme. (b) The desired force curve (c) The system block diagram of the low-level controller.

where $\varphi(t)$ is the gait phase; $P(t)$ is the gait percentage; n is the cumulative number of the current cycle. The event indicating the start of the gait was recorded as the maximum hip flexion angle. When both $\dot{\theta}(t_i) < 0$ and $\dot{\theta}(t_{i-1}) > 0$ are satisfied at the t_i moment, the t_i moment is the start of each gait cycle, at which point the current phase $\varphi(t_i)$ is set to 0. It is worth noting that $P(t)$ is only the predicted percentage value, not the actual value. Its error is mainly affected by the AHO's learning parameters and the input signal's stability. The performance of the upper-level controller is verified by a treadmill experiment in Sect. 4 of this paper.

Many researchers have customized mathematical models to generate desired force curves based on the approximate pattern of joint biological moments [9,11]. This device uses a similar scheme to generate the desired force curve of the exoskeleton by fitting a sine function, as shown in Fig. 2(b), where the black line represents the desired force curve of the exoskeleton and the red line represents the biological moment curve of the hip joint. The desired force curve is designed based on the pattern of the biological moment curve. The assistance starts at 0% of the gait phase and reaches a peak force of 125 N at 17%, after which the force begins to decrease until it drops to 0 N at 35% of the gait phase. The Bowden cables remain tensioned, but the force is 0 N for the rest of the gait cycle. In actual working conditions, it is defined that the force of the exoskeleton can be considered as $0\,\mathrm{N}$ when the data of the load cell is less than $5\,\mathrm{N}$.

3.2 Low-Level Controller

The soft thigh braces will produce nonlinear deformation when stretched, which significantly increases the control difficulty of the system. This paper proposes a PID controller based on feedforward compensation to track the desired force trajectory accurately.

The system block diagram of the low-level controller is shown in Fig. 2(c). $L_c(\theta)$ is the critical cable length corresponding to the thigh swing angle θ, which is the length of the tension Bowden cable when the force is $0\,\mathrm{N}$; k_{exo} is the stiffness of the exoskeleton, and the value is the ratio of the actual force F_a to the amount of change in the critical cable length ΔL_c; $L_c(\theta)$ and k_{exo} are two easily identifiable quantities in the system, which are used to design the feedforward controller.

The PID input signal of the system is the actual force deviation e_F, and the output is the cable length variation ΔL, which is related as follows:

$$\Delta L = K_P e_F + K_I \int e_F + K_D \dot{e}_F + L_c(\theta) - L_a + \frac{\dot{F}_d}{k_{exo}} \qquad (6)$$

where the actual force deviation is:

$$e_F = F_d - F_a \qquad (7)$$

K_P, K_I and K_D are the proportional, differential and integral coefficients of the PID controller, respectively. L_a is the actual cable length obtained by converting the measured value of the motor encoder. In actual operation, it is found that the direct input of cable change length can easily lead to instability factors such as motor stalling, so the cable length change speed v_d is used as input:

$$v_d = \Delta L/(rT_c) \qquad (8)$$

where r is the pulley radius at the motor's output and T_c is the control period of the system.

4   Experiment

4.1 Experimental Protocol

The experimental protocol includes two main experiments. In the first experiment, the performance of the controller was evaluated in a treadmill test. Then kinematic and metabolic experiments were performed to determine the metabolic impact of the exoskeleton. Four healthy male subjects (age 23.0 ± 0.7 years, mass $69.5 \pm 2.8\,\mathrm{kg}$, height $1.78 \pm 0.03\,\mathrm{m}$, and mean $\pm$ standard deviation (SD)) participated in the study. All participants had no history of musculoskeletal or neurological diseases. All participants signed informed consent forms before the start of the experiment.

One of the four subject (age 22.0 year, mass 73 kg, height 1.84 m) participated in the first experiment. Firstly, to evaluate the control accuracy of the high-level controller, the subject wore the SH-Exo and walked on treadmill at 4 km/h for 3 min, then increased the speed to 5 km/h during the walking state, continued walking for 3 min and then stopped the experiment. The exoskeleton sends the gait division data to the PC during the experiment in real time through Bluetooth.

For the low-level controller, the control performance of the two controllers was compared at a speed of 4.5 km/h. The subject first walked on the treadmill wearing the SH-Exo with the PID controller for 5 min. After a 5-minute rest, the subject walked on the treadmill again for 5 min, wearing the SH-Exo with the PID controller based on feedforward compensation. The desired and measured force during a stable state were recorded under different control strategies (Fig. 3).

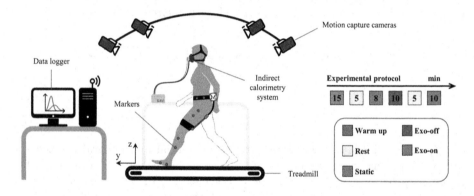

Fig. 3. The experimental platform and procedure

In the kinematic and metabolic experiment, four subjects walked on a treadmill at 4.5 km/h under two experimental conditions. The testing procedure was as follows:

1) Warm-up: Walk on a treadmill for 15 min at a speed of 4.5 km/h.
2) Sit down and rest for 5 min.
3) Static: Stand on a treadmill for 8 min to measure the basal metabolic rate.
4) Exo-off: Wear the exoskeleton and walk on a treadmill at a speed of 4.5 km/h for 10 min without assistance.
5) Sit down and rest for 5 min.
6) Exo-on: Wear the exoskeleton and walk on a treadmill at a speed of 4.5 km/h for 10 min with assistance.

Metabolic rate was assessed through indirect calorimetry (K4b2, Cosmed, Italy) for three conditions: Static, Exo-off, and Exo-on. Further, The carbon dioxide and oxygen data were gathered from the last two minutes of each condition using the Brockway equation to calculate the metabolic rate. The net metabolic rate was obtained by subtracting the metabolic rate of static from the total metabolic rate of walking. Lower limb motions were measured by a reflective marker motion capture system (NOKOV Motion Capture System, China), and joint angles were calculated from measured lower limb motions using inverse kinematics by software(MATLAB, MathWorks).

4.2 Experiment Results and Analysis

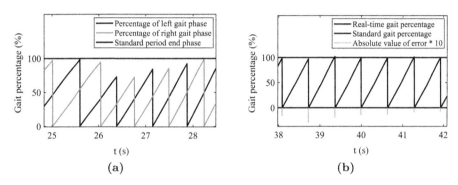

(a)   (b)

Fig. 4. The high-level controller performance analysis. (a) Gait percentage estimation when walking speed changes. (b) Gait percentage error when walking speed is stable.

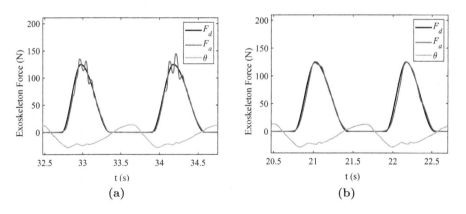

(a)   (b)

Fig. 5. The low-level controller performance analysis. (a) The control effects of the PID controller. (b) The control effects of the PID controller based on feedforward compensation.

Control Performance Assessment. Figure 4(a) shows the results of gait division for subjects walking from a walking speed of 4 km/h gradually accelerating to a speed of 5 km/h, where the blue and orange lines represent the percentage of gait phase for each leg, respectively, and the black line represents the end of the standard cycle. It was easy to find that the AHO quickly adapted to the new walking speed after about 2.5 s when the walking speed was changed.

Figure 4(b) shows the absolute error between the real-time gait percentage estimated by AHO and the standard gait percentage during walking. Specifically, the absolute error of AHO's calculation of the gait period during gait stability is less than 5% in all cases. Therefore, the high-level control experiments show that the AHO can quickly adapt to the new gait speed with high accuracy when changing the walking speed. In addition, the controller is set to implement assisted force control only when the absolute error of the gait phase percentage is satisfied below 10%, ensuring the wearer's safety in case of gait instability.

The control effects of the PID controller and the PID controller based on feedforward compensation are shown in Fig. 5(a) and Fig. 5(b), respectively. The blue line F_d represents the desired force; the red line F_a represents the actual force; the yellow line θ represents the hip angle. It can be found that the PID controller has a significant control error, while the control error near the peak force is reduced significantly after adding feedforward compensation. In the 5-minute experiment, the average force deviation RMSE values for the PID control and the PID control based on the feedforward compensation are 6.0774 and 4.5322, respectively. It can be found that the control accuracy of the PID controller based on the feedforward compensation is significantly improved compared to that of the PID controller.

Kinematics and Metabolic Rate. As shown in Fig. 6, in the treadmill experiment, there were some differences in the kinematics of each joint, except for the peak ankle plantarflexion angle, which remained essentially constant. Compared to the Exo-off condition, the peak extension angle of the hip joint increased, and the peak flexion angle decreased; the peak ankle dorsiflexion angle decreased, and the knee flexion angle decreased slightly during the whole gait cycle.

Our initial results suggest that the device does not appear to disrupt normal walking kinematics drastically. It makes sense that the hip trajectories should be shifted toward extension since the exoskeleton exerts a force on the thigh in the extension during approximately one-third of the gait cycle. Interestingly, the kinematics of the other two joints of the lower limb were also affected when assisting the hip joint, suggesting that the subjects actively changed the kinematics of the other joints to maintain normal gait when the hip joint kinematics changed.

The net metabolic rate of the four subjects are presented in Fig. 7(a), and Fig. 7(b) shows the average of the net metabolic rate of all subjects. The results show that the average net metabolic rate in the Exo-on condition was reduced by $5.3 \pm 0.7\%$ (mean $\pm$ SEM; paired t-test, p $= 0.014$) for walking compared to the

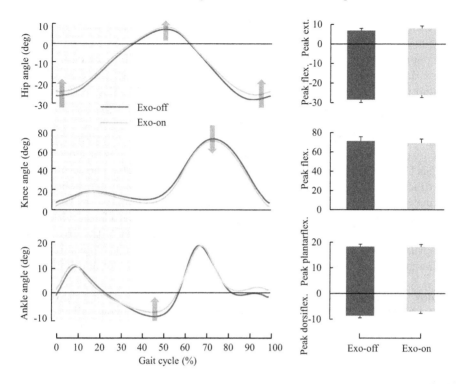

Fig. 6. Joint kinematics in the treadmill experiment

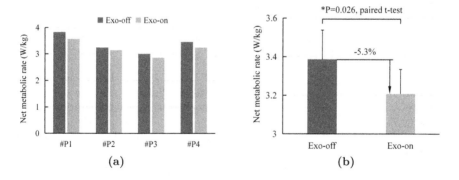

Fig. 7. Metabolic rate in the treadmill experiment. (a) The net metabolic rate of all subjects. (b) The average net metabolic rate.

Exo-off condition, which confirms the efficacy of the hip assistance in reducing the metabolic cost of walking.

5   Conclusion

This paper presents a soft hip exoskeleton (SH-Exo) for daily walking of healthy people, from aspects of the design concept, mechanical structure, control strategy and performance evaluation, which effectively provides an assisted force for hip extension through an actuation system with flexible Bowden cable. A control strategy based on AHO is proposed to achieve gait division and gait phase recognition. In order to reduce the metabolic energy of human walking, a control strategy of PID controller based on feedforward compensation is proposed, which realizes the goal of tracking the desired force curve accurately. The results of the experiment show that the SH-Exo significantly reduces the metabolic cost of walking by an average of 5.3% in the Exo-on condition compared to the Exo-off condition. Future work will be devoted to the study of exoskeleton with multimode switching. In addition, to improve the assistance effect of the exoskeleton, the optimal assistance force curve will be obtained based on the optimization of the human motion model to reduce more metabolism of the human body.

Acknowledgment. The authors would like to gratefully acknowledge the reviewers comments. This work is supported by National Natural Science Foundation of China (Grant No. 52075180), and the Fundamental Research Funds for the Central Universities.

References

1. Meng, Q., et al.: Flexible lower limb exoskeleton systems: a review. NeuroRehabilitation **50**, 1–24 (2022)
2. Li, Z., Deng, C., Zhao, K.: Human-cooperative control of a wearable walking exoskeleton for enhancing climbing stair activities. IEEE Trans. Industr. Electron. **67**(4), 3086–3095 (2019)
3. Awad, L.N., Esquenazi, A., Francisco, G.E., Nolan, K.J., Jayaraman, A.: The rewalk restore^{TM} soft robotic exosuit: a multi-site clinical trial of the safety, reliability, and feasibility of exosuit-augmented post-stroke gait rehabilitation. J. Neuroeng. Rehabil. **17**(1), 1–11 (2020)
4. Quinlivan, B.T., et al.: Assistance magnitude versus metabolic cost reductions for a tethered multiarticular soft exosuit. Sci. Robot. **2**(2), eaah4416 (2017)
5. Gregorczyk, K.N., et al.: The effects of a lower body exoskeleton load carriage assistive device on oxygen consumption and kinematics during walking with loads. Technical report, ARMY NATICK SOLDIER CENTER MA (2006)
6. Walsh, C.J., Endo, K., Herr, H.: A quasi-passive leg exoskeleton for load-carrying augmentation. Int. J. Humanoid Rob. **4**(03), 487–506 (2007)
7. Asbeck, A.T., De Rossi, S.M., Holt, K.G., Walsh, C.J.: A biologically inspired soft exosuit for walking assistance. Int. J. Robot. Res. **34**(6), 744–762 (2015)
8. Kim, J., et al.: Autonomous and portable soft exosuit for hip extension assistance with online walking and running detection algorithm. In: 2018 IEEE International Conference on Robotics and Automation (ICRA), pp. 5473–5480. IEEE (2018)
9. Kim, J., et al.: Reducing the metabolic rate of walking and running with a versatile, portable exosuit. Science **365**(6454), 668–672 (2019)

10. Yin, K., Pang, M., Xiang, K., Chen, J., Zhou, S.: Fuzzy iterative learning control strategy for powered ankle prosthesis. Int. J. Intell. Robot. Appl. **2**(1), 122–131 (2018)
11. Cao, W., Chen, C., Hu, H., Fang, K., Wu, X.: Effect of hip assistance modes on metabolic cost of walking with a soft exoskeleton. IEEE Trans. Autom. Sci. Eng. **18**(2), 426–436 (2020)
12. Seo, K., Lee, J., Lee, Y., Ha, T., Shim, Y.: Fully autonomous hip exoskeleton saves metabolic cost of walking. In: 2016 IEEE International Conference on Robotics and Automation (ICRA), pp. 4628–4635. IEEE (2016)
13. Neumann, D.A.: Kinesiology of the Musculoskeletal System-e-Book: Foundations for Rehabilitation. Elsevier Health Sciences (2016)
14. Righetti, L., Buchli, J., Ijspeert, A.J.: Dynamic Hebbian learning in adaptive frequency oscillators. Phys. D **216**(2), 269–281 (2006)
15. Yan, T., Parri, A., Ruiz Garate, V., Cempini, M., Ronsse, R., Vitiello, N.: An oscillator-based smooth real-time estimate of gait phase for wearable robotics. Auton. Robot. **41**(3), 759–774 (2017)

Design and Control of a Portable Soft Exosuit by Musculoskeletal Model-Based Optimization

Nianfeng Wang[(✉)] [iD], Zicong Wang [iD], Zitian Li, Shuhao Xia,
and Xianmin Zhang

Guangdong Key Laboratory of Precision Equipment and Manufacturing Technology,
School of Mechanical and Automotive Engineering, South China University of
Technology, Guangzhou 510640, People's Republic of China
menfwang@scut.edu.cn

Abstract. Universally applicable ankle assistance profiles can be generated through musculoskeletal model-based optimization, which can be applied to lightweight assistance conditions like unpowered exoskeletons and home rehabilitation. However, the effect of model-calculated optimal profiles on the energetics and kinematics of human walking still needs to be verified. Here, a portable soft exosuit was developed to apply model-based optimized moments and proportional biological moments to the ankle joint for comparison experiments. A low-level control strategy based on Gaussian process optimization was applied to each participant to track the target experimental moment accurately. Six participants walked on a treadmill at $1.25\,\mathrm{ms}^{-1}$ under one unpowered and two powered conditions, where metabolic costs and joint kinematics were measured. Compared with the Exo-off condition, the optimal assistance exosuit significantly reduced metabolic cost by an average of 6.23%, while the proportional condition was 2.09%. This study presents a simulation and optimization design paradigm using local musculoskeletal modeling to develop new assistance patterns more efficiently.

Keywords: Exosuit · Walking assistance · Wearable robotics

1 Introduction

Wearable robots have been developed to augment strength and reduce effort during people's daily activities, and they have shown great potential in numerous areas [1–3]. Reducing metabolic costs during human walking with ankle exoskeletons is a vital application of wearable robots. In recent years, significant breakthroughs have been made in the structural design of unpowered exoskeletons [4] and the assistive strategies of autonomous exoskeletons [5,6]. However, the human-machine coupling model is so complicated that the general optimal assistance profile of the ankle exoskeleton and its biomechanical principles of

H. Yang et al. (Eds.): ICIRA 2023, LNAI 14268, pp. 386–397, 2023.
https://doi.org/10.1007/978-981-99-6486-4_34

metabolic reduction at the muscle and even neurological levels still need to be clarified.

Some researchers have proposed personalized assistance based on metabolic cost and joint kinematics [7–9], achieving significant metabolic reductions during walking. The average profiles obtained from online optimization may only partially reflect the actual situation due to the limitation of sample size and parameter scale. In addition, it is difficult to analyze the underlying biomechanical mechanisms based on these individualized results.

Simplified musculoskeletal models of the ankle joint were proposed to estimate the effect of exoskeleton assistance at the muscle level [10, 11], and the optimal assistance profiles were calculated through the model [12]. Parametrically defined musculoskeletal properties and more optimizable variables allowed the model to generate resolvable optimal assistance profiles. However, many exciting results and viewpoints from the simulation model have yet to be verified by related experiments.

In this paper, a portable soft exosuit was developed to verify the effect of musculoskeletal model-based optimized ankle assistance on the energetics and kinematics of human walking. First, the optimal and the proportional profiles were generated through the musculoskeletal model. Then the design of the hardware system and control system of the exosuit was described in detail. Finally, a comparison experiment was conducted between the proportional and the optimal profiles.

2   Methods

2.1   Musculoskeletal Model-Based Assistance Profile Generation

An ankle joint musculoskeletal model based on the Hill-type muscle model was applied to reflect the biomechanical dynamics of the ankle joint during human walking (Fig. 1a). The muscle force F_{Muscle} and the length of the muscle-tendon unit L_{MTU} can be calculated by inputting the measured total ankle moment, exoskeleton moment, and ankle joint angle into the musculoskeletal geometric relationship (Fig. 1b and Fig. 1c). The length of the tendon L_{Tendon} can be calculated through the tendon stiffness-force property (Fig. 1d). By subtracting this length from L_{MTU}, we can obtain the length of the muscle L_{Muscle}. Differentiating with respect to time gives the muscle velocity V_{Muscle}. The muscle activation can be calculated through the muscle dynamics (Fig. 1d). The metabolic cost of muscle can be calculated through the muscle energetics (Fig. 1e).

Then, the metabolic cost of the plantarflexors was minimized as the objective function for optimizing the ankle joint assistance moment and set the following constraints based on the biomechanical characteristics of the ankle joint: (i) the sum of exoskeleton moment and muscle tension moment is less than the total moment, (ii) the exoskeleton moment less than a certain proportion of the total moment and (iii) the exoskeleton moment only acts during 10%–65% of the gait cycle.

A standard genetic algorithm is applied to solve the optimization problem above. In order to speed up convergence and make the results more reasonable, downsampling and interpolation are used to accelerate the optimization process and smooth the moment profile. Thus, the optimized assistance profile curve can be calculated. Details about the musculoskeletal model and optimization of the assistance profile can be found in [11, 12].

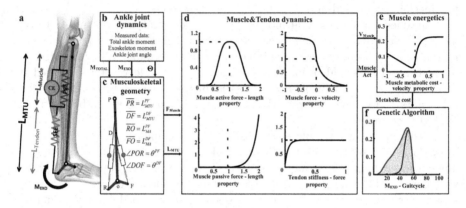

Fig. 1. Generation of the assistance profile from musculoskeletal model. (Color figure online)

2.2   Soft Exosuit Design and Arrangement

The design of the soft exosuit refers to the solution provided in [5], and the exoskeleton system has been made lightweight and easy to wear, providing good portability and comfort for the user (Fig. 2). The total weight of the system is 3.9 kg, including four parts: control module, actuator units, sensing system, and textiles elements.

To avoid distal mass distribution, the main part of the exosuit is positioned near the center of mass of the body (Fig. 2a). The soft exosuit uses a STM32F4 microcontroller to read sensor data, detect gait percentage and perform real-time control at a rate of 100 Hz. Two high power-mass ratio motors (EC-4pole 305013, Maxon, Switzerland) connected to a gearbox of ratio 79:1 (GP 32 HP 326666, Maxon, Switzerland) driving 33-mm radius pulleys, which can provide up to 12 Nm of peak torque. An incremental encoder (HEDL 5540-110514, Maxon, Switzerland) that operates at 500 counts per revolution measures motor position. A servomotor driver (EPOS4-520885, Maxon, Switzerland) controls each motor in a closed loop. The #100 Dyneema is used as the inner cable of the Bowden cable assembly, wrapped in the Bowden housing, delivering a controlled assistance force from the waist to the ankle (Fig. 2b). For force-based speed control, the force level transmitted to the user is monitored utilizing a load sensor (AT8301, AUTODA, China) at the end of the Bowden cable (Fig. 2d). Briefly, the force measured in real-time is differentiated from a predefined target force to calculate the motor output speed. Two inertial measurement units IMUs (JY901, Wit-motion, China) bound in front of the thighs (Fig. 2b) are used to estimate the real-time gait percentage during walking to match the value of the target force. The entire system is powered by a lithium polymer battery with a nominal voltage of 24 V and a capacity of 6800 mAh, which lasts approximately 5 km when the exosuit is actuated with a peak force of 200 N per step.

Textile elements can be divided into three parts (Fig. 2b and Fig. 2d): trunk, lower extremity, and feet. The trunk section is primarily designed to support the weight of the exosuit using a combination of shoulder straps and waist belts, similar to a backpack's carrying system, which provides good comfort for the wearer. The lower extremity part is a band sewn with tight pants to reduce the number of adjustable elastic bands and improve the efficiency of wearing. The upper end of the band is connected to the waistband to form the upper anchor point, while the lower end ends near the knee on the calf to form the lower anchor point. These two anchor points define the path of the transmitted force, highlighted in red. The Foot section (Fig. 2d) is a foot sleeve integrated with a force sensor that can be worn inside shoes without modifying the original shoe structure. An equivalent force sensor installation method is used to avoid the inconvenience caused by sensor interference with the human body during walking.

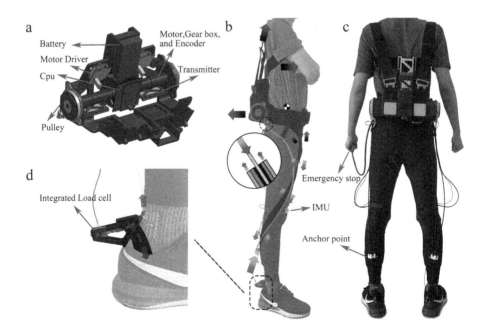

Fig. 2. Soft exosuit. (a) CAD of actuation system, (b) The load path specified by the textile elements, (c) Exosuit arrangement, (d) Foot sleeve with a force sensor. (Color figure online)

2.3   Soft Exosuit Control Strategy

The exosuit control strategy used in this study can be divided into two levels:
(i) the high-level control design inspired by the biomechanics of human walking
and (ii) the low-level implementation of force-based velocity control (Fig. 3).

(i) The high-level control profile was defined by the simulation of the ankle
joint musculoskeletal model described above (Fig. 1f), the blue curve is the
proportional biological moment, and the red curve is the optimized moment
restricted within the blue area. The Adaptive Hopf Oscillator (AHO) [13] estimates real-time gait percentage to determine when to apply assistance force
during human walking. IMUs bound on the thigh can collect the swing angle
of the thigh. When the frequency of human walking becomes stable, the IMUs
can output a stable periodic signal. The Adaptive Hopf Oscillator (AHO) can
synchronize its frequency with human walking and adapt to changes in human
walking frequency, achieving adaptive stride detection. Dividing the integral of
the learned angular frequency over time by 2π gives the current gait percentage.

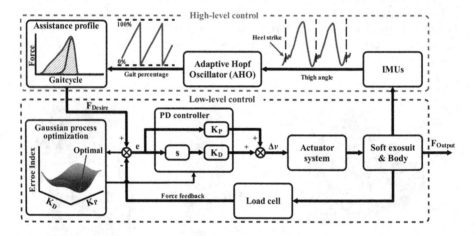

Fig. 3. Schematic of the over all control strategy.

(ii) The low-level control uses a PD controller for force-based velocity control, a simple method shown to have good control performance [1], provided that
control parameters are properly configured. The human-machine system of the
soft exoskeleton and wearers is complex, and the relevant physical factors of different subjects vary greatly and are difficult to measure, which poses a challenge
in determining control parameters. A sample-efficient method based on Gaussian processes has been developed to identify the exosuit control parameters
that minimize the control error. After evaluating a certain number of control
parameters, a generation is formed, and the gaussian process optimization is
used to calculate the next generation of control parameters to be tested. The
initial search space was predefined based on practical experience, from which

nine sample points were evenly selected as the initial sample set. If a subsequent prediction point occurs on a non-zero edge of the search space, the corresponding dimension will be extended beyond the edge in the following prediction to increase the search space. During optimization, 12 steps of data are collected for each test. The control error of the integer gait percentage obtained by spline interpolation is calculated for each step. The error index E is the weighted average of control errors according to desired force. When the Euclidean distance between the latest predicted point and any sample point is less than 1, the one with the smallest error index is the optimal result. For the implementation of proportional moment and optimal moment, it is necessary to identify the PD controller parameters separately.

2.4   Experimental Protocol

Six healthy male adults (age, 23.0 ± 0.7 years; mass, 69.5 ± 2.8 kg; height, 1.7 ± 0.03 m; mean $\pm$ SD) participated in this study. All participants provided written, informed consent before participating in the study. The study's nature and possible consequences were explained before obtaining consent. The experiments in this study were divided into two parts, firstly identifying the control parameters for each subject using Gaussian process optimization and then comparing the metabolic exertion and kinematic effects on the body with proportional and optimal moment assistance. All participants attended three experimental sessions: a training session, an optimization session, and a testing session. In every session, participants walked on a treadmill at 1.25 ms^{-1} under three experimental conditions: one powered-off and two active. During the testing session, participants began with a 10 min warm-up period where they experienced the two active experimental conditions. Then an 8-min stand still was applied to measure basal metabolic rate after a 5-min break. After the static condition, the participants underwent the three experimental conditions, each 5 min in length; the order of the experimental conditions was randomized, and a 5-min break was given between the two conditions. All energetics and biomechanics measurements were conducted during the testing session (Fig. 4).

Metabolic rate was assessed using an indirect measurement method (K4b2, Cosmed, Italy) in four conditions: static, proportional assistance, optimal assistance, and Exo-off. In addition, carbon dioxide and oxygen data were collected from the last two minutes of each condition, and the metabolic rate was calculated using the Brockway equation. The net metabolic rate was obtained by subtracting the static metabolic rate from the average metabolic rate during walking. Lower limb kinematics was measured by a reflective marker motion capture system (NOKOV Motion Capture System, China).

3   Results

3.1   Optimal and Proportional Assistance Profiles

As shown in Fig. 5a, the proportional moments were calculated by multiplying the total moment by 5% to 15%, while the optimal moments were calculated

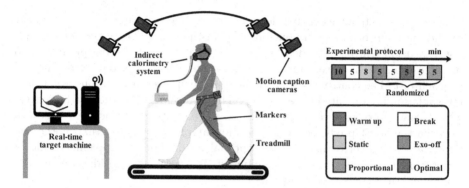

Fig. 4. Experimental platform and protocol.

by a genetic algorithm under the constraint of the corresponding proportional moment. The optimal moments were concentrated between 35% and 65% of the gait cycle, corresponding to the phase when the ankle joint reaches maximum dorsiflexion to toe-off during walking. As the selected proportion increased, the peak points of the optimal moments gradually shifted from almost the same as the proportional moments to slightly after the proportional moments at 1–2%. The peak values of the optimal moments were increasingly smaller than the proportional moments.

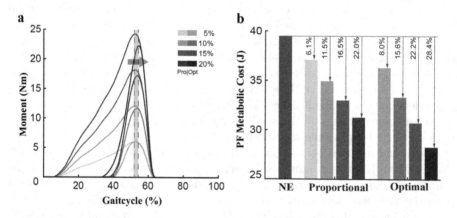

Fig. 5. Simulation results of (a) assistance profiles and (b) PF metabolic costs.

The metabolic cost of plantarflexors, with the assistance of the proportional and optimal moments during walking, can be calculated using the ankle joint musculoskeletal model (Fig. 5). As the selected proportion increased, the PF metabolic cost with optimal moments decreased significantly lower than that with the proportional moments. A non-linear relationship was observed between the reduction of PF metabolic cost and the increase in the proportion, indicating a gradual decrease in the efficiency of the assisting moment.

3.2 Gaussian Process Optimization and Control Performance

The results of the Gaussian process optimization and the control performance of the assistance force for a representative subject are shown in Fig. 6. For each condition, the average duration of the Gaussian process optimization process was 168 steps, which was approximately 4 min, to meet the convergence requirements. Optimal control parameters varied for subjects or conditions, but all were located within the initial search space. Compared to the target assistance force, both the proportional assistance force (RMSE = 0.40 N) and the optimal assistance force (RMSE = 0.15 N) achieved control performance that met the experimental requirements.

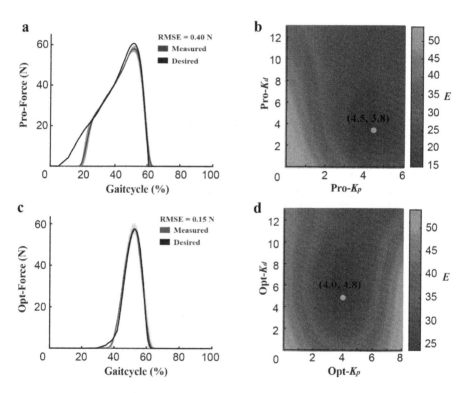

Fig. 6. Results of gaussian process optimization and control performance.

3.3 Metabolic Rates

Results and statistical analysis of the metabolic cost of six participants in the text section are shown in Fig. 7. The proportional condition of subject 5 had a higher reduction in net metabolic cost than the optimal condition, and the proportional condition of subject 6 had an increase in metabolic cost. The average basal metabolic rate during standing was $1.26 \pm 0.16\,\mathrm{Wkg^{-1}}$. The average metabolic rate of the Exo-off condition was $3.55 \pm 0.18\,\mathrm{Wkg^{-1}}$. The average metabolic rate of the proportional condition was $3.46 \pm 0.14\,\mathrm{Wkg^{-1}}$. The average metabolic rate of optimal condition was $3.40 \pm 0.18\,\mathrm{Wkg^{-1}}$. Net metabolic cost of the proportional condition and optimal condition was separately $3.43 \pm 2.09\,\%$ (mean $\pm$ s.e.m, paired t-test, p $= 0.135$) and $6.23 \pm 0.78\,\%$ (mean $\pm$ s.e.m, paired t-test, p < 0.01) lower than the Exo-off condition. The net metabolic cost of the optimal condition was $2.70 \pm 2.06\,\%$ (mean $\pm$ s.e.m, paired t-test, p $= 0.232$) lower than the proportional condition.

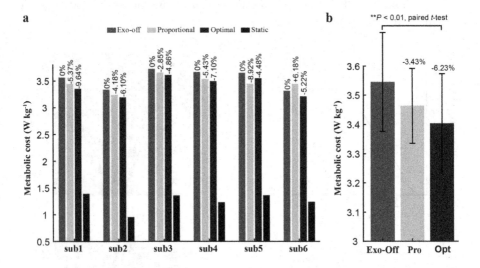

Fig. 7. Metabolic rate results of (a) each subject and (b) average.

3.4 Joint Kinematics

The results of hip, knee, and ankle joint kinematics are presented in Fig. 8. Significantly lower peak ankle dorsiflexion angles were reported in the optimal and proportional condition concerning the Exo-off condition (paired t-test, p < 0.05). Moreover, the peak ankle plantarflexion angles of the two were significantly lower than the Exo-off condition (paired t-test, p < 0.05). Additionally, significantly lower hip extension angles peak were reported in the optimal and proportional condition with respect to the Exo-off condition (paired t-test, p < 0.05). No other significant differences were reported in joint kinematics.

4 Discussion

The optimal moment profiles calculated from the optimization of the musculoskeletal model are consistent with the contraction characteristics of the muscle-tendon unit during human walking [14]. The consistency helps to maintain

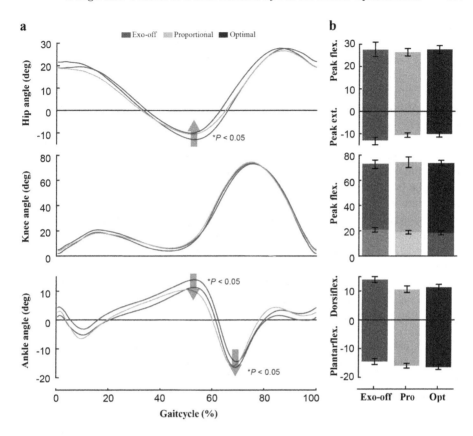

Fig. 8. Changes in joint kinematics with optimal and proportional assistance.

low muscle concentric contraction velocity to reduce energy consumption, as described by the muscle metabolism cost-velocity property (Fig. 1e). Additionally, the concentrated assistance moment avoids interfering with the tendon's storage of mechanical energy during dorsiflexion, which helps to reduce muscle velocity during push-off. The optimal moment profiles are similar to the generic optimal moments obtained by averaging individualized profiles [7,9]. Therefore, the optimal moment profile is likely to be effective in real-world experiments.

For both proportional and optimal moments, the ratio between the reduction in PF muscle metabolic cost calculated by the model and the magnitude of the external assistance decreases as the assistance magnitude increases. This suggests that the efficiency of external assistance may decrease with increasing magnitude. Due to the limitations of the local model, it is unclear whether there is a 'sweet spot' in the assistance efficiency of exosuit to achieve a significant global metabolic reduction at a lower level of assistance magnitude. Research about assistance based on measured muscle dynamics has achieved high levels of efficiency [15], which was achieved using local musculoskeletal modeling of the ankle joint to predict assistance moments.

Using Gaussian process optimization to identify the optimal control parameters for each participant is reported as a simple and efficient low-level control solution, with convergent results obtained through just a few minutes of the online optimization process. The control performance of the modified proportional force and optimal force meets the requirements of the comparison experiment.

Compared to the 5% proportional profile, the average moment of the optimal profile with the same amplitude is only 50%. However, it achieves significant metabolic benefits with relatively low forces. Consistently, previous studies have found that assisting dorsiflexion during human walking can reduce maximum dorsiflexion angle, resulting in the reduction of tendon stretch and energy storage. Applying force too early further unloads the force of the muscle-tendon unit, not only reducing tendon energy storage but also passively increasing the displacement of muscle fascicles. As a result, the plantarflexor muscles need to increase their contraction effort and velocity during mid-late stance to compensate for the extra energy and displacement, which disrupts the normal tuned muscle-tendon dynamics. According to the muscle metabolic cost-velocity property (Fig. 1e), high muscle velocity results in a less economical condition. Therefore proportional moments are not efficient assistance profiles. The optimal moments partially replace the force generated by the centripetal contraction of the plantarflexor muscles without weakening tendon energy storage during the isometric contraction of muscles. Therefore, the optimal moments achieved better metabolic reduction benefits.

5   Conclusion

This paper developed a soft exosuit to apply musculoskeletal model-based optimized and proportional biological assistance to the ankle joint. A low-level control strategy based on Gaussian process optimization was proposed to accurately track the target experimental moment. The results demonstrate that the model-calculated optimal moments have a significant advantage in metabolic benefit. Although many fundamental research and development limitations remain in musculoskeletal modeling, ankle joint biomechanics, exosuit development, and control, this study demonstrates the simulation and optimization design paradigm based on local musculoskeletal modeling, which can reduce the cost and time required to develop new assistance patterns. The preliminary design of the soft exosuit and limited metabolic and kinematic experiments are presented in this paper. In future work, muscle-level experiments such as muscle activation and ultrasound measurements will be completed to delve into the underlining biomechanical mechanisms.

Acknowledgment. The authors would like to gratefully acknowledge the reviewers comments. This work is supported by National Natural Science Foundation of China

(Grant No. 52075180), and the Fundamental Research Funds for the Central Universities.

References

1. Siviy, C., et al.: Opportunities and challenges in the development of exoskeletons for locomotor assistance. Nat. Biomed. Eng. **7**, 1–17 (2022)
2. Xia, S., Wang, N., Chen, B., Zhang, X., Chen, W.: Nonlinear stiffness mechanism designed by topology optimization reduces backpack vibration. Int. J. Mech. Sci. **252**, 108345 (2023)
3. Wang, N., Lao, K., Zhang, X.: Design and myoelectric control of an anthropomorphic prosthetic hand. J. Bionic Eng. **14**(1), 47–59 (2017)
4. Collins, S.H., Wiggin, M.B., Sawicki, G.S.: Reducing the energy cost of human walking using an unpowered exoskeleton. Nature **522**(7555), 212–215 (2015)
5. Asbeck, A.T., De Rossi, S.M., Holt, K.G., Walsh, C.J.: A biologically inspired soft exosuit for walking assistance. Int. J. Robot. Res. **34**(6), 744–762 (2015)
6. Kim, J., et al.: Reducing the energy cost of walking with low assistance levels through optimized hip flexion assistance from a soft exosuit. Sci. Rep. **12**(1), 11004 (2022)
7. Zhang, J., et al.: Human-in-the-loop optimization of exoskeleton assistance during walking. Science **356**(6344), 1280–1284 (2017)
8. Ding, Y., Kim, M., Kuindersma, S., Walsh, C.J.: Human-in-the-loop optimization of hip assistance with a soft exosuit during walking. Sci. Robot. **3**(15), eaar5438 (2018)
9. Slade, P., Kochenderfer, M.J., Delp, S.L., Collins, S.H.: Personalizing exoskeleton assistance while walking in the real world. Nature **610**(7931), 277–282 (2022)
10. Sawicki, G.S., Khan, N.S.: A simple model to estimate plantarflexor muscle-tendon mechanics and energetics during walking with elastic ankle exoskeletons. IEEE Trans. Biomed. Eng. **63**(5), 914–923 (2015)
11. Wang, N., Zhong, Y., Zhang, X.: An improved model to estimate muscle-tendon mechanics and energetics during walking with a passive ankle exoskeleton. In: Yu, H., Liu, J., Liu, L., Ju, Z., Liu, Y., Zhou, D. (eds.) ICIRA 2019, Part I. LNCS (LNAI), vol. 11740, pp. 83–96. Springer, Cham (2019). https://doi.org/10.1007/978-3-030-27526-6_8
12. Wang, N., Li, Z., Zhong, Y., Zhang, X.: Assistive torque of ankle exoskeleton based on a simple biomechanical model and a genetic algorithm. In: Liu, X.-J., Nie, Z., Yu, J., Xie, F., Song, R. (eds.) ICIRA 2021, Part I. LNCS (LNAI), vol. 13013, pp. 780–790. Springer, Cham (2021). https://doi.org/10.1007/978-3-030-89095-7_74
13. Righetti, L., Buchli, J., Ijspeert, A.J.: Dynamic Hebbian learning in adaptive frequency oscillators. Phys. D **216**(2), 269–281 (2006)
14. Farris, D.J., Sawicki, G.S.: Human medial gastrocnemius force-velocity behavior shifts with locomotion speed and gait. Proc. Natl. Acad. Sci. **109**(3), 977–982 (2012)
15. Nuckols, R.W., Lee, S., Swaminathan, K., Orzel, D., Howe, R.D., Walsh, C.J.: Individualization of exosuit assistance based on measured muscle dynamics during versatile walking. Sci. Robot. **6**(60), eabj1362 (2021)

Structural Design and Stiffness Characteristics of a Passive Variable Stiffness Joint

Keming Liu[ID], Bai Chen[✉][ID], Ziyu Liao[ID], Tianzuo Chang[ID], Jiajun Xu[ID], and Zhendong Tu[ID]

School of Mechanical and Electrical Engineering, Nanjing University of Aeronautics and Astronautics, Nanjing, China
chenbye@nuaa.edu.cn

Abstract. Supernumerary robotic limbs(SRLs) are new type of wearable robots. In order to achieve safe and stable operations for the SRLs, a tendon-driven passive variable stiffness joint(pVSJ) integrated into the shoulder joint of the SRLs is presented, which can output different stiffness and improve the safety of human-robot interaction. The stiffness change of the pVSJ is achieved by winding a tendon around pulleys to drive the flexible element to stretch. In the non-operating state, the stiffness characteristics of the pVSJ can be changed by adjusting the pre-tension of the flexible element, the winding method of the tendon, and replacing the flexible element. A mathematical model is established for the tendon-driven pVSJ to reveal its stiffness characteristics. The model is verified through quasi-static experiments. The experimental results show that there is an obvious hysteresis phenomenon during low torque loading. The hysteresis range is 20.8%-32.5%. The angular range of the loading hysteresis of the pVSJ is negatively related to the spring preload, spring stiffness, the number of working branches, and it is positively related to the rope diameter. The unloading process basically conformed to the theoretical model, with a maximum relative error of 3.4%. Therefore, the exact stiffness output can be achieved by first increasing and then decreasing the joint torque to reach the target torque.

Keywords: Flexible joints · Passive variable stiffness joints · Stiffness model · Supernumerary robotic limbs · Human-robot safety

1 Introduction

Supernumerary Robotic Limbs (SRLs) are new type of wearable robots with independent movement capabilities that can greatly enhance the wearer's abilities in activities, operations, and sensing [1–3]. However, the independence and strong human-robot integration of SRLs pose significant challenges to human safety [4]: the large overlap between the SRLs and the wearer's body makes it easy to collide with the body and cause injury. To address the above human-robot safety issues, making the joints of SRLs flexible is an effective solution [5]. Hasanen et al. [6] used actively variable stiffness joints in SRLs to assist stroke patients in completing hand-to-mouth tasks, utilizing their inherent flexibility and buffering capability to greatly reduce the harm caused by human-robot collisions

H. Yang et al. (Eds.): ICIRA 2023, LNAI 14268, pp. 398–409, 2023.
https://doi.org/10.1007/978-981-99-6486-4_35

during the task. However, the SRLs system is fixed to a chair, and the researchers don't need to consider the burden of SRLs on the body. Its weight and volume are both large [7], making it unsuitable for SRLs worn on the body.

Passive Variable Stiffness Joint (pVSJ) is a type of joint that can achieve different stiffness outputs through the deviation angle of the structure [8]. Its equivalent stiffness does not require extra driving units for adjustment. Compared with active variable stiffness actuators, this stiffness adjustment method greatly reduces the weight of the joint and can be well applied to the lightweight requirements of SRLs worn on the human body [9]. According to the driving mode, pVSJ can be classified into an active pVSJ [10–13] and a passive pVSJ [14–16]. There are more studies on human-robot interaction safety and torque control in the active pVSJ. In response to human-robot safety issues, some pVSJs have been designed to have a negative load to stiffness correlation [11] which enables robot joints to maintain high rigidity in normal operation to ensure positioning accuracy. At the same time, rigidity can be suddenly decreased in the event of a collision, to reduce impact force and achieve safety of human-robot collisions [17]. Passive pVSJ is mainly applied in fields such as assistance and gravity compensation. In assistance, the pVSJ is used to adapt to [16] or imitate [15] the movement of a certain part of the human body. For example, the joint stiffness increases to provide support assistance when the upper limb of the human body enters the support phase. When the upper limb of the human body enters the swing phase, the joint stiffness becomes extremely low, causing little obstruction to the movement of the upper limb. In the field of gravity compensation, the pVSJ is designed to match the target torque-deflection curve as closely as possible, in order to accurately compensate for the torque generated by gravity under different postures of human limbs or robotic limbs [14].

In summary, the detailed design of pVSJ in different scenarios needs to be based on their own task requirements, and there is no unified design paradigm or evaluation criteria. The pVSJ is widely used, but there is no precedent for integrating pVSJ into SRLs. Therefore, developing a pVSJ application is of great significance for SRLs to improve the safety of human-robot interaction.

The paper presents a tendon-driven pVSJ design for the joint of the SRLs, which achieves different stiffness outputs and provides buffering and shock absorption effects in case of accidental collision between human and the SRLs. The stiffness characteristics of pVSJ can be adjusted in three ways. The pVSJ has a compact structure, light weight, and a positive correlation between load and stiffness, which can meet the needs of SRLs. The main contributions of the paper are as follows: 1) A pVSJ is proposed for lightweight SRLs to improve the human-robot safety; 2) The theoretical model of the static stiffness of the pVSJ is developed and verified experimentally; the experimental results show that there is low-torque hysteresis in the loading process and the unloading process is basically in line with the theoretical model. This provides an important basis for the accurate output of the subsequent joint stiffness.

2 Design Principles of the Tendon-Driven pVSJ

2.1 Design Index for the Tendon-Driven pVSJ

Our previous research developed a rigid waist the SRLs to assist in thin-wall support tasks [18]. In order to improve the stability of the SRLs' support and to guarantee the safety of human-robot interaction at work, it is necessary to design a pVSJ for the SRLs. Based on requirements during the process of thin-wall support, the paper proposes the design criteria for the pVSJ at the joint of the SRLs. Table 1 summarizes the design indicators for pVSJ. The stiffness of the flexible joint is required to be positively correlated with the torque, as the joint can maintain a low stiffness under low loads to better absorb the impact during the swing process of the SRLs. K is the systematic stiffness of joints.

Table 1. Design specifications for pVSJ

Items	Design indicators of pVSJ
Maximum torque of the joints	$2N \cdot M$
systematic stiffness of joints	$1.0 - 3.4\ Nm/rad$
System lightweighting meets strength verification	200–243 g, $E \geq 1.2\ Gpa$
The collision safety issue during the swinging process	$K \propto \theta$

2.2 Basic Principles of Variable Stiffness

The design of the tendon-driven pVSJ is based on a special four-bar linkage mechanism [19], as shown in Fig. 1(a). In this mechanism, the length of the rack is 0, and rods 1 and 3 are mounted on the base through a pin joint at point A. Flexible rod 2 connects rods 1 and 3 to pin joints at points B and C, respectively.

The tension in the flexible rod 2 is denoted by F, and the joint torque required for balance is denoted by τ. Based on the principle of virtual work and Hooke's law, the following can be obtained

$$\tau = l_1 \sin \alpha \cdot F = L_1 \cdot F \tag{1}$$

$$L_1 = l_1 \sin \alpha = \frac{l_1 l_3 \sin \theta}{l_2} = \frac{l_1 l_3 \sin \theta}{\sqrt{l_1^2 + l_3^2 - 2 l_1 l_3 \cos \theta}} \tag{2}$$

$$F = k(l_2 - l_{2,0}) + F_0 = k \cdot (l_2 - l_3 + l_1) + F_0 \tag{3}$$

l_1, l_2, and l_3 represent the lengths of connecting rod 1, 3, and flexible rod 2 respectively. k is the stiffness of the flexible rod 2. θ is the torsion angle between connecting rod 1 and 3, while L_1 is the equivalent lever arm. $l_{2,0}$ represents the length of flexible coupling rod 2 when the tension in rod 2 is $\theta = 0$. At this moment, the tension in rod 2 is F_0.

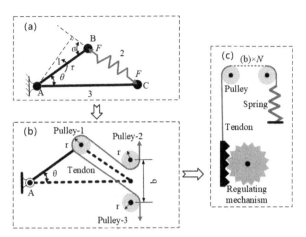

Fig. 1. The process of pVSJ. (a) The special circumstances of a four-link mechanism; (b) A set of working branches using pulleys and the tendon to realize the pVSJ; (c) Conceptual design of the pVSJ.

The above four-bar linkage mechanism can be realized through pulleys and a tendon. Figure 1(b) shows a basic tendon-driven pVSJ working branch. Multiple sets of working branches are connected in series, with one end connected to an elastic element to replace flexible coupling rod 2. The other end connected to an adjusting mechanism to configure the pre-tension of the elastic element, thus forming a tendon-driven pVSJ as shown in Fig. 1(c).

At this point, the stiffness of the flexible rod 2 is the equivalent stiffness of the tendon in series with the spring, which is calculated as

$$k = \frac{k_t \cdot k_s}{k_t + k_s} \tag{4}$$

k_t is the stiffness of the spring and k_s is the stiffness of the tendon.

r is the radius of the pulley represented. b is the distance between the centers of pulley 2 and pulley 3. The change in the length of flexible coupling rod 2 is represented by the deformation of the spring under the tension of the tendon. For the same deflection angle θ, the correspondence is influenced by the number of branches used in the joint. Therefore, the deformation amount δl of the spring and the equivalent force arm L of the mechanism can be represented as

$$\delta l = 2N(l_2 - l_{2,0}) = 2N(l_2 - l_3 + l_1) \tag{5}$$

$$L = 2NL_1 \tag{6}$$

According to formulas (1), (2), (3), (5), (6), the tension force a of the tendon and the joint torque b used to balance the tension force are respectively given by

$$F = k \cdot \delta l + F_0 = 2Nk \cdot (l_2 - l_3 + l_1) + F_0 \tag{7}$$

$$\tau = L \cdot F = 2NL_1 \cdot (2Nk \cdot (l_2 - l_3 + l_1) + F_0) \tag{8}$$

Therefore, the stiffness model of pVSJ is as follows

$$K = \frac{\partial \tau}{\partial \theta} = 2Nk \cdot (\frac{\partial l_2}{\partial q} + \frac{\partial L}{\partial q} \cdot (l_2 - l_3 + l_1)) + F_0 \frac{\partial L}{\partial q} \tag{9}$$

From the stiffness model of the tendon-driven pVSJ, it can be seen that, under the condition of the geometric parameters of the mechanism being determined, the stiffness model is affected by the number of branches N, the pre-tension force F_0 of the springs, and the equivalent stiffness k of the mechanism. Therefore, it has three ways to adjust the stiffness characteristics. Depending on the space constraints required by the shoulder joint of the SRLs and the size of the motor, the appropriate mechanism geometry parameters are selected as shown in Table 2.

Table 2. Geometric parameters of tendon-driven PVSJ

Parameter	Specification	Value(mm)
r	Pulley radius	5.0
d	Tendon diameter	1.0
b	Center distance of pulleys 2 and 3	14.8
l_1	The length of bar 1	6.0
l_3	The length of bar 3	22.8

The stiffness-deflection curves under the three adjustment methods are shown in Fig. 2(a), (b), and (c). The choice of spring stiffness, preload and number of working branches in Fig. 2 are all constrained by the joint dimensions. The joint stiffness of a part of the pVSJ has a tendency to change from "hardening" to "softening", that is, the stiffness increases and then decreases with the deflection angle of the joint, but due to the limitation of the tendon stretching range, the mechanism with a large preload, high spring stiffness and a large number of working branches only has a hardening region, which can meet the design requirements of the pVSJ: the joint stiffness is positively related to the load.

In the range of stiffness adjustment, the minimum output stiffness of the pVSJ occurs in the no-load condition. In this case, the output stiffness of the pVSJ is positively related to the number of operating branches, but does not vary with the spring stiffness. Under load, the maximum output stiffness of the pVSJ is positively related to the number of working branches and the spring stiffness, but does not vary significantly with different spring preloads.

According to the range of joint stiffness requirements: $1.0 - 3.4 N \cdot M / rad$, a pVSJ with the following parameters can be selected as a flexible joint for use in thin-walled work with the SRLs' support: $F_0 = 20N, k \geq 6 N/mm, 2 \leq N \leq 3$.

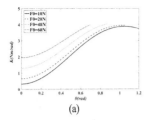
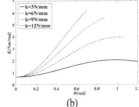
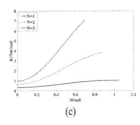

(a)   (b)   (c)

Fig. 2. Simulation of the stiffness model and constraint conditions of the tendon-driven pVSJ. (a) Variation curve of pVSJ stiffness when adjusting pre-tension force with N = 2 and k = 6 N/mm; (b) Variation curve of pVSJ stiffness when adjusting spring stiffness with N = 2 and F_0 = 20 N; (c) Variation curve of pVSJ stiffness when changing the winding method of the tendon with F_0 = 20 N and k = 6 N/mm.

3 Structural Design of the Tendon-Driven pVSJ

The detailed structural design of the tendon-driven pVSJ is shown in Fig. 3. It consists of a motion coupling module and a pre-tension force adjustment module, which are respectively used to transmit power and adjust the stiffness characteristics of the joint. The input shaft is fixedly connected to the drive motor flange, and the output connecting member is fixedly connected to the output flange. The input shaft can drive the output connecting member to rotate under the action of the drive motor and the variable stiffness adjustment mechanism. Due to joint space constraints, the pVSJ uses two sets of working branch pulleys. Each branch composed of a tendon wrapped around three pulleys, with one pulley on the input flange and two pulleys on the output flange. The tendon wrapped around the pulleys is used to couple the motion from the input shaft to the output flange. One end of the tendon is connected to the tension spring, and the other end is fixed to the pre-tension force adjustment module.

The spring support is installed on the output flange to fix one end of the spring. The output flange is designed with a special groove at the installation position of the spring support, which allows the placement of springs with an outer diameter of less than 12 mm and a stretching range of 50 mm. The tendon and spring are fixed by an aluminum sleeve, which also has a limit function. When the aluminum sleeve is stretched to the contact position with the pulley, the spring will no longer stretch.

In the pre-tension adjustment module, the hollow bolt and matching nut are installed on the mounting hole on the output flange side. The tendon passes through the threading hole of the hollow bolt. The end of the tendon is fixed to the tail end of the hollow bolt using an aluminum sleeve through compression. A compression spring is placed between the head of the hollow bolt and the matching nut to prevent the nut from loosening due to insufficient tension in the tendon.

The tendon-driven pVSJ integrates all components into a compact cylindrical space with a radius of 48 mm and a height of 60mm. Its main components are made of nylon, with a total weight of only 227 g, meeting the weight requirements and further reducing the burden on the body during the work of the SRLs.

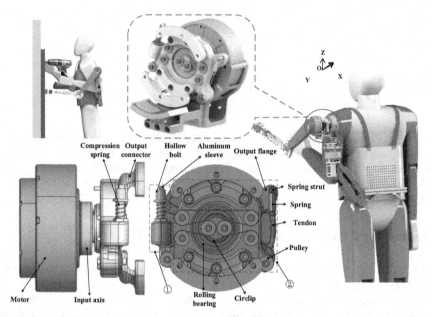

Fig. 3. The SRLs and structure design of pVSJ. ①The motion coupling module; ②The pre-tension force adjustment module.

4 Tendon-Driven pVSJ Performance Test

4.1 Experimental Platform for pVSJ

In order to verify the static stiffness characteristics of the tendon-driven pVSJ, an experimental platform shown in Fig. 4 was designed for quasi-static testing. One end of the tendon-driven pVSJ was fixed to the experimental substrate, and the other end was connected to a static torque sensor, with the pendulum, incremental encoder, and the other end of the static torque sensor also connected.

The high-level control was implemented on the host computer using SIMULINK, while the low-level real-time control was operated on the target machine using the MATLAB XPC system. Communication between the host and target machines was achieved through TCP/IP. Feedback data from the torque sensor and encoder was transmitted to the target machine through a data acquisition system, and the host computer could monitor these feed-backs in real-time. In the experiment, the pendulum was rotated with an extremely low frequency, and the torque was applied to the output shaft of the tendon-driven pVSJ through the pendulum's offset. The torque sensor measured the torque value, and the encoder measured the deflection angle of the pVSJ.

4.2 Test of Static Stiffness Characteristics

Five sets of loading and unloading static stiffness experiments were set up, in order to test the effect of spring preload, spring stiffness, number of working branches and tendon diameter on the static stiffness characteristics of the pVSJ. Experiment 0 was a

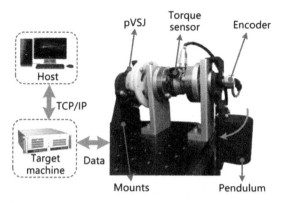

Fig. 4. Tendon-driven pVSJ stiffness characteristic testing experimental platform

control group, where the pVSJ was set up with the following parameters: a spring with a stiffness of 6 N/mm and a tendon with a diameter of 1.2 mm, two sets of working branches and an adjusted spring preload of 20 N. The other four experiments were based on the first group and changed a certain parameter: Experiment 1 changed the spring preload to 40 N and 60 N; Experiment 2 used a spring with a stiffness of 12 N/mm; Experiment 3 was equipped with a set of working branches; Experiment 4 used a tendon with a diameter of 0.8 mm. In addition, the spring preload of the pVSJ was set by means of a tensiometer. The results of the test experiments are shown in Table 3.

4.3 Discussion of Experimental Results

As shown in Table 3(a), (c), (e) and (g), there is a significant hysteresis in the actual torque deflection curve at the initial rotation during the loading experiment; Under high loads, the actual torque deflection curve basically conforms to the theoretical model. This is due to the partial position of the tendon not being able to overcome static friction for rotation at low loads. In this case, the torque value increases slowly and the actual stiffness is much lower than the theoretical stiffness. After overcoming static friction by rotating a certain angle, the transmission tendon quickly moves to its normal position, causing a sudden change in the mechanism stiffness and a rapid increase in torque value. The hysteresis of the loading process relative to the unloading process can be expressed in terms of e_h, which is calculated as

$$e_h = \frac{\max(\tau_l(\theta) - \tau_{ul}(\theta))}{\tau_{\max}} \tag{10}$$

$\tau_l(\theta)$ and $\tau_{ul}(\theta)$ represent the measured torque during loading and unloading respectively, and $\tau_{\max}$ represents the maximum measured torque. e_h for each group of loading experiments is shown in Table 4.

The extent to which hysteresis occurs varies somewhat with different parameter variations. As the spring preload increases, the hysteresis angle of the pVSJ gradually decreases and the amount of hysteresis further increases. The lower the stiffness of the

Table 3. The torque-deflection curves for the pVSJ with different conditions

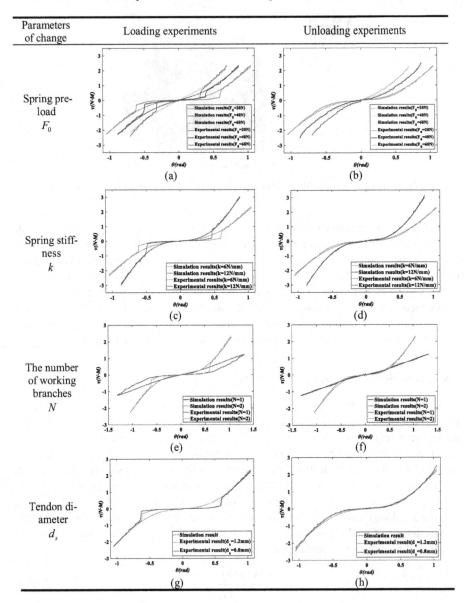

Parameters of change	Loading experiments	Unloading experiments
Spring pre-load F_0	(a)	(b)
Spring stiffness k	(c)	(d)
The number of working branches N	(e)	(f)
Tendon diameter d_s	(g)	(h)

flexible element used, the greater the angle of hysteresis at pVSJ, but there is no significant difference in the amount of hysteresis. For a given number of working branches, the hysteresis phenomenon almost runs through the entire loading process of pVSJ. The relative hysteresis amount in the unloading process reached 32.5%. It indicates that the fewer the number of working branches, the more obvious the hysteresis phenomenon.

In order to further explore the influence of different tendon diameters on the hysteresis phenomenon in the static stiffness characteristics of pVSJ, tendons with diameters of $d = 0.8$ mm were used for experiment. As can be seen from the Fig. 5(g), the larger the tendon diameter, the greater the loading hysteresis and the smaller the hysteresis angle range of pVSJ. On the other hand, the smaller the tendon diameter, the smaller its ultimate tensile strength, so in practical applications, a smaller diameter tendon can be selected to expand the range of torque output while satisfying the maximum tensile force requirement.

As shown in Table 3(b), (d), (f) and (h), during unloading, the torque deflection curve basically conforms to the torque deflection model. Its maximum absolute error is represented by, and its maximum relative error is represented by e_s. Its calculation formula is as follows

$$e_s = \frac{e_{a\,\text{max}}}{\tau_{\text{max}}} \tag{11}$$

$e_{a\,\text{max}}$ and e_s for each group of unloading experiments are shown in Table 4. The errors under different parameters during unloading are small and do not vary much. Therefore, the accurate output of stiffness can be achieved by first increasing the output torque moderately and then reducing it to the torque corresponding to the matching stiffness.

Table 4. Errors in static stiffness testing

Projects	$e_h(\%)$	$e_{a\,\text{max}}(N \cdot M)$	$e_s(\%)$
Experiment 0 (control group,$F_0 = 20N$,$k = 6N/mm$,$N = 2$,$d_s = 1.2mm$)	21.4	0.073	3.2
Experiment 1 ($F_0 = 40N$)	25.6	0.065	2.8
Experiment 1($F_0 = 60N$)	26.4	0.084	3.4
Experiment 2($k = 12N/mm$)	20.8	0.062	2.9
Experiment 3($N = 1$)	32.5	0.035	2.5
Experiment 4($d_s = 0.8mm$)	24.8	0.071	3.1

5 Conclusions

A tendon-driven pVSJ integrated shoulder joint on the SRLs is designed to achieve different stiffness outputs and ensure safety in human-robot interaction. Compared to previous research on this type of flexible joint [19], the pVSJ designed in this paper uses a hollow bolt structure for fixing the tendon and adjusting the preload of the spring, making it more compact and further extending its application scenario; the stiffness model of the pVSJ is verified and the hysteresis pattern during loading is studied in depth.

The stiffness of the pVSJ is changed through the extension and contraction of flexible components driven by the tendon wrapped around pulleys. The output stiffness has the characteristic: stiffness is positively related to the input load. In non-working state, the stiffness characteristics can be changed in three ways, including adjusting the pre-tension of the flexible components, changing the number of working branches, and replacing the flexible components. Its weight is only 227 g, which is 6% lighter than the original rigid joint and can meet the requirements of lightweight for the SRLs' system.

The mathematical model of the pVSJ is further built. The system stiffness is affected by the equivalent spring stiffness of the pVSJ, the number of working branches, and the pre-tension force of the spring. The pre-tension force of the spring is positively correlated with the output stiffness of the mechanism under no-load conditions. At the same angle, the output stiffness of pVSJ is positively related to the equivalent spring stiffness and the number of working branches.

To verify the stiffness mathematical model of the tendon-driven pVSJ, a test platform is constructed for quasi-static experiments. The experimental results show that there is an obvious hysteresis phenomenon during the loading process of the pVSJ, especially in the low torque loading process. The hysteresis range is 20.8%–32.5%. The angular range of the loading hysteresis of the pVSJ is negatively related to the spring preload, spring stiffness and number of working branches, and positively related to the tendon diameter. pVSJ loading hysteresis increases as the spring preload and the number of working branches increases. The result of unloading process basically conforms to the theoretical model, and the maximum relative error is 2.5%–3.4%. Therefore, the accurate output of stiffness can be achieved by first increasing the output torque moderately and then reducing it to the torque corresponding to the matching stiffness when the SRLs support thin wall.

In future research, this work will be conducted on topics such as crash damping effects, crash safety control strategies, and impedance control of support based on the previous research.

Acknowledgement. This work was supported by the National Natural Science Foundation of China (U22A20204 and 52205018), the Fundamental Research Funds for the Central Universities, China (NP2022304).

References

1. Tong, Y., Liu, J.: Review of research and development of supernumerary robotic limbs. IEEE/CAA J. Autom. Sinica **8**, 929–952 (2021)
2. Yang, B., et al.: Supernumerary robotic limbs: a review and future outlook. IEEE Trans. Med. Robot. Bionics **3**, 623–639 (2021)
3. Dominijanni, G., et al.: The neural resource allocation problem when enhancing human bodies with extra robotic limbs. Nat. Mach. Intell. **3**, 850–860 (2021)
4. Tsagarakis, N.G., et al.: A compact soft actuator unit for small scale human friendly robots. In: 2009 IEEE International Conference on Robotics and Automation(Kobe), pp. 4356–4362 (2009)
5. Vanderborght, B., et al.: Variable impedance actuators: a review. Robot. Auton. Syst. **61**, 1601–1614 (2013)
6. Hasanen, B.B., et al.: Novel supernumerary robotic limb based on variable stiffness actuators for hemiplegic patients assistance. In: Proceedings of the 2022 IEEE/RSJ International Conference on Intelligent Robots and Systems (2022)

7. Awad, M.I., et al.: Passive discrete variable stiffness joint (pDVSJ-II): modeling, design, characterization, and testing toward passive haptic interface. J. Mech. Robot. **11**, 011005 (2019)

8. Wolf, S., et al.: Variable stiffness actuators: review on design and components. IEEE/ASME Trans. Mechatron. **21**, 2418–2430 (2016)

9. Petit, F., Dietrich, A., Albu-Schaffer, A.: Generalizing torque control concepts: using well-established torque control methods on variable stiffness robots. IEEE Robot. Automat. Mag. **22**, 37–51 (2015)

10. Qian, Y., et al.: Design, modelling, and control of a reconfigurable rotary series elastic actuator with nonlinear stiffness for assistive robots. Mechatronics **86**, 102872 (2022)

11. Park, J.-J., Song J.B.: Safe joint mechanism using inclined link with springs for collision safety and positioning accuracy of a robot arm. In: 2010 IEEE International Conference on Robotics and Automation(Anchorage), pp. 813–818 (2010)

12. Van Ham, R., et al.: MACCEPA, the mechanically adjustable compliance and controllable equilibrium position actuator: design and implementation in a biped robot. Robot. Auton. Syst. **55**, 761–768 (2007)

13. Chen, T., Casas, R., Lum, P.S.: An elbow exoskeleton for upper limb rehabilitation with series elastic actuator and cable-driven differential. IEEE Trans. Robot. **35**, 1464–1474 (2019)

14. Balser, F., et al.: A novel passive shoulder exoskeleton designed with variable stiffness mechanism. IEEE Robot. Autom. Lett. **7**, 2748–2754 (2022)

15. Liu, Y., et al.: A low-cost single-motor-driven climbing robot based on overrunning spring clutch mechanisms. Int. J. Adv. Robot. Syst. **19** (2022)

16. Zhou, T., et al.: Reducing the metabolic energy of walking and running using an unpowered hip exoskeleton. J. NeuroEng. Rehabil. **18**, 95 (2021)

17. Park, J.-J., et al.: Safe link mechanism based on nonlinear stiffness for collision safety. Mech. Mach. Theory **43**, 1332–1348 (2008)

18. Liao, Z., et al.: A human augmentation device design review: supernumerary robotic limbs. IR **50**, 256–274 (2023)

19. Li, Z., Chen, W., Bai, S.: A novel reconfigurable revolute joint with adjustable stiffness. In: 2019 International Conference on Robotics and Automation (ICRA), pp. 8388–8393 (2019)

A Development Control and HRI
of Supernumerary Robotic Limbs Based on ROS

Qian Zheng⬡, Ziyu Liao⬡, Bai Chen⁽⊠⁾⬡, Tianzuo Chang⬡, Zhicong Zhang⬡,
and Hongtao Wu

School of Mechanical and Electrical Engineering, Nanjing University of Aeronautics and
Astronautics, Nanjing, China
chenbye@nuaa.edu.cn

Abstract. This paper design a supernumerary robotic limbs (SRLs) to autonomously assist a human, and proposes a human-robot interaction (HRI) mode based on gesture to control for SRLs. To realize the automatic continuous motion of SRLs, this study developes a control system and simulation platform for SRLs based on robot operating system (ROS). The developed system can automatically generate different trajectories according to recognized gestures, and realize the autonomous and continuous motion of SRLs based on the established kinematic model. Moreover, a PID-based trajectory tracking control is implemented to enhance the performance of SRLs' system. Finally, this paper showes that the feasibility of the developed control system through simulations and experiments, and this study also evaluates the performance of the proposed HRI mode via the users' questionnaires, which provides a reference for the development of wearable robot technology in the future.

Keywords: Human-robot interaction · Robot operating system · Control system · Supernumerary robotic limbs

1 Introduction

The state-of-art wearable robotics technology called supernumerary robot limbs (SRLs) which can augment human's perception, operation and other capabilities through additional robotic limbs which will be worn on the human body [1, 2]. Unlike exoskeletons and conventional manipulators, the additional robotic limbs of SRLs are independent kinematic structure, which require the new cooperation mode of human-robot interaction (HRI). Since the distance between the user and SRLs is very short, the control system requires higher safety and reliability than conventional wearable robot [3]. Therefore, this study established the control system and simulation platform of SRLs based on robot operating system (ROS), which is a convenient and efficient control system.

Nowadays, the researchers develop various HRI modes for SRLs. Fu et al. [4] use a gaze signal to control SRLs with human demonstration data. SRLs moves following the gaze information and reaches near to the position of the target. Iwasaki et al. [5, 6] propose a point command operation method called the "face vector", which control the SRLs according to position of the 3-dimensional coordinates target point. However, these interfaces can only achieve point-to-point movement of SRLs, which don't require the trajectory of the movement. Meantime, there must be an object at the target position to guide SRLs to move. Sasaki et al. [7, 8] propose a non-manual control interface to control the SRLs via the motion of foot. This mode requires the operator to sit on a chair and cannot move. Mahdi et al. [9] control the SRLs through the visual tracking equipment to track the trajectory of the user's hip, shoulder, elbow and wrist, which requires significant movement of the body and causes human disturbance. The control mode for the SRLs requires being able to adjust to the flexible environment. Thus, we proposed an HRI based on the gestures to direct control the overall movement of SRLs.

In recent years, many researchers have studied the kinematics and trajectory planning of the robots based on the ROS. Sergio et al. [10] present an interfacing of a robotic arm with a motion planner and a 3D viewer (Rviz), which is used to manipulate and grip objects to transport them from one location to another using Robot Operating System (ROS). Sana et al. [11] deal with Yaskawa robots controlling the ROS for teleoperation tasks, and propose an improved version of the standard ROS-based control. The trajectory tracking and latency are improved. Xu et al. [12] use ROS to build the robot control system, and the simulation of robot motion planning and experimental verification. The development of robotic limbs through ROS has gradually matured. At the same time, SRLs requires high real-time and autonomy, it is a good choice to use ROS to build the control system.

The rest of this paper is organized as follows. The mechanical design of a SRLs is presented together with the kinematic modeling in Sect. 2. An autonomy HRI mode of SRLs based on gesture recognition, simulation platform of SRLs based on ROS and a PID controller are proposed in Sect. 3. In Sect. 4, the kinematic model was verified and the feasibility and effectiveness of the control system are verified by experiments. Then, the performance of the proposed the HRI mode is evaluated via the users' questionnaires. Finally, the conclusion and the future work are proposed in Sect. 5.

2 The Frameworks of SRLs

2.1 Hardware Platform of SRLs

Based on the kinematic performance and human-robot factor indices, the prior studies design a waist-mounted SRLs, which has an additional robotic limb with 4 -DOFs able to augment human's perception, operation and other capabilities [13]. The hardware platform of SRLs is shown in Fig. 1. The robotic limb is designed as the human-like configuration, the shoulder joint has 2 DOFs and is driven by DC motors. The elbow is one DOF rotation joint which is driven by a DC motor. The wrist is also one DOF which is actuated by a servo. The opening and closing of the gripper are controlled by another servo. The driven layer of SRLs is controlled by CAN and UART communication based on the Raspberry Pi. The control input signal comes from the surface electromyography (sEMG) via the gForcePro which is a sEMG acquisition device. Furthermore, the support base of robotic limb is mounted on a wearable backpack with a shell and cushion. The shell comprises polypropylene plastic to protect the human body during collision accidents. Additionally, an air cushion is installed between the human body and the protective shell to improve wearing comfort.

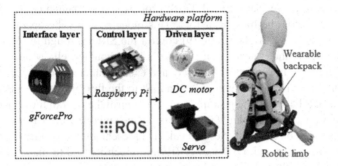

Fig. 1. Hardware platform of SRLs

2.2 Kinematic Modeling of SRLs

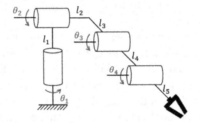

Fig. 2. Simplified kinematic model of SRLs

Table 1. D-H parameter of SRLs

Link	a_i (mm)	α_i (°)	d_i (mm)	θ_i (°)
1	0	$\pi/2$	l_1	θ_1
2	l_3	0	l_2	θ_2
3	l_4	0	0	θ_3
4	l_5	0	0	θ_4

To achieve the position control of SRLs and validate the simulation platform, it is necessary to analyse and model the kinematic structure of the robotic limb [14]. At the same time, trajectory planning based on ROS needs to use Kinematics model. The simplified model is shown in Fig. 2. The D-H parameter is shown in Table 1.

The transformation matrix based on D-H parameter of two adjacent links can be expressed as:

$$i-1 T_i = \begin{bmatrix} c\theta_i & -c\alpha_i s\theta_i & s\alpha_i s\theta_i & a_i c\theta_i \\ s\theta_i & c\alpha_i c\theta_i & -s\alpha_i c\theta_i & a_i s\theta_i \\ 0 & s\alpha_i & c\alpha_i & d_i \\ 0 & 0 & 0 & 1 \end{bmatrix} \tag{1}$$

The pose and position of SRLs' gripper can be calculated by the transformation matrix as follows:

$$^0T_4 = {}^0T_1 {}^1T_2 {}^2T_3 {}^3T_4 = \begin{bmatrix} c_1 c_{234} & -c_1 s_{234} & -s_1 & -l_2 s_1 + c_1(c_2 l_2 + c_{23} l_4 + c_{234} l_5) \\ s_1 c_{234} & -s_2 s_{234} & c_1 & l_2 c_1 + s_1(c_2 l_3 + c_{23} l_4 + c_{234} l_5) \\ -s_{234} & c_{234} & 0 & l_1 - l_3 s_2 - l_4 s_{23} - l_5 s_{234} \\ 0 & 0 & 0 & 1 \end{bmatrix} \tag{2}$$

where: $c_i = \cos\theta_i$, $s_i = \sin\theta_i$, $c_{ijk} = \cos\theta_i \cos\theta_j \cos\theta_k$, $s_{ijk} = \sin\theta_i \sin\theta_j \sin\theta_k$.

3 Developed Control System Based on ROS

The control architecture for the SRLs is shown in Fig. 3. The control system is implemented in the robotic operating system (ROS), which includes a complete path planning for the SRLs, computing the inverse kinematics, trajectory generation, and controller design. Furthermore, the surface electromyography signal as input control signals while wearing the SRLs.

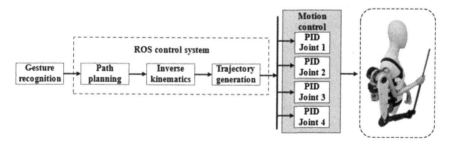

Fig. 3. An overall system control architecture of SRLs

The control system consists of four motors, controllers (servo motor, HT-04, CAN 3), (servo, UART, 1) and encoders (incremental encoder). Moreover, a graphical interface is developed using a combination of Python and ROS that can be used to choose the various types of control modes, tune control parameters, sending high level control commands and real-time logging of data. A CAN bus communication is adopted as the communication method between ROS and HT-04, while a UART bus communication is adopted as the communication method between ROS and servo.

3.1 HRI Model of SRLs

In this study, an HRI mode of SRLs is proposed, which establishes the relationship between the gestures and the movement of SRLs, as shown in Fig. 4. The candidate gestures include wrist flexion (WF), wrist extension (WE), fist clench (FC), palm stretching (PS), and rest (RT). This mode is focus on the movement of SRLs' gripper, so each gesture is mapped only to the movement direction of SRLs. Specifically, the FC gesture controls the gripper to move backward, and the WE gesture controls the gripper to move forward. The gesture WF controls the gripper to move upward, and the rotate movement is controlled by the gesture PS. The gesture RT is the transition gestures in the switching process of each gesture, and the SRLs will stop at the current position during the gesture RT. Furthermore, the control of the gripper is not in this HRI mode, the opening and closing of gripper is directly controlled by the programming from the user input.

In this study, surface electromyographic signal (sEMG) is obtained from the forearm muscle groups of the user via the gForcePro. The gForcePro armband has built-in 8-channel highly sensitive EMG sensor. To avoid the excessive loss of essential information of sEMG signals, 200 Hz was used as the sampling frequency. During the experiment, the armband slid up along the forearm until there was no space between the electrodes and the skin. The armband switch was oriented consistently upward.

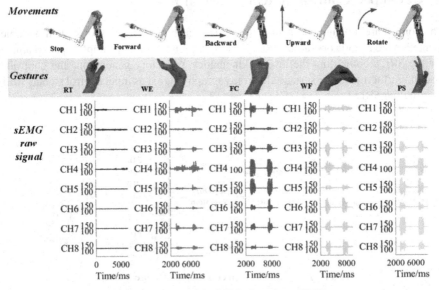

Fig. 4. HRI model of SRLs based on sEMG.

During the data acquisition process, each subject sits on a chair, and his arm naturally sagges. There are five gestures in total. Among them, the gesture RT is the excessive interval state of the other four gestures to reduce the impact of muscle fatigue. The action time and rest time lasts for 5 and 3 s respectively, and each action lasts for 10 times. The relationships between the collected sEMG signals and the corresponding gestures as shown in Fig. 4.

10 subjects are asked to repeat 10 times for each gesture. A total of 500 samples from the five gestures are collected for each subject. These samples are divided into two groups, and each group occupies half samples. One group is used to train the classifier, the other is used for the test classifier. The gesture recognition method is developed based on AI training algorithm of the gForcePro armband. When finish all target gestures data recording, the gForceAPP will upload the data and the model will be built on cloud server. Then, when user makes a gesture, the gForcePro will output the recognition result based on the AI training model. And the recognition result as a publish node to send to the ROS, the linear trajectory planning node as a subscribe node receives the information and conducts trajectory planning.

3.2 PID Controller

PID correction is a closed-loop control that is widely used in industry and academic research because it is simple to apply and provides good results. The proportional, integral, and derived actions comprise the PID control law. The objective of feedback control is to reduce the error signal; the difference between the measured value and the reference value. The proportional action is to generate an action that varies proportionally to the error signal. The advantage of the integral controller is that it eliminates the regulation error which persisted with a proportional regulator alone. The derived action makes it possible to anticipate the future variations of the measurement signal by applying a proportional action to its rate of variation. The derived action has a predictive effect [15].

The output of the PID controller is given by Eq. (3).

$$Output = K_p e(t) + K_i \int_0^t e(t)dt + K_d \frac{de(t)}{dt} \tag{3}$$

where, $e(t)$ is the error between the simulation angle and the actual angle. The simulation angle is obtained from the planned trajectory through the inverse solution of Kinematics. The actual angle is obtained from motor feedback. Output is the motor input torque.

3.3 ROS Control System

Figure 5 shows the overall control system of SRLs based on ROS. The gesture information node needs to communicate with the linear trajectory planning node. The coarse interpolation points are obtained after linear interpolation, and the angular information of the four joints of the SRLs are generated through the calculation of the open motion planning library (OMPL) of Moveit and the kinematics solver. Joint angle information is published to virtual joints in Rviz to control the motion of virtual robot. At the same time, the information of path points are sent to the joint controller to control the rotation of the real joint.

Configuring the Moveit package includes the following steps: import the URDF model, generate the self-collision detection matrix, creat a robot planning group, set the zero position.

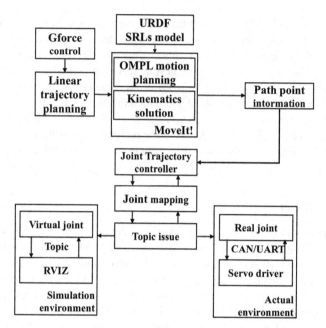

Fig. 5. ROS control flow chart.

4 Experiment and Discussion

4.1 Kinematic Model Verification

To verify the kinematic model, the deviation between the actual and theoretical position of the robot end-effector is measured. The actual position can be determined by measuring the position of the target ball, while the theoretical can be calculated by D-H model. The laser tracker used in the measurement process and the installation position of the target ball are shown in Fig. 6(a).

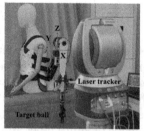   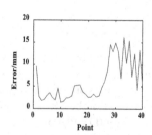

(a) The set setup of calibration experiment   (b) The result of calibration experiment

Fig. 6. Laser tracker and target ball installation position (a), the deviation between the actual and theoretical position of the robot end-effector (b).

The deviation between the actual and theoretical position of the robot end-effector is shown in Fig. 6(b). The max position error is 16.14 mm and the average position error is 6.14 mm. The end positions of SRLs in the actual are basically consistent with the calculated end positions. The correctness of the simulation model is verified.

4.2 The Simulation and Experiment of the SRLs

To verify the feasibility and effectiveness of the established control system, we have carried out simulation and experiment on SRLs. The user wears a robot and is asked to make four gestures. After the robot recognizes the user's gestures, it carries out corresponding trajectory planning. Then, the SRLs moves in the virtual environment of Rviz and the actual robot completes the corresponding movement, shown in Fig. 7.

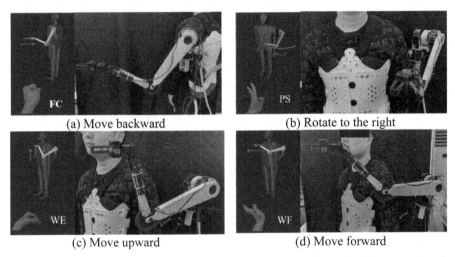

(a) Move backward   (b) Rotate to the right

(c) Move upward   (d) Move forward

Fig. 7. The motion of supernumerary robot limbs in simulation and actual environment when the user makes a gesture.

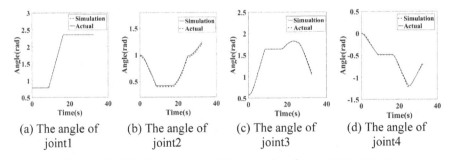

(a) The angle of   (b) The angle of   (c) The angle of   (d) The angle of
joint1   joint2   joint3   joint4

Fig. 8. The SRLs' trajectory tracking control performance assessment

We have selected joint angle trajectories to evaluate the system's performance. The pair of set value of the robot and the actual value of each joint angle is shown in Fig. 8.

Table 2. Statistical analysis of PID control method using RMES value

Value	Joint1	Joint2	Joint3	Joint4
RMES(rad)	0.0085	0.0210	0.0131	0.0165

As can be seen from Fig. 8, in the actual process of SRLs' movement, the movement of the SRLs is smooth, and the distance error between the tracking trajectory and the simulation trajectory is also small. The joint angle trajectories are recorded, and the whole system is evaluated upon the tracking performance of all joints represented by the root mean square (RMSE) value shown in Table 2. It is noted that the SRLs' system is able to satisfactorily track the reference trajectories and show average RMSE values of 0.0085 rad, 0.0210 rad, 0.0131rad, and 0.0165 rad for the four joints, respectively.

4.3 HRI Evaluation

Ten participants (8 male, 2 female) voluntarily join the simulation experiment of HRI. Participants' age ranged from 22 to 29-year-old (Mean = 25.5, STD = 5.0). No participants experience any physical disabilities and all have fully functional right arms. All participants provide their informed consent prior to starting the study and are informed about the procedure and the approximated length of the study.

Table 3. Subjects were asked to rate the questionnaire on a 7-likert scale. Five questions were prepared about HRI based on EMG signal.

Types	Q#	Questionnaire
HRI based on EMG signal	Q1	I feel that using EMG signals can accurately interact
	Q2	I feel that using EMG signals takes a lot of time
	Q3	I feel that gestures are easy to muscle fatigue
	Q4	I feel HRI requires little spirit
	Q5	I feel easy and relaxed during HRI

At the end of experiment, participants are asked to rate the questionnaire on a 7-Likert scale. Five questions are prepared about HRI based on EMG signal, which are shown in Table 3. The questions are proposed based on three indicators of HRI. Q1 and Q2 correspond to robustness. Q3 and Q4 correspond to awareness. Q5 corresponds to adaptability. For each of the statements, the participants are asked to rate how much it held true for them on a 7-point Likert scale from -3("not at all true for me") to 3 ("very true for me"). Figure 9 shows the throughput for each question across all participants. Most participants believe that the sEMG signal recognition is accurate, and it takes little time and spirit to control the virtual SRLs. Most participants feel easy and relaxed during HRI, but half of participants feel that making gestures is very tired.

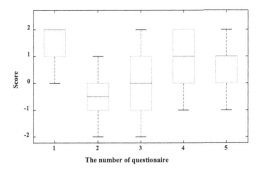

Fig. 9. Score of questionnaire on the sense of HRI.

4.4 Comepared with State-of-the-Art Works

The movement time and distance error of HRI mode are compared with the state-of-the-art Works, and the result is presented in Table 4. Considering the safety of the user, the speed of the motor is set at 0.25 rad/s, so movement takes a long time. The movement time of our system is 32 s, which is include two parts: an execution time of 27.5 s and a lag of 462 ms. The 462 ms includes gesture making and gesture recognition, while 27.5 s contains trajectory planning and trajectory execution time which accounts for the majority. The movement time of "The motion of foot" and "Gaze" are short because the motor speed is fast and the movement distance is short. Although the movement time of our system is a bit lower, this is perhaps not surprising given the safety of controlling the motor at a very low speed with the gesture. The distance error of the SRLs is 1.61 cm. The most of the error is caused by human disturbance and the lag between tracking and actuation to communicate.

Table 4. Movement time and distance error of compared with state-of-the-art works for HRI of SRLs.

HRI Model	Movement Time	Distance Error
Proposed method	32 s	1.61 cm
The motion of foot [7, 8]	2.5 s	7 cm
"face vector" [5, 6]	42 s	6.7 cm
Gaze [4]	0.2 s	2.8 cm

5   Conclusion and the Future Work

In this paper, a 4-DOFs SRLs is designed which is worn on the waist of human body to assist in grasping or in the holding of an object. Meanwhile, an HRI mode based on arm gestures, a simulation platform developed based on ROS and a PID-based trajectory tracking control are proposed. The feasibility and effectiveness of the control system are verified by simulation and experiments. According to subjective feedbacks from the user tests, most participants consider that accurate control of SRLs can be achieved with less time and effort. Overall, the control system and HRI mode of the SRLs are feasible.

This article mainly verifies the feasibility of gesture as HRI method for SRLs, which pay less attention to the gesture recognition and whether the gesture recognition error. Subsequent work will focus on the accuracy of gesture recognition and gesture formulation based on application. Regarding future work, more attention will be paid to the actual SRLs. SRLs weight is about 5.9 kg, the experiments with other subjects about quantify stress and ergonomics will be performed. Meanwhile, improving the lag between tracking and actuation to communicate in less than 462 ms consistently, is necessary for reducing the movement error of the SRLs. Even with the limitations of our study and our exploratory prototype, the SRLs with gesture remapping would create a space for exploring and reimaging what the human body could do.

Acknowledgement. This work was supported by the Fundamental Research Funds for the Central Universities (Grant No. NP2022304), the National Natural Science Foundation of China (Grant No. 52105103).

References

1. Liao, Z., Chen, B., Chang, T., Zheng, Q., Liu, K., Lv, J.: A human augmentation device design review: supernumerary robotic limbs. Industr. Robot: Int. J. Robot. Res. Appl. **50** (2022)
2. Yang, B., Huang, J., Chen, X., Xiong, C., Hasegawa, Y.: Supernumerary robotic limbs: a review and future outlook. IEEE Trans. Med. Robot. Bionics **3**, 623–639 (2021)
3. Tong, Y., Liu, J.: Review of research and development of supernumerary robotic limbs. IEEE/CAA J. Automatica Sinica **8**(5), 929–952 (2021)
4. Fan, Z., Lin, C., Fu, C.: A gaze signal based control method for supernumerary robotic limbs. In: 2020 3rd International Conference on Control and Robots (ICCR), Tokyo, Japan pp. 107–111 (2020)
5. Iwasaki, Y., Iwata, H.: A face vector - the point instruction-type interface for manipulation of an extended body in dual-task situations. In: 2018 IEEE International Conference on Cyborg and Bionic Systems (CBS), Shenzhen, China, pp. 662–666 (2018)
6. Iwasaki, Y., Takahashi, S., Iwata, H.: Comparison of operating method of extra limbs in dual tasks: point and path instruction. In: 2022 IEEE/SICE International Symposium on System Integration (SII), Narvik, Norway, pp. 171–176 (2022)
7. Sasaki, T., Saraiji, M., Fernando, C., Minamizawa, K., Inami, M.: MetaLimbs: multiple arms interaction metamorphism. In: ACM SIGGRAPH 2017 Emerging Technologies, pp 1–2 (2017)
8. Saraiji, M., Sasaki, T., Kunze, K., Minamizawa, K., Inami, M.: MetaArms: body remapping using feet-controlled artificial arms. In: Proceedings of the 31st Annual ACM Symposium on User Interface Software and Technology (UIST '18), pp. 65–74 (2018)
9. Khoramshahi, M., Morel, G., Jarrassé, N.: Intent-aware control in kinematically redundant systems: Towards collaborative wearable robots. In: 2021 IEEE International Conference on Robotics and Automation (ICRA), Xi'an, China, pp. 10453–10460 (2021)
10. Hernandez, S., Maldonado, C., Marin, A., Rios, H., Vazquez, H., Palacios E.: Design and implementation of a robotic arm using ROS and MoveIt. In 2017 IEEE International Autumn Meeting on Power, Electronics and Computing (ROPEC), Ixtapa, Mexico, pp. 1–6 (2017)

11. Baklouti, S., Gallot, G., Viaud, J., Subrin, K.: On the improvement of ROS-based control for teleoperated yaskawa robots. Appl. Sci. **11**, 7190 (2021)
12. Xu, T., Liu, H., Huang, R., Yao, Z., Xu, J.: Research on motion trajector planning of industrial robot based on ROS. In: 2022 7th International Conference on Automation, Control and Robotics Engineering (CACRE), Xi'an, China, pp. 58–62 (2022)
13. Liao, Z., et al.: Collaborative workspace design of supernumerary robotic limbs base on multi-objective optimization. J. Braz. Soc. Mech. Sci. Eng. **45**, 354 (2023)
14. Chang, T., Jiang, S., Chen, B., Liao, Z., Lv, J., Liu, D.: Design of supernumerary robotic limbs and virtual test of human–machine interaction safety. In: Tan, J. (ed.) Advances in Mechanical Design. Mechanisms and Machine Science, vol. 111, pp. 2027–2045. Springer, Singapore (2022). https://doi.org/10.1007/978-981-16-7381-8_127
15. Gull, M., et al.: A 4-DOF upper limb exoskeleton for physical assistance: design, modeling, control and performance evaluation. Appl. Sci. **11**, 5865 (2021)

Hybrid APFPSO Algorithm for Accurate Model-Free Motion Control of a Knee Exoskeleton

Zunmei Tian, Haojie Liu$^{(\boxtimes)}$, Chang Zhu, Wei Meng, and Quan Liu

Artificial Intelligence and Rehabilitation Robotics Laboratory, School of Information Engineering, Wuhan University of Technology, Wuhan 430070, China
lhj1989@whut.edu.cn

Abstract. The motor-driven rehabilitation robots can not only simplify the traditional onerous treatment, but also effectively promote the nerve remodeling of patients. The model-free adaptive control algorithm is a data-driven intelligent control algorithm, and it is widely used in rehabilitation robots. However, it faces difficulties with parameter tuning and optimization. This paper proposes an improved particle swarm optimization algorithm to optimize controller parameters, which utilizes tent chaotic mapping to initialize the population and introduces mass into the gravity migration strategy. The original force between two particles is replaced with the attraction and repulsion of the artificial potential field, which calculates the improved perturbation that updates the algorithm's position and automatically optimizes the control parameters. The experimental results demonstrate that the proposed algorithm can improve the accuracy of trajectory tracking at different amplitude angles compared to the original algorithm, which shows that it gains good potential in motion control of rehabilitation robot.

Keywords: Rehabilitation robot · Model-free control · Particle swarm optimization algorithm · Tent chaotic mapping · Gravity migration strategy

1 Introduction

Most incapacitated patients lack exercise, which can lead to secondary health risks [1–5]. Recently, knee exoskeleton has helped more and more patients recover, and achieved good therapeutic effect. Quasi-direct actuation [6–9] provides a possible solution for the design of compact and lightweight knee exoskeletons. However, there are some factors that reduce control accuracy between knee exoskeleton and human body, which makes it difficult to establish the control model. Model-free adaptive control (MFAC) algorithm has been widely used in the control of knee exoskeleton. However, the lack of systematic and effective methods for optimizing control parameters limits its control precision. A new

H. Yang et al. (Eds.): ICIRA 2023, LNAI 14268, pp. 422–431, 2023.
https://doi.org/10.1007/978-981-99-6486-4_37

tuning method [10] which used the nonlinear virtual reference feedback tuning (VRFT) algorithm to automatically determined all parameters of the data-driven model-free adaptive control algorithm. Reference [11] designed a model-free learning adaptive control (MFLAC) based on pseudo-gradient concepts and optimization procedure by a particle swarm optimization (PSO) approach, which adopted constriction coefficient and Henon chaotic sequences (CPSOH). Reference [12] uses iterative feedback tuning (IFT) and Reference [13] uses related-based tuning (CbT). The paper is organized as follows: Sect. 2 describes and explains the algorithm framework. Section 3 gives the simulation and experimental verification of the algorithm. Section 4 analyzes and summarizes the achievements of this paper and the future development direction.

2   Method

Particle swarm optimization (PSO) is one of the most widely used meta-heuristic algorithms based on swarm intelligence [14]. Gravity random walk (GRW) method can be combined with PSO algorithm, in which each individual has four attributes: position(X), height(h), energy(Ep), and mass(m) [15]. The meta-heuristic algorithm based on swarm intelligence is assumed to consist of N individuals. The position of i individual in the t th iteration can be defined as (1).

$$X_i^t = [x_{i1}^t, ..., x_{id}^t, ..., x_{iD}^t], i = 1, 2, ..., N \tag{1}$$

According to the law of conservation of mechanical energy, the energy of an object can be calculated by (2)

$$E_{pi} = m_i g h_i \tag{2}$$

$$E_{pi} = |fitness(X_i) - fitness(\varphi)| \tag{3}$$

$$h_i = \frac{\|X_i - \beta\|_2}{\|\beta - \varphi\|_2} + \varepsilon \tag{4}$$

For the minimization problem, φ^t and β^t can be obtained by formula $\beta^t = \min_{j \in \{1,...,N\}} fitness(X_j^t)$, $\varphi^t = \max_{j \in \{1,...,N\}} fitness(X_j^t)$. For the maximization problem, φ^t and β^t can be obtained by formula $\beta^t = \max_{j \in \{1,...,N\}} fitness(X_j^t)$, $\varphi^t = \min_{j \in \{1,...,N\}} fitness(X_j^t)$.and ε is a very small constant.$\|\cdot\|_2$ is the Euclidean distance between two individuals.

$$m_i^t = \frac{E_{pi}^t}{h_i^t \times g^t} \tag{5}$$

where g^t is the energy constant of the t iteration .

$$g^t = |fitness(\beta^t) - fitness(\varphi^t)| \tag{6}$$

Aiming at the problem of path planning, the artificial potential field(APF) is composed of the gravitational potential field generated by the planning end point and the repulsive potential field caused by environmental obstacles [16]. Inspired by this, we consider using the gravitational potential field and the repulsive potential field to update the position of each particle, and establish a suitable fitness function, so as to find the position of the new particle under the action of gravity and repulsive force.

In the traditional APF, the expression of the attractive potential field function is

$$U_{att}(X) = \frac{1}{2}K_{att}\rho(X, X_{goal})^2 \tag{7}$$

where K_{att} is the positive proportional gain factor, X is the position coordinates of mobile robot,X_{goal} is the location coordinates of the target point, and $\rho(X, X_{goal}) = \|X - X_{goal}\|_2$ is the Euclidean distance between the robot and the target.The corresponding attractive force function is

$$F_{att}(X) = -\nabla U_{att}(X) = -\frac{1}{2}K_{att} \cdot \nabla \rho^2(X, X_{goal}) = -K_{att}(X - X_{goal}) \tag{8}$$

Here, it is assumed that the four parameters of optimization belong to different vector directions.

$$F_{atti}(X) = -K_{att}(i - i_{goal}), i = x, y, z, u \tag{9}$$

where, x, y, z and u respectively represent optimized parameters η, μ, ρ and λ.

In the traditional APF, the expression of the repulsive potential field function is

$$U_{rep}(X) = \begin{cases} \frac{1}{2}K_{rep}(\frac{1}{\rho(X, X_{obs})} - \frac{1}{\rho_0})^2, if\rho(X, X_{obs}) \leq \rho_0 \\ 0, if\rho(X, X_{obs}) > \rho_0 \end{cases} \tag{10}$$

where K_{rep} is the proportional gain factor of repulsive potential field, ρ_0 is the maximum influence distance of obstacle repulsive potential field.The corresponding repulsive force function is

$$F_{rep}(X) = -\nabla U_{rep}(X) = \begin{cases} K_{rep}\left(\frac{1}{\rho(X, X_{obs})} - \frac{1}{\rho_0}\right)\left(\frac{1}{\rho(X, X_{obs})^2}\right)\frac{X - X_{obs}}{\|X - X_{obs}\|}, if\rho(X, X_{obs}) \leq \rho_0 \\ 0, if\rho(X, X_{obs}) > \rho_0 \end{cases} \tag{11}$$

The repulsive force in each direction is calculated by the following formula

$$F_{repi}(X) = \begin{cases} K_{rep}\left(\frac{1}{\rho(X, X_{obs})} - \frac{1}{\rho_0}\right)\left(\frac{1}{\rho(X, X_{obs})^2}\right)\frac{i - i_{obs}}{\|X - X_{obs}\|}, if\rho(X, X_{obs}) \leq \rho_0 \\ 0, if\rho(X, X_{obs}) > \rho_0 \end{cases}, i = x, y, z, u \tag{12}$$

The robot will avoid obstacles and move towards the target in the direction of the combined attraction and repulsion. The resultant force can be expressed as

$$F(X) = -\nabla U(X) = F_{att}(X) + F_{rep}(X) \tag{13}$$

Based on the calculation formula of disturbance in [15], the calculation formula of disturbance in this paper is derived as

$$a_{ji}^t = F_{ji}^t/(m_{ji}^t + \varepsilon), j = x, y, z, u \tag{14}$$

where j represents the four directions of the corresponding four parameters. Finally, the random disturbance a_{ji}^t of variable dimension by individual i in the t-th iteration is added to the position update equation.

$$X_{ji}^{t+1} = X_{ji}^t + V_{ji}^{t+1} + a_{ji}^t, j = x, y, z, u \tag{15}$$

where x,y,z,u are the column vectors of vector X and X_{ji}^{t+1} represents the position update of the ith individual, in the j direction, at the t+1 iteration. In this paper utilizes tent chaotic mapping to initialize the population and enhance the algorithm's performance during the exploration stage.

$$x^{t+1} = tent(x^t) = \begin{cases} 2x^t, 0 \leq x^t < 0.5 \\ 2(1-x^t), 0.5 \leq x^t < 1 \end{cases} \tag{16}$$

The pseudo code of APFPSO algorithm is shown in Algorithm 1.

Algorithm 1. Artificial Potential Field PSO algorithm.

Require: I/O model of simulation system
Ensure: the optimal parameters
 1: **Initialize** all parameters and maximum iterations
 2: Tent Chaotic map initializes the positions of all particles;
 3: **for** $t = 1 \rightarrow maxIter$ **do**
 4:     Evaluate each particle according to the fitness function
 5:     Find the optimal particle and the worst particle
 6:     Calculate the energy, height and mass of each particle by (3), (4) and (5), respectively.
 7:     Calculate the energy constant by (6)
 8:     Calculate the gravitational and repulsive forces by (9),(12) respectively.
 9:     Calculate the total interaction force on each particle by (13).
10:     Calculate the random disturbance of each particle by (14).
11:     Update the position of all particles using the formula (15)
12:     Check whether each particle is out of bounds, and if so, randomly initialize the position of the pollen
13: **end for**

---

3   Experiment Results

3.1   Experimental Setup

The actuators used in the experiment included a custom high torque density brushless DC motor with a rated torque of 16N·m, a peak torque of 48 N·m, a reduction ratio of 6:1, a weight of (730g ± 20g), and a compact structure of (94 mm × 52 mm).

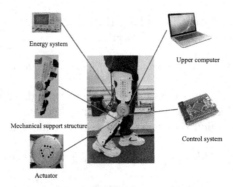

Fig. 1. Experimental platform of the single joint rehabilitation robot.

Figure 1 shows the experimental device of a single joint rehabilitation robot. The control program SISO-MFAC is implemented using LabVIEW. The control signal generated by the program is transmitted to the motor through CAN communication, and then the motor returns to the actual motion position in real time, which is then used by the control program to calculate the input torque of the motor in the next step, thus forming a closed-loop control system. To evaluate the effectiveness of a control system, four types of errors are defined below.

$$MAE = \frac{1}{m} \sum_{k=1}^{m} |\theta_d(k) - \theta(k)|, \quad k = 1, 2, \cdots, m \tag{17}$$

$$AVME = \max(|\theta_d(k) - \theta(k)|), \quad k = 1, 2, \cdots, m \tag{18}$$

$$RMSE = \sqrt{\frac{1}{m} \sum_{k=1}^{m} (\theta_d(k) - \theta(k))^2}, \quad k = 1, 2, \cdots, m \tag{19}$$

$$PCCs = \frac{1}{N-1} \sum_{i=1}^{N} \left(\frac{X_i - \mu_X}{\sigma_X}\right) \left(\frac{Y_i - \mu_Y}{\sigma_Y}\right) \tag{20}$$

3.2 Improved Particle Swarm Optimization Algorithm Analysis

Simulation. To facilitate comparative analysis, a typical nonlinear system model presented in literature was selected as the simulation model in this paper. The input-output relationship of this model can be expressed as follows:

$$y(k+1) = \begin{cases} \frac{y(k)}{1+y^2(k)} + u^3(k), k \leq 500 \\ \frac{y(k)y(k-1)y(k-2)u(k-1)(y(k-2)-1)+a(k)u(k)}{1+y^2(k-1)+y^2(k-2)}, k > 500 \end{cases} \tag{21}$$

The expected output is

$$y^*(k+1) = \begin{cases} 0.5 \times (-1)^{round(k/500)}, k \leq 300 \\ 0.5 \sin(k\pi/100) + 0.3 \cos(k\pi/50), 300 < k \leq 700 \\ 0.5 \times (-1)^{round(k/500)}, k > 700 \end{cases} \tag{22}$$

This paper selects the following fitness function:

$$J = \int_0^\infty (t|e(t)|+10(y(t+1) - y(t)) + 0.001u^3)dt + 2t_u \qquad (23)$$

MFAC parameter optimization algorithm based on improved particle swarm optimization algorithm was written with MATLAB. The flow chart of the algorithm was shown in Fig. 2 and then simulation was conducted based on the optimization parameters. The results of MFAC parameter optimization of APFPSO algorithm and the convergence process of fitness function are shown in Fig. 3a and Fig. 3b where Katt=0.1, Krep $= 100,\rho_0 = 25$. GRWPSO is in literature [15], and PSO is the original algorithm.

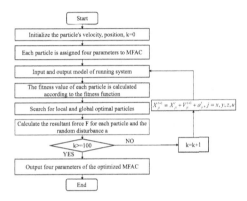

Fig. 2. APFPSO algorithm optimization flow chart of MFAC parameters.

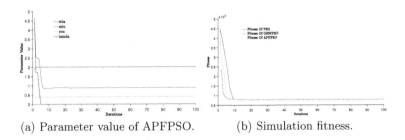

(a) Parameter value of APFPSO.   (b) Simulation fitness.

Fig. 3. APFPSO parameter optimization process

Figure 3a and Fig. 3b demonstrate that the three particle swarm optimization algorithms, namely PSO, GRWPSO, and APFPSO, converge after 10, 15, and 6 iterations respectively, reaching the optimal fitness value. Although the fitness function of APFPSO has the highest value at the beginning, its convergence result is comparable to that of PSO and GRWPSO after the sixth iteration. Therefore, it can be observed that the algorithm possesses a higher explorative capability in the early stages as well as quicker convergence speed in later stages.

The simulation results in Fig. 4 show that, compared with the reference parameter $[\eta, u, \rho, \lambda] = [1, 1, 0.6, 1]$, the parameter $[\eta, u, \rho, \lambda] = [2, 0.8869, 0.4, 0.01]$ iterated by the APFPSO algorithm brings less overshoot and oscillation after the simulation.

The overshoot of the two groups of parameters under simulation is 79.24%, 66.1%, respectively. The corresponding overshoot is reduced by 13.14% after 500 steps. Although the input-output relationship has changed, the model and time-varying parameters of the object have also changed. Meanwhile, when the expected output changes at the 700th step, 750th step, 850th step and 950th step, the overshoot is greatly reduced to zero, and the change of the expected output is also overcome.

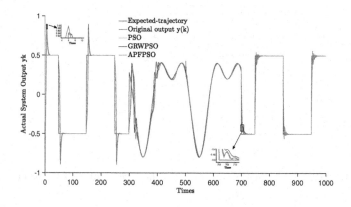

Fig. 4. Simulation result.

In Table 1 the average values of Mean Absolute Error(MAE), Root Mean Square Error(RMSE) and Pearson correlation coefficient(PCCs) were calculated for 19 times of random training.

Table 1. Analysis of simulation results.

Algorithm	MAE	RMSE	PCCs	AVME
PSO	0.0436	0.1434	0.9526	0.9732
GRWPSO	0.0406	0.1404	0.9544	0.9732
APFPSO	0.0397	0.1401	0.9548	0.9401

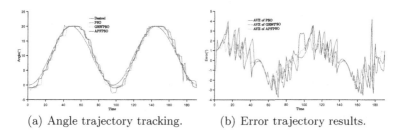

(a) Angle trajectory tracking.   (b) Error trajectory results.

Fig. 5. The desired angle amplitude $= 20°$

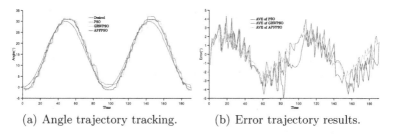

(a) Angle trajectory tracking.   (b) Error trajectory results.

Fig. 6. The desired angle amplitude $= 30°$.

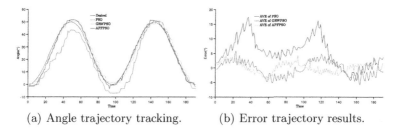

(a) Angle trajectory tracking.   (b) Error trajectory results.

Fig. 7. The desired angle amplitude $= 50°$.

3.3 Analysis of Position Tracking Results

In order to ensure the effect of rehabilitation, the robot should move within a reasonable range of the knee joint. Considering the need to ensure smooth and safe movement in lower limb movement, sinusoidal signal was selected in this experiment, and the frequency was 1.01 Hz. Under no-load conditions, set the desired angles to $20°$, $30°$, and $50°$.

Fig. 5, 6 and 7 are the angular trajectory and error trajectory when the expected angular amplitude is $20°$, $30°$ and $50°$, respectively. In the angular trajectory curve, the blue curve represents the desired Angle of the joint. The brown curve represents the control effect of SISO-MFAC after setting parameters of PSO, the yellow curve represents the control effect of SISO-MFAC after setting parameters of GRWPSO, and the purple curve represents the control effect of SISO-MFAC after setting parameters of APFPSO.

The required angular amplitude is changed to verify the control effect of the algorithm in each suitable range. It can be seen from the experimental results that APFPSO has higher performance in parameter setting according to the AVE error curve drawn and the experimental bar chart of three amplitude.

Figure 8 shows four errors of position tracking under three parameter setting controls from the perspective of data. It can be seen that PCCs of APF is always greater than PSO and GRWPSO, while AVME, MAE and RMSE are all smaller than PSO and GRWPSO. With the error of PSO as the benchmark, the AVME of APFPSO decreases by 46.49%, 18.36% and 75.33%, and the RMSE decreases by 29.67%, 29.41% and 75.45%, respectively, when the amplitude is 20°, 30° and 50°. In addition, it can be observed that the errors of the three parameter Settings increase with the increase of the expected angular amplitude.

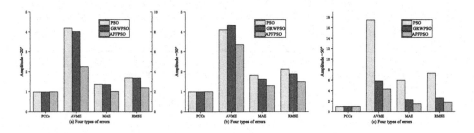

Fig. 8. Error results.

4   Conclusion

In this paper, a PSO optimization algorithm based on the combined force of mass and artificial potential field to update the position perturbation is proposed to realize the automatic optimization of the parameters η, μ, ρ and λ of SISO-MFAC, and simulation experiments are designed to improve the overharmonic jitter and verify the effectiveness and feasibility of the method. At the same time, SISO-MFAC control based on APFPSO parameter setting is carried out in the actual robot system. The maximum error of AVME is reduced by more than 70% compared with the parameter setting based on PSO, and the maximum error of RMSE is reduced by more than 70% compared with the parameter setting based on PSO. In the future, we plan to increase the load and implement real-time parameter settings for better tracking control.

Acknowledgement. This work is supported by the National Natural Science Foundation of China under Grant 52075398 and 52275029.

References

1. Booth, F., Roberts, C., Laye, M.: Lack of exercise is a major cause of chronic diseases. Compr. Physiol. **2**, 1143–1211 (2012)

2. Knight, J.: Physical inactivity: associated diseases and disorders. Ann. Clin. Lab. Sci. **42**, 320–37 (2012)

3. Baylor, C., Yorkston, K., Jensen, M., Truitt, A., Molton, I.: Scoping review of common secondary conditions after stroke and their associations with age and time post stroke. Top. Stroke Rehab. **21**, 371–82 (2014)

4. Sezer, N., Akkuş, S., uğurlu, F.G.: Chronic complications of spinal cord injury. World J. Orthop. **6**, 24–33 (2015)

5. Jensen, M., Truitt, A., Schomer, K., Yorkston, K., Baylor, C., Molton, I.: Frequency and age effects of secondary health conditions in individuals with spinal cord injury: a scoping review. Spinal Cord **51**(12), 882–892 (2013)

6. Wensing, P.M., Wang, A., Seok, S., Otten, D., Lang, J., Kim, S.: Proprioceptive actuator design in the MIT cheetah: Impact mitigation and high-bandwidth physical interaction for dynamic legged robots. IEEE Trans. Robot. **33**(3), 509–522 (2017)

7. Yu, S., et al.: Design and control of a high-torque and highly backdrivable hybrid soft exoskeleton for knee injury prevention during squatting. IEEE Robot. Autom. Lett. **4**(4), 4579–4586 (2019)

8. Long, Y., Peng, Y.: Design and control of a quasi-direct drive actuated knee exoskeleton. J. Bionic Eng. **19**(3), 678–687 (2022)

9. Huang, T.H., et al.: Modeling and stiffness-based continuous torque control of lightweight quasi-direct-drive knee exoskeletons for versatile walking assistance. IEEE Trans. Robot. **38**(3), 1442–1459 (2022)

10. Roman, R.C., Radac, M.B., Precup, R.E., Petriu, E.M.: Data-driven model-free adaptive control tuned by virtual reference feedback tuning. Acta Polytechnica Hungarica **13**(1), 83–96 (2016)

11. dos Santos Coelho, L., Coelho, A.A.R.: Model-free adaptive control optimization using a chaotic particle swarm approach. Chaos Solitons Fractals **41**(4), 2001–2009 (2009)

12. Hjalmarsson, H., Gunnarsson, S., Gevers, M.: A convergent iterative restricted complexity control design scheme. In: Proceedings of 1994 33rd IEEE Conference on Decision and Control, vol. 2, pp. 1735–1740. IEEE (1994)

13. Karimi, A., Mišković, L., Bonvin, D.: Convergence analysis of an iterative correlation-based controller tuning method. IFAC Proc. Volumes **35**(1), 413–418 (2002)

14. Poli, R., Kennedy, J., Blackwell, T.M.: Particle swarm optimization. Swarm Intell. **1**, 33–57 (1995)

15. Jiahao, F.: Research on swarm intelligence-based metaheuristic algorithm for unconstrained single object optimization problem. Ph.D. thesis, Jilin University (2022)

16. Koren, Y., Borenstein, J., et al.: Potential field methods and their inherent limitations for mobile robot navigation. In: ICRA, vol. 2, pp. 1398–1404 (1991)

The Influence of Task Objectives and Loads on the Synergies Governing Human Upper Limb Movements

Shumin Wang[1], Xiongfei Zheng[1], Ting Zhang[2], Jiejunyi Liang[1], and Xiufeng Zhang[3]([✉])

[1] School of Mechanical Science and Engineering, Huazhong University of Science and Technology, Wuhan 430074, China
[2] School of Mechanical and Electric Engineering, Soochow University, Suzhou 215131, China
[3] National Research Center for Rehabilitation Technical Aids, Beijing 100176, China
zhangxiufeng@nrcrta.cn

Abstract. The human upper limbs exhibit a multitude of daily functional behaviors, yet these diverse movements arise from a limited set of invariant units—synergistic bases comprising basic motion primitives. However, as human movements necessarily entails interaction with the external environment factors such as task objectives and loads may impact the synergies, thereby compromising the control of the wearable robotics based on those laws. Elucidating the influence of external factors on the synergies governing human upper limb movements presents an urgent yet unresolved challenge. The present study employed principal component analysis (PCA) to identify the distinct synergies for movements associated with differing task objectives. Comparison revealed that, for reaching movements and transferring movements, the factors exerting the greatest impact on synergies are displacement of the distal endpoints and hand grasping. For varied loads, analysis of overall similarity across synergies under different loads revealed how motion synergies changes with increased loads.

Keywords: Upper limbs · Motion synergies · Loads

1 Introduction

Motion synergies indicate that the different degrees of freedom (DoFs) among limbs are not independent of one another, and they are coupled to ensure coordinated movements of the human limbs [1]. Motion synergies are often applied in the design and control of anthropomorphic machines such as prostheses, rehabilitative exoskeletons, and assistive exoskeletons [2]. Despite the proliferation of wearable robots, human-machine interaction with these systems continues to be hampered by inadequate anthropomorphism and dexterity. In particular, undifferentiated application of the concept of common motion primitives for control exacerbates environment interaction issues for wearable

---

S. Wang and X. Zheng—Contributed to the work equally and should be regarded as co-first authors.

© The Author(s), under exclusive license to Springer Nature Singapore Pte Ltd. 2023
H. Yang et al. (Eds.): ICIRA 2023, LNAI 14268, pp. 432–450, 2023.
https://doi.org/10.1007/978-981-99-6486-4_38

robots, especially under changing external conditions. Hence, study and elucidation of the intrinsic laws of motion manifested during human interaction with the environment, and application of these laws for control of wearable robots, may enhance rehabilitation outcomes [3] and quality of life for individuals with limb disabilities and other users.

To explore the synergies of the human upper limb movements and elucidate the mechanisms underlying their generation, researchers worldwide have conducted extensive investigations. Employing motion capture system, Bockemuehl et al. obtained spatial movement data across 10 DoFs for the arm and shoulder girdle during natural movements, extending synergy research into three dimensions. Their experiment collected single-hand capture motion data across 16 distinct trajectories [4]. By using PCA, these data revealed stable synergies of high information coverage among joints. Computational results showed that the original 10 redundant DoFs could be replaced by 3 principal components (PCs) without losing most motion information. Averta et al. proposed a dynamic means of describing human movements that incorporates time as a variable in synergies, demonstrating the temporally variant nature of synergies in human upper limb movements. Their experiment selected 30 distinct grasping target movements and recorded movement data across 7 DoFs for the right arm [5]. Extracting PCs at different points during movements and calculating temporal deviations clarified that human upper limb movement trajectories could be reconstructed through a linear combination of several major time-related functions. However, the above methods for studying motion synergies have focused solely on common motion primitives based on multi-movement averaging to maximize coverage of motion information, ignoring the impact of differences across various movement tasks and task demands.

Therefore, the presented study investigated the influence of factors such as task objectives and task demand on motion synergies. First, to obtain experimental data most representative of the impact of varied task objectives and task demands on synergies, we designed two experiments. The first experiment established a movement task with actions selected to achieve maximum coverage of upper limb motion range and hand prehension type. The second experiment, using the same actions, established a movement experiment under different loads by incrementally increasing the loads as an experimental variable. Second, to establish a dataset of multi-degree-of-freedom natural upper limb movements [6], we converted the raw data into angular displacement data across DoFs of the upper limbs. According to the relationship between points and the spatial coordinate system, we established the coordinate system and its matrix representation to obtain transformation matrices between different coordinates. Using Euler angle inverse solution, we obtained motion data under different task objectives and loads, establishing a dataset of upper limb movements. Thirdly, to explore the factors influencing multi-degree-of-freedom synergies of the upper limbs under different task objectives and their relative impacts, we conducted a comparative analysis of the synergies manifested in motion under different task objectives. Through PCA, we obtained synergies for motion data grouped by task objective [7]. Based on the variation in variance accounted for by synergies across groups and comparison of synergies, we confirmed that for reaching movements and transferring movements, the factor exerting the greatest influence was the motion path of the end effector. Finally, to clarify the influence of load on synergies, we described how synergies changed with load using load as the sole variable. Through the variance accounted for distribution and similarity of the synergies obtained by PCA, we elucidated how motion synergies became more similar and dissimilar with increasing load, revealing the influence of load on multi-degree-of-freedom synergies of the upper limbs.

In summary, this study explored the factors influencing multi-degree-of-freedom synergies of the upper limbs during experimental actions derived from daily tasks, as well as their relative impacts. We demonstrated that the first influence was the motion path of the upper limb end effector. We investigated the influence of load on motion synergies using load as a variable. An analysis of the similarity between synergies under different loads revealed factors impacting multi-degree-of-freedom synergy movements of the upper limbs under different loads.

2 Methodology

We used coordinate transformation method and Euler angle inverse solution to obtain seven-degree-of-freedom joint angular motion data for the upper limbs and extracted synergies by PCA. By comparing synergies and groupings under different task objectives and loads, we analyzed the influencing factors and relative impacts.

2.1 Calculation of Angular Displacement Data

We converted the three-dimensional data of the observed points collected in the experiment into angular displacement to quantify upper limb joint movements. Using coordinate transformation method, we calculated the rotation angle of the coordinate system relative to the coordinate axes within each time interval. Specifically, we regarded the upper limbs as a complete kinematic chain (shoulder joint three DoFs, elbow joint two DoFs and wrist joint two DoFs), where the movements of each joint followed the principle of relative motion. By calculating the changes in the coordinates of each observed point between two adjacent time intervals, we obtained the angular displacement of each joint within those time intervals. Then, using the method of solving simultaneous equations, we calculated the absolute angular displacement of each joint within each time interval.

Assuming that three observed points are not collinear, numbered $A(x_A, y_A, z_A)$, $B(x_B, y_B, z_B)$, $C(x_C, y_C, z_C)$. The origin O is on the line formed by points A and B. Set up the coordinate system as shown in Fig. 1.

The matrix expression of the established coordinate system is

$$
\begin{cases}
\vec{y} = \overrightarrow{AB} \\
\vec{x'} = \overrightarrow{OC} \\
\vec{z} = \vec{x'} \times \vec{y} = \overrightarrow{OC} \times \overrightarrow{AB} \\
\vec{x} = \vec{y} \times \vec{z} = \overrightarrow{AB} \times \overrightarrow{OC} \times \overrightarrow{AB} \\
H = [\vec{x}\ \vec{y}\ \vec{z}] \times \begin{bmatrix} \frac{1}{|\vec{x}|} & 0 & 0 \\ 0 & \frac{1}{|\vec{y}|} & 0 \\ 0 & 0 & \frac{1}{|\vec{z}|} \end{bmatrix}
\end{cases}
\tag{1}
$$

The base coordinate system in the initial state is specified as H_1, and the moving coordinate system to be sought is specified as H_2.

Before the motion, there is a matrix transformation between the base coordinate system and the moving coordinate system to be sought, i.e. $H_2 = H_1 \times {}^1_2T$.

After the motion, the base coordinate system and the coordinate system to be sought are respectively noted as $H_{1'}$, $H_{2'}$, and the mutual relationship remains unchanged $H_{2'} = H_{1'} \times {}^1_2T'$.

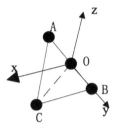

Fig. 1. Three-point spatial coordinate system.

When the motion occurs only in the base coordinate system, the transformation relationship between the coordinate system to be found and the base coordinate system does not change, i.e. ${}^1_2T = {}^1_2T'$.

When the coordinate system is in motion with respect to itself, there is a transformation matrix T. The transformation matrix after motion is equal to the transformation matrix when the target coordinate system does not produce motion multiplied by the transformation matrix of the target coordinate with respect to itself, that is ${}^1_2T' = {}^1_2T \times T$.

Combined, the rotation of the target coordinate system on itself results in

$$\begin{cases} {}^1_2T = (H_1)^{-1} \times H_2 \\ {}^1_2T' = (H'_1)^{-1} \times H'_2 \\ T = ({}^1_2T)^{-1} \times {}^1_2T' \end{cases} \tag{2}$$

Since the permutation matrix can be split to perform the multiplication cross of the rotation matrix around the coordinate axes, Eq. (3) is obtained in a fixed order [8].

$$T = Y_1X_2Z_3 = \begin{bmatrix} c_1c_3 + s_1s_2s_3 & c_3s_1s_2 - c_1s_3 & c_2s_1 \\ c_2s_3 & c_2c_3 & -s_2 \\ c_1s_2s_3 - c_3s_1 & c_1c_3s_2 + s_1s_3 & c_1c_2 \end{bmatrix} \tag{3}$$

where c_i represents the cosine of the i-th rotation angle $\cos\theta_i$, and s_i represents the sine of the i-th rotation angle $\sin\theta_i$. Subsequently, the range of angle values is determined according to the joint and the direction of the determined coordinate axis, and the data points beyond the limit position are discarded. For the purpose of description noting T as R:

$$T = R = \begin{bmatrix} r_{11} & r_{12} & r_{13} \\ r_{21} & r_{22} & r_{23} \\ r_{31} & r_{32} & r_{33} \end{bmatrix} \tag{4}$$

The inverse solution gives,

$$\begin{cases} \theta_1 = Atan2(r_{13}, r_{33}) \\ \theta_2 = Atan2(-r_{23}, r_{22}/c_3) \\ \theta_3 = Atan2(r_{21}, r_{22}) \end{cases} \tag{5}$$

Equation (3–5) always holds when the rotation angle is not equal to $\pm\pi/2$. Since the experiment data acquisition frequency was 100 Hz, the time interval between two data acquisitions was very short (0.01 s). Within this time interval, it was difficult for the upper limb joint rotation angle to reach $\pm\pi/2$, so Eq. (3–5) could be used to calculate the joint angle.

2.2 Extraction of Synergies

The goal of PCA [9] is to perform a linear combination between variables for a set of non-linearly correlated variables, and to explain the set of variables with the combined model, which generally has fewer model variables than the original variables, i.e., it achieves dimensionality reduction [10].

Define the data to be analyzed X, where there are n variables $X_1, X_2, , X_n$, each of which is obtained by m observations, i.e.

$$X = \begin{bmatrix} X_1 \, X_2 \cdots X_n \end{bmatrix} = \begin{bmatrix} x_{11} & x_{12} & \cdots & x_{1n} \\ x_{21} & x_{22} & \cdots & x_{2n} \\ \vdots & \vdots & \ddots & \vdots \\ x_{m1} & x_{m2} & \cdots & x_{mn} \end{bmatrix} \tag{6}$$

In this paper, we use the eigenvalue decomposition of PCA. Suppose Σ is the variance-covariance matrix of the data set, corresponding to the eigenvalue-eigenvectors $(\lambda_1, e_1), (\lambda_2, e_2), \cdots, (\lambda_n, e_n)$, where $\lambda_1 \geq \lambda_2 \geq \cdots \geq \lambda_n$. The i-th PC is

$$Y_i = (X - \overline{X})e_i = e_{i1}(X_1 - \overline{X_1}) + e_{i2}(X_2 - \overline{X_2}) + \ldots + e_{n1}(X_n - \overline{X_n}), i = 1, 2, \ldots n \tag{7}$$

The variance and covariance are respectively

$$\begin{aligned} Var(Y_i) &= e'_i \sum e_i = \lambda_i \\ Cov(Y_i, Y_k) &= e'_i \sum e_k = 0, i \neq k \end{aligned} \tag{8}$$

The first PC has the maximum variance. Each PC obtained by PCA corresponds to a variance contribution, which indicates its ability to express information in the data set. In some unserious situation, the first PC can be compared directly.

2.3 Comparison of Similarity and Clusters

By comparing the similarity and clustering grouping of synergies under different task objectives, we obtain the influence factors and relative influence degrees under different task objectives.

(1) Similarity between variables

The similarity between variables is used to show the relationship between the proximity of two groups of data, including cosine similarity, Pearson Correlation Coefficient, Jaccard coefficient, etc. Generally the larger the coefficient, the higher the similarity. Assume two variables X, Y have the sample values $(x_1, x_2, \ldots, x_n)$, $(y_1, y_2, \ldots, y_n)$.

Combining the advantages, disadvantages and applicability of each similarity measure, this study uses the extended Pearson correlation coefficient [11] for cosine similarity,

$$r = \frac{\sum_{i=1}^{n}(x_i - \bar{x})(y_i - \bar{y})}{\sqrt{\sum_{i=1}^{n}(x_i - \bar{x})^2}\sqrt{\sum_{i=1}^{n}(y_i - \bar{y})^2}} \tag{9}$$

(2) Clustering method

There are two main approaches to cluster analysis, hierarchical clustering and non-hierarchical clustering [12]. Considering the size and content of the data in this paper, the hierarchical clustering method is mainly used. The goal of hierarchical clustering is to partition and aggregate several groups of objects to be determined into new combinations, using distance values as a metric.

The specific procedure for hierarchical clustering of objects with N objectives is:

(a). Take N targets and form an $N \times N$ distance matrix $D = \{d_{ij}\}$, where the element d_{ij} denotes the distance between the i-th target and the j-th target.
(b). Find the two different targets U and V that are closest in distance from the distance matrix with the distance d_{UV} and grouped as (UV).
(c). Remove the rows and columns corresponding to UV from the matrix, add the grouping (UV), and calculate the distance value again to get the new matrix.
(d). Repeat steps (b) and (c) (N-1 times) until all targets are grouped into one grouping, and record the result of each grouping and the distance value at the time of grouping.

3   Upper Limb Motion Synergy Data Acquisition Experiment

This study employed an optical motion capture system (Vicon MX) from Vicon Metrics Limited (Oxford, UK) with a real-time sampling frequency of 100 Hz. The system consisted of multiple high-speed infrared cameras and other hardware devices. The Vicon system used Vicon Vegas sensors with proprietary patents, which offered high resolution, high capture frequency, and good three-dimensional reconstruction. The cameras collected real-time changes in the reflective markers. Using software, we obtained real-time change data for the coordinates of the reflective markers during the experiment. We determined the joint motion coordinate system using three points to determine one coordinate system and calculated joint angular displacement data using the Euler angle inverse solution. There are various ways to express motion states. In this study, we used joint angular displacements to represent the motion state. Because the range of external conditions that can influence movements is very broad, this experiment was designed from two perspectives—different daily tasks and loads—to determine influencing factors and degrees of influence for subsequent calculations.

A total of 14 Marker points were used for upper limb motion data collection, corresponding to the body parts, shoulder joint, elbow joint and wrist joint, as shown in Fig. 2.

The basic principle of the experiment was that the markers would not move and remained in a relatively stable state when only the upper limbs were active. We used three markers on the chest and back. For three motion parts, namely the shoulder, elbow, and wrist, at least one coordinate axis coincided with the actual rotation axis to facilitate calculation. The markers on the upper arm and shoulder together established the shoulder joint motion coordinate system. Considering that the skin and skeleton were not completely rigid during movements, the distance between them could not be too close to avoid insignificant performance and too far to avoid mutual influence between the elbow joint markers. Therefore, we placed the markers at the middle position of the arm length. The same rationale applied to the forearm markers.

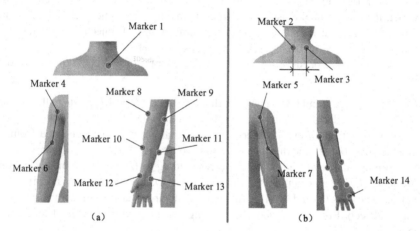

Fig. 2. Marker point location schematic. (a) The front view. (b) The back view.

3.1 Multi-task Objective Experiment

On the one hand, the muscles of arm and hand are largely shared during movement. On the other hand, most hand muscles have attachment points on the forearm. When the hand moves, both types of muscles are driven, affecting the arm movements. Therefore, hand movements directly affect arm work. According to the degree of hand involvement, the experimental actions were divided into three categories [5]: (1) reaching movements, (2) transferring movements, and (3) tool-mediated actions. Manipulation actions could not be classified or planned to meet the control variable standards and were not considered in this experiment. Reaching movements and transferring movements are a fundamental component of functional movements required for daily life. The actions selected in this experiment are highly correlated with human independent motor ability, which is helpful to extract upper limb synergies. The focus was on reaching and transferring movements. Literature [13] used the extreme position and control variable method, they obtained the workspace that the forearm could achieve. Based on the initial sitting position, daily actions in the upper limb motion space were selected to obtain eight target actions for the first category. According to the literature [14–16], hand grasping actions were classified into 16 types based on features such as finger involvement and the size and shape of the grasped object. According to the grasping action and sitting action, seven target actions were selected for the second category. The specific classification is shown in Fig. 3.

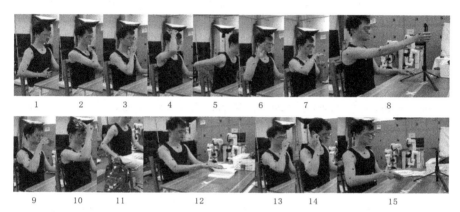

Fig. 3. Experimental action paradigm. 1 Touch the belly; 2 Touch left shoulder; 3 Make a quiet sign; 4 Touch the head; 5 Touch the back of waist; 6 Greet; 7 Make a pause sign; 8 Touch the front of chest; 9 Drink water; 10 Wear a hat; 11 Lift a bag; 12 Turn a page; 13 Eat food; 14 Ring up; 15 Put a plate.

Initial State: The sitting position was selected as the initial position with the palms facing down and naturally placed on the table. To reduce the motion errors caused by body size, the distance between the front chest and the table was the length of the subject's forearm, as shown in Fig. 4.

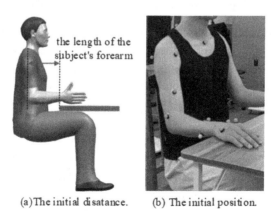

(a)The initial disatance.   (b) The initial position.

Fig. 4. Experimental Initial state. (a) The initial distance. (b) The initial position.

Experimental Process: Starting from the initial state, the subjects completed the actions sequentially according to the order shown in Fig. 4(b). After completing each target action, the initial state was restored as one set of data. 15 experimental actions were repeated 10 times for each subject as the experimental data for one person. The experiment did not strictly specify the time, but to prevent subject fatigue, there was at least a 5-s pause between each action.

Experimental Subjects: 10 healthy adults with a dominant right hand participated in this experiment. The anthropometric data of the subjects are shown in Table 1. Before the experiment, each subject was informed of the experimental content.

Table 1. Body size data of subjects in experiments with different task objectives.

Number	Height	Arm length	Forearm length	Upper arm length	Shoulder breadth
1	180 cm	62 cm	29 cm	30 cm	42 cm
2	174 cm	73 cm	26 cm	29 cm	47 cm
3	175 cm	72 cm	28 cm	33 cm	45 cm
4	187 cm	75 cm	30 cm	26 cm	47 cm
5	175 cm	73 cm	29 cm	25 cm	29 cm
6	179 cm	72 cm	29 cm	25 cm	34 cm
7	173 cm	70 cm	27 cm	24 cm	31 cm
8	178 cm	75 cm	30 cm	27 cm	30 cm
9	183 cm	75 cm	31 cm	26 cm	30 cm
10	167 cm	68 cm	25 cm	25 cm	28 cm

3.2 Experimental Setup of Upper Limb Movements Under Different Loads

Before the experiment, the Vicon system and marker positions remained unchanged.

Experimental Equipment: The experiment used 0.5 kg, 1 kg, and 2 kg dumbbells as loads. The dumbbells were placed in a briefcase as loads, as shown in Fig. 5. The empty briefcase without added dumbbells was considered No. 1. Subsequently, 0.5 kg was added each time. The maximum mass of the load equipment was 4 kg, and it was numbered 2 to 9 in sequence for record keeping.

Experimental Subjects: 10 healthy adults with right-handed dominance aged 22 to 26 years were informed of the experimental content in advance, shown in Table 2.

Experimental Process: Experimental Action 11 was selected from the experimental actions in Sects. 3.1. In order to ensure that the motion trajectory of the entire experimental movement was relatively consistent, the experimental route was required to be the same, and the initial point, end point and key way points of the entire movement process were set in advance on the reference object and remain unchanged. To reduce

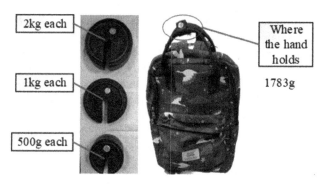

Fig. 5. Load equipment.

Table 2. Body size data of subjects in experiments with different loads.

Number	Height	Arm length	Forearm length	Upper arm length	Shoulder breadth
1	180 cm	62 cm	29 cm	30 cm	42 cm
2	174 cm	73 cm	26 cm	29 cm	47 cm
3	175 cm	72 cm	28 cm	33 cm	45 cm
4	187 cm	75 cm	30 cm	26 cm	47 cm
5	176 cm	74 cm	29 cm	28 cm	46 cm
6	184 cm	75 cm	28 cm	30 cm	46 cm
7	173 cm	70 cm	27 cm	24 cm	31 cm
8	178 cm	75 cm	30 cm	27 cm	30 cm
9	182 cm	74 cm	31 cm	27 cm	30 cm
10	168 cm	69 cm	25 cm	26 cm	28 cm

errors introduced by the subject's body size, the subject's hands were naturally placed on the knees as the initial state. The initial point (or end point) of the load device was in front of the subject's feet. During the experiment, the subject needed to move the load device to the right side of their body. Placing both hands back on the knees was considered a complete experimental action. The subjects with nine different loads to completed specified experimental actions. Each load was repeated 10 times as the data for one person.

4 Analysis of the Influence Factors and the Corresponding Effects on Motion Synergies

By coordinate transformation and Euler angle inverse solution on the collected experimental data, seven-degree-of-freedom joint angle data were obtained. PCA was used to respectively extract the coordination rules of seven DoFs and five DoFs in multi-joint upper limb motion, obtaining changes in motion synergies classified by action type. Through similarity comparison and cluster analysis of the synergies obtained, the main factors influencing the synergies were found to be the overall process of the action, the grasping situations of the hand, and the complexity of the actions in the experiment.

The load was selected as a further object of study to explore the synergies of multi-degree-of-freedom upper limb motion. Based on the synergies of the seven DoFs of upper limb motion, the synergies implied in the five DoFs of upper limb motion was explored in depth. The similarity between synergies was analyzed to reveal the influencing factors of multi-degree-of-freedom synergy motion of the upper limbs under different loads.

4.1   Analysis of Motion Synergies Under Multi-task Objectives

A total of 14 Marker points are selected in the experiment, and the data are recorded in each frame corresponds to the coordinates of the Marker points at that moment. The original data matrix x_i at moment i can be expressed as:

$$x_i = [x_{i,1}, x_{i,2}, x_{i,3}, \cdots, x_{i,3\times n}], n = 14 \qquad (10)$$

where $[x_{i,3\times j-2}, x_{i,3\times j-1}x_{i,3\times j}]$ represents the coordinate values of the j-th Marker at moment i. Three coordinate systems are formed by 14 points (every 3–4 points form one), corresponding to shoulder joint, elbow joint and wrist joint, respectively.

A single action is repeated m times, then the data set X is represented as:

$$X = \begin{bmatrix} x_1 \\ x_2 \\ \vdots \\ x_m \end{bmatrix} \qquad (11)$$

The joint angular displacement data of the upper limbs are obtained according to the calculation in multi-task objective experiments, and the motion state is represented by the angular displacement corresponding to each moment of freedom to obtain the state matrix y_i at moment i:

$$y_i = [y_{i,1}, y_{i,2}, \cdots, y_{i,n}], n = 7 \qquad (12)$$

where $y_{i,j}$ represents the angular displacement of the j-th joint degree of freedom at the i-th moment, with m sampling points in one sampling. The state data after the k-th sampling is represented as:

$$Y_k = \begin{bmatrix} y_1 \\ y_2 \\ \vdots \\ y_k \end{bmatrix} \qquad (13)$$

Then, the state data for PCA:

$$Y = \begin{bmatrix} y_1 \\ y_2 \\ \vdots \\ y_m \end{bmatrix} \approx \begin{bmatrix} \eta_{1,1} & \eta_{1,2} & \cdots & \eta_{1,h} \\ \eta_{2,1} & \eta_{2,2} & \cdots & \eta_{2,h} \\ \vdots & \vdots & \ddots & \vdots \\ \eta_{m,1} & \eta_{m,2} & \cdots & \eta_{m,h} \end{bmatrix} \begin{bmatrix} \alpha_1 \\ \alpha_2 \\ \vdots \\ \alpha_h \end{bmatrix} + \overline{Y}, h \le n \qquad (14)$$

where the matrix $\alpha_i = \begin{bmatrix} \delta_{i,1} & \delta_{i,2} & \cdots & \delta_{i,n} \end{bmatrix}$ denotes the correspondence between the i-th PC and the joint DoFs, and η_i denotes the corresponding weights of the selected PC at moment i.

A widely view is that the upper limbs have seven DoFs. In practical applications, if seven DoFs motion synergies are used for control, the overall fault tolerance rate of the system will be low due to the characteristics of the synergies themselves (variance ratio less than 100%). If the mechanism design is directly based on the synergies of the seven DoFs of the upper limbs, there will always be deviation between the mechanical structure and the target position after the completion of the movement, and the lack of additional adjustment ability will not be able to achieve the work goal for the mechanism. Therefore, the collaborative cognition of the upper limb movement focuses on the three DoFs of the shoulder joint and the two DoFs of the elbow joint, and the wrist joint can be independently designed to consider the wrist separately and analyze the synergies of five DoFs of the upper limbs.

Considering that the seven DoFs in the upper limbs have a calibration effect, the seven DoFs were first analyzed. The variance ratios were calculated according to the numbering in the experiment, as shown in Fig. 6.

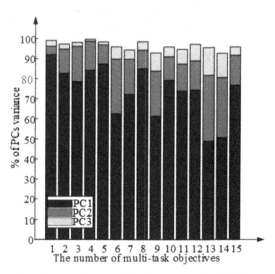

Fig. 6. Variance ratios of seven-degree-of-freedom synergies in 15 groups of movements.

A variance ratio of 80% is used as the criterion for judging whether the synergies can effectively reproduce the motion. It can be seen that the variance ratio of the first synergies fluctuate greatly, with a minimum of 45.15% and a maximum of 92.05%, indicating that the first synergies can directly replace the motion process of the corresponding group. In 15 groups of actions, the variance ratio of 5 groups is greater than 80%, indicating that at least the first synergies can be used to explain most of the motion information in these 5 groups of actions. When the first 2 synergies (the first and second synergies) are selected, the minimum variance ratio is 83.71% and the maximum is 98.57%. When the first 3 synergies are selected, the maximum variance ratio reached 99.63%, close to 100%. This means that in the seven DoFs upper limb motion, at least the first two synergies can be selected to effectively reconstruct the motion information of most actions. Judging from the range of variance ratios, the maximum difference between transferring movements and reaching movements, that is, whether the hand grasps or not, will affect the motion synergies of the upper limbs. It is speculated that the contraction of hand muscles affects the upper limb motion.

Compared with seven DoFs, five DoFs of the upper limbs omitted two DoFs: wrist flexion/extension and wrist abduction/adduction.

The motion data of five DoFs were grouped according to the actions to calculate the synergies and variance ratios, as shown in Fig. 7(a). At this time, a variance ratio exceeding 80% requires at least the first two synergies. For the first three synergies, the variance ratio of about 1/2 of the actions exceeded 99%, close to 100%. When high precision is required in applications, the first three synergies can be considered to reproduce motion. The variance ratios of the first three synergies of the five DoFs were compared with those of the seven DoFs, as shown in Fig. 7(b). In reaching movements, the variance ratios of the first three synergies are relatively close in numerical values and trends, indicating that the wrist has little effect on the synergies. In transferring movements, the trends remained close, but significant differences appeared in the numerical values in the latter half of the transferring movements. Combined with the differences between reaching movements and transferring movements, it is speculated that such differences will

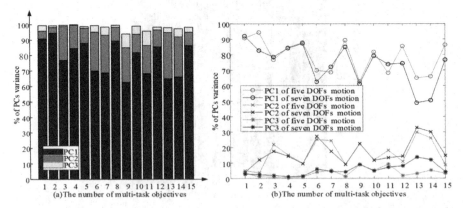

Fig. 7. (a) Variance ratios of the five-degree-of-freedom synergies in 15 sets of movements; (b) Schematic diagram of the variance ratios of the first three synergies in seven and five DoFs.

become more apparent when hand movements increase. Comparing the data of seven DoFs and five DoFs shows that wrist movements do affect motion synergies. However, according to the changes in the variance ratio of the first type of action, the influence of wrist movements is limited.

The distribution of the first synergies shows that in addition to the differences between reaching movements and transferring movements, there is another factor affecting the motion synergies. Similarity comparison and cluster analysis using the first synergies are shown in Fig. 8.

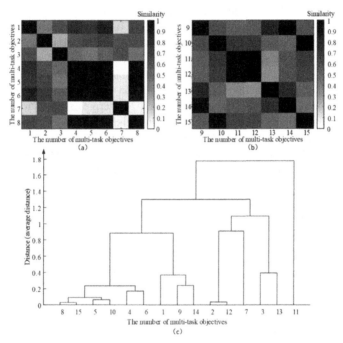

Fig. 8. (a) The similarity of first synergies in arrival action; (b) The similarity of first synergies in delivery action; (c) The clustering grouping results of first synergies.

According to the similarity in Fig. 8(a) and 8(b), it is not difficult to find that there are indeed influencing factors that cause differences in the synergies of the same type of actions, not just different variance ratios. The 15 groups of actions are grouped according to the first synergies, using the average distance as the grouping basis, shown in Fig. 8(c). According to the grouping results, the first synergies with the shortest distance do not necessarily belong to the same type of action, such as actions 8 and 15. Action 8 is a reaching movement and action 15 is a transferring movement. The common point between the two actions is that the hand passes through roughly the same position, that is, the overall action process is roughly the same. Within the experiments, the first element of the synergies is the action process without the hand. In addition, whether the hand participates in grasping and the specific requirements of the action will have a certain impact, with a relatively lower impact. However, the degree of influence of the latter two lacks a comparison with control variables, and cannot be compared for the time being.

4.2 Analysis of Motion Synergies with Different Loads

In the load experiment, the external load mass was changed as the experimental independent variable to find the changes in motion synergies caused by changes in load mass. The synergies of seven DoFs motion of the upper limbs have not been widely used. Only preliminary cognition of seven DoFs is enough. The five DoFs motion has a wider application and needs to be calculated and analyzed from a mathematical level.

The motion of seven DoFs of the upper limbs can be effectively reconstructed using the first 2 synergies. Similarly, when the load changed, the synergies under 9 different loads were calculated in sequence. The variance ratios of the first 3 synergies under 9 different loads is shown in Fig. 9. The minimum variance ratio of the first 3 synergies is 84.25%. In addition, the first 2 synergies reach a reproduction rate of 80% in 6 conditions of 9 different loads. Therefore, the first 3 synergies are selected to represent the corresponding motion. The empty equipment weighs 1783 g. For each load group, the load increased by 500 g. Based on the first group, the second, fourth and eighth groups had the largest differences according to the total variance of the first 3 synergies. In terms of mass difference, except for the second group, the total mass of the other two groups was close to twice the total mass of the first group. It is speculated that the influence of motion synergies of two groups is related to the relative difference between different loads.

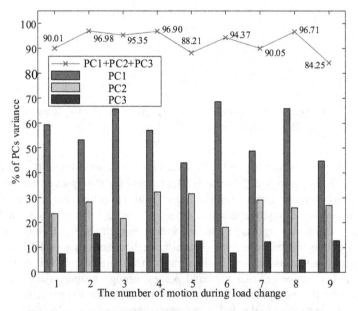

Fig. 9. Variance ratios of the first three synergies in seven DoFs.

The synergies of five DoFs of the upper limbs have a wide range of applications. An analysis of variance ratios was carried out. Groups were made according to load as the independent variable to calculate the corresponding synergies and variance ratios for each group.

The data under different task goals shows that the first 3 synergies of the five DoFs upper limb motion can reconstruct more than 90% of the information (the minimum value of group SA is 94.3197%). With 80% as the limit, only the first 2 synergies are required. According to different loads, the corresponding PCs were extracted, as shown in Fig. 10. The total variance ratio of the first 2 synergies reaches an average of 90.1122%, with a maximum of 96.1502% and a minimum of 82.8141%, exceeding 80%. This means that for occasions where high accuracy is not required, the first 2 synergies can be directly used to represent the motion under the corresponding load. For the first 3 synergies, the average variance ratio is 96.1722%, with a minimum of 91.2507%, exceeding 90%. This means that under a single load, the first 2 synergies can achieve effective reconstruction of motion, and the first 3 synergies further increase the degree of reconstruction. Further consideration will be given to the specific situation of synergies between joints under different loads.

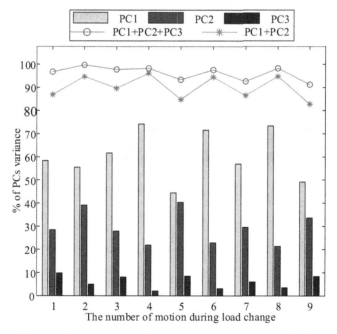

Fig. 10. Variance ratios of the first three synergies in five DoFs.

Pearson's coefficient is used to compare the similarity of the first 3 synergies under different loads, as shown in Fig. 11(a–c). The mean similarity of the first synergies is 0.7750, the second synergies is 0.7943, and the third synergies is 0.5876. In the first and second synergies, the similarity between most groups fluctuates around 0.70, indicating that the synergies under different loads are still close. However, the low similarity in the third synergies means that the synergies that supplements information show differences. When the load changed, the adjustment method adopted by the limbs deviated.

In the synergies of five DoFs motion, the first to fifth elements correspond to shoulder abduction/adduction, shoulder internal/external rotation, shoulder flexion/extension, elbow pronation/supination and elbow flexion/extension respectively. According to the correspondence between the coefficients in the coordinate system and the DoFs of the joints, the elements of the synergies were divided into two groups (1–3 and 4–5), forming a three-dimensional vector in the shoulder joint coordinate system and a two-dimensional vector in the elbow joint coordinate system. The length of the vector represents the degree to which the shoulder joint and elbow joint participate in the motion in the synergies. Since the synergies were standardized during calculation, the square of the vector modulus was used as a quantitative description of the proportion of the shoulder and elbow joints in the synergies, as shown in Fig. 11(d–e).

As shown in the three curves in Fig. 11, the degree of participation of the shoulder and elbow joints in the first synergies is relatively small, and the variation was small under low loads. It is believed that the first group of synergies is relatively stable when the load changed. Supplementary to the first synergies, the shoulder joint accounts for the main motion in the second synergies. Initially, the proportion of the shoulder joint is almost 1. However, the conclusions of the first and the second synergies do not apply to the third synergies. The third synergies supplements the motion reconstruction ability of

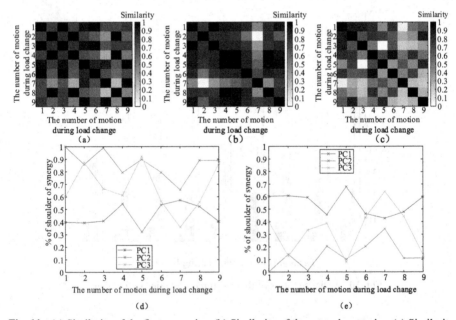

Fig. 11. (a) Similarity of the first synergies; (b) Similarity of the second synergies; (c) Similarity of the third synergies; (d) Percentage of shoulder joints in the first three synergies; (e) Percentage of elbow joints in the first three synergies. In (d) and (e), number 1 represents mass 0. Number 2 represents mass 0.5 kg. Each cell is increased by 0.5 kg. The number 9 represents maximum mass 4.0 kg.

the first two groups of synergies. It has a smaller variance ratio than the second synergies and is of less importance, belonging to secondary motion.

The muscles involved in a single motion are roughly unchanged. When the load exceeds a certain range, the physical properties (contraction rate, etc.) of the muscles differ from each other. Considering only the load factor, the properties of the muscles themselves change, and the degree of difference between the muscles also changes. As one of the factors affecting motion synergies, changes in the contraction rate of different muscles will lead to changes in synergies. In this experiment, since the loads affect all participating muscles, the final synergies changes significantly under the influence of muscles on each other.

5   Conclusion

To explore the synergies between the multi-degree-of-freedom movements of the upper limbs, starting from the daily functional activities of the human upper limbs, the upper limb movements were classified according to the workspace and hand grasp. Experimental paradigms were designed. According to the experimental data, the joint motion angles were calculated, and the synergies of the seven DoFs and five DoFs multi-joint movements of the upper limbs were extracted by PCA, respectively. Analysis of the synergies showed that the main factor affecting the synergies under multiple task goals was the movement path of the distal end of the upper limbs. To explore the synergies of upper limb movements under different loads, an upper limb movement experiment with different load masses under a single action was designed. Based on the synergies between the seven DoFs movements of the upper limbs, the synergies contained in the five DoFs movements of the upper limbs were further explored. The similarity between synergies was analyzed to reveal the influencing factors of multi-degree-of-freedom synergy movements of upper limbs under different loads. Loads change the properties of muscles and the differences between muscle group properties, thereby affecting the synergies of upper limb movements. The experimental results show that loads lead to changes in motion synergies.

Acknowledgements. This research was funded by the National Key R&D Program of China (2020YFC2007800) granded to Huazhong University of Science and Technology, and the National Natural Science Foundation of China (52005191).

References

1. Bernstein, N.A.: The Coordination and Regulation of Movements. Pergamon Press, New York (1967)
2. De Looze, M.P., Bosch, T., Krause, F., Stadler, K.S., O'sullivan, L.: Exoskeletons for industrial application and their potential effects on physical work load. Ergonomics **59**(5), 671–681 (2016)
3. Plaza, A., Hernandez, M., Puyuelo, G., Garces, E., Garcia, E.: Lower-limb medical and rehabilitation exoskeletons: a review of the current designs. IEEE Rev. Biomed. Eng. **16**, 278–291 (2021)

4. Bockemühl, T., Troje, N.F., Dürr, V.: Inter-joint coupling and joint angle synergies of human catching movements. Hum. Mov. Sci. **29**(1), 73–93 (2010)
5. Averta, G., Valenza, G., Catrambone, V., Barontini, F., Scilingo, E.P., Bicchi, A.: On the time-invariance properties of upper limb synergies. IEEE Trans. Neural Syst. Rehabil. Eng. **27**(7), 1397–1406 (2019)
6. Huang, B., Xiong, C., Chen, W., Liang, J., Sun, B.Y., Gong, X.: Common kinematic synergies of various human locomotor behaviours. R Soc Open Sci. **8**(4), 210161 (2021)
7. Jarque-Bou, N.J., Vergara, M., Sancho-Bru, J.L., Gracia-Ibanez, V., Roda-Sales, A.: Hand kinematics characterization while performing activities of daily living through kinematics reduction. IEEE Trans. Neural Syst. Rehabil. Eng. **28**(7), 1556–1565 (2020)
8. Wang, K., Li, J., Shen, H.: Inverse dynamics of a 3-DOF parallel mechanism based on analytical forward kinematics. Chin. J. Mech. Eng. **35**(05), 307–316 (2022)
9. Hotelling, H.: Analysis of a complex of statistical variables into principal components. Columbia Uni. **24**(6), 417–431 (1933)
10. Dominici, N., Ivanenko, Y.P., Cappellini, G., d'Avella, A., Mondi, V., et al.: Locomotor primitives in newborn babies and their development. Science **334**(6058), 997–999 (2011)
11. Johnson, R.A., Wichern, D.W.: Applied Multivariate Statistical Analysis. Sixth Edition, pp. 524–542 (2008)
12. Johnson, S.C.: Hierarchical clustering schemes. Psychometrika **32**(3), 241–254 (1967)
13. Abdel-Malek, K., Yang, J., Brand, R., Tanbour, E.: Towards understanding the workspace of human limbs. Ergonomics **47**(13), 1386–405 (2004)
14. Santello, M., Flanders, M., Soechting, J.F.: Postural hand synergies for tool use. J. Neurosci. **18**(23), 10105–10115 (1998)
15. Lenarcic, J., Umek, A.: Student member: simple model of human arm reachable workspace. IEEE Trans. Syst., Man, Cybern. **24**(8), 1239–1246 (1994)
16. Kyota, F., Saito, S.: Fast grasp synthesis for various shaped objects. In: Computer Graphics Forum, vol. 31. Wiley, Hoboken (2012)

Design and Development of Wearable Upper Limb Soft Robotics for Load Lifting Task Assistance

Sibo Cheng[1], Huaiyu Na[1], Kaifeng Zheng[1], Haopeng Ou[1], Ning Jia[2], Xingda Qu[1], and Xinyao Hu[1(✉)]

[1] Institute of Human Factors and Ergonomics, College of Mechatronics and Control Engineering, Shenzhen University, Shenzhen, China
huxinyao@szu.edu.cn
[2] Chinese Center for Disease Control and Prevention, National Institute of Occupational Health and Poison Control, Beijing, China

Abstract. Work-related musculoskeletal disorders (WMSDs) pose a significant concern in several industries, especially those involving manual or repetitive tasks. Wearable assistive robotics technology has emerged as a potential solution to prevent WMSDs. Current exoskeletons are bulky and heavy, have certain drawbacks that can limit their effectiveness. Alternatively, soft robotics technology provides a non-invasive, ergonomic, and adaptable approach. This paper introduced the design and development of wearable soft robotic system aiming for load lifting task assistance. The system design, Pneumatic Artificial Muscles (PAMs) design, and wearable design aspects were presented. A preliminary system evaluation test was carried out. The results indicate that this system is effective in reducing the muscle activities. Therefore, it can be potentially used for preventing muscle fatigue around shoulder joint, under repetitive and load-carrying work tasks.

Keywords: Wearable robotics · Soft robot · Upper limb augmentation · Ergonomics

1 Introduction

Work-related musculoskeletal disorders (WMSDs) pose a significant concern in several industries, especially those involving manual or repetitive tasks. Such disorders can lead to chronic pain, reduced productivity, and increased healthcare expenses. Upper limb disorders have been reported as the most common type of WMSD, with prevalence rates ranging from 41.5% to 76.8% across different countries and industries [1–3].

Wearable assistive robotics technology has emerged as a potential solution to prevent WMSDs [4]. However, exoskeletons, which are bulky and heavy, have certain drawbacks that can limit their effectiveness. They can restrict joint motion, require a power source, and be uncomfortable to wear for long periods of time, leading to skin irritations and

---

S. Cheng and H. Na—Contributed equally to this work.

© The Author(s), under exclusive license to Springer Nature Singapore Pte Ltd. 2023
H. Yang et al. (Eds.): ICIRA 2023, LNAI 14268, pp. 451–460, 2023.
https://doi.org/10.1007/978-981-99-6486-4_39

pressure sores. Although exoskeletons can reduce users' acute physical stress, their long-term impact on workers' health remains unclear [5].

Alternatively, soft robotics technology provides a non-invasive, ergonomic, and adaptable approach to assist human body movements. Wearable soft robotics use materials that match the human musculoskeletal system's modulus, enabling natural movements without impeding performance. Actuation is usually achieved pneumatically, making it safe for human interaction. Additionally, wearable robotics structures can be customized for better fitting to human body segments. Soft robotics have been designed to assist with shoulder movements [6], upper limb flexion [7], and wrist flexion [8]. However, previous studies have mainly focused on assisting individuals with limited mobility or rehabilitation, with no exclusive focus on designing wearable soft robotics to support body areas during occupational settings for WMSD prevention.

The development and implementation of soft robotic technology have the potential to revolutionize occupational health and safety, providing a practical and cost-effective solution for preventing and managing WMSDs. However, this potential is yet to explore. This study presents the initial prototype of a wearable soft robotic that aims to assist healthy individuals in work environments. The system includes untethered pneumatic-powered assistive components, mounted on an on-shelf protective jacket designed to transmit forces efficiently while ensuring user comfort. The exosuit can support users during both isometric and dynamic tasks with the aid of a wearable inertial measurement unit (IMU) sensing system. The effectiveness of this exosuit is evidenced by the considerable reduction in user muscular activity and fatigue observed in the experiments.

2 Materials and Methods

2.1 System Design

System Overview
This wearable soft robotic system is designed to provide assistive torque when people are performing manual load-lifting tasks. The system overview is depicted in Fig. 1. A on-shelf textile-based protective jacket was implemented as the basis of the wearable system. This protective jacket was originally designed for motorcyclist protection. It has plastic pads designed at different body parts for protective purposes. Those plastic pads allow the pneumatic artificial muscles (PAMs) to be firmly anchored on designed locations. On top of them, customized anchor structures and reinforcing layer are designed to allow the assistive forces generated by the PAMs to be effectively transferred to the human body. Four customized McKibben PAMs were used for actuation. They are powered by a portable pneumatic control system which consists a miniature air compressor, a customized air tank, an embedded control system, and a battery. Three customized inertial measurement units (IMUs) were used for body motion sensing and providing real-time input signals for system control. The entire system is powered by a 24 V lithium batteries. The entire system has the weight of 4.25 kg. The assistive part only weights 2.55 kg (protective jacket = 1.3 kg, battery = 0.4 kg). The cost of the entire system is approximately 700 RMB (100 USD).

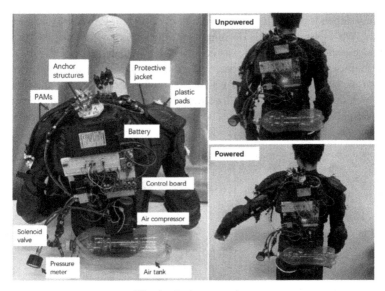

Fig. 1. System overview

Pneumatic Artificial Muscles (PAMs)

The PAMs are responsible to generate the assistive forces. A McKibben design was chosen because it is by far the most widely used and low-cost PAM solution [9]. This kind of PAM can deform according to pressure change and provide linear assistive force at the should joint. The design and manufacture of the PAM are shown in Fig. 2(a) and (b). There are four design factors that can affect the generated force, including the length of the PAM, the outer-shell materials, the inter-tube diameter, and the changes in air pressure. The length of the PAM was designed as 30 cm each, based on the anthropometric shoulder and upper arm data of Chinese adult males. To test the rest designing factors, six different PAM designs, including two outer-shell materials, i.e., the metal mesh and the nylon mesh, and three inter-tube diameters, $\phi18$ mm, $\phi16$ mm, $\phi12$ mm (Fig. 2(c)), were tested under different pressure levels ranged from 0–0.026 MPa. The testing results were shown in Fig. 2(d). The results show that the metal outer shell with the inter-tube diameters of $\phi18$ mm has the highest force-pressure ratio. It can generate approximately 50 N (note that this is up to the measurement limits of the force gauge used in the experiment) at the air pressure level of 0.12 MPa. However, the metal mesh deformed suffered unevenly during the testing experiment. It also resulted in abrupt changes in the PAM deformation which could potentially have a negative effect on the PAM control. Therefore, the nylon outer shell with the inter-tube diameters of $\phi18$ mm was chosen. The test also shows that when the air pressure is increased beyond 0.2 MPa, it had only a small effect on the PAM deformation and assistive forces. Therefore, the pressure level was set at 0.2 MPa for further application.

Wearable Design

One major design concern of this wearable robotic system is to allow the PAMs to provide ergonomically correct assistance to the user while they are performing the lifting task.

This mainly depends on the layout regarding how different PAMs are anchored on the body parts. We adopted a bionic design where three PAMs were designed to simulate the deltoid muscle, and one PAM was designed to simulate the musculi supraspinatus since these muscle groups are involved and prone to injuries during load-lifting tasks. The layout of those PAMs locations was determined based on some preliminary tests, during which different PAM anchor locations were tested and their combined assistive effects were observed and optimized. The finalized design was shown in Fig. 3.

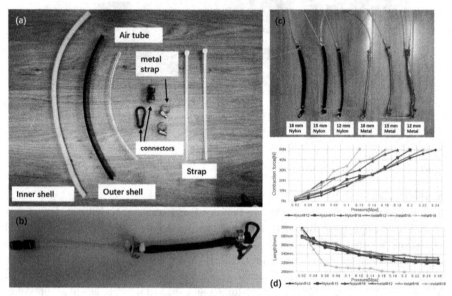

Fig. 2. (a) The components of the PAM; (b) the manufactures PAM; (c) six different PAM designs; (d) the contraction forces and changes in lengths for different PAM designs.

Another design concern is whether the force generated by the PAMs can be effectively transferred to the human body. To solve this problem, customized and 3D-printed anchor structures were made to allow the PAMs to be firmly anchored at the designed locations. The details of those anchor structures are depicted in Fig. 4. However, when the anchor structures were mounted directly on the textile-based cloth, part of the force generated by the PAMs can still be absorbed by the textile material and demise the assistive impact. To minimize such effect, a carbon-fiber reinforcing layer (300 mm × 100 mm × 0.5 mm) was designed and connected with the textile-based cloth, where the anchor structures can be mounted on (Fig. 5(a)). The anchor structures are fixed onto the reinforcing layer on the protective suit with M3 screws and nuts. A 12 mm-diameter U-shaped pipe buckle was used to align the PAMs. Finally, in order to ensure that the arm can be effectively pulled up, a customized splint structure (length 150 mm, width 90 mm) is designed. The structure can be fixed through four nylon straps with a width of 20 mm. A magnetic snap on its lower part makes it easy to wear through the arm. Sponges are used at the inner side to improve the comfortability (Fig. 5(b)).

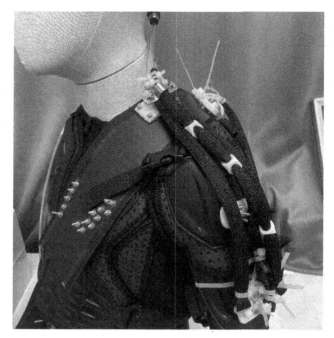

Fig. 3. PAMs placement

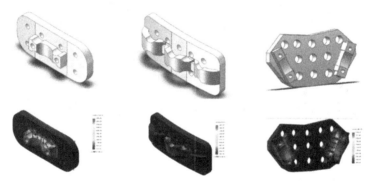

Fig. 4. Design of anchor structure. The finite element analysis results (below) show that the expected stress will not be beyond the stress limitation of the design materials.

The final design concern is the system's portability and wearability. The portability largely depends on the air source. Given that the required air pressure level is 0.2 MPa, a miniature air compressor was used which can provide instant air pressure up to 0.25 MPa. However, this type of air compressor is limited by its airflow speed. Therefore, an air tank is necessary to provide continuous air pressure. Two air tank designs were tested, including an on-shelf stainless air tank (500 ml) and a low-cost plastic air tank (500 ml) made from a disposable drink bottle (Fig. 6). They were both pumped and tested under repeated PAM deformation conditions to examine their capability to retain

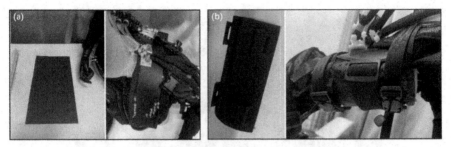

Fig. 5. (a) Design and implementation of the carbon-fiber reinforcing layer to assist the force transfer; (b) design and implementation of the splint structure to support the arm lifting

the air pressure level. The results show that the PAM deformation will decrease after repeated deformation cycles. However, the low-cost plastic air tank has a much lower decreasing rate compared to the stainless air tank, indicating a better air pressure level capability. Besides that, the plastic air tank is much lower cost. Therefore, the plastic air tank is chosen. Since the plastic air tank is also very light. A two-liter Coca-Cola drink bottle was used for further application. It can provide sufficient input air into the pneumatic system.

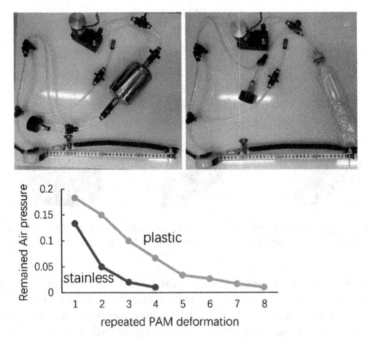

Fig. 6. Comparison of different air tank design

Sensing and Control

The schematic diagram for the sensing and control system is shown in Fig. 7. The control is electrical control is divided into two modules: the pneumatic control module and the sensor module. The sensor module utilizes the BNO-055 9-axis IMU sensor for posture detection. The pneumatic control module uses the ESP32 system on chip (SOC) as the main control chip. It receives commands and changes the GPIO pin levels. Through the gate driver circuit connected to the MOSFET, it controls the solenoid valves to achieve pneumatic control. The entire system is connected to a WiFi network generated by the same router, ensuring that all devices are within the same local area network (LAN).

Three IMUs were installed on the waist, lower arm and wrist respectively to estimate the arm lifting angle. When the Angle was detected to reach the threshold value, the electromagnetic valve was opened, the pneumatic muscle was shortened, and the anchoring device was pulled to raise the arm.

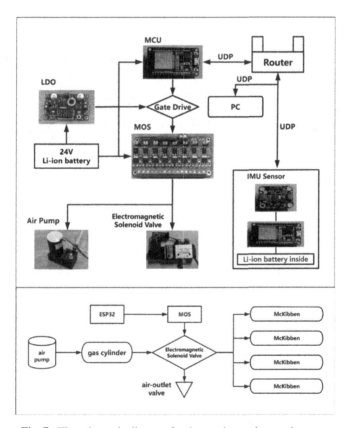

Fig. 7. The schematic diagram for the sensing and control system

2.2 System Evaluation

In order to verify the effect of this system on reducing the muscle fatigue, EMG sensors were used to monitor muscle activities of supraspinatus muscle, posterior deltoid muscle bundle, middle deltoid muscle bundle and anterior deltoid muscle bundle. In order to strengthen the fit between the EMG sensor and the human body, conductive adhesive is used to enhance the conductivity after the EMG sensor is installed on the human body, and binding is used to tighten the fixation to prevent falling off and strengthen the fit between the sensor and the human body (Fig. 8).

Two load-lifting conditions were tested, including arm lifting without additional weight and arm lifting with 2 kg weight. During the test, the participant was sitting upright and lift the weight with the arm sideways (Fig. 8).

The EMG signals generated under the testing conditions were compared. The hypothesis to be tested is that with the assistance of this wearable soft robotic system, the muscle activities of the corresponding muscle groups can be reduced.

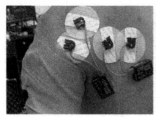

Fig. 8. The experiment set-up.

3   Results and Discussion

The EMG results under different testing conditions were shown in Fig. 9. The results show that the muscle activities were different between arm lifting without additional weight and arm lifting with 2 kg weight. It is clear that additional load-carrying requires higher muscle contractions. The EMG amplitudes for all tested muscle groups reduced significantly when the wearable robot is providing assistive force. Such reduction can be found in both testing conditions.

The results indicate that the robotic system is effective in reducing the muscle activities. Therefore, it can be potentially used for preventing muscle fatigue around shoulder joint, under repetitive and load-carrying work tasks.

The objective of this study is to introduce a novel wearable soft robotic system that aims to provide assistance in load lifting tasks. The system design encompassed the conceptualization and realization of the wearable soft robotic system. Detailed considerations were given to the overall structure, key components arrangement, and control system. By integrating robotic technologies and employing ergonomic principles, a robust and efficient system was devised to effectively assist users in load lifting tasks.

This study highlights the potential of soft robotics in preventing work-related musculoskeletal disorders. The detrimental impact of work-related musculoskeletal disorders on workers' health and productivity is well-documented. This study shows how soft robotic systems can be leveraged to alleviate the strain on the musculoskeletal system during occupational activities.

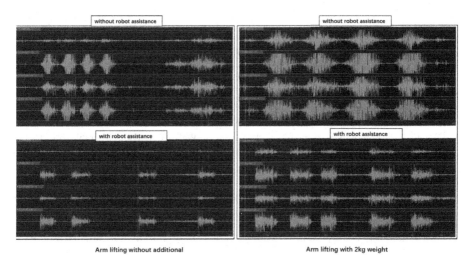

Arm lifting without additional   Arm lifting with 2kg weight

Fig. 9. Comparison of EMG signals under different testing conditions. The different color lines indicate different muscle groups, including (from the top to the bottom) supraspinatus muscle, posterior deltoid muscle bundle, middle deltoid muscle bundle and anterior deltoid muscle undle. (Color figure online)

4   Conclusion

This paper presents the design and development of a wearable soft robotic system specifically designed to assist in load lifting tasks. The system encompasses various aspects including system design, PAM design, and wearable design considerations. A preliminary evaluation test was conducted to assess the efficacy of the system. The obtained results indicate that this innovative system effectively mitigates muscle activities, thereby demonstrating its potential in alleviating muscle fatigue around the shoulder joint during repetitive and load-carrying work tasks. Further research and refinement of the system are warranted to fully explore its potential benefits in occupational settings.

Acknowledgement. This research is in part supported by the National Key R&D Program - Research on Key Technologies and Intervention Strategies for the Prevention and Control of Work-related Diseases and Occupational Injuries [2022YFC2503205] and the Shenzhen Science and Technology Program [JCYJ20210324093005015].

References

1. Lim, M.C., et al.: Prevalence of upper limb musculoskeletal disorders and its associated risk factors among janitorial workers: a cross-sectional study. Annal. Med. Surg. **73**, 103201 (2021)
2. Okezue, O.C., Anamezie, T.H., Nene, J.J., Okwudili, J.D.: Work-related musculoskeletal disorders among office workers in higher education institutions: a cross-sectional study. Ethiop. J. Health Sci. **30**(5), 715–724 (2020)
3. Govaerts, R., et al.: Prevalence and incidence of work-related musculoskeletal disorders in secondary industries of 21st century Europe: a systematic review and meta-analysis. BMC Musculoskelet. Disord. **22**(1), 751 (2021)
4. De Bock, S., et al.: Benchmarking occupational exoskeletons: an evidence mapping systematic review. Appl. Ergon. **98**, 103582 (2022)
5. Bär, M., Steinhilber, B., Rieger, M.A., Luger, T.: The influence of using exoskeletons during occupational tasks on acute physical stress and strain compared to no exoskeleton - a systematic review and meta-analysis. Appl. Ergon. **94**, 103385 (2021)
6. O'Neill, C.T., Phipps, N.S., Cappello, L., Paganoni, S., Walsh, C.J.: A soft wearable robot for the shoulder: design, characterization, and preliminary testing. In: 2017 International Conference on Rehabilitation Robotics (ICORR), pp. 1672–1678. IEEE (2017)
7. Samper-Escudero, J.L., Gimenez-Fernandez, A., Sánchez-Urán, M.Á., Ferre, M.: A cable-driven exosuit for upper limb flexion based on fibres compliance. IEEE Access **8**, 153297–153310 (2020)
8. Chiaradia, D., Tiseni, L., Xiloyannis, M., Solazzi, M., Masia, L., Frisoli, A.: An assistive soft wrist exosuit for flexion movements with an ergonomic reinforced glove. Front. Robot. AI **7**, 595862 (2021)
9. Chou, C.-P., Hannaford, B.: Measurement and modeling of McKibben pneumatic artificial muscles. IEEE Trans. Robot. Autom. **12**(1), 90–102 (1996)

A Novel Lower Limb Rehabilitation Exoskeleton Combined with Wheelchair

Xinzhili Chen, Dong Yuan, Xiaodong Qin, Jiahong Liu, Minchao Liu, Liugang Zhao, Yiyou Li, Sen Huang, Yao Guo, and Bo Li[✉]

Chongqing University of Technology, Chongqing 400000, NJ, China
libo_doctor@163.com

Abstract. To help people with lower limb weakness or disability rehabilitation, this paper develops a novel system of lower limb rehabilitation exoskeleton combined with wheelchair. The lower limb exoskeleton is set with 6 degrees of freedom including hip joints, knee joints and ankle joints on the basis of human anatomy. The range of rotation angle and torque of each degree of freedom are determined according to human gait analysis. Based on these analyses, we designed the hip, knee and ankle joint structures. To make the exoskeleton combined with wheelchair which was designed according to the Chinese standard of electric powered wheelchair, we designed an integrated mechanism of wheelchair and exoskeleton. Based on the integrated mechanism, a posture transformation mechanism to assist patients change between standing and sitting posture was designed. Embedded control system was established to control the whole system to do posture transformation and gait training. Taking into account the lower limb weakness or disability, we chose passive target tracking control. Finally, we simulated the gait training and posture transformation, which verified that the system could stably perform transformation and walking gait process, and it could effectively track the predetermined trajectory during gait training.

Keywords: Lower-limb Exoskeleton · Wheelchair · Rehabilitation · System Design

1 Introduction

Many people have motor dysfunction of lower limb due to cerebral apoplexy and spinal cord injury. They are difficult to walk, or even only stay in bed. For alleviating these problems and facilitating the independent life of patients, it is important to provide them with safe and reliable assistive devices.

Wheelchair is used as the main auxiliary equipment for patients whose lower limbs is weak or disabled. Patients who use wheelchairs for a long time have less opportunities to exercise their own lower limbs, which leads to paralyze the lower body and decrease physical function, and it is also easy to cause problems such as hip joint pain, pressure ulcers, urolithiasis, and drainage difficulty [1, 2]. To avoid these problems, according to clinical medicine, people with lower limb weakness or disability can compensate or reorganize nerve tissue function, coordinate joint muscles, improve exercise ability, and improve or even restore walking function by properly maintaining standing or even simple walking. Lower limb exoskeleton can help the lower limb disabled people standing and walking.

There are some of commercialized exoskeleton robots including HAL [1, 3], ALEX [4–6], Indego [7, 8], Ekso [9], ReWalk [10–12], all of which have the function of helping people with disabilities to stand and walk. Nevertheless, they cannot provide sufficient stability for patients during walking independently. Long time of gait training will lead to excessive fatigue and difficulty in keeping balance.

In this study, we designed a system of lower limb rehabilitation exoskeleton combined with wheelchair which could meet the necessity of long-time gait training and sitting for rest, and it could also help users to get up and sit down stably without crutches. There is an integrated mechanism to connect the exoskeleton for lower limb rehabilitation with the electric wheelchair for traveling. Based on the mechanism, we established the embedded control system which was used to control the whole system.

2   Mechanism Design

2.1   Lower Limb Exoskeleton Mechanism Design

Overall Mechanism Design. The system of lower limb rehabilitation exoskeleton combined with wheelchair is a wearable robot system for patients with lower limb weakness or disability. The structure of the exoskeleton should be designed based on the anatomic structure of human lower limbs.

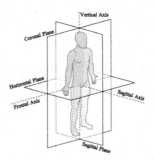

Fig. 1. Human anatomy model.

According to human anatomy, there are three mutually perpendicular reference surfaces and reference axes set on human model (see Fig. 1). Each human lower limb has 8 degrees of freedom (DOF) based on human kinematics, including 3 hip joints, 2 knee joints and 3 ankle joints. Considering that the motion of human lower limbs on the sagittal plane plays an important role during human gait locomotion, we only determined the DOF of the hip, knee and ankle joints on the sagittal plane [13]. The following Table 1 gives the range of locomotion angles of human lower limb joints on the sagittal plane which can be obtained on the basis of motion anatomy.

Table 1. The range of motion angles of human lower limb joints.

Joint	Degrees of freedom	Human range of motion
Hip	Extension/Flexion	120°/30°
Knee	Extension/Flexion	10°/140°
Ankle	Plantarflexion/Dorsiflexion	50°/30°

According to human gait analysis, the gait locomotion during walking shows a periodic law. The trajectory of two lower limbs is similar, and the phase is half a period. This study only analyzes the gait of one lower limb, and obtains the motion data of one leg during lower limb walking according to the standard gait database of the International Society of Biomechanics (see Fig. 2).

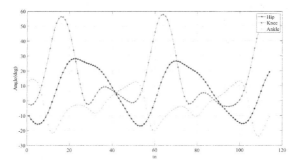

Fig. 2. Lower limb joint rotation angle.

We designed the structure of exoskeleton combined with those data (see Fig. 3). Each leg of the exoskeleton has three rotational DOF (i.e., hip, knee, and ankle) in the sagittal plane. Considering that the patients cannot provide power to move, we set the hip joint and knee joint as active driving joints. For meeting the height of different people, adjustable connecting rods are set near the hip joints and knee joints, and supporting rods are set near the ankle joints, so that the exoskeleton can be adapted to the patients of different anthropometric parameters, and ensure human-machine collaboration. The following Table 2 gives range of locomotion angle of each joint of the exoskeleton which is determined after taking into consideration posture transformation between standing and sitting.

Hip Joint Structure. The hip joint is set at the position between the thigh and connecting rod (see Fig. 3). We installed high torque motors on the hip joints to drive whole lower limb to lift and swing. Through using Opensim to simulate the walking of human model with a height of 180 cm and a weight of 100 kg, we confirmed that the driving torque of the motor cannot lower than 60 Nm (see Fig. 4).

To avoid the motor output shaft directly bearing high torque, we set up a tension spring connected to the motor and the motor mounting (see Fig. 5). A is tension spring fixed end on the motor mounting, B is the wire rope fixed end on the thigh, and the

Table 2. Rotation range of each exoskeleton joint.

Joint	Degrees of freedom	Human range of motion
Hip	Extension/Flexion	110°/20°
Knee	Extension/Flexion	5°/90°
Ankle	Plantarflexion/Dorsiflexion	20°/20°

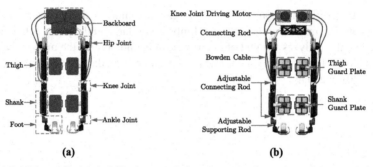

(a)   (b)

Fig. 3. 6-DOF lower limb rehabilitation exoskeleton: (a) The front view of the exoskeleton; (b) The back view of the exoskeleton

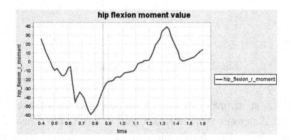

Fig. 4. Torque of hip joint.

distance from point A is the farthest in motion. C and D are respectively the wire rope fixed end positions on the thigh when the leg lifts and swings.

The expansion amount of the tension spring can be obtained by the cosine theorem formula:

$$\Delta L_{life} = L_{AB} - L_{AC} = L_{AB} - \sqrt{R^2 + (L_{AB} - R)^2 - 2R(L_{AB} - R)\cos(180 - \alpha)} \quad (1)$$

$$\Delta L_{swing} = L_{AB} - L_{AD} = L_{AB} - \sqrt{R^2 + (L_{AB} - R)^2 - 2R(L_{AB} - R)\cos(180 - \beta)} \quad (2)$$

where ΔL_{life} and ΔL_{swing} are the stretching amount of the tension spring when the leg is lifted forward and swings backward respectively, L_{AB}, L_{AC} and L_{AD} are the distances of

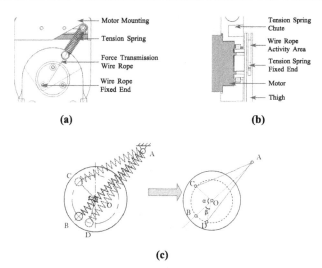

(a)   (b)

(c)

Fig. 5. Gravity compensation device: (a) The front view of the structure; (b) The side sectional view; (c) The geometric simplification diagram of the device.

AB, AC and AD respectively, and R is the rotation radius of the fixed end of the tension spring on the motor.

Knee Joint Structure. To reduce the weight of the exoskeleton the load torque of the hip joint, we designed a Bowden cable to drive mechanism (see Fig. 3 and Fig. 6). There are driving motors of the knee joint set on the back, which is connected with input end spooling wheel. The output end spooling wheel is connected with the knee joint. The installation method of Bowden cable is that wind Bowden cable around the input end and output end spooling wheel, and then pressed in the inner groove by bolts and gaskets. This method can also make the side of the coil pre-wrapped by the input end spooling wheel unwrapped when the motor rotation exceeds the limited range, so that the Bowden cable can break away from the extrusion of the gasket and prevent the knee joint from exceeding the limited angle, thus protecting the joint.

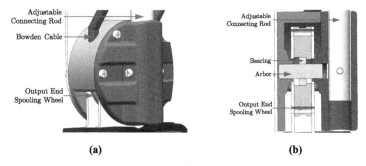

(a)   (b)

Fig. 6. Knee joint structure: (a) Three-dimensional structure; (b) Sectional view.

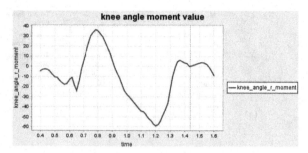

Fig. 7. Knee joint torsion.

On the basis of gait simulation by Opensim, the output shaft torque of the motor which is used to drive knee joint cannot be lower than 58 Nm (see Fig. 7).

Ankle Joint Structure. We set a baffle on the outer shell of the foot component to avoid the ankle joints to rotate over its motion range leading to damage patients. A torsion spring is used to reset the ankle joint, and provide feelings of grip force for patients by its elastic force during walking so that promoting the rehabilitation (see Fig. 8). A rigid material at the bottom of the foot plays a supporting role during gait training. A shoe sleeve produced by flexible material and is hinged on the rigid brace. A buckle is set on the shoe sleeve to locate the foot of patients.

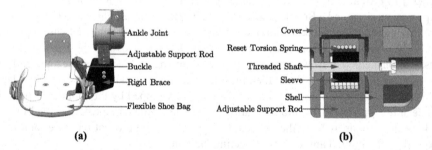

Fig. 8. Foot structure: (a) Three-dimensional diagram of foot structure; (b) Ankle joint sectional view.

2.2 Integrated Wheelchair Mechanism Design

Overall Mechanism. The overall wheelchair mechanism (see Fig. 9) includes the following main mechanisms: an integrated mechanism for combining with the exoskeleton, a posture transformation mechanism for assisting the patient to transform between standing and sitting posture, and a moving mechanism for driving the wheelchair. On the basis of Chinese standard of electric powered wheelchair, we determined these parameters of the wheelchair: its total length is not more than 1200 mm, total width is not more than 700 mm, and total height is not more than 1090 mm.

(a)   **(b)**

Fig. 9. Overall wheelchair mechanism: (a) Three-dimensional diagram of wheelchair mechanism; (b) Side view of wheelchair mechanism.

Integrated Mechanism Design. A combination framework is set on the wheelchair, which can help combine exoskeleton with wheelchair (see Fig. 10). To ensure that the exoskeleton is tightly installed on the wheelchair, we used a spring-loaded release pin to locate the exoskeleton. The center of gravity of the human body will move up and down during walking, so we installed the slide rail on the integrated mechanism and connect the exoskeleton with the slide rail through the shell of spring-loaded release pin to ensure that the center of gravity of the exoskeleton and the human body move synchronously during walking, so as to improve the wearing comfort.

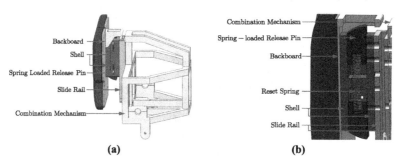

(a)   **(b)**

Fig. 10. Integrated mechanism: (a) The whole mechanism diagram; (b) Sectional view of the part of spring-loaded release pin.

Posture Transformation Mechanism. We designed the posture transformation mechanism trough the combination framework and the linear actuator. The mechanism drives the combination frame to rise and fall through the linear actuator movement, so as to support patients to stand or sit down. The backboad remains vertical during the posture transformation process, so that ensure the patients upper body vertical, reduce psychological pressure on patients, and avoid the safety accident caused by the violent shaking of the upper body.

Figure 11 shows a simplified model diagram of the system when it is transforming the posture. Where the thigh and calf of the exoskeleton are simplified as component 1 and component 2 respectively, the backboard and combination framework of the exoskeleton are simplified as component 3, the wheelchair seat is simplified as component 4, and the linear actuator is simplified as component 5 and component 6.

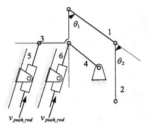

Fig. 11. Principle of posture transformation mechanism between standing and sitting postures.

Moving Mechanism. The moving mechanism (see Fig. 12) is mainly used to drive the wheelchair and carry the weight of the whole system. The whole structure of the mechanism is triangular, which can ensure the stability of the wheelchair. We designed a bearing beam at the rear wheel to distribute the load. To maintain the stability of the wheelchair during travel, we designed a damping mechanism at the rear wheel of the wheelchair to keep at least three wheels remain on the ground. On the basis of the data of rear wheel driving obtained from the motion analysis of SolidWorks (see Fig. 13), we obtained that rear wheel driving torque cannot be less than 17 Nm.

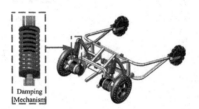

Fig. 12. Moving mechanism.

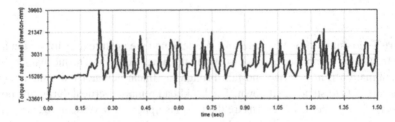

Fig. 13. Moving torque variation of rear wheel motor.

2.3 Overall Mechanism System

Based on the exoskeleton and wheelchair mechanism designed above, we used integrated mechanism to combine them, and then set up the whole overall mechanism of lower limb rehabilitation exoskeleton combined with the wheelchair system (see Fig. 14). The overall mechanism has two types of posture. The posture of setting and standing can be transformed between each other throw the progress shown in Fig. 14(b)).

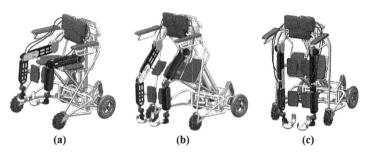

(a)   (b)   (c)

Fig. 14. Overall mechanism of lower limb rehabilitation exoskeleton combined with wheelchair system: (a) Setting posture; (b) Transformation progress; (c) Standing posture.

3 Control System

3.1 Hardware Design

Based on above analysis, we developed the hardware of the embedded control system (see Fig. 15). A STM32F429IGT6 board is served as the embedded controller of the system. The integrated deceleration servo motors MYACTUATOR RMD X6-s2 (rated power of 132 W, maximum torque of 39 Nm, weight of 0.6 kg and nominal speed of 70 rpm) and RMD X10-s2 (rated power of 400 W, maximum torque of 120 Nm, weight of 1.1 kg and nominal speed of 160 rpm) which integrates the encoder and driver, and exchanges information with STM32 through controller area network (CAN) are respectively set as the driving motors of hip joint and knee joint to meet the requirement of joint torque. A brushed digital current (DC) motor (rated power of 250 W, maximum torque of 18 Nm, weight of 2.82 kg and nominal speed of 120 rpm) is used to be the driving motor of the wheelchair, which can be driven by an AQMD3620NS actuator. Due to the requirement of the control system stability, we chose motion processing sensor (MPU6050) to collect the motion speed of the wheelchair, and set a thin film pressure sensor on the back to collect the pressure between human body and backboard. To support the gravity of the wheelchair and patients, we chose the linear actuators whose thrust reached 2000 N. The relay module is used to control the voltage direction, so that control the linear actuators to extend and retract.

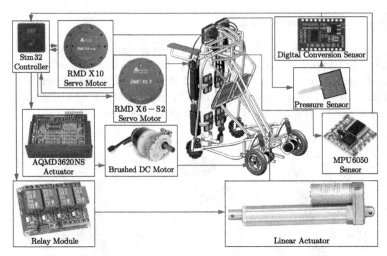

Fig. 15. Hardware design of embedded control system.

3.2 Gait Rehabilitation Training Control

Considering patients with lower limbs weakness or disability, we adopted passive training method to train patients, that was helping patients track the target trajectory for gait training through the exoskeleton repeated tracking control (see Fig. 16).

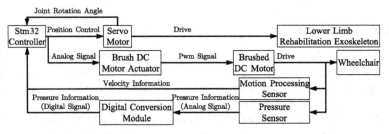

Fig. 16. Hardware design of control system.

The control principle of the lower limb rehabilitation exoskeleton is as follows: transforming the planned target trajectory into discrete data, and writing to STM32 controller; then the controller sends message of position control command to the servo motor to rotate to the planned angle position through CAN communication; the encoder inside the motor feeds back the information of the rotation angle of the motor shaft to the controller through CAN communication, so as to realize the semi-closed loop control of the patients hip joints and knee joints angle.

To set the trajectory, according to Fig. 2, we extracted data of 50 units (one gait period) and performed Fourier fitting on the motion data of knee joint and hip joint:

$$\theta(t) = \sum_{n=1}^{N} A_n \sin(B_n t + C_n) \tag{3}$$

where $\theta(t)$ is the rotation angle of the hip joint and the knee joint at different times, A_n, B_n, C_n are fitting parameters, N is the number of fitting terms, $t \in [0, 2]$ is the normalized time. Fourier fitting of the hip joint and knee joint at $N = 6$ and $N = 5$, respectively, to obtain the trajectory equations of the hip joint and the knee joint with respect to time (the equation curve is shown in see Fig. 17).

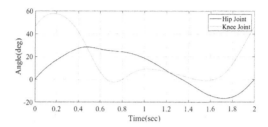

Fig. 17. Active driving joint trajectory.

To avoid the resistance caused by the weight of the wheelchair during gait training, we also designed a wheelchair control system (see Fig. 16). The embedded control system keeps the contact force between patients and backboard at a predetermined range to make the wheelchair move following patients.

The control principle of driving wheelchair is as follows: the contact force information between the backboard and the back of users is collected by the film pressure sensor, and the data is sent to the STM32 controller after AD conversion through the digital conversion module; the controller calculates the control speed of the wheelchair through the contact force information, then converts the data of speed into analog voltage signal, and transmits the signal to the DC motor actuator; actuator outputs the PWM signal to drive the brushed DC motor to move at a planned speed, thereby controlling the forward speed of the wheelchair; the motion processing sensor installed on the wheelchair combination framework feeds back the wheelchair speed information to the STM32 controller to adjust the control signal of the wheelchair, so as to realize the closed-loop control of the wheelchair speed.

3.3 Posture Transformation Control

The control system structure shown in Fig. 18 is designed for controlling posture transformation mechanism. Its principle is as follows: after receiving the signal given by the user, the STM32 controller outputs signal to control the relay, and then the relay controls the voltage direction, thereby controlling the expansion of the linear actuator, so as to help patients stand and sit; the motion processing sensor installed on the combination frame feeds back the lifting speed information frame to STM32 controller; STM32 controller calculates the time it takes to complete this action through the maximum extension and contraction of the push rod, and adjusts the speed of the joint motor, so that each joint motor rotates to the specified angle when the linear actuator reaches the push stroke.

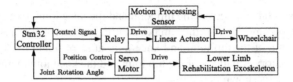

Fig. 18. Basic principle of posture transformation control.

During the posture transformation of the system, the calves need to always remain perpendicular to the ground to prevent the patient from tilting and even falling. The controller needs to ensure the angle relationship:

$$|\theta_1(t)| = |\theta_2(t)| \tag{4}$$

where $\theta_1(t)$ is the angle between thigh and backboard at time t, and $\theta_2(t)$ is the angle between thigh and calf at time t (see Fig. 11).

4   Simulation

4.1   Gait Rehabilitation Training Simulation

In this study, the whole model of the system of lower-limb exoskeleton combined with wheelchair was simulated by gait training. After importing the model into Adams, the main part was simplified and retained. The mass of the human body was equivalent to the backboard, thigh and calf, and the drive of the hip joints and knee joints was set according to controlling position for 5 s simulation. In the simulation process, the system can move forward stably, and the swing of the exoskeleton is close to the human walking gait. The trajectory data of hip joint and knee joint obtained by simulation are imported into MATLAB to compare with the preset trajectory (see Fig. 19). We found that the simulation results deviate from the predetermined trajectory very little, which proves that the system can closely track the preset trajectory and maintain the overall stability during the training process.

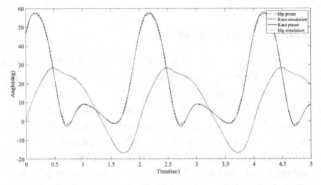

Fig. 19. Comparison of simulation results and preset trajectories.

4.2 Posture Transformation

The simulation analysis of the sitting posture transformation mechanism was carried out. The model was imported into SolidWorks, and some redundant parts were also deleted for Motion analysis. In the simulation, the hip joint and knee joint were set as rotating motors, and the linear actuator was a linear motor. The whole simulation process was 6.4 s, the expansion speed of linear actuator was set to 40 mm/s, and the rotation speed of hip joint and knee joint was set to 1.8 rpm. After simulation, we found that $|\theta_1(t)|$ was approximately equal to $|\theta_2(t)|$, and the hip joints and knee joints can be rotated close to 90° when the linear actuator reached the stroke, and then stopped (see Fig. 20). After the human body weight was equivalent to the model for simulation, the whole system still completed the deformation stably in the process of posture transformation.

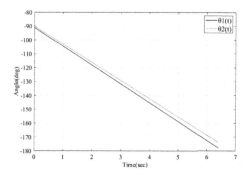

Fig. 20. The variation between $\theta_1(t)$ and $\theta_2(t)$ during process of posture transformation.

5 Conclusion

In this paper, we developed a system of lower limb rehabilitation exoskeleton combined with wheelchair, which aimed to assist patients with lower limb weakness or disability to rehabilitate. On the basis of human anatomy and human gait analysis, we determined the number of DOF of exoskeleton to be 6, which included 2 hip joints, 2 knee joints and 2 ankle joints. We determined that the motion of the hip joints and knee joints from extension to flexion is respectively −20°–110° and −90°–5°, and the motion of the ankle joints from dorsiflexion to plantarflexion is −20°–20°. To meet the height requirements of different patients, the exoskeleton can be adjusted longitudinally. For making the exoskeleton combined with a wheelchair which was designed based on the Chinese standard of electric powered wheelchair, we designed an integrated mechanism of wheelchair and exoskeleton. To support patients to stand up and sit down, a posture transformation mechanism was designed to facilitate patients transform postures between standing and sitting. We developed embedded control system to control the whole system do gait training and posture transformation. The simulation experiments of gait training and posture transformation proved that the system could closely track the preset trajectory of human gait during the gait training process and maintained the stability during gait training and posture transformation process.

Acknowledgments. This work was funded by Chongqing Science and Technology Commission of China (cstc2020jcyj-msxmX0398), Science and Technology Research Program of Chongqing Municipal Education Commission (KJZD-K202001103, KJQN202201169), the Scientific Research Foundation of Chongqing University of Technology (2019ZD61), and the graduate student Innovation Project of Chongqing (NO. CYS21466). Supported by action plan for quality development of Chongqing University of Technology graduate education (Grant No. gzlcx20233409).

References

1. Kenta, S., Gouji, M., Hiroaki, K., Yasuhisa, H., Yoshiyuki, S.: Intention-based walking support for paraplegia patients with Robot Suit HAL. Adv. Robot. **21**(12), 1441–1469 (2012)
2. Sumit, D., Shankar, M., Vikas, P.: Design of a reconfigurable wheelchair with stand-sit-sleep capabilities for enhanced independence of long-term wheelchair users. Technol. Disabil. **30**(3), 135–151 (2018)
3. Tomoyuki, U., et al.: Feasibility and safety of Robot Suit HAL treatment for adolescents and adults with cerebral palsy. J. Clin. Neurosci. **68**, 101–104 (2019)
4. Sai, K.B., Seok Hun, K., Sunil, K.A., John, P.S.: Robot assisted gait training with active leg exoskeleton (ALEX). IEEE Trans. Neural Syst. Rehabilit. Eng. **17**(1), 2–8 (2009)
5. Sai, K.B., Seok Hun, K., Sunil, K.A., John, P.S.: Novel gait adaptation and neuromotor training results using an active leg exoskeleton. IEEE/ASME Trans. Mechatron. **15**(2), 216–225 (2010)
6. Rand, H., Lauri, B., Xin, J., Siddharth, C., Joel, S., Sunil K.A.: Gait adaptation using a cable-driven Active Leg Exoskeleton (C-ALEX) with post-stroke participants. IEEE Trans. Neural Syst. Rehabilit. Eng. **28**(9), 1984–1993 (2020)
7. Ryan, J.F., Hugo, A.Q., Michael, G.: Preliminary evaluation of a powered lower limb orthosis to aid walking in paraplegic individuals. IEEE Trans. Neural Syst. Rehabilit. Eng. **19**(6), 652–659 (2011)
8. Ryan, J.F., Hugo, A.Q., Spencer, A.M., Kevin, H.H., Clare, H., Michael, G.: A preliminary assessment of legged mobility provided by a lower limb exoskeleton for persons with paraplegia. IEEE Trans. Neural Syst. Rehabilit. Eng. **22**(3), 482–490 (2014)
9. Eliza, S.: Good-bye, wheelchair. IEEE Spectr. **49**(1), 30–32 (2012)
10. Gabi, Z., Harold, W., Manuel, Z., Israel, D., Ayala, B., Alberto, E.: Safety and tolerance of the ReWalk™ exoskeleton suit for ambulation by people with complete spinal cord injury: a pilot study. J. Spinal Cord Med. **35**(2), 96–101 (2012)
11. Esquenazi, A., Talaty, M., Packel, A., Saulino, M.: The ReWalk powered exoskeleton to restore ambulatory function to individuals with thoracic-level motor-complete spinal cord injury. Am. J. Phys. Med. Rehabil. **91**(11), 911–921 (2012)
12. Jaewook, K., Yekwang, K., Seung-Jong, K.: Biomechanical task-based gait analysis suggests ReWalk gait resembles crutch gait. Appl. Sci. **12**(24), 12574 (2022)
13. Bingshan, H., Hongyang, Y., Hongrun, L., Yongjie C.: Design of mechanism and control system for a lightweight lower limb exoskeleton. In: 2018 3rd International Conference on Control, Robotics and Cybernetics (CRC), pp. 26–28. IEEE, Penang (2018)

Biomechanical Design and Evaluation of a Lightweight Back Exoskeleton for Repetitive Lifting Tasks

Sen Huang, Xinzhili Chen, Liugang Zhao, Yiyou Li, Dong Yuan, Minchao Liu, Jiahong Liu, and Bo Li$^{(\boxtimes)}$

Chongqing University of Technology, Chongqing 400000, NJ, China
libo_doctor@163.com

Abstract. Repetitive and high-strength lifting tasks increase the risk of work-related musculoskeletal disorders (Wmsds) in the back and arms. To provide arms and back assistance for workers in repetitive lifting tasks, we developed a lightweight back exoskeleton (LBE). We analyzed the human kinematics, statics, and dynamics of lifting tasks to provide a theoretical basis for the design of the LBE. We designed the arm and back assistant modules. The energy storage mechanism set on arm assistant module is used to do passive assistance. The Bowden cable-driven mechanism based on the series elastic actuator set on back assist module is adopted to do active assistance. The electromyography (EMG) of the left and right biceps brachii (BB) and lumbar erector spinae (LES) were measured to evaluate the arms and back assistance effects of the LBE. When wearing the LBE during repetitive lifting tasks, the average EMG of the BB and LES decreased by 15.15% and 28.25%, respectively. The results demonstrated that the LBE could alleviate muscle fatigue for repetitive lifting tasks.

Keywords: Lifting Tasks · Back Exoskeleton · Muscle Activity · Arm Assist · Back Assist

1 Introduction

Manual materials handling (MMH) activities that need workers to repetitively lift heavy objects usually result in work-related musculoskeletal disorders (WMSDs) [1], especially in the human back and arms. WMSDs affect the health of workers and increase the economic costs of enterprises. It is necessary to assist the repetitive lifting tasks.

Back exoskeletons have proved to enhance human strength, reduce muscle force, prevent WMSDs, and improve work efficiency [2]. It can be classified as 'passive' or 'active' according to the actuators [3]. Passive exoskeletons use different energy storage mechanisms, such as gas springs [4], torsion springs [5], and carbon fiber [6] to assist in lifting by translating potential energy into kinetic energy. However, the assistance torque provided by the passive exoskeletons is related to the bending angle of the torso, which results in a limited assist effect. Active exoskeletons use powered actuators to assist the worker in repetitive lifting tasks [7, 8]. Active exoskeletons can provide greater power,

H. Yang et al. (Eds.): ICIRA 2023, LNAI 14268, pp. 475–488, 2023.
https://doi.org/10.1007/978-981-99-6486-4_41

but they have a more complicated and heavier system [9]. For example, the weight of the waist-assist exoskeleton, H-WEXv2, and Xotrunk is 5 kg, 5.5 kg, and 6.5 kg, respectively.

To address the above problems, we designed a lightweight back exoskeleton (LBE) combined with the technological advantages of passive and active exoskeletons which could assist the arms and back respectively. The LBE consists of arm and back assistant modules. The energy storage mechanism set on arm assistant module is used to do passive assistance. The Bowden cable-driven mechanism based on the series elastic actuator set on back assist module is adopted to do active assistance. Furthermore, this paper analyzes the potential effects of the exoskeleton considering both factors of lifting height and whether to wear the exoskeleton or not.

2 Biomechanical Analysis

2.1 Kinematics Analysis of Lifting

To study the motion characteristics of lifting, we used the Vicon motion capture system (Oxford Metrics Limited, UK) to capture the 3D coordinates of reflection markers. The system consists of 10 MX cameras, which can achieve a resolution of 16 million pixels with a full capture speed of 120 fps. To prevent obstruction of the marker point used for measuring the hip joint, the initial arm position was tilted forward by about 20°. Seven reflective markers were attached to the skin of the subjects, which were captured by the camera system to record the kinematic data of human movements. The position of the reflective markers and the lifting process were shown in Fig. 1(a). The height and weight of the 24-year subject were 1.75 m and 60 kg, respectively.

Fig. 1. The lifting process of human (a) and the position of the reflective markers (b)

The hip and knee joint angles were calculated by vector dot product, and the calculation formula can be expressed as:

$$\theta_i = \arccos \frac{P_n P_{n-1} P_n P_{n+1}}{\|P_n P_{n-1}\| \|P_n P_{n+1}\|} \tag{1}$$

The P is the position of the reflective markers. The central point (P_{n-1}, P_n, P_{n+1}) of the two joints corresponding to each segment represents the angle between the two spatial vectors corresponding to the two adjacent segments, as shown in Fig. 1(b).

We obtained the range of motion of the elbow and hip joints during lifting by Matlab software. As shown in Fig. 2, the flexion angles of the hip and elbow joints are in the range of 15.3–102.6° and 102.9–136.6° respectively. These data provide a theoretical basis for static analysis and dynamic simulation during lifting.

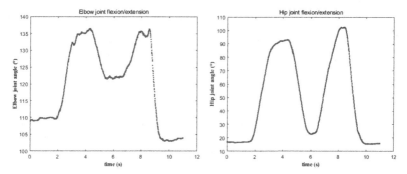

Fig. 2. The angle motion range of the elbow and hip joints of the human

2.2 Statics Analysis of Lifting

Due to the involvement of multiple muscle groups in lifting motion, the mechanism of the lifting motion is very complex. The lifting motion mainly occurs in the sagittal plane. To simplify the analysis, we established a static model, as shown in Fig. 3. In the module, we assumed that the forces acting on the sagittal plane were symmetrical. According to the force and moment balance, we analyzed the forces exerted on the forearm and L5/S1 joint during lifting [7].

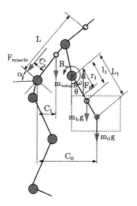

Fig. 3. The simplified static model with lifting

The torque exerted on the elbow joint by the box can be expressed as:

$$R_e = m_b g l_1 \sin \theta + m_0 g L_1 \sin \theta \tag{2}$$

where l_1 is the length of the proximal elbow joint, L_1 is the length of the forearm, and θ is the angle between the upper arm and the forearm.

The muscle force of the biceps brachii (BB) can be calculated as:

$$F_B = \frac{m_b g l_1 \sin \theta + m_0 g L_1 \sin \theta}{r_1 \sin \omega_1} \tag{3}$$

where ω_1 is the inclined angle of the BB and upper arm, and r_1 is the distance from the muscle attachment to the shoulder joint.

According to static equilibrium, the sum of the moments at the L5/S1 disc must be zero, which can be obtained:

$$m_0 g C_0 + m_{total} g C_1 = F_{muscle} C_2 \qquad (4)$$

where C_0 is the horizontal distance from the center of mass of the box to the L5/S1 joint, C_1 is the horizontal distance from the center of mass of the upper body to the L5/S1 joint, and C_2 is the distance from the erector spinae to the L5/S1 joint. The m_{total} is the mass of the head, arms, and trunk. m_b is the mass of the forearm and m_0 is the mass of the box. The α is the sagittal trunk flexion angle.

The forces exerted by the erector spinae (ES) can be obtained:

$$F_{muscle} = \frac{m_0 g C_0 + m_{total} g C_1}{C_2} \qquad (5)$$

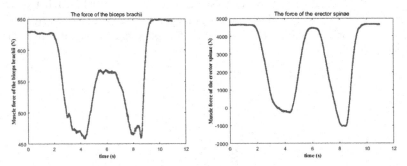

Fig. 4. The forces of the BB and the ES

We assumed that the mass of an adult human body is $m = 60$ kg and the height is $H = 1.75$ m. The distance $L = 0.6$ m from the center of mass of the head and neck to the L5/S1 joint. The mass of the box is $m_0 = 15$ kg. According to the literature [10], we have $C_0 = Lcos\alpha$, $C_1 = 0.626Lcos\alpha$, $L_1 = 0.146H$, $l_1 = 0.06278H$, $m_b = 0.016 m$, $m_{total} = 0.678 m$, the value of C_2 is usually 5 cm, $r_1 = 0.06 m$, $\omega_1 = 80°$. By substituting these values into Formula (3) and Formula (5), we obtained the forces of the BB and the ES.

As shown in Fig. 4, when the human lifted a 15 kg load, the forces exerted by the BB and the ES were calculated to be 650 N and 4683 N, respectively. As the weight of the load increased, the forces on the BB and the ES also gradually increased. When the muscles of the arm and back bear greater force, leading to muscle fatigue and even greater damage.

2.3 Dynamics Simulation of Lifting

To further investigate the characteristics of human lifting motion, we obtained the hip and elbow joints motion trajector by Vicon motion capture system. Inputing these motion trajectories into the SolidWorks, then obtained the torque of the elbow and hip joints, as shown in Fig. 5.

The simulation results showed that the maximum torque of the elbow joint of the subject was approximately 14.8 N·m, while the maximum torque on the elbow joint reached about 129.3 N·m. It can be found that human joints bear larger torque, which could potentially lead to injury of joints.

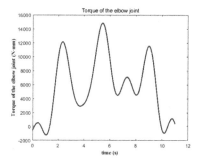 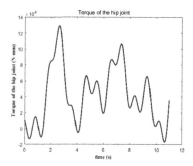

Fig. 5. Torque of elbow and hip joints

3   Mechanical Structure and Control Design

3.1   Analysis of Exoskeleton Design Theory

When the subject wears the LBE to lift a box, the Bowden cable-driven mechanism based on a series elastic actuator outputs the torque to pull up the torso and support the arms, keeping the legs and upper limbs upright and enabling the arms to hold the box, as shown as Fig. 6. The total mass of the LBE is neglected in the following analysis for it is lightweight, and all the definitions are assumed as the same as the former section described [11].

The flat spiral spring output the assistance force F_{arm}. The tension spring output the assistance force F_{lumbar}. The motor output the assistance torque R_{Asist}. According to static equilibrium, the torque balance formula of the forearm can be obtained:

$$F_B^* r_1 \sin \omega_1 = m_b g l_1 \sin \theta + m_0 g L_1 \sin \theta - F_{Arm} \sin\left(90° - \theta_2 + \gamma\right) L_1 \sin \theta \quad (6)$$

where γ is the angle between the forearm and the wire rope.

According to static equilibrium, the torque balance formula of the back can be obtained:

$$m_0 g C_0 + m_{total} g C_1 = F_{muscle}^* C_2 + 2R_{Assist} + 2F_{lumbar} C_3 \quad (7)$$

where C_3 is the distance from the assistance force F_{lumbar} to the L5/S1 joint.

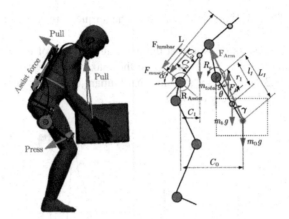

Fig. 6. The assistant principle of the LBE

According to Formulas (2–7), the assistance ratio (AR) for the ES and BB can be obtained:

$$ AR_B = 1 - \left(\frac{F_B^*}{F_B}\right) \quad AR_{muscle} = 1 - \left(\frac{F_{muscle}^*}{F_{muscle}}\right) \tag{8}$$

To avoid excessive assistance that could lead to muscle hypertrophy [12], we chose an assistance ratio of $AR_B = 30\%$ for the BB and $AR_{muscle} = 40\%$ for the ES during lifting. For the arm assistant module, we chose a flat spiral spring model [$b * h * r * l$ of 7 * 0.3 * 13 * 920 mm] as an energy storage mechanism. For the back assistant module, we chose a tension spring [$d * D_O * L$ of 1.2 * 12 * 100 mm], with a spring stiffness of 2.5 N/mm and a DC brushless motor (RMD-X8) both as a powered actuator, which has a nominal torque of 9 N·m.

3.2 Mechanical Structure

The overall mechanical structure of the LBE consists of a back assistant module, an arm assistant module, and an adjustable mechanism, as shown in Fig. 7. The weight of the LBE is 5 kg. The back assistant module consists of a Bowden cable-driven mechanism and a singular series elastic element. The Bowden cable-driven mechanism consists of a double-wire winch, Bowden cable, gears, motor output shaft, hip assistant winch, and DC brushless motors. One end of the bionic spine is fixed on a double-wire winch, and the other end is connected to a tension spring by a wire rope. One end of the Bowden cable is fixed on the double-wire winch, and the other end is fixed on the hip assistant winch. The double-wire winch is connected to the large gear through the motor output shaft. The large gear promotes pinion gear. The motor is connected to the pinion gear.

The hip assistant winch has the freedom of flexion/extension in the sagittal plane, which can stimulate the Bowden cable-driven mechanism to assist the back during bending. The adjustable mechanism is designed for the different height groups of wearers. There is a thigh baffle of the LBE to ensure closely combined with the human and to reduce the damage to the thigh when the wearer bends.

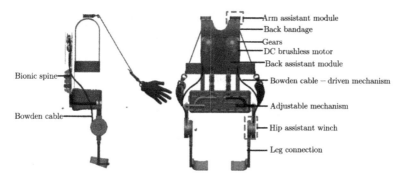

Fig. 7. The overall mechanical structure of the LBE

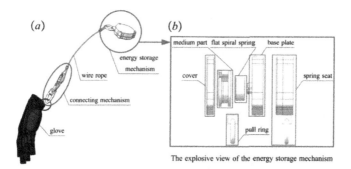

Fig. 8. The detailed arm assistant module

The arm assistant module consists of an energy storage mechanism, connecting mechanism, wire rope, and glove, as shown in Fig. 8(a). One end of the wire rope is fixed on the energy storage mechanism, and the other end is fixed on the glove. The energy storage mechanism has a cover, medium part, flat spiral spring, base plate, and pull ring, as shown in Fig. 8(b). The energy storage mechanism can be restored to the initial state under the restoring force of the flat spiral spring after the completion of the repetitive lifting tasks.

3.3 Dynamic Module Analysis

To obtain the dynamic characteristics of the LBE system and then achieve accuracy control of the LBE movement, we established the human-exoskeleton coupling dynamic model by Lagrange equation [11], as shown in Fig. 9.

The X-Y Cartesian coordinate system is established with Point O as its origin. m_1 is the mass of the upper limbs and LBE, and m_2 is the mass of the arms. m_3 is the mass of the box, and l_1 and l_2 are the distance of the LBE and arms.

The Lagrange equation can be expressed as

$$\frac{d}{dt}\left(\frac{\partial k}{\partial \dot{\theta}_i}\right) - \frac{\partial k}{\partial \theta_i} + \frac{\partial u}{\partial \theta_i} = \tau_i \tag{9}$$

The relative position from system i-1 to system i is represented by transformation matrix:

$$
{}_{i}^{i-1}T = \begin{bmatrix}
c\theta_i & -s\theta_i & 0 & \alpha_{i-1} \\
s\theta_i c\alpha_{i-1} & c\theta_i c\alpha_{i-1} & -s\alpha_{i-1} & -s\alpha_{i-1}d_i \\
s\theta_i s\alpha_{i-1} & c\theta_i c\alpha_{i-1} & c\alpha_{i-1} & c\alpha_{i-1}d_i \\
0 & 0 & 0 & 1
\end{bmatrix} \tag{10}
$$

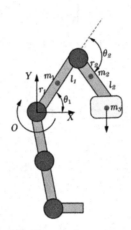

Fig. 9. The simplified human dynamics model with lifting

The transformation matrix of relative position from the system i to system 0

$$
{}_{N}^{0}T = {}_{1}^{0}T {}_{2}^{1}T {}_{3}^{2}T \cdots {}_{N}^{N-1}T \tag{11}
$$

The centroid position vector of the trunk, arms, and box can be obtained:

$$
{}_{1}^{0}\vec{P} = \begin{bmatrix} r_1 c\theta_1 \\ r_1 s\theta_1 \\ 0 \end{bmatrix} \quad
{}_{2}^{0}\vec{P} = \begin{bmatrix} l_1 c\theta_1 + r_2 c(\theta_1 - \theta_2) \\ l_1 s\theta_1 - r_2 s(\theta_1 - \theta_2) \\ 0 \end{bmatrix}
$$

$$
{}_{3}^{0}\vec{P} = \begin{bmatrix} l_1 c\theta_1 + l_2 c(\theta_1 - \theta_2) \\ l_1 s\theta_1 - l_2 s(\theta_1 - \theta_2) \\ 0 \end{bmatrix} \tag{12}
$$

The centroid velocity vector of the trunk, arms, and box can be obtained:

$$
{}_{1}^{0}\vec{V} = \begin{bmatrix} -r_1 s\theta_1 \dot{\theta}_1 \\ r_1 c\theta_1 \dot{\theta}_1 \\ 0 \end{bmatrix} \quad
{}_{2}^{0}\vec{V} = \begin{bmatrix} -l_1 s\theta_1 \dot{\theta}_1 - r_2 s(\theta_1 - \theta_2)(\dot{\theta}_1 - \dot{\theta}_2) \\ l_2 c\theta_1 \dot{\theta}_1 + r_2 c(\theta_1 - \theta_2)(\dot{\theta}_1 - \dot{\theta}_2) \\ 0 \end{bmatrix}
$$

$$
{}_{2}^{0}\vec{V} = \begin{bmatrix} -l_1 s\theta_1 \dot{\theta}_1 - l_2 s(\theta_1 - \theta_2)(\dot{\theta}_1 - \dot{\theta}_2) \\ l_2 c\theta_1 \dot{\theta}_1 + l_2 c(\theta_1 - \theta_2)(\dot{\theta}_1 - \dot{\theta}_2) \\ 0 \end{bmatrix} \tag{13}
$$

The centroid angular velocity vector of the trunk, arms, and box can be obtained:

$$
{}^0_1\vec{\omega} = \begin{bmatrix} 0 \\ 0 \\ \dot{\theta}_1 \end{bmatrix} \quad
{}^0_2\vec{\omega} = \begin{bmatrix} 0 \\ 0 \\ \dot{\theta}_1 + \dot{\theta}_2 \end{bmatrix} \quad
{}^0_3\vec{\omega} = \begin{bmatrix} 0 \\ 0 \\ \dot{\theta}_1 + \dot{\theta}_2 \end{bmatrix} \tag{14}
$$

The v_i ($i = 1,2$) is the centroid velocity of the cartesian coordinate system, the J_i is the torque of rotational inertia of the cartesian coordinate system. We assumed that the plane of O point was zero potential energy surface. If the friction between the human and the exoskeleton is not taken into account, the total kinetic energy K and the potential energy u of the human-exoskeleton power system can be described as follows:

$$
K = \sum_{i=1}^{2} \frac{1}{2}\left(m_i v_i^2 + J_i \dot{\theta}_i^2\right) \quad u = \sum_{i=1}^{3} m_i g {}^0_i \vec{P}_y \tag{15}
$$

The partial derivative of K can be obtained by:

$$
\begin{aligned}
\frac{\partial K}{\partial \theta_i} &= \frac{1}{2}\frac{\partial J_{11}}{\partial \theta_i}\dot{\theta}_1^2 + \frac{\partial J_{12}}{\partial \theta_i}\dot{\theta}_1\dot{\theta}_2 + \frac{1}{2}\frac{\partial J_{22}}{\partial \theta_i}\dot{\theta}_2^2 (i = 1, 2) \\
\frac{\partial K}{\partial \dot{\theta}_i} &= J_{1i}\dot{\theta}_1 + J_{i2}\dot{\theta}_2 (i = 1, 2)
\end{aligned} \tag{16}
$$

Formulas (13–14) are brought into Lagrange Eq. (7)

$$
\begin{aligned}
\begin{bmatrix} T_1 \\ T_2 \end{bmatrix}
&= \begin{bmatrix} \left(m_1 r_1^2 + I_{1,2,3} + m_2(l_1^2 + r_2^2) + m_3(l_1^2 + l_2^2) + 2(m_2 l_1 r_2 + m_3 l_1 l_2 c_1)\right) & 0 \\ -\left(m_2 r_2^2 - I_2 + m_3 l_2^2 - I_3 + (m_2 l_1 r_2 + m_3 l_1 l_2)c_1\right) & 0 \end{bmatrix}\begin{bmatrix} \ddot{\theta}_1 \\ \ddot{\theta}_2 \end{bmatrix} \\
&+ \begin{bmatrix} 0 & -\left(m_2 r_2^2 - I_2 + m_3 l_2^2 - I_3 + m_2 l_1 r_2 + m_3 l_1 l_2 c_1\right) \\ 0 & m_2 r_2^2 + I_2 + m_3 l_2^2 + I_3 \end{bmatrix}\begin{bmatrix} \ddot{\theta}_1 \\ \ddot{\theta}_2 \end{bmatrix} \\
&+ \begin{bmatrix} 0 & (m_2 r_2 + m_3 l_2)l_1 s_1 \\ -(m_2 r_2 + m_3 l_2)l_1 s_1 & 0 \end{bmatrix}\begin{bmatrix} \dot{\theta}_1 \\ \dot{\theta}_2 \end{bmatrix} \\
&+ \begin{bmatrix} -2(m_2 l_1 r_2 + m_3 l_1 l_2)s_1 & 0 \\ 2(m_2 l_1 r_2 + m_3 l_1 l_2)s_1 & 0 \end{bmatrix}\begin{bmatrix} \dot{\theta}_1\dot{\theta}_2 \\ \dot{\theta}_2\dot{\theta}_1 \end{bmatrix} \\
&+ \begin{bmatrix} (m_1 r_1 + m_2 l_1 + m_3 l_1)gc_1 + (m_2 r_2 + m_3 l_2)gc(\theta_1 - \theta_2) \\ (m_2 g r_2 + m_3 g l_2)c(\theta_1 - \theta_2) \end{bmatrix}
\end{aligned} \tag{17}
$$

When wearers lift a heavy box, the box is always vertically downward, and the geometric relationship is $\theta_2 = \pi/2 + \theta_1$, substituting into the Formula (15), we get

$$
\begin{aligned}
[T] &= \left[m_1 r_1^2 + I_1 + m_2 l_1^2 + m_3 l_1^2 + 4(I_2 + I_3)\right]\left[\ddot{\theta}_1\right] \\
&+ \left[(m_1 g r_1 + m_2 g l_1 + m_3 g l_1)c_1\right]
\end{aligned} \tag{18}
$$

3.4   Control System

The electronics hardware system of the LBE is shown in Fig. 10. It consists of a system control board, motor control board, actuator module, and expansion module. Each actuator module is powered by a voltage of 48 V, rated power 160 W motor, in series connection with a tension spring. The motor control board includes a motor driver (BLDC PMSM FOC) and sensors. The inertia measurement unit (IMU) sensor is used to detect trunk motion conditions. We used the OLED interactive module of the system control board to achieve human-computer interaction. To satisfy the requirements of the manual lifting tasks, we chose the battery YSN-2402500 which is placed in the back assistant module. We used the STM32F03C8T6 control board as the controller of the control system whose working voltage is 3.3–5 V [7].

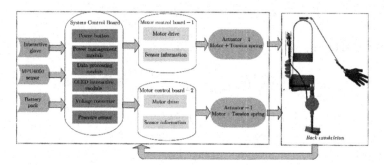

Fig. 10. The electronics hardware system of the LBE

Without considering friction of the bandage and bowden cable, the dynamic equation of the LBE can be described by

$$T = D(q)\ddot{q} + H(q, \dot{q})\dot{q} + G(q) \tag{19}$$

where $q, \dot{q}, \ddot{q} \in R^N$ is the joint angles, velocities and accelerations respectively, $D(q)$ is the inertial matrix, $H(q, \dot{q})$ is the centripetal force and coriolis force, $G(q)$ is the moment formed by gravity, T is the moment or force applied to each joint.

Passive control methods offer simplicity and reliability. However, they may have limitations in adaptability, real-time adjustment, and design constraints, such as PID control, fuzzy control, and EMG control. Active control methods offer flexibility, adaptability, and precise control, but they are more complex, such as control methods based on force sensor or EMG sensor. We adopted the PID control method based on IMU sensor.

PID controller provides an assistant torque T at each joint in the assistant process of the LBE. The principle of PID control can be defined as

$$T = K_p \cdot \Delta q + K_i \cdot I + K_d \cdot D \tag{20}$$

$$\Delta q = q_d - q \quad I = \int_{t_1}^{t_2} \Delta q(t) dt \quad D = \frac{d\,\Delta q}{dt} \tag{21}$$

where q_d and q are the desired trajectory and actual trajectory of the controlled joint respectively. Δq is the trajectory error, I is the error integral, and D is the error integral derivative of the error. K_P, K_i, and K_d are the proportion-gain, integral gain, and differential gain of the PID controller respectively.

The parameters of the controller are defined by the Critical Gain Method. It involves identifying the critical gain (K_c) which can be used to determine the proportional, integral, and derivative gains (K_P, K_i, and K_d). When the system response approaches the critical stable state, the critical gain value is recorded. Using the critical gain value to calculate the other PID parameters: $K_P = (0.5–0.7K_c)$, $K_i \approx 3K_c$, and $K_d = 1/3K_c$.

K_P affects the proportion of control output to the error signal. K_i eliminates steady-state errors and K_d enables the controller to anticipate and react to changes in the error signal.

The control block of the LBE is shown in Fig. 11.

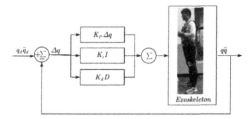

Fig. 11. The control block of the PID controller of the human-exoskeleton system

4 Tests

4.1 Experiment Protocol

The Electromyographic (EMG) signals can reflect human muscle activity [7]. Therefore, the lumbar erector spinae (LES) of the back and biceps brachii (BB) of the arms were selected as the evaluation object [13]. Three healthy males participated in this experiment (year: 23 ± 1, weight: 70 ± 2 kg, height: 175 ± 3 cm). The subjects signed informed consent before the experiment. A 16-channel NO-raxon-DTS wireless surface EMG acquisition system (Noraxon, USA) was used to measure the EMG signals of the human body during repetitive lifting. The EMG signal data were collected at a 1500 Hz sampling rated by MR 23 software of the workstation. We used a disposable bipolar electrode patch. The position of the patch is the left and right side of the LES and the BB, as shown in Fig. 12(a). Before the patch, the skin surface was clear with 75% medical alcohol to clean up oil pollution. After the skin was dry, the electrode pad was patched.

Before the experiment, subjects were familiarized with both the LBE and testing process. One lifting cycle included the following four steps: (1) the subjects stretched the wire rope of the arms assistant module and bent down to pick up a 5 kg box ([W * D * H of 45 * 34 * 27 cm] with handles on both sides [24 cm]) on the floor; (2) lifting the box to an upright position while holding the load close to the body with flexed elbows;

Fig. 12. The position of the test muscle (a) and the lifting process (b)

(3) pausing for 2 ~ 3 s, put the load down to the floor again; (4) returning to the original upright posture, the lifting process is shown in Fig. 12(b). Subjects were required to perform 5 lifting cycles for each load in one min. Loads are 5 kg, 10 kg, and 15 kg respectively. A load lift was completed and the subject rested for 20 min.

4.2 Results

The collected original EMG signals were filtered (20 Hz–300 Hz), and rectification and root mean square values (RMS, 500 ms) were processed. According to the initial statistical analysis, there were no significant differences in average EMG between the left and right side, which could be combined to calculate the average. The test results of the three subjects were averaged. The assistance efficiency of the LBE expressed as

$$\eta = 1 - \frac{E_w}{E} \tag{22}$$

where E and E_w are the average EMG of the subjects lifting the load without and with the LBE, respectively.

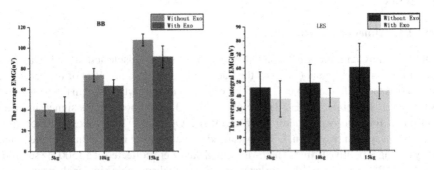

Fig. 13. The average EMG (uV) of the BB and LES with\without LBE

Figure 13 shows the average EMG of BB and LES for lifting 5 kg to 15 kg load respectively under wearing the exoskeleton or not. The statistical test results are shown in Table 2. The LBE significantly reduced the activities of the BB and LES. When subjects wear the LBE and lift 5 kg to 15 kg, the muscle activity of the LES reduction ranged by 17.24–28.25%. The muscle activity of the BB reduction ranged by 7.23–15.15% when wearing the LBE and lifting 5 kg to 15 kg. From Table 1, the decreasing rate of muscle

Table 1. The statistical data of the BB and LES average EMG

		5 kg	10 kg	15 kg	5 kg	10 kg	15 kg
		LES			BB		
Without Exo (uV)	Average	45.69	49.05	60.41	40.09	73.77	107.63
	Sd	11.63	13.69	17.60	5.73	6.45	5.80
With Exo (uV)	Average	37.81	38.60	43.34	37.19	63.03	91.33
	Sd	13.15	6.62	5.64	15.62	6.41	10.52
	Efficiency (%)	−17.24	−21.31	−28.25	−7.23	−14.56	−15.15

activities of the BB and LES increased with the weights of the load increasing. The experimental results indicate that wearing the LBE can reduce muscle fatigue of the BB and LES in repetitive lifting tasks.

5 Conclusions

The purpose of this study was to describe the design of the LBE for back and arms assistance during repetitive lifting tasks. Human kinematics, static, and dynamic analysis provided a theoretical basis for the design of the exoskeleton system. The LBE consists of arm and back assistant modules. The energy storage mechanism set on arm assistant module is used to do passive assistance. The Bowden cable-driven mechanism based on the series elastic actuator set on back assist module is adopted to do active assistance. IMU sensor was used to detect wearers' motion intention. PID controller was used to control the output torque of the motors, so as to achieve real-time assistance during the repetitive lifting tasks.

The assistance effect and design rationality of the LBE are verified by the tests of the LBE. We found that wearing the LBE to lift 15 kg load, the muscle activity of the BB and LES decreased by 15.15% and 28.25%, respectively. The results demonstrated that the LBE could alleviate muscle fatigue for repetitive lifting tasks. Future work will conduct more tests on LBE to evaluate the performance of the exoskeleton. We will further research the method to reduce the muscle fatigue of human in repetitive lifting tasks by optimizing the structure of LBE.

Acknowledgments. This work was funded by Chongqing Science and Technology Commission of China (cstc2020jcyj-msxmX0398), Science and Technology Research Program of Chongqing Municipal Education Commission (KJZD-K202001103, KJQN202201169), the Scientific Research Foundation of Chongqing University of Technology (2019ZD61), and the graduate student Innovation Project of Chongqing (NO. CYS21466). Supported by action plan for quality development of Chongqing University of Technology graduate education (Grant No. gzlcx20232123).

References

1. Roveda, L., Savani, L., Arlati, S.: Design methodology of an active back-support exoskeleton with adaptable backbone-based kinematics. Int. J. Ind. Ergon. **79**(3), 102991 (2020)
2. Toxiri, S., Matthias, N., Lazzaroni, M.: Back-support exoskeletons for occupational use: an overview of technological advances and trends. IISE Trans. Occup. Ergonom. Human Fact. **6**, 1–13 (2019)
3. De Looze, M.P., Bosch, T., Krause, F.: Exoskeletons for industrial application and their potential effects on physical work load. **59**(5), 671–681 (2016).
4. Alemi, M.M., Geissinger, J., Simon, A.A.: A passive exoskeleton reduces peak and mean EMG during symmetric and asymmetric lifting **47**, 25–34 (2019)
5. Baltrusch, S.J., Van, D.J.H., Koopman, A.S.: SPEXOR passive spinal exoskeleton decreases metabolic cost during symmetric repetitive lifting. Eur. J. Appl. Physiol. **120**(2), 401–412 (2020)
6. Schmalz, T., Colienne, A., Bywater, E.: A passive back-support exoskeleton for manual materials handling: reduction of low back loading and metabolic effort during repetitive lifting. IISE Trans. Occup. Ergonom. Human Fact. **10**(1), 7–20 (2022)
7. Yong, X., Yan, Z.F., Wang, C.: Ergonomic mechanical design and assessment of a waist assist exoskeleton for reducing lumbar loads during lifting task. Micromachines **10**(7), 1–18 (2019)
8. Dong, J.H., Lim, H., Park, S.: Singular wire-driven series elastic actuation with force control for a waist assistive exoskeleton, H-WEXv2. IEEE/ASME Trans. Mechatron. **2**(25), 1026–1035 (2020)
9. Lazzaroni, M., Fanti, V., Sposito, M.: Improving the efficacy of an active back-support exoskeleton for manual material handling using the accelerometer signal. IEEE Robot. Automat. Lett. **7**(3), 7717–7721 (2022)
10. Winter, D.A.: Biomechanics and Motor Control of Human Movement, 4th edn. John Wiley & Sons Inc, Hoboken (2005)
11. Ji, X.J., Wang, D., Li, P.: SIAT-WEXv2: a wearable exoskeleton for reducing lumbar load during lifting tasks. Complexity **2020**, 1–12 (2020)
12. Graham, R.B., Agnew, M.J., Stevenson, J.M.: Effectiveness of an on-body lifting aid at reducing low back physical demands during an automotive assembly task: assessment of EMG response and user acceptability. Appl. Ergon. **40**(5), 936–942 (2009)
13. Almenara, M., Cempini, M., Gómez, C.: Usability test of a hand exoskeleton for activities of daily living: an example of user-centered design. Disabil. Rehabil. Assist. Technol. **12**(1), 84–96 (2017)

Biomechanical Design, Modeling and Control of an Ankle-Exosuit System

Liugang Zhao, Sen Huang, Yiyou Li, Xinzhili Chen, Dong Yuan, Minchao Liu, Jiahong Liu, Xiaodong Qin, Han Cui, and Bo Li[✉]

Chongqing University of Technology, Chongqing 400000, NJ, China
libo_doctor@163.com

Abstract. To improve the walking abilities of the ankle patients with locomotion impairment, a biomimetic Ankle-Exosuit was designed based on the muscle-tendon-ligament model. The Ankle-Exosuit assisted ankle plantarflexion by exerting a force parallel to the muscle to reduce plantar flexor activation and enhance lower extremity walking endurance. The bandage locomotion could be effectively reduced by the designed lacing mechanism. We established the coupled kinematic model of human-exosuit. To determine the opening and closing times of the ankle plantarflexion assistance, a threshold detection algorithm was proposed for the recognition of heel-off (HO) and toe-off (TO). A trajectory generator according to the fusion of the coupled kinematic model and trajectory generation function was developed. Comparison experiments based on the measurements of the surface electromyographic (sEMG) signals demonstrated that when wearing the Ankle-Exosuit, the locomotion activation of the gastrocnemius muscles (GM) and soleus muscles (SM) decreased by 11.09% and 6.5%, respectively. The proposed Ankle-Exosuit can decrease muscle fatigue to achieve effective walking assistance.

Keywords: Ankle-Exosuit · Gait recognition · Coupled kinematic model · Trajectory generator

1 Introduction

The ankle plays an imperative part in walking and running activities. However, gait abnormalities [1], and muscular weakness [2], are prevalent problems in ankle locomotion impaired patients. Lower extremity exoskeleton that augments ankle locomotion performance and decreases muscle activation has continuously attracted investigation.

Lower extremity exoskeleton can be divided into rigid and soft exoskeleton. In the previous research, most of these assistive devices are active rigid lower extremity exoskeletons [3]. HAL, [4] ReWalk, [5] and Ekso GT™ [6], are typical rigid lower extremity exoskeletons. These rigid exoskeletons implement human-exoskeleton locomotion couple by rigid link mechanism and assist mobility by directly drive. However, the rigid link mechanism and powerful motors dominate the gait of the wearer, it enforces the walking pattern, results in limited movement flexibility. In contrast to rigid lower extremity exoskeleton, the soft lower extremity exoskeleton is characterized by compact size, lightweight, and locomotion flexibility [7].

© The Author(s), under exclusive license to Springer Nature Singapore Pte Ltd. 2023
H. Yang et al. (Eds.): ICIRA 2023, LNAI 14268, pp. 489–502, 2023.
https://doi.org/10.1007/978-981-99-6486-4_42

The research team of Harvard University proposed biological muscle-tendon-ligament model [8], and virtual anchor technique [9], to design flexible lower extremity exoskeleton. Their model and technique provided inspirations for the design of the Exo-Suit [10], Myosuit [11], etc. However, because to the presence of shear pressures in the assistance process, problems like as bandage locomotion and assistance lag arise, which must be addressed. In addition, the human-exosuit control system is another key technology that need to be considered.

Ding, et al. [12] used a control strategy of iterative learning to update the position profile of the actuator, which provided assistance by controlling the start time, peak time and peak size of the control force. Harvard University enhanced accuracy of the aided trajectory tracking by using a force-position hybrid control technique [10] and a guide position controller [13]. The above controls were designed mainly according to human-exosuit interaction information, which did not consider human-exosuit coupling kinematic and kinetic. The development of flexible lower extremity exoskeleton needs to consider not only control performance but also the entire human-exosuit system [14].

To solve the above problems, we developed an Ankle-Exosuit based on the muscle-tendon-ligament model, designed a trajectory generator according to the coupled kinematic model of human-exosuit and threshold detection algorithm to achieve effective walking assistance.

2   Ankle-Exosuit Mechanism Design

2.1   Biomechanics of Ankle Locomotion

This section introduced the biological principles of ankle locomotion, which was an important guidance for the biomimetic design of the Ankle-Exosuit and the surface electromyographic (sEMG) experiments.

The soleus muscles (SM) and gastrocnemius muscles (GM) contributed 93% of the plantarflexion moment during natural ankle walking [15]. In contrast, the remaining muscle contributed only 7%. The primary muscle groups contribute to plantarflexion movement of the ankle (Fig. 1), and the total force for these muscle groups can be described by

$$\Sigma F_{ma} = F_{gm} + F_{hm} + F_{others} \tag{1}$$

In the equation, F_{gm} represents the force given by the GM, F_{hm} represents the force produced by the SM, F_{others} represents the sum of the other muscle forces, ΣF_{ma} represents the combined force of the helpful muscle groups. We presumed that the GM and Achilles tendon junction was the floating anchor point $A_r(A_l)$ and the heel subcutaneous capsule mimic was the fixed anchor point $B_r(B_l)$. We imitated the morphology and function of biological muscle-tendon-ligament structures by using the Bowden cable. The typical length of the Achilles tendon in adult males is around 15 cm, and the Bowden cable was initially set at 18 cm to accommodate displacement error. We indirectly provided a portion of the force in the form of a Bowden cable.

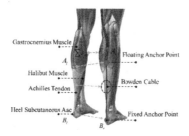

Fig. 1. Biomechanical analysis of ankle locomotion.

2.2 Mechanism Design

The Ankle-Exosuit was developed to assist human locomotion and increase lower extremity walking endurance by reducing muscle activation (Fig. 2), its full mass was approximately 2.5 kg. Two DC servo motors with reducers and servo drivers were positioned at the waist and connected to pulleys, and Bowden cable transmitted torque to the ankles of wearer. Two pairs of plantar pressure sensor insoles measured the force of human-exosuit interaction information while walking and communicated the data to a control board attached to the actuator module with wire. A lithium polymer battery was built into the driver module to power the Ankle-Exosuit.

Human load affects metabolic rate and muscle weariness during walking. In order to reduce the weight of the system, mechanical structure of the Ankle-Exosuit was concentrated on modular, integrated, and lightweight design. Compared with other flexible lower extremity exoskeletons, The Ankle-Exosuit is more flexible to wear, more convenient to carry and less bound movement, which is mainly due to the design and implementation of a rapid tethering mechanism. The driving module and calf strap was designed as follows.

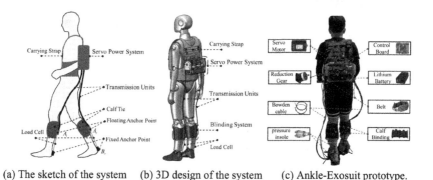

(a) The sketch of the system   (b) 3D design of the system   (c) Ankle-Exosuit prototype.

Fig. 2. Mechanism design of the Ankle-Exosuit

(1) Actuation design
 The Ankle-Exosuit has developed an actuation unit (Fig. 3). To accommodate individualized wear and assistance, we strongly emphasized drive mass and size being

as light and tiny as feasible. The drive assembly was 256 mm long, 168 mm high, and 104 mm broad. The actuation unit includes two DC electric integrated torque servo motors (42AIM30, 0.4 kg) and a planetary gearhead (OKD42PLEK50, 0.35 kg, 50:1 reduction). The motor integrated a 15-bit absolute encoder and servo driver (YZ-AIMD). The system was powered by a lithium battery (44800 mAh, 24 V, 0.41 kg) with its own emergency switch, which can provide nearly 480 min of continuous power to the drive system, which was enough to meet the demand for a more extended range without having to change power sources or recharge midway. The drive system can provide a maximum of 15 NM of extra torque.

The Bowden cable winder comprised a pulley (inner diameter 22 mm, outside diameter 60 mm, thickness 9 mm), a standard bearing (inner diameter 8, outer diameter 14 mm, thickness 4 mm), and support bar (Fig. 3). The Bowden cable sheath was fastened to the end cap of pulley with a cap screw and has an inner diameter of around 1.5 mm and an outer diameter of approximately 5 mm. It was grease-filled to decrease friction and Bowden cable energy transfer loss. The Bowden cable (cable diameter 1.2 mm, load capacity 40.8 kg) was wound on the pulley through the end cover hole, and the Bowden cable head was secured in the pulley groove with double screws, with enough clearance between the end cover and the Bowden cable head to prevent the Bowden cable head from rubbing violently against the end cover.

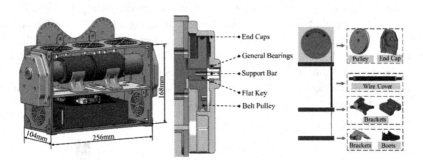

Fig. 3. Drive mechanical design and Bowden cable unit

(2) Flexible bandage design

A functional bandage component for the newly wrapped calf in the Ankle-Exosuit system is shown in Fig. 4. Its total mass was about 0.22 kg. The carrier features a waist belt and a tether strap for simply attaching the actuator to the waist belt. The calf strap has a rapid tethering mechanism to adapt various calf shapes and sizes. The bandage's inner layer, which touches the skin of wearer closely, was constructed of sponges and mesh. The sponge improves comfort and reduces skin abrasion from the bandage, while the mesh's honeycomb surface increases friction between the bandage and the skin. The sponge absorbs perspiration from the calf via the honeycomb pores to prevent slippage under load.

The heel and middle of the shoe contain textile straps linked to the calf bandages to strengthen operating stability of the calf bandages. The far-end of Bowden cable was linked to a fixed anchor on the heel. Meanwhile, the proximal sheath was attached to a floating anchor on the calf bandage, which was operated by an actuator that compressed the Bowden cable to deliver a mechanical force to the ankle.

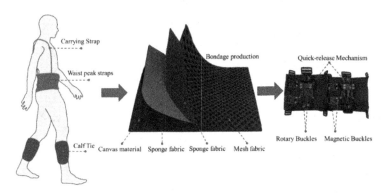

Fig. 4. Flexible bandage design.

3   Human and Ankle-Exosuit Coupled Kinematic

We established a human ankle joint and the Ankle-Exosuit coupling relationship through the lower extremity biokinetic mechanism and derived the ankle joint change angle and motor rotation angle model to support the assistance trajectory generation and tracking of the Ankle-Exosuit.

The geometric link between the angular position of the Ankle-Exosuit pulley q_a and the angular position of the ankle joint θ_a may be represented as depicted in Fig. 5.

$$R_P(q_a - q_{a0}) = r_a(\theta_a - \theta_{a0}) \tag{2}$$

where R_P is the radius of the pulley, q_a is the output angle of the servo motor, q_{a0} is the initial position of the servo motor, r_a is the distance between the center of rotation of the ankle and the fixed anchor of the same heel, θ_a is the plantarflexion angle of the ankle, θ_{a0} is the initial angle of plantarflexion of the ankle joint, $\Delta\theta_a = \theta_a - \theta_{a0}$, $\cdot\theta_1$ is the angle between the initial length of the standing Bowden cable and the foot, that is

$$\theta_1 = arccos\frac{r_c^2 + l_{a1}^2 + r_a^2 - l_{a0}^2}{2r_a\sqrt{r_c^2 + l_{a1}^2}} \tag{3}$$

The ankle plantarflexion locomotion can be simplified to a rotation around the center of rotation. Therefore, the arc traversed by the ankle for the center of rotation was equal to the arc traversed by the pulley. The kinematic model of the ankle joint was obtained by transforming Eq. (2).

$$\theta_a = \frac{R_P}{r_a}(q_a - q_{a0}) + \theta_{a0} \tag{4}$$

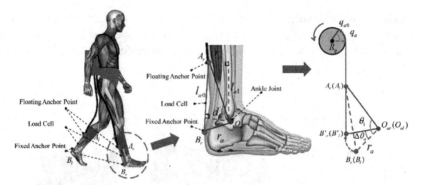

Fig. 5. Coupling relationship between human ankle joint and the Ankle-Exosuit.

4 Gait Recognition

The goal of gait recognition is to aid in decision-making. In this paper, we use a threshold real-time gait phase detection algorithm [16, 17], which detects the mean pressure in the foot-ground contact area using a plantar pressure sensor to achieve heel-off (HO) and toe-off (TO) gait event recognition (see Fig. 6a), with the goal of the controller sending the appropriate assistance start and end commands.

4.1 Gait Analysis

A single gait cycle was separated into seven stages by classifying two contiguous contacts of the ipsilateral heel as an entire cycle, respectively, loading response (LR), middle stance (MSt), terminal stance (TSt), pre-swing (PSw), initial swing (ISt), middle swing (MSw), terminal swing (TSw) (see Fig. 6a). We identified the instant heel strike to the ground as the gait behavior during the weight-bearing response period since it only accounts for roughly 2% of the cycle. The gray region represents the foot pressure recording area, while the orange-red area represents the assistance area. The assistance begins when the heel leaves the ground and finishes when the medial forefoot leaves.

The grey and orange-red areas are the plantarflexion (PF) intervals of the ankle (Fig. 6b), with the grey area muscles passively performing negative work to overcome the energy impact of the environment in order to maintain walking stability and the orange-red area muscles actively performing positive work to change the position and posture of the foot, at this moment, the force exerted by the muscles on the ankle joint is explosive and transient. Practical ankle joint support during active, positive muscular action may minimize muscle fatigue and energy consumption. Therefore, our selection of the orange-red region as the assistance interval is consistent with the biology of lower extremity locomotion.

4.2 Real-Time Gait Detection

A pair of plantar pressure sensors were used to recognize the stride of the HO the ground. Plantar pressure sensors were placed into a boot as a shoe insole, measuring the

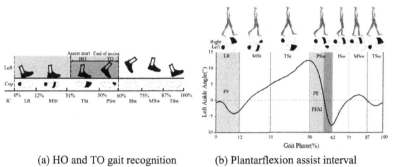

(a) HO and TO gait recognition   (b) Plantarflexion assist interval

Fig. 6. Gait analysis of the lower extremity.

contact forces between the foot and the ground. To filter the impact of the environment on the foot pressure measurement, we employed Kalman filtering or complementing filtering methods [18–20] to process the data obtained by the plantar pressure sensors. The microcontroller in the drive unit collected signals from all the sensors by wire. The number and type of sensors was reconfigured to suit different walking experiments and project development requirements.

Each plantar pressure sensor was divided into three areas (Fig. 7), with three pressure points in the forefoot (FF) and pressure values recorded as F_{ff1}, F_{ff2} and F_{ff3}. The middle foot (MF) has two pressure points and the pressure values are noted as F_{ff4} and F_{mf5}. The rear foot (RF) has three pressure points and the pressure values were noted as F_{rf6}, F_{rf7} and F_{rf8}, accounting for 40%, 30% and 30% of the total foot length, respectively [21]. The HO sign was the rapid drop of the pressure signal value in the heel region, and the mean value of the signal in this area must fulfill the following relationship.

$$\begin{cases} \sum_{i=6}^{8} F_{rfi} < 3\varepsilon_r \\ \sum_{i=4}^{5} F_{mfi} < 3\varepsilon_m \\ \sum_{i=1}^{3} F_{ffi} > 3\varepsilon_f \end{cases} \tag{5}$$

where ε_r is the heel strike (HS) detection threshold, ε_m is the foot flat (FF) detection threshold, ε_f is the TO detection threshold. The TO satisfies the following expression:

$$\sum_{i=6}^{8} F_{rfi} + \sum_{i=4}^{5} F_{mfi} + \sum_{i=1}^{3} F_{ffi} < 3(\varepsilon_r + \varepsilon_f + \varepsilon_m) \tag{6}$$

In order to avoid the influence of the environment and the wearer on the signal acquisition of the plantar pressure sensor, the Ankle-Exosuit conducts a 5-s threshold self-test each time it is powered on. After each gait detection during assistance, threshold updates take place.

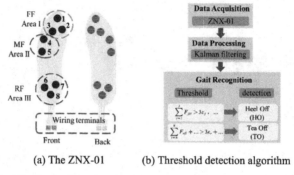

(a) The ZNX-01   (b) Threshold detection algorithm

Fig. 7. Lower extremity locomotion intention recognition

5 Control System Design

Due to the effect of the nonlinear features of the flexible material, the intrinsic character-istics of the drive, and the energy loss of the transmission parts, providing exact help to the wearer at the correct gait phase and the proper assistance interval is a huge issue. In this study, we demonstrated that PID position control, based on the ankle joint kinematic model and overrides locomotion signal input, efficiently guaranteed the precise tracking of the assist trajectory and decreased the additional delay to enhance the stability of human-exosuit cooperative control.

5.1 Controller Design

The Ankle-Exosuit generated auxiliary forces by contracting the Bowden cable, using a PID position controller to change the position of the Bowden cable. We proposed a loco-motion control strategy based on a biological model of lower extremity locomotion that can adjust the human gait cycle, amplitude, and contour to suit individualized wearing needs, allowing the assistance trajectory of the position controller to adapt to the natural gait trajectory of human body and enabling active human participation in the assistance. Different from other exosuits control strategies, we emphasized the introduction of the coupling model of human and the Ankle-Exosuit into the control loop, and integrated the Fourier function to fit the OpenSim walking simulation data to generate an assistance trajectory that conforms to the ankle joint locomotion law.

We developed a system consisting of high-level, middle-level, low-level controllers, a human and the Ankle-Exosuit system, as seen in Fig. 8. The high-level controller, the outer layer, detects support phase gait events in the gait cycle based on foot plantar pressure sensor measurements. The middle-level controller combines the ankle joint coupling locomotion control model and the OpenSim simulation data to generate the desired position trajectory. The low-level controller, an inner layer, runs closed loop position control on motor position for the actuation system to track the desired cable position trajectories generated by the middle-level controller. The low-level controller controls the value of the output voltage (U_{com}) by correcting the position error (P_{err}), and reduces the error of the Bowden cable output position (P_{cable}) and the desired position trajectory value (P_{value}). The human and the Ankle-Exosuit control system adjusts the Bowden cable assistance trajectory to assist the locomotion gait of the wearer.

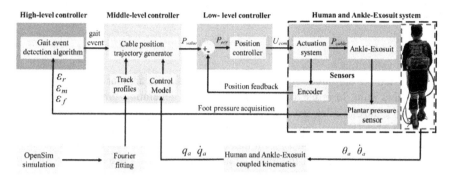

Fig. 8. Schematic block diagram of the Ankle-Exosuit controller. The diagram shows the human and the Ankle-Exosuit system (blue), sensor system (orange), high-level controller (gray), middle-level controller (yellow) and low-level controller (green). The high-level controller completes the gait intention recognition through the threshold detection algorithm, and detects the gait event according to the measured value of the foot pressure sensor. The middle-level control generates the desired assistance trajectory based on the coupling model, trajectory generation function and gait events. The low-level control adjusts the position output of the actuator system to track the desired trajectory generated by the middle-level controller. (Color figure online)

In order to achieve personalized wearing assistance requirements and adapt to different walking gait of wearers, we obtained a gait cycle ankle angle from OpenSim simulation, normalized the coordinates and fitted it to $\theta_{fa}(t)$ by Fourier function, and transformed $\theta_{fa}(t)$ into a generic trajectory generation function by parametric processing.

$$\theta_a(t) = A_a\theta_{fa}\left(\frac{1}{T}t\right) + B_a \tag{7}$$

where $\theta_a(t)$ is the ankle joint angle, A_a is the amplitude, T is the gait period, B_a is the joint angle offset, and $\pm\frac{T}{2}$ is the phase difference between the left and right leg.

According to Eqs. (4) and (7), the model of the ankle joint trajectory generator can be expressed as

$$q_a(t) = \frac{r_a}{R_p}\left(A_a\theta_{fa}\left(\frac{1}{T}t\right) + B_a\right) - \frac{r_a}{R_p}\theta_{a0} + q_{a0} \tag{8}$$

5.2 Trajectory Generator Model Validation

(1) Model parameters calculation

We used the statistical method of sampling to select 10 typical participants from 100 participants with different height and weight, measured and calculated the model parameters, and determined the model parameters by calculating the mean value to increase the accuracy of the model parameters. The model parameters are shown in Table 1.

Table 1. List of model parameters

Symbols	R_p	l_{a0}	r_a	r_c	l_{a1}
Value (mm)	30	180	84	58	192

(2) Model validation

We varied the amplitude A_a, the gait period T and the angular displacement B_a of the ankle joint. In order to verify the trajectory generation function and the locomotion control model, we displayed the joint locomotion trajectories produced by the trajectory generation function across five gait cycles by altering the values of amplitude A_a, gait period T, joint angular displacement B_a of the ankle joint. The locomotion trajectory of the ankle joint was precisely replicated by the trajectory generation function (Fig. 9).

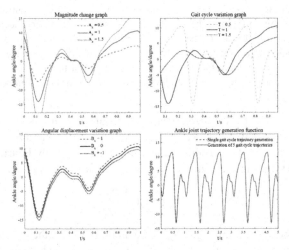

Fig. 9. Verification result of the trajectory generation function

The locomotion trajectory of the input motor was synchronized with the ankle-assisted trajectory (Fig. 10), the rationality of the trajectory generator model was proved..

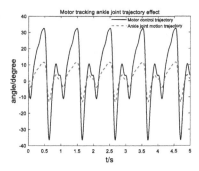

Fig. 10. Angle relationship between Ankle joint and motor.

6 Experiments

In order to evaluate the efficacy of the Ankle-Exosuit, muscle activation is compared unworn the Ankle-Exosuit by the sEMG experiments. A treadmill, a set of sEMG device (Noraxon-DTS series wireless sEMG recording device, USA), and a host computer for data reception (MR23 software) made up most of the experimental apparatus (Fig. 11).

The sEMG assessment experiments included three healthy adult individuals (age = 24 ± 2 years, height = 170 ± 10 cm, weight = 65 ± 10 kg). The two groups of experiments were separated by 10 min to ensure that the muscles could recover sufficiently. Before starting the sEMG experiments, the subjects were informed about the detailed experimental procedure. Six pairs of disposable electrode pads were placed on the surface of six muscles (medial and lateral GM and SM of the left and right legs), which had been previously cleaned with alcohol to allow measurement of the fatigue level of the gastrocnemius and hamstrings muscles. The sEMG acquisition frequency was set to 1500 Hz and the acquisition time was 2 min. The sEMG signal was input to the PC and low-pass filtered, rectified and normalized. We selected the maximum sEMG signal values for 100 gait cycles and summed the GM and HM of the left and right legs to find the mean and standard deviation.

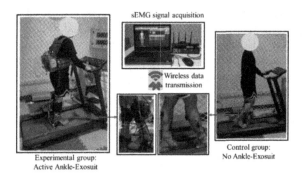

Fig. 11. Subjects wore Ankle-Exosuit with EMG tester for walking test on a treadmill.

The sEMG experiments demonstrated that while wearing the Ankle-Exosuit for ankle gait assistance, the amount of activation of both the GM and SM was reduced, with the GM displaying the most significant performance (Fig. 12). Compared with the unworn the Ankle-Exosuit, the activation rate of the GM muscle and the SM decreased by 11.08% and 6.5%, respectively.

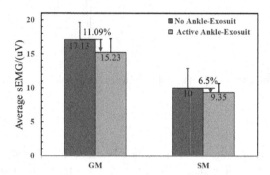

Fig. 12. Comparison of sEMG signals between the experimental and control groups.

7   Conclusion

In this study, we developed an Ankle-Exosuit system to achieve effective walking assistance. A biomimetic Ankle-Exosuit was designed based on the muscle-tendon-ligament model by analyzing biomechanics of the ankle joint. Meanwhile, the bandage locomotion can be effectively reduced by the designed lacing mechanism. The human-exosuit coupled kinematic model was established. Recognition of HO and TO was implemented by threshold detection algorithm. The generation of ankle-assisted trajectory was achieved by the fusion of the coupled kinematic model and trajectory generation function. The Ankle-Exosuit provided assistance to the ankle joint after completing the gait recognition. The assistance trajectory tracking error was reduced by PID feedback control.

Three volunteers participated in the sEMG experiments to assess the auxiliary performance of the Ankle-Exosuit. Comparison experiments demonstrated that when wearing the Ankle-Exosuit, the locomotion activation of the GM and SM decreased by 11.09% and 6.5%, respectively. Conclusively, this comprehensive study indicates that the Ankle-Exosuit system has the ability to reduce muscle activation to enhance human walking endurance, showing great potential to assistance walking in ankle patients with locomotion impairment.

Acknowledgements. This work was funded by Chongqing Science and Technology Commission of China (cstc2020jcyj-msxmX0398), Science and Technology Research Program of Chongqing Municipal Education Commission (KJZD-K202001103, KJQN202201169), the Scientific Research Foundation of Chongqing University of Technology (2019ZD61), and the graduate student Innovation Project of Chongqing (NO. CYS21466). Supported by action plan for quality development of Chongqing University of Technology graduate education (Grant No. gzlcx20233426).

References

1. Olney, S.J., Rsichards, C.: Hemiparetic gait following stroke. Part I: Characteristics. Gait Posture **4**(2), 136–148 (1996)
2. Moriello, C., Finch, L., Mayo, N.E.: Relationship between muscle strength and functional walking capacity among people with stroke. J. Rehabil. Res. Dev. **48**(3), 267–275 (2011)
3. MAili, P., Salvo, F.D., Caserio, M.: Neurorehabilitation in paraplegic patients with an active powered exoskeleton (Ekso). Digit. Med. **2**(4), 163 (2016)
4. Jansen, O., Grasmuecke, D., Meindl, R.C.: Hybrid assistive limb exoskeleton HAL in the rehabilitation of chronic spinal cord injury: proof of concept; the results in 21 patients. World Neurosurg. **110**, e73–e78 (2018)
5. Hong, E., Gorman, P.H., Forrest, G.F.: Mobility skills with exoskeletal-assisted walking in persons with SCI: results from a three center randomized clinical trial. Front. Robot. AI **7** (2020)
6. Milia, P., De Salvo, F., Caserio, M.: Neurorehabilitation in paraplegic patients with an active powered exoskeleton (Ekso). Digit. Med. **2**(4), 163 (2016)
7. Ding, Y., Galiana, I., Asbeck, A..T.: Biomechanical and physiological evaluation of multi-joint assistance with soft exosuits. IEEE Trans. Neural Syst. Rehabilit. Eng. **25**(2), 119–130 (2017)
8. Park, Y.L., Chen, B.R., Perez-arancibia, N.O.: Design and control of a bio-inspired soft wearable robotic device for ankle-foot rehabilitation. Bioinspir. Biomim. **9**(1), 016007 (2014)
9. Wehner, M., Quinlivan, B., Aubin, P.M.: A lightweight soft exosuit for gait assistance. In: Proceedings of the 2013 IEEE International Conference on Robotics and Automation, F, 2013. IEEE (2013)
10. Awad, L.N., Bae, J., O'Donnell, K.: A soft robotic exosuit improves walking in patients after stroke. Sci. Transl. Med. **9**(400), eaai9084 (2017)
11. Schmid, K., Duarte, J.E., Grimmer, M.: The myosuit: bi-articular anti-gravity exosuit that reduces hip extensor activity in sitting transfers. Front. Neurorobot. **11** (2017)
12. Ding, Y., Gallana, I., Siviy, C.: IMU-based iterative control for hip extension assistance with a soft exosuit. In: Proceedings of the 2016 IEEE International Conference on Robotics and Automation (ICRA), F, 2016. IEEE (2016)
13. Lee, G., Ding, Y., Bujanda, I.G.: Improved assistive profile tracking of soft exosuits for walking and jogging with off-board actuation. In: Proceedings of the 2017 IEEE/RSJ International Conference on Intelligent Robots and Systems (IROS), F, 2017. IEEE (2017)
14. Walsh, C.: Human-in-the-loop development of soft wearable robots. Nat. Rev. Mater. (2018)
15. Haxton, H.A.: Absolute muscle force in the ankle flexors of man. J. Physiol. **103**(3), 267–273 (1944)
16. Li, Y.D., Hsiao-Wecksler, E.T.: Gait mode recognition and control for a portable-powered ankle-foot orthosis. Proceedings of the 2013 IEEE 13th International Conference on Rehabilitation Robotics (ICORR), F, 2013. IEEE (2013)
17. Bae, J., De Rossi, S.M.M., O'Donnell, K.: A soft exosuit for patients with stroke: feasibility study with a mobile off-board actuation unit. In: Proceedings of the 2015 IEEE International Conference on Rehabilitation Robotics (ICORR), F, 2015. IEEE (2015)
18. Gallagher, A., Matsuoka, Y., Ang, W,-T.: An efficient real-time human posture tracking algorithm using low-cost inertial and magnetic sensors. In: Proceedings of the 2004 IEEE/RSJ International Conference on Intelligent Robots and Systems (IROS) (IEEE Cat No. 04CH37566), F, 2004. IEEE (2004)
19. Marins, J.L., Yun, X., Bachmann, E.R.: An extended Kalman filter for quaternion-based orientation estimation using MARG sensors. In: Proceedings of the 2001 IEEE/RSJ International Conference on Intelligent Robots and Systems Expanding the Societal Role of Robotics in the the Next Millennium (Cat No 01CH37180), F, 2001. IEEE (2001)

20. Foxlin, E.: Inertial head-tracker sensor fusion by a complementary separate-bias Kalman filter. In: Proceedings of the IEEE 1996 Virtual Reality Annual International Symposium, F, 1996. IEEE (1996)
21. Chevalier, T.L., Hodgins, H., Chockalingam, N.: Plantar pressure measurements using an in-shoe system and a pressure platform: a comparison. Gait Posture 31(3), 397–399 (2010)

A Binocular Vision Based Intelligent Upper Limb Exoskeleton for Grasp Assisting

Yiyou Li, Liugang Zhao, Sen Huang, Xinzhili Chen, Dong Yuan, Minchao Liu, Xiaodong Qin, Fangcao Hu, Changhong Wang, Qiusheng Zhao, and Bo Li[✉]

Chongqing University of Technology, Chongqing 400000, NJ, China
libo_doctor@163.com

Abstract. Assisting patients with upper limb motor dysfunction to complete activities of daily living can improve their quality of life. This paper develops a binocular vision-based upper limb exoskeleton to assist grasping. The mechanism adopts a modular design to reduce the complexity of the joint. The cable-driven actuators were used to improve system compliance. A binocular vision-based detection and location system was developed, which adopted a depth camera and deep learning detection algorithm to identify and locate objects. The frame of the target object detected by the master computer was sent to the trajectory controller, then the trajectory controller controlled the cable-driven actuator to approach the target object by calculating the inverse kinematics of the multi-joint mechanism. Grasping experiments demonstrated that the system could effectively assist patients with upper limb dysfunction in recognizing and locating target objects.

Keywords: Upper limb exoskeleton · Cable-driven · Binocular vision · Visual recognition · Grasp assistance

1 Introduction

Neurological disorders such as Parkinson's, stroke, and spinal cord injury result in motor dysfunction of the upper limb [1–3]. The upper limb motor dysfunction causes the patient to lose self-care ability [4–6]. The upper limb exoskeleton is an effective device to assist patient to independently implement activity of daily life.

At present, the upper limb exoskeleton mainly challenges the human-machine motion compatibility and interaction [7–9]. Cui et al. developed an upper limb exoskeleton (CAREX-7) to regulate hand forces and moments to assist in dexterous hand manipulation. The CAREX-7 existed motion incompatibility issues between the exoskeleton and human joints [10, 11]. To enhance the performance of human-machine interaction and motion compatibility, Perry et al. designed a 7DOF rehabilitation exoskeleton with a cable drive and a zero-clearance reverse drive gearbox to reduce inertia and stiffness [12]. None of the above exoskeletons had developed effective human-machine interaction, which needs the intervention of others.

Gull Ahsan et al. proposed a novel wheelchair-assisted upper limb exoskeleton using a tongue-based interface with semi-autonomous control [9, 13, 14]. Tongue control can

© The Author(s), under exclusive license to Springer Nature Singapore Pte Ltd. 2023
H. Yang et al. (Eds.): ICIRA 2023, LNAI 14268, pp. 503–517, 2023.
https://doi.org/10.1007/978-981-99-6486-4_43

assist patients with upper limb motor dysfunction control the exoskeleton and requires the user to adapt to this control mode after prolonged tongue training. The exoskeleton uses HSV color recognition and RANSAC technology to implement feature extraction and target recognition functionalities. The feature extraction visual recognition method is not applicable to other target objects and has several limitations. Deep learning extends the data model by introducing methods such as learning semantics to recognize more different target objects.

In this paper, we present an upper limb exoskeleton assisted grasping system based on visual recognition and localization. A binocular vision-based detection and location system was developed, which used a depth camera and deep learning detection algorithm to identify and locate objects. The frame of the target object detected by the master computer was re-sent to the trajectory controller, and the trajectory controller controlled the cable-driven actuator to approach the target object by calculating the inverse kinematics of the multi-joint mechanism.

2 Development of Upper Limb Exoskeleton System

The structure of the upper limb exoskeleton-assisted grasping system designed in this paper is shown in Fig. 1. It consists of the upper limb exoskeleton mechanics, a master computer (vision system), and a slave computer (controller, and motor). The functions of the system mainly include image processing, visual recognition and positioning of the master computer, kinematic solving, and PID control of the slave computer.

The upper limb exoskeleton uses the depth camera to precisely identify and locate the target object. The frame of the target object detected by the master computer was re-sent to the trajectory controller, and the trajectory controller controlled the cable-driven actuator to approach the target object by calculating the inverse kinematics of the multi-joint mechanism. The cable-driven of upper limb exoskeleton then propels the user's upper limb to approach and capture the target item to conduct the auxiliary positioning and grasping function.

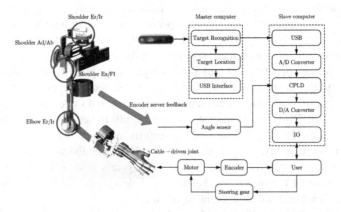

Fig. 1. Upper limb exoskeleton control system based on visual detection

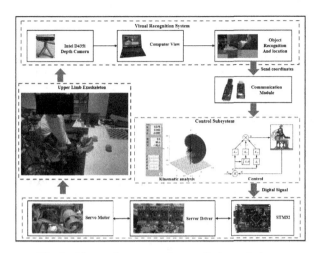

Fig. 2. Electronic system of upper limb exoskeleton

The parts of the control system, including the motors, controllers, encoders, and force sensors, are shown in Fig. 2. The system can measure the rotation angle of each joint and calculate the spatial position of the actuating end. The controller can read the rotation angle of each joint of the upper limb exoskeleton in real-time. The motor driver is connected to the controller through the analog output channel. The slave controller and master computer interact via the USB port. Computer vision mainly performs target recognition and target localization.

The depth camera is used to recognize the target object, and the depth information is aligned with the color information to obtain the rough position information of the target object in the scene. The improved D-H algorithm is used to establish the kinematic model and analyze the relative positional relationship between the target object and the world coordinate system. Then, based on the inverse kinematic solution, the rotation angle of each joint is calculated and transmitted to the controller to drive the exoskeleton.

To enhance the comfort of human-computer interaction, a human-computer interaction interface for user cognitive decision-making is developed using vision technology, which can display visual detection information and provide decision cognition for the user to grasp the target object in real time.

3 Mechanism and Control System

3.1 Mechanism Design

The overall structure of the upper limb exoskeleton is shown in Fig. 3. It mainly consists of the cable-driven system, shoulder joint, elbow joint, upper arm, forearm, etc. To assist patients in daily tasks and improve their quality of life, computer vision technology is integrated to an already developed upper limb exoskeleton [15]. The drive system and control device are located on the back of the backplate, and the mechanisms of the system are designed in a modular way to reduce the complexity of the joints. While ensuring that the upper limb exoskeleton is able to perform its motor functions, it must also be comfortable for the patient to wear.

The movable structure is designed in the shoulder, forearm, and small arm parts, such as the yellow indication arrow position in the figure, which can be applied to different human upper limb sizes. The joint limiting structure is then created to make sure that the exoskeleton's joint rotation angle stays within the human joint movement range throughout the action, thus improving the compatibility of human-computer motion. To ensure human-exoskeleton locomotion compatibility, the corresponding joint axes of the human and the exoskeleton should be aligned [6]. Based on the above requirements, a four-DOFs upper limb exoskeleton was designed, which includes shoulder joint adduction/abduction, internal/external rotation and flexion/extension, and elbow joint flexion/extension.

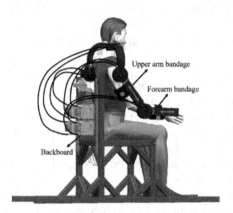

Fig. 3. Design of Upper limb exoskeleton structure

3.2 Kinematic Analysis

The upper limb exoskeleton's kinematic model is based on a modified D-H algorithm [16]. To obtain the spatial relationship between the corresponding links of each joint and, ultimately, the composite transformation matrix of the executive end of the upper limb exoskeleton and the world coordinate system, four kinematic parameters are used to describe the spatial relationship between two adjacent links.

The structural parameters allow the kinematic model of the upper limb exoskeleton to be constructed, as shown in Fig. 4. The D-H parameters of the upper limb exoskeleton are shown in Table 1, where d_1 and d_2 represent the upper arm and forearm joint lengths, respectively.

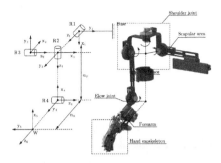

Fig. 4. Coordinate system layout of upper limb exoskeleton

Table 1. D-H Parameter

i	∂_{i-1}	a_{i-1}	d_i	θ_i
1	0	0	0	θ_1
2	$-pi/2$	0	0	$\theta_2 - pi/2$
3	$-pi/2$	0	d_1	θ_3
4	$pi/2$	0	0	θ_4
5	$-pi/2$	0	d_2	0

In the parameter table, d_i and θ_i signify the offset and joint angle from x_{i-1} to x_i., while ∂_{i-1} and a_{i-1} denote the distance and torsion angle from z_{i-1} to z_i.

$$
{}^{i-1}_{i}T = \begin{bmatrix}
c\theta_i & -s\theta_i & 0 & \alpha_{i-1} \\
s\theta_i c\alpha_{i-1} & c\theta_i c\alpha_{i-1} & -s\alpha_{i-1} & -s\alpha_{i-1}d_i \\
s\theta_i s\alpha_{i-1} & c\theta_i s\alpha_{i-1} & c\alpha_{i-1} & c\alpha_{i-1}d_i \\
0 & 0 & 0 & 1
\end{bmatrix}
\tag{1}
$$

The kinematic equations of the upper limb exoskeleton can be established for an upper limb exoskeleton with n degrees of freedom after defining the linkage coordinate system and acquiring the associated D-H parameters. The conformal transformation matrix of the executive end of the upper limb exoskeleton with the world coordinate system is obtained by multiplying the chi-square transformation matrices between neighboring connecting rods of each joint, as illustrated in Eq.

$$
{}^{0}_{n}T = {}^{0}_{1}T {}^{1}_{2}T {}^{2}_{3}T \cdots {}^{n-1}_{n}T
\tag{2}
$$

where is the neighboring coordinate system's flush transformation matrix. Equation (3) is the flush transformation matrix between the executive end of the upper limb exoskeleton and the world coordinate system, which can be inferred from Table 1's D-H parameters and the composite transformation matrix Eqs. (1) and (2).

$$
{}_5^0T = \begin{bmatrix} a_{11} & a_{12} & a_{13} & p_x \\ a_{21} & a_{22} & a_{23} & p_y \\ a_{31} & a_{32} & a_{33} & p_z \\ 0 & 0 & 0 & 1 \end{bmatrix} \tag{3}
$$

The inverse kinematics can be used to control the upper limb exoskeleton in the desired posture and determine the angle of each joint based on the upper limb exoskeleton's known posture after obtaining the chi-square transformation matrix between the executive end and the world coordinate system.

$$
\theta_1 = atan2(p_y - d_5 a_{23}, p_x - d_5 a_{13}) \tag{4}
$$

$$
\theta_3 = atan2(\pm\sqrt{(a_{21}c_1 - a_{11}s_1)^2 + (a_{23}c_1 - a_{13}s_1)^2}, a_{21}s_1 - a_{22}c_1) \tag{5}
$$

$$
\theta_4 = atan2(\frac{a_{23}c_1 - a_{13}s_1}{s_3}, \frac{a_{11}s_1 - a_{21}c_1}{s_3}) \tag{6}
$$

$$
\theta_2 = \varphi - atan2(d_3 + d_5 c_4, \pm\sqrt{p_z^2 + (p_x c_1 + p_y s_1)^2 - (d_3 + d_5 c_4)^2}) \tag{7}
$$

Workspace analysis is an important feature that influences the structural design of the upper limb exoskeleton. The workspace of the upper limb exoskeleton was analyzed using a kinematic model. Given the position of any point in the workspace, it was determined whether the actuating end of the exoskeleton could reach the target position. Therefore, we used MATLAB software for simulation analysis and evaluated the workspace of the upper limb exoskeleton within the bounded range of the joints based on a Monte Carlo algorithm to collect 30,000 sets of samples, as shown in Fig. 5b.

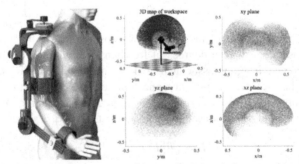

(a)human-exoskeleton system (b)upper limb exoskeleton workspace

Fig. 5. Upper limb exoskeleton simulation model

3.3   Exoskeleton Control System

Due to factors such as bending deformation of the sheath and friction of the components, there is a position error between the actual position and the desired position during the movement of the patient's upper limb driven by the upper limb exoskeleton. To ensure that the actual position is consistent with the desired position, an angle encoder is installed at the movable joint position to measure the actual angle of joint rotation. The exoskeleton drive system consists of a drive motor and a Bowden wire, and the joint position is controlled by a PID control algorithm. The control framework of the upper limb exoskeleton is shown in Fig. 6, and this control system is implemented in Windows system operation.

The master computer vision frame identifies and locates the coordinates of the target object position, and uses inverse kinematics to calculate the angle that each joint needs to rotate when the exoskeleton actuating end reaches the target position, and transmits the joint rotation angle to the possible sensing system through the USB serial port, and the controller controls the motor to drive the upper limb exoskeleton to drive the patient's upper limb to move to the target object position. Before the upper limb exoskeleton performs the assisted task, the hand-eye calibration of the exoskeleton actuating end and camera position is required to ensure the accuracy of grasping.

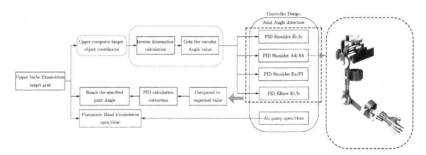

Fig. 6. Upper limb exoskeleton Control the structure

The drive module for the upper limb exoskeleton is placed towards the back of the platform to lessen the strain it places on the patient's hand. The power for the shoulder and elbow joints is provided by four motors that are fixed to the back plate bracket. Bowden cables and pre-tensioners convey the power to the joints, and each rotating joint has encoders built in to make it easier to detect the rotation angle of the corresponding joint.

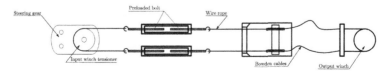

Fig. 7. Bowden cable-based actuation system

Due to the joint required by each active joint being different, the relationship between the human active joint and the maximum human torque is summarized in the reference [17]. To improve the power-to-mass ratio and power-to-volume ratio, a Bowden cable-based drive system was designed as shown in Fig. 7.

The system consists of an input winch, an output tiller, and a preload module. The input winch is driven by a motor and the output tiller rotates to drive the active joint, and the Bowden cable consists of a sheath and a wire rope. The relative movement of the wire rope within the sheath can transmit motion and force to ensure accurate, fast, and stable desired movement. Its pre-tensioning process can be divided into two stages, the first stage is to adjust the position of the sliding slider on the fixed base by changing the rotation depth of the bolt; the second stage is to adjust the length of the tensioner on the wire rope. In the process of power transmission, there is a position error between the actual position and the desired position due to the bending deformation of the sheath and the friction of the components. To ensure that the actual position is the same as the desired position, an angle encoder is installed at the joint position to measure the actual position.

The kinetic model of the upper limb exoskeleton can be described as:

$$\tau = D(q)\ddot{q} + H(q, \dot{q})\dot{q} + G(q) + \tau_d \tag{8}$$

where $q\dot{q}\ddot{q} \in R^N$ denote the joint angle, velocity, and acceleration, respectively, D is the inertia matrix, H is the Gauche force vector, G is the gravity vector, and τ_d denotes the unknown external disturbance. In this paper, the PID control algorithm is used to achieve the position control of the joint, as shown in Fig. 8.

$$\Delta\theta = \theta_i - \theta_0 \tag{9}$$

$$I = \int_{t_1}^{t_2} \Delta\theta(t)dt \tag{10}$$

$$D = \frac{d\Delta\theta}{dt} \tag{11}$$

The PID control law is:

$$u = K_p \cdot \Delta\theta + K_i \cdot I + K_d \cdot D \tag{12}$$

θ_i θ_o is the actual location and the desired location of the controlled joint. $\Delta\theta$ I the position error, I is the error integral and D is the error derivative. K_p, K_i, and K_d are proportional, integral, and derivative gains of the PID controller, respectively.

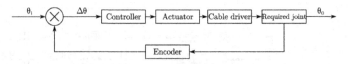

Fig. 8. Diagram of the control structure

4 Computer Vision Module

4.1 Modeling of Binocular Vision Technology

In this study, the IntelD435i depth camera is used to identify and locate the target objects using binocular vision technology. Figure 9 shows the technical principle of binocular stereo vision, in which O_L and O_R denote the left and right optical centers of the depth camera, respectively, and the distance between the optical centers is L. The Y coordinates of their projection distances are equal. It is assumed that there are two imaging points, P_1 and P_2, at point P in space.

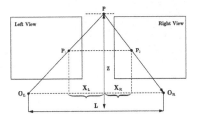
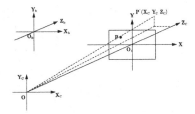

Fig. 9. The principle of binocular stereo vision

Fig. 10. Principle of camera projection

Where X_L and X_R are the distance of the target point in the X-direction of the left and right camera optical center imaging, respectively, and Z is the depth distance from the target point to the center of the binocular camera.

In the process of camera imaging, the pixel coordinate system, image coordinate system, camera coordinate system, and world coordinate system need to be converted. The camera imaging principle is shown in Fig. 10. The pixel coordinate system and the camera coordinate system can be represented by the chi-square matrix as follows:

$$
\begin{bmatrix} u \\ v \\ 1 \\ 1 \end{bmatrix} = \frac{1}{Z_C} \begin{bmatrix} \frac{1}{d_x} & 0 & u_0 & 0 \\ 0 & \frac{1}{d_y} & v_0 & 0 \\ 0 & 0 & 0 & 0 \\ 0 & 0 & 0 & 1 \end{bmatrix} \begin{bmatrix} f_x & 0 & 0 & 0 \\ 0 & f_y & 0 & 0 \\ 0 & 0 & 1 & 0 \\ 0 & 0 & 0 & 1 \end{bmatrix} \begin{bmatrix} x_c \\ y_c \\ z_c \\ 1 \end{bmatrix}
\tag{13}
$$

where u, v denotes the rows and columns of pixels in the image, u_0 and v_0 denote the pixel coordinates of the target point, d_x and d_y denote the vector values of unit pixels on the horizontal and vertical axes. x_c, y_c, and z_c denote the intermediate coordinates for locating the target object by camera identification, f_x and f_y are the internal parameters of the depth camera, and the calibration process is required next.

4.2 Eye-to-Hand Calibration

To accurately grasp the target object, eye-to-hand calibration is required to convert the exoskeleton executive end coordinate system to the world coordinate system with the camera coordinate system. A label is placed on the wrist joint position at the executive end of the exoskeleton, and the wrist is part of the arm closest to the gripper. Without precise calibration, the arm was set to its initial state, and we manually placed the arm on a straight line, pointing to the ground, as the initial state and the configuration of each joint were set to zero. This is a way to obtain accuracy without measurement or calibration, which can be compensated by a tag mounted on the wrist, as shown in Fig. 11.

Fig. 11. Eye to hand calibration system

We manipulate the arm to a specific pose by looking at the wrist-mounted tag, obtain the pose of the end-effector through a tag-to-end-effector transformation, and then model the pose of the end-effector as a hand-eye transformation of the fixed arm configuration, which consists of the angle of each joint.

4.3 Target Detection

In the initial stages of building the system, the proposed Yolov4 algorithm was used to detect and locate the target object. However, the visual framework was not able to stably identify the detection during the process of recognizing the target object. To address this issue, Yolov5 was introduced along with Mosaic data enhancement and automatic learning anchor framework. As a result, subsequent Yolo series algorithms have higher detection rates and accuracy. The Yolov7 neural network has a fast detection rate and can predict the whole picture information while extracting image features [18]. This makes it suitable for the detection and localization of target objects by upper limb exoskeletons.

In this study, the Yolov7 target detection algorithm is used to detect and localize the target object that the patient wants to grasp. The depth camera is positioned on the left side of the wheelchair and pointed towards the area in front of the user. Figure 12 illustrates the visual recognition process which involves acquiring a large number of target object images using the depth camera, training the acquired dataset through the Yolov7 network model architecture, solving the pixel coordinates of the target object in the video stream using the coordinate function, and combining the depth information from the RGB-D camera to obtain the Cartesian coordinates of the target object.

4.4 Target Grasp

The target object is grasped by the vision system's final component, which also places a cup and a tennis ball on the table. A visual interface is developed based on the vision

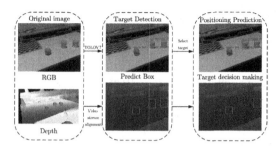

Fig. 12. Target recognition process

system for the user to give commands to grasp the target objects, as shown in Fig. 13. When the user clicks on the screen to select the target object to be recognized, the target object recognition box will switch from green to blue. It is up to the user to decide whether to grasp the detected target object, and the motor can be controlled by clicking on the command to drive the upper limb exoskeleton to locate and grasp that target object.

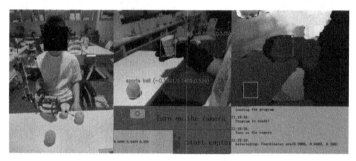

Fig. 13. Target grasping is the coordinate relationship between the positioning and direction of the execution end and the target object

5   Grasp Experiment

This paper focuses on building an intelligent assisted grasping system for the upper limb exoskeleton based on binocular vision. To verify the effectiveness of the built system and the control performance of the exoskeleton, the target object grasping experiment is used to track the trajectory of each joint angle of the upper limb exoskeleton and to analyze whether the control performance of the upper limb exoskeleton can help patients with upper limb impairment to grasp objects by comparing the theoretical trajectory with the actual motion trajectory of the exoskeleton.

In this study, two grasping tasks were chosen to evaluate the accuracy of upper limb exoskeleton grasping, namely grasping a paper cup and a sphere. As shown in Fig. 14, the experiment result was demonstrated that the system can achieve the task of grasping water cups. For each task, 10 grasping experiments were performed by the 2 subjects, who were seated in a wheelchair wearing the upper limb exoskeleton and followed the desired joint angle trajectories. The joint angle trajectories were recorded, and the tracking performance of all joints of the entire exoskeleton system was evaluated based on the root mean square representation over 10 experiments.

Table 2 presents the statistics for assessing the motion performance of the human-worn upper limb exoskeleton. For the water cup grasping task, the mean RMSE values for the four joints were 0.2719 rad, 0.2904 rad, 0.6233 rad, and 0.5450 rad, respectively. The variance of the mean RMSE for the other 10 experiments corresponding to the four joints were 4.518×10^{-4}, 1.410×10^{-4}, 7.740×10^{-6}, and 1.090×10, and the results indicated that the fluctuations of RMSE values were within the acceptable range of variation, indicating that the exoskeleton was able to perform the grasping normal task of grasping the water cup (Figs. 15, 16, and 17).

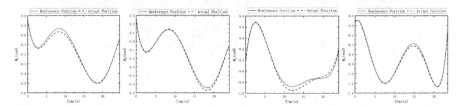

(a)   (b)   (c)   (d)

Fig. 14. Demonstration of normal drinking task: (a) initial position, (b) exoskeleton moves to the grasping position, (c) Grab and pick up the glass, (d) the drinking position.

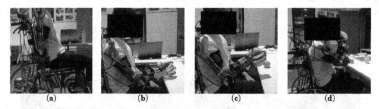

Fig. 15. Grasping trajectory evaluation of an upper limb-assisted exoskeleton in a drinking task.

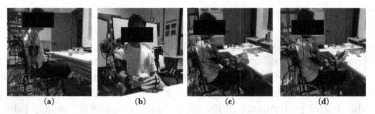

(a)   (b)   (c)   (d)

Fig. 16. Demonstration of an object pick-up task: (a) initial position, (b) moving over the target, (c) exoskeleton moves to a grasping position and holds the object, (d) picking the object up.

The tracking performance of the shoulder joints required to grasp the spherical object was significantly improved compared to the first task. As can be seen in Table 2, the

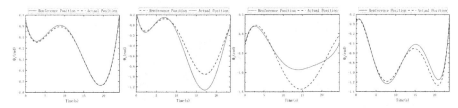

Fig. 17. Grasping trajectory evaluation of an upper limb assisted exoskeleton in ball grasping task.

Table 2. Statistical analysis of PID control method using RMSE value for the performance assessment of the wheelchair exoskeleton

Joints	Average RMSE	Max RMSE	Min RMSE	Variance RMSE	Average RMSE	Max RMSE	Min RMSE	Variance RMSE
	Drinking Task				Object Picking Task			
Joint1	0.2719	0.3159	0.1998	4.518×10^{-4}	0.2430	0.2492	0.2386	7.440×10^{-6}
Joint2	0.2904	0.3061	0.2738	1.410×10^{-4}	0.5548	0.5622	0.5470	2.020×10^{-5}
Joint3	0.6233	0.6277	0.6189	7.740×10^{-6}	0.5995	0.6034	0.5939	7.880×10^{-6}
Joint4	0.5450	0.5572	0.5214	1.090×10^{-4}	0.6543	0.6740	0.6355	1.350×10^{-4}

accuracy of shoulder joint 2 and shoulder joint 3 was significantly improved for the second grasping task when performing the water cup grasping task. For the grasping spherical object task, the average RMSE values of the four joints were 0.2430 rad, 0.5548 rad, 0.5995 rad, and 0.6543 rad, respectively. The variance of RMSE for the other 10 experiments was 7.440×10^{-6}, 2.020×10^{-5}, 7.880×10^{-6}, and 1.350×10^{-4}, respectively, which indicate that the fluctuations of RMSE values are small and within the acceptable variation range, indicating that the exoskeleton can perform the task of grasping a normal grasping spherical object.

Successfully completed 7 out of 10 water cup grasping tasks, with an average grasping time of 60 s each. In the task of grasping a spherical object 6 out of 10 times were successfully completed with an average grasping time of 80 s each time. In the experiments where the grasping objects were not successful, we found that the structural gap of the upper limb exoskeleton and the choice of control method may affect the grasping accuracy of the exoskeleton system.

According to the experimental results in Fig. 18, grasping the average RMSE value of shoulder joint 1 was much lower than the other three joints for the two different tasks, and grasping spherical objects tended to be more difficult and the control scheme more complicated than grasping a water cup when controlling the exoskeleton to perform the grasping task. Because of the small size of the spherical object, it usually requires

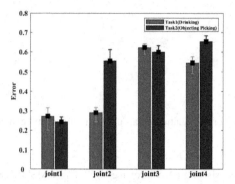

Fig. 18. Bar diagram of the RMSE with variance from 10 trials for each task.

the exoskeleton's wrist to rotate, thus changing the exoskeleton's grasping posture. In contrast, the bottle can be controlled to drive the exoskeleton to grasp the palm without turning the wrist of the exoskeleton. We designed the shoulder joint of the exoskeleton to include shoulder flexion, abduction/adduction, and external/internal rotation, where the rotation of the shoulder joint replaces the rotation of the wrist joint.

6   Conclusion

This paper presented an upper limb exoskeleton assisted grasping system based on visual recognition and localization. The mechanism system adopts a modular design to reduce the complexity of the joint. The relative frame between the grasping end of the upper limb exoskeleton and the base coordinate system is obtained by kinematic model. The frame of the target object detected by the master computer was sent to the trajectory controller. The trajectory controller controlled the cable-driven actuator to approach the target object by calculating the inverse kinematics of the multi-joint mechanism. A visualization interface is developed for the user to decide on the cognitive grasping target and achieve the assisted grasping function. Grasping experiments demonstrated that the system could effectively assist individual to complement activities of daily living.

This binocular vision-based servo control system will provide new ideas and methods to address the field of upper limb exoskeleton assisted grasping.

In the future, the aim is to achieve a more accurate estimation of the end position of the arm, enabling the motion control to be more precise, and we will improve the grasping accuracy in complex environments.

Acknowledgments. This work was funded by Chongqing Science and Technology Commission of China (cstc2020jcyj-msxmX0398), Science and Technology Research Program of Chongqing Municipal Education Commission (KJZD-K202001103, KJQN202201169), the Scientific Research Foundation of Chongqing University of Technology (2019ZD61), and the graduate student Innovation Project of Chongqing (NO. CYS21466), Supported by an action plan for quality development of Chongqing University of Technology graduate education (Grant No. gzlcx20222047).

References

1. Altenburger, R., Scherly, D., Stadler, K.S.: Design of a passive, iso-elastic upper limb exoskeleton for gravity compensation. ROBOMECH J. **3**(1), 12–19 (2016)
2. Gopura, R.A.R.C., Bandara, D.S.V., Kiguchi, K., Mann, G.K.I.: Developments in hardware systems of active upper-limb exoskeleton robots: a review. Robot. Auton. Syst. **75**, 203–220 (2016)
3. Kim, B., Deshpande, A.D.: An upper-body rehabilitation exoskeleton Harmony with an anatomical shoulder mechanism: design, modeling, control, and performance evaluation. Int. J. Robot. Res. **36**(4), 414–435 (2017)
4. Kwakkel, G., Kollen, B.J., Krebs, H.I.: Effects of robot-assisted therapy on upper limb recovery after stroke: a systematic review. Neurorehabil. Neural Repair **22**(2), 111–121 (2008)
5. Kiguchi, K., Kado, K., Hayashi, Y.: Design of a 7DOF upper-limb power-assist exoskeleton robot with moving shoulder joint mechanism. In: 2011 IEEE International Conference on Robotics and Biomimetics, pp. 2937–2942 (2011)
6. Li, J.F., Cao, Q., Dong, M.J., Zhang, C.Z.: Compatibility evaluation of a 4-DOF ergonomic exoskeleton for upper limb rehabilitation. Mechan. Mach. Theory 156, 104146–104164 (2021)
7. Gull, M.A., Bai, S., Bak, T.: A review on design of upper limb exoskeletons. Robotics **9**(1), 16–51 (2020)
8. Thogersen, M., Gull, M.A., Kobbelgaard, F.V., Mohammadi, M., Bengtson, S.H., Struijk, L.N.S.A.: EXOTIC - a discreet user-based 5 DoF upper-limb exoskeleton for individuals with tetraplegia. In: IEEE 3rd International Conference on Mechatronics, Robotics and Automation (ICMRA), Electronic Network, pp. 79–83 (2020)
9. Gull, M.A., et al.: A 4-DOF upper limb exoskeleton for physical assistance: design, modeling, control and performance evaluation. Appl. Sci. **11**(13), 5865–5878 (2021)
10. Cui, X., Chen, W., Jin, X., Agrawal, S.K.: Design of a 7-DOF cable-driven arm exoskeleton (CAREX-7) and a controller for dexterous motion training or assistance. IEEE/ASME Trans. Mechatron. **22**(1), 161–172 (2017)
11. Mao, Y., Agrawal, S.K.: Design of a cable-driven arm exoskeleton (CAREX) for neural rehabilitation. IEEE Trans. Rob. **28**(4), 922–931 (2012)
12. Perry, J.C., Rosen, J., Burns, S.: Upper-limb powered exoskeleton design. IEEE/ASME Trans. Mechatron. **12**(4), 408–417 (2007)
13. Bengtson, S.H., et al.: Computer vision-based adaptive semi-autonomous control of an upper limb exoskeleton for individuals with tetraplegia. Appl. Sci. Basel **12**(9), 4374–4398 (2022)
14. Thogersen, M.B., Mohammadi, M., Gull, M.: A: user-based development and test of the EXOTIC exoskeleton: empowering individuals with tetraplegia using a compact, versatile, 5-DoF upper limb exoskeleton controlled through intelligent semi-automated shared tongue control. Sensors **22**(18), 6919–6942 (2022)
15. Liu, M., Li, B., Ning, Q.: Design of an upper limb exoskeleton to assist disabled individuals. In: IEEE 3rd International Conference on Service Robotics Technologies, Chengdu, pp. 63–67 (2022)
16. Rocha, C.R., Tonetto, C.P., Dias, A.: A comparison between the Denavit-Hartenberg and the screw-based methods used in kinematic modeling of robot manipulators. Robot. Comput. Integrat. Manuf. **27**(4), 723–728 (2011)
17. Rebelo, J., Sednaoui, T., den Exter, E.B., Kruger, T., Schiele, A.: Bilateral robot teleoperation a wearable arm exoskeleton featuring an intuitive user interface. IEEE Robot. Automat. Magaz. **21**(4), 62–69 (2014)
18. Wang, C.Y., Bochkovskiy, A., Liao, H.Y.M.: Yolov7: trainable bag-of-freebies sets new state-of-the-art for real-time object detectors. arXiv e-prints (2022)

Perception and Manipulation
of Dexterous Hand for Humanoid Robot

Contact Force and Material Removal Simulation for a Virtual Robotic Polishing Platform

Mubang Xiao, Xiao Luo, and Ye Ding[✉]

State Key Laboratory of Mechanical System and Vibration, School of Mechanical
Engineering, Shanghai Jiao Tong University, Shanghai, China
{xiaomb,y.ding}@sjtu.edu.cn

Abstract. It is of great potential for robots to replace human workers in manual finishing tasks using the deep reinforcement learning (DRL) technique. However, due to the high cost of the trial-and-error learning process in the real world, it is important to pre-train virtual robots in a physical simulation platform with high fidelity and then transform the learned policies to real robots. In this paper, we aim to develop a physical simulation platform tailored to robotic polishing, combining real-time contact force solving and material removal visualization. The platform can simulate the transient contact impulse and the static contact pressure distribution between the compliant polishing tool and the rigid workpiece with arbitrary shapes. A hierarchical reinforcement learning scheme for robotic polishing is also presented to learn path and force planning policies leveraging haptic and visual feedback.

Keywords: Robotic polishing · contact modeling · deep reinforcement learning

1 Introduction

Training robots to accomplish complex contact-rich tasks using deep reinforcement learning (DRL) is an emerging direction in recent years. Researchers successfully trained robots to grasp complex 3D objects, insert a peg into a hole [1], or walk stably in an unstructured environment [2]. Inspired by these works, this paper aims to apply the DRL technique to robot automatic polishing [3], making sense of haptic and visual feedback.

Due to the high cost of the trial-and-error learning process in the real world, it is a trend to pre-train the robots in a physical simulation platform and then transfer the gained knowledge to the real hardware [4]. A simulation platform with high fidelity could close the sim-to-real gap. Therefore, the main objective of this paper is to develop a virtual robotic polishing platform that can generate haptic and visual sensory data efficiently.

The haptic sensory data provides contact forces and contact point location information of the robot and the environment. The robot is expected to react

H. Yang et al. (Eds.): ICIRA 2023, LNAI 14268, pp. 521–532, 2023.
https://doi.org/10.1007/978-981-99-6486-4_44

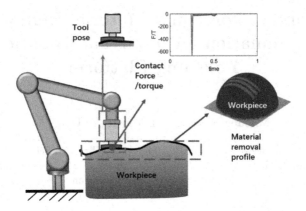

Fig. 1. The multimodal sensory data generated in robotic polishing, including the contact force (haptic feedback) and the material removal depth (visual feedback).

to the haptic feedback, adapting its impedance parameters or reference trajectories to maintain a desired contact force. The key part of generating haptic information for robotic polishing or other robot manipulation tasks is solving the multi-body contact dynamics. In multi-body contact dynamics, the contact bodies cannot penetrate each other. The penalty-force methods [5,6] employ the virtual spring-damper model to compute the contact forces. These penalty-force methods have clear physical meanings, but they use very small simulation time-step to ensure stability. The constraint-based methods [7,8] could simulate the rigid-body contacts more efficiently. The complementary conditions of the contact points are utilized to compute the normal contact impulses. Then, Coulomb's friction cone constraints and the maximum dissipation principle are used to compute the tangential contact impulses.

As for the visual sensory data, it provides observations of the relative pose between the tool and the workpiece and also measures which extent the workpiece is polished. The robot is expected to know which part of the workpiece is over-polished and which part is lack-polished, and then to plan a proper polishing path and normal contact force to improve the polishing accuracy. Based on the material removal model, the material removal depths on the workpiece surface can be mapped into a standard "gray image" which can be easily set as the input of a deep convolutional neural network (DCNN) for further low-dimensional representation learning [1].

Our contributions are summarized as follows: 1) develop a virtual robotic polishing platform considering robot contact dynamics, contact pressure distribution, and material removal process; 2) propose a hierarchical DRL scheme for the robotic polishing task utilizing multimodal sensory data. Performing the detailed training leaves in the future work.

2   Background of Contact Dynamics

In this section, an efficient per-contact iteration method developed by Hwangbo et. al [9] is reviewed. As shown in Fig. 1. The articulated robot has n serial links and a tool installed at its end-effector. The contact dynamics of the robot is written as

$$M(q)\dot{u} + h(q, u) = \tau + J_c(q)^T f_c \qquad (1)$$

where $q \in \Re^n$ is the joint angles, $u \in \Re^n$ is the joint velocities, $M(q)$ is the robot mass matrix and $h(q, u)$ is the nonlinear forces. $\tau \in \Re^n$ is the joint actuation torques and $f_c = [f_{c1}, \cdots, f_{cN}]^T \in \Re^{3N}$ are the contact forces at the contact points O_i $(i = 1, \cdots, N)$. Subscript i represents the i_{th} contact. $J_c(q) = [J_{ci}, \cdots, J_{cN}]^T \in \mathbb{R}^{3N \times n}$ denotes the contact jacobians from the joint velocities u to the contact velocity v_i given in the contact frame $\{O_i\}$. The x and y axes of the contact frame span the tangent plane at the contact point, the z-axis is parallel to the contact normal of the environment.

The collision between robot and environment is assumed as inelastic and the normal contact velocities at the contact points will decay to zero to prevent further penetrations. To avoid solving the non-differentiable dynamics, the contact dynamics Eq. (1) is rewritten in the discrete form

$$\begin{aligned} M(q^-)(u^+ - u^-) &= (\tau - h(q^-, u^-))\Delta t + J_c^T \lambda \\ u^+ &= u^- + M^{-1}\{(\tau - h(q, u^-))\Delta t + J_c^T \lambda\} \end{aligned} \qquad (2)$$

where Δt is the simulation time-step. The signs $+$, $-$ denote the states at the next and the current time-steps, respectively. $\lambda = f_c \Delta t \in \mathbb{R}^{3N}$ represents the contact impulses. In Eq. (2), the contact impulses λ are remained to be solved.

The per-contact iteration algorithm solves only one contact impulse at a time while keeping other contact impulses constant. It computes the contact impulses iteratively until the solutions are converged. Describing the contact dynamics in each contact frame by multiplying the contact jacobian matrix J_{ci} on Eq. (2)'s left, the contact impulse λ_i can be written as an affined form

$$v_i^+ = c_i + A_i \lambda_i \qquad (3)$$

where $v_i^+ = J_{ci} u^+$ is the i_{th} contact velocity at the next time-step, $c_i = J_{ci} u^- + J_{ci} M^{-1}(\tau - h(q, u^-))\Delta t + J_{ci} M^{-1} J_{cj}^T \lambda_j$ $(i \neq j)$ is the current contact velocity plus the velocity change caused by the joint torques, nonlinear forces, and contact impulses at other contact points. $A_i = J_{ci} M^{-1} J_{ci}^T$ is the inverse of the robot's mass matrix expressed in the i_{th} contact frame. Subscripts T, N or x, y, z are used to represent the tangential and normal components. The complementary conditions at each contact point are stated as below

- Distance complementary condition:
  $0 \leq g_i \perp \lambda_{i,N} \geq 0$
- Velocity complementary condition:
  if $g_i = 0$, then $0 \leq v_{i,N} \perp \lambda_{i,N} \geq 0$

where g_i is the gap distance. In practice, a small drift in the position-level constraint is allowed. It can be verified that the normal contact impulse $\lambda_{i,N}$ is positive only when the gap distance g_i and the normal contact velocity $c_{i,N}$ in Eq. (3) are non-positive.

Assuming the normal contact impulse is positive and the tangent contact velocity is non-zero, the tangential contact impulse $\lambda_{i,T}$ can be calculated based on the Coulomb's friction cone constraint and the maximum dissipation principle:

- Coulomb's friction cone constraint:

$\|\lambda_{i,T}\| \leq \mu \lambda_{i,N}$ or $\lambda_{i,x}^2 + \lambda_{i,y}^2 \leq \mu^2 \lambda_{i,z}^2$

If the contact impulse $\lambda_i^{v=0}$ that achieves zero contact velocity is in the Coulomb's friction cone, the contact bodies will be in stick contact. Otherwise, the contact bodies will slide and the solution of $\lambda_i^{v=0}$ should be projected onto the Coulomb's friction cone. The maximum dissipation principle indicates that the contact impulse is to minimize the kinetic energy at the contact point, i.e.,

- Maximum dissipation principle:

$$\lambda_i^* = \arg \min v_i^{+^T} A_i^{-1} v_i^+, \ \lambda_i \in C_i \tag{4}$$

where C_i is the feasible set of the i_{th} contact impulse formed by the velocity complementary condition and the Coulomb's friction cone constraint. If the inverse mass matrix A_i is full rank, the maximum dissipation principle (4) leads to a convex optimization problem with a unique solution.

There are two trival contact cases: when the contact is open, the contact impulse is simply zero; when the two contact bodies are in stick contact, the contact impulse is the unconstrained solution of Eq. (3), i.e., $\lambda_i^{v=0} = -A_i^{-1} c_i$. For the nontrival contact case, two equality constraints should be enforced:

$$h_1(\lambda_i) = v_{i,z}^+ = A_{i(r3)} \lambda_i + c_{i,z} = 0, \ h_2(\lambda_i) = \lambda_{i,x}^2 + \lambda_{i,y}^2 - \mu^2 \lambda_{i,z}^2 = 0 \tag{5}$$

According to the first-order Karush-Kuhn-Tucker (KKT) condition, if λ_i is the optimal solution of Eq. (4), the gradient of the kinetic energy $E = v_i^{+^T} A_i^{-1} v_i^+$ should be zero in the unconstrained space, which is given by $\eta = \nabla h_1 \times \nabla h_2$. The optimization problem is equivalent to finding λ_i satisfying

$$\frac{\partial E}{\partial \lambda_i} \eta = 0 \iff (A_i \lambda_i + c_i) \eta = 0 \tag{6}$$

It is observed [9] that by representing the tangential contact impulses $[\lambda_{i,x}, \lambda_{i,y}]$ as polar coordinates $[r\cos\theta, r\sin\theta]$ and then substituting them into the equality constraints given by Eq. (5), the contact impulse λ_i can be written as a function of the polar angle θ only. To obtain the global minimum solution θ, an efficient bisection method is applied to find the zero-cross point of Eq. (6). The initial guess of θ is chosen as the polar angle of the unconstrained solution: $\theta^0 = \text{atan2}(\lambda_{i,y}^{v=0}, \lambda_{i,x}^{v=0})$. The initial search interval is bisected and the subinterval is selected where the function sign changes. The optimal θ is found when the desired precision is met. The rest contact points can be handled in the same procedure successively using the updated contact impulses.

3   Contact Pressure and Material Removal

During the polishing process, the workpiece material within the contact interface is removed by the abrasive rotating tool. According to the Preston equation, the material removal depth is equal to the contact pressure multiplies the tool dwell time. Therefore, it is necessary to know the contact pressure distribution to simulate the material removal depths over the workpiece surface. However, existing constraint-based methods for rigid-body contact simulation could not report the contact pressure distribution. A practical way to acquire the contact pressure is to compute the static normal contact force between tool and workpiece using the constraint-based method, and then analyze the tool deformation as a static problem given the computed normal contact force.

3.1   Contact Pressure Distribution

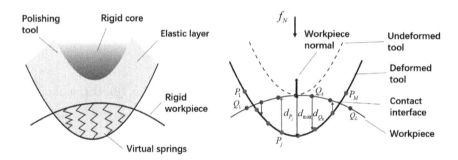

Fig. 2. Left, the overview of the quasi-rigid polishing tool. Right, the deformation of the polishing tool under normal contact force f_N.

For describing the tool deformation, a quasi-rigid body assumption is adopted [6] which assumes the tool can undergo modest deformation in the vicinity of the contact point while its basic shape is preserved. As can be seen in Fig. 2, the polishing tool can be regarded as a rigid core covered with an elastic layer. The elastic layer is assumed as an array of massless springs that are parallel to the tool surface normal. The static normal contact force can be obtained based on the contact dynamics model by setting the contact velocities $J_{ci} u^-$ as zero, which means the system is static and the normal contact force balances the joint actuation torques and nonlinear forces such as gravity. Suppose the static normal contact force is obtained as f_N, the integration of the contact pressure within the contact interface equals to f_N.

Now, a simple nonlinear stress-strain law [10] is adopted to describe the normal contact pressure p generated by the deformation of the elastic spring

$$p = E(\frac{|d|}{H})^\beta \tag{7}$$

where E and β are the nonlinear material modulus and the stress-strain power index, which can be identified through tool loading tests. H is the elastic layer thickness and d is the contact depth. For tool points not in contact, d is set as zero. Suppose there are M virtual springs corresponding to the M sampled tool points (see Fig. 2), the resultant normal contact force can be calculated by summing all the contact pressures:

$$F_N = \sum_{j=1}^{M} p_{P_j} \cdot \Delta S_{P_j} = \sum_{j=1}^{M} E(\frac{|d_{P_j}|}{H})^{\beta} \cdot \Delta S_{P_j} \tag{8}$$

where ΔS_{P_j} is the weighted area of the sampled tool point P_j. For a meshed tool surface, the weighted area is the average area of its adjacent meshes. The tool points are projected onto the implicit workpiece surface embedded in the sampled point cloud along the workpiece normal. This projection is based on the moving least squares (MLS) approach [5], where the unstructured point cloud is fitted locally using the plane or polynomial function. The contact depths d_{P_j} can be estimated via the MLS approach given the maximum contact depth d_{max} at the initial contact point O_i. The normal contact force can be written as a nonlinear scalar function of d_{max} according to Eq. (8)

$$F_N = F_N(d_{max}) = f_N \tag{9}$$

The Newton-Raphson method can be used to solve Eq. (9). It can obtain the solution in a few iteration steps.

3.2 Material Removal Profile

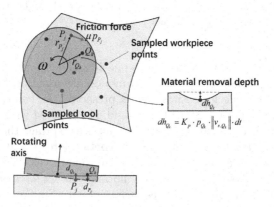

Fig. 3. Illustration of the rotating polishing tool. The resulting material removal depth at the sampled workpiece point Q_k is dh_{Q_k}.

The material removal depth can be simulated by utilizing the Preston equation. When the polishing tool is moving on the workpiece, the tool dwell time

dt at a workpiece point is the reciprocal of the tool feedrate v_f. The instaneous material removal depth equals

$$dh = K_p \cdot p \cdot \|v_s\| \cdot dt \tag{10}$$

where K_p is the material removal coefficient. Suppose there are L sampled workpiece points, the contact pressure p_{Q_k} and the tool sliding velocity v_{s,Q_k} for the sampled workpiece point Q_k are given by

$$(p_{Q_k}, v_{s,Q_k}) = (E(\frac{|d_{Q_k}|}{H})^\beta, \omega \times r_{Q_k}) \tag{11}$$

where d_{Q_k} is the distance from the sampled workpiece point Q_k to the tool bottom surface along the workpiece normal, as shown in Fig. 3. Note that the tool has displaced a normal distance d_{max} under the static normal contact force f_N. r_{Q_k} is the vector from the tool's rotating axis to the sampled workpiece point Q_k. ω is the rotating angular speed. As the polishing tool often has a simple analytical shape (spherical or cylindrical), d_k can be solved by calculating the point-surface distance directly without using the MLS approach. If the sampled workpiece point is not in contact with the polishing tool, the contact pressure and the tool sliding speed are set as zero. The final material removal profile is obtained by accumulating the material removal depths for all the time-steps:

$$h_{Q_k} = \sum_{i=1}^{T} dh_{Q_k}|_{t=t_i} \ (k = 1, \dots, L) \tag{12}$$

where T is the final time-step.

4   Hierarchical Learning Scheme

In this section, we present a hierarchical reinforcement learning scheme to train dynamic polishing policies based on DRL. The scheme's overview is illustrated in Fig. 4. A high-level controller is trained to output the next tool location and nominal contact force. A low-level controller is trained to output the joint actuation torque command. The two controllers are trained according to the received rewards produced by the developed polishing simulation platform.

4.1   High-level Controller

In typical robotic polishing processes, the goal g_H is to achieve uniform material removal depths on the workpiece. Specifically, the expected value of the material removal depths should equal to E_h, and the standard deviation of the material removal depths should be smaller than σ_h.

The material removal profile is a kind of visual feedback in the 3D space. To flatten the material removal profile as a standard 2D image, we view the material removal profile from the $+z$ axis. As can be seen in Fig. 5, the x and y axes are the same as the workpiece frame and the origin is chosen as the tool

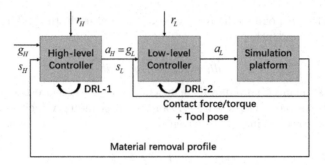

Fig. 4. Hierarchical learning scheme of the robotic polishing task.

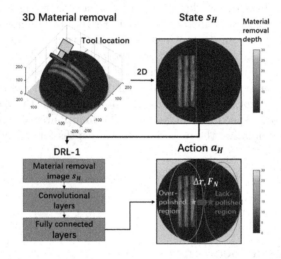

Fig. 5. The overview of the high-level controller. The 3D material removal profile (up-left) is transformed into a 2D gray image (up-right) which is set as the input of a deep convolutional neural network. (Color figure online)

location. Then, the material removal profile is scaled into a gray image with $I \times I$ pixels. The gray value at a pixel equals to the material removal depth at the corresponding workpiece point. For the pixels that are not belong to the workpiece, the gray values are set as E_h, which means they do not needed to be polished yet. Finally, we normalize the gray image via dividing the gray values by E_h. The low-dimensional representations of the high-dimensional material removal profile can be learnt from a deep convolutional neural networks.

During the polishing, the robot investigates the material removal profile to make the best actions. Two actions a_H can be performed by the robot to achieve the material removal goal: the next tool location $\Delta r = [\Delta x, \Delta y] \in \mathbb{R}^2$ and the normal contact force $f_N \in \mathbb{R}$ (see Fig. 5). Considering the policy network can only output the pixel of the next tool location $[\Delta I_x, \Delta I_y]$, the displacement output should times the scaling size of the workpiece to obtain the actual tool motion $[\Delta x, \Delta y]$. The contact force output f_N is determined by the nearby material removal depths and the expected material removal depth. Once the robot performs such an action, the material removal profile is updated according to the mateiral removal model Eq. (12), and thus a new visual state s_H is generated. The reward for the high-level controller should be designed to encourage the tool to move from the over-polished region to the lack-polished region. For example, the high-level reward r_H can be designed as follows

$$r_H = w \cdot \sum_{k=1}^{L} \mathrm{sgn}(E_h - h_{Q_k}) e^{\frac{|E_h - h_{Q_k}|}{\sigma_h}} \cdot dh_{Q_k} \tag{13}$$

where w is a weight coefficient, dh_{Q_k} and h_{Q_k} are the instantaneous and the accumulated material removal depth at the workpiece point Q_k. This reward reflects the deviation between actual and expected material removal depths.

4.2 Low-level Controller

The actions output by the high-level controller including the next tool location Δr and the normal contact force f_N are set as the goal of the cascaded low-level controller, i.e., $a_H = g_L$. The observed low-level state s_L should contain the tool location given in the workpiece frame and the contact force/torque sensed by the end-effector. Some advanced deep learning techniques have already shown successes in estimating the relative pose between two 3D objects from the RGB images [11]. With these techniques, the RGB image capturing the pose information of tool and workpiece is selected as the visual part of the input state s_L. A multimodal fusion module [1] can be employed to encode and fuse the visual and contact force states, as shown in Fig. 6.

For a torque-driven robot [12], the action a_L is chosen as the task-space tool reference trajectory $\hat{x}$ and the adaptive impedance parameters $[k_p, k_d]$. This selection of the action a_L was found to be effective in many contact-rich tasks [2]. In the adaptive impedance controller, the output joint actuation torques are given by $\tau = J_e^T(k_p(\hat{x} - x) + k_d(\dot{\hat{x}} - \dot{x}))$, where J_e is the Jacobian of the end-effector and the derivative of the reference trajectory $\dot{\hat{x}} = 0$. The reward for the low-level controller can be designed to encourage the tool to reach the next tool location Δr at a given feed rate v_f and maintain the normal contact force f_N. For example, the low-level reward r_L can be designed as

$$r_L = w_v(\hat{v}_f \cdot \frac{\Delta r}{\|\Delta r\|} - v_f)^2 + w_f(\hat{f}_N - f_N)^2 \tag{14}$$

where $\hat{v}_f$ and $\hat{f}_N$ are the actual feed velocity and normal contact force. w_v and w_f are the weight coefficients penalizing the path and force tracking errors, respectively. Last but not least, it is observed [1] that compared to the high-level controller, the low-level controller should be run and trained at a higher frequency to perform the contact-rich task more robustly.

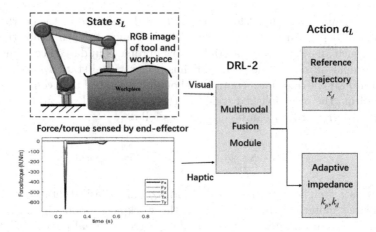

Fig. 6. The overview of the low-level controller. The RGB image of tool and workpiece, the contact force are set as the visual and haptic input states, respectively. The policy network outputs the task-space reference trajectory and adaptive impedances.

5   Simulation Examples

We built the virtual robotic polishing platform on Matlab 2020a for some simple demonstrations. The polishing robot is chosen as Puma560. The collision bodies of the serial links are modeled as cylinders with the radii of 40 mm and with the lengths of 431.8 mm. The polishing tool is modeled as a cylinder with the radius of 50 mm and with the height of 50 mm. The workpiece is modeled as a sphere with the radius of 300 mm and its center is fixed at $[500, -100, -100]$ mm in the robot base frame. The simulation time-step Δt is set as 0.01 s.

5.1   Haptic Data Simulation

When the links or the tool collides with the environment, the contact point undergoes a transient contact impulse. To show this force transition, we investigate the articulated robot is moving with constant actuation torques $\tau = [0, -20, 0, 0, 0, 0]$ N/m. The initial joint angles are set as $q_0 = [0, \pi/2, -\pi, 0, 0, 0]$ and the initial joint velocities are set as zero. Figure 7 depicts the robot configuration and the contact point locations at different time steps. The contact force/torque sensed by the robot end-effector is also plotted in Fig. 7.

5.2   Visual Data Simulation

The contact pressure and the material removal parameters are identified through the tool loading and the robotic polishing experiments [10]. The nonlinear material modulus $E = 0.84Mpa$, the stress-strain power index $\beta = 0.89$, and the material removal coefficient $K_p = 0.0238$. Figure 8 depicts the 3D material removal profiles and their 2D images with 200×200 pixels. It can be seen that

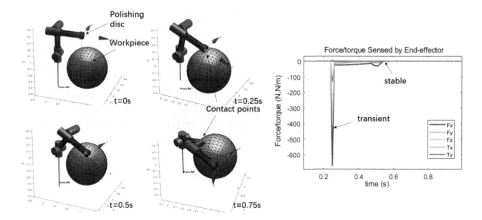

Fig. 7. The robot configurations and the contact point locations at different time steps t=0 s, 0.25 s, 0.5 s, 0.75 s. The actuation torques are set as $\tau = [0, -20, 0, 0, 0, 0]$ N/m. The The contact force/torque sensed by the end-effector is shown on the right.

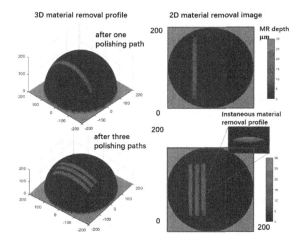

Fig. 8. The 3D material removal profiles and their 2D images after the first and the third parallel polishing paths.

there are three material removal stripes generated on the workpiece. Each stripe consists of successive instaneous material removal profiles with blade shapes due to the non-uniform contact pressure distributions.

6   Conclusion

In this article, a simulation platform tailored to the deep reinforcement learning of robotic polishing policies is presented. A rigid-body contact dynamics model is employed to compute the contact force between the torque-driven articulated robot and the workpiece. A quasi-rigid body assumption and a nonlinear stress-strain law are used to compute the contact pressure distribution between the compliant polishing tool and the workpiece with arbitrary shapes, which lays the basis of the material removal simulation. A hierarchical reinforcement learning scheme for intelligent robotic polishing is developed, where the high-level and low-level controllers receive haptic (contact force) and visual (material removal profile, tool pose relative to the workpiece) feedback from the simulation platform and are responsible for the polishing path/force planning and controlling, respectively. Future work includes improving the rendering of the robotic polishing process and choosing proper deep neural network structures. The ultimate goal is transferring the learned polishing policies to a real torque-driven robot.

References

1. Lee, M.A., et al.: Making sense of vision and touch: learning multimodal representations for contact-rich tasks. IEEE Trans. Robot. **36**(3), 582–596 (2020)
2. Tsounis, V., Alge, M., Lee, J., Farshidian, F., Hutter, M.: DeepGait: planning and control of quadrupedal gaits using deep reinforcement learning. IEEE Robot. Autom. Lett. **5**(2), 3699–3706 (2020)
3. Zhu, D., et al.: Robotic grinding of complex components: a step towards efficient and intelligent machining - challenges, solutions, and applications. Robot. Comput. Integr. Manuf. **65**, 101908 (2020)
4. Bin Peng, X., Andrychowicz, M., Zaremba, W., Abbeel, P.: Sim-to-real transfer of robotic control with dynamics randomization. In: Proceedings - IEEE International Conference on Robotics and Automation, pp. 3803–3810 (2018)
5. Pauly, M., Pai, D.K., Guibas, L.J.: Quasi-rigid objects in contact. In: Proceedings of the 2004 ACM SIGGRAPH/Eurographics Symposium on Computer Animation, pp. 109–119 (2004)
6. Song, P., Kraus, P., Kumar, V., Dupont, P.: Analysis of rigid-body dynamic models for simulation of systems with frictional contacts. J. Appl. Mech. Trans. ASME **68**(1), 118–128 (2001)
7. Horak, P.C., Trinkle, J.C.: On the similarities and differences among contact models in robot simulation. IEEE Robot. Autom. Lett. **4**(2), 493–499 (2019)
8. Negrut, D., Serban, R., Tasora, A.: Posing multibody dynamics with friction and contact as a differential complementarity problem. J. Comput. Nonlinear Dyn. **13**(1), 1–6 (2018)
9. Hwangbo, J., Lee, J., Hutter, M.: Per-contact iteration method for solving contact dynamics. IEEE Robot. Autom. Lett. **3**(2), 895–902 (2018)
10. Xiao, M.B., Ding, Y., Fang, Z., Yang, G.: Contact force modeling and analysis for robotic tilted-disc polishing of freeform workpieces. Precis. Eng. **66**(May), 188–200 (2020)
11. Kokic, M., Kragic, D., Bohg, J.: Learning task-oriented grasping from human activity datasets. IEEE Robot. Autom. Lett. **5**(2), 3352–3359 (2020)
12. Zhang, J., Zhang, B.: An iterative identification method for the dynamics and hysteresis of robots with elastic joints. Nonlinear Dyn. **111**, 13939–13953 (2023)

Soft Humanoid Hand with C-Shaped joint and Granular-Jamming Palm

Haoxian Zheng[1], Bin Fang[2(✉)], Junxia Yan[1], Huaping Liu[2], and Fuchun Sun[2]

[1] School of Mechanical Engineering, Jiangnan University, Wuxi, China
[2] Department of Computer Science and Technology, Tsinghua University, Beijing, China
fangbin@tsinghua.edu.cn

Abstract. In this paper, we propose a soft humanoid hand with a C-shaped joint and granular-jamming palm. The C-shaped joint with spring steel strip has low forward stiffness and can be easily bent, while its inherent elasticity enables it to return to its original position. The reverse stiffness of the joint is higher, providing strong support. The granular-jamming palm endows the soft humanoid hand with superhuman capabilities. Then the required bending moment for joint bending was derived through theoretical analysis of the C-shaped joint. The experimental platform was built, and the grasping, adhesion, and weight-bearing experiments were carried out. The results demonstrate the superior performance of the soft humanoid hand with a C-shaped joint and granular-jamming palm.

Keywords: Soft humanoid hand · C-shaped joint · Granular-Jamming Palm · theory analysis · grasping

1 Introduction

In recent years, the development of robot technology has progressed rapidly, and more industries are beginning to introduce robot technology into their production and work [1, 2]. Traditional end-effectors can only achieve single functions, which makes them rarely meet the requirements of complex tasks. However, dexterous hands have the characteristics of high flexibility and strong operation ability, which makes them have broad application prospects in national defense, medical care, rescue, aerospace, and industrial production [3].

The functions of dexterous hands are mainly determined by the fingers. Flexible fingers can effectively improve the flexibility of dexterous hands. Therefore, research on the fingers of dexterous hands, especially the study of finger joint structures, is crucial. According to the finger joints and transmission modes of dexterous hands, they can mainly be divided into three types: rigid joint dexterous hands, flexible joint dexterous hands, and soft joint dexterous hands.

Rigid joint dexterous hands use linkage mechanisms to connect with motors or directly drive joint movement with motors. Once the motor position is determined, all linkage positions and joint angles will be fixed, such as the i-Limb hand [4], Bebionic hand [5], Michelangelo hand [6], Taska hand [7], Mia hand [8], and Vincent hand [9].

© The Author(s), under exclusive license to Springer Nature Singapore Pte Ltd. 2023
H. Yang et al. (Eds.): ICIRA 2023, LNAI 14268, pp. 533–545, 2023.
https://doi.org/10.1007/978-981-99-6486-4_45

Dexterous hands using this type of joint have advantages such as compactness, high grasping force, and high control precision. However, rigid joint dexterous hands are not friendly to human-robot interaction and have limited adaptability. Flexible-jointed dexterous hands refer to hands with flexible transmission and surface materials. Many humanoid dexterous hands use these types of joints, such as the Hannes Hand [10], KIT Hand [11], X-Hand [12], and Soft Hand [13]. This humanoid dexterous hand is called a flexible dexterous hand, which is usually underactuated and driven by the driving tendon ropes wrapped around the joint axis or the pulleys on the joint axis. The disadvantage of these dexterous hands is that the tendons that drive finger flex-ion need to be decoupled, the joint structure at the joint needs to be complex, and additional devices need to be installed to ensure reverse support. The fingers of soft jointed dexterous hands are mostly designed as integrated units, such as pneumatic flexible dexterous hand [14], Soft Neuroprosthetic Hand [15], RBO Hand2 [16], and Pneumatic bionic hand [17]. Generally, pneumatic, or hydraulic drive is used to bend the dexterous fingers by applying air or hydraulic pressure to the fingers, to simulate the bending of human fingers. The disadvantage is that the joints have poor bearing capacity and the gripping force of the bent fingers is insufficient.

Currently, most humanoid hands pay little attention to the design of the palm's structural functionality. Alternatively, they only focus on studying individual aspects such as emulating gecko palms, particle jamming effects, and pneumatic suction cups to achieve a single adhesion function. However, the application of these features in combination on humanoid hands has yielded poor results, serving merely as auxiliary functions during finger grasping processes. In this study, we leverage the particle jamming effect on humanoid hands to endow the palm with active degrees of freedom, thereby achieving superhuman hand functionality.

The rigid joint dexterous hand has the characteristics of compactness, high grip force, and high control accuracy, but it is not user-friendly for gripping fragile objects. The flexible joint dexterous hand and soft joint dexterous hand have flexibility and adaptability. When enveloping objects, they can adapt to the target surface with the minimal contact stiffness. However, the reverse load-bearing capacity of these two types of joints is usually insufficient. Additionally, the grasping force of soft joint dexterous hands is usually inadequate. Furthermore, most existing dexterous hands replicate the functions of human hands with less focus on the palm. We designed a palm-adherent structure based on the principle of particle jamming to endow the dexterous hand with superhuman hand functions. Therefore, this paper proposes a C-joint finger and a palm-adhering structure design for a super-functional soft humanoid hand.

2 Structure Design and Analysis

2.1 Overall Design of Dexterous Hand

The dexterous hand consists of five fingers and fourteen joints, with a range of motion from 0 to 90° and automatic reset function after forward bending. The solid parts are all 3D printed using nylon material, and driven by LA10-021D/P miniature linear motors and tendon transmission to achieve the flexion motion of the fingers. The surface of the fingers is covered with silicone gel similar to human skin, which serves as the skin of the dexterous hand. The size, kinematics, and range of motion of the dexterous hand are designed to be humanoid. The use of C-shaped joints reduces structural complexity, and the palm adopts the principle of particle blocking to give the dexterous hand with the ability to adhere to objects, making it more suitable for grasping small and delicate objects, and increasing the freedom and multi-tasking capability of the dexterous hand.

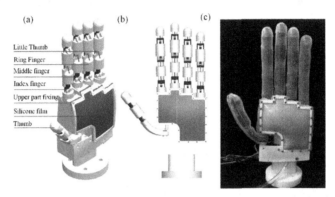

Fig. 1. Overall design model of the soft humanoid hand. (a) The constituent components of the soft humanoid hand. (b) A three-dimensional illustration of the soft humanoid hand. (c) A physical prototype of the soft humanoid hand.

The LA10-021D/P miniature linear servo drive and the DMS-MG90 steering motor are built into the humanoid hand. The driver weighs only 21 g and is 66 mm long. The DMS-MG90 steering motor weighs 9 g, forcing the thumb to swing to the inside of the palm, and the miniature linear servo drive forces the fingers to bend through tendon cables. The pulley assembly increases the stroke of the miniature linear servo drive. A smaller miniature linear servo drive was selected and integrated into the palm of the hand, which not only provided the stroke required to bend the fingers of the prosthesis, but also minimized the overall size of the humanoid hand. The total weight of the hand is 622 g, with a height of 230 mm and a width of 90 mm. Typically, the goal of a humanoid hand is not only to replicate the shape of a human hand, but also to replicate its basic functions. With this in mind, we designed the humanoid hand shown in Fig. 1, using a C-joint finger design to simplify the structure and weight, all of which are intended to improve the overall reliability of the structure, while meeting the adaptability and stability requirements for gripping, and adding the ability to adhere to the palm, giving the dexterous hand superhero functionality. The proposed humanoid hand has 17 degrees of freedom.

2.2 C-Shaped Joint Design

The finger joints of a dexterity hand should have a range of motion of 0–90°, provide reverse support, and have a reset function after forward bending. Therefore, the joint largely determines the flexibility of the fingers. However, existing joint structures are complex and difficult to meet the requirements of reverse support, or require additional devices.

By using C-shaped spring plates to connect two joints, the phalanges are 3D printed with nylon material and C-shaped holes are reserved on the end faces of the phalanges for fixing the spring plates. The spring steel sheets undergo radial elastic deformation in the C-shaped holes and form a C-shaped cross section between the two hinges, which is called a C-shaped hinge. Table 1 lists the basic parameters required for making joints using spring steel sheets, which are determined by the manual size and machining accuracy.

Table 1. The Basic Parameters of Spring Steel Sheets

	Spring Steel
Length	35 mm
Width	17 mm
Height	0.1 mm
Breaking Strength	735 MPa
Yield Strength	430 MPa
Elongation	10%
Density	7.85 g/cm^3

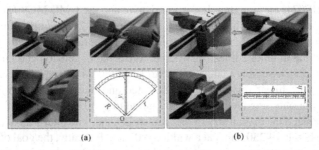

(a)   (b)

Fig. 2. Bending of joints in both flexion and extension directions. (a) When the C-shaped joint is bent in the opposite direction, the cross-section at the midpoint becomes a C-shaped section. (b) When the C-shaped joint is bent in the forward direction, the cross-section at the midpoint becomes a rectangular section.

When C-shaped spring steel plates are used as joints, the cross section at the center of the spring steel plate is not always a standard C-shaped cross section. As shown in Fig. 2(b), when the finger is bent, the finger joint tends to move in the negative z-axis direction. Therefore, the joint has less resistance to the bending force of the finger and is easier to bend. This ability of the joint to resist bending is called forward stiffness, and the cross-section of the spring steel sheet at the center is rectangular. As shown in Fig. 2(a), when the finger is not bending, the finger joint tends to move in the positive z-axis direction. At present, the cross section of the spring steel plate at the center is in a standard C-shape. The joint has greater resistance to the bending force of the finger, making it difficult to bend. This ability of the joint to resist bending is called reverse stiffness.

The designed joints allow the fingers to have good flexion during grasping tasks, meeting the requirements of gripping. The low positive stiffness that needs to be overcome during positive bending enables the fingers to bend smoothly, while the high negative stiffness that needs to be overcome during non-bending movements enables the fingers to provide strong negative support. In addition, the spring steel sheet has the characteristic of self-restoration, allowing it to automatically return to its original position after bending. Unlike most humanoid flexible and dexterous hands, this design of a bidirectional stiffness joint for a humanoid flexible and dexterous hand has greater negative support, solving the problem of insufficient negative grip strength of the fingers, and meeting the needs of daily enveloping grasp and holding. Figure 3(a) shows the joint design process, Fig. 3(b) shows the composition of the various parts of the index finger, and Figs. 3(c)–(d) show the size of the thumb and index finger. Except for the thumb, the structures of the other four fingers are the same, and only the structure of the index finger is shown here.

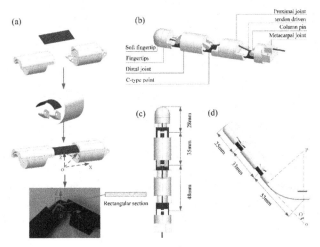

Fig. 3. Finger design. (a) The joint section's components and the assembly process. (b) Composition of the designed finger. (c) Dimensions of the various parts of the finger in detail. (d) Dimensions of each portion of the thumb, as well as the angle of departure.

2.3   Granular-Jamming Palm Design

In this paper, the granular jamming effect was utilized in the design of the hand palm, and a hand palm structure with variable stiffness and adhesion function was proposed, as shown in Fig. 4(a). The hand palm structure consists of a jamming chamber, granular fill, silicone membrane, and upper fixed part. A groove was designed on the palm as the jamming chamber for granular fill, and the silicone membrane was used as a sealing film to close the jamming chamber and prevent the granular fill from leaking out. The silicone membrane was fixed to the palm surface with an upper fixed component that has M2 screw holes reserved on both the component and the palm. The silicone membrane was secured to the palm with a circle of screws to complete the adhesion hand palm structure.

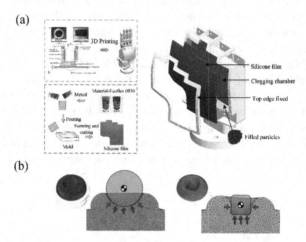

Fig. 4. Granular-Jamming Palm structure. (a) Assembly process of the Granular-Jamming Palm. (b) Principle of particle blockage adhesion. (Color figure online)

The design of a variable stiffness particle adsorption palm in this paper endows dexterous hands with degrees of freedom beyond human hands, making them more flexible during interactive operations with small-volume objects. As shown in Fig. 4(b), the principal diagram of particle adsorption is displayed. When the palm is not under negative pressure, the particles in the blocking chamber are in a loose state and can flow freely. When the target object is pressed into the blocking chamber, the particle adsorption palm will envelop the target object. Then, through negative pressure, the particles change from a loose state to a compact state, the stiffness of the particle adsorption palm increases, and it can firmly grip the target object. Figure 4(b) shows the force states of gripping a sphere and a cylinder, where the black arrows represent the suction force of particles under negative pressure on the object, and the red arrows represent the clamping force of particles in a compact state on the side of the object. By changing the positive and negative pressure, the stiffness of the palm can be altered to complete the process of grasping and releasing objects based on the sensation.

3   C-Shaped Joint Theory Analysis

The paper demonstrates a significant difference in the stiffness of the finger in the forward and backward directions using a C-shaped joint, with greater support for the backward direction and fulfilling the forward flexion action. This section will provide a detailed derivation of the forward and backward stiffness of the C-shaped joint based on the theory of thin shells.

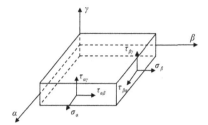

Fig. 5. Mid-surface differential element.

The middle part of the C-shaped joint is the most prone to unstable deformation. Taking a thin shell differential element from the middle section of the spring steel C-shaped joint for internal force analysis, as shown in Fig. 5, the height of the differential element is $d\gamma$, and the mid-surface is $d\alpha \times d\beta$. The forces acting on each side face can be divided into three stress components in three directions. On the cross section perpendicular to the α direction, with a width of $B_1 d\beta$ and a height of $d\gamma$, the three stress components are σ_α, $\tau_{\alpha\beta}$, $\tau_{\alpha\gamma}$; on the cross section perpendicular to the direction of β, with a width of h and a height of $B_2 d\alpha$, the three stress components are σ_β, $\tau_{\beta\alpha}$, $\tau_{\beta\gamma}$. According to assumption 3, $\sigma_\gamma = 0$.

On the cross-section perpendicular to the direction of α, the internal forces per unit length of the mid-surface of the differential element are:

$$M_\alpha = \frac{1}{B_1 d\beta} \int_{-\frac{h}{2}}^{\frac{h}{2}} \sigma_\alpha (1 + \frac{\gamma}{R_\beta}) \gamma (B_1 d\beta) d\gamma = \int_{-\frac{h}{2}}^{\frac{h}{2}} \sigma_\alpha (1 + \frac{\gamma}{R_\beta}) \gamma d\gamma \qquad (1)$$

Similarly, it can be deduced that the internal forces per unit length of the differential element at its center in the direction perpendicular to the y-axis are: M_β.

Where M_α and M_β refer to bending moment. As shown in Fig. 6, it is a schematic diagram of the distribution of internal forces on the differential element.

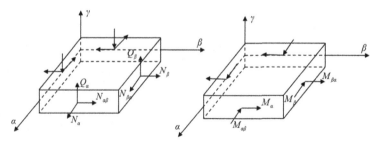

Fig. 6. Internal force distribution of a differential element. (a) Force distribution. (b) Moment distribution.

The C-shaped spring steel sheet joint can be regarded as an open half-cylindrical shell. Based on Love's theory [18], the expression for the bending strain component in the middle surface of the shell is as follows:

$$x_\alpha = \frac{1}{B} \frac{\partial}{\partial \alpha} \left(\frac{u}{R_\alpha} - \frac{1}{A} \frac{\partial w}{\partial \alpha} \right) + \frac{1}{AB} \left(\frac{v}{R_\beta} - \frac{1}{B} \frac{\partial w}{\partial \beta} \right) \frac{\partial A}{\partial \alpha} \tag{2}$$

$$x_\beta = \frac{1}{B} \frac{\partial}{\partial \beta} \left(\frac{v}{R_\beta} - \frac{1}{B} \frac{\partial w}{\partial \beta} \right) + \frac{1}{AB} \left(\frac{u}{R_\alpha} - \frac{1}{A} \frac{\partial w}{\partial \alpha} \right) \frac{\partial B}{\partial \alpha} \tag{3}$$

$$x_{\alpha\beta} = \frac{A}{B} \frac{\partial}{\partial \beta} \left(\frac{u}{AR_\alpha} - \frac{1}{A^2} \frac{\partial w}{\partial \alpha} \right) + \frac{B}{A} \frac{\partial}{\partial \alpha} \left(\frac{v}{BR_\beta} - \frac{1}{B^2} \frac{\partial w}{\partial \beta} \right) \tag{4}$$

where A and B refer to lame constant; α, β and γ refer to spatial surface coordinate axes; u, v, w represent the displacement of a point P on the middle surface of the shell in the directions of the three coordinate axes of the surface; u_1, v_1 and w_1 refer to the displacement of a point P on the middle surface of the shell moving to point P_1 in the directions of the three coordinate axes of the surface.

The paper analyzes a differential element taken from the surface of the C-shaped joint of the spring steel strip. The differential element is made of isotropic material and satisfies the generalized Hooke's law. Assuming that the stress component along the normal direction of the middle surface is much smaller than the stress component in the direction perpendicular to the normal, it can be ignored and understood as if the load is directly applied to the middle surface, and there is no interaction of forces between the layers of the curved shell. The stress-strain relationship of the shell becomes:

$$\varepsilon_\alpha = \frac{1}{E} \left[\sigma_\alpha - \mu \sigma_\beta \right] \tag{5}$$

$$\varepsilon_\beta = \frac{1}{E} \left[\sigma_\beta - \mu \sigma_\alpha \right] \tag{6}$$

$$\varepsilon_\gamma = \frac{\mu}{E} (\sigma_\alpha + \sigma_\beta) \tag{7}$$

$$\varepsilon_{\alpha\beta} = \frac{\tau_{\alpha\beta}}{G} \tag{8}$$

Further derivation leads to the expression for stress of the shell:

Combining Eq. 3 with the internal force equation of the shell 1 and the generalized Hooke's law mentioned above, the internal forces per unit length of the middle surface of the differential element on the cross-section perpendicular to the direction are obtained as:

$$M_\alpha = D \left[\kappa_\alpha + \mu \kappa_\beta + \frac{1}{R_\beta} (\varepsilon_\alpha + \mu \varepsilon_\beta) \right] \tag{9}$$

The expression is the same on the cross-section perpendicular to the β direction, and it is not repeated here. Where κ_α and κ_β refer to the curvature changes of the coordinate curves α and β; χ refer to torsion parameter; D refer to bending stiffness: $D = Eh^3/12(1 - \mu^2)$.

The above formula is complex and cumbersome, but it accurately describes the internal force of the thin shell element, which h/R is much smaller than 1 in the thin shell theory. Novozhilov derived a more concise and accurate formula for the internal force equation from the perspective of the deformation energy.

$$M_\alpha = D(\kappa_\alpha + \mu\kappa_\beta) \tag{10}$$

$$M_\beta = D(\kappa_\beta + \mu\kappa_\alpha) \tag{11}$$

The bending moment per unit length of the middle section of the joint of the C-shaped section is related to the changes in curvature κ_α and κ_β of the middle surface of the shell. Therefore, the formula for calculating the bending moment per unit length of the middle section of the joint of the C-shaped section is:

$$M = D(\kappa_l + \mu\kappa_t) \tag{12}$$

The large deformation of the C-shaped joint cross-section of the spring steel plate occurs during bending, and the curvature a and b cannot be directly obtained. Therefore, it is impossible to calculate the critical bending moment that occurs during large deformation. However, the finite element method provides convenience for calculation. Through finite element simulation of joint bending in both directions, the results show that the reverse stiffness is much greater than the forward stiffness, reaching 36 times larger.

4 Experimental

Human hands can be combined into various gestures. Therefore, the dexterity of the hand to freely form a variety of gestures like the human hand, implies that the dexterous hand has a high degree of anthropomorphism.

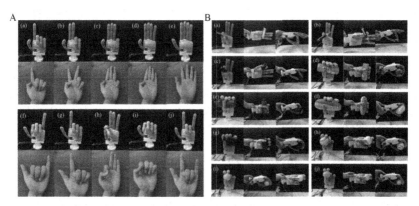

Fig. 7. Gesture and grasping experiment. A Ten hand gesture actions. B Ten different grasping actions for physical objects.

As shown in Fig. 7.A, the designed dexterous hand completed 10 sets of gesture trials. The upper part of the figure shows the gestures of the dexterous hand, while the lower part shows the corresponding human gesture actions. The experiments showed that this 5-finger dexterous hand has a high level of anthropomorphic characteristics and can perform various gesture actions such as "1", "2", "3", "4", "5", "6", "8", "OK", "fist" and "I love you" like human hands. The fingers have good independent movement and coordination abilities and can arbitrarily combine different digital shapes. Corresponding dexterity tests were conducted on each part of the dexterous hand, and the results showed that the dexterous hand has good dexterity, stability and reliability.

As shown in Fig. 7.B, we conducted grasping experiments on 10 different types of objects, and the results showed that the dexterous hand has good grasping ability.

To verify the rationality of the proposed joint, force testing was conducted on the C-shaped joint fingers as shown in Fig. 8.A The results showed that the maximum backward stiffness of the joint was 728 Nmm, and the maximum forward stiffness was 20 Nmm. There was a large difference in stiffness between forward and reverse directions. Figure 8.B shows four different objects and shapes of non-enveloping grasping experiments. The experimental results showed that the designed C-shaped joint has a large backward supporting force, and the dexterous hand can have a non-enveloping grasping ability like that of a human hand.

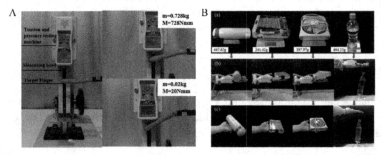

Fig. 8. Finger joint experiment. A. Display of maximum bending moment for measured flexion-extension stiffness. B. Experiment on finger reverse support performance of anthropomorphic hand.

As shown in Fig. 9, the silicone film on the surface of the palm is in a normal tension state in normal conditions. When the palm approaches the target object in working conditions, the object is completely trapped in the particle jamming palm. Then, by using a vacuum pump to suck the air out of the gaps between the particles in the palm, the particles become tightly packed and complete the "suction" action. The experiment shows that this highly functional design has good adhesion ability for picking up small objects and is an effective design solution for a dexterous hand that surpasses human functionality.

Figure 10 shows the ability of the dexterous hand to perform multi-task operations. Figure 10(a) shows the dexterous hand performing two hand gesture actions of grasping and adhesion. Figure 10(b) shows the dexterous hand performing other multi-task interactions while grasping an object. The experiment verified the effectiveness of the design of the dexterous hand.

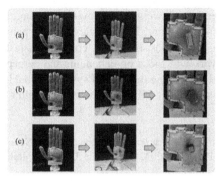

Fig. 9. Palm adhesion experiment. (a) Adhesion of pen caps. (b) Adhesion of bottle caps. (c) Adhesion of small cubes.

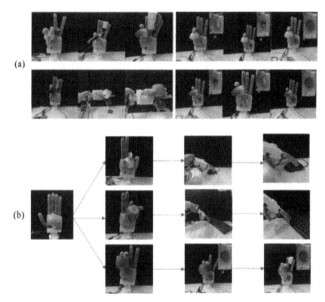

Fig. 10. Interactive operation experiment. (a) Two types of task operations. (b) Multi-task interactive operation.

5 Conclusion

In this paper, we proposed the soft humanoid hand with a C-shaped joint and a granular-jamming palm. The bending moment change formula for forward and reverse bending of the C-shaped joint was derived through theoretical analysis. The results show that the reverse stiffness is much greater than the forward stiffness, implying that the flexible and dexterous hand is convenient for grasping during forward bending and has strong support during reverse bending. We built an experimental platform and conducted experiments on grasping, gestures, palm adhesion, and weight-bearing with the flexible and dexterous hand. Compared with traditional flexible and dexterous hands, the C-shaped joint structure has a simple, lightweight, and low-cost design, and solves the problem of weak reverse stiffness of the joint. The particle-adhesive palm endows the dexterous hand with superhuman capabilities, making it convenient, fast, and flexible to grasp small objects. Future work will focus on enhancing the perceptual capabilities of the soft humanoid hand and optimizing the control system to enable the dexterous hand to have active sensing capabilities. It will be applied in the field of prosthetics for people with disabilities.

Acknowledgement. This work was supported by the National Natural Science Foundation of China (Grant No. 62173197, U22B2042), Tsinghua University Initiative Scientific Research Program with 2022Z11QYJ002.

References

1. Ren, T., et al.: Novel bionic soft robotic hand with dexterous deformation and reliable grasping. IEEE Trans. Instrum. Meas. **72**, 1–10 (2023). Art no. 7502110. https://doi.org/10.1109/TIM.2023.3248098
2. Pozzi, L., Gandolla, M., Pura, F., et al.: Grasping learning, optimization, and knowledge transfer in the robotics field. Sci. Rep. **12**(1), 1–11 (2022)
3. Chen, Y., Zhao, H., Mao, J., et al.: Controlled flight of a microrobot powered by soft artificial muscles. Nature **575**(7782), 324–329 (2019)
4. Van Der Niet, O., van der Sluis, C.K.: Functionality of i-LIMB and i-LIMB pulse hands: case report. J. Rehabil. Res. Dev. **50**(8), 1123–1128 (2013)
5. Medynski, C., Rattray, B.: Bebionic prosthetic design. In: Myoelectric Controls/Powered Prosthetics Symposium (MEC), pp. 279–282 (2011)
6. Luchetti, M., Cutti, A.G., Verni, G., et al.: Impact of michelangelo prosthetic hand: findings from a crossover longitudinal study. J. Rehabil. Res. Dev. **52**(5), 605–618 (2015)
7. Widehammar, C., Lidström Holmqvist, K., Hermansson, L.: Training for users of myoelectric multigrip hand prostheses: a scoping review. Prosthet. Orthot. Int. **45**(5), 393–400 (2021)
8. https://www.prensilia.com/portfolio/mia/
9. Schulz, S.: First experiences with the vincent hand. In: Myoelectric Symposium, pp. 14–19 (2011)
10. Laffranchi, M., Boccardo, N., Traverso, S., et al.: The Hannes hand prosthesis replicates the key biological properties of the human hand. Sci. Robot. **5**(46) (2020)
11. Weiner, P., Starke, J., Rader, S., et al.: Designing prosthetic hands with embodied intelligence: the KIT prosthetic hands. Front. Neurorobot. **16** (2022)
12. Xiong, C.H., Chen, W.R., Sun, B.Y., et al.: Design and implementation of an anthropomorphic hand for replicating human grasping functions. IEEE Trans. Rob. **32**(3), 652–671 (2016)
13. Li, H., Ford, C.J., Bianchi, M., et al.: BRL/Pisa/IIT SoftHand: a low-cost, 3D-printed, under-actuated, tendon-driven hand with soft and adaptive synergies. IEEE Robot. Autom. Lett. **7**(4), 8745–8751 (2022)
14. Tian, M., Xiao, Y., Wang, X., et al.: Design and experimental research of pneumatic soft humanoid robot hand. In: Kim, J.H., Karray, F., Jo, J., Sincak, P., Myung, H. (eds.) Robot Intelligence Technology and Applications 4. AISC, vol. 447, pp. 469–478. Springer, Cham (2017). https://doi.org/10.1007/978-3-319-31293-4_37
15. Gu, G., Zhang, N., Xu, H., et al.: A soft neuroprosthetic hand providing simultaneous myoelectric control and tactile feedback. Nat. Biomed. Eng. 1–10 (2021)

16. Deimel, R., Brock, O.: A novel type of compliant and underactuated robotic hand for dexterous grasping. Int. J. Robot. Res. **35**(1–3), 161–185 (2016)
17. Chen, C., Sun, J., Wang, L., et al.: Pneumatic bionic hand with rigid-flexible coupling structure. Materials **15**(4), 1358 (2022)
18. Love, A.E.H.: A Treatise on the Mathematical Theory of Elasticity, pp. 28–197. Dover Pub, New York (1944)

Design of a Three-Finger Underactuated Robotic Gripper Based on a Flexible Differential Mechanism

Xiantao Sun[1], Changsheng Gan[1], Wenjie Chen[1(✉)], Weihai Chen[2], and Yuanyuan Liu[1]

[1] School of Electrical Engineering and Automation, Anhui University, Hefei 230601, China
wjchen@ahu.edu.cn
[2] School of Automation Science and Electrical Engineering, Beihang University, Beijing 100191, China

Abstract. Adaptive grippers are widely used in industrial automation, manufacturing, and other applications where objects being handled are often irregular in shape or size. Cost and control complexity are the two critical considerations in the design process of an adaptive gripper. To address these problems, a novel single-input-three-output (SITO) flexible differential mechanism with a two-degree-of-freedom (two-DOF) flexure hinge is proposed to develop a single-drive adaptive gripper that is low-cost and easy-to-control. This paper introduces the grasping structure and working principle of the proposed gripper before conducting the finite element simulation on the flexure hinge. Based on the analysis results, a gripper prototype is fabricated and tested to evaluate its grasping performance on various irregular objects. The experimental results show that this gripper is highly adaptive and capable of grasping objects of various shapes, making it a promising solution for industrial automation, manufacturing, and related robotic applications, etc.

Keywords: Underactuated Gripper · Adaptive Grasping · Differential Mechanism · Flexure Hinge

1 Introduction

The robotic gripper is an automated tool that can mimic many motions and functions of human hands, allowing it to grasp and manipulate objects based on pre-programmed actions. In automated operations, the effective use of grippers is crucial to achieve the grasping and releasing of objects, which can be classified into standard and irregular shapes according to their geometry of the objects. Standard objects are relatively easy to operate, while irregularly shaped objects are more common and requires the gripper to be adaptive. With the diversified development of the market, the customized production mode of high-mix low-volume (HMLV) has increasingly become the norm. Therefore, there is an urgent need for an adaptive gripper that can adapt to objects with different shapes, sizes, and stiffness. Overcoming the key technical challenges in developing

© The Author(s), under exclusive license to Springer Nature Singapore Pte Ltd. 2023
H. Yang et al. (Eds.): ICIRA 2023, LNAI 14268, pp. 546–557, 2023.
https://doi.org/10.1007/978-981-99-6486-4_46

such an adaptive gripper has both theoretical significance and potential for practical applications.

Automated assembly processes typically rely on two methods of supplying objects, namely floating supply via conveyors or trays, and fixed supply via special fixtures. In the case of floating supply, precise positioning of objects is not required during the grasping process since the object can move freely and towards the gripper center under the action of gripping force. This approach is typically best suited for objects with regular geometry. However, in industrial applications, irregularly shaped objects are more common, and they are usually supplied through fixed fixtures, which can result in positioning errors between the gripper and objects in the process of grasping. To address this issue, robotic companies often incorporate a visual sensor to obtain positional information of objects and then adjust the position and posture of the robot arm accordingly to reduce their relative errors. However, this approach can increase the system cost and meanwhile reduce the real-time performance, and it also has high requirements for the accuracy of the visual sensor. In many industrial scenarios, it may be necessary to develop specialized grippers for irregularly shaped objects to meet different grasping requirements. However, switching between different grippers during grasping can reduce production efficiency and increase the system cost. Thus, in automated operations, there is an increasing tendency to use adaptive grippers to reduce the grasping difficulty, improve efficiency, and enhance adaptability to various objects.

Recent research has categorized grippers into two types, i.e., fully-actuated and underactuated grippers, based on the relationship between the number of gripper motors and degrees of freedom. Fully-actuated grippers, such as Utah/MIT hand [1], the DLR hand [2], and the Shadow hand [3], etc., have five fingers that allow for independent control of each finger joint. However, these grippers are limited by their complex control, as well as a large number of motors and sensors, which limits their commercial development and widespread use in industrial markets. At present, only universities, research institutes and a few companies are conducting relevant research about fully-actuated grippers.

For the other type of gripper, underactuated gripper typically has fewer motors than its DOFs, making them easy to control while grasping objects and leading to their widespread development. According to their different underactuated principles, various types of underactuated grippers have been developed with the tendon drive [4–8], multi-linkage drive [9–12], and gear drive [13, 14], etc. These grippers usually add springs in the passive joints to avoid incoherent motions of these joints, allowing for better control of many joints with fewer motors. However, this can also lead to new problems, such as difficulty in controlling each joint independently and uncertainty in position when grasping irregular objects. Underactuated grippers can adapt the object shape and size by applying force to actuate the joints, resulting in the passive and enveloping grasping. Although these grippers can adapt to different objects, it is challenging to precisely grasp small and irregularly shaped objects.

So far, many underactuated grippers have been developed for different grasping tasks. For example, Nishimura et al. [15] proposed the design guidelines and control strategies for aligning the fingertip positions, and designed a gripper with special finger structure that exerts force to push objects towards the gripper center and locate their position accurately. Chen et al. [16] developed a new type of mandibular gripper with anthropomorphic characteristics that can exert specific force on cylindrical assembly objects with various surface materials and can precisely locate or turn during high-speed movement. Harada et al. [17] proposed a combined structure gripper with two shape-adaptive mechanisms, one of which is a granular interference mechanism and the other one is a single-wire driven multi-finger mechanism. This design allows the position and posture of the grasped object to remain unchanged. Hsu et al. [18] designed an intelligent self-locking underactuated set with a parallel actuator. The system adopts a differential gear to adjust the power distribution between the gripper and brake, and the lock is triggered when the power reaches the required grasping force. Nie et al. [19] combined an inner gripper using a crank slider mechanism for precise positioning and an outer gripper using a parallel four-bar linkage for stable clamping. This design provides a low-cost solution for positioning and grasping objects, but it is limited to grasping cylindrical objects and objects with cylindrical holes. Sun et al. [20] used an X-shaped linkage-based differential mechanism and two seesaws to design a single-actuator four-finger adaptive gripper to effectively grasp irregular-shaped flat objects without the use of any sensors.

On the other hand, some researchers have incorporated soft materials into gripper designs, taking advantage of their unique material properties to improve adaptive grasping performance. This gripper theoretically has infinite passive DOFs and can grasp objects without any damage. There is no doubt that its adaptive characteristics are the best compared the above two adaptive grippers. For instance, Yang et al. [21] drew inspiration from the shape and movement of sea anemones to develop a soft gripper with multiple flexible arms to adapt to various target sizes. Achilli et al. [22] designed a modular structure by using soft materials such as thermoplastic polyurethane to improve the adaptability to the object shapes and sizes. However, due to the easily deformable characteristics of the soft materials, this gripper has disadvantages such as insufficient rigidity, low load capacity, and poor grasping stability.

Based on the above requirements, the paper proposes the design of a novel three-finger adaptive gripper with one active input and three passive outputs. The gripper adopts a SITO flexible differential mechanism. Three fingers of the gripper are connected in parallel relative to the differential mechanism, but their motions do not interfere with each other, allowing for the adaptive grasping. In addition, the material characteristics of the flexure hinge are utilized to maintain the center position after grasping.

2 Mechanical Structure

The CAD model of the proposed three-finger underactuated gripper is shown in Fig. 1. It mainly consists of three parts, i.e., motor driver, differential mechanism, and finger structure. The gripper is connected to the robotic arm by a flange during use. The motor driver provides the power and control strategies for the specific grasping motions. A flexible differential mechanism is connected to the stepping motor and moves up/down with the motor, distributing the driving force to the three fingers through a two-DOF flexure hinge and three pairs of crossing cables. Each finger with the parallel four-link structure is connected to the output end of the differential mechanism through tables. The gripper can automatically adapts to the shape and size of the grasped object based on the adaptive characteristic of this novel flexible differential mechanism.

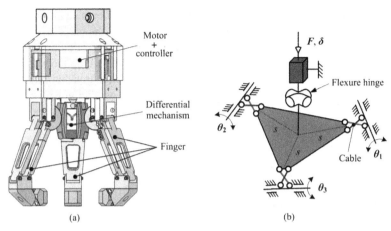

(a)   (b)

Fig. 1. (a) CAD model and (b) schematic of the three-finger underactuated gripper. (Color figure online)

2.1 Motor Driver

The driving part includes a linear stepping motor and a controller. The motor indicated in yellow and the entire circuit part are mounted on the blue bracket, as show in Fig. 1. The selected stepping motor is a Haydn 43000 series linear motor that operates on a DC 5 V voltage, offers a maximum stroke of 19.05 mm, and generates a driving force of up to 300 N. The control board has an isolation module, a controller module, and a driver module. The system control diagram is illustrated in Fig. 2.

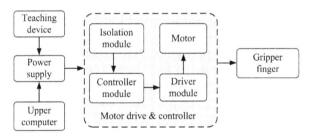

Fig. 2. System control flow chart.

2.2 Finger Structure

The finger structure of the proposed gripper is shown in Fig. 3(a). The gripper has three fingers spaced 120° apart from each other. The three fingers have the structure of a parallel four-link mechanism and are fixed on the gripper base. The flexible cable is utilized to connect the fingers to the differential mechanism. Since the cable has a large stiffness in the axial direction but a very small stiffness in the bending direction, it is strong enough to pull the finger up and down. One end of the cable is fixed on a semi-circular pulley attached to the four-link mechanism while the other end of the cable is connected to the flexure hinge. In addition, the cables are wrapped around the circular surface of the pulley. When the pulley rotates, the cable always keep tighten within the whole rotation range. The parallel four-link mechanism of the finger is used to transfer the motion and power from the motor to the fingers. It also can generate a parallel grasping motion on the fingertip when the motor pushes or pulls it. Therefore, the vertical motion of the motor can be converted into the horizontal motions of the fingers.

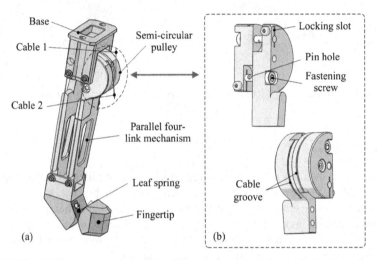

Fig. 3. (a) Finger structure, and (b) different viewpoints the semi-circular pulley.

The detailed structure of the semi-circular pulley is shown in Fig. 3(b). As mentioned earlier, two cables are required to achieve the opening and closing operations of the fingers. Therefore, there are two cable grooves on the pulley to guide the cable motion. One end of two cables is fixed on the pin holes located on the upper and lower fastening screws. The cable tension can be adjusted by rotating the fastening screws. After adjusting the tension, the locking slot is tightened and does not rotate to maintain the set cable tension.

It can be seen that the fingertip is connected to the parallel four-link mechanism by the two cross leaf springs. This design can provide a relative soft rotary compliance but keep large linear stiffness in the vertical and horizontal directions. Which can help the gripper better to adapt to different shaped objects. The modular design of the fingertip also allows for handling different materials by changing different fingertips. In addition, mounting cross leaf spring on the fingertip can also provide a necessary compliance for the insertion operation.

2.3 Flexible Differential Mechanism

As shown in Fig. 4(a), in this design, the differential mechanism acts as an intermediate motion/force transmission unit, which can balance the driving force into the three fingers.

It is equipped with one input motion from the linear motor and three output motions of three fingers, and consists of a flexure hinge and three brackets for mounting the cables. Each bracket is connected to one finger by two cross cables, as shown in Fig. 4(b).

The flexure hinge is a two-DOF universal joint, which is made from two perpendicular notch flexures. This design can avoid complexity of the motion transmission mechanism, ensuring compact size of the designed gripper. In addition, the flexure hinge also possesses the built-in stiffness that can ensure the differential mechanism return back to its original position after tilting.

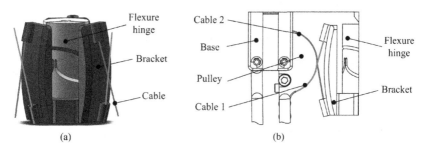

(a)   (b)

Fig. 4. (a) Differential mechanism, and (b) the connection between the finger and flexure hinge.

3   Working Principle of Adaptive Grasping

3.1   Planar Analysis of Grasping Motion

The differential mechanism in the proposed adaptive gripper serves as the transfer mechanism that converts the input from the motor into the outputs of the three fingers while also balancing the force distribution between fingers to establish a stable grasping force closure. As shown in Fig. 5, the flexure hinge can provide two flexible DOFs, namely the rotation about the x-axis and y-axis (denoted as ψ_x and ψ_y). This design idea of this flexure hinge is mainly inspired by the traditional universal joint, its detailed analysis can be found in [23].

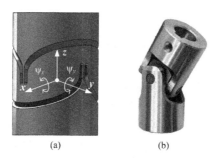

(a)   (b)

Fig. 5. (a) CAD model of the two-DOF flexure hinge, and (b) traditional universal joint.

Based on the finger function described above, we first analyze the adaptive grasping process of the gripper using a two-dimensional structure diagram. Initially, the gripper center is not aligned with that of the workpiece, as shown in Fig. 6(a). First, the linear motor moves upwards, which drives the differential mechanism to move. As a result, the cable 1 connected to the differential mechanism bracket moves upwards. The semicircular pulley on the finger mechanism rotates counterclockwise around its center, driven by the pulling force of the cable 1, causing the fingertips to move towards the center. It is noted that the cable 1 bears the large tension force while the cable 2 bears the very small tension force in this process.

When the right finger touches the object as shown in Fig. 6(b), the rotation angles of the two fingers are denoted as θ_1, and the distance of the motor shaft is d_1. Subsequently, when the motor shaft continues to move upwards, the right finger stops moving since it is restricted by the object. At the same time, the flexure hinge rotates θ_0 around the rotation center until the other finger also touches the object, and the motor stops moving, as shown in Fig. 6(c).

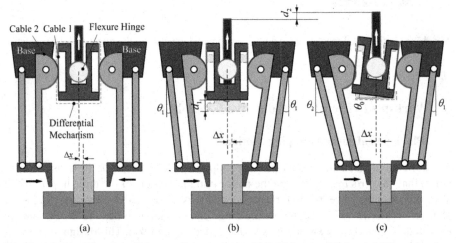

Fig. 6. Adaptive grasping of the two-finger gripper. (a) Initial state, (b) the right finger touches the object, and (c) two fingers touch the object.

3.2 Spatial Analysis of Grasping Motion

According to the planar motion analysis of the above two-finger adaptive gripper, the grasping states of the similar three-finger gripper can be divided into the following two cases to discuss the relationship between the finger motions and the motor motion.

Case 1: If the grasped object is regular and symmetrical, and the center of the gripper is aligned with the center of the object, there will be no deflection in the flexure hinge. The kinematic modeling is very simple in this case.

Case 2: When the grasped part is irregular or the centers of the gripper and the part do not align, the motions of the three fingers can be classified into three types. The first type occurs when one finger touches the object first, and the other two fingers subsequently touch the object at the same time. The second type occurs when two fingers touch the object at the same time, followed by the third finger. In fact, the motions of the two types are identical and are similar to the motions of the two-finger gripper. The third type occurs when the three fingers touch the object at different times, as depicted in Fig. 7. The initial state is illustrated in Fig. 7(a), where the center M of the grasped object and the center m of the gripper are not aligned. The three fingers move towards the center to close, driven by the motor. As shown in Fig. 7(b), the finger 1 first touch the object, and the flexure hinge does not deform before this time. Then, as the other two fingers continue to move, the flexure hinge start to deform until the finger 2 contacts with the object. Finally, all fingers contact with the object. It can be seen that the motor motion can be divided into three stages, and the flexible hinge undergoes two times of deformation in different directions. It can be seen that the maximum deformation of the flexure hinge determines the adaptive range of the gripper.

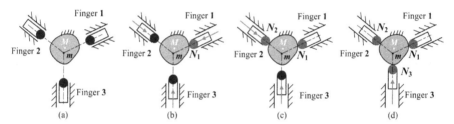

Fig. 7. Adaptive grasping of the three-finger gripper. (a) Initial state, (b) one finger touches the object, (c) two fingers touch the object, and (d) three fingers touch the object.

4   Flexure Hinge Design

4.1   Flexure Hinge Structure

A flexure hinge is a component that can significantly deform under an external force/torque. It is usually made from a piece of metal material by the wire electrical discharge machine (WEDM) to produce various structures with different DOFs in a small size. Compared with the conventional rigid joints, the flexure hinge does not require lubrication and can provide stable motion with high precision. Additionally, it can return to its initial state through its own elasticity after the external force/torque is removed. However, the deformation is mainly concentrated at the notch, so the notch stiffness becomes the most critical factor in the hinge design. In theory, the stiffness of the flexure hinge along the y- or z-axis can be estimated as $K = EI / l$, where E is the Young modulus of the material, I is the second moment of area, and l is the length of the thin beam in the flexure hinge as shown in Fig. 8.

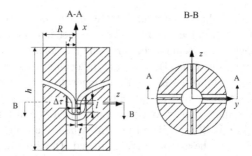

Fig. 8. Cross sections of the flexure hinge.

The key geometric parameters of the two-DOF flexure hinge are shown in Fig. 8. The hinge has a height of h, an inner diameter of r, an outer diameter of R, the notch has a width of $\Delta \tau$, a length of l, and a gap of t between the incision. By comprehensively analyzing the required adaptive range of the gripper, the geometrical parameters of the flexure hinge are determined and listed in Table 1.

Table 1. Geometrical parameters of the two-DOF flexure hinge.

Symbol	R	r	h	t	l	$\Delta \tau$
Unit	mm	mm	mm	mm	mm	mm
Value	20	4	30	0.5	3	1

4.2 Finite Element Simulation

A flexure hinge utilizes the deformation of thin-walled members for the motion or force transmission. Therefore, during the design phase, it is crucial to pay special attention to ensure that the deformation or stress of the thin-walled members remains within the permissible limit of the material to guarantee reliable motion. In this section, the finite element simulations of the two-DOF flexure hinge will be performed with Ansys Workbench for performance evaluation.

According to the geometric parameters listed in Table 1, the 3D model of the flexure hinge is established in Solidworks, and then the model is imported into ANSYS Workbench. The material is selected as stainless steel with the elastic modulus of 193 GPa, the Poisson's ratio of 0.3, and the allowable stress of 207 MPa. During the simulation, the bottom of the flexure hinge is fixed, and the other end is subjected to a 100 N/mm torque. The flexure hinge is meshed, and the eight weakest surfaces are selected for additional mesh refinement, with a mesh size of 0.5 mm to ensure the simulation accuracy. The simulation results including the deformation and stress distribution are shown in Fig. 9. It can be seen that the flexure hinge can withstand a large deformation within the allowable range of stress, which is very beneficial to the adaptive grasping characteristics of the gripper.

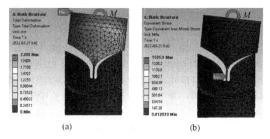

(a)   (b)

Fig. 9. Finite element simulation results. (a) Deformation, and (b) stress distribution.

5   Adaptive Grasping Experiments

After completing the gripper design, a prototype of the proposed three-finger gripper is fabricated and the adaptive grasping functions will be evaluated. The gripper is mounted on the UR5 robot arm. It is noted that no sensors are used in the grasping process. A series of objects with different shapes or sizes are selected as the grasped objects to verify the grasping performance of the gripper.

The self-adaptive grasping experimental results are shown in Fig. 10, showcasing various common everyday objects and irregularly shaped 3D printed objects. The objects range in size, from the largest object measuring more than 8 cm by 8 cm to the smallest object measuring less than 2 cm by 2 cm. These experiments demonstrate the efficiency of the gripper to grasp objects with differing shapes and sizes, including irregularly shaped objects.

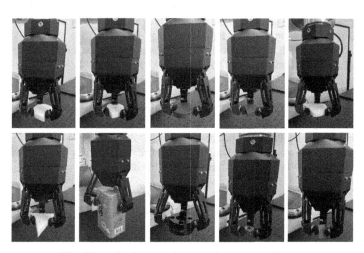

Fig. 10. Adaptive grasping tests for various objects.

6 Conclusions

In the paper, a SITO underactuated robotic gripper is designed by introducing a flexure hinge into the novel flexible differential mechanism. The gripper structure and working principle are introduced in detail. Based on the characteristics of the gripper, some adaptive grasping experiments are carried out to verify the gripper performance. Experiments show that the gripper can grasp a wide range of objects and can adapt to their shape changes. In the future, this gripper will be used for robotic assembly.

Acknowledgement. This work was supported in part by the National Key Research and Development Program of China under Grant 2022YFB4702501, and in part by the National Natural Science Foundation of China under Grant 52005001.

References

1. Jacobsen, S.C., Wood, J.E., Knutti, D.F., et al.: The UTAH/MIT dextrous hand: work in progress. Int. J. Robot. Res. **3**(4), 21–50 (1984)
2. Grebenstein, M., Chalon, M., Hirzinger, G., et al.: Antagonistically driven finger design for the anthropomorphic DLR hand arm system. In: International Conference on Humanoid Robots, Nashville, TN, USA, pp. 609–616 (2010)
3. Ochan, A.: Shadow delivers first hand. Ind. Rob. Int. J. **32**(1), 15–16 (2005)
4. Dollar, A.M., Howe, R.D.: Joint coupling design of underactuated hands for unstructured environments. Int. J. Robot. Res. **30**(9), 1157–1169 (2011)
5. Ciocarlie, M., Hicks, F.M., Holmberg, R., et al.: The velo gripper: a versatile single-actuator design for enveloping, parallel, and fingertip grasps. Int. J. Robot. Res. **33**(5), 753–767 (2014)
6. Aukes, D.M., Heyneman, B., Ulmen, J., et al.: Design and testing of a selectively compliant underactuated hand. Int. J. Robot. Res. **33**(5), 721–735 (2014)
7. Catalano, M.G., Grioli, G., Farnioli, E., et al.: Adaptive synergies for the design and control of the Pisa/IIT SoftHand. Int. J. Robot. Res. **33**(5), 768–782 (2014)
8. Odhner, L.U., Jentoft, L.P., Claffee, M.R., et al.: A compliant, underactuated hand for robust manipulation. Int. J. Robot. Res. **33**(5), 736–752 (2014)
9. Laliberte, T., Birglen, L., Gosselin, C.: Underactuation in robotic grasping hands. Mach. Intell. Robot. Control **4**(3), 1–11 (2002)
10. Birglen, L.: Type Synthesis of Linkage-Driven Self-Adaptive Fingers (2009)
11. Yamaguchi, K., Hirata, Y., Kosuge, K.: Underactuated robot hand for dual-arm manipulation. In: 2015 IEEE/RSJ International Conference on Intelligent Robots and Systems, Hamburg, Germany, pp. 2937–2942 (2015)
12. Kang, L., Seo, J.T., Yoon, D., et al.: Design of a 3-DOF linkage-driven underactuated finger for multiple grasping. In: 2019 IEEE/RSJ International Conference on Intelligent Robots and Systems, Macau, China, pp. 5608–5613 (2019)
13. Ozawa, R., Mishima, Y., Hirano, Y.: Design of a transmission with gear trains for underactuated mechanisms. IEEE Trans. Robot. **32**(6), 1399–1407.1 (2016)
14. Zhang, W., Che, D., Liu, H., et al.: Super under-actuated multi-fingered mechanical hand with modular self-adaptive gear-rack mechanism. Ind. Robot. Int. J. (2009)
15. Nishimura, T., Tennomi, M., Suzuki, Y., et al.: Lightweight high-force gripper inspired by chuck clamping devices. IEEE Robot. Autom. Lett. **3**(3), 1354–1361 (2018)

16. Chen, F., Cannella, F., Canali, C., et al.: In-hand precise twisting and positioning by a novel dexterous robotic gripper for industrial high-speed assembly. In: 2014 IEEE International Conference on in Robotics and Automation, Hong Kong, China, pp. 270–275 (2014)

17. Harada, K.: Proposal of a shape adaptive gripper for robotic assembly tasks. Adv. Robot. **30**(17/18), 1186–1198 (2016)

18. Hsu, J., Yoshida, E., Harada, K., Kheddar, A.: Self-locking underactuated mechanism for the robotic gripper. In: IEEE International Conference onAdvanced Intelligent Mechatronics, Munich, Germany, pp. 620–627 (2017)

19. Nie, K., Wan, W., Harada, K.: A hand combining two simple grippers to pick up and arrange objects for assembly. IEEE Robot. Autom. Lett. **4**(2), 958–965 (2019)

20. Sun, X., Wang, C., Chen, W., Chen, W., Yang, G., Jin, Y.: A single-actuator four-finger adaptive gripper for robotic assembly. IEEE Trans. Industr. Electron. **70**(12), 12555–12565 (2023)

21. Yang, J., Ren, C., Yang, C., et al.: Design of a flexible capture mechanism inspired by sea anemone for non-cooperative targets. Chin. J. Mech. Eng. **34**(1), 1–13 (2021)

22. Achilli, G.M., Valigi, M.C., Salvietti, G., Malvezzi, M.: Design of soft grippers with modular actuated embedded constraints. Robotics **9**(4), 105 (2020)

23. Teo, T.J., Yang, G., Chen, I.M.: A large deflection and high payload flexure-based parallel manipulator for UV nanoimprint lithography: part I. Model. Anal. Precis. Eng. **38**(4), 861–871 (2014)

Design and Development of a Composite Compliant Two-finger Gripper

Tong Guan[2,3], Shujie Tang[2,3], Genliang Chen[1,2(✉)], Wei Yan[2,3], Junjie Luo[2,3],
and Hao Wang[1,3]

[1] State Key Laboratory of Mechanical Systems and Vibration, Shanghai Jiao Tong University,
Shanghai 200240, China
{leungchan,wanghao}@sjtu.edu.cn
[2] Meta Robotics Institute, Shanghai Jiao Tong University, Shanghai 200240, China
{tongguan,sjtang,ywgump,luojunjie0001}@sjtu.edu.cn
[3] Shanghai Key Laboratory of Digital Manufacturing for Thin-Walled Structures, Shanghai Jiao
Tong University, Shanghai 200240, China

Abstract. This paper proposes a composite compliant two-finger gripper for compliant assembly. During the interaction between grasped objects and the environment, objects can be stably grasped with rigid fingertips, and the flexible structure of the fingers can be passively deformed to achieve passive compliance. Additionally, flexible sensors installed on the finger can actively sense the deformation of the finger and calculate the environmental interaction force of the grasped object, thereby enabling the realization of active compliance. The prototype of the compliant gripper is developed using easily obtainable materials and simple manufacturing methods. Using the principal axes decomposition of the structural compliance method, the flexible beams of the finger are approximated as one hyper-redundant multi-body system. The kinetostatic model and sensing model of the compliant gripper are derived, and the Newton-Raphson method is used to obtain the equilibrium configuration of the flexible beams and the interaction force of the grasped object. A verification experiment demonstrates the validity of the proposed perception method in sensing the interaction force on the grasped object.

Keywords: Compliant Gripper · Composite Compliance · Kinetostatics Analysis · Interaction Force Sensing

1 Introduction

In recent years, robots have been applied in various fields including industrial automation, medical and health care, agricultural mechanization, and social services [1]. Using different kinds of end effectors, robots can complete different tasks such as grasping, assembly, picking, grinding, and polishing [2–4]. A noteworthy and common characteristic of these tasks is that the manipulator must be in contact with the environment, which necessitates compliant control to improve the precision and safety of the interaction [5].

© The Author(s), under exclusive license to Springer Nature Singapore Pte Ltd. 2023
H. Yang et al. (Eds.): ICIRA 2023, LNAI 14268, pp. 558–567, 2023.
https://doi.org/10.1007/978-981-99-6486-4_47

Compliant control refers to the robot implementing a pre-determined task in contact with the environment by complying with the environment. Presently, there are three primary types of compliance used in manipulators: passive compliance, active compliance, and composite compliance. Passive compliance is primarily achieved by introducing flexible materials at the joints of the fingers or wrists of the manipulator, thereby imparting compliance to the manipulator. The RCC mechanism is a typical example of a passive compliance device [6]. Passive compliance typically incorporates a specialized structural design tailored to its application scenario, resulting in limited versatility. Active compliance involves actively controlling the contact between the device and the environment based on feedback information from sensors that perceive the assembly state. Active compliance is typically divided into two types: impedance control and force-position hybrid control [7, 8]. The impact force generated during interaction cannot be effectively buffered solely by active compliance due to the influence of sensor measurement errors. Composite compliance integrates the aforementioned two compliance methods, thereby leveraging the advantages of both. However, it is accompanied by the challenge of complex structural design. [9].

The Fin-ray gripper is a flexible gripper that utilizes the principle of fin-ray, derived from the way a fish fin deforms when it contacts an object. The bionic finger, created based on this principle, comprises two longitudinal flexible skeletons connected at one end and a transverse rigid support for the fingertip of the longitudinal skeleton. This finger possesses strong adaptability and flexibility [10–12]. In this paper, the arrangement of the longitudinal flexible beams on both sides of the fin-ray gripper is changed from a V-shaped arrangement to an equidistant arrangement, which enhances fingertip flexibility, enabling the passive assembly of the grasped object. On this basis, the flexible sensor on the finger senses the interaction force of the grasped object, thus realizing compound compliance that combines active and passive compliance.

The structure of this paper is as follows: Sect. 2 provides the design and fabrication of the compliant gripper, Sect. 3 gives the kinetostatics model of the compliant gripper, Sect. 4 presents the interaction force sensing model based on the flexible sensor, and Sect. 5 verifies the above model through interaction force sensing experiments. Finally, conclusions are drawn in Sect. 6.

2   Finger Design and Fabrication

The composite compliant gripper designed in this paper is composed of two symmetrically arranged compliant fingers. Each finger consists of a rigid fingertip, a finger base, a rigid rib, two rigid connectors, four flexible beams, and flexible sensors attached to the inner flexible beams. There are two mutually perpendicular flexible beams connected by rigid connectors on the inner and outer sides of the finger. The lower part of the flexible beams is attached to the finger base at a 45° angle, while the upper part connects to the rigid fingertip. A rigid rib is installed between the two rigid connectors and connected with the rigid connectors through passive joints. During interaction with the environment, the designed compliant gripper structure ensures stable grasping from three aspects, the rigid fingertip, the flexible beams with passive compliance, and the rigid ribs, which provide increased grasping force and structural stability.

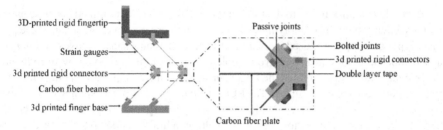

Fig. 1. Structure of the compliant finger

In order to achieve basic functions while simplifying the manufacturing process, both the flexible beams and the rigid ribs are constructed using carbon fiber beams, while 3D printing technology is utilized to fabricate the rigid fingertip, rigid connectors, and finger base. To establish a compact and simple passive joint, long tapes as wide as the ribs are applied to both sides of the rigid rib, with longer tape parts adhered to each other and connected to the rigid connectors. A narrow gap between the rigid connector and the rigid rib enables the latter to rotate around the connection point at the gap, creating a pair of passive joints. Strain gauges, developed in our previous work [13], are attached to the carbon fiber beams on the inside to facilitate the implementation of flexible sensor functionality. Figure 1 depicts the structure of the flexible finger, implemented using the above-described approach.

3   Kinetostatic Modeling

This section presents the kinetostatic modeling of the compliant gripper, wherein the compliant behavior of the fingers is primarily generated by the flexible beams positioned on both sides. When the gripper grasps an object and interacts with its surroundings, the pose variation of the fingertip results in the deformation of the flexible beams. Thus, the problem of object pose and interactive force perception can be reformulated as the problem of equilibrium configuration of the flexible beams. To address the issue of deformation reconstruction and load sensing for large deformed flexible beams, the flexible links are represented by hyperredundant linkages composed of rigid bodies that are joined by passive elastic joints based on our prior work [14–16]. Grounding on the principal axes decomposition of the structural compliance matrix, the passive elastic joint is treated as a spatial 6-DOF linkage with rigid bodies and passive elastic joints. For the carbon fiber beams, the effects of shearing and compression are neglectable compared to the bending one, enabling the simplification of the unit as a torsion spring.

The equivalent model of the compliant finger is analyzed below. To simplify the model, the four flexible beams on the inner and outer sides of the finger are treated as one composite flexible beam for the purposes of solution. The rigid connectors and fingertips are considered as rigid joints. The connection between the inner flexible beam and the finger base of the compliant finger is regarded as the beginning of the composite flexible beam, while the connection between the outer flexible beam and the finger base is considered as the end of the single flexible beam.

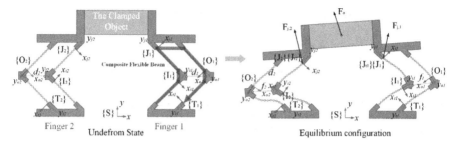

Fig. 2. Mechanism approximation of the compliant gripper.

To determine the equilibrium state of the flexible gripper when clamping an object interacting with the environment, several factors must be considered simultaneously. These include the geometric constraints at the end of the flexible beams, the force equilibrium between the joints, the length constraints of the rigid ribs, the geometric constraints of the rigid fingertips, and the force equilibrium of the grasped object, as illustrated in Fig. 2. It should be noted that this paper assumes that two fingers are connected by a single-degree-of-freedom gripper and that the distance between the two fingers is known. With this in mind, the kinetostatics model can be established as follows:

$$
C(\mathbf{x}) =
\begin{bmatrix}
\mathbf{y}_1 \\
\mathbf{y}_2 \\
\tau_1 \\
\tau_2 \\
d_{r,1} \\
d_{r,2} \\
\mathbf{g}_{j1} \\
\mathbf{g}_{j2} \\
\mathbf{B}
\end{bmatrix}
=
\begin{bmatrix}
(\ln(\mathbf{g}_{t,1}^{-1}\mathbf{g}_{st,1}))^{\vee} \\
(\ln(\mathbf{g}_{t,2}^{-1}\mathbf{g}_{st,2}))^{\vee} \\
K_1\theta_1 - J_1^{\mathrm{T}}\mathbf{F}_1 - (J_{1,1}^{T} - J_{O,1}^{T})\mathbf{F}_{r,1} - J_{j,1}^{T}\mathbf{F}_{j,1} \\
K_2\theta_2 - J_2^{\mathrm{T}}\mathbf{F}_2 - (J_{1,2}^{T} - J_{O,2}^{T})\mathbf{F}_{r,2} - J_{j,2}^{T}\mathbf{F}_{j,2} \\
d_1 - d_{1,0} \\
d_2 - d_{2,0} \\
(\ln(\mathbf{g}_{j,1}^{-1}\mathbf{g}_{sj,1}))^{\vee} \\
(\ln(\mathbf{g}_{j,2}^{-1}\mathbf{g}_{sj,2}))^{\vee} \\
\mathbf{F}_{j,1} + \mathbf{F}_{j,2} - \mathbf{F}_{os}
\end{bmatrix}
\tag{1}
$$

where $\mathbf{x} = [\theta_1^T, \theta_2^T, \mathbf{F}_1^T, \mathbf{F}_2^T, f_1, f_2, \mathbf{F}_{j,1}^T, \mathbf{F}_{j,2}^T, \mathbf{F}_o^T]^T$ represents the variables of the problem. Here $\theta_1 = [\theta_{1,1}, \theta_{1,2}, \ldots, \theta_{1,N_1}]^T$, $\theta_2 = [\theta_{2,1}, \theta_{2,2}, \ldots, \theta_{2,N_2}]^T \in \mathbb{R}^{N \times 1}$ are the joint displacement vectors of the flexible beams of two fingers, $\mathbf{F}_1, \mathbf{F}_2 \in \mathbb{R}^{6 \times 1}$ are the external wrenches at the end of flexible beams. $f_1, f_2 \in \mathbb{R}$ represent the magnitudes of the internal forces of the rigid ribs. Because the rigid ribs can be regarded as two-force rods, the direction of its internal forces is along the ribs. $\mathbf{F}_{j,1}, \mathbf{F}_{j,2} \in \mathbb{R}^{6 \times 1}$ represent the grasping wrenches at the joints of fingertips. $\mathbf{F}_o \in \mathbb{R}^{6 \times 1}$ denotes the interaction force. $\mathbf{g}_{st,1}, \mathbf{g}_{st,2} \in SE(3)$ represent the poses of the end frame $\{T_1\}$, $\{T_2\}$ with respect to $\{S\}$, and $\mathbf{g}_{t,1}, \mathbf{g}_{t,2} \in SE(3)$ are the target poses of the former, respectively. $(\ln(\mathbf{g}_{t,1}^{-1}\mathbf{g}_{st,1}))^{\vee}, (\ln(\mathbf{g}_{t,2}^{-1}\mathbf{g}_{st,2}))^{\vee} \in \mathbb{R}^{6 \times 1}$ denote the pose deviation of the current pose of the end frame from its target one. $\tau_1, \tau_2 \in \mathbb{R}^{N \times 1}$ represent the resultant moments in the joint spaces of the two fingers, which consists of four parts, namely, the torque of each joint, the end load, the internal reaction force of the rigid joint, and the clamping wrench at the fingertip, which can be expressed as:

$$\begin{cases} \tau_1 = K_1\theta_1 - J_1^T\mathbf{F}_1 - (J_{I,1}^T - J_{O,1}^T)\mathbf{F}_{r,1} - J_{j,1}^T\mathbf{F}_{j,1} \\ \tau_2 = K_2\theta_2 - J_2^T\mathbf{F}_2 - (J_{I,2}^T - J_{O,2}^T)\mathbf{F}_{r,2} - J_{j,2}^T\mathbf{F}_{j,2} \end{cases} \tag{2}$$

where $K_1 = \mathrm{diag}(k_{1,1}, k_{1,2} \cdots, k_{1,N})$, $K_2 = \mathrm{diag}(k_{2,1}, k_{2,2} \cdots, k_{2,N}) \in \mathbb{R}^{N \times N}$ represent the joint stiffness matrices of the approximated mechanisms. $J_1 = [\boldsymbol{\xi}_{1,1}, \boldsymbol{\xi}_{1,2}, \cdots, \boldsymbol{\xi}_{1,N}]$, $J_2 = [\boldsymbol{\xi}_{2,1}, \boldsymbol{\xi}_{2,2}, \cdots, \boldsymbol{\xi}_{2,N}] \in \mathbb{R}^{6 \times N}$ represent Jacobian matrices of the flexible beams. $J_{I,1} = [\boldsymbol{\xi}_{1,1}, \cdots, \boldsymbol{\xi}_{1,N_L}, \mathbf{0}, \cdots, \mathbf{0}]$, $J_{O,1} = [\boldsymbol{\xi}_{1,1}, \cdots, \boldsymbol{\xi}_{1,N_O}, \mathbf{0}, \cdots, \mathbf{0}] \in \mathbb{R}^{6 \times N}$ are the Jacobian matrices of $\{I_1\}$, $\{O_1\}$ with respect to $\{S\}$. $J_{j,1} = [\boldsymbol{\xi}_{1,1}, \cdots, \boldsymbol{\xi}_{1,N_j}, \mathbf{0}, \cdots, \mathbf{0}] \in \mathbb{R}^{6 \times N}$ is the Jacobian matrix of the fingertip. $J_{I,2}, J_{O,2}, J_{j,2} \in \mathbb{R}^{6 \times N}$ can be obtained in the same way. $\mathbf{F}_{r,1} = f_1\mathbf{W}_1 \in \mathbb{R}^{6 \times 1}$ is the internal reaction force of the rigid rib. $\mathbf{W}_1 = [\mathbf{r}_{I,1} \times \mathbf{u}_1, \mathbf{u}_1]^T \in \mathbb{R}^{6 \times 1}$ is the is the corresponding wrench. Here $\mathbf{u}_1 = (\mathbf{r}_{I,1} - \mathbf{r}_{O,1})/d_1$ represents the unit vector from the left joint to the right joint of the rib of finger 1. $\mathbf{r}_{I,1}, \mathbf{r}_{O,1} \in \mathbb{R}^{3 \times 1}$ indicate the position vectors of the joints on the left and right sides of the rib of finger 1. $d_1 = \|\mathbf{r}_{I,1} - \mathbf{r}_{O,1}\| \in \mathbb{R}$ indicates the distance between the joints on the left and right sides of the rib. $\mathbf{F}_{r,2} \in \mathbb{R}^{6 \times 1}$ can be obtained in the same way. $d_{r,1} = d_1 - d_{1,0} \in \mathbb{R}$ indicates the deviation of the distance between the joints on both sides of the rib and the length of the rib, and $d_{r,2}$ can be obtained in the same way. $g_{sj,1}, g_{sj,2} \in SE(3)$ represent the poses of the fingertip frames $\{J_1\}$, $\{J_2\}$ with respect to $\{S\}$. $g_{j,1}, g_{j,2} \in SE(3)$ are the target poses of the former. $(\ln(g_{j,1}^{-1}g_{sj,1}))^\vee$, $(\ln(g_{j,2}^{-1}g_{sj,2}))^\vee \in \mathbb{R}^{6 \times 1}$ denote the pose deviations of the current pose of the fingertip frame from its target one. $\mathbf{B} = \mathbf{F}_{j,1} + \mathbf{F}_{j,2} - \mathbf{F}_{os} \in \mathbb{R}^{6 \times 1}$ indicates the torque deviation at the fingertips of two fingers. Here $\mathbf{F}_{os} = Ad(g_o^{-1}(\theta_1))^T\mathbf{F}_o \in \mathbb{R}^{6 \times 1}$ transfers the interaction force into a wrench with respect to $\{S\}$. $Ad(\cdot)$ is the adjoint operator that converts the elements of $SE(3)$ from the standard form of 4×4 to the form of 6×1. $g_o \in SE(3)$ represent the poses of the point of interaction force with respect to $\{S\}$.

The number of equations and unknowns are both $2N+32$, Since the gripper is a planar mechanism, the number of equations and unknowns are both $2n+17$ after simplification. The Newton-Raphson method is employed to effectively solve these equations. Gradient matrix can be written as:

$$\nabla_C = \begin{bmatrix} \frac{\partial \mathbf{y}}{\partial \theta} & O & O & O & O \\ \frac{\partial \tau}{\partial \theta} & \frac{\partial \tau}{\partial \mathbf{Ft}} & \frac{\partial \tau}{\partial \mathbf{f}} & \frac{\partial \tau}{\partial \mathbf{F_j}} & O \\ \frac{\partial \mathbf{d}}{\partial \theta} & O & O & O & O \\ \frac{\partial \mathbf{y_j}}{\partial \theta} & O & O & O & O \\ O & O & O & \frac{\partial \mathbf{B}}{\partial \mathbf{F_j}^T} & \frac{\partial \mathbf{B}}{\partial \mathbf{F_o}} \end{bmatrix}_{(2n+17) \times (2n+17)} \tag{3}$$

O is all-zero matrix. Then, the interaction force of the grasped object and the equilibrium configuration of the gripper can be solved through a gradient-based algorithm:

$$\mathbf{x}^{(k+1)} = \mathbf{x}^{(k)} + (\nabla_C^{(k)})^{-1}C^{(k)} \tag{4}$$

where the subscript k denotes the k_{th} iterative step. The equation will be solved iteratively until the residual reach the setting number which is near zero.

4 Interaction Force Sensing Model

In Sect. 3, we present a methodology for determining the deformation of flexible beams and the interaction force through the identification of the grasped object's pose. However, in practical scenarios, the grasped object's pose may not be readily available. To address this challenge, we employ a model-based approach to reconstructing the large deformations of slender flexible beams through strain gauges, which was developed in our prior work [13]. Specifically, by measuring the resistance of the strain gauges, we can obtain the local curvature information of the flexible beams. We extend the constraint equation and gradient matrix by incorporating the curvature information, leading to the development of a sensing model:

$$
C_s(\mathbf{x}) =
\begin{bmatrix}
\mathbf{y}_1 \\
\mathbf{y}_2 \\
\tau_1 \\
\tau_2 \\
d_{r,1} \\
d_{r,2} \\
\mathbf{B} \\
\mathbf{S}
\end{bmatrix}
=
\begin{bmatrix}
(\ln(\mathbf{g}_{t,1}^{-1}\mathbf{g}_{st,1}))^{\vee} \\
(\ln(\mathbf{g}_{t,2}^{-1}\mathbf{g}_{st,2}))^{\vee} \\
\mathbf{K}_1\theta_1 - \mathbf{J}_1^{\mathsf{T}}\mathbf{F}_1 - (\mathbf{J}_{1,1}^{T} - \mathbf{J}_{O,1}^{T})\mathbf{F}_{r,1} - \mathbf{J}_{j,1}^{T}\mathbf{F}_{j,1} \\
\mathbf{K}_2\theta_2 - \mathbf{J}_2^{\mathsf{T}}\mathbf{F}_2 - (\mathbf{J}_{1,2}^{T} - \mathbf{J}_{O,2}^{T})\mathbf{F}_{r,2} - \mathbf{J}_{j,2}^{T}\mathbf{F}_{j,2} \\
d_1 - d_{1,0} \\
d_2 - d_{2,0} \\
\mathbf{F}_{j,1} + \mathbf{F}_{j,2} - \mathbf{F}_o \\
S_e\theta - s
\end{bmatrix}
\tag{5}
$$

By comparing (1), it can be seen that the unknown variables of the two models are the same, the difference is that $\mathbf{g}_j \in \mathbb{R}^{6\times 1}$ in the constraint item is replaced by $\mathbf{S} \in \mathbb{R}^{m\times 1}$. Here $\mathbf{S} = S_e\theta - s$ represents the constraints on the bending information collected by the strain gauges. $\mathbf{s} = [s_{1,0}, \cdots s_{m,0}]^T \in \mathbb{R}^{m\times 1}$ Indicates the angle of each strain gauge. $S_e \in \mathbb{R}^{m\times n}$ is a constant matrix related to the position of strain gauges. m is the number of strain gauges. In order to solve the model, $m \geq 6$ needs to be guaranteed, and we choose $m = 8$ to reduce the error. The Jacobian matrix of the sensing model is similar to (3):

$$
\nabla_{C_s} =
\begin{bmatrix}
\frac{\partial \mathbf{y}}{\partial \theta} & \boldsymbol{O} & \boldsymbol{O} & \boldsymbol{O} & \boldsymbol{O} \\
\frac{\partial \tau}{\partial \theta} & \frac{\partial \tau}{\partial \mathbf{Ft}} & \frac{\partial \tau}{\partial \mathbf{f}} & \frac{\partial \tau}{\partial \mathbf{F}_j} & \boldsymbol{O} \\
\frac{\partial \mathbf{d}}{\partial \theta} & \boldsymbol{O} & \boldsymbol{O} & \boldsymbol{O} & \boldsymbol{O} \\
\frac{\partial \mathbf{S}}{\partial \theta} & \boldsymbol{O} & \boldsymbol{O} & \boldsymbol{O} & \boldsymbol{O} \\
\boldsymbol{O} & \boldsymbol{O} & \boldsymbol{O} & \frac{\partial \mathbf{B}}{\partial \mathbf{F}_j} & \frac{\partial \mathbf{B}}{\partial \mathbf{F}_o}
\end{bmatrix}_{(2n+19)\times(2n+17)}
\tag{6}
$$

The difference is the fourth row is updated. All block but the first one yield to zeros. The first block $\partial \mathbf{S}/\partial\theta$ is the constant matrix $S_e \in \mathbb{R}^{8\times 1}$. The approach used for obtaining the solution is similar to that presented in Sect. 3:

$$
\mathbf{x}^{(k+1)} = \mathbf{x}^{(k)} + (\nabla_{C_s}^{(k)})^{+}C_s^{(k)}
\tag{7}
$$

where $(\nabla_{C_s}^{(k)})^{+}$ is the pseudo-inverse of ∇_{C_s}.

5 Experiment Verification

In this section, we present an experimental setup aimed at validating the precision of the interactive force perception method, as illustrated in Fig. 3. The setup consists of two fingers symmetrically positioned on a horizontal slide table, a set of perception system, a Six-dimensional force sensor, an 80 mm × 40 mm × 20 mm square object, and a vertical three-degree-of-freedom slide table.

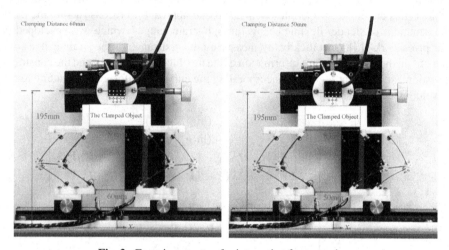

Fig. 3. Experiment setup for interaction force sensing.

Initially, the position of the horizontal slider is adjusted to ensure minimal contact between the finger and the object. At this point, the distance between the bases of the two fingers is set to be equal to the length of the clamped object, which is 80 mm. T, the horizontal slider is adjusted inward to simulate two gripping scenarios. In the first scenario, the distance between the bases of the two fingers is set to 60 mm, while in the second scenario, it is set to 50 mm. For each of these gripping scenarios, the position of the square object is manipulated using the three-degree-of-freedom sliding stage. This manipulation allows the force-measuring point of the force sensor, highlighted by the yellow dot in Fig. 3, to be positioned at various locations indicated by the white dots in the same figure. The distance between each position point and its adjacent upper, lower, left, and right points is 5 mm. The force-measuring point of the force sensor is positioned 8.25 mm above the installation surface and initially set at a height of 74 mm. During the movement of the square object, the readings from the force sensor and the corresponding strain gauges are recorded at each location. The tighter the gripper clamps the target object, the smaller the interaction space, resulting in a difference in the number of position points between the two gripping scenarios.

Figure 4 illustrates the deviation between the measured interaction force and the induced value when clamped at 60 mm. Specifically, at 18 test positions, the absolute errors for the two-plane forces and the torque around the z-axis (perpendicular to the x-y plane in Fig. 3) are recorded as 0.97 N, 2.76 N, and 0.18 Nm, respectively. Similarly, Fig. 5 depicts the deviation between the measured interaction force and the induced value when clamped at 50 mm. At 14 test positions, the absolute errors for the two-plane forces and the torque around the z-axis are measured to be 1.42 N, 1.41 N, and 0.10 Nm, respectively.

The primary reason for these errors lies in the calibration of the strain gauges. The calibration process establishes a relationship between the output voltage and the bending angle of the strain gauge through linear fitting. However, errors may arise during this calibration process, resulting in inaccuracies in force sensing. These errors, in turn, affect the accuracy of the sensing model.

The absolute errors in force measurements are small in both directions, but the vertical direction exhibits a larger error. This is attributed to the initial application of a horizontal gripping force on the gripper. Consequently, the deformation caused by the horizontal force during the experiment is more significant, leading to more accurate force sensing in the horizontal direction. Additionally, it is observed that the compliant gripper's sensing of torque has a relatively larger error. This can be attributed to the calculation of torque relying on the predicted pose of the grasped object. However, due to the inherent errors in the predicted pose of the grasped object, the error in perceived torque is amplified through the combined effect of these two errors. Consequently, the error in perceived torque is larger. Nevertheless, the overall trend aligns with the actual scenario.

By comparing the results of the two groups of experiments, it becomes evident that as the gripper clamps the object more tightly, the perception accuracy increases.

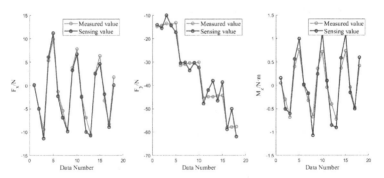

Fig. 4. Comparison between the measured and sensing interaction force when clamping 60mm

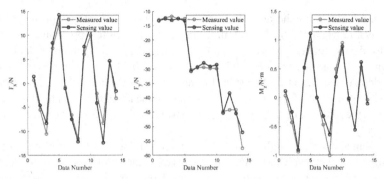

Fig. 5. Comparison between the measured and sensing interaction force when clamping 50mm

6 Conclusion and Outlook

In this paper, a composite compliant two-finger gripper is proposed. When the grasped object interacts with the environment, the flexible beams of the finger can be passively deformed to achieve passive compliance in the assembly process. At the same time, the flexible sensors installed on the compliant fingers can actively sense the deformation of the compliant fingers, which can be used to derive a sensing model to calculate the interaction force on the grasped object, enabling active compliance. Kinetostatic model and sensing model are derived using a discretization-based method. And the proposed model is verified by experiments in two gripping scenarios. When the clamping distance is set at 60 mm, the absolute errors of the two-plane force and torque around the z-axis are measured as 0.97 N, 2.76 N, and 0.18 Nm, respectively. Similarly, when the clamping distance is reduced to 50 mm, the absolute errors of the two-plane force and torque around the z-axis are observed to be 1.42 N, 1.41 N, and 0.10 Nm, respectively.

In future work, we will design the driving part of the gripper, build the real-time force sensing system and optimize the parameters.

Acknowledgement. This research work was supported in part by the National Key R&D program of China under the Grant 2019YFA0709001, and the National Natural Science Foundation of China under the Grant 52022056.

References

1. Rubio, F., Valero, F., Llopis-Albert, C.: A review of mobile robots: concepts, methods, theoretical framework, and applications. Int. J. Adv. Robot. Syst. **16**(2) (2019)
2. Nahavandi, S., Uddin, M.J., Nasu, Y., Trinh, H., Saadat, M.: Automated robotic grinding by low-powered manipulator. Robot. Comput.-Integrat. Manuf. **23**(5), 589–598 (2007)
3. Li, L., Yu, S., Sun, W.: Design of flexible pressure sensor applied to mechanical gripper. IEEE Sens. J. **22**(16), 15793–15801 (2022)
4. Cheng, C., Fu, J., Su, H., Ren, L.: Recent advancements in agriculture robots: benefits and challenges. Machines **11**(1), 48 (2023)
5. Wang, W., Loh, R.N., Gu, E.Y.: Passive compliance versus active compliance in robot-based automated assembly systems. Ind. Robot Int. J. 48–57 (1998)

6. Whitney, D.E.: What is the remote centre compliance (RCC) and what can it do?. In: Proceedings of the 9th International Symposium on Industrial Robots, Washington, DC, pp. 135–152 (1979)
7. Roveda, L., Vicentini, F., Pedrocchi, N., Tosatti, L.M.: Force-tracking impedance control for manipulators mounted on compliant bases. In: IEEE International Conference on Robotics and Automation (ICRA), pp. 760–765 (2014)
8. Raibert, M.H., Craig, J.J.: Hybrid position/force control of manipulators. ASME. J. Dyn. Syst. Meas. Control 103(2), 126–133 (1981)
9. Su, J., Liu, C., Li, R.: Robot precision assembly combining with passive and active compliant motions. IEEE Trans. Industr. Electron. 69(8), 8157–8167 (2021)
10. Ali, M.H., Zhanabayev, A., Khamzhin, S., Mussin, K.: Biologically inspired gripper based on the fin ray effect. In: 5th International Conference on Control, Automation and Robotics (ICCAR), pp. 865–869 (2019)
11. Crooks, W., Vukasin, G., O'Sullivan, M., Messner, W., Rogers, C.: Fin ray® effect inspired soft robotic gripper: from the robosoft grand challenge toward optimization. Front. Robot. AI 70 (2016)
12. Crooks, W., Rozen-Levy, S., Trimmer, B., Rogers, C., Messner, W.: Passive gripper inspired by Manduca sexta and the Fin Ray® Effect. Int. J. Adv. Rob. Syst. 14(4), 1729881417721155 (2017)
13. Luo, J., Xun, Y., Yao, J., Chen, G., Wang, H.: Sensor-based reconstruction of slender flexible beams undergoing large-scale deflection. In: IEEE/RSJ International Conference on Intelligent Robots and Systems (IROS), pp. 6936–6943 (2022)
14. Chen, G., Zhang, Z., Wang, H.: A general approach to the large deflection problems of spatial flexible rods using principal axes decomposition of compliance matrices. ASME J. Mech. Robot. 10(3), 031012 (2018)
15. Chen, G., Wang, H., Lin, Z., et al.: The principal axes decomposition of spatial stiffness matrices. IEEE Trans. Rob. 31(1), 191–207 (2015)
16. Chen, G., Kang, Y., Liang, Z., Zhang, Z., Wang, H.: Kinetostatics modeling and analysis of parallel continuum manipulators. Mech. Mach. Theory 163, 104380 (2021)

A Novel Skill Learning Framework for Redundant Manipulators Based on Multi-task Dynamic Movement Primitives

Yuming Ning, Tuanjie Li$^{(\boxtimes)}$, Cong Yao, and Yonghua Huang

School of Mechano-Electronic Engineering, Xidian University, Xi'an 710071, China
tjli@mail.xidian.edu.cn

Abstract. Skill learning is a frontier problem in intelligent robot systems, which aims to make robots efficiently learn manipulation skills from human demonstration. In this paper, we propose a novel robot skill learning framework based on multi-task dynamic movement primitives (MT-DMPs) to improve the operation efficiency of redundant manipulators, which is mainly composed of sub-task segmentation module, parameter setting module, robot skill learning module and pose optimization module. We describe the design steps of the proposed framework in detail as follows: 1) Finite State Machine (FSM) is used to divide multiple tasks into a sub-task sequence, thus forming the state transition diagram for the robot to perform multiple tasks. 2) An exponential decay function is introduced to improve the basic DMPs, and the design flow for instantiating robot skills is summarized. 3) Velocity Directional Manipulability (VDM) is introduced as the evaluation index of robot motion performance, and a pose optimization model suitable for redundant manipulators is established. Finally, we build an experimental platform based on the Robot Operating System (ROS), and carry out a series of experiments. The results show that our proposed skill learning framework can improve the efficiency and accuracy of autonomous operation of redundant manipulators.

Keywords: Skill learning · Multi-task dynamic movement primitives · Pose optimization model · Robot Operating System

1 Introduction

With the continuous development and improvement of electronic information technology and manufacturing process, the production steps and manufacturing requirements of high-tech products become more and more complex. To meet the requirements of processing and testing in new high-tech products development, "Replacing humans with robots" has become an inevitable trend in the future industrial development [1, 2]. 7-DOF redundant manipulators have good motion performance and operational flexibility, so they are widely used in intelligent manufacturing, warehouse logistics, biomedicine, and other modern industrial fields [3, 4], as shown in Fig. 1. However, 7-DOF redundant manipulators are also facing emerging challenges, mainly in the following aspect:

© The Author(s), under exclusive license to Springer Nature Singapore Pte Ltd. 2023
H. Yang et al. (Eds.): ICIRA 2023, LNAI 14268, pp. 568–578, 2023.
https://doi.org/10.1007/978-981-99-6486-4_48

1) Inefficient motion planning [5]. 7-DOF redundant manipulators are commonly used in complex unstructured environments, and traditional motion planning algorithms such as random sampling, heuristic learning and neural network have the problems of long motion planning time and low success rate of planning, which will lead to the low operation quality and the operation blocking.

2) Poor real-time performance for multi-task learning and execution [6]. Up to now, the research on robot skill learning mainly focuses on end-to-end reinforcement learning algorithms, which have the problems of long pre-training time, poor motion robustness, and only suitable for a single task, so they cannot be used in engineering practice.

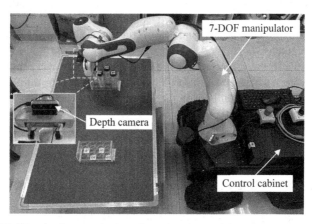

Fig. 1. The 7-DOF redundant manipulator is performing a pick-and-place task autonomously.

Therefore, it is of great significance to find a robot skill learning method suitable for continuous multi-task execution to promote the development and application of redundant manipulators.

Robot skill learning is one of the core problems for redundant manipulators. Up to now, many scholars have carried out extensive research on the methods of robot skill learning, and it can be divided into two categories according to different methods. The first is ones based on the artificial intelligence algorithms, such as deep reinforcement learning (DRL) [7], artificial neural network (ANN) [8], heuristic learning (HL) [9], etc. Liu et al. focus on the assembly-oriented industrial grasping scenarios, and propose a digital twin-enabled approach that realizes the effective transfer of DRL algorithms to physical robots [10]. Sun et al. adopt a modularized strategy to design a robotic reinforcement learning system, which can learn navigation and grasping together automatically [11]. Zeng et al. propose a human-in-the-loop learning-control approach based on end-to-end neural network model, which can acquire compliant grasping and operating skills of a multi-fingered dexterous hand [12]. Lin et al. present a graph neural network (GNN) policy architecture, which can solve complex long-horizon manipulation problems for robotic manipulators [13]. Duque et al. propose a motion skill segmentation method based on heuristic learning [14]. However, the first type of robot skill learning methods has the problems of long offline training time and poor robustness, so it is difficult to be used in engineering practice. The second is ones based on imitation learning, such as dynamical system (DS) [15], dynamic movement primitives (DMPs) [16], probabilistic movement primitives (ProMPs) [17], etc. Among them, DMPs and its variants have become the mainstream algorithms of robot skill learning due to their simple modeling and strong versatility [18]. Li et al. propose a skill learning strategy based on DMPs for human-robot cooperative manipulation, which can react compliantly to robot interaction with human subjects [19]. Yu et al. propose a robot skill learning framework considering both motion and impedance features, which employs DMPs to model motion and impedance features simultaneously [20]. Fang et al. present a rotation-invariant dynamical-movement-primitive method for learning interaction skills [21]. Zhang et al. develop a robot learning system based on DMPs and broad neural network (BNN), which can reuse the motion controller that has been learned [22]. However, the above studies are only limited to single-task learning, and do not consider multi-task autonomous learning for robotic manipulators.

Therefore, due to the limitations in the above studies, a novel robot skill learning framework is proposed based on multi-task dynamic movement primitives (MT-DMPs), and the main contributions are listed in the following:

1) A novel robot skill learning framework based on MT-DMPs is proposed, and the design steps and working principle of the framework are described in detail.
2) The working principle and derivation process of each sub-module are given. Among them, we focus on the sub-task segmentation module based on Finite State Machine (FSM), the robot skill learning module based on DMPs, and the pose optimization module based on Velocity Directional Manipulability (VDM).
3) An experimental platform is built based on the Robot Operating System (ROS), and the effectiveness of the proposed skill learning framework is verified by prototype experiments.

2   Robot Skill Learning Framework

In this paper, we propose a novel robot skill learning framework based on multi-task dynamic movement primitives (MT-DMPs), as shown in Fig. 2. The framework is composed of sub-task segmentation module, parameter setting module, robot skill learning module and pose optimization module.

The main working principle of the proposed framework is as follows.

1) When the executive program is started, FSM is used to divide multiple tasks into a sub-task sequence.
2) Parameter setting module outputs the target pose, scaling factor and other parameters to the DMPs-based robot skill learning module.
3) VDM-based pose optimization module optimizes the pose of the robot and outputs the optimized pose to the robot actuator.
4) When the last subtask ends, actuating signals Signal_1 and Signal_2 will activate the next subtask unit until all tasks are executed by the robot.

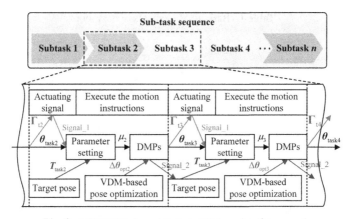

Fig. 2. MT-DMPs-based Robot skill learning framework

2.1 FSM-Based Sub-task Segmentation Module

As one of the theoretical models of state machine, FSM is a mathematical model that describes a finite number of states and the transitions and actions between these states [23]. It has the advantages of easy writing, convenient debugging and high operating efficiency. FSM is a commonly used model for industrial design, computer and mathematical logic design, and it can describe the operation process of the robot intuitively and clearly. Its basic elements include state, action, event and transition. The difficulty of FSM application lies in extracting basic elements from application objects and constructing FSM model. Based on the behavior characteristics of autonomous operation of redundant manipulators, the FSM-based behavior decision system model based on FSM is designed in this paper. Pick-and-place task in Fig. 1 as an example, and the basic FSM elements of the robot are shown in Table 1. To describe the above model more intuitively, its state transition diagram is shown in Fig. 3.

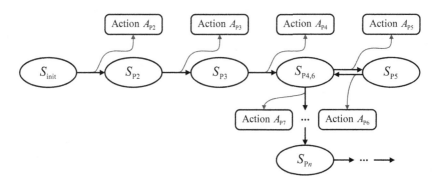

Fig. 3. FSM state transition diagram of the robot performing a pick-and-place task

Table 1. Basic FSM elements of the robot

Basic elements	Symbol
State	$S_{\text{init}}, S_{P2}, S_{P3}, S_{P4,6}, S_{P5}, \cdots, S_{Pn}$
Action	$A_{P2}, A_{P3}, A_{P4}, A_{P5}, A_{P6}, A_{P7}, \cdots, A_{Pn}$
Event	Signal_1, Signal_2
Transition	State transition function $Tran\,()$

2.2 DMPs-Based Robot Skill Learning Module

In this section, we introduce DMPs to design the skill learning module. The basic principle of DMPs is to learn the mapping function of position y and velocity $\dot{y}$ to acceleration $\ddot{y}$ respectively from the teaching trajectory [16]. For the robot system, if the position y_t and velocity $\dot{y}_t$ at time t are known, DMPs can calculate the expected acceleration $\ddot{y}_t$ online, and then obtain the expected position $(y_t + \Delta t \dot{y}_t)$ and velocity $(\dot{y}_t + \Delta t \ddot{y}_t)$ at the next moment Δt. Here, we will build the second-order DMPs system to obtain a smooth robot joint trajectory, and its working principle can be summarized in Fig. 4.

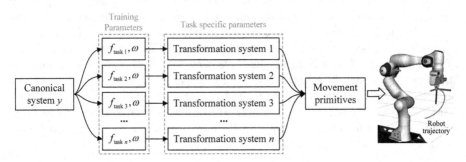

Fig. 4. Schematic diagram of DMPs system

The mathematical model of the second-order DMPs system can be obtained, as shown in formula (1). The DMPs system can guarantee the independent motion characteristics of each robot joint.

$$\begin{cases} \tau \ddot{y} = \alpha_z(\beta_z(g - y) - \dot{y}) + f(x, g) \\ f(x, g) = \dfrac{\sum\limits_{i=1}^{N} \omega_i \cdot \psi_i}{\sum\limits_{i=1}^{N} \psi_i} x(g - y_0) \\ \psi_i = \exp\left(-h_i(x - c_i)^2\right) \end{cases} \tag{1}$$

where the disturbance term $f(x, g)$ is composed of a series of kernel functions, τ is a temporal scaling factor, g is the delayed goal function. α_z, β_z are time constants, ψ_i is the kernel function and ω_i is the weight, h_i is the variance of the kernel function, c_i is the center point of the ψ_i. ω_i can be described by formula (2).

$$\omega_i = \frac{S^T \Gamma_i f_{target}}{S^T \Gamma_i S} \tag{2}$$

where,

$$S = \left[x_{t1}(g - y_0) \; x_{t2}(g - y_0) \cdots x_{tP}(g - y_0) \right]^T \tag{3}$$

$$\Phi_i = \begin{bmatrix} \psi_i(t_1) & 0 & \cdots & 0 \\ 0 & \psi_i(t_2) & \cdots & 0 \\ \vdots & \vdots & \ddots & \vdots \\ 0 & 0 & \cdots & \psi_i(t_P) \end{bmatrix} \tag{4}$$

$$f_{target} = \left[f_{target}(t_1) \; f_{target}(t_2) \cdots f_{target}(t_P) \right]^T \tag{5}$$

Here, we can summarize the workflow of DMPs-based robot skill learning module, as shown in Fig. 5.

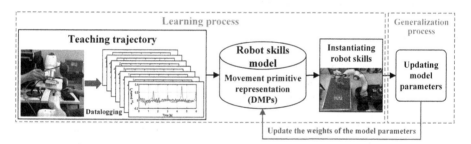

Fig. 5. Schematic diagram of the DMPs-based robot skill learning module

In addition, an exponential decay function is introduced to optimize the acceleration curve to prevent the acceleration jump during the initial movement of the robot. The exponential decay function is described by formula (6).

$$\tau \dot{x} = -\alpha_x x \tag{6}$$

Because the position P_k^* of the robotic end-effector is not a definite value, we introduce the convergence factor $\mu_m \in (0, 1]$ to guide the robotic end-effector to reach the target point, as shown in formula (7).

$$P_k^* = P_k(t_0) + \mu_m \cdot \left(T_{T_{k-1}} - P_k(t_0) \right) \tag{7}$$

where k indicates the task number, $T_{T_{k-1}}$ is the input target pose.

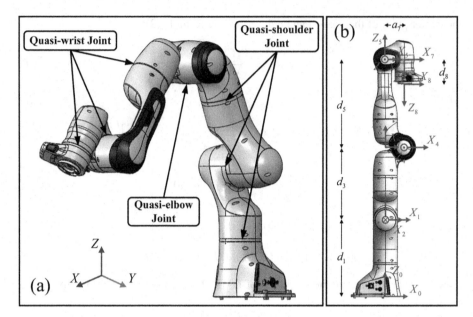

Fig. 6. The 7-DoF manipulator: (a) Simulation model. (b) D-H coordinate system.

2.3 VDM-Based Pose Optimization Module

In this section, the D-H method [24] is used to establish the spatial coordinate system of the 7-DOF redundant manipulator, which is used to describe the spatial pose relationship between the coordinate system of two adjacent connecting rods of the manipulator, as shown in Fig. 6.

Based on the D-H coordinate system and geometric parameters of the 7-DoF manipulator, the pose conversion relationship T_7^0 can be described by formula (8).

$$T_7^0(\theta) = \prod_{i=1}^{7} T_i^{i-1} = \begin{bmatrix} R_7^0(\theta) & P_7^0(\theta) \\ 0 & 1 \end{bmatrix} \tag{8}$$

where $R_7^0(\theta)$ and $P_7^0(\theta)$ represent the robot posture and robot end-effector position, respectively.

VDM [25] is introduced as the optimization index to establish a novel search criterion. Firstly, we establish the conversion relationship between the joint vector θ in joint space and the pose vector $\mathbf{x}$ in operational space, as shown in formula (9).

$$\dot{x} = \begin{bmatrix} v \\ \omega \end{bmatrix} = J(\theta)\dot{\theta} = \begin{bmatrix} J_v \\ J_\omega \end{bmatrix} \dot{\theta} \tag{9}$$

where $\dot{x}$ represents the generalized velocity matrix of the robot end-effector in operational space, $\dot{\theta}$ represents the joint velocity matrix of the robot in joint space. v and ω represent the linear velocity and angular velocity of the robot end-effector. $J(\theta)$ is the velocity Jacobian matrix of the robot.

Secondly, the unit sphere in joint space can be described by formula (10), and we can obtain the generalized velocity ellipsoid of the robot in the operational space, as shown in formula (11).

$$\dot{\theta}^T \dot{\theta} = 1 \tag{10}$$

$$\dot{x}^T \left(J(\theta) J^T(\theta) \right)^{-1} \dot{x} = 1 \tag{11}$$

To describe the motion performance of the robot in its motion direction, we define the motion velocity of the robot end-effector as $\dot{x} = Mp$, and substitute the motion velocity $\dot{x}$ into formula (11), and the VDM of the robot can be described by formula (12).

$$M = \left[p^T \left(J(\theta) J^T(\theta) \right)^{-1} p \right]^{-1/2} \tag{12}$$

where M is the VDM of the robot along the direction p.

Finally, based on the above description, the pose optimization problem can be described as the mathematical programming model as follows:

$$\begin{cases} \text{Find } \boldsymbol{\theta} = \begin{bmatrix} \theta_1 & \theta_2 & \cdots & \theta_7 \end{bmatrix}^T \\ \max \ M(\boldsymbol{\theta}) = \left[p^T \left(J(\theta) J^T(\theta) \right)^{-1} p \right]^{-1/2} \\ s.t. \ \ T_7^0(\boldsymbol{\theta}) = \prod_{i=1}^{7} T_i^{i-1}, \ \text{ forward kinematic equation} \\ \theta_i \in \begin{bmatrix} \theta_{i,\min}, & \theta_{i,\max} \end{bmatrix}, \ i = 1, 2, \ldots, 7 \end{cases} \tag{13}$$

The adaptive PSO algorithm [26] is used to solve the optimization model in formula (13), and the robot with the optimal motion performance and the corresponding joint angles can be obtained.

3 Experiment and Analysis

In this section, we build an experimental platform based on ROS, and carry out a series of prototype experiments to verify the effectiveness of the proposed skill learning framework. To ensure the correctness of the experimental conclusion, the experimental platform of all contrast experiments is consistent (Experimental platform: Intel Core i7-10750H with 16G of memory, software version: Ubuntu 18.04 LTS + ROS Melodic).

To analyze the learning precision and efficiency of the robot skills learning method proposed in this paper, a series of experiments are performed using MT-DMPs and the algorithms proposed in [16] and [27], respectively, and the experimental results are compared. We set the particle number $m = 70$, inertia weight $\omega = \mathbf{0.3}$, learning factors $c_1 = 1.5$, $c_2 = 1.5$, iteration stop condition $\lambda \geq 0.6$.

The experimental content is that the 7-DOF manipulator can perform a pick-and-place task autonomously after skill learning. Figure 7 shows the experimental results

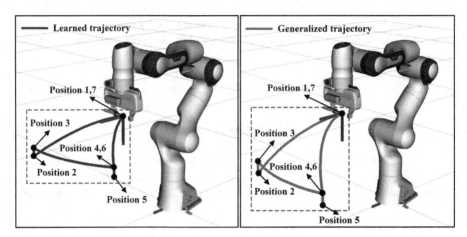

Fig. 7. Robot trajectory generalizations: (a) Learned trajectory. (b) Generalized trajectory.

of the robot trajectory generalizations, including learned trajectory and generalized trajectory.

Figure 8 shows the experimental results of the robot pick-and-place skill learning in the real-world. From Fig. 8, we can see that the robot can accurately place test tubes into the glass rack through our proposed skill learning method. To avoid the occasionality of the experimental results, each group is tested 20 times and its average value is taken as the final result. The experimental data is summarized in Table 2, including the execution time, the value of VDM, and success rate.

Fig. 8. The experimental results of the robot pick-and-place skill learning in the real-world

From Table 2, we can see that the proposed robot skill learning method (MT-DMPs) shows a significant improvement compared with the other two algorithms. Compared with DMPs and DMPs-PCC, the execution time is reduced by 36.2% and 8.1%, respectively, and the VDM is improved by 34.8% and 8.3%, respectively. Moreover, the success rate of our method has reached 100%, indicating that the proposed skill learning method can make the robot obtain better operation accuracy.

Table 2. Contrastive data of the prototype experiments

Algorithm	Execution time	VDM	Success rate (%)
DMPs [16]	26.0177	0.610	65%
DMPs-PCC [27]	18.0514	0.759	95%
MT-DMPs	16.5954	0.822	100%

4 Conclusion

In this paper, we propose a novel robot skill learning framework based on MT-DMPs to improve the operation efficiency of redundant manipulators, which is mainly composed of sub-task segmentation module, parameter setting module, robot skill learning module and pose optimization module. We describe the design steps of the proposed framework in detail, and show the working principle and derivation process of each sub-module. Among them, we focus on the sub-task segmentation module based on FSM, the robot skill learning module based on DMPs, and the pose optimization module based on VDM. Finally, we build an experimental platform based on ROS, and the effectiveness of the proposed skill learning framework is verified by proto-type experiments. The experimental results show that our method can effectively improve the operation accuracy and working efficiency of the robot.

References

1. Knudsen, M., Kaivo-Oja, J.: Collaborative robots: frontiers of current literature. J. Intell. Robot. Syst. Theory Appl. **3**(2), 13–20 (2020)
2. Gualtieri, L., Rauch, E., Vidoni, R.: Emerging research fields in safety and ergonomics in industrial collaborative robotics: a systematic literature review. Robot. Comput.-Integr. Manuf. **67**, 101998 (2021)
3. Alambeigi, F., Sefati, S., Armand, M.: A convex optimization framework for constrained concurrent motion control of a hybrid redundant surgical system. In: 2018 Annual American Control Conference (ACC), pp. 1158–1165 (2018)
4. Pham, A.D., Ahn, H.J.: High precision reducers for industrial robots driving 4th industrial revolution: state of arts, analysis, design, performance evaluation and perspective. Int. J. Precis. Eng. Manuf. Green Technol. **5**(4), 519–533 (2018)
5. Tamizi, M.G., Yaghoubi, M., Najjaran, H.: A review of recent trend in motion planning of industrial robots. Int. J. Intell. Robot. Appl. 1–22 (2023)
6. Lu, Z., Wang, N., Yang, C.: A constrained dmps framework for robot skills learning and generalization from human demonstrations. IEEE/ASME Trans. Mechatron. **26**(6), 3265–3275 (2021)
7. Li, X., Liu, H., Dong, M.: A general framework of motion planning for redundant robot manipulator based on deep reinforcement learning. IEEE Trans. Ind. Inform. **18**(8), 5253–5263 (2021)
8. Xu, C., Wang, M., Chi, G., et al.: An inertial neural network approach for loco-manipulation trajectory tracking of mobile robot with redundant manipulator. Neural Netw. **155**, 215–223 (2022)

9. Ding, G., Liu, Y., Zang, X., et al.: A task-learning strategy for robotic assembly tasks from human demonstrations. Sensors **20**(19), 5505 (2020)

10. Liu, Y., Xu, H., Liu, D., et al.: A digital twin-based sim-to-real transfer for deep reinforcement learning-enabled industrial robot grasping. Robot. Comput.-Integr. Manuf. **78**, 102365 (2022)

11. Sun, C., Orbik, J., Devin, C.M., et al.: Fully autonomous real-world reinforcement learning with applications to mobile manipulation. In: Proceedings of the 5th Conference on Robot Learning (PMLR), pp. 308–319 (2022)

12. Zeng, C., Li, S., Chen, Z., et al.: Multifingered robot hand compliant manipulation based on vision-based demonstration and adaptive force control. IEEE Trans. Neural Netw. Learn. Syst. 1–12 (2022). https://doi.org/10.1109/TNNLS.2022.3184258

13. Lin, Y., Wang, A.S., Undersander, E., et al.: Efficient and interpretable robot manipulation with graph neural networks. IEEE Robot. Autom. Lett. **7**(2), 2740–2747 (2022)

14. Duque, D.A., Prieto, F.A., Hoyos, J.G.: Trajectory generation for robotic assembly operations using learning by demonstration. Robot. Comput.-Integr. Manuf. **57**, 292–302 (2019)

15. Zeng, C., Yang, C., Cheng, H., et al.: Simultaneously encoding movement and sEMG-based stiffness for robotic skill learning. IEEE Trans. Ind. Inform. **17**(2), 1244–1252 (2020)

16. Ijspeert, A.J., Nakanishi, J., Hoffmann, H., et al.: Dynamical movement primitives: learning attractor models for motor behaviors. Neural Comput. **25**(2), 328–373 (2013)

17. Frank, F., Paraschos, A., Smagt, P., et al.: Constrained probabilistic movement primitives for robot trajectory adaptation. IEEE Trans. Robot. **38**(4), 2276–2294 (2021)

18. Saveriano, M., Abu-Dakka, F.J., Abu-Dakka, A., et al.: Dynamic movement primitives in robotics: a tutorial survey. arXiv preprint arXiv:2102.03861 (2021)

19. Li, J., Li, Z., Li, X., et al.: Skill learning strategy based on dynamic motion primitives for human–robot cooperative manipulation. IEEE Trans. Cogn. Dev. Syst. **13**(1), 105–117 (2020)

20. Yu, X., Liu, P., He, W., et al.: Human-robot variable impedance skills transfer learning based on dynamic movement primitives. IEEE Robot. Autom. Lett. **7**(3), 6463–6470 (2022)

21. Fang, B., Wei, X., Sun, F., et al.: Skill learning for human-robot interaction using wearable device. Tsinghua Sci. Technol. **24**(6), 654–662 (2022)

22. Zhang, Y., Li, M., Yang, C.: Robot learning system based on dynamic movement primitives and neural network. Neurocomputing **451**, 205–214 (2021)

23. Park, H.W., Ramezani, A., Grizzle, J.W.: A finite-state machine for accommodating unexpected large ground-height variations in bipedal robot walking. IEEE Trans. Robot. **29**(2), 331–345 (2012)

24. Hartenberg, R.S., Denavit, J.: A kinematic notation for lower-pair mechanisms based on matrices. J. Appl. Mech. **77**(2), 215–221 (1955)

25. Hu, S., Yang, Q., He, L., Tan, X.: Mechanism parameters optimization of bionic frog jumping robot based on velocity directional manipulability measure. J. Beijing Univ. Aeronaut. Astronaut. **3**, 351–356 (2012)

26. Sancaktar, I., Tuna, B., Ulutas, M.: Inverse kinematics application on medical robot using adapted PSO method. Eng. Sci. Technol. Int. J. **21**(5), 1006–1010 (2018)

27. Ning, Y., Li, T., Du, W., et al.: Inverse kinematics and planning/control co-design method of redundant manipulator for precision operation: design and experiments. Robot. Comput.-Integr. Manuf. **80**, 102457 (2023)

Research on Configuration Optimization of Space Robot for Satellite Capture

Shanxiang Fang[1,2](✉) and Tuan Hei[2]

[1] Department of Mathematics and Theory, Peng Cheng Laboratory, Shenzhen 518055, China
[2] School of Mechanical, Electronic and Control Engineering, Beijing Jiaotong University,
Beijing 100044, China
fangshx@bjtu.edu.cn

Abstract. In the satellite capture task of space robot, when the target satellite is in the operational space, the manipulator needs to be adjusted to the capture configuration for successful capture. Based on the demand for comprehensive adaptability of the manipulator during adjustment in complex environments, an average maneuverability index is designed in this paper, which could reflect the comprehensive dexterity of the manipulator during adjustment from the initial state to the capture state, and could be used to select the optimal capture configuration. By numerical simulation, the proposed configuration optimization strategy can make the space robot have the strongest dexterity in the process of adjusting the initial configuration to the capture configuration, so as to improve the success rate of capturing the target satellite by using space robot in complex environment.

Keywords: Space Robot · Satellite Capture · Configuration Optimization

1 Introduction

The technology of in-orbit robot capture is to use the space server to approach the target satellite and capture the space target with the robot arm [1–3]. On the basis of successful proximity tracking, the target satellite will be in the operating space of the space robot arm. To achieve capture, it is necessary to adjust the robotic arm to the capture configuration [4, 5]. Due to the redundant properties of the arm of the space robot, there may be infinite sets of configuration solutions to complete the task when operating for a certain target in the reachable space. Therefore, it is necessary to put forward the optimal index to select the configuration of the solution set.

At present, there have been many studies on the optimization strategies for redundant robot operation configurations for different task scenarios and objectives. In order to improve the safety of head collision between flexible robots and human bodies in man-machine cooperative operation, Meng et al. [6] established an equivalent model of head collision and proposed robot safety indexes. The gradient projection algorithm is used to reduce the safety risk index, and the optimization goal is man-machine cooperation security, solving the problem of safety configuration optimization in the continuous path of robots. Guo et al. [7] established a dynamic model before and after the collision to

H. Yang et al. (Eds.): ICIRA 2023, LNAI 14268, pp. 579–588, 2023.
https://doi.org/10.1007/978-981-99-6486-4_49

solve the problem of base pose changes caused by collision during target capture. With the goal of minimizing the impact on robot angular momentum during the collision, they proposed a numerical method of optimal configuration planning based on particle swarm optimization. Zhao et al. [8] adopts the normal distribution improved Monte Carlo method to solve the workspace of the 9-DOF redundant serial robot, and selects the optimal configuration of the redundant robot with the operability and reachable space as the optimal objective. Yang et al. [9] analyzes the impact of dual arm coupling on the operability of the task arm in a dual arm space robot system. The configuration of the dual arm space robot is selected with the optimization objectives of operability and minimum attitude disturbance of the base.

According to the above research, most of the existing configuration optimization methods of robotic arms can only be applied to specific scenarios and only select the optimal configuration at a certain moment in the task. However, when the shape of the target satellite or the environment is relatively complex in the capture task, the adjustment and adaptability of the manipulator in the motion process are highly required. Therefore, the conventional method is not suitable for the optimization of robotic arm configuration before satellite capture. Based on the demand for comprehensive adaptability of the manipulator during adjustment in complex environments, an average maneuverability index is designed in this paper, which could reflect the comprehensive dexterity of the manipulator during adjustment from the initial state to the capture state, and could be used to select the optimal capture configuration.

2   Construction of the Mapping Between Reachable End Pose and Configuration Set for Space Robots

2.1   Kinematic Model of Space Robot

According to the method proposed by Denavit Hartenberg to describe the motion relationship rules of mechanism [10], the space connection relation of two adjacent connecting rods is described by four variables: rod length a, offset d, twist angle α and rotation angle q. The homogeneous transformation matrix is used to describe the position and pose relationship between the coordinate systems of each connecting rod.

The 7-DOF SSRMS space robot used in the International Space Station is taken as the research object in this paper. According to the DH parameter method, the DH coordinate system is established in combination with the 7-DOF redundant manipulator structure, as shown in Fig. 1. DH parameters were calculated on the basis of DH coordinate system and structural data, and DH parameters were obtained in Table 1.

The transformation matrix of the coordinate system ($\{i\}$ and $\{i + 1\}$) of adjacent connecting rods is shown in Eq. (1):

$$^{i-1}_{i}\mathbf{T} = \mathbf{Rot}(X, \alpha_{i-1})\mathbf{Trans}(X, a_{i-1})\mathbf{Rot}(Z, q_i)\mathbf{Trans}(Z, d_i)$$

$$= \begin{bmatrix} cq_i & -sq_i & 0 & a_{i-1} \\ sq_i c\alpha_{i-1} & cq_i c\alpha_{i-1} & -s\alpha_{i-1} & -d_i s\alpha_{i-1} \\ sq_i s\alpha_{i-1} & cq_i s\alpha_{i-1} & c\alpha_{i-1} & d_i c\alpha_{i-1} \\ 0 & 0 & 0 & 1 \end{bmatrix} \tag{1}$$

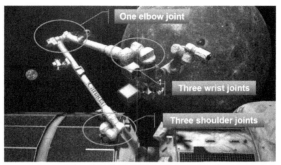

(a) The 7-DOF SSRMS space robot

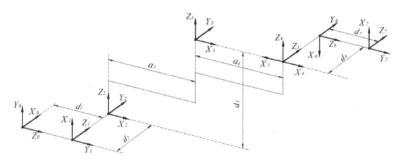

(b) The DH coordinate system

Fig. 1. The DH coordinate system of 7-DOF SSRMS space robot.

Table 1. DH parameter table of space robot.

Connecting rod i	$q_i/°$		a_i/m	$\alpha_i/°$	d_i/m
	Straightened state	Folded state			
1	90	90	0	0	0.6
2	90	90	0	90	0.5
3	0	90	0	-90	0.5
4	0	180	5	0	0.5
5	180	90	5	0	0.5
6	-90	-90	0	0	0.5
7	180	180	0	-90	0.6

The transformation matrix of the end coordinate system {7} relative to the base coordinate system {0} on the base can be obtained by multiplying the transformation matrices of the connecting rod in sequence:

$$_{7}^{0}\mathbf{T} = _{1}^{0}\mathbf{T}_{2}^{1}\mathbf{T}_{3}^{2}\mathbf{T}\cdots_{6}^{5}\mathbf{T}_{7}^{6}\mathbf{T} = _{1}^{0}\mathbf{T}(q_1)_{2}^{1}\mathbf{T}(q_2)_{3}^{2}\mathbf{T}(q_3)\cdots_{7}^{6}\mathbf{T}(q_7) \qquad (2)$$

The position vector $\mathbf{P}$ represents the position of the end connecting rod, and the rotation matrix $\mathbf{R} = [\mathbf{n} \, \mathbf{o} \, \mathbf{a}]$ represents the orientation of the end connecting rod. Equation (2) can be written as Eq. (3).

$$\begin{bmatrix} {}_7^0\mathbf{R} & {}^0\mathbf{P}_7 \\ 0 \; 0 \; 0 & 1 \end{bmatrix} = {}_1^0\mathbf{T}(q_1) \, {}_2^1\mathbf{T}(q_2) \cdots {}_7^6\mathbf{T}(q_7) \tag{3}$$

The above equation is the kinematic equation of the space robot, which represents the relation between the pose of the end of the connecting rod and the joint variable.

2.2 Construction of the Mapping Between Reachable end Pose and Configuration Set

After the space robot completes the satellite approximation tracking, the target satellite will be in the reachable space at the end of the manipulator. At this moment, the relative posture between the space robot and the target satellite needs to be maintained, and the posture relationship between the manipulator base and the target satellite is fixed as $\mathbf{T}_{cap}$. In order to adjust the space robot from the initial configuration to the capture configuration, the inverse solution is needed. However, the inverse solution operation of redundant manipulator usually has infinite solutions, and the calculation method is complex. In this paper, the Hash Map method is used to construct the mapping between the end pose and the configuration set of the manipulator. After the target pose is determined, the corresponding configuration set can be found in the mapping.

In order to quickly determine the capture configuration, The Hash table H is constructed for the mapping relationship between the end pose and the configuration of the manipulator.

$$H = \left\{ {}_n^0\mathbf{T} : \mathbf{M}_q \right\} \tag{4}$$

where, ${}_n^0\mathbf{T}$ represents the transformation matrix of the end system of the manipulator relative to the base system, $\mathbf{M}_q$ represents the set of space robot's configurations. Each set of space robot's configurations is composed of n joint angles. Since the joint of the actual manipulator has rotation limit, the joint limit matrix is set as Eq. (5).

$$\mathbf{q}_{limit} = \begin{bmatrix} q_{1\,min} & q_{2\,min} & q_{3\,min} & q_{4\,min} & q_{5\,min} & q_{6\,min} & q_{7\,min} \\ q_{1max} & q_{2max} & q_{3max} & q_{4max} & q_{5max} & q_{6max} & q_{7max} \end{bmatrix} \tag{5}$$

where, $q_{i\,min}$ represents the minimum joint limit of joint i, $q_{i\,max}$ represents the maximum joint limit of joint i. q is rasterized as Eq. (6).

$$q_i = q_{i\,min} + (q_{i\,max} - q_{i\,min})k/K_i \tag{6}$$

where, $K_i = (q_{i\,max} - q_{i\,min})/\lambda$, λ is the angle step size of rasterization.

By combining the rasterized joint angles of n joints, arbitrary discrete joint angle combinations are obtained: $\mathbf{q} = \begin{bmatrix} q_1 \cdots q_i \cdots q_n \end{bmatrix}$.

The forward kinematics equation of the space robot can be used to calculate the end pose ${}_n^0\mathbf{T}$ of the manipulator. ${}_n^0\mathbf{T}$ is used as the key value of the Hash table, and q is inserted into the configuration set corresponding to ${}_n^0\mathbf{T}$ in the map H.

After determining the position and posture of the target satellite, the transformation matrix $\mathbf{T}_{cap}$ of the end of the capturing configuration manipulator relative to the base system of the space robot can be easily calculated. Then, the corresponding configuration set is searched directly in the mapping H according to the key value $\mathbf{T}_{cap}$, and the configuration set of the manipulator that can meet the acquisition task can be obtained.

3 Configuration Optimization and Path Planning Based on Optimal Average Operability

The space robot discussed in this paper has redundancy, and a end transition matrix can correspond to multiple configurations. Therefore, it is necessary to optimize the alternative capturing configurations according to the motion characteristics of the space robot. The operation configuration with the optimal average operability during configuration adjustment can be selected as the final capturing configuration.

3.1 Maneuverability Index

In this section, the maneuverability index of a single configuration is given based on the kinematic model. By solving the Jacobian matrix of the manipulator with differential transformation method, the influence of each joint motion on the end motion of the manipulator can be obtained.

Considering the joint action of all joints, the relationship between joint angular velocity and end linear/angular velocity can be obtained as follows:

$$\begin{bmatrix} v \\ \omega \end{bmatrix} = \mathbf{J} \begin{bmatrix} \dot{q}_1 \\ \dot{q}_2 \\ \vdots \\ \dot{q}_n \end{bmatrix} \tag{7}$$

It can be simplified into the equation:

$$\mathbf{V} = \dot{\mathbf{P}} = \mathbf{J}(\mathbf{q})\,\dot{\mathbf{q}} \tag{8}$$

where, $\mathbf{V}$ is the velocity vector, $\dot{\mathbf{P}}$ is the derivative of the pose of the end of the manipulator, $\dot{\mathbf{q}}$ is the angular velocity vector of the joint. It can be deduced from Eq. (3):

$$v = \mathbf{J}(\mathbf{q})\,\dot{\mathbf{q}} \tag{9}$$

In the above equation, the Jacobian matrix $\mathbf{J}(\mathbf{q})$ represents the generalized transmission ratio from the joint rotational velocity to the end operating velocity. Based on the angle of each joint of the space robot $q_1, q_2, \ldots, q_n$, the singular values

$\sigma_1, \sigma_2, \ldots, \sigma_m(\sigma_r)$ of the Jacobian matrix can be obtained, and the kinematic performance indexes related to the singular values of the Jacobian matrix $\mathbf{J}(\mathbf{q})$ can be obtained.

Maneuverability was used to characterize the kinematic performance of the manipulator in different configurations. The mathematical expression of maneuverability was shown as Eq. (10). The greater the maneuverability, the stronger the motion ability of the manipulator in this configuration.

$$\xi(\mathbf{q}) = \sigma_1 \sigma_2 \cdots \sigma_m \tag{10}$$

3.2 Optimization of Capture Configuration Based on the Highest Average Maneuverability

Since the inverse configuration set $\mathbf{M}_q$ corresponding to a end pose of a redundant robot contains multiple groups of configuration solutions, it is necessary to evaluate and optimize the configurations in the $\mathbf{M}_q$. Considering that the space robot needs to adjust from the initial configuration to the capture configuration, it may be restricted by the environment during the adjustment process, which requires higher maneuverability of the manipulator. Therefore, the average maneuverability is adopted as the Basis of optimization.

According to the improved S-shaped velocity trajectory planning algorithm [11], the smooth interpolation function $q(t)$ of the manipulator adjusting from the initial configuration to the capture configuration can be obtained.

Average maneuverability can be calculated according to S-shaped planning algorithm and Eq. (10):

$$\xi_{avg} = \int_{t_0}^{t_f} \xi(q(t))dt / (t_f - t_0) \tag{11}$$

Then the average maneuverability $\mathbf{M}_{\xi_{avg}}$ corresponding to $\mathbf{M}_q$ can be obtained, and the capture configuration with the highest average maneuverability can be obtained by comparison. $\mathbf{q}_{cap}$ is the capture configuration with optimal operability.

$$\mathbf{q}_{cap} = \arg\max \xi_{avg}(q) \left(q \in \mathbf{M}_{\xi_{avg}} \right) \tag{12}$$

The capturing configuration of the average optimal maneuverability corresponding to the reachable terminal pose is unique and not affected by other factors. The calculation of this section can be completed before the start of approximation tracking, and the mapping H of reachable end pose and configuration set can be transformed into the mapping H_{cap} of reachable terminal pose and optimal capture configuration.

$$H_{cap} = \left\{ {}_n^0\mathbf{T} : \mathbf{q}_{cap} \right\} \tag{13}$$

To sum up, the optimization of the capture configuration is completed in the case that the relative pose of the target satellite and the space robot is known. On this basis, the joint sequence adjusted to the optimal operational configuration is obtained by using the path planning method, and the configuration adjustment is completed.

4 Simulation Analysis of Capture Configuration Adjustment

In order to verify the validity of the proposed configuration optimization method of space robot for satellite capture, numerical simulation is carried out.

Assuming that the end capture pose of space robot is known, the mapping between any group of reachable end-pose and the configuration set of the space robot can be obtained by using the mapping method above. The configuration set satisfying the end pose can be obtained by using MATLAB toolbox based on $\mathbf{T}_{cap}$. Let $\mathbf{T}_{cap} = [4.335\ 1.668\ 2.434\ -0.594\ 2.234]$. Joint 7 is uniformly discretized in the interval $[-90, 90]$ as a fixed angle, and the space robot can be transformed into a 6-DOF robot for reverse solution, and 1448 configuration sets will be obtained. Then, path planning is performed for configurations in the optional configuration set, and the initial joint angle was set as $\mathbf{q}_0 = [10\ 20\ 30\ 40\ 50\ 60\ 70]$ (°). Joint angular path planning is carried out respectively, and the results are shown in the figure.

Figure 2 shows the joint angle sequence of joints 1–7 from the initial configuration to any configuration planning in the capture configuration set when the improved S-type trajectory planning method is adopted. There are 1448 curves in each figure, and each curve conforms to the joint motion law of the improved S-shaped smooth trajectory planning.

Of all the configurations that satisfy the capture condition, the maximum average maneuverability is calculated to be 156.846, and the corresponding operational configuration is $[-93.16\ 0.36\ 53.48–58.64\ 157.68\ 59.42\ -26.14]$ (°). In this case, the dexterity of the space robot is the strongest in the process of adjusting the initial configuration to the capture configuration, and the success rate of capturing the target satellite in the complex environment will be improved.

Finally, joint angle and joint angular velocity adjusted to the optimal operable configuration according to the improved S-shape trajectory planning are shown in Fig. 3. The smooth motion of space robot can be guaranteed during configuration adjustment.

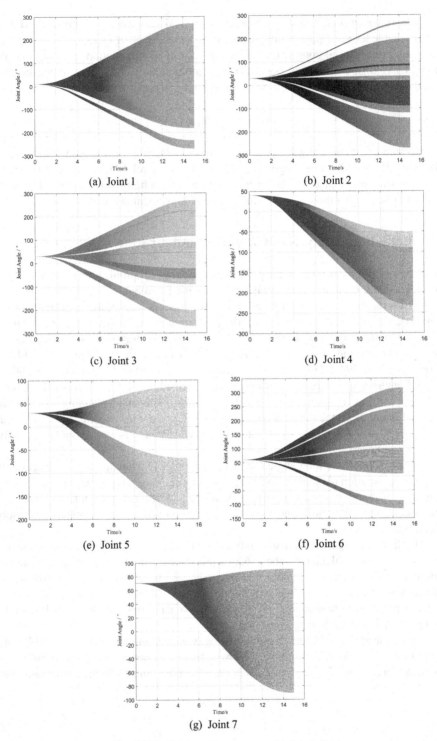

(a) Joint 1

(b) Joint 2

(c) Joint 3

(d) Joint 4

(e) Joint 5

(f) Joint 6

(g) Joint 7

Fig. 2. The joint angle sequence of joints 1–7.

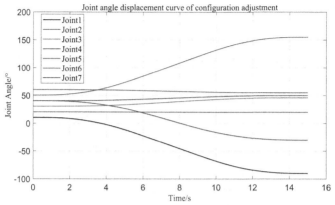

(a) Joint angle displacement curve of configuration adjustment

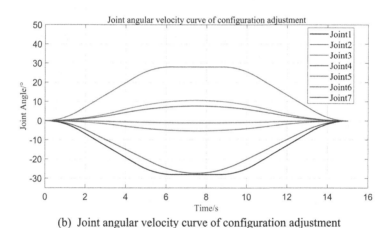

(b) Joint angular velocity curve of configuration adjustment

Fig. 3. Joint angle and angular velocity curves adjusted to the optimal capture configuration.

5   Conclusion

The configuration optimization strategy of space robot for satellite capture proposed in this paper aims to optimize the operational configuration of the space robot before capturing the satellite, so as to improve the success rate of satellite capture. The designed mapping method for reachable end pose and configuration sets can take the calculation offline and improve the efficiency of the calculation during task execution. The optimized operation configuration scheme based on the optimal average maneuverability can optimize the operation configuration of the manipulator during the adjustment process, so as to improve the adaptive ability of the space robot during the capturing process. Finally, the feasibility and effectiveness of the proposed configuration optimization strategy for the satellite capture mission is verified by numerical simulation.

Acknowledgments. This work was supported by the the Fundamental Research Funds for Central Universities of China under Grant 2018YJS135.

References

1. Aaron, B.: Technological wonder and strategic vulnerability: satellite reconnaissance and American national security during the cold war. Int. J. Intell. Counter Intell. **33**(2), 328–353 (2020)
2. Liu, X., Cai, G., Wang, M., et al.: Contact control for grasping a non-cooperative satellite by a space robot. Multibody Syst.Dyn. **50**(2), 119–141 (2020)
3. Akhloumadi, M., Ivanov, D.: Influence of satellite motion control system parameters on performance of space debris capturing. Aerospace **7**(11), 160 (2020)
4. Fu, X., Ai, H., Chen, L.: Repetitive learning sliding mode stabilization control for a flexible-base, flexible-link and flexible-joint space robot capturing a satellite. Appl. Sci. **11**(17), 8077 (2021)
5. Xu, W., Meng, D., Liu, H., et al.: Singularity-free trajectory planning of free-floating multiarm space robots for keeping the base inertially stabilized. IEEE Trans. Syst. Man Cybern.-Syst. **49**(12), 2464–2477 (2019)
6. Meng, D., Wang, X., Liang, B., et al.: Safe configuration optimization of flexible joint manipulator based on equivalent model of head collision. Jiqiren/Robot **4**(39), 523–531 (2017)
7. Guo, W., Wang, T.: Pre-impact configuration optimization for a space robot capturing target satellite. J. Astronaut. **36**(04), 390–396 (2018)
8. Zhao, Z., Xu, Z., He, P., et al.: Configuration optimization of nine degree of freedom super-redundant serial manipulator based on workspace analysis. J. Mech. Eng. **55**(21), 51–63 (2017)
9. Yang, S., Wen, H., Jin, D.: Trajectory planning of dual-arm space robots for target capturing and base manoeuvring. Acta Astronaut. **164**(9), 142–151 (2019)
10. Fang, S., Zhang, Q., Cheng, W., et al.: Research on path planning of robotic ultrasonic surface strengthening for turbine blade based on dynamic response of ultrasonic surface strengthening. Adv. Mech. Eng. **11**(12), 3: 1–9 (2019)
11. Fang, S., Zhang, Q., Zhao, H., et al.: The design of rare-earth giant magnetostrictive ultrasonic transducer and experimental study on its application of ultrasonic surface strengthening. Micromachines **9**(98), 1–13 (2018)

Multifunctional Wound Monitoring Sensor Based on Laser-Induced Graphene

Huaping Wu$^{(\boxtimes)}$, Jiachao Sun, Zhendong Liu, Ye Qiu, and Ye Tian

College of Mechanical Engineering, Zhejiang University of Technology,
Hangzhou 310023, China
wuhuaping@gmail.com

Abstract. The chronic wound monitoring has attracted significant attention due to its crucial role in promoting treatment and shortening treatment cycles. However, developing wound monitoring sensors to achieve a multifunctional sensory system with high sensitivity remains a grand challenge, which is attributed to the difficulty of integrating multiple sensors simultaneously without causing signal coupling. Here, we propose a novel wound monitoring sensor based on laser-induced graphene. The sensor not only has the characteristics of flexibility and stretchability, but also can monitor a variety of wound information (i.e., pH, strain). With the structural design of multifunctional sensing schemes, the multifunctional sensory system deconvolutes multiple sensing characteristics of the monitoring process and thus holds impressive behavior for measurement and warning of wound tearing. As a proof-of-concept demonstration, the multifunctional sensor based on laser-induced graphene realizes the intelligent monitoring of wound status varying in pH and strain, paving the way for the development of microsurgery robots, human-machine interfacing, and advanced prosthetics.

Keywords: wound monitoring · flexible pH sensor · strain sensor · laser induced graphene

1 Introduction

In recent years, with the wide application of various sensors in wearable devices, higher requirements have been placed on miniaturization, flexibility, and stability of sensing materials and devices [1–5]. In addition, people also want wearable sensors to have as many functions as possible to meet the needs of different fields [6]. In daily production and life, it is inevitable that wounds appear on the skin due to trauma of various reasons. Wounds can be roughly divided into chronic wounds and acute wounds [7]. Chronic wounds are not only difficult to treat and have a long recovery period, but severe chronic wounds can also cause amputations and even endanger patients' lives [8]. Therefore, it is of great scientific significance and social value to develop and develop wearable flexible sensors that can effectively monitor the status of chronic wounds [9].

Enormous demand and promising prospects for bioinspired intelligent robotics have led to notable progress in wound monitoring [10, 11]. At present, the wound monitoring

H. Yang et al. (Eds.): ICIRA 2023, LNAI 14268, pp. 589–596, 2023.
https://doi.org/10.1007/978-981-99-6486-4_50

sensors developed by scholars often have a single function. They can only monitor a single information of the wound, and cannot accurately measure the true state of the wound. In addition, the current wound monitoring sensors developed have not effectively monitored and warned of the wound tear, and the secondary tear of the wound is also one of the important reasons for the difficult healing of the wound. Therefore, this paper proposes a new type of wound monitoring sensor based on laser-induced graphene. The sensor not only has the characteristics of flexibility and stretchability, but also can monitor a variety of wound information (pH and strain).

Here, A layer of porous graphene was prepared on the surface of polyimide film by laser induced graphene method. The porous graphene is then transferred to the surface of the polydimethylsiloxane by the viscosity of the polydimethylsiloxane when it is not solidified. Under the stretching deformation, porous graphene will form a large number of gap cracks on the surface, which can be used to monitor whether the wound is stretched, so as to give the wound a stretch warning. Furthermore, an electrochemical workstation was used to electroplate a layer of metallic copper on the surface of the laser-induced graphene, and the resistance-temperature characteristics of metallic copper were used to determine the temperature change of the wound. Through the structural design of soft and hard combination, the interference of strain on the temperature sensor is isolated, making the pH sensor measurement more accurate. Besides, the pH of the wound was monitored based on the electrochemical properties of polyaniline, and the effect of different electropolymerization conditions on the performance of the pH sensor was studied. The integration of the multifunctional sensing system is demonstrated to realize intelligent monitoring the wound, revealing its potential as a promising strategy for soft robotics, human-machine interfaces, and neuroprosthetics.

2   Preparation and Performance Testing of Flexible Strain Sensors

The experiments utilized laser scanning to produce porous graphene which was subsequently transferred onto PDMS; the wires were eventually connected and encapsulated. The preparation steps and physical structure of the flexible strain sensor are depicted in Fig. 1a and Fig. 1b respectively. Raman spectroscopy is commonly used to detect and analyze material properties, with the method being highly accurate for nano-carbon materials. In this study,

Raman spectroscopy was utilized to detect and analyze the laser-induced graphene. The characteristic peaks of the Raman spectra of laser-induced graphene are similar to those of graphene, with the study material produced having three main graphene peaks [12]. A higher D peak intensity represents graphene defects, whereas a higher intensity of the G peak indicates a lower number of graphene layers. Therefore, Raman spectroscopy was utilized to identify that the material produced in this study was laser-induced graphene [13]. The surface morphology of laser-induced graphene after the transfer is displayed in Fig. 1d, illustrating a porous sheet-like stacked structure similar to graphene produced in other studies [14, 15].

When a flexible sensor is stretched, the resistance changes as the porous graphene on the substrate surface develops cracks visible to the naked eye. The change in resistance is used to deduce the change in strain. It is important to note here that very small strains

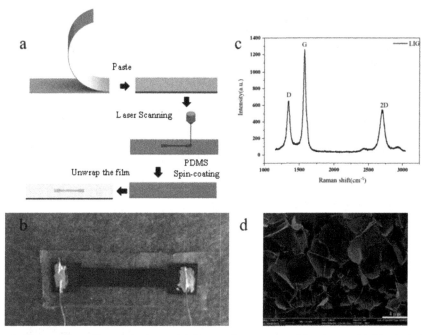

Fig. 1. Preparation of strain sensors. (a) Preparation process of the sensor. **(b)** Physical view of the sensor. **(c)** Raman spectral analysis of laser-induced graphene. **(d)** Surface morphology of laser-induced graphene after transfer.

can cause cracks in the graphene, so the strain sensor prepared in this study is highly sensitive and very suitable for human detection.

The strain-resistance curve of the sensor is shown in Fig. 2a, where the strain sensor sensitivity GF is 164.80 for the strain range 0–25% and 504.20 for the strain range 25–38%. When the sensor is in the high strain region, the crack expands as the strain increases, so that even a very small strain can cause a large change in the crack and therefore a large change in resistance. The strain sensitivity is selected according to the different strain situations, so that the detection accuracy will be more accurate. The linearity of the strain sensor can be divided into two regions, the linearity of the whole sensor is about 92%, in the 0–25% region the linearity of this sensor is 97.27%, in the 25–38% region the linearity is 99.5%. Figure 2b shows the minimum detection limit of the flexible strain sensor prepared in this paper. The minimum detection limit of the strain sensor is 0.3% strain.

In addition to being sensitive to strain, the flexible sensor prepared in this study is also sensitive to angle change. The angle-current change diagram is shown in Fig. 2c, where it should be noted that the current change is more pronounced at the beginning of the angle change, and gradually decreases as the angle bend increases. The main reason for this phenomenon is that as the bending angle gradually increases, the resistance of the flexible sensor gradually increases, while the current gradually decreases, and therefore the current change gradually decreases.

The flexible strain sensor prepared in this paper has excellent and stable repeatability, as shown in Fig. 2d, at larger strains (25%), the flexible strain sensor prepared in this paper has good repeatability, which lays a good foundation for the application of the flexible strain sensor.

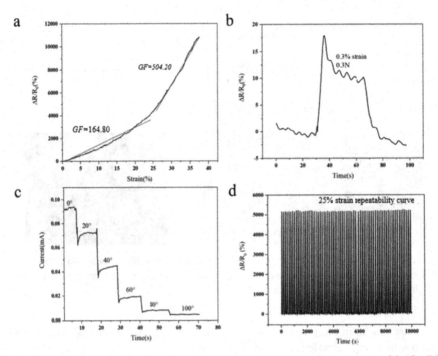

Fig. 2. Performance testing of flexible strain sensors. (a) Strain-resistance curve of the flexible strain sensor. **(b)** Minimum detection limit of the flexible strain sensor. **(c)** Angular detection of the flexible strain sensor. **(d)** Repeatability experiment of the flexible strain sensor.

3   Preparation and Performance Testing of Flexible pH Sensors

The materials mainly used in the flexible pH sensor prepared by this paper are polyaniline (PANI), and electrochemical synthesis of polyaniline is adopted [16]. As shown in Fig. 3b, the silver part on the left is the reference electrode, which is made of Ag/AgCl silver paste and the surface is modified with PVB. The dark green part on the right is the working electrode, which is mainly made of polyaniline nanowires. The black serpentine band part is laser-induced graphene which mainly serves to connect the electrode with the copper wire. The sensor length is about 25 mm and its width does not exceed 10 mm.

The linearity and error of the pH flexible sensor prepared by this research in measuring pH buffer solutions with pH values of 4 to 10 are shown in Fig. 3a. It is found that the flexible pH sensor prepared by this research has good linearity, with a linearity of up to 99.9% and a sensing error of less than 5%. Figure 3b is a staircase diagram showing the continuous monitoring of pH changes in the solution by the flexible pH sensor. It can be seen from the figure that the flexible pH sensor developed in this paper can monitor different pH values stably and respond quickly to changes in pH in the solution. The flexible pH sensor developed in this paper targets long-term monitoring of wounds, so the stability of the sensor is crucial. As shown in Fig. 3c, the flexible pH sensor monitored pH buffer solutions with pH values of 4, 7, and 10 for up to 12 h, and the maximum drift was less than 3%.

This research also performed stretching tests on the flexible pH sensor and tested its performance under stretching conditions. Figure 3d shows the monitoring of pH values under stretching conditions, where pH buffer solutions with pH values of 4, 7, and 10 were monitored, and the flexible pH sensor was stretched with a stretching test device. It was found from the test that the stretching strain did not affect the pH monitoring results, and it could still monitor pH values normally even at strains as high as 35%.

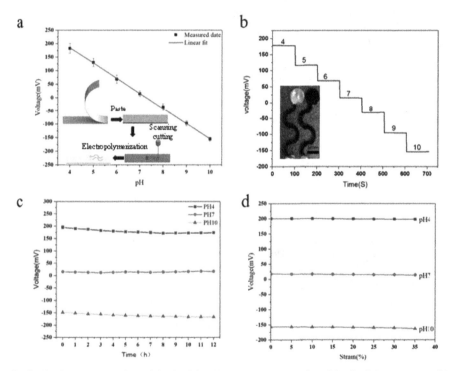

Fig. 3. Performance testing of the flexible pH sensor. (a) Linearity of the flexible pH sensor. (b) Flexible pH sensor's detection ladder. (c) Stability of the flexible pH sensor. (d) Tensile stability of the flexible pH sensor.

4 Research on Laser-Induced Graphene-Based Flexible Wound Monitoring Sensors

The flexible wound monitoring sensor consists of a pH sensor on the front and a strain sensor on the back, with a polydimethylsiloxane substrate as illustrated in Fig. 4a. By monitoring the strain status of the wound, the flexible wound strain monitoring sensor from this study, presented in Fig. 4b, can accurately and timely detect wound strain and provide an early warning of wound tearing. The experimental data depicted in Fig. 4b validates the feasibility of utilizing the flexible wound strain monitoring sensor in wound tear warnings. As illustrated in Fig. 4c, the wound monitoring sensor displays its capability to effectively distinguish between different pH buffer solutions by injecting them using an injection pump into a simulated human skin wound. The wound monitoring sensor displayed in Fig. 4c can be applied in pH monitoring of wounds as evidenced by the experimental data. Figures 4d shows the effect of strain on the pH sensing unit of the pH monitoring unit of the flexible wound monitoring sensor. The wound monitoring sensor was stretched to 5%, 10%, and 15% strain using a stretching device then the pH monitoring performance of the flexible temperature sensor was tested. It can be seen from the figures that the pH monitoring unit in the flexible wound monitoring sensor is completely unaffected by strain and can operate normally at a certain strain.

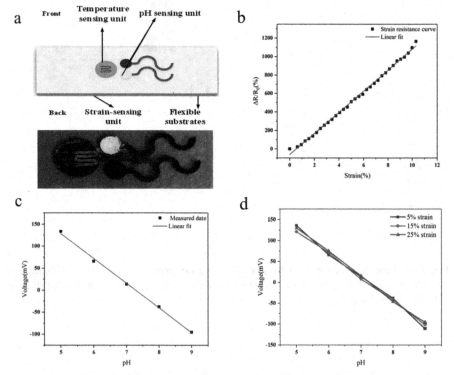

Fig. 4. Performance testing of the flexible strain sensor. (a) Flexible wound monitoring sensor structure design and physical. (b) Human-like skin wound strain monitoring. (c) Human-like skin wound pH monitoring. (d) Flexible wound monitoring sensor pH monitoring strain stability test.

5 Conclusion

In summary, we demonstrated a multifunctional sensory system utilizing the laser-induced graphene with high sensitivity to sense multiple information (i.e., pH, and strain), enabling the sensing modules to realize real-time monitoring of chronic wounds. Through the reasonable structural design, finite element analysis, and experimental research, a flexible multi-functional sensor for pH and strain was prepared for real-time monitoring of wound status. The sensor can not only monitor wound healing information, provide guidance for doctors' treatment, but also monitor the strain at the wound in time to remind patients to avoid secondary laceration injuries. This research provides a strategy toward multifunctional measurements and would broadly benefit many fields, especially for intelligent soft robotics, minimally invasive surgery, and electronic prostheses.

References

1. Babu, A., Aazem, I., Walden, R., Bairagi, S., Mulvihill, D.M., Pillai, S.C.: Electrospun nanofiber based TENGs for wearable electronics and self-powered sensing. Chem. Eng. J. Rev. **452**, 139060 (2023)
2. Hu, L., et al.: Hydrogel-based flexible electronics. Adv. Mater. Rev. **35**(14) (2023)
3. Ma, R., Xu, Z., Wang, X.: Polymer hydrogel electrolytes for flexible and multifunctional zinc-ion batteries and capacitors. Energy Environ. Mater. Rev. Early Access 2023
4. Miao, J., Fan, T.: Flexible and stretchable transparent conductive graphene-based electrodes for emerging wearable electronics. Carbon **202**, 495–527 (2023)
5. Swan, M.: Emerging patient-driven health care models: an examination of health social networks, consumer personalized medicine and quantified self-tracking. Int. J. Environ. Res. Publ. Health **6**(2), 492–525 (2009)
6. Say, R., Murtagh, M., Thomson, R.: Patients' preference for involvement in medical decision making: a narrative review. Patient Educ. Couns. **60**(2), 102–114 (2006)
7. Roy, S., Sen, C.K.: miRNA in wound inflammation and angiogenesis. Microcirculation **19**(3), 224–232 (2012)
8. Milne, S.D., Connolly, P., Al Hamad, H., Seoudi, I.: Development of wearable sensors for tailored patient wound care. In: 36th Annual International Conference of the IEEE-Engineering-in-Medicine-and-Biology-Society (EMBC), Chicago, IL, pp. 618–621 (2014)
9. Frykberg, R.G., Banks, J.: Challenges in the treatment of chronic wounds. Adv. Wound Care **4**(9), 560–582 (2015)
10. Sani, E.S., Wang, C.R., Gao, W.: A soft bioaffinity sensor array for chronic wound monitoring. Matter **4**(8), 2613–2615 (2021)
11. Wang, L.R., Zhou, M.Y., Xu, T.L., Zhang, X.J.: Multifunctional hydrogel as wound dressing for intelligent wound monitoring. Chem. Eng. J. **433**, 134625 (2022)
12. Dresselhaus, M.S., Jorio, A., Hofmann, M., Dresselhaus, G., Saito, R.: Perspectives on carbon nanotubes and graphene Raman spectroscopy. Nano Lett. **10**(3), 751–758 (2010)
13. Sun, B.H., et al.: Gas-permeable, multifunctional on-skin electronics based on laser-induced porous graphene and sugar-templated elastomer sponges. Adv. Mater. **30**(50), 1804327 (2018)
14. Carvalho, A.F., et al.: Laser-induced graphene strain sensors produced by ultraviolet irradiation of polyimide. Adv. Function. Mater. **28**(52), 1805271 (2018)

15. Peng, Z.W., et al.: Flexible boron-doped laser-induced graphene microsupercapacitors. ACS Nano **9**(6), 5868–5875 (2015)
16. Delvaux, M., Duchet, J., Stavaux, P.Y., Legras, R., Demoustier-Champagne, S.: Chemical and electrochemical synthesis of polyaniline micro- and nano-tubules. Synth. Met. **113**(3), 275–280 (2000)

Soft Fingertip with Sensor Integrated for Continuous In-hand Manipulation

Xiaolong Ma[1], Zhenwu Guo[1], Yangqing Ye[2], and Guanjun Bao[2(✉)]

[1] China Jiliang University, Hangzhou, China
[2] Zhejiang University of Technology, Hangzhou, China
gjbao@zjut.edu.cn

Abstract. The human hand's fingers are capable of precise manipulation due to the abundance of neural receptors in them. These receptors provide interactive feedback to the brain in real-time. However, complex sensors are difficult to integrate into the fingers of a robotic hand due to space limitations. To address this issue, a separation of sensor and perception approach was adopted, resulting in the design of a soft fingertip with a cavity structure, the cavity is connected to the sensor through an air tube. By squeezing the cavity balloon, the internal air pressure changes, which can be detected by a pressure sensor. This allows for the grasping force to be perceived. The simulation reveals when the compression exceeds 1/3 of the total thickness, the Hertzian model fails. The experiments involving two fingers manipulating an object demonstrated that real-time feedback of finger-tip force enables cooperative movement between the two fingers. The experiment involving three fingers rotating a soft paper cup showed that real-time feedback of finger force can achieve force closure of three fingers during operation and enable continuous in-hand operation. These experimental results indicate that the designed soft fingertip can be effectively applied to multi-finger cooperative manipulations, laying the foundation for dexterous manipulation of multi-fingered hands.

Keywords: Continuous manipulation · Cooperating manipulation · Contact force · Sensor · Soft fingertip

1 Introduction

To ensure the force closure of multiple fingers in real-time during the manipulation of a multi-fingered robot dexterous hand, it is essential to have real-time feedback of the contact force through force perception at the finger end. One common practice is to embed force sensors in the fingertips to identify the magnitude of the contact force [1, 2]. The embed sensor in the robotic hand can be used to distinguish the degree of fruit maturity when picking fruits [3].

Although mechanical hands with embedded sensors achieve stable grasping, there are still some challenges in the multi-finger dynamic manipulation of objects. These challenges include: 1) providing real-time and accurate feedback on contact force through

© The Author(s), under exclusive license to Springer Nature Singapore Pte Ltd. 2023
H. Yang et al. (Eds.): ICIRA 2023, LNAI 14268, pp. 597–607, 2023.
https://doi.org/10.1007/978-981-99-6486-4_51

sensors embedded at the fingertips [4, 5]; 2) ensuring stable and sensitive output of contact force data [6]; 3) during continuous in-hand manipulation, the controller needs to calculate the position of the contact points between multiple fingers, the allowable range of contact forces, and ensure force closure [7, 8]. In this work, we tried to address these three issues.

Inspired by the softness of human fingers, circular or hemispherical tips are commonly used in the design of dexterous robotic hand fingertips [9]. This design offers the advantage of directing contact force towards the center of the circle at any contact point on the finger surface. However, it also presents challenges in accurately perceiving force due to the uniaxial force direction of traditional force sensors [10]. To address this issue, we propose a new design for the fingertip that incorporates a hemispherical shape with a hollow center, resulting in a finger that more closely resembles the softness of the human hand.

Various sensors are commonly embedded in the fingertip, such as piezoresistive [11, 12], piezoelectric [13], capacitive [14], visual [15], and multimodal sensors [16]. However, some of these sensors present challenges in achieving consistent data output. Piezoresistive and capacitive sensors, for instance, can be difficult to calibrate and may produce inconsistent data. Piezoelectric sensors only provide output signals at the moment of contact and disengagement, limiting their usefulness in continuous force sensing. Capacitive sensors are susceptible to interference factors and are greatly affected by the material of the object being contacted. Visual sensors are time-consuming in image processing [17]. Finally, the complex structure of multimodal sensors makes them difficult to manufacture, leading to high prices.

2   Development of the Soft Fingertip

2.1   The Structure of Soft Fingertip with Sensor Integrated

The size of the dexterous humanoid robot hand is remarkably similar to that of a human hand. However, due to the narrow space between the fingers, it is challenging to install a force sensor. Instead of using a traditional embedded force sensor [9], a soft, hollow air bag structure was designed for the finger tips. This innovative design allows for the change in air pressure generated by the force of the air bag being compressed to reflect the change in contact force. Figure 1(a) shows the components of the soft fingertip with the pressure transducer connected to the hemispherical sphere airbag, which could be easily manufactured in fingertip.

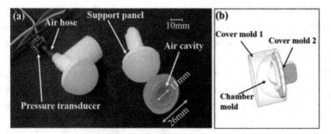

Fig. 1. Overview of the soft fingertip structure. (a) The components of the soft fingertip. (b) 3D-printed mold is used to fabricate soft fingertip

To enable accurate perception of force along the finger face in any normal direction, the contact part between the soft finger and the object is designed as a hemispherical shape. The inner cavity has a radius of 5.5 mm, while the outer cavity boasts a radius of 13 mm. Moreover, soft silicone fingers have been utilized to ensure that the finger's shape changes in accordance with the external outline of the object. The air pressure transducer generates electrical charge proportional to the air pressure inside the hemisphere.

2.2 Fabrication of Soft Fingertip

To made the soft fingertip, a silicone pouring technology was adopted. Firstly, the mold was designed by using a 3D design software, the lower and upper covers of the mold were printed by a 3D printer machine. To facilitate bubble spillover during pouring, eight holes with diameter of 1 mm were distributed along the circumference of the top cover. The top cover was designed as hemispherical protrusions, with a radius of 5.5 mm. The lower cover was concave with a radius of 13 mm. The preparation of the fingertip is achieved by mixing an equal weight of the two-part silica gel parts A and B [Ecoflex0050 1A 1B] as recommended by the manufacturer, Smooth-On USA. The mixed liquid silica gel was carefully poured into the cover mold 1. Then the cover mold 2 was combined with the cover mold 1 [18]. The combined mold was put into a vacuum box with a vacuum pump of Mastercool 90066-2V-220 (Mastercool, Inc., Randolph, NJ). The pressure inside the vacuum box dropped from 0.101 MPa to 0.011 MPa (absolute pressure) to precipitate small bubbles from the liquid silica gel. Twenty minutes later, the assembled mold was taken out of the vacuum box and placed in an oven at 50 °C for curing. Two hours later, the silica gel air cavity in the mold could be taken out as a solid body. Each sample was inspected using a light source projected on the sample to observe possible air bubbles. Figure 2(a) shows a final sample that has been discarded owing to the presence of many bubbles, and Fig. 2(b) shows a qualified soft fingertip. A convex ring was designed on the surface of the support plate for mount and seal the soft fingertip, as shown in Fig. 2(c).

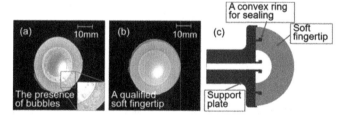

Fig. 2. Example of soft fingertip inspected with backlight. (a) The presence of bubbles in the fingertip, which was discarded owing to the presence of many bubbles in the silica gel. (b) A qualified soft fingertip. (c) A convex circle is designed on the support plate for sealing, connecting to the soft fingertip.

2.3 Contact Force Sensing Properties

Many modeling of the mechanical contact force of hemispherical and hemicylindrical soft fingertips have been proposed [9]. The Hertzian contact model is one of the classical linear elastic models [19]. The two hard contacting surfaces are squeezed, its performance like linear elastic materials. While Tatara experimentally revealed that the Hertzian contact model is not valid in the case of a large deformation for nonlinear elastic materials with $a/R \geq 0.3$ [20] (where R is the radius of a hemispherical soft fingertip and a is the pressed depth), A contact model between hemispherical soft fingertip and rigid body is proposed.

Assuming that the height of the sphere l is a variable, it decreases as the contact force increases. The maximum thickness of the sphere is l_0, external radius is R, the contact radius is a and depth of contact is d. We assumed that the contact depth should be less than the radius of the hemisphere and the deformation area should be less than the contact radius. The hemisphere deformed in the uniaxial direction, using the modulus of $\tilde{E} \approx kE$, where $\tilde{E}$ is the elasticity coefficient, E is the Young's modulus of the material and k is an empirical number, usually $k = 1,000$.

As shown in Fig. 3, the axial displacement $z(r)$ of the contact surface is a function of radius r [19, 20]:

$$z(r) = \frac{\pi \sigma(0)}{4\tilde{E}a}(2a^2 - r^2) = \frac{\pi \sigma(0)a}{2\tilde{E}} - \frac{\pi \sigma(0)r^2}{4\tilde{E}a}, \quad -a \leq r \leq a \tag{1}$$

where $\sigma(0) = \tilde{E}\frac{d}{l_0} = (\frac{\tilde{E}F}{\pi l_0 R})^{1/2}$ is the maximum stress exists at the center of the contact area between the soft finger and object, a is the contact radius.

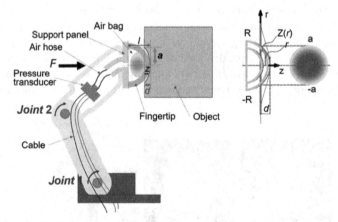

Fig. 3. Overview of robotic finger in contact with a cubic box, including a hemispherical soft fingertip, air pressure sensor, and its internal structure.

In the condition of $d \ll R$, the geometric constraint can be approximated to

$$z(r) = d - \frac{r^2}{2R}, \quad -a \leq r \leq a \tag{2}$$

Combining Eq. (1) and (2) yields

$$d = \frac{\pi \sigma(0)a}{2\tilde{E}}, \quad \frac{1}{R} = \frac{\pi \sigma(0)}{2\tilde{E}a} \tag{3}$$

From Eq. (3), we can obtain:

$$a^2 = Rd \tag{4}$$

We can obtain the relationship of a from d, which can be measured using a pressure sensor for force feedback.

$$\begin{cases} F = p \cdot (\pi \cdot a^2) \\ p_{20}V_0 = p_{21}V_1 \end{cases} \tag{5}$$

where p_{20} indicates the initial air pressure inside the cavity, p_{21} represent the pressure after the soft finger contacts with object.

2.4 Simulation of Contact Characteristics Between Soft Fingertip and Object

The model of the soft finger and grasped object was constructed using the finite element analysis software Abaqus. The contact type between the fingertip and the object was a soft contact, whereby the finger end model was simplified as a semicircular sphere, and the object was simplified as a rigid plate. This simplification is a common method used to model the contact between a soft finger and an object.

Figure 4 depicts the finite element model of a rectangular plate with the dimensions 0.5 mm × 30 mm × 25 mm, alongside the finite element model of a semi-cylindrical finger end with a radius of 10 mm. Due to the metal plate being harder than the finger end, the deformation of the metal plate is negligible. The material of the plate is elastic steel, with a density of 7850 kg/m^3, Poisson's ratio of 0.3, and Young's modulus of 210000 MPa, C3D8R hexahedral elements, the plate is meshed with 600 units, each element with a length of 1 mm, a width of 1 mm, and a thickness of 0.5 mm.

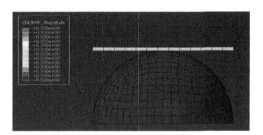

Fig. 4. The Meshing of soft fingertip model

In the software, we set the material is rubber, the model type is hyper-elastic constitutive, with parameters set as follows: rubber density is 1.1 g/cm^3. The finger end was meshed with C3D8RH and C3D6H elements, while the connection type between the soft finger and the object is static general nonlinear. The connection mode was defined as surface to surface, and the friction coefficient was set at 0.5, which is typically used for contact between silicone rubber and plastic materials. Additionally, all nodes on the upper surface of the fingertip are fixed in place.

To verify the accuracy of the material parameters incorporated in the soft finger constitutive model, a combined simulation and experimental testing of finger material characteristics was carried out. The simulation involved fixing the spherical bottom surface of the fingertip and applying vertical pressure on the object pressed into the fingertip. The relationship between the contact force and pressing distance as illustrated in Fig. 5. The relationship curve derived from the simulation bears a resemblance to that from the experiment, with a relative error of under 3%, within 3 mm of the pressing depth. This confirms the accuracy of the material parameters utilized in the finite element model.

As can be seen from the comparison diagram depicting simulation and experimental curves, the finite element curve and experimental curve are essentially consistent when the deformation of the soft finger is less than 3 mm. However, when the deformation of the finger exceeds 3 mm, a deviation between the finite element curve and experimental curve arises. Moreover, the simulated contact pressure is greater than the pressure obtained by theoretical calculation at the same deformation. The difference between the two becomes increasingly larger as the deformation escalates. This outcome arises as the compression exceeds 1/3 of the total thickness, and the Hertzian model fails in agreement with reference [20]. As a result of this effect, more force is needed to produce a small amount of compression deformation in the soft finger ending. This force is also the reason behind the rapid increase in contact pressure when the deformation of the finger end exceeds 3 mm. Figure 6 shows the pressure cloud map of the pressing surface of the soft fingertip.

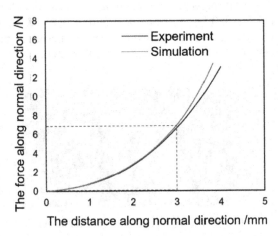

Fig. 5. The Normal force and normal compression displacement curves

The comparative analysis of simulation and experimental results in order to evaluate the applicability of the proposed theory. Results showed that the theory has a certain range of application; specifically, when the deformation is less than 1/3 of the total thickness, the relationship between contact force and deformation of the fingertip can be accurately described. Figure 6 illustrates the accuracy of the theoretical predictions at various depths of deformation: (a) the depth of 1 mm, (b) the depth of 2 mm, and (c) the

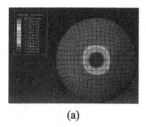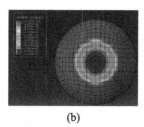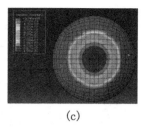

(a)   (b)   (c)

Fig. 6. The cloud images depict the pressure distribution on the contact surface at various depths of deformation. (a) The depth of deformation d0 = 1 mm, (b) the depth of deformation d0 = 2 mm, (c) the depth of deformation d0 = 3 mm.

depth of 3 mm. These results provide valuable insights into the pressure distribution on the soft fingertip during forward pressing. The pressure distribution diagram in Fig. 6 (a) (b) and (c) clearly demonstrate that the maximum contact force is located in the center of contact, with subsequent decrease in contact force as one moves towards the edge, until reaching zero force at the contact edge. This phenomenon can be explained through the differential model of the soft fingertip, observed where the strain of the micro-element in the center of contact is the largest, resulting in the corresponding maximum contact pressure. Conversely, the micro-element at the contact edge does not compress and deform, resulting in zero contact pressure. These simulate results will aid in further understanding of contact mechanics and improve the development of soft fingertip.

3   The Experiments: Manipulating Rigid Object with Two Soft Fingertips

Manipulating an object by two fingers is a challenging task because it requires cooperating the constraint forces to avoid slipping. The process requires the dynamic manipulation of the object under different contact forces and joint positions. The contact force should be controlled in a proper range to grasp the square object, but not too much to lose the balance of the two fingers.

To ensure that the object remained safely secured throughout manipulation, the grasp force was adjusted using a force control algorithm. This algorithm was based on independent finger controllers. During the experiment, the robotic hand was initially placed in an open configuration, and the fingers then closed gradually until the fingertips made contact with the object.

The evaluation results are presented in Fig. 7, where two fingers were tasked with picking up a square object. The left finger was designated the active finger, while the right fingertip followed the left fingertip motion through adjusting contact forces. The left finger was responsible for pushing the object in a left-to-right direction, while the contact forces between the fingertip and object were recorded and fed back into the controller. The right finger moved in the same direction as the left finger to reduce contact force.

When the left finger moved upward, the contact forces simultaneously decreased at both fingertips. The contact forces are shown in Fig. 8(b) and were used by the controller to detect upward or downward movements. The right finger's motion followed the left

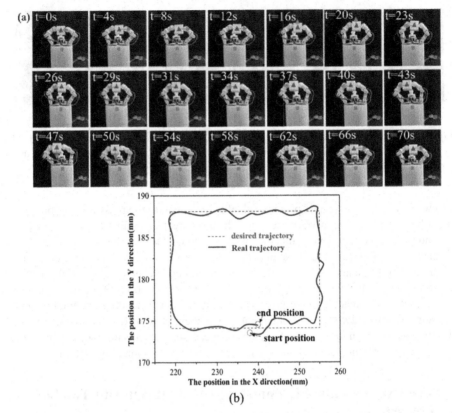

Fig. 7. Manipulating experiment: (a) The snapshots of manipulating a square object. The photos were taken at time intervals of six seconds. (b) Fingers manipulating the object along a rectangular trajectory (42 mm × 14 mm), showing the trajectory of the object (blue solid curve) and expected trajectory (red dashed curve). (Color figure online)

finger for an upward movement in a right-to-left direction, as evidenced by the contact forces shown in Fig. 8(c).

Despite the successful manipulation of the object along the desired trajectory, undesired errors were encountered, as shown in Fig. 7(b). Specifically, the start point's position was (236, 173), and the end point's position was (240, 174). The horizontal and vertical distance errors were 9.5% and 7.14%, respectively. One reason for these errors is that the soft fingertip materials slightly deform, resulting in slower restoration to the initial state when the contact force is reduced. This phenomenon can be observed in Fig. 8(a) (b). Overall, the results demonstrate the potential of the proposed system, but further improvements may be necessary to achieve higher accuracy.

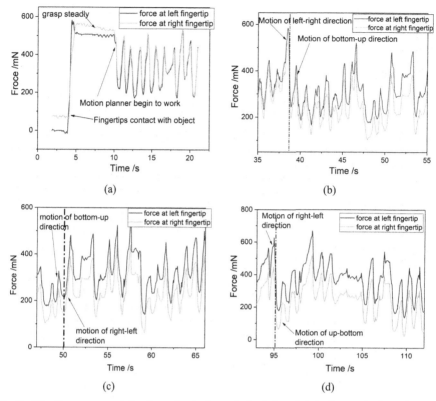

Fig. 8. The force curves at the fingertip. (a, b, c, d) the left and right fingers in four directions motion.

4 Conclusion

Inspired by the human fingertip, the robot hand has soft and deformable soft fingertips for stable grasping as well as continuous in-hand manipulation. Therefore, a soft fingertip with a force sensor integrated was proposed and employed in a three-fingered robot hand prototype.

The main contributions of this work can be summarized as follows. 1) The airbag type force sensor can detect force from any acting point on its body, which is highly significant for the robot hand to perform grasping, especially manipulating. 2) The sensor acts as a force transducer, as well as the fingertip, which facilitates the proposed sensor embedded soft fingertip to feel objects while manipulating them. 3) The sensor-based soft fingertip enables the robot hand to perform physical impedance control, which significantly reduces the precision requirement on the position and orientation of the fingertip. 4) The interaction between the soft fingertip and its target can perceive the softness of the object by the analysis of the sensed force using a machine learning method, which could improve the grasping and manipulating without additional sensors. 5) All the aforementioned advances rely on the simple mechanism and structure of the sensor-embedded soft fingertip, which also features itself with low cost, small size, and light weight.

References

1. Guanjun, B., et al.: Soft robotics: academic insides and perspectives via bibliometric analysis. Soft Rob. **5**(3), 229–241 (2018)
2. Schmitz, A., Maggiali, M., Natale, L., Bonino, B., Metta, G.: A tactile sensor for the fingertips of the humanoid robot icub. In: IEEE/RSJ International Conference on Intelligent Robots and Systems (IROS), pp. 2212–2217 (2010)
3. Chitta, S., Piccoli, M., Sturm, J.: Tactile object class and internal state recognition for mobile manipulation. In: IEEE International Conference on Robotics and Automation, pp. 2342–2348 (2010)
4. Li, Z., Hsu, P., Sastry, S.: Grasping and coordinated manipulation by a multifingered robot hand. Int. J. Robot. Res. **8**(4), 33–50 (1989)
5. Kim, I., Nakazawa, N., Inooka, H.: Control of a robot hand emulating human's hand-over motion. Mechatronics **12**(1), 55–69 (2002)
6. Fan, S., Gu, H., Zhang, Y., Jin, M., Liu, H.: Research on adaptive grasping with object pose uncertainty by multi-fingered robot hand. Int. J. Adv. Robot. Syst. **15**, 1–16 (2018)
7. Han, L., Trinkle, J.C.: Dextrous manipulation by rolling and finger gaiting. In: Proceedings. 1998 IEEE International Conference on Robotics and Automation, vol. 1, pp. 730–735 (1998)
8. Pfanne, M., Chalon, M., Stulp, F.: Object-level impedance control for dexterous in-hand manipulation. IEEE Robot. Autom. Lett. **5**, 2987–2994 (2020)
9. Bakhy, S.H.: Modeling of contact pressure distribution and friction limit surfaces for soft fingers in robotic grasping. Robotica **32**, 1005–1015 (2014)
10. Kappassov, Z., et al.: Tactile sensing in dexterous robot hands-review. Rob. Auton. Syst. **74**, 195–220 (2015)
11. Büscher, G., Koiva, R., Schürmann, C., Haschke, R., Ritter, H.J.: Flexible and stretchable fabric-based tactile sensor. In: IEEE/RSJ International Conference on Intelligent Robots and Systems (IROS 2012) (2012)
12. Wu, K., et al.: Research of a novel miniature tactile sensor for five-finger dexterous robot hand. In: Proceedings of IEEE International Conference on Mechatronics Automation, Xi'an, China, August 2010, pp. 422–427 (2010)
13. Teshigawara, S., Shimizu, S., Tadakuma, K., et al.: High sensitivity slip sensor using pressure conductive rubber. Sensors 988–991 (2009)
14. Kew Lee, H., Chung, J., Chang, S.-I., Yoon, E.: Normal and shear force measurement using a flexible polymer tactile sensor with embedded multiple capacitors. Microelectromech. Syst. 934–942 (2008)
15. Lambeta, M., Chou, P.W., Tian, S., et al.: DIGIT: a novel design for a low-cost compact high-resolution tactile sensor with application to in-hand manipulation. IEEE Robot. Autom. Lett. **5**(3), 3838–3845 (2020)
16. Qiu, Y., et al.: Bioinspired, multifunctional dual-mode pressure sensors as electronic skin for decoding complex loading processes and human motions. Nano Energy **9**(78), 105337 (2020)
17. Church, A., James, J.W., Cramphorn, L., Tactile model O: fabrication and testing of a 3D-printed, three-fingered tactile robot hand. Soft Robot. 1–17 (2020)
18. Marechal, L., et al.: Toward a common framework and database of materials for soft robotics. Soft. Robot. **8**, 284–297 (2020)

19. Hertz, H.: On the Contact of Rigid Elastic Solids and on Hardness. Chapter 6: Assorted Papers. MacMillan, New York (1882)
20. Tatara, Y.: Large deformations of a rubber sphere under diametral compression: part 1: theoretical analysis of press approach, contact radius and lateral extension. JSME Int. J. **36**, 190–196 (1993)

Author Index

H. Yang et al. (Eds.): ICIRA 2023, LNAI 14268, pp. 609–611, 2023.
https://doi.org/10.1007/978-981-99-6486-4

Printed in the United States
by Baker & Taylor Publisher Services